THE MAKING OF

CREEPSHOW 2

LEE KARR

**FOREWORD BY
PRODUCER DAVID BALL**

Plexus, London

British Library Cataloguing in Publication Data
A catalogue record for this book is available from
the British Library

ISBN-13: 978-0-85965-572-9

Book design by Coco Balderrama
Front cover, back cover, and spine design by Rick Catizone
Front cover and title page original new artwork copyright © 2022
Rick Catizone
Back cover artwork by Ron Frenz
Creepshow 2 one sheet poster imagery from spine copyright ©
Lakeshore Entertainment (Vine Alternative Investments) and RLJ
Entertainment
Creepshow title font trademark Taurus Entertainment Company
Original quotes from Richard P. Rubinstein featured in this publication
copyright © 2022 RPR
Printed in India by Replika Press PVT Limited

Contents

Foreword by David Ball

In the real world of movie making, and I exclude the money-no-object Hollywood blockbuster or franchise, research and planning need to be extensively completed to have the remotest chance of delivering the film on time and budget. The bottom line will almost never change once the investment has been insured and the green light given. Obviously there can be an occasional variance when a higher paid actor agrees to play and the financiers and/or sales people believe the actor reduces their risk, but this is usually the only reason for an increase in the budget. So, we have a locked figure to make the film and there will never be a dime more, creating a torrent of pressure from day one until delivery, with the producer's neck firmly in the noose.

All films are different in terms of shape, size, visual requirement or budget but the intensity of bringing all the pieces together with military precision remains the same; I often liken it to attempting to complete a jigsaw upside down. When I received the screenplay for *Creepshow 2* in May 1986, it appeared on first reading to be straightforward and I relished the challenge of reuniting with the team from its predecessor - and *Day of the Dead* - once again teaming up with creative movie giants Stephen King and George A. Romero.

Straightforward it wasn't from day one, with limited funding (not much more than half the original *Creepshow* budget) and beset by nightmare level problems to overcome. We'd agreed to extend a courtesy to Stephen by shooting one of the three stories in his home town of Bangor, Maine and being predominantly a night shoot it was last on the schedule. Good weather was required for the other two segments, so we choose a solid dry

Below: David Ball and director Michael Gornick (left) flank screen legend Dorothy Lamour on the set of *Old Chief Wood'nhead* in Humboldt, Arizona – October 1986. (courtesy of Michael Felsher)

Above: David Ball and executive producer Richard P. Rubinstein(right) during a Bangor, Maine Chamber of Commerce party celebrating the production of *Creepshow 2* coming to town – November 1986. (courtesy of Michael Felsher)

location in Prescott, Arizona only to be washed out by torrential rain whilst trying to shoot *The Raft* and putting us a week behind schedule whilst generating reams of paper to keep the head honchos off our backs. Being a week late arriving in Bangor to be welcomed by an earlier than usual fall of snow whilst not having a leading lady signed up compounded our problems, making it physically the hardest assignment most of us would ever go through, requiring the bravest of attitudes from cast and crew.

Braver still is Lee Karr's exhausting mission to unearth the incredible events occurring during the making of *Creepshow 2*. Experienced by the publication of *The Making of George A. Romero's Day of the Dead*, Lee has spent years slowly unravelling every piece of the complex jigsaw and putting pen to paper in spectacular detail. One tends to forget some of the anecdotes over time but Lee's research and total commitment to this book bring the whole thing home as if it were yesterday, something I would have been unable to do. Congratulations Lee for supplying a cherished memory and a mesmerizing read; a must for horror fans – correction, movie buffs worldwide.

David Ball

Producer *Creepshow 2*

June 2020

Preface

So, why are you writing a book about *Creepshow 2*? It's a fair question. Well, let's see, how did this all come about?

Shortly after the publication of *The Making of George A. Romero's Day of the Dead* in 2014, a fellow Romero enthusiast contacted me and suggested we work together on a book about the making of that film's predecessor, *Dawn of the Dead*. I loved the idea, of course, but I only wanted to do it if the producer of the film, Richard P. Rubinstein, gave his official stamp of approval and was involved in a significant way. For a few months Richard considered the idea and as he did, I took the time to conduct interviews with a handful of members from the production. It was all very exciting and something I was very passionate about. In the end, Richard decided not to go forward with it and because of that, my desire to continue working on the potential book quickly dissipated. However, the itch to work on something new would not go away and so I began to consider other options. I knew I wanted to stay in the Romero sandbox – particularly with Laurel, his former production company – that was certain.

In October 2015 I approached a good friend who just happened to be the director of *Creepshow 2*, Michael Gornick, to see how he'd feel if I wrote a book about the making of his feature film and hopefully receive his blessing to do so. I knew I had an ally in Mike, a true supporter, and that he wouldn't let me down. And he most certainly did not. He stopped by my apartment not long after that first talk to drop off his production files: his script and shot lists, storyboard art, call sheets, handwritten notes, etc. It was a treasure trove of information and he entrusted me with it all. Not only that but he devoted himself to the project by being available for as many interviews as needed – at least eight in-depth discussions for this book. Likewise with producer David Ball, someone I knew I could turn to for knowledge. David is a sage when it comes to film production and has a sharp recollection of his time on *Creepshow 2* and with

Above: Outside the master of horror Stephen King's Bangor, Maine abode with my better half, Renee – April 2017.

Laurel in general. Knowing that I had the support of these two gentlemen made the decision an easy one.

What would turn out to be not so easy was the pushback I received from some of the crew, specifically the makeup effects team. To say this was disappointing doesn't begin to cover it, frankly. In my previous book about the making of *Day of the Dead* there is a quote from one member of the makeup effects unit about another – a quote that I sincerely thought nothing of when I placed it in the book – which upset the person the quote was regarding. To make matters worse, I had sent the manuscript to this individual before the book's publication and nothing was ever said, which tells me he didn't bother to actually read it. All of this came to light not long after the book's release and it turned into a very painful lesson for me. He wanted no part of this book and as a show of solidarity, the other members of the makeup effects team followed along, all declining to be interviewed. So, in full disclosure, the exhaustive detail I would have preferred to have in this book regarding the makeup effects work is lacking. It is covered, but it's not as in-depth as I had envisioned.

Contrast that bitter disappointment though with the experience I had with assistant director Kato Wittich and production manager Charles Carroll. I discuss this further into the book but they too had some issues with my *Day* book regarding how their relationship was framed in it. But rather than shun my newest endeavor, they instead agreed to speak with me again, under mutually agreed parameters, and in my opinion helped to make me a more empathetic and understanding writer. That too is a lesson learned, one that I truly value.

Writing this book has also opened up new friendships for me with some of the people involved, which is something I did not anticipate. Cast members Holt McCallany, Don Harvey, and Domenick John Sportelli are wonderful guys whom I've gotten to know over the last six years. It just so happened that during the writing of this book, Holt came to town to shoot the first two seasons of *Mindhunter* for Netflix, which afforded me the opportunity to tag along and spend some time with him and Michael Gornick at a couple of Pittsburgh Pirates games. Visiting the set of *Mindhunter*

Above: Your humble author, age 14, calling from his hometown into CNN's *Larry King Live* to ask Stephen King if George Romero was making *Pet Sematary* – April 1986.

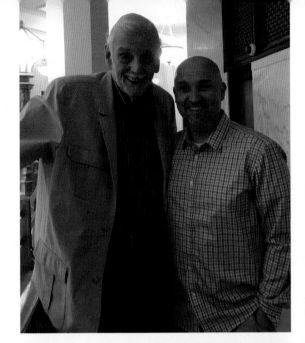

Above: Hanging out with star Holt McCallany(left) and director Michael Gornick(center) at PNC Park in Pittsburgh, PA – July 2018.
Below: With Michael Gornick recording an audio commentary for Shout Factory's release of the original 1982 *Creepshow* – August 2018. (all photos courtesy of Lee Karr)

Above: With the legend himself: the late, great George A. Romero, who would sadly pass away three months later – April 2017.
Below: Re-enacting an iconic moment from *The Raft* at Granite Basin Lake in Prescott, Arizona – December 2017.

and then being treated to dinner by Holt, all on the same night, is a prime example of how incredibly generous a guy he is. Don Harvey and Domenick John Sportelli each participated in a small *Creepshow 2* reunion that I organized for Chiller Theatre in New Jersey in 2017. Sitting at a dinner table afterwards and engaging in conversation with them both is a special memory, one that came about because of this book project.

And Richard Rubinstein insists that I now call him Richard, not Mr. Rubinstein.

It took well over five years to research and write this book, something I also did not anticipate. I figured, having had the experience of writing the book on *Day,* that perhaps things would be quicker and easier this time around; it was anything but. From dealing with cast and crew who didn't want to participate, to wrestling with the complexities of a film that endured severe weather issues – meaning pinpointing filming dates was rather tough – to confronting my own self-doubt about whether I could actually pull something like this off again, there were substantial challenges to overcome and much work to be done.

I first saw *Creepshow 2* during its opening weekend in May 1987 at the Tara Cinemas, formerly the Weis Cinema Centre, in Savannah, Georgia. My Mom dropped me off at my favorite cinema that day, like she so often did, and I sat in the same auditorium in which I had first watched *Superman: The Movie, The Empire Strikes Back, Raiders of the Lost Ark, Return of the Jedi, Indiana Jones and the Temple of Doom, The Return of the Living Dead,* and *Aliens* in. So, *Creepshow 2* is up there for me with some of the most memorable films I saw at the theater when I was young and impressionable. It's a film that truly grows on you, and you find yourself appreciating its charms even more upon repeated viewings. To learn years later just how steep of a mountain to climb making this film was makes my appreciation for it even greater. As you'll see in the pages to come, the production was beset with problems and the fact that it turned out as good as it did is a testament to the people who were there each day turning lemons into lemonade. That's not an easy thing to do, but this dedicated cast and crew did just that.

Lee Karr

Pittsburgh, PA

June 2021

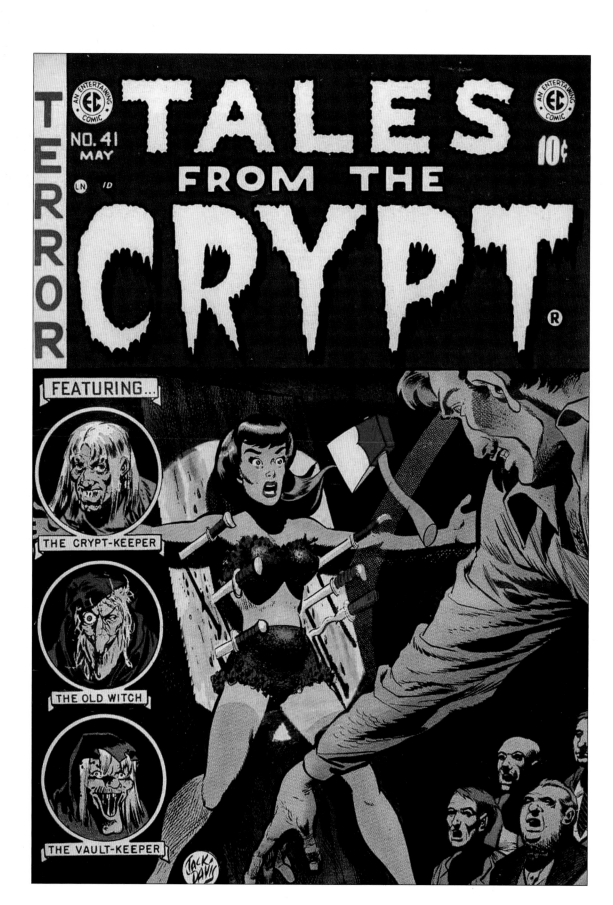

8

Chapter 1 Two Creeps Are Better Than One

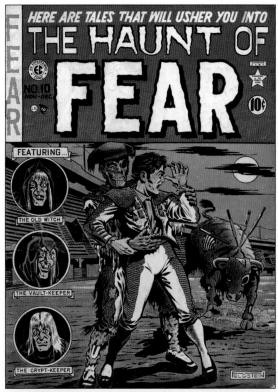

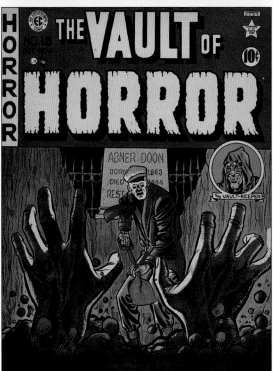

A LAUREL COMIC IS A MORAL COMIC. That catchy tagline, conjured from the mind of author Stephen King, would adorn the back of crew t-shirts during the 1981 Pittsburgh filming of Laurel Entertainment's *Creepshow*. An ode to the notorious E.C. comic books of the 1950's, *Creepshow* paid tribute to grotesque titles such as *Tales from the Crypt*, *The Vault of Horror*, and *The Haunt of Fear*. With stories like *The Thing from the Grave!*, *Doctor of Horror*, and *The Living Mummy!* E.C.'s tales operated with their own ghoulish sense of morality where evil doers received their just desserts in a variety of morbid ways. Director George A. Romero and writer Stephen King both grew up on the lurid comics and sought to bring the visceral shocks and scares that the comics provided, and that they so enjoyed as kids, to a new generation, only this time on the big screen.

"My mom hated those gruesome E.C. comics of the fifties, but she let me read them...until the nightmares started," King is quoted as saying. "Nightmares where people were on baseball teams disemboweling the bad guys and lining the base paths with their intestines. That was one of my favorites. They used his head for the ball and this one eye was bulging out as the bat hits it. That's when she said, 'OK, that's enough', and started taking them away. And that's when I started buying them and putting them under my bed." **(1)**

"I was only allowed to read things like *Pogo* and *Donald Duck*," Romero told *Cinefantastique* magazine. "I smuggled the E.C's in, though! I'd go somewhere with them and listen to some Alan Freed!" **(2)**

Originally known as "Educational Comics" for titles such as *Picture Stories from the Bible* and *Picture Stories from American History*, "Entertaining Comics", or E.C., would gain notoriety in the early 1950's for its graphically violent horror comics. Publisher William Gaines and his top editor, Al Feldstein, along with artists like Johnny Craig, Graham Ingels, Jack Kamen, and Jack Davis (a Georgia boy, like your humble author) helped to introduce a new type of macabre "forbidden fruit" to members of the "Silent Generation", as well as to "Baby Boomers".

In his fantastic 1981 non-fiction book *Danse Macabre*, a meditation on the horror genre's popularity, Stephen King spoke to the lasting impression that the E.C. comics had on him. "Those horror comics of the fifties still sum up for me the epitome of horror, that emotion of fear that underlies terror, an emotion which is slightly less fine, because it's not entirely of the mind," writes King. "Horror also invites a physical reaction by showing us something which is physically wrong." **(3)**

Indeed, the pages of E.C. comics provided plenty of imagery which could be considered "physically wrong":

Far left and left above and below: E.C. titles such as *Tales from the Crypt*, *The Haunt of Fear* and *The Vault of Horror* would create quite a controversy during the early 1950's. (copyright William M. Gaines Agent, Inc.)

Above: William Gaines(left) and Al Feldstein pose with some of E.C.'s popular titles in their New York City office. (copyright William M. Gaines Agent, Inc.)

be-headings, dismemberments, and other ghastly sights were on display each issue. And yet, while E.C. comics were known for this type of over the top violence, there was oddly enough a sense of morality and justice that was at the heart of many of their stories, as warped as it might be. "It wasn't necessarily that good triumphed over evil, because the triumph was not necessarily good," recalled Al Feldstein. "But something happened that gave a kind of morality to it - twisted, I must admit - but a morality." **(4)**

"In the old E.C. comics the guilty were always punished," said Stephen King to *Fantastic Films* magazine. "That was the traditional American view of morality; even our novels and other writings, which were considered great literature, tended to be that way. Then, after World War I and World War II, we started to get the idea that, although the cause of 'good' won, the 'good' also got their guts blown out or died from inhaling gas. Also there was the murder of five million Jews. You have to keep in mind that the people involved in this, William Gaines, Al Feldstein, were Jewish. I don't know what they would say about it, but it's significant to me that biblical 'Good over Evil' comics became 'horror' comics after the Holocaust. It was the last gasp of the romantic idea that evil is punished by the forces of good. They couldn't justify that idea anymore, so what you started to get in the E.C.'s was the story that the wife really does kill her husband and run off with her lover...they bash the poor guy over the head and drop him into the lake with bricks wired to his feet. And they get away with it. So you have to introduce a supernatural element to get the scales back into balance." **(5)**

Interestingly enough Al Feldstein addressed such notions in a 1981 interview, one in which even he found it difficult to say what their motivations might have truly been at the time. "But *primarily* - and that's why I want to leave the analyzing to you people - *primarily*, while reflecting our personal feelings and maybe reflecting a lot of our unconscious feelings, these stories that Bill (Gaines) and I wrote were commercial ventures to produce a magazine that would entertain people and *sell*," Feldstein told *Squa*

Tront magazine. "To get to the nitty gritty of what we were feeling, or what our personal lives were like is something that's difficult for me to do, especially thirty years later." **(6)**

Much like the doomed victims of the comics themselves, E.C.'s popular horror titles would die a grim death by the mid 50's. In April 1954 a U.S. Senate Subcommittee was held in New York City to examine juvenile delinquency, with particular attention paid to the comic book industry. One of the individuals to testify during that investigation was psychiatrist Dr. Fredric Wertham, author of the just published *Seduction of the Innocent*, which was a study of "the influence of comic books on today's youth". Wertham's theories contended that the violence portrayed in comics like the ones published by E.C. could inspire children to act out in a similar fashion.

"It is my opinion, without any reasonable doubt and without any reservation, that comic books are an important, contributing factor in many cases of juvenile delinquency," Wertham asserted. "There arises the question, what kind of a child is affected? And I say again without any reasonable doubt and based on hundreds and hundreds of cases of all kinds that it is primarily the normal child. Mr. Chairman, American children are wonderful children, we give them a chance they act right. And it is senseless to say that all these people who get into some kind of trouble with the law must be abnormal or there must be something very wrong with them. As a matter of fact the most morbid children that we have seen are the ones who are least affected by comic books because they are wrapped up in their own fantasies." **(7)**

Wertham even suggested that reading comic books prevented children from using "proper reading techniques", meaning moving from left to right on the page, and went as far as to say that the issue of comic books or "crime comic books", as he defined them, was a "public health problem". During his testimony, Wertham openly stated for the record his view of comic books as being "smut and trash" and illustrated this point by showcasing the story *Foul Play*, the gruesome baseball revenge tale published the year prior in *The Haunt of Fear*, which Stephen King admits was one of his favorites.

None of this, as you can imagine, sat well with E.C. publisher William Gaines, who volunteered to speak in front of the Senate Subcommittee to refute Wertham's notions. "Our American children are for the most part normal children. They are bright children," Gaines testified. "But those who want to prohibit comic magazines seem to see instead dirty, twisted, sneaky, vicious, perverted little monsters who use the comics as blueprints for action. Perverted little monsters are few and far between, they don't read comics. The chances are that most of them are in schools for retarded children. What are we afraid of? Are we afraid of our own children? Do we forget that they are citizens, too, and entitled to the essential freedom to read? Or do we think our children so evil, so vicious, so simple minded that it takes but a comic magazine story of murder to set them to murder, of robbery to set them to robbery?"

Perhaps his best salvo though was directed squarely at the good doctor himself - Wertham. "I was the first publisher in these United States to publish horror comics. I'm responsible, I started them," read Gaines from his prepared statement. "Some may not like them; that's a matter of personal taste. It would be just as difficult to explain the harmless thrill of a horror story to a Dr. Wertham as it would be to explain the sublimity of love to a frigid old maid." **(8)**

Sadly, less than a year later, after public backlash and the creation of the new Comics Code Authority, E.C. ended publication of the horror titles. No longer would graphic carnage mixed with silly puns from the Vault Keeper or the Old Witch be available on newsstands for impressionable youths to devour. "Well, there were a lot of parent groups, the Catholic church was incensed at that point, there were some Protestant groups, and the idea just got around and appealed to everybody, that the problems they were having with kids came from comic books," Gaines told *The Comics Journal* in a 1983 interview. "And I can understand, after all, kids all of a sudden, after being relatively well-behaved, maybe were starting to misbehave. The people in the 50's didn't *begin* to know what was coming in the 60's and 70's (laughter), but at the time they may have been upset by what they thought was dreadful behavior, and I guess they were all looking around for the first scapegoat. In this world, nobody wants to be blamed for anything, so they picked on somebody." **(9)**

Not long afterwards, Gaines began concentrating solely on the enormously successful publication for which he would end up being best remembered for: *Mad* magazine.

Just prior to a summer of 1979 get-together - one which would prove to be the genesis for *Creepshow* (we'll get to that shortly) - Stephen King, George Romero, and Romero's producer and business partner, Richard Rubinstein, had also huddled up regarding King's popular novel, *'Salem's Lot.* Concerned with the number of vampire related projects coming down the Hollywood pipeline and not wanting to be late to the party, as well as being impressed by Romero's quirky vampire tale, *Martin,* Warner Brothers approached Romero and Rubinstein about their interest in reworking one of the many already commissioned scripts for *'Salem's Lot,* including one penned by King himself. "So, I was pretty excited about it," Romero said to *Fantastic Films.* "And I spoke to Steve on the phone then went up to visit him. That's when we met. He was excited about the process of doing *'Salem's Lot;* I wanted to go back to his screenplay. So we got to know each other." **(10)**

That phone call from Romero would be quite a moment for the up-and-coming novelist, a moment he promptly shared with his wife, Tabitha. "I dropped my pants...! I mean, I couldn't believe it, man," King told *Starburst* magazine. "I just walked in and said, 'Do you know who called me on the phone today? George f***ing Romero...called me on the telephone. You hear me?' And she said, 'Who's that?' And I said, '*Night of the Living Dead*...the movie you walked out of because you were so scared!'" **(11)**

Unfortunately for King and Romero *'Salem's Lot* would end up in the hands of another film-maker, Tobe Hooper, and in a different format than had originally been envisioned as well - a harbinger of things to come for the dynamic duo. "We bowed out of that as soon as we found out they wanted to do it as a TV mini-series instead," Romero is quoted as saying in *Cinefantastique* magazine. "I wasn't going to Burbank to make a TV movie." **(12)**

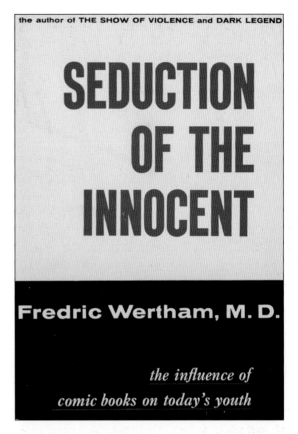

Above: Dr. Fredric Wertham's book, *Seduction of the Innocent,* was a major nail in the coffin for the E.C. horror titles. (copyright 1954, Rinehart & Company)

An aside from that original meeting, and a fateful one at that, was an offer made to Romero and Rubinstein by King. In a story which has become legend, King offered up his novels, whose rights were still available, and told Romero to take his pick of the litter. That pick was the massive post-apocalyptic tale, *The Stand.*

The idea for *Creepshow* would be born during a 1979 summer get-together when Romero and Rubinstein would return to Maine, this time with their families, and pay a visit to King's summer home in Center Lovell. The meeting would center on ideas for a horror project which they could produce as a way of gaining momentum for what their true end game was: an adaptation of King's *The Stand.* "We talked about making *The Stand* as a feature but realized it would be a tough sell given the for sure high budget cost when compared with our low budget credentials," says Richard Rubinstein. "Steve then suggested he had an idea for a medium budget anthology feature film inspired by the 1950's E.C. Comics. George liked the idea. I asked Steve if he had a title in mind. He responded *Creepshow.* I asked Steve how long it would take him to write a script and he answered two months. 58 days later Steve's first original screenplay was on my desk."

Creepshow would be more than just an attempt by King and Laurel to curry favor with major studio backing, however.

It was also born out of love, a love for things that go bump in the night. And as far as Stephen King was concerned, this was an opportunity to really scare audiences like never before. "The way I described *Creepshow* to George originally was when they show the movie, they shut the doors and not let anybody out," said King to *Pittsburgh* magazine. "And when it was over, people are gibbering and crawling up the aisle with JuJubes in their hair because they've been trying to cram themselves under the seats. To which George says, 'I hear you talking.'" **(13)**

For King the prospect of working with Romero was an especially exciting opportunity. His admiration for Romero would appear in print in late 1979/early 1980 when he penned an article for *Rolling Stone* magazine about the year in movies. In the "The Horrors of '79" King would discuss the abundance of genre films or films with dark and heavy subject matters released that year. In particular he paid attention to a low budget independent film you might have heard of - *Dawn of the Dead* - ranking it ahead of such respected films that year as *The Deer Hunter*, *Apocalypse Now*, and *Alien* as the best film of 1979. "For unreal horror, no movie released in 1979 can top George Romero's *Dawn of the Dead* - the finest horror film of the year, perhaps of the decade," King enthusiastically wrote. But he would not stop there and went even further with his praise for *Dawn's* director. "Romero may well be *the* director of the Seventies; even more than Coppola, he gives us that exciting sense of a unified vision, an idea dovetailing neatly with creative bent and emotional commitment." **(14)**

The admiration wasn't just a one-way street though, as Romero admired King's talents just as much. In the afterword to *Fear Itself: The Horror Fiction of Stephen King*, Romero described the feeling each time he picked up a newly released King novel. "I eagerly enter the pages of a new Stephen King book with lighthearted joy and great expectations; not unlike the feelings I remember having as a kid entering an amusement park," Romero wrote. "He knows the same people I know, he's been to the same gas station, the same Seven-Eleven, he listens to the same rock and roll that's on my local AM band, and I know damn well he's been to an amusement park not too far from my hometown. I hear ya, Steve, and I love ya, and I'm not afraid to say it." **(15)**

Now it should be noted that the idea of creating a horror anthology inspired by the works of E.C. Comics was certainly nothing new. In the early 1970's, Milton Subotsky's production company, Amicus, produced film adaptations of *Tales from the Crypt* and *The Vault of Horror*. And while the adaptations were well crafted and fun, featuring well known stars, they weren't exactly what King and Romero had in mind for their potential comic book movie. "Neither George Romero nor I felt the Subotsky films worked very well," King told *Heavy Metal* magazine in 1980. "We'd like to do five or six or seven pieces, short ones, that would just build up to the punch, wham the viewer, and then you'd go on to the next one." **(16)** Interestingly enough years later Subotsky would co-produce King adaptations such as *Cat's Eye* and *Maximum Overdrive*.

Not long after that meeting in which the idea for *Creepshow* was spawned Romero and Rubinstein would enter a three-picture agreement with Salah and Richard Hassanein's United Film Distribution Company, who had released the highly successful *Dawn of the Dead* for the self-described "Cecil B. DeMilles of Pittsburgh". The deal would produce Romero's updated version of the Arthurian legend, *Knightriders*, the final installment of Romero's living dead trilogy, *Day of the Dead*, and nestled in between those two the E.C. inspired comic book come to life, *Creepshow*. Meanwhile, King would continue cranking out best-sellers such as *Firestarter*, *Cujo*, *Christine*, and *Pet Sematary*. Funny enough, King would set *Christine*, the story of a haunted 1958 Plymouth Fury, in Pittsburgh and dedicated the book to Romero and his wife at the time, Christine Forrest Romero. Down the road, Romero's name would become attached to the screen adaptation of *Pet Sematary* as well. Development, however, of *The Stand* as a theatrical would turn out to be too tough of a nut for the trio to crack and by 1985 Romero left the production company he helped form with Rubinstein, Laurel Entertainment. Eventually *The Stand* would be produced for television in 1994, but without Romero's involvement. Frustratingly, a similar fate was also visited upon Romero with *Pet Sematary* in 1989.

Released in November 1982 *Creepshow* would prove to be a moderate success, both at the box office and with critics. It was the number one movie in America in its opening weekend and would gross back its entire shooting budget of nearly eight million dollars in its first five days of release alone. By its second weekend, however, it would be bested by a re-release of *The Empire Strikes Back* and by the third week lagged behind *E.T.*, which was in its 25th week of release! Reviews were mixed, with probably no better example of this than the difference of opinion between well-known critics, Roger Ebert and Gene Siskel. Reviewing the film for the *Chicago Sun-Times* Ebert said, "Romero and King have approached this movie with humor and affection, as well as with an appreciation of the macabre." **(17)**

His counterpart, Siskel, however, writing in the *Chicago Tribune*, was a little less kind. "*Creepshow* joins two masters of horror - film-maker George Romero and novelist Stephen King - and proves that two minds are not necessarily better than one. In fact, it is hard to believe that either man would have made such a bad film working without the other." **(18)**

Despite those mixed reviews and modest box office returns almost immediately plans were set in motion to produce a sequel. "Steve King and I both feel the same way; and we've made a sort of private pact, that if we get the chance, we will do another," Romero told *Fangoria* magazine. "There are a number of things we'd really love to do, some that would require a little more money...if the opportunity presents itself." **(19)**

The key word in that quote is "money". That issue - the need for more of it - might be as synonymous with the film career of George Romero as even, say...zombies! Having enough of a budget was always an obstacle for the gifted artist and when it came to the sequel for the comic book come to life his view, in the opinion of this author, was completely justified. "The original *Creepshow* was the only movie that I directed that ever made it to number

one on the *Variety* charts," says Romero. "So, I thought *Creepshow 2* should have had some respect and some better treatment *budgetarily* than it did. And that was it. I just thought at every corner there was something that went wrong, there was something with the budget that wasn't there, and blah, blah, blah."

By late winter/early spring of 1983 Laurel Entertainment was already beginning to set the table for *Creepshow II*, as it was referred to then, with Roman numerals. But instead of Romero being at the helm again, there was thought of giving someone else a shot behind the camera. "Ideally, we'd like to get to a point where there's a picture a year from George and I, and one picture a year from another writer-director," Richard Rubinstein said to *Fangoria* magazine. "Laurel would in such a case act as an umbrella, raise the money, provide the production expertise and a seasoned crew with the kind of experience that would provide a first-time director with the kind of support he'd need in that situation." **(20)**

Now, while Rubinstein and Romero were certainly looking to expand and give other talented artists opportunities at directing, one of the possible reasons why Romero decided to take a back seat this time around was due to his interest in a potential new superhero project with a very well-known comic book company. Laurel, looking to branch out from strictly horror related fare, had negotiated a deal with the then Editor-in-Chief of Marvel Comics, Jim Shooter, who also happened to be a Pittsburgh native, on a new superhero character entitled *Copperhead*, sometimes

Above: Horror icons George Romero(left) and Stephen King during the 1981 filming of *Creepshow* in Pittsburgh, PA. (copyright 1981, Laurel-Show, Inc. / 1982, Warner Brothers, Inc.)

referred to as *Hero of the Century*, and later to be known as *Mongrel*. "Somebody at Marvel, I don't know who it was, some executive, met Rubinstein,'" recalls Shooter. "Anyway, the first thing I knew about it was that I was asked to participate in a meeting with George Romero, Richard Rubinstein, the president of the company, Jim Galton, and I think - *I think* - Alice Donenfeld."

During that initial meeting things began slowly, with little to no progress on ideas, and that's when Romero decided to break the ice. "George Romero, he said - I don't know the exact words, but more or less - 'Screw this. Hey, Jim, let's go to lunch.' So, I said, 'Yeah, fine. Let's go.' So, anyway, the meeting broke up and George and I went off to have lunch. It was a little favorite place of ours, just right around the corner, so I took him there. And we just sat there and we were talking and he was talking about things that had crossed his mind - various, random thoughts and stuff; nothing coherent. I mean, neither of us had a real coherent idea at that point. But, then I said some things and he said some things, so we go back and forth," Shooter says. "Anyway, so we cooked up the basis of this idea about something in the future with a character who was half man, half robot - a theme which I had done before - and basically the very, very foundations of an idea."

From there Shooter and Romero would continue to exchange ideas, something not lacking in Romero's fertile

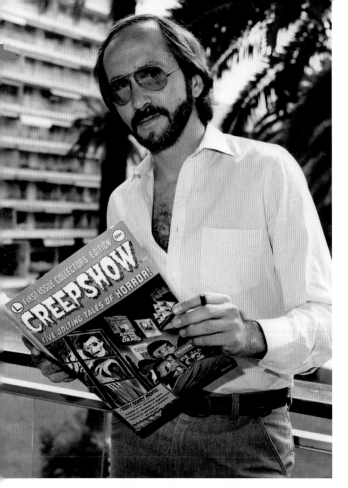

Above: Laurel Entertainment President, Richard P. Rubinstein, would shepherd *Creepshow 2* through development hell from 1984 until 1986 before finally striking a deal with Bob Rehme at New World Pictures. (courtesy of Lee Karr)

imagination. But it soon became apparent to Shooter that it would be his duty to rein in George's concepts and structure them into something cohesive. "See, now, at that point I thought that, well, you know, I'm the creative guy and George knows the business; he'll be the guy who puts the nuts and bolts in, right? Just the opposite," admits Shooter. "I mean, George, can't say enough good (things) about him, but he is not a technician, you know? I mean, he had a million ideas, all kinds of ideas, millions of them - not well organized. And so I found myself being the architect. So, most of the things in *Mongrel* were at least based on stuff that George said. But, I was the one who came up with the reasons for stuff and I added to them and then I strung it together and made it work. And George, kind of weirdly...I mean, we came up with the idea of this future law enforcement guy in a time where there was sort of almost civil war and anarchy and all that stuff. And, I thought he was a good guy. Now, here's the thing: see, George is kind of a little to the Left of Karl Marx, you know. So, his first take on it was kind of like *V*, the anarchist. The people who were just like completely, you know, far to the Left were the good guys. And, I thought, 'You know, I don't want the Republicans to be the good guys, but gee that's a little extreme. I mean, sorry, but I was trying to split it down the middle here.' And I'll give you an example: George's first title for the work was *Copperhead Conquers the Warhawks*.

So, okay, you've gotta be on the side of these radical Leftists and conquer the Republicans? I'm like, 'What? Uhhh...' First of all that title, I think, was, sorry, kind of small time - *Copperhead Conquers the Warhawks*. I mean, that sounds like something that, you know, New World Pictures at their lousiest would make. I'm serious, man. It was, like, you couldn't make a Canon film out of that. Anyway, I said, 'Wait a minute. Wait a minute. How about we take these elements and we play with them?' You know, no one's the good guys. There are these guys that think this and there are those guys that think that. And the ending is going to be this guy who starts out being on the government's side, eventually realizes that's not a good side. And then he gets on the other side and then he eventually realizes that's not a good side. And the big grand ending is that there's no choice but for *him* to take over."

Now, just for the sake of clarity, while it might sound like Shooter was slightly critical of Romero and his take on the project that would be a misrepresentation of how Shooter viewed the Pittsburgh horror icon. He understood, just as much as say a Stephen King, the caliber of talent he was working with in Romero. "He'll smoke you, man. He's very, very...I don't know, brilliant, I guess, is a good word. What it does is it challenges you and then you gotta rise to their level and fire all your guns and try to keep up. But, he's one of those guys. And I've sat with some 'bigger' names and I thought, 'Yeah, whatever. I can do what this guys does, no problem.' But with George, I mean, there's stuff he was just coming up with and I was like, 'I would have never have thought of it', you know," says Shooter. "Because the thing is, George came up with all kinds of stuff: a creature called the Myrmidon, because Achilles' soldiers were called Myrmidons. You know all this great stuff that I had to find a way to make it work. But, a lot of it was just brilliant and would have been tremendous visuals, *tremendous* visuals."

The project was something that excited Romero a great deal and had it come to fruition, who knows what could have happened with Romero's career? Maybe he would have had the type of resume Sam Raimi eventually created years after *The Evil Dead* when he helmed his *Spider-Man* trilogy? Unfortunately we'll never know as the project would languish in limbo for several years before eventually dying just before a similar themed project would hit screens in 1987, *Robocop*. "I'm really looking forward to seeing you...and *really* looking forward to working on this," wrote Romero in a letter to Shooter at the time. "It's our (Laurel's) favorite project...and it seems to be getting a lot of favorable interest." **(21)**

Besides the potential project with Marvel, Romero had other irons in the fire which would prevent him from directing this go around. Thanks to Laurel acquiring a two-million-dollar fund upon going public in 1980 the up-and-coming production company had some money in the coffers and decided to utilize that money on various properties. One of those was *The Sisterhood*, a 1982 novel by Michael Palmer about a group of nurses who form a "secret society" to end the suffering of patients in a Boston hospital through euthanasia. Another was an adaptation by Romero of Mary Shelley's classic *Frankenstein*, a film which Romero saw

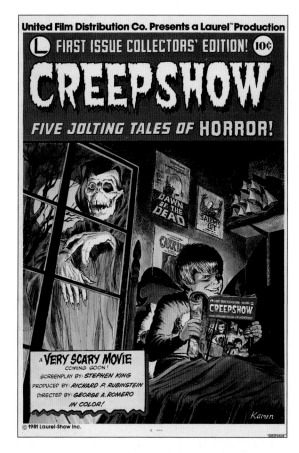

Above: The teaser poster for the original *Creepshow*, featuring brilliant artwork from famed E.C. artist Jack Kamen, would be discarded by Warner Brothers for a new theatrical poster featuring Joann Daley's equally as brilliant design. (copyright 1981, Laurel-Show, Inc. / 1982, Warner Brothers, Inc.)

and loved as a youth in one of its re-releases. And lastly, of course, there was *Day of the Dead*, which Romero was scripting during this period.

And on top of all of that there was a feeling of having already accomplished what he had wanted with the original *Creepshow*. "I guess I felt all along that I had done it," Romero told *The Film Journal* in 1987. "Stephen and I really enjoyed working on the first one. We had a lot of fun with it, but neither one of us was greatly enthused about doing it again. For no reason other than that it's just sort of a one-trick pony. I just felt that we had designed the format for it and it's like a TV series. If it ever gets to Part Four, if we get an itchy finger, we might be able to step back in and do it again." **(22)**

So, with that in mind and with Romero's plate already overflowing, that meant someone else would need to be chosen to step behind the camera and direct. And that's where it got interesting.

In April of 1983, just six months after the release of *Creepshow*, George Romero drafted a five-page letter to Laurel's senior vice president and head of production and finance, David Vogel. The letter, encouraged by Richard Rubinstein, would place Romero officially on record for who he believed to be the best candidate, or candidates, to helm *Creepshow II*. The letter reads much like a Romero script: very descriptive, written in a more personal and less formal tone, with a dash of wit and humor thrown in for good measure. But besides being his typically fun and lighthearted self, Romero is also frank and brutally honest about his perceptions of each candidate. For Romero there were four potential successors and he ranked them in the following order: 1) John Harrison, 2) Tom Savini, 3) Michael

Gornick, and if necessary 4) Tommy Lee Wallace.

In Romero's eyes Harrison was the most polished of the three Laurel in-house candidates, viewed almost like a "politician", to quote Romero. Words like "flexible" and "resilient" are used to describe him and without question Harrison was Romero's preferred choice. "When George and I were having dinner in New York one evening, the subject came up. It was early days and I don't think the project was fully green-lit. He did ask if I'd be interested. Nothing definite," says Harrison. "By the time it was, I may have been involved with several things on the west coast. Memory is a little foggy on the chronology."

Regarding Savini, Romero felt he ranked second due to his name recognition and should he succeed as director that could serve the company well many times over in the future. Savini had already proven himself a master makeup effects artist, as well as working in front of the camera as an actor and stuntman. Logically his next step would be to direct and Savini was enthusiastic about that possibility. "If you had the choice of being just an actor, just a special effects guy, just a film-maker, or all of the above, you know, I would want to choose all of the above. And all of the above is available when you direct," Savini stated in the *Fangoria* magazine video documentary *Scream Greats*. "What was the line in *All That Jazz*? 'To be on the wire is to be alive, the rest is waiting.'" **(23)**

That brings us to number three on Romero's list, the man

Above: The May 4, 1983 advertisement in *Variety* for future Laurel Entertainment productions, including the first appearance of Jack Kamen's *Creepshow 2* teaser art in black and white.

who would indeed direct the film, Michael Gornick. Before I go into detail discussing Romero's critiques and analysis of him and why he placed third in the initial running I want to take a moment to speak to the caliber of person Michael Gornick is. Had it not been for Michael, I would have never known about the existence of Romero's letter. At a certain point, very early on, Michael came to me and presented the letter telling me that if I was going to tackle this project and do a thorough job then I should know about it. Frankly, the letter hurt him. But that feeling of hurt didn't prevent him from allowing me access to it and making use of it in these pages. He is the definition of a "stand-up guy", willing to do anything to help a friend. "He's a very good guy. I tell you I could call Mike up today and say, 'Mike, I got a flat on the 405. Will you come up and help me out?' And he would be here," laughs George Romero. But hyperbole aside, Romero is absolutely correct. That's the kind of man I've personally always known Michael Gornick to be.

In discussing Gornick, Romero would express a level of apprehension regarding his emotions and whether he felt he could keep them in check, especially with a major studio such as Warner Brothers involved and peering around the corner, which they were at this point. "The potential 'stress points' that I'm referring to are: reactions to criticism; capacity to 'juggle' creatively without feeling threatened; and capacity to make objective decisions under the 'fire' of big-finance," explained Romero. "I have a hard time with these, myself, but I've seen Mike come close to 'walking' under such pressures in his capacity as D.P., and in 'Post'."

Romero continued his evaluation believing that a smaller project, with less involvement from higher ups, would best serve Gornick at that particular time. "This is not a statement about talent. I think we should find a project for Mike on which his exposure would be lessened; something, for example, which is financed by Salah (Hassanein) alone, so that 'us kids' are basically running it except for one or two 'Papal visits'," Romero wrote. **(24)**

As mentioned, Romero's letter was a painful and disheartening reality for Gornick to confront. Their relationship went back to the days of The Latent Image, the production company Romero had formed prior to Laurel, and knowing Romero's real feelings was sobering for Gornick. "Probably as disappointing as hearing Mom and Dad talk about you; in this case - Dad. And realizing that he may have had low to no confidence in you, in that one aspect," confides Gornick. "I mean, to learn that he had some reservations in terms of, I guess, what might be called my 'creativity' really hurt. It had to hurt, you know? It's like realizing, 'Wow. That's what you think about me, Dad? That's too bad. Can we talk?'"

Ultimately, Romero's view of who was best suited to direct speaks for itself. "Mike was one of the best friends that I ever had in the business! I mean, we used to sit in a mixing room and chat and have these great conversations all the time. And then, you know, all of a sudden...I don't know. I shouldn't say," Romero confides. "But anyway, I just wouldn't want to get back into that controversy right now (laughs). And that's it. If you have a document that shows that, then that's exactly...those basically are my same feelings, even today."

The letter would also discuss potential "hired guns", other genre directors outside the Laurel team, that either had been suggested by David Vogel or contemplated by Romero in some form or fashion. Big names such as Wes Craven (*The Hills Have Eyes*), Sean Cunningham (*Friday the 13th*), and Joe Dante (*The Howling*) are mentioned in passing, while lesser known talents such as James Glickenhaus (*The Exterminator*), Allan Arkush (*Rock 'n' Roll High School*), and Ulli Lommel (*The Boogey Man*) were also given consideration. But for Romero, his top choice for an outside talent would fall with John Carpenter disciple, Tommy Lee Wallace.

"*Halloween III* was a 'not-so-hot'...but the problem was *mostly* in the script. There is a good bit of 'theatricality' in it...check it out," Romero suggested. "The biggest single reason that makes me trust Wallace, is the fact that he was Carpenter's editor on John's hottest stuff. That makes him the only guy, on either list, to have worked on films that are *truly* GOOD...bordering on great." **(25)** It's noteworthy that Romero remarks that Wallace, having worked on films like *Halloween* and *The Fog* for John Carpenter, was the only candidate who had worked on something that was "truly good...bordering on great", considering that Gornick, Harrison, and Savini had all worked in some capacity for Romero on *Dawn Of The Dead* and *Creepshow*. It gives you an insight into how Romero viewed his own work in the genre and as an artist in general.

Another interesting revelation from the letter is Stephen King's perception of the original *Creepshow* and the level of violence on display in the film. According to Romero,

King relayed his thoughts on the matter through written notes and expressed a desire for more "blood and guts" this time around, a notion Romero didn't necessarily agree with. "He said something to me like: 'Audiences will walk in expecting the fun scares that they got in the first film... we should take 'em off guard and kick 'em in the kidneys with some real gross-out violence',", wrote Romero. "I don't think Steve was ever really pleased about the amount of 'lightheartedness' in CREEP 1...and I suppose that somewhat of a 'shift' toward a higher 'gross-out' level might make CREEP II do better at the old-B.O. than it would if it were a pure imitation of its ancestor, but I opt for sticking with the basic 'style' of the original." **(26)**

"I remember Steve wanted *Creep 2* to be more graphic," confirms Richard Rubinstein.

Just a few months after the release of *Creepshow*, February 1983, word was already spreading in industry trades like *Variety* that Laurel was in talks with Warner Brothers to release a sequel to the modest box office hit. By March, in that same trade publication, it would be publicly announced that Romero would officially step away from the director's chair this time for the planned sequel.

In May 1983, Laurel Entertainment placed a nine-page advertisement in *Variety*'s 26th International Film Annual for their upcoming film projects and included in that spread was the first artwork for the recently announced *Creepshow 2*. Just as they had done with the original *Creepshow*, Laurel hired former E.C. artist Jack Kamen to create the advertising art (and in the opinion of this author, he did a superior job to his already iconic art from the original). Kamen's art showed the Creep, the ghoulish spectre last seen peering through young Billy's bedroom window as he read his *Creepshow* comic book in the dark by flashlight, this time working a newsstand holding up a copy of the newest issue of *Creepshow* as an enthralled Billy looks on.

One interesting side note regarding Laurel's relationship with Jack Kamen is the one he shared with Richard Rubinstein. "Jack Kamen is a very close friend of my father's. When I was born, in Brooklyn, Jack and his wife lived next door to my parents," Rubinstein shared with *Fangoria* magazine. "I used to sit on his lap while he did E.C. work." **(27)**

These were heady times for Richard Rubinstein's Laurel Entertainment. During this period numerous projects and ideas were in the works, including one with John Harrison called *Imagine That!* Other possibilities included a cable TV talk show with John Wilcock, one of the co-founders of *The Village Voice,* and an untitled script by Carol Marner about a female New York City police officer leading an investigation into a woman rapist who preys on men. Another potential idea floating around the Laurel offices during this period involved 3-D technology. Romero was even in preparations to write a brief ten-minute screenplay to utilize as a test of the new 3-D system, which his longtime financiers, Salah and Richard Hassanein of United Film Distribution, were involved in. Of course, rumors had swirled during this time that possibly *Day of the Dead* would be a candidate for 3-D, but that never materialized. And originally Romero had considered doing one of the episodes for the first *Creepshow* in 3-D, back when the project was first being

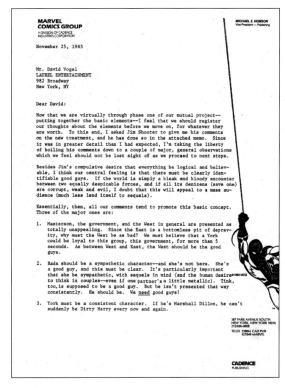

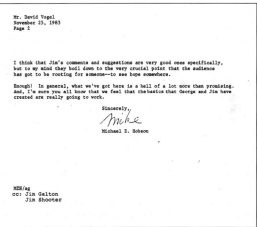

Above: November 1983 letter from Marvel Comics' vice president of publishing, Michael Hobson, to Laurel Entertainment's David Vogel regarding the joint superhero project George Romero and Jim Shooter were working on. (courtesy of Jim Shooter)

formulated in 1979. Laurel even had interests in entering the world of off-Broadway productions! It was a diverse and eclectic strategy that Rubinstein had in mind for his young company.

Much like the decision of who would be best to direct *Creepshow 2*, the story of its screenplay and the path it took to reach the screen is equally fascinating. Five stories, like the original film. No, make it four stories. This story is in, that one's out - eventually ending with three stories. Man, where should I begin with this subject?

April 12, 1983

TO: David Vogel
From: George Romero
Re: Directors for CREEPSHOW II
CC: Richard Rubinstein, Michael Gornick

Dear David,

Richard has suggested that it might be appropriate for me to offer a list of my suggestions for CREEPSHOW II directors. Since I responded to him in a "closed" memo, I'm sending this off to you directly.

First of all, my "list" is small, and, I have "verbalized" it, to both you and Richard, but I admit I haven't "presented" my views in a cohesive package, so here goes: First choice: John Harrison, Second choice: Tom Savini, Third Choice: Michael Gornick, and Fourth (should we have to go with somebody more "credentialed") Tommy Lee Wallace.

The reason I pick Harrison over Gornick: Mike might not be emotionally ready (particularly on his first time out) to deal with the pressure. I'm not saying we shouldn't give him a chance. In fact, now that he has aggressively expressed his desire, we definitely <u>should</u> give him a chance. But to "try" him on a project where Warners is directly involved, might not serve us, or the project <u>or</u> Mike. This is not a statement about talent. I think we should find a project for Mike on which his exposure would be lessened; something, for example, which is financed by Salah alone, so that "us kids" are basically running it except for one or two "Papal visits".

The potential "stress points" that I'm referring to are: reactions to criticism; capacity to "juggle" creatively without feeling threatened; and capacity to make objective decisions under the "fire" of big-finance. (I have a hard time with these, myself, but I've seen Mike come close to "walking" under such pressures in his capacity as D.P., and in "Post".)

Mike has always held himself in check, cooled himself down, and come back to perform at his customary 150% level, but to make his first picture be one that's this much of a "fishbowl" could endanger the degree of "smooth ness" with which the production comes off, and could wind up being a disserv-ice to Mike himself. (It is vitally important that things at least "appear" to go smoothly. This is the first "deal" that has Salah spooning bucks into a film without me directing. If it "goes down" easily, we can expect to make other non-Romero deals "go down" easily.)

Harrison is supremely flexible and resilient, if he's nothing else. He's a "Polit-ician" and he has "managed"; his corporate and producing background will make it easier for him to relate to "Mark the Shark", who, I understand, is our Warner Bros. contact (In fact John knows Mark). John is just as familiar with the material as Mike. Plus, if John directs, we get the benefits of both talents, because Mike can contribute, in the million other ways that he usually does, even if he doesn't "shoot". I fully respect the sensitivity of the political issue here, and I agree that, should it work out with John, Mike needs to be given a position of authority.

I rank Savini above Mike (again, not considering talent) but simply because of his "<u>name</u>" value. He's actually "better known" (on a retail level) than any of the directors I've seen on the "lists" that have come through here. Did you ever see an eight page spread on James Glickenhaus?

Savini just might be "acceptable" because of his name. He certainly has no "self confidence" problem (in fact, that's his biggest drawback, but you've been able to keep him reasonably in check). And if he "comes through", he could (again because of his "name") become somebody we could easily "bank" again and again.

John, Tom and Mike, in that order, comprise what I will refer to, from here on, as our "Inside Team". People who intimately know the material, and our working style. People who are "relatives", "family", if you will. People from whom we can expect a higher degree of loyalty; who are more likely to stick with us after the fact and become "bankable" in an ongoing way. All other candidates, I will call "Hired Guns". Now, of course, we might "luck out" and find some outsider who "falls in love" with our style, but everybody in this category is an "unknown entity". And even personal interviews can't give us enough information as to "what they're really like". (Hliddal turned out to be fine, Giuliano turned out to be a jerk.)

Besides, most of the "suggested" people are already getting some degree of work, are likely to be more expensive than our "Insiders", and, most importantly, are likely (if they're good) to want to put too much of their own stamp on a film which MUST be imitative, stylistically, of the "motherfilm".

On this subject of who's "good" (in my opinion, of course)...let me respond to your "lists":

Craven, Cunningham, Dante, Lieberman and Sholder are the "cut-em-up-in-the-woods" boys. That's not quite true of Dante, and his work is the best of the batch, with Cunningham running an "inconsistant" second, but "my socks-have-still-been-on" after seeing films by any of the five candidates. (In the case of Sholder, I just noticed that you include ALONE IN THE DARK in your bracket labeled "PBS Dramas"...I'm talking about ALONE IN THE DARK, the theatrical "slice and dicer". Am I wrong and the bracket right, or vice-versa?) Anyway, most of these films "suque", and the good ones employ a "nitty-gritty" naturalism which is anathema to the "theatricality" of a film like CREEPSHOW. (Dante is the only one who shows more pizazz, but he's likely to be "out of reach...and "difficult".)

Lommel's BOGEY MAN was interesting in a brooding kind of way, but slow and un-suspenseful. I don't know Lord's foreign titles, but VISITING HOURS was wretched! Rosenthal proved he couldn't imitate a clear-cut predecessor when he couldn't even imitate the simplistic "kill-him-and-he-keeps-coming" drum-beat of HALLOWEEN (actually it was a synthesizer beat).

Roth I don't know at all (never saw any of the titles). James (get that boy a press agent) Glickenhaus is a "revenge" director of singularly incoherent films. (THE SOLDIER does have some uniquely "nasty" violence in it, but it's really un-glued.) Tommy Wallace I'll get to later, so that completes "LIST #2.

LIST #1: Despite your note, which protested that there was no particular "preferential" order intended, I notice that Harrison is found in the last position (where his credits appear as particularly inadequate after the other entries). Tommy Wallace is on the "reject" list (Savini and Gornick didn't even make that).

I'll take them in backwards order. (That puts John "first", but you know my opinion there, so let's move on...) ...to Peter Crane. THE SIEGE OF 31, AUGUST was quite warm, actually, and there were some very intelligent shot selections (important when you're doing a "40-shot 4-day wonder"). It's hard to tell much, though, from this kind of production, because so much of the "style" (lighting, number of shots, etc.) is subject to "formula" and to the influence of a "mill-hand" support staff. (While 31, AUGUST has a nice "theatrical" look and feel, ALL television is more "theatrical" than it is "nitty".) Anyway...super hard to judge, but I "suspect" this is a bright and diligent guy who we should keep our eyes on. Did we get his name from Garber? I understand he did the effects on this. (By the way, I couldn't find the Paul Lynch segment, "advertised" in your note, on the tape.)

Flynn is the "Vendetta King" in my book, too, but we don't want "meanness" do we? (Steve might. Witness his notes about wanting more "blood and guts" in CREEP II. He said something to me like: "Audiences will walk in expecting the fun scares that they got in the first film...we should take 'em off guard and kick 'em in the kidneys with some real gross-out violence".) I don't think Steve was ever really pleased about the amount of "lightheartedness" in CREEP I...and I suppose that somewhat of a "shift" toward a higher "gross-out" level might make CREEP II do better at the old-B.O. than it would if it were a pure imitation of its ancestor, but I opt for sticking with the basic "style" of the original. Let me know what you think. As you know, I happen to believe that the stories themselves are more fun, E.C. and more fun - as a whole body - than the stories in CREEP I...but then Steve's not writing the screenplay, so his dialogue, style, etc., will be missing.) Anyway, Flynn may be the "last of the good B directors", but we don't need his "nasti-ness"...nor are we making a B picture, in the usual sense (at least in style... we're talking about a comfortable schedule...a lot of shots...our kind of production values...and..."theatricality", I keep coming back to that word.)

Freedman, I'd say "no" to. BORDERLINE was "way total dull" and KANSAS CITY BOMBER was "like skanky to the max". (Also, Ed told me that Freedman was a semi nurd.)

Arkush...Pretty good. I liked DEATHSPORT's outrageousness (borrowed and copied from Bartell's DEATH RACE 2000...copied pretty well). ROCK AND ROLL HIGH SCHOOL is lots of fun, and HEARTBEEPS is warm and somewhat "theatrical"...I don't see anything that relates to "scariness", though, or "suspense", so...who can tell?

Franklin: Who knows about PSYCHO II? PATRICK was "ok", but again (he looked down as the lights came up) my socks were still on.

That covers LIST #1. Officially, and "for the record" (just so nobody can say that I never even "reacted" to the suggestions) I'll say that, of the names on the "LISTS", my "top three" would be Wallace, Arkush, Crane. Of course, if Dante became available, we'd have to consider it, though I'd resist strongly if it meant paying "large dollars" (if we're gonna pay "BIG", let's go after a "BIG" name).

I said I'd get back to Tommy Wallace. HALLOWEEN III was a "not-so-hot"... but the problem was mostly in the script. There is a good bit of "theatrical-ity" in it...check it out. The biggest single reason that makes me trust Wall-

ace, is the fact that he was Carpenters editor on John's hottest stuff. That makes him the only guy, on either list, to have worked on films that are truly GOOD...bordering on great...(qualifiers: Some of Flynn's work is really good, although outside the genre. I think Dante is a really good director, but the films he's gotten so far have not been.) Tommy's worked INTIMATELY on bitchin' stuff with a bodacious director (HALLOWEEN was like awesome.) He's a "stylist" (and he was Art Director on ASSAULT ON PRECINCT 13, so he has an understanding of design, which is important in CREEPSHOWs).

Anyway, that's why Tommy's my choice in terms of "Hired Guns". (He's also a real easy guy and a total non-Hollywood type who would LOVE to work in an environment unencumbered by bull shit.)

Bottom line...I'd like to keep it in the family. I think we'll be best served by an "Insider". I understand that I'm making a deal with myself, here. I understand that both Salah and Warners have to agree. My feeling is that we could ultimately "sell" someone like Harrison to Salah, assuming we put in a real effort to that effect, and don't fold at first resistance. I think I could sell him with a phone call...subject to Warners approval, of course. (DAD: "I'll say yes if your mother says yes." MOM: "I'll say yes if your father says yes.") As to Warners...I dunno. "Mark the Shark" might...he just might...go for the idea, based on our rapport with Harrison in terms of work-ing style and creative "sympathy" (especially if we wind up having to do a "square-dance" around whatever union problems arise because of Warners "up front" involvement. I also realize that if we can't "dance" the unions, that could knock our "Insiders" out of the box totally, unless they can get into DGA and are inclined to do so.)

It's a matter of "salesmanship"...(we've gotta sell what we want, in order to get what we want). It's a matter of not bowing to the first line of defense. It's a matter of pushing. We just might score. Given that the other "creative" controls are being so carefully horded by Warners, the director might not be so important to them. I think they feel, ultimately, that we're not going to get a "GREAT" director on this project...and I think they must realize (as we should) that most of these other guys (the "Hired Guns") are either un-proven or are proven...to be "hacks"! If Warners insists on a "Hired Gun", they're insisting on the basis of "experience" purely...it seems that we can "back up" our "Insiders" with OUR experience...we can, in essence, "guarantee" their performance with our own "in-house" capacities.

I realize that in trying to measure "Insiders" against "Hired Guns", I'm compar-ing apples to oranges in the sense that with the "Insiders", I'm using "personal-ity" and "familiarity" as criteria, whereas I'm discussing "Hired Guns" (and often rejecting them) on the basis of "talent". (The "BIZ" seems to create this kind of dilemma. I mean...GANDHI having to go up against TOOTSIE? Really!!!) But ALL WE KNOW from the "Hired Guns" is their work (except for a few hours of meetings in a couple of cases). And I point out that the work could LIE!

MOST of what we know from the "Insiders" is "personal", but we know it well from being involved very closely with all of these folks for a long, long time. PLUS their "talents", while none have a "credit" for directing a feature, are not "unknown" to us (they've each actually "directed" sequences in my films and in others). Their instincts are good, in all cases, and they've each been around the set "a whole bunch".

"The stories were all there as possibilities. Steve threw this whole bundle of stories at George, so they were available; how we parceled them out was up to us," recalls Michael Gornick. "That's how trusting Steve was. Can you imagine this world renowned author putting so much trust in to a place...I mean it shows a lot of respect for George, obviously."

For the longest time the belief has been that just like the first *Creepshow* its sequel was to have five stories, with a wraparound segment as well. *The Cat from Hell*, *Old Chief Wood'nhead*, *The Raft*, *Pinfall*, and *The Hitchhiker* would be the five tales showcased in the script. This has been the scuttlebutt amongst fans for years and George Romero himself is even on record having stated so! "Right after the original *Creepshow*, Steve agreed to do *Creepshow II*. Not to do the screenplay, but he contributed five stories," Romero is quoted as saying in the book *Dark Visions*. "A couple of them were published stories, *The Cat from Hell* and *The Raft*, and a couple of them were just idea sketches that he had. From that material I wrote a screenplay for *Creepshow II*, which was composed of five stories and a wraparound, just like the original *Creepshow*." (28)

Now, here's where it gets interesting and a bit confusing as well. In researching this book I gained access to three different screenplays. One was the production script, which contained just the three filmed stories and the wraparound. We all know those to be *Old Chief Wood'nhead*, *The Raft*, and *The Hitchhiker*, so we'll put that aside. The other two scripts were early drafts from 1984. The first 127-page draft, dated January 10, 1984 contained four stories, not five. Those stories were *The Raft*, *The Hitchhiker*, *Pinfall*, and *Old Chief Wood'nhead*. The second 112-page draft is not cover dated, however its date of registration with the United States copyright office is May 23, 1984. And like Romero's first draft, it too contains only four stories, not five. Those stories were *Old Chief Wood'nhead*, *The Raft*, *Pinfall*, and *The Cat from Hell*. Now, how curious is that? Was there ever a script that contained all five stories? If so, I could not locate one. A search with the U.S. copyright office turned up nothing. In fact, I was surprised to find out that the first draft wasn't in their database either, only the second draft.

Some of the key players involved with the production, unfortunately, were not much help here. Stephen King, forget it. I have as much chance of interviewing King as I do becoming the Mayor of Pittsburgh. Michael Gornick only had his production script. Richard Rubinstein was nice enough to answer some of my questions, but I used

In the interest of "selling" my perspective, which I intend to fight for, to both "outside" and "inside" parties...I don't want to see a "LIST" go out of here yet, to either Salah or to Warners. We shouldn't "publish" anything at all until we have a united front behind a "First Choice"...we can back up from there.

I'm sure we'll get "LISTS" from "them" (THEM! THEM! AAAAAAARGH!). But what do you think those lists are going to look like? They'll be the "Who's Who" of Slice-N-Dice. Unless there's some "favoritism" going on somewhere, we might be able to overthrow their "catalogs" for the reasons I've cited above.

Finally...and this is my MAIN point, really...ALL of the "Hired Guns" (including Tommy Lee), being UNKNOWN ENTITIES to us, we have no reason to go in "selling" them...even to the extent of throwing their hats into the ring. If we're going to wind up with an outsider (whose politics we don't know, who's disciplines we don't know, who's style we can only interpret from sources that are not "all-telling")...LET WARNERS MAKE THE PICK! Or at least, let's us make the pick from their list (if, and only if, they insist... at gunpoint). In other words, if something's gonna go wrong, let it be "on them", not on us. Our "Insiders" we can cover for if there's a problem. (We could cover for a "Hired Gun" too, but why should we use up our energies on somebody we don't know...and don't "owe"...and suppose the problem runs the other way...suppose it's OUR fuck-up we have to cover. The "Insiders" are likely to give us a hand in that regard, rather than "blow the whistle" on us.) As I said...this project going off "smoothly" is very, very important to us...and to you, David, in terms of "selling" you as producer on MARVEL and on other "bigger" projects.

I understand that a more experienced director might also cause things to go smoother, but there's a higher likelihood of the reverse. I also understand that my views "are not necessarily the views of this station or its affiliates". You know that I'm always open to discussion on this, but I don't want to see any "gun jumping" damage done to my candidates because we make premature statements to Salah or to Warners. I don't want to wind up arguing over something that's already a fait accompli because somebody already made an "informal" arrangement over breakfast. I'm sorry, but I know how these things can go when you "business-side guys", Laurel's primary negotiators, want to "influence" things in a direction for whatever reason. That's why I want us to make our internal decision before speaking to anyone on the outside.

I know this is your first project as Producer, David...well, welcome to your first "hassle"...(I shouldn't say that, maybe there's no hassle here at all...we'll talk in N.Y. in the beginning of May, unless this winds up having to be decided sooner than that, in which case, there's always the telephone.)

All the best...hope I didn't mess up your day.

Pages 18-21: George Romero's 5 page letter to Laurel Entertainment's David Vogel regarding who would be the best choice for the director's chair on *Creepshow 2*. (courtesy of Michael Gornick)

up my allotted time with him. David Vogel never returned any requests for an interview. David Ball wasn't involved at that point with the production. That leaves the man who wrote the screenplay himself, George Romero. What would he recall about those early drafts? "I don't even remember that! I don't, man," says Romero. "I mean, somebody came around recently with some sort of a script that was supposedly the fourth story. I don't know, was it...what did they not do? They did *Wood'nhead,* right?"

There was one other option I considered, but I just couldn't bring myself to ask because of the sensitive nature of the request. Romero's former wife, Christine, who I have a friendly relationship with, had once mentioned to me that she had taken a large portion of George's work related possessions and placed them in storage for their daughter, Tina, to have one day. Could George's original passes at the script and Stephen King's notes that he sent to George for those scripts be in there? Possibly, yes. However, George passed away during the writing of this

book and I felt it would be too intrusive, so I just couldn't bring myself to ask such a thing. And as fate would have it, most of George's files were donated by his family to the University of Pittsburgh for posterity for the George A. Romero Archival Collection in Pittsburgh. During the late editing stages of this book I was able to gain access to some of those archival files and sadly I was unable to find any notes or different versions of the screenplay.

As for King, he too is on record regarding the script. In an insightful 1989 interview from the book *Feast of Fear*, King spoke with *The Zombies That Ate Pittsburgh* author Paul Gagne about the process of creating the film's screenplay. "I sat down and did sort of a notebook. I don't know how other people's film treatments look, but I knew what we were after, particularly after the first film. I pretty much scripted the wraparound story, where this kid is chased by a bunch of juvenile delinquents, except they changed it from live action to animation. It follows what I did pretty closely though. In terms of the stories, I wanted to start off with a Jack Davis kind of story. It was about a dead bowling team," King told Gagne. "Anyway, I put down about seven or eight ideas. Then I did sort of the same thing I did with George when he and I first got together - I just asked him to pick whatever he liked. The notes I sent him were pretty detailed, and they even had some dialogue, but George really carried it off. He scripted four, including the bowling story, the hitchhiker story, *The Raft*, which is based on one of the short stories in *Skeleton Crew*, and *Chief Wood'nhead*, an original story about a wooden Indian that comes to life. I had actually started that one as a short story, but it fit the film perfectly so we used it there. Anyway, George sent me the script, and I suggested some cuts and some changes, and some of them were made and some were not. He's a darn good writer." **(29)**

As King mentioned, the script for *Creepshow 2* was a combination of previously published material, along with some original story concepts. King had done the same thing with the first film incorporating the stories *Weeds* (*The Lonesome Death of Jordy Verrill*) and *The Crate* into that film's script, both of which had originally appeared in adult magazines, *Cavalier* and *Gallery*, respectively. And speaking of men's magazines, I guess there's no better place to start our breakdown of the history and background of each story than by spotlighting one with quite a history in the pages of men's magazines. It's perhaps the oldest one from King's library related to the film - *The Raft*. I say oldest because while *The Raft* wouldn't officially see publication until its appearance in the November 1982 issue of *Gallery* magazine, according to King the story dated back to the late 1960's when he was on a beach one day and noticed a wooden float out on the water. After putting to paper quite a gruesome little tale, King would eventually try it out on a live audience. "I remember reading the story at a coffee house," King told *The Twilight Zone* magazine. "And having people almost throw up." **(30)**

The Raft tells the story of four college students - Deke, Randy, LaVerne, and Rachel - from the fictional Horlicks University in Pittsburgh who decide to take a late day jaunt out to Cascade Lake to "say good-bye to summer". Instead they end up saying good-bye to their lives as a mysterious, dark organism floating in the lake stalks and eventually devours each one by one. The characters are archetypal: Deke is the jock, Randy is the brain, Rachel is the cute, but shy girl, and LaVerne is more of the sexy, party girl type. King's story is at times funny - the joking between Deke and Randy and their habit of calling each other Pancho and Cisco is enjoyable and relatable - but for the most part the tale is truly horrifying as the situation becomes very dire for the protagonists.

In his 1985 book *Skeleton Crew*, a collection of short stories, including *The Raft*, King discussed in the book's "Notes" section the origin of the story. "I wrote this story in the year 1968 as *The Float*," wrote King. "In late 1969 I sold it to *Adam* magazine, which - like most of the girlie magazines - paid not on acceptance but only on publication. The amount promised was two hundred and fifty dollars." **(31)** The reason King mentions that sum of money is because in the spring of 1970 he would find himself in a bit of legal trouble with the town of Orono, Maine for confiscating traffic road cones. Apparently King had hit a few which damaged his vehicle and he took out his displeasure by rounding up as many as he could and placing them into the back of his station wagon. The story goes that King was eventually charged with petty larceny, fined $250, and given seven days to come up with the money or else face 30 days in jail. It was then that King would receive his "deus ex machina", as he phrased it, when a check for $250 arrived in the mail from *Adam* magazine for his story of *The Float*. "It was like having someone send you a *real* Get Out of Jail Free card," King wrote. **(32)** This apparently meant that the story was now in print, but according to King he never received a copy from the publisher and never found one on a newsstand as well. To this day, no one has ever reported possessing a copy or having read the story in the magazine.

King is also on record when he was interviewed by Richard Wolinsky and Lawrence Davidson for the Berkeley, California radio show *Probabilities* in 1979 as saying that Doc Lowndes, a well-known editor of science-fiction and fantasy publications, who had previously published other King stories, had purchased *The Float*, but the story never ran because his magazines went under.

Years later, King would decide to revisit the story. "Somewhere along the way I lost the original manuscript, too," King wrote in *Skeleton Crew*. "I got to thinking about the story again in 1981, some thirteen years later. I was in Pittsburgh, where the final *Creepshow* editing was going on, and I was bored. So I decided to have a go at re-creating that story, and the result was *The Raft*. It is the same as the original in terms of event, but I believe it is far more gruesome in its specifics." **(33)** It's very interesting that King revamped the story during the making of *Creepshow* because in an interview with Paul Gagne published in 1989's *Feast of Fear,* King briefly mentions possible stories that could have made their way into the original *Creepshow* screenplay, *The Float* being one. Ultimately, of course, King would reject the idea.

As previously mentioned, *The Raft* would make its first appearance in print inside the pages of *Gallery* magazine in November 1982. Rather than publish it the standard way inside its pages, the publisher opted to print it as an insert, a mini novel, if you will, complete with an illustrated

cover. And the gentleman responsible for creating the art for that cover was Peter Catalanotto, who would take an understated approach for the horror tale. "I wasn't familiar with Stephen King's work although I knew of him from the huge success of *Carrie* and *Salem's Lot*," recalls Catalanotto. "I wanted the image for *The Raft* to be more ominous than scary. The sunglasses left on the empty raft atop dark water conveyed something wasn't right. I think a good illustration lures the reader to the story. With a title like *The Raft* it was pretty clear what to showcase. The teens in the story were mere fodder for the terror. I respected that the art director let me do something subtle as opposed to scantily clad teens screaming and cowering."

Catalanotto would use watercolor, his preferred medium, to create the image, and layered it to give it a richer feel. "Often I work dark to light, the opposite of how water color is taught, where I'll scrub away paint to achieve a soft glow," says Catalanotto. "The water around the 'blob' on the upper right of the raft was scrubbed away to accent the evil darkness."

The following summer, in June 1983, the story would appear again, this time in the pages of *The Twilight Zone* magazine, featuring beautiful color artwork for the front cover of the issue, as well as an atmospheric black and white illustration from David Klein inside. It's interesting to note that going from the pages of a nudie magazine to the more tame pages of a sci-fi/fantasy/horror fiction periodical might seem a bit strange, but *The Twilight Zone* fell under the umbrella of Montcalm Publishing, the same publisher of *Gallery*.

Two years later in 1985 the story would resurface once more in *Skeleton Crew*, published by G.P Putnam's Sons. Apparently in the interim, King took the time to polish a few things about the story or perhaps reinserted what had possibly been edited out from *Gallery* and *The Twilight Zone*; while there's nothing earth shatteringly different about the story, there are little changes made throughout that are of interest to the hardcore fan. Some of the subtle, yet noticeable, differences featured in the *Skeleton Crew* version of the story include the album resting on Randy's stereo, which is no longer a new Triumph album, but instead a new Night Ranger one. Most of the song lyrics and remembrances in Randy's mind, such as the TV show *Route 66* towards the end of the story, are in place here, while a good bit were removed in the *Gallery* and *The Twilight Zone* versions. And lastly, in the *Gallery* and *The Twilight Zone* versions, Randy simply looks at the dark creature in the water and says, "Show me something pretty", before the inevitable takes place. However in *Skeleton Crew* he asks the creature to sing with him to Gary U.S. Bonds' hit *School is Out*, "I can root for the Yankees from the bleachers...I don't have to worry 'bout teachers...I'm so glad that school is out...I am gonna... sing and shout." He then whispers, "Do you love?", before accepting his fate.

An interesting sidenote regarding the 1985 *Skeleton Crew* release was that an alternate limited edition, Stephen King signed version of just 1000 copies was released by Scream Press featuring illustrations from artist J.K. Potter. *The Raft*, of course, is featured with truly gruesome black and white imagery of a bloodied Deke (presumably) being pulled down through the raft's boards, his chest torn open and rib cage exposed.

The next story we'll cover is *The Cat from Hell*, one that has quite a long history in print before its eventual bow on the silver screen in another Richard P. Rubinstein production, 1990's *Tales from the Darkside: The Movie*.

The story of *The Cat from Hell* centers around a hitman named John Halston, who has been summoned to the Connecticut countryside mansion of old man Drogan, a wealthy shut-in who is in need of Halston's services. The target of the deadly contract in which they enter upon is a cat, a "hellcat" as it is referred to. According to Drogan, the cat was responsible for the deaths of his sister, Amanda; her friend, Carolyn Broadmoor; and a hired family servant, Richard Gage. Fearing the cat is a demon sent to punish him for his family's deadly pharmaceutical experimentations on felines, Drogan desperately turns to the hired assassin to solve his problem. In the end, as you might suspect, the cat winds up taking the contract killer out instead - and in gruesome fashion, no less.

Like *The Raft*, King's *The Cat from Hell* would begin its life in print in the pages of an adult magazine, this time *Cavalier*. In the "Sunset Notes" section of his 2008 book *Just After Sunset*, another collection of his short stories, which featured *The Cat from Hell*, King touched on the genesis of the story about the vicious "hellcat" with a taste for murder. "It came about in an amusing way," King writes. "The fiction editor of *Cavalier* back then, a nice guy named Nye Willden, sent me a close-up photograph of a hissing cat. What made it unusual - other than the cat's rage - was the way its face was split down the middle, the fur on one side white and glossy black on the other. Nye wanted to run a short story contest. He proposed that I write the first five hundred words of a story about the cat; they would then ask readers to finish it, and the best completion would be published. I agreed, but got interested enough in the story to write the entire thing." **(34)**

The opening portion of *The Cat from Hell* would appear in the March 1977 issue of *Cavalier* magazine, along with the contest announcement mentioned by King. Readers would need to complete King's story, with a minimum of 1500 words and no more than 4000. The winner would receive $500 and his or her story would be published that summer in *Cavalier*. King's grisly conclusion to the tale would appear three months later in the June 1977 issue of the magazine. That September, the winning entry, written by Phil Bowie, who initially submitted his winning entry under a pseudonym, would be published just as *Cavalier* promised. Later that year, in December, the second place winner, Marc Rains, would see his version of the story's conclusion printed in *Gent* magazine, a "sister" publication of *Cavalier*. Suffice it to say that both winning stories were very different than the one King himself concocted, but it was certainly an interesting gimmick by the publisher. And it would end up being a worthwhile gimmick for Bowie who would go on to a long freelance writing career, with several novels to his name.

As years passed, *The Cat from Hell* would end up in several anthologies including *Tales of Unknown Horror* in 1978, *Magicats!* in 1984, *Twists of the Tale: An Anthology*

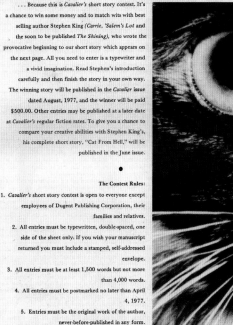

Here's one story you'll have to finish yourself:

... Because this is *Cavalier's* short story contest. It's a chance to win some money and to match wits with best selling author Stephen King (*Carrie, 'Salem's Lot* and the soon to be published *The Shining*), who wrote the provocative beginning to our short story which appears on the next page. All you need to enter is a typewriter and a vivid imagination. Read Stephen's introduction carefully and then finish the story in your own way. The winning story will be published in the *Cavalier* issue dated August, 1977, and the winner will be paid $500.00. Other entries may be published at a later date at *Cavalier's* regular fiction rates. To give you a chance to compare your creative abilities with Stephen King's, his complete short story, "Cat From Hell," will be published in the June issue.

●

The Contest Rules:

1. *Cavalier's* short story contest is open to everyone except employees of Dugent Publishing Corporation, their families and relatives.
2. All entries must be typewritten, double-spaced, one side of the sheet only. If you wish your manuscript returned you must include a stamped, self-addressed envelope.
3. All entries must be at least 1,500 words but not more than 4,000 words.
4. All entries must be postmarked no later than April 4, 1977.
5. Entries must be the original work of the author, never-before-published in any form.
6. The judges will be the editorial staff of Dugent Publishing Corporation, whose decisions will be final.

CAVALIER : 23

Above: The contest page for Stephen King's *The Cat from Hell*, featured in the March 1977 issue of *Cavalier* magazine. The story, originally featured in an early version of the *Creepshow 2* screenplay, would eventually hit screens in 1990's *Tales from the Darkside: The Movie*. (copyright 1977, Dugent Publishing Corp.)

of *Cat Horror* in 1996, and the previously mentioned *Just After Sunset* in 2008. Interestingly enough the film adaptation featured in 1990's *Tales from the Darkside: The Movie* would be directed by none other than John Harrison.

The third story in our examination is *The Hitchhiker*. Now, discussing this story and its history is a little more difficult because it was never published like *The Raft* and *The Cat from Hell* and King has never really spoken a great deal about its background publicly, at least that I'm aware of.

The Hitchhiker is the tale of Annie Lansing, an adulterous wife on her way home one evening after a session with her gigolo, who accidentally hits a man hitchhiking on the interstate. Her decision to leave the man for dead on the side of the road comes back to haunt her, literally, for the duration of the story, as the hitchhiker continues to reappear, terrorizing her as she desperately attempts to make her way home. Looking worse as the night goes by, taunting Annie with, "Thanks, lady. Thanks for the ride." The hitchhiker finally delivers Annie's comeuppance in the garage of her home.

An interesting difference from Romero's script to the eventual completed film is that the story takes place in Romero's western Pennsylvania rather than King's Maine, with Romero mentioning Interstate 79, instead of I-395, and the hitchhiker instead looking to make his way to Harrisburg rather than Dover.

According to the U.S. copyright office, *The Hitchhiker* was registered on September 7, 1983. It is registered alongside the other stories featured in the film, including the wraparound segment, with the odd exception of *The Cat from Hell*, which isn't found anywhere relating to a motion picture until a date of execution of May 27, 1987. This was when it was to be incorporated into *Tales from the Darkside: The Movie*, which was still a couple of years from beginning its production. *The Hitchhiker* is listed as "Text" for the type of work, as are the other stories, and is registered as three pages long. It was meant to be a possible replacement story in the original *Creepshow* for *They're Creeping Up On You*. If so, wouldn't it be much longer than three pages? Yes, you would think. So, a bit of mystery remains regarding its background - sort of like the hitchhiker himself.

With this being the case, it's interesting to wonder if King was influenced by the classic radio play of the same name written by Lucille Fletcher (*Sorry, Wrong Number*) in the early 1940's. In the radio drama, performed by the legendary Orson Welles, a man, Ronald Adams, is driving from New York City across country to California and encounters a hitchhiker on the side of the road. At first, he sees him on the Brooklyn Bridge, then later on the Pennsylvania Turnpike (interesting to note that Adams remarks during the story that he "had a good night's sleep in Pittsburgh"), and later on in Ohio. After continuing to see the mysterious hitchhiker, who is desperately attempting to flag Adams down during his trip, Adams eventually decides to pick up a woman in need of a ride to keep him company for the rest of the drive. After seeing the man yet again while driving through Texas, Adams nearly has an accident while behind the wheel. In a panic, the woman flees the car, having never seen the hitchhiker herself. Adams, fearful he could be losing his mind, stops at a payphone in New Mexico to call home to his mother and it is then that he learns the shattering truth. A woman answers the phone and informs Adams that his mother was hospitalized for a nervous breakdown over the death of her son, Ronald, who was killed several days prior in a car accident on the Brooklyn Bridge.

Fletcher's chilling story was born out of a real life incident that occurred in 1940 when she and her husband, Bernard Herrmann - yes, the same Bernard Herrmann who would go on to compose the scores for such classic films as *Citizen Kane*, *The Day the Earth Stood Still*, *Psycho*, and *Taxi Driver* - were driving and saw a man on the Brooklyn Bridge and then later on the Pulaski Skyway. After that, they never saw him again, but it inspired Fletcher to pen the story for Orson Welles as a ghost tale a year later for his popular radio show. Welles would go on to perform the story several times, complete with a haunting musical score by Bernard Herrmann. "A story doesn't have to appeal to the heart, it can also appeal to the spine," Welles said in his 1942 radio introduction to the story. "Sometimes you want your heart to be warmed and sometimes you want your spine to tingle. The tingling, it's to be hoped, will be quite audible as you listen tonight to *The Hitchhiker*." **(35)**

Two decades later, in 1960, Rod Serling would adapt the story for his new anthology television show *The Twilight Zone*, this time changing the lead to a female.

The next tale on our ghoulish ledger is a classic E.C. style narrative of macabre vengeance, *Old Chief Wood'nhead*. Like *The Hitchhiker*, the story of *Old Chief Wood'nhead* was an original one and had never been published. And also like *The Hitchhiker,* King hasn't really spoken much publicly about the story, which makes delving into its background and origin a little bit of a challenge as well.

Old Chief Wood'nhead tells the tale of Ray and Martha Spruce, an elderly couple who run a general store - complete with a cigar store Indian out front - in the dying town of Dead River. Ray Spruce, always the optimist, believes in his small western town and the people in it. Many of the downtrodden townsfolk are in debt to him for his kindness and for allowing them to make purchases from his store without the means to pay at the time. One of those people is Benjamin Whitemoon, a local tribesman, who brings to the Spruces a collection of treasured jewelry from his tribe as collateral for the debt his people owe. Later that evening, the Spruces are victims of a vicious robbery by a young gang of hoodlums, looking to make themselves a score before heading to California. One of the young punks is Sam Whitemoon, nephew of Benjamin, who murders the couple over the Indian treasure - "the keys to the city of Los Angeles", as he puts it. The group of thugs never makes their getaway to Hollywood though as the old cigar store Indian comes to life and hunts each one of them down delivering retribution in the manner only a Native American warrior could.

The two-page text for *Old Chief Wood'nhead* was registered with the U.S. copyright office, again, with the other stories in September of 1983. It is important to remember that King mentioned to Paul Gagne in *Feast of Fear* that he initially began *Old Chief Wood'nhead* as a short story.

Perhaps the most celebrated story from the early drafts of *Creepshow 2*'s screenplay is one that wouldn't make it into the movie and as of this writing has yet to be adapted for film - *Pinfall*. The story is easily the most E.C.-inspired tale from either of the *Creepshow* films. It is King's tip of the hat to *Foul Play* - one of the most notorious stories from the E.C. archives, the same story that prompted his mother to take away his horror comics, and the same one that Dr. Fredric Wertham would spotlight in his book *Seduction of the Innocent* as well as in front of the U.S. Senate Subcommittee on juvenile delinquency in 1954.

Narrated by the Crypt-Keeper himself, *Foul Play* is about a heated baseball playoff game between Central City and Bayville for the "Bush League" pennant. Central City's star pitcher, Herbie Satten, is so obsessed with winning said pennant that he executes a murderous plot in which he takes out Bayville's star second baseman, Jerry Deegan, by sliding into second base while attempting to steal and spiking him with poisoned spikes on his cleats. The scheme works as Satten strikes out the disoriented Deegan to end the game and Central City wins the pennant. Immediately upon striking out, Deegan drops dead right on the baseball diamond. Afterwards it is discovered by Bayville's team doctor that Deegan was poisoned and the culprit is Herbie Satten. Bayville brain-storms their own plot to avenge Deegan by luring Satten to the stadium, appealing to his

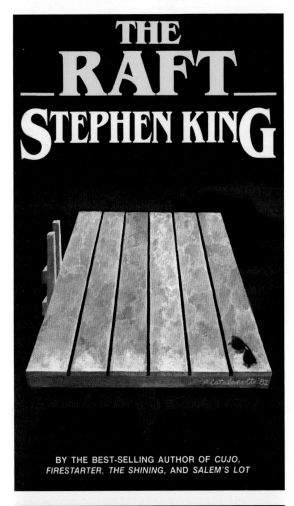

BY THE BEST-SELLING AUTHOR OF *CUJO*,
FIRESTARTER, *THE SHINING*, AND *SALEM'S LOT*

inflated ego, a big mistake for ole Herbie. The story ends with a Grand Guignol flourish as the Bayville team "play ball" with the remains of Mr. Herbert Satten: his heart is home-plate, his intestines line the base paths, and his head is the ball. "Herbie, the pitcher, went to *PIECES* that night and was taken *OUT*...out of *EXISTENCE* that is!" cackled the Crypt-Keeper at the end of the gruesome tale. **(36)**

A one-page piece of text for *Pinfall* was registered with the U.S. copyright office in September 1983. The man responsible for turning that text into the story that would become *Pinfall* was, of course, George Romero. "I wrote it from a couple of pages that Steve had sketched out. It was my total favorite," Romero told *Cinefantastique* magazine. "It was like the old E.C. baseball story where they used the guy's body parts for the base bags. It was that kind of grim humor. It was my *fave*! I thought it had the best, funniest characters. And I thought it was the best suited for the comic book premise." **(37)**

Pinfall is the hilarious and morbid tale of two rival bowling teams at the Big Ten Lanes bowling alley: the Regi-Men, a snooty band of white-collar types led by the obsessive Reggie Rambeaux, and the Bad News Boors, a group of drunken slobs led by the coarse Chooch Mandolino. The story really kicks into gear when J. Frederick MacDugal, the tenth wealthiest man in the world, and also an avid bowler, passes away and leaves a large sum of prize money for the Big Ten Lanes team that has the highest score at the end of the season. After falling behind Chooch and the Boors in the rankings, Reggie decides to ensure victory for his Regi-Men by making sure the Boors are no longer a factor in the competition. The Boors vehicle is sabotaged by the Regi-Men, ultimately leading to their deaths, as the aptly named boorish bowlers lose control of their van, plummeting down a cliff in a fiery crash. The murderous Regi-Men never see the fruits of their diabolical labor though as they are paid a late night visit at the bowling alley by the re-animated and burnt-to-a-crisp corpses of the Bad News Boors. The story concludes with the Boors drinking bloody beers and bowling Reggie's head down the lane to take out the pins, which in this case are the arms and legs of the Regi-Men.

The humor in Romero's script is silly and broad; the dialogue and character descriptions that much sillier and that much broader. For instance, he describes Chooch Mandolino as a *"Donkey Kong* look-alike" and the Regi-Men are portrayed as "Moonie-like clans on *Family Feud*". Another example would be one day during "training" the Regi-Men are out jogging and Reggie leads them in a classic military style limerick by shouting, "There was an old guy named Dave, who kept a dead whore in a cave, he'd often admit, 'I'm a bit of a shit, but think of the money I save.'"

And much like he did with *The Hitchhiker*, Romero can't help but sneak in a wink and a nod to his beloved Pittsburgh as towards the end of the story he describes the Big Ten Lanes bowling alley as looking like "Three Rivers Stadium after a Steelers loss"; it's simply classic Romero,

Above left: The cover for the mini novel of Stephen King's *The Raft*, with art by Peter Catalanotto, featured in the November 1982 issue of *Gallery* magazine. (copyright 1982, Montcalm Publishing Corp.) **Below left:** The June 1983 issue of *The Twilight Zone* magazine with Stephen King's *The Raft* gracing the cover. (copyright 1983, TZ Publications, Inc.)

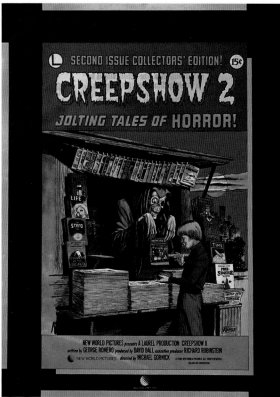

describing a scene so on the nose in only the way he could. Romero is truly in his element with the story and he doesn't hold back. As you read the script you get the feeling that the author is having a very good time writing it. And, of course, at the end there's zombies and all the fun that they bring. It's a fantastic and fitting tribute to the legend of E.C. comics. "I really thought *Pinfall* could be the topper," says Michael Gornick. "It's a wonderful story, wonderful story."

And tying it all together in a nice little bow is the wraparound story of young Billy and his adventures with a gang of bullies. King's three-page wraparound would be registered with the U.S. copyright office in September 1983, listed officially as "Creepshow II - frame story". As King mentioned earlier in his interview with Paul Gagne, the wraparound segment scripted by Romero pretty much stayed faithful to his initial outline and was originally intended to be live action. It is noteworthy that in Romero's first draft of the screenplay, the wraparound was more in line with the original *Creepshow* as Billy's story bookends the film. However, in his second draft, Romero would change things up by interweaving Billy's story between segments, which is how it would eventually unfold in the completed film.

In the story, our hero, Billy, is pursued by a gang of ruffian kids who are out to terrorize the young *Creepshow* comic book enthusiast who has just picked up an important package from the local post office. Inside the package is the answer to all of Billy's problems - Venus flytrap bulbs. As the bullies pursue their prey through the streets of Elmville they eventually end up in a deserted clearing where Billy has laid a deadly trap for them. Suddenly, monstrous Venus Flytraps appear and devour the hoodlums as young Billy looks on with a devilish grin: "Giant Venus flytraps. They eat meat!"

Eventually, due to cost-cutting and time-saving measures, the wraparound story would be changed to animation. This decision would actually appeal to Michael Gornick, who viewed the extra animation as a fitting tip of the hat to the old E.C. comics. "What I wanted to do is really expand by another 60% the animation," says Gornick. "So, even though it was kind of a wrap-around material at some point it would take its own form and body and become a little more of a story about boy Billy, in animated form. So that in essence, when you finally watch the motion picture you'd feel like you've watched four live action motion pictures (if you include *Pinfall*) or anthology stories and then this major animation piece that wrapped it around and kind of tied it all together and gave homage to the E.C. comics, you know, which is what I've always thought this was all about from day one. Which I didn't think *Creepshow 1* gave enough of a bow to and I thought we did more so in *Creepshow 2*."

Above left: The November 2, 1983 *Variety* advertisement by Laurel Entertainment announcing that Warner Brothers would again handle distribution duties for them for the upcoming *Creepshow 2*. Six months later Warner Brothers would unfortunately back out. **Below Left:** A 1986 advertisement in *Screen International* for New World's upcoming *Creepshow 2*, featuring Jack Kamen's amazing full color teaser artwork.

So, with the project now having a screenplay, this brings us to perhaps the most arduous aspect of the process - the financing. And for *Creepshow 2*, securing financing would be a multi-year journey.

In November 1983, one year after the release of the original *Creepshow*, Laurel Entertainment would place a full-page ad in *Variety* announcing that Warner Brothers would once again distribute Laurel's live action horror comic book. And as with the first film, Salah Hassanein, along with Richard Rubinstein this time, would serve as executive producer. The budget was set at $4.5 million with production being forecast for the spring and summer of 1984, with *Day of the Dead* to follow in the summer and fall. However, by April 1984 it was announced in that same industry trade, *Variety*, that Warner Brothers was no longer involved with the project and Laurel was producing the feature as an independent. Eventually Salah Hassanein would drop out as well, basically leaving the project in limbo until 1986 when New World Pictures stepped in and offered to produce the film.

"On *Creepshow 2* - this is how I remember it - I think Warner's probably had the right of first refusal for the sequel and passed on it and dropped out a few months later. That's what I think would have happened because when they get the right to distribute the first one, they usually get an option if there's any sequels," says Richard Hassanein of United Film Distribution Company, who financed the original *Creepshow*. "Then New World got involved and we did license it to them. And as I remember we didn't want to do it because George (Romero) didn't want to direct it and Warner Brothers had dropped out. And New World came around and we just made the deal."

So, basically from 1984 until 1986 the project languished in what you might describe as turnaround hell. It was then that a company known for its history in the exploitation field, New World Pictures, swooped in to save the day. What is a little ironic regarding New World entering the picture is the prior history that Laurel had, or I should say *didn't* have, with the company due to perceived differences with New World's founder Roger Corman, who left the company in 1983 when he sold to new ownership. "We've had several meetings with them, and we've never been able to distribute anything through New World," Romero told *Fantastic Films* in 1979. "As nearly as I can determine, it's simply because Roger thinks that I'm almost a competitor, which is silly, really, because I'm talking about a distribution branch outfit." **(38)**

What truly made the difference in the case of New World was its CEO, Bob Rehme, a veteran of the industry and someone who appreciated the genre for its ability to turn a quick buck. "I think what happened is that we had a relationship with Bob Rehme, who was running New World at the time, and we were talking about doing some projects and Bob was a fan of the genre at a certain price and New World, it was sort of in their sweet spot at the time," says *Creepshow 2* associate producer, Mitchell Galin. "And we just started a conversation about...I think he asked, 'Are you guys looking to do another *Creepshow*?' And I think it sort of evolved in that way. I remember going out to – Richard (Rubinstein) and I - going to L.A. and meeting with Bob and discussing it. And basically Bob was very much a man of his word and very quick to do things, he was a decisive decision-maker, and essentially it came down to that if the movie could be done on a certain budget based on the stories that we proposed to him, which did include obviously some Stephen King stories, that they were willing to finance the movie. And it happened almost as quickly as that."

Hailing from Cincinnati, Ohio Bob Rehme has spent his entire working life in the motion picture industry, starting out initially as a theater usher when he was a teenager and then later working his way into theater management. From there, Rehme went to work for United Artists and Paramount Pictures as a publicist. After some time owning a chain of drive-in movie theaters in Ohio, he eventually wound up in Los Angeles working for Roger Corman at New World Pictures. However, running Avco/Embassy Pictures during the late 1970's and early 1980's would cement his name in the industry. Avco/Embassy was home to some of the best quality genre fare released during that era, with titles such as *Phantasm*, *Scanners*, and *The Howling* on its resume. Following his tenure with Avco/Embassy, Rehme would move to Universal Studios where he ran their distribution and marketing division, overseeing the releases of films such as *E.T., The Thing,* and *Halloween III*. Later he would be promoted to head of production and oversaw such genre titles as *Videodrome*, *Psycho II*, and *Jaws 3-D*. Rehme truly enjoyed and respected these types of pictures and without a doubt, he would be the man most responsible for making *Creepshow 2* a reality at his old stomping grounds, New World Pictures.

"When I got involved in running companies and came to make modest budget pictures I thought that the simple thing to do was to make thrillers like *Creepshow 2* and I made a lot of those," says Rehme. "I had worked at New World in the 70's as the sales manager for Roger Corman and I moved from there to Embassy Pictures and then to New World. And *Creepshow 2* was one of those. I made pictures like that. I made pictures like *The Fog* and *Escape from New York* and *Prom Night*; I mean, just an endless number of these pictures. Because I felt that they were modest budgets and the studios weren't really focusing on those kind of pictures at that time. And they weren't expensive to make and they were basically 'review proof', you know, they didn't have to be great. I couldn't ensure how they were going to turn out, so it was all about the story, the title, and how well you could make a picture like that. So, that's what we did. And I found out that *Creepshow*, the rights to a sequel would be available. I don't know if I called George Romero or who I called, but we got the rights and we made the movie. And that's what happened. It's that simple."

And despite the fact that there were still some details to iron out and some hurdles to clear before it was all official, one thing was now certain: *Creepshow 2* had a place to call home.

Chapter 2 Laurel - CST, Inc.

Even though things wouldn't be officially consummated between Laurel and New World until July 17, 1986 when the film contract was finally signed, pre-production was well underway on *Creepshow 2*. On May 19, New World development executive Randy Levinson penned a two-page memo to New World's senior vice president of motion picture production, Paul S. Almond, breaking down the film's script and offering story suggestions for each segment. It's interesting to note that by this point *Pinfall* was already removed from the screenplay, which Levinson references. "The *Creepshow II* screenplay favorably compares to the original *Creepshow*," wrote Levinson. "With the omission of the bowling alley tale, this *Creepshow* actually flows a lot more smoothly than the first one." **(1)**

Some of his observations and suggestions included drawing out the deaths of the murderous punks in *Old Chief Wood'nhead*, making some of the teens from *The Raft* a little more "villainous or pranksterish" – Levinson's phrasing – since it felt unfair that these nice kids suffered such a horrible fate, and perhaps switching the genders of the driver and the hitcher in *The Hitchhiker*, since there was "a very conservative and somewhat outdated morality" – again, Levinson's words – to the story, what with the cheating wife getting her nasty comeuppance and all.

Perhaps his most important note was in regards to the wraparound story and the Venus flytrap and how that would play in the film. Levinson was concerned about the cost of making it seem believable and dangerous, but was also leery that it could come off as too derivative to the Audrey II puppet from the upcoming remake of *Little Shop of Horrors*, which was due in theaters later that year. That note of caution, coupled with a desire by Michael Gornick to have more animation, more than likely led to the decision to switch the sequence to animation because, within a month's time, it was decided that the best course of action would be to animate the majority of the wraparound story. Proposals were sent to Richard Rubinstein and George Romero, explaining the need to do so due to time and budget constraints. After meeting with animator Rick Catizone on June 9 Michael Gornick – who was Laurel's choice to now direct the picture, but had yet to be formally approved by the film's bonding company, Film Finances – would draft a two-page memo on June 17 to George Romero respectfully expressing the need to revise the wraparound material quickly and efficiently and to also keep the parameters of the material at nine minutes/pages. Gornick included brief excerpts from Romero's script with strategic points to amend the material and estimates of length of time for each. Basically it was a helpful road map for Romero to follow, making his job easier.

And quickly getting back to the screenplay being chopped down to three stories from four, Mitchell Galin would offer an interesting notion as to why three was the magic number. "Well there was a feeling that if we did things on an odd number in an anthology that theoretically the odds of more people liking the movie than not were

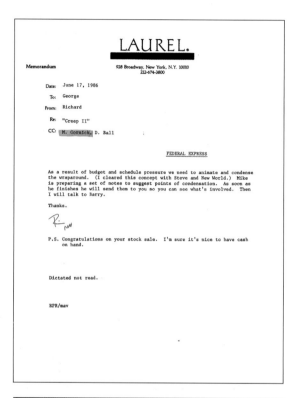

increased, with the notion that if you like two out of the three stories then they liked the movie," he explains. "If they liked two out of four stories then they'd come away saying, 'Yeah, the movie was okay', there was like almost a balance with it. There was a theory, I'm not saying its fact, but that's the theory that we were operating on. We did the same thing with the *Tales from the Darkside* movie."

Above: Laurel memo from Richard Rubinstein informing George Romero that *Creepshow 2*'s wraparound segment would now be animated – June 1986. (courtesy of Michael Gornick) **Below:** Producer David Ball with the late actor Joe Pilato(left) during principal photography for George A. Romero's *Day of the Dead* in late 1984. (courtesy of Joe Pilato)

"He'd have a better pulse on it than I would. I don't know. As a moviegoer I don't know if it would have affected me either way," says Michael Gornick. "I think as a moviegoer though if *Creepshow 1* had five, I'm wondering why aren't there five here? It just always feels like a little lesser because you don't have five. You know? So, anyway, I tried to make up that margin by putting more animation, figuring that's the truth of it, it's basically born out of the comic book and drawing."

David Ball, who served as co-producer on *Day of the Dead*, would now step in as producer for *Creepshow 2*. In truth, his duties were all but the same, as he functioned as the on-set producer for both features. After proving himself on the original *Creepshow* where he entered late in the game to get that production back on track, as well as on *Day of the Dead,* Richard Rubinstein felt at ease with Ball's style and reached out to the diligent and resolute Brit for the comic-book-come-to-life sequel. "Rubinstein called me and said, 'We've got a deal to do *Creepshow 2*', I said, 'Yeah, okay,'" remembers Ball. "He said, 'but we haven't got the budget. We've only got four million dollars.' And I said, 'Well, blimey', I said to him, 'Richard, that's a BIG ask after spending seven on the first one.' He said, 'Yeah, but this one's only three stories with an animated wrap around.' I said, 'Yeah, but animation, Richard, is slow and time consuming.' You know? So, I had a budget of four million dollars and I got on a plane and I went to New York and we set the whole thing up in New York."

Born in London, England in 1948 David Ball has always had a photographic memory for numbers, something he inherited from his mother. He would attend college in Hertfordshire, not far from where he went to school as a young boy in north London. As a youth he was surrounded by family and friends who had a passion for the arts, in particular music. "I was the only member of a large family who didn't play an instrument," Ball laughs. "I was too busy kicking the soccer ball around the fields." His father was an organist and pianist and his siblings played piano and guitar. His best mate in school was musician Alan Warner, who would go on to become one of the founding members of The Foundations, famous for their hit songs *Baby, Now That I've Found You* and *Build Me Up Buttercup*. Like most kids he was a movie lover, taking in a lot of westerns due to his father's love of the genre.

Immediately upon finishing school Ball would begin utilizing the head for numbers he possesses. "My first job on leaving school was as a trainee accountant and it wasn't very highly paid," he recalls. "I had to go to college, day-college, night school, and all that. And I was doing pretty well, but it was in a chemical manufacturing company that used to manufacture cosmetics. You know Oil of Olay? Well, they used to make that." Not long after, Ball would be involved in a major automobile accident, one that put him out of work for nearly nine months. After recovering he returned to work doing labor intensive jobs such as heavy pipe work just to earn a little money, while most of his friends were working for the studios doing a variety of things. At their suggestion Ball would apply for a trainee accountant position at Elstree Studios and by the end of 1969 he was hired. "So, I got the job and within a week I

Above: David Ball, seen here next to actress Jeremy Green during filming of *The Raft*, would suffer the loss of his brother during pre-production for *Creepshow 2*. The steadfast producer would throw himself into his work to cope with the tragedy. (courtesy of Michael Felsher) **Below:** Laurel memo from David Ball to music legend Les Reed regarding his interest in tackling the score for *Creepshow 2* – June 1986. (courtesy of Michael Gornick)

realized that I was over qualified because my credentials were so much more than was required; which meant that I didn't find the work very stimulating," says Ball. "So, I decided to set about finding out how the money was spent. And I'd say to the accountant, 'Can I go on the set and have a look?' And he'd say, 'Oh, we don't go on the set. You don't need to do that.' So, I'd go on the set from 8:15

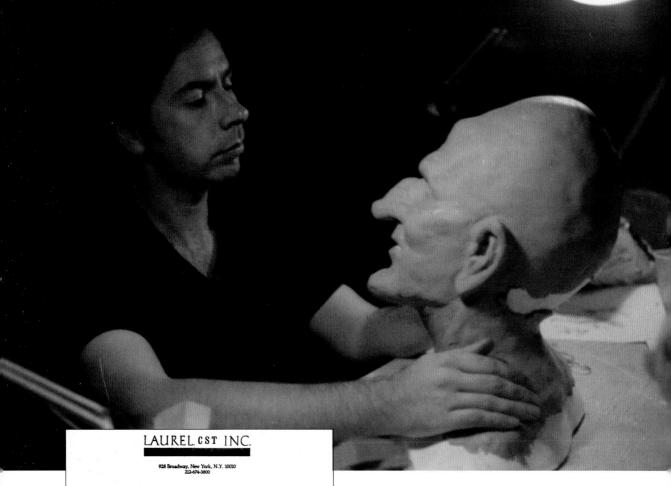

Above: Original makeup effects lead Ed French, seen here on location in Arizona inspecting his version of the Creep, would face many struggles during his abbreviated time on the production. (courtesy of Father William Kosco) **Below:** Laurel memo to Tom Savini, who was on location filming *The Texas Chainsaw Massacre Part 2*, from David Ball seeking the horror legend's input regarding the makeup effects for *Creepshow 2*. (courtesy of Michael Gornick)

in the morning until I was due in the office at 9. Then I'd go on the set from 1:30 until 2. Then I'd go on the set from 5 until 5:30 or 6. I was inquisitive and I wanted to learn so I could understand the expenditure thing."

Ball worked as an accountant on a string of TV shows and films including a couple of Freddie Francis genre pictures, *The Legend of the Werewolf* and *The Ghoul*. It was during this period that Ball, annoyed at watching how much money production managers wasted and also desiring to learn even more about the industry, decided to teach himself how to break a script down and make a shooting schedule. In the meantime he continued his accounting duties on more TV shows and features like *The New Avengers* with Patrick Macnee and *Sunburn* with Farrah Fawcett. Of note for all the hardcore horror junkies out there he even performed accounting duties on Lucio Fulci's 1981 horror film *The Black Cat*.

Around this same time the tenacity that Ball had shown in teaching himself some of the duties of a production manager would bear fruit when he was given the opportunity to fill that position on a film shot in Mexico called *Cattle Annie and Little Britches* starring Burt Lancaster, Rod Steiger, and Diane Lane. The film would turn out to be a memorable and key entry in Ball's resume. Again, it was the first feature in which he would serve as production manager, but the film would also allow him the chance to showcase his eye for detail and cost cutting measures to notable higher ups when he hammered out some contract details. "So, I got in the office at like three o'clock in the afternoon and they said, 'You have to go to the Telex room at the hotel', so I went there.

Above: A 22 year old Michael Gornick, circa 1970, when he was an airman and motion picture sound specialist at Los Angeles Air Force Station. (courtesy of Michael Gornick) **Below:** Michael Gornick would hone many technical skills while working on *The Winners* sports documentary series with George Romero and Richard Rubinstein.

So, I was still there at midnight cracking out this contract," remembers Ball. "And occasionally I'd say, 'Well, shouldn't you add this?', and they'd say, 'Oh, yeah, good idea'...'Do you think this is necessary?'...'No, you're right. We don't.' So, the contract was done for Salah Hassanein's company, which was United Artists Theater Circuit. And I think Salah took quite a shine to me, you know. And that was that."

The shine that Hassanein had taken to Ball would lead to his fateful entrance into the operations of Laurel Entertainment when he was contacted by Hassanein's United Film Distribution Company to travel to Pittsburgh, Pennsylvania in the latter portion of 1981 to oversee the finances for the lagging production of *Creepshow*. The assignment would also provide Ball the chance to be a body double of sorts for one of the movie's biggest stars in the film's most infamous scene from *They're Creeping Up On You* when the production's famous special makeup effects artist "bugged" him about assisting with a favor. "Fuckin' Tom Savini, the bastard," laughs Ball. "I was always generally nosey, I wanted to see what was happening; I was always nosey. So, I went in his place one day and I said, 'How you doing, Tom?' He said, 'Hi, David. I'm good', he said, 'You know what? You're the same size as E.G. Marshall.' I said, 'Well, does that make me lucky or

unlucky?' He said, 'It depends which way you look at it. I'm gonna use your body for his body mold. Are you up for it?' And I said, 'Yeah, I'm up for it.'"

A few years later, of course, Ball would return to co-produce the last of George Romero's *Dead* films, *Day of the Dead*, which brings us up to speed with *Creepshow 2*.

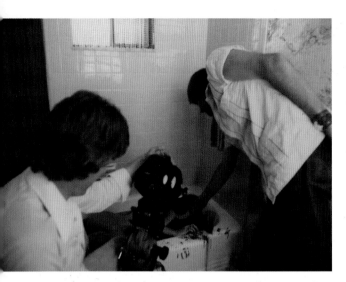

Above: George Romero directs actress Elayne Nadeau during her death scene while Michael Gornick, serving his first stint as director of photography, stands by waiting to film on the set of *Martin* in 1976. (courtesy of Michael Gornick)

Above: Original ad slick for George A. Romero's *Martin* which ran in London's *Evening Standard* in November 1979.

Beginning a new film project is a time of many emotions. There's the excitement for starting something new, but there's also knowing that you're about to dive into a long and intensive period where your attentions will be monopolized. So, anything outside the norm that occurs, especially something deeply personal, can test a human being. Shortly after pre-production began on *Creepshow 2* Ball would receive some tragic news from home. "I'd been on the picture about two weeks, I suppose, and then I heard the sad news that my brother had died," shares Ball. "So, I flew home for his service. And then shed a few tears, had a few beers with the family, and got back on a plane. My philosophy has always been life goes on. He was my best buddy and he's still my best buddy, if you like." And as many people do who suffer a blow such as losing a loved one, Ball turned to what he knew best to help him through – his work. "I think it helps a great deal if you've got something you can turn your attention to when you're having a dark hour," he says. "Yeah, I think it did help me. In fact, I probably worked harder on *Creep 2* because I really needed to get it out of my head."

Ball was busy with an assortment of tasks during this time, including reaching out to a potential composer for the score. Famed songwriter Les Reed, who was responsible for some of Tom Jones' biggest hits like *It's Not Unusual* and *Delilah*, was contacted by Ball in mid-June 1986 about composing the score for an early February 1987 session. "I'd never met Les Reed in my life," says Ball. "But he'd written so many hits for so many people and his orchestral stuff was superb."

"David Ball contacted me through a mutual friend in the film business, he was excited about his new film called *Creepshow 2* of which he was producing with direction by Michael Gornick, for New World Pictures in 1986," recalls Reed. "David had witnessed some of my film music and obviously thought that this subject was right up my street

as from an early age, I have been interested and indeed involved in the supernatural."

Asking Reed to score the picture was an interesting choice for the production as they chose to go in a very different direction than the original which, while featuring snippets from library tracks, was mainly scored by John Harrison. Apparently Harrison was never a consideration as no one from the production approached him about scoring the sequel. "I had moved to L.A. at the time and was busy with my projects there," says Harrison. "And I think Mike Gornick wanted to put his own stamp on the project, which I fully understand and applaud."

One aspect of choosing Reed, besides his obvious talent and musical skills, was the fact that he was located in the U.K. Early on Ball knew he wanted to take the post-production to his native England, which is indeed what happened, as it was simply a numbers game. "Purely financial," says Ball. "Also, the style of working in L.A. is completely different to the style of working in London. For example, on the sound side you have a sound editor per reel and then an assistant and a cutting room. You've got so many people; you've got so many different ears producing a soundtrack, that's why these things don't work. So, I said up front, before we started shooting, I said to Rubinstein, 'Post-production is going to London because I don't have the money anymore.' I've got to put what I put on the screen and after *The Raft* I had to inform everybody post-production will be London. I had one editor and one assistant, one sound editor and one assistant. Okay, the editor and the sound editor came on location. You know why? Because I couldn't have looping or ADR on edits in America in the '80's when you didn't have digital technology, so if I needed any lines of dialogue my sound editor recorded them on the way to the airport with the actors. So, we left America with an entirely clean dialogue track."

Another task addressed during this hectic time was who would tackle the makeup effects. Initially the choice would

Above: Michael Gornick rides sidecar with biker Bill "Butchie" George during filming of George A. Romero's *Dawn of the Dead* in early 1978. (courtesy of Michael Gornick)

go to Ed French, an artist who had done a fair amount of work for Laurel's syndicated television series, *Tales from the Darkside*. French, whose background included some acting as well, would be tapped to head up the effects crew and was also slated to play the Creep character seen book-ending the film, a role eventually given to Tom Savini. The quality of French's work at that time was not quite on par with say a Tom Savini, however his relationship with Michael Gornick, who French had previously worked with, and the time served working for Richard Rubinstein's company, Laurel Entertainment, had given him an in road.

French's work up to that point, outside of *Tales from the Darkside*, consisted basically of cult and exploitation titles: *Nightmares in a Damaged Brain* (aka *Nightmare*), *Sleepaway Camp*, and *C.H.U.D*. One of the more intriguing titles on his resume isn't a film he actually worked on, rather one he helped via advertising when he created the special makeup effects for the infamous *Bloodsucking Freaks* poster. The chance to work on a feature film for Laurel, a sequel to *Creepshow* no-less, was a big break for the rising effects artist.

"My opportunity to helm the special makeup effects for *Creepshow 2* came about as a direct result of working with director Michael Gornick on Laurel Entertainment's anthology series *Tales from the Darkside*," French writes in a statement he provided for this book. "In fact my work on the pilot episode, *Trick or Treat* (directed by Bob Balaban), was largely instrumental in launching the series into TV syndication. The show put me on the map as an up-and-coming special makeup effects artist. It was a wonderful

opportunity and enormously satisfying creatively. Many of the teleplays that I contributed FX makeup to were directed by Michael and penned by George Romero. I was very excited when I met with Michael and producer Richard Rubinstein to discuss my participation in *Creepshow 2*. I always loved the E.C. horror comics from the early 1950's with the jaw-dropping twist endings and black humor. Certainly William Gaines's groundbreaking comic books have provided ample inspiration for film-makers over the years. Their influence can be seen as early as the 1960's in *Dr. Terror's House of Horrors* and *The Torture Garden*, horror compilations made by British horror outfit Amicus. Later, in the '70's, Amicus made *The Vault of Horror* and *Tales from the Crypt*, two anthologies that were directly adapted from stories published in the infamous comics. I enjoyed all these films, but I thought the first *Creepshow* significantly upped the ante for stylish horror compilation films and I felt jazzed about the prospect of working on scripts by the tag-team of terror, author Stephen King and director George A. Romero. What could be better?"

Of note regarding French's hiring is a letter sent to Tom Savini from David Ball in mid-June 1986. Savini, who was busy at the time working on the sequel to Tobe Hooper's *The Texas Chainsaw Massacre* in Austin, Texas, had been previously contacted by Ball to discuss his thoughts on French for the job. What exactly was said by Savini to

Above: Riding on the back of an ATV Michael Gornick captures up close action during the filming of George A. Romero's *Knightriders* in the summer of 1980. (courtesy of Michael Gornick) **Below:** Michael and Michele Gornick at the wedding of George and Christine Romero during late summer 1980. (courtesy of Michael Gornick)

Ball isn't known, but whatever it was it apparently wasn't flattering, as Ball makes reference to it in the letter. "In general, I do not care to hear of technicians being maligned before their work has been seen," wrote Ball. "But your initial reservation has been duly noted." **(2)**

One of the rare times that Savini has addressed this subject – quite candidly, I might add – was in a lengthy 1988 interview that appeared in the late Chas. Balun's horror fanzine, *Deep Red*. "I thought I was going to do *Creepshow 2*," Savini told interviewer Dennis Daniel. "I was working on *Texas Chainsaw Massacre 2* at the time and Laurel called me and asked if I could recommend someone to do the effects on *Creepshow 2*. I said, 'That's a strange question. Why

aren't you asking me?' They said that Richard Rubinstein, the head of Laurel, didn't want to tie me up 'cause he wanted me to direct some *Tales from the Darkside* episodes. I said I could direct *Tales* and supervise and design the effects for *Creepshow 2*. They wound up spending maybe twice what they would have paid me with the problems they had using the person they did. I told them, 'This person can't do it unless he has top-notch help.'" **(3)**

"Tom and I had some direct conversations," admits Michael Gornick on the subject of French's hiring. "He told me flatly that Ed didn't have the – Ed had the ability – he didn't have the stamina. And he wasn't a kind of supervisor or maestro of his people; that he had a very strong ego, he was more singularly involved in terms of his work. He wouldn't involve other people. And much of that came to light during the shoot. But I loved Ed because, you know, he had incredible talent and I was willing to take the gamble. I thought, 'Well, we could work with this, we can actually help Ed.' And I thought if he had a diverse enough crew like he wound up having that he would acquiesce, he would give up duties, he would give up much of what he felt was part of his need, creative need, to his crew. He wouldn't necessarily be the only figure. So, Tom just warned me. Tom thought also that he was maybe weak technically – I'm not sure about that."

Location scouting was also underway and one of the initial spots scouted would end up becoming the eventual area for filming – Prescott, Arizona. Founded in 1864, one year after the discovery of gold in the nearby Bradshaw Mountains, Prescott would become the first capital of Arizona Territory. In its infancy Prescott was a classic frontier town, complete with drunken bar brawls and gunfights, whose saloons were hangouts for legends of the old west like Wyatt Earp and Doc Holliday. The town would prove itself to be quite resilient after surviving a great fire in 1900 that destroyed most of the business district. As the community matured and grew over time it would become an attractive locale for film production with movies like *How the West Was Won* (1962), *Billy Jack* (1971), and Sam Peckinpah's *Junior Bonner* (1972) having been shot there.

"Prescott's a really beautiful setting. And it's a real old western town. I mean, the main street is called Whiskey Row and there really was like all these saloons; there's beautiful mountains," says assistant production manager Debra Tanklow. "It's not like the Arizona you think of; it's hilly, and pine forests – they had this Ponderosa pine forest. I remember driving over this mountain to a town called Skull Valley. I mean, it was really a cool place to be."

With favorable weather forecasts provided to the production by Accuweather things were certainly looking good for Prescott as a landing spot for the production, despite the fact that scouting for other regions in the west would go on in areas near Santa Fe, New Mexico and Provo, Utah.

Monday, June 23, 1986 would be a pivotal date in the production time-line of *Creepshow 2*. This was the day that Laurel would meet with representatives from Film Finances, the company retained to insure the film with a completion bond.

Above: Michael Gornick, with his longtime assistant cameraman, Tom Dubensky, during filming of the original *Creepshow* in 1981. (courtesy of Michael Gornick)

Above: Original ad slick for George A. Romero's *Knightriders*, featuring a bonus co-feature of *Dawn of the Dead*, which ran in *The Los Angeles Times* in April 1981.

The meeting was held at Laurel's Manhattan offices on Broadway and consisted of producer David Ball, director Michael Gornick, production manager Charles Carroll, and Film Finances representative Kurt Woolner. The meeting would last 5 hours, from 3PM until 8PM, and would cover a wide array of subjects. Woolner had gone through the proposed budget with a fine tooth comb questioning everything from the $538,000 allocated for the film's story rights, screenplay, executive producer, and development fees to the $25,950 which was budgeted for hair and makeup, a number Woolner felt was too low by a couple of thousand dollars. Woolner also raised concerns over things which would indeed become issues during the filming, such as the blob from *The Raft* and working on the water in general, plus weather cover for the Arizona portion of filming. He

was mildly concerned about potential issues of inclement weather for *The Hitchhiker* segment as well, since it would be shot last and in late fall in Maine. Despite those concerns and questions, for the most part, Woolner was satisfied with Laurel's responses and presentation and returned to Los Angeles where he would issue a letter of intent to bond the film, pending final approval from managing director Richard Soames, thus putting the onus on New World to now sign the contract with Laurel and make it all official.

Film Finances was incorporated in 1950 in response to the financial plight suffered in the late 1940's by England's film industry. While for the most part being an insurer, Film Finances would also need to be proficient in film production, meaning having experienced producers at the ready to oversee a production if necessary. Over time they would expand globally to countries like Australia, Canada, and the United States. In the early 1980's they would successfully help to repair the professional image of Francis Ford Coppola when they bonded his two youth films *The Outsiders* and *Rumble Fish*, after the struggles Coppola endured going over budget on *Apocalypse Now* and *One from the Heart*.

"All the distributor wants to know is, number one, if they're putting up money and guaranteeing money they want to know that they get delivered a first rate movie. A bond company has no interest in anything other than the film being delivered. So, they don't care about creative nuance, they wanna just make sure it gets done," explains Mitchell Galin. "The film-maker wants to make his film creatively satisfying, understanding that he's gotta make certain compromises relating to budget. A bond company's only objective is, 'Here's the script, we're delivering the script, as long as it's deliverable and you've delivered a ninety-five-minute movie with the essence of this script, then we're done.' And how it gets done and whether it's commercially successful is not of their interest. They get their percentage of the budget to insure it and that's what they do and that's their business."

One of the more important facets of the meeting with Film Finances was that the final stamp of approval for director Michael Gornick was given. Gornick's latest *Tales from the Darkside* episode, *The Circus,* was viewed allowing Kurt Woolner to see the type of work Gornick was capable of. "Those *Tales from the Darkside*s, I think they were made for something ridiculous like $115,000 a show or something," says David Ball. "And Gornick did a few of those and he knew about discipline. And so when it came to bonding the picture Film Finances, who I had worked with many, many times, they asked me, 'What about Mike Gornick? What about this director guy?' I said, 'He's solid as a rock! He's solid as a rock. You don't have to worry about him.' And they said, 'Okay, David. If you say he's solid we'll buy it.' And he got a bond."

The viewing of the episode also demonstrated the capabilities of Ed French both as a makeup effects artist and as an actor, since French had played the vampire character in the episode. Very noteworthy here is that the episode's director of photography, Jon Fauer, was apparently the initial choice for cinematographer for *Creepshow 2* as the viewing of the episode was intended to showcase

Above: Original ad slick for an amazing George A. Romero double bill – *Creepshow* and the infamous R-rated cut of *Dawn of the Dead* – which ran in the New Jersey newspaper *The Record* in May 1983. **Below:** Michael Gornick films Tim Dileo's death scene in George A. Romero's *Day of the Dead,* shot on Sanibel Island, Florida in December 1984. (courtesy of Michael Gornick)

his work as well. The reasons for his departure from the upcoming production aren't known. Fauer has gone onto a very successful career as the publisher of *Film and Digital Times*, authored a dozen books on the subject of cinematography, and teaches advanced cinematography at Columbia University Graduate School of the Arts.

Another point of interest from the meeting was that Prescott, Arizona was discussed and by all accounts was now indeed the choice for the production's base.

As discussed the meeting with Film Finances solidified the decision of who would be the director for *Creepshow 2* and that man would indeed be Laurel Entertainment's diligent and always reliable "utility man", Michael Gornick.

Born at home on November 23, 1947 Michael George Gornick, named after his father, was raised in Trafford, Pennsylvania, the youngest of three children born to Croatian immigrants. His grandfather, Thomas Michael, had come to the United States on a visa and worked in the steel mills of Pittsburgh, Pennsylvania and Youngstown, Ohio and on occasion would send for his wife, Catherine, to visit him in the U.S. She would eventually become pregnant and while visiting her husband in Braddock, Pennsylvania gave birth to Gornick's father – thus making him a naturalized citizen. After he had reached the age of reason Gornick's father returned to the U.S., since he was already naturalized, and took up residence in Braddock. A few years later he sent for his wife, Mary Veronica, and started a family in the Pittsburgh area, eventually settling in Trafford. It was there in that small Western Pennsylvania town that his youngest child would discover a fascination with cameras and moving pictures.

"Oh, it was idyllic. I mean, it was almost like Mayberry R.F.D.," Gornick fondly recalls about Trafford. "We were self-sustained. We had our own supermarkets. We had motion picture theaters – one, the McBride. And while it wasn't grand, it was an event each and every week, and also during the week. It ran seven days a week, first run motion pictures. Most importantly for me, Hammer stuff, I really enjoyed. So, that was like kind of our main source of entertainment, the McBride Theatre; very, very friendly people – community people. One could run upstairs and watch the projectionist and that was when I first got my peek behind the scenes. That was my main source of entertainment. Television to some degree, but there was something intriguing about motion pictures and still photography I kind of got attached to – my sister was kind of a shutter bug. And I had an immense curiosity at the time – even as a kid – as to what was happening inside this magic box. Early in life I was able to make some sort of association between the magic box and what I could see on the screen. I thought, 'Hmm, I know you capture this image somehow and then in turn at some point it goes on to this big screen that I'm watching where I can watch *The Three Stooges*, I can watch all my favorites.' So, I was kind of curious, but I knew there was some association."

Right: Michael Gornick directing on the sets of Laurel's syndicated TV series *Tales from the Darkside*: with Bruce Davison from *The Word Processor of the Gods*, Jerry Stiller from *The Devil's Advocate*, and William Hickey from *The Circus*. (courtesy of Michael Gornick)

Above: *Creepshow 2*'s rookie production designer, Bruce Miller, relaxes on the beach at Granite Basin Lake during filming of *The Raft*. (courtesy of Angela Nogaro) **Below:** *Creepshow 2*'s costume designer Elieen Sieff-Stroup visiting the Dead River location from *Old Chief Wood'nhead*. (courtesy of Rebecca Mayo)

As was touched upon Gornick was the youngest of three children. His late brother, Thomas, and his sister, Caroline, were much older than him and by the time he reached his formative years they were already out of the house, leaving Gornick with the feeling of being an only child in many respects. Thomas, who was 15 years older than his brother, would become a priest and fans of the original *Creepshow* might recognize him from his cameo on the television set as Father Martin Burdik in *The Lonesome Death of Jordy Verrill* segment. "That was an actual sermonette that my brother did on a local Wheeling, West Virginia station, I believe," Gornick says.

The Catholic faith wouldn't just play a large part in his brother's life, but in his own as well while growing up. Gornick believes that very much like the McBride Theatre it contributed to his desire to be in the field of entertainment one day. "Okay, this is deep in my soul. Okay? You were asking me how I got involved or how did you develop an interest in the entertainment industry, so called. Right, how do you do this? And I swear it goes back to my days as an altar boy," he says. "Now, I grew up in the old pre-Vatican II Catholic Church. So it was full of beautiful ceremony, the incenses, smoke. The altar was a sacred area; it was almost like the altar of King David. Only a select few could enter the sanctuary and I was one of those people! I was the altar boy who went with the celebrant to the altar and we spoke in another language – it was Latin. And it was all ceremony. You rang bells and you emerged with the sacristan, you came out of the altar, and everyone's attention was on you! I mean, it was glorious. It was sacred, but it was almost like a stage play; almost like an old morality tale you were playing out."

And it was in high school that Gornick would further develop that fascination with the stage. "Luckily one of my guidance counselors who was named Alice Giglio, who was actually a graduate of the theater arts department from CMU (Carnegie Mellon University), she would annually have a stage event called 'The Command Performance' and she developed my interest in stage work and acting – possibly directing, but at that point it was mainly acting – and opened up my world," he explains. "Because she was my guidance counselor and my natural course of studies were, 'Mike, you're excellent at math and science. You'll probably want to study engineering.' So, she and I talked about this and I said, 'Yeah, I know, I probably should be an engineer, but could I do something in the arts perhaps?' And she said, 'Well, why don't you split it down the middle? You could think about something like meteorology?' And I said, 'Yeah, okay. Let's try that.'" (laughs)

After receiving a scholarship to attend Penn State, through an organization associated with mining engineers, Gornick experienced some harrowing visits to mining facilities causing him to rethink his plans, ultimately steering him in a completely different direction. "So, I actually stayed on at Penn State, gave up my scholarship in mining engineering, and went directly into...at that point in time they had something called Broadcast Studies and it was wonderful because it was very diverse, you could take courses in journalism, theater arts – it was a palette that you could choose from. And that's what I did. I joined the Department of Arts and Architecture and I majored in broadcasting."

While there Gornick drifted towards theater arts and that's where most of his attention was spent, rather than the journalistic side of things. He did, however, try his hand at making films including working on the award winning *They Keep Going Back*, a film about miners and the mining industry in Scranton, Pennsylvania. "So, yeah, I did some film-making, but I just loved theater arts," he says. "And had it not been for the Vietnam War where I was given a 2-S deferment and had to join after I got out of college I probably would have emphasized and gone more directly into theater arts. I loved the live stage."

As Gornick alluded to, the military would play a part in his life after graduating college. The Vietnam War was still being waged in Southeast Asia and if you were given a 2-S deferment, as Gornick explained, it meant you could attend college, but once you left school you were either drafted or you could enlist. Gornick's hopes were that President Nixon would find a way to end the war before he would graduate, but that did not come to pass. "Literally the day I was packing up my things at Penn State to put in my car

I got a draft notice," Gornick recalls. "My mom called and said, 'You've been drafted', and I said, 'Okay'. And on the way back I stopped at an Air Force recruiter thinking I don't want to go to the Army, I don't want to go to the Marines; I don't want to be just simply drafted. I want to have some choice in the matter if I can. So, I stopped at an Air Force recruiter and said, 'What do you have? Can I make motion pictures or do some broadcasting in the Air Force?' He said, 'Sure!', and I said, 'Okay'. So, the difference being that had I just simply been subject to the draft it would have been two years, when I enlisted with a service like the Air Force it became a commitment of four years. So, that's a trade-off."

After completing basic training in San Antonio, Texas the Air Force would indeed honor their word as Gornick would find himself stationed in Los Angeles, California. There he would work a great deal on motion picture sound, a talent that would later get his foot in the door with a particular production company in Pittsburgh. He would perform editorial work as well, physically cutting film. Part of his work in L.A. included working on what could best be described as propaganda reports for Congress. "At that time what we were doing is President Nixon's big plan was the 'Vietnamization' of the war, which means he was turning the war over to the Vietnamese, who were quite capable – but they weren't," says Gornick. "And unfortunately my Air Force team over there, who were actually filming a lot of this, a lot of it was staged. I mean, we were trying to show how they could pilot aircraft and it was all simulations pretty much, just as I later did myself in motion picture work; a lot of fire footage that was, you

Above: Ed French in his Brooklyn loft/studio during the makeup effects prep for *Creepshow 2* – summer 1986. (courtesy of Michael Gornick) **Below:** Howard Berger's designs for Tom Wright's character from *The Hitchhiker*, seen here in Ed French's Brooklyn loft/studio – summer 1986. (courtesy of Michael Gornick)

know, actually American fighters flying. So, we made these so called Congressional reports to show how well the war was going. And it wasn't. It wasn't."

Gornick would spend two years in Los Angeles until being reassigned to Lowry Air Force Base in Denver, Colorado. Finding the lack of work there to be unfulfilling, Gornick decided to do something about it. "So, about a year into that I petitioned my Congressman, John Herman Dent from Jeanette, Pennsylvania, at that point and said, 'Look, I'm wasting time here. I'm wasting taxpayer money. I'd like to go back and rejoin society,'" he recalls. "The war was starting to wind down then, you know, we realized there was no hope in Vietnam. And so he granted and found me what they call an 'early out' and I was dismissed."

Above: Howard Berger, Greg Nicotero, and Everett Burrell in Prescott, Arizona. (courtesy of Rebecca Mayo)

A key sidebar about his time in Denver was a film he went to see one day, a film that would introduce him to the work of a man he would one day become a close collaborator of. "I became a regular moviegoer due to my boredom. (laughs) But anyhow at one point, yeah, I saw *Night of the Living Dead* – blew me away. I thought, 'Wow, it's so well crafted. Who is this guy?,'" says Gornick about a Pittsburgh film-maker named George Romero. "So, I was fascinated. It was very well done. It was a very believable cast – for the most part the acting was superb. And so when I got back to Pittsburgh I had a true interest in who made this and how they made this."

After leaving the Air Force Gornick would return to Pittsburgh to visit his mother (his father had passed away several years prior) and to take a breather before eventually planning to return to Los Angeles where he intended to try his luck in the film industry. But before doing so he would make a telephone call that would derail those plans all together. "So, I still had this fascination about this amazing motion picture that I had seen and at that point it had good box office and had put Pittsburgh literally on the motion picture map so I thought, 'I gotta see these guys, see what it's all about,'" recalls Gornick. "I put in a phone call and said, 'Hi, I'm Mike (laughs). I'm in from Denver on the way back to L.A. Just wanted to stop by and say hi! Is that possible?' And, as I remember, I think it was Bonnie Hinzman, who later married Bill Hinzman, and whose brother is Nick Mastandrea, 'grip extraordinaire', and said, 'Yeah, come on down.' So I did! Came down one afternoon, figuring I'd get to meet this guy Romero. And indeed came into the office but discovered soon after being there that George was prepping at the time for a film called *The Crazies*, so he wasn't going to be in the office.

But I met some of his staff: a guy named Vince Survinski, and Bonnie, and his general manager Al Croft, and his sales person there Walton Cook."

During his visit to The Latent Image offices Gornick was offered the opportunity to work as a boom operator on the aforementioned new project that George Romero was filming in nearby Evans City, Pennsylvania called *The Crazies*. That opportunity would unexpectedly allow Gornick to showcase more of his varied talents as a film technician. "Actually, during the course of *The Crazies* I probably boomed and operated maybe a week," says Gornick. "And at some point, George being George, always engaging in conversation on set, talking about everything but the motion picture itself that he's producing, but he said to me at one point, 'Say, man. Can you shoot?' And I said, 'Yeah, I can shoot.' So, I explained to him what I had done in the Air Force, did some cutting, and so forth. He said, 'Well, we have this commercial gig going on back in Pittsburgh for a company called Disston Tools. It's kind of a drag, but we gotta shoot it', and I said, 'Okay'. He said, 'Would you be interested in going back and doing this thing?' And I said, 'Yeah, of course!'"

Gornick's work would make a favorable impression on Romero who decided to keep him around The Latent Image for potential future projects. It was then that he was introduced to the laid-back atmosphere of 247 Fort Pitt Blvd. "It felt kind of chaotic," says Gornick. "It was more of a personification of George – very relaxed, very cool: if you got there at eight in the morning? 'That's cool'; if you got there at eleven? 'That's fine'; if you stepped in on George during the course of one of his telephone conversations? 'That's alright. Come on in, man. You have any smokes?' So it was very, very loose. Some of that was great. Some of that was frustrating to me because I'm a structured person. And at the time he had endless employees, I'm not sure they were all getting paid or not."

The chaos and lightheartedness at The Latent Image was a bit surprising for Gornick as he wondered when the next project would come along. Romero was busy editing *The Crazies* for release and would often edit the film at home, rather than The Latent Image facilities on Fort Pitt Blvd, which meant the atmosphere would be even looser than it typically was. "And so there was no George, there was just this chaotic activity. There was speculation about future projects, but I could see no advancement toward a project," recalls Gornick. "Luckily very soon, like maybe a week into my stay there, George had an old project called *Jack's Wife* that starred Ray Laine, a college friend of his, and it was in a state of disrepair: it needed cutting, it needed prepared for distribution, meaning that eventually the negative had to be cut and so it was just in shambles. And George had zero interest in doing that because his current project was *The Crazies* and he was staying with that. And little to none of the people at The Latent Image at that time had any interest, neither any ability, to do any of this. So, again, George came to me one day and said, 'Say, man. Would you be interested

in working on the sound shit for *Jack's Wife*?'"

Those carefree early days at The Latent Image were about to come to an end though with the introduction of Romero's new producer Richard Paul Rubinstein. Romero and Rubinstein met when the aspiring New York producer, complete with Wall Street credentials, was working on an article on Romero related to the upcoming release of *The Crazies* for the industry trade publication *Filmmakers Newsletter*. The two quickly hit it off and realized that perhaps they could help one another. "I'm inherently a gambler and I bet on George because I thought his level of creative talent combined with his enthusiasm for writing and directing feature films was special," says Rubinstein. "On the other hand it was also clear that his 'business' skill-set was not as developed. On a more personal level I was impressed by his unwillingness to go personally bankrupt because he had guaranteed bank loans in connection with some of his prior movies that had not been repaid."

"He brought instant structure to everything," Gornick says about Rubinstein's arrival. "Initially it was somewhat painful because it was so loose and so chaotic that it felt unfamiliar. But he brought a kind of structure and a financial plan, I guess, business plan, to the company and to George and

Below: Mike Trcic working diligently inside the EFXACO in Prescott, Arizona. (courtesy of Father William Kosco)

1850 to the close of the century, it is generally agreed that the carving of tobacconists' Indians reached its peak in the 1890s. Some cast-metal figures appeared in the late eighties; they were expensive but, because of their weight, were not as easily stolen as the wooden Indians. Figure 124 is of cast zinc, with a wrought-iron bow. The heroic pose of the chieftain returning from the hunt (119) is unique

Above left and right: Reference pages of historical cigar store Indian statues. Chief Wood'nhead's look was created by borrowing from several different designs. (courtesy of Michael Gornick). See Chapter 3.

held out some promise for proceeding with investment by others, as opposed to self-financing; which, I think, is the key issue. Richard brought that whole new possibility to George, rather than George taking the risk, throwing the dice."

With Rubinstein now on board, The Latent Image would take a back seat to a new image and a new name as well. Before teaming up with Rubinstein, George Romero had registered the corporate name of Laurel Tape & Film, Inc., named after Pennsylvania's state flower. Not wanting to spend the several hundred dollars it would cost to form a new company they decided to use Laurel as the name of their new joint venture (Rubinstein would later form The Laurel Group in New York City – a subsidiary of his first company The Ultimate Mirror – a separate company all together from Laurel Tape & Film). And one of the first projects they'd produce together would be a series of television sports documentaries. The sports docs would serve as a way for Laurel to generate some cash flow, helping to solidify their fledgling new company, but also keep Romero working, honing his technical skills. "So we did, we made a series of sports documentaries called *The Winners* and that was a deal structured by Richard early in the game," Gornick says. "He discovered a need that ABC had in terms of providing material post-*Monday Night Football*, in the mountain states and the west coast. ABC needed material and they thought, 'How natural; sports documentaries, one hour before the evening news.' And so thus we were contracted to do these shows called *The Winners* and we had to seek out high profile athletes, obviously, ABC wanted quality."

Laurel would continue producing the sports docs for a couple of years before returning Romero back to the world of feature films with *Martin*. The small, intimate portrait of a

mentally disturbed young man who believes he's afflicted with the curse of vampirism wasn't a box office success at all, receiving limited distribution through New York producer and exhibitor Ben Barenholtz's Libra Films. Termed an "in-betweener" by the late Barenholtz, Romero's low budget character study would be all but impossible to successfully promote. "You know, *Martin* was a very difficult film to distribute. We tried different campaigns...it just did not – DID NOT – click with audiences...some critics didn't like it at all," Barenholtz explains. "If it was just a vampire film it would have been (easier), but it was much more than that. So, it didn't satisfy that audience that much and it didn't satisfy the art film, the sort of 'artsy', audience either because it was too bloody for them and not bloody enough for the other. So, it was stuck somewhere in between and that's very difficult to market."

"It was another one of the...almost a classic failure, in terms of George's whole lineage starting back, right after *Night of the Living Dead* – *There's Always Vanilla* and *The Crazies* and here comes another one, you know," says Gornick. "Everyone thought, 'Wow, another dud.'"

Interestingly, the ever-so-brief pairing of Laurel and Libra nearly led to an ongoing partnership between the two according to Barenholtz. "We basically had an agreement to form a joint company, you know, Richard in charge of production and me being in charge of distribution," he says. "I don't know, I think Richard decided it wasn't feasible or it was more of a financial thing, whatever."

Above: Stunt coordinator Taso Stavrakis, seen here with longtime friend Tom Savini at Disney World during a break from the Florida portion of filming for *Day of the Dead* in December 1984. (courtesy of Taso Stavrakis)

Laurel's next feature though would be the one the company was longing for from the beginning, a sequel to Romero's groundbreaking debut *Night of the Living Dead*. 1978's *Dawn of the Dead* would become an international box office hit and bring even more critical acclaim for Romero. The film's financial success brought about a three picture agreement for Laurel with *Dawn*'s distributor, Salah Hassanein's United Film Distribution Company. The deal would also help Rubinstein take the next step in his vision when he decided to go public and file with the Securities & Exchange Commission to form Laurel Entertainment in April of 1980. But as it turns out for Gornick it would change the dynamics of the company he had grown up with. "You know, this dredges up a lot of emotions though, I gotta tell you," admits Gornick. "It was the beginning of the end. I'll explain to you: exciting by concept because we were offered a three picture deal by Salah Hassanein – United Film Distribution – and it meant all kinds of what I anticipated to be new freedoms in terms of budget, new equipment. It was...it was glorious. And I thought it would be the beginning of a new age for the then Laurel Tape & Film. It also paralleled to be the start of Richard Rubinstein's attempt to form a public company called Laurel Entertainment. And Richard saw it, more to his advantage, as a way to hype the new over the counter stock, which was Laurel Entertainment, by declaring that he had a three-picture deal with Salah Hassanein and a future in significant motion pictures. So, there were these two parallel forces at work: one was my innocent thoughts about creating a new kind of Latent Image/Laurel Tape & Film in Pittsburgh, a new grand studio. And Richard – and I found later George – attempting to form a public company, something that had different kinds of significance than simply film-makers in Pittsburgh."

Laurel Entertainment would become a reality in the summer of 1980 while the filming of Romero's next feature, *Knightriders*, was taking place. Gornick would learn of the news on set from Laurel's at the time financial vice president, David Vogel. For some time Gornick was under the impression that as the outfit grew and became more successful that he, along with other key contributors, would be participants in that growth and success. "But as it turns out when it was finally formulated I was excluded. And Richard and George explained to me that I would always probably be available to be employed by Laurel Entertainment, but I wouldn't be 'intimate' to the company. They were principal share-holders, along with Richard's father, some other investors," Gornick says. "I was offended and I had plans that after we shot *Knightriders* that I probably should find other employment. Because it was kind of a hurt, you know; a disappointment."

Thankfully, Gornick didn't leave the company and would stay on for the entire duration of Laurel's existence. He would go on to serve as director of photography on the original *Creepshow* and the third installment of the *Dead* trilogy, *Day of the Dead*. He would serve as the post-production supervisor on all of Laurel's theatrical efforts as well and showed incredible flexibility and a willingness to do whatever had to be done to get the finished product in the can. "You know, I was kind of like what Hollywood calls a mule, where you work for a studio out there, you do what you're told; it's a labor. And working for George was just that, you were kind of

Above: Business card for Taso Stavrakis' company The New York City Stunt League. (courtesy of Taso Stavrakis) **Below:** Taso Stavrakis (aka Sir Ewain) in full jousting gear as part of the Hanlon-Lees Action Theater. (courtesy of Taso Stavrakis)

a mule," Gornick confides. "I wasn't the figure-head; I wasn't the 'George Romero'. But happily enough, yeah, if you want the negative cut, yeah I'll do it. If you want me to direct, I'll do it. If you want me to shoot, I'll do it. I'll be an actor; just a lot of fun. You're that mule – you take that task and do it. But yeah, I developed incredible diversity."

Being a mule for Romero would certainly pay off with the ingraining of a wealth of knowledge and experience onto Gornick's resume. Besides the cinematography and post-production work, Gornick was also afforded the opportunity to direct for *The Winners* sports documentaries, helming several episodes including ones on Pittsburgh Steelers players Terry Bradshaw and Rocky Bleier. That experience would come in handy when Gornick was given the chance years later to direct for the new syndicated television series that Laurel was producing called *Tales from the Darkside*. Gornick would direct four episodes during the show's four seasons – all shot in New York – and had an enormous desire to ensure his episodes were stand-outs. "I had incredible intensity because I wanted to make it good and so I studied and schemed," says Gornick. "The beauty of the *Tales from the Darkside* series is that it demanded complete discipline. You basically had three days to shoot. You had sixty setups – and I mean setups – that's all you had. You could try to glean as many shots out of those sixty setups as you could; your budget was very limited. And if you had any kind of makeup, or preparation for makeup, that was part of your time on set with your actors. Couldn't be better, it just called upon your full discipline to focus and get it done."

It was also around this period of time that George Romero began plans to leave Laurel Entertainment. Having corporate responsibilities, as well as Laurel's concentration on the new TV show, just wasn't particularly appealing to the Pittsburgh auteur. Prior to the production of *Day of the Dead* Romero knew that he would be leaving Laurel Entertainment to basically freelance as a writer and director (that would become official in June of 1985). Those days for Gornick were personally difficult as he felt his relationship with Romero starting to deteriorate over his perceived loyalty to Laurel. "George's parting shot to me before he formally left the old Latent Image, the old Laurel Tape & Film in Pittsburgh, was a conversation that we had over the phone and I said, 'George, are you splitting, man? Because Vince (Survinski) and I are wondering,'" recalls Gornick. "And he said, 'Yeah, man. I'm splitting, that's it. I'm going to Sanibel.' He said, 'What are you up to?', and I said, 'George, I've got to stay, I need to provide. I've got three kids now and it's not bad for me.' And he said to me, 'Man, it's hard to believe that you don't have enough cash yet.' And it was silence because I didn't know what to say to George. It's like, 'No. George, I worked for you two and a half years for $375 a month. You know, I barely cracked $1000 dollars when I shot your first motion picture.' So, he didn't know, he didn't understand. And that's his perspective. So that was, in essence, our parting shot."

And while Romero seemingly felt slighted by the allegiance Gornick displayed to Laurel, that show of faith wasn't lost on others who also worked with him and knew him well. "Mike was much appreciated and respected by me for his work ethic, loyalty, and skill set," says Richard Rubinstein. "He continued to work for Laurel in New York City for years afterward."

"It was very easy to work with Michael because Michael was somebody that I knew basically as a man who made the trains run smoothly," says Laurel's trusted casting director Leonard Finger. "He was the 'go to guy' on productions and the person who was involved with the daily routines of making things happen properly. He was not a prima donna. He was a person who was a brass tax, nuts and bolts kind of a guy, who was willing to listen to pretty much anything."

"I love Mike, he's a lovely guy. I've got a lot of time for Mike Gornick," says David Ball. "He's probably THE unsung hero of Laurel Entertainment. You know, he did every movie and then he did the *Darkside* stuff. He's one of the big roots of Laurel Entertainment, you know, and you have to respect that because most of it is self-tuition. And to reach that stage in your life where you're revered and respected through self-tuition shows how hard you must have worked as a youngster. And I have to take my hat off to that."

And despite the faith and backing of both Ball and Rubinstein, coupled with the excitement of being able to finally direct a feature film, doubts from Romero's letter about who would be best suited for the project still lingered for Gornick. Those feelings of being a so-called runner-up to John Harrison and Tom Savini and not being the favorite gnawed at him, but he also knew that this was a big opportunity and it was one that would give him a break from the harsh grind of *Tales from the Darkside*. "All those things kind of weighed against me in terms of feeling terribly enthusiastic about the project," he says. "But all the while knowing that it will get me out of New York, it kind of satisfied my ultimate dream which is to direct a motion picture."

Creepshow 2 was making progress during its pre-production – a bit on the slow side, mind you, but progress nonetheless – with important positions being filled. However, it was still in need of key personnel including a production designer and costume designer. On Laurel's previous three features those duties were handled respectively by the husband and wife team of Cletus and Barbara Anderson, longtime friends of George Romero. However, in this particular case their services were not retained. "I think the primary reason was because they were too cheap," says veteran costume designer Barbara Anderson. "So they hired our assistants instead."

As Anderson so bluntly states, for these crucial positions Laurel would in fact turn to their young apprentices. And while they were young, they were certainly not lacking in skill and talent. "It was a big step. I'm not sure if we even knew where we were going to shoot at the time," recalls Bruce Miller about landing the job of production designer. "I was one of the main designers in Pittsburgh, along with Cletus, who I don't think wanted to do it because George (Romero) was not involved. And since I had been his art director for so many projects, I guess to some extent, Laurel thought I was a cheap choice for them."

"Well, here's the thing. I had been the costume designer on *Sleepaway Camp* and then I did a TV series with Bruce, I did *Moving Right Along*, which was a little TV series for WQED," recalls Eileen Sieff-Stroup on the opportunity to become costume designer. "So, when this came along I was really excited that they asked me because I was trying to do more design work. You know, I was going back and forth; I still hadn't kind of settled into my supervisor on 'big movies' role, which is sort of what I did most of my career. And so it was a step up for me, but it was really nice because it was within 'the family'."

Above: Leonard Finger, Laurel Entertainment's steadfast casting director, seen here in his Manhattan office. (courtesy of Leonard Finger)

Bruce Alan Miller grew up in Solon, Ohio – a suburb of Cleveland – with a passion for architecture and theater beginning in high school. He attended college at the University of Virginia where he concentrated on theater, after having not particularly enjoyed the architecture program. He would receive his BA and then followed that up by getting accepted into the University of Minnesota where he earned his Master of Fine Arts degree in their theater design program. After graduation he went to work for the Minnesota Opera Company as technical director, designing one show a year. Miller would work there for seven years until being hired by the Pittsburgh Public Theater in a similar capacity, but after a little over a year in Pittsburgh he was let go. "I only was there for a year and a half. In my personal life I used to think I'd take two steps up the ladder and then fall back one step," Miller says about the setback. "So, my second year at the public theater was one of those fall back things. The first year was fantastic; the second year was very difficult."

Things were about to change for Miller however. During his time at the Pittsburgh Public Theater he became acquainted with Cletus Anderson, who learned of his departure from the public theater and offered Miller a job

Above: The Creep himself, Tom Savini, seen here as Arthur in George A. Romero's *Martin* in 1976. (courtesy of Michael Gornick)

on George Romero's upcoming feature, *Knightriders*. "I was available and so he hired me to be his assistant which I then did for seven or eight years while I was in Pittsburgh," says Miller. "So, *Knightriders* was our first show, and then *Creepshow*, a lot of public television stuff – when public television in Pittsburgh was a booming operation. *You and Your Tax Form*, I think I did that for three years at WQED; worked with Zilla Clinton (George Romero's veteran production manager) a lot."

From there Miller would continue his relationship with Laurel serving as art director on the pilot episode of *Tales from the Darkside* and the third installment of Romero's zombie opus, *Day of the Dead*, before getting his opportunity as production designer on *Creepshow 2*. "I probably didn't realize what it was doing for my career at the time, but looking back at it, it certainly has opened doors for me...lots of doors actually," admits Miller. "So, I would say it gave me a career to tell you the truth."

Eileen Mae Sieff-Stroup would grow up in Churchill, Pennsylvania, a suburb of Pittsburgh. She began sewing around the age of four and by eleven was sewing customer's clothes in her family's tailor shop in the nearby borough of Wilkinsburg. It was shortly before graduating high school that she decided what her career pursuit

would be. "So, I pretty much was gonna go do costumes – that was it," recalls Sieff-Stroup. "And around my senior year in high school I said to my mom, 'You know what, they're having an open house at CMU, I want to go. That's where I want to go to school. I think I'm gonna go study costume design.'"

Getting into Carnegie Mellon University would prove to be an impressive accomplishment for Sieff-Stroup. She had mostly concentrated on academic classes in high school, rather than drawing, so at her CMU interview her art was greeted less than enthusiastically. However, after pulling out some of the costumes she had created from her own designs, she was accepted by the school. And it was during her time at CMU that a big opportunity would present itself. "And then while I was there Barbara (Anderson) asked me to work on *Creepshow*," she says. "You know, she'd asked a couple of other people, they weren't available and then she asked me and I was trying to decide what I was going to do after school. I was gonna maybe go back to graduate school at CMU, I got accepted, and I got *Creepshow* and I was like, 'Oh, no graduate school for me. I just want to go do movies.' And then that launched me."

After *Creepshow* Sieff-Stroup would move to New York City and like her fellow crew member, Bruce Miller, she'd work on the pilot episode of *Tales from the Darkside,* as well as Romero's third zombie film *Day of the Dead*. After those she worked for costume designer Hilary Rosenfeld on the low budget feature *Flight of the Spruce Goose*, which interestingly enough featured George Romero in a small acting role as the character "Gromero". Following that project she followed Rosenfeld to Tennessee where she would work on one of the most underrated films of the 1980's. "Then I got to go on to *At Close Range*, which was like a dream," she says. "It was incredible. It was an incredible job because of all the fantastic acting."

An interesting side note to Sieff-Stroup's decision to accept the job for *Creepshow 2* was the film she turned down to do so, one that is considered iconic to a generation of females who grew up in the 1980's. "So, when I had finished *At Close Range*, Hilary, the costume designer, was going off to do another movie, *Dirty Dancing*, and she asked me to go with her. And David (Ball) called me to work on *Creepshow 2*," she remembers. "But I wanted to be a costume designer, so I did *Creepshow 2* instead of doing *Dirty Dancing*. But I was not sorry because *Dirty Dancing* was a really hard movie."

As mentioned before, the contract with New World wouldn't officially be signed until July 17. This was three weeks after the meeting with the bonding company, Film Finances, and would thus create a slight delay regarding the start of principal photography which was now scheduled for Monday, September 15, 1986. This put a little more pressure on the production from the jump because they were looking at an eight week scheduled shoot which would now push into late Fall, ending around the first week of November, with an answer print delivery date of March 15, 1987. Delays with New World would become a much bigger issue later during production when the Annie Lansing role, from *The Hitchhiker* segment, turned into a bit of a fiasco, which we'll get to later.

Dealing with New World was a much different experience for Laurel compared to past dealings with more "Mom and Pop" distributors such as United Film Distribution Company. And for David Ball the difference was stark. "Chalk and cheese, man. Chalk and cheese," he says. "UFD, Salah Hassanein, he'd ask you a question...he's very direct, Salah, very, very direct; very hard business man, but fair. And he would ask you a question and you'd give him an answer and that would be it, over and done with. New World? Impossible: vice president of this, vice president of that, head of in charge of this, deputy assistant, bloody vice president in charge of this, vice president in charge of that. You know? It was difficult – very difficult people."

Besides costing the production roughly $10,000, the delay would also prevent Laurel from hiring more makeup effects technicians to assist Ed French with his prep, which they eventually did when they brought Greg Nicotero, Howard Berger, Everett Burrell, and Mike Trcic on board – all veterans of Laurel's previous feature, *Day of the Dead*. Nicotero had made a good impression on Richard Rubinstein with his effective management of Tom Savini's makeup effects department on that film, so Rubinstein was hoping for something similar on *Creepshow 2*. The arrival of the upstart effects assistants though would create problems with the effects lead, French. "What had happened is this one producer asked us to come in and supervise Ed, but Ed was never told that we were there to supervise Ed," Howard Berger said in Anchor Bay's 2004 *Nightmares in Foam Rubber* DVD featurette. "So, Greg and I would be very forceful on how we wanted things done and then Ed would – you know, as he should, not knowing what the situation was – be very forceful back. And it became a very huge struggle, especially a struggle between Greg and Ed." **(4)**

French, upon learning from Nicotero that the younger effects crew weren't just there as help, but were there to monitor the progress and quality of the effects preparation as well, wasn't too enthused. The prep would go on though in French's Brooklyn, New York loft/studio despite the awkwardness of the situation. And then a conversation with the film's director and Nicotero would elevate tensions. "And I got myself into a lot of trouble because I remember talking to Michael Gornick and Michael said, 'How's everything going there?' I said, 'It's hard for me to say. I'm not quite sure how we're gonna utilize some of this stuff. I'm not quite sure how these things are gonna play,'" said Nicotero in that same Anchor Bay DVD featurette. "That set off a whole series of alarm bells and the next thing I know I was called a 'spy' and was banned from the workshop." **(5)**

Around this time a visit from David Ball, Michael Gornick, and Bruce Miller to French's loft/studio would prove to be a heated and volatile encounter. French was responsible for creating what would be "the blob" for *The Raft* segment and had teamed up with mechanical effects expert Ken Walker on a bladder machine that would be used to create the illusion of this living, amorphous lake creature. Effects assistant Matt Marich, who would be brought in later once the team was in Arizona, remembers the device and how ingenious it actually was. "So, originally Ed French had this very neat little system set up where it was kind of like a floating black bladder; much like the Dick Smith bladder

DOMENICK JOHN

SIZE____ HT____ SHOE____
HAIR____ EYES____ BORN____
AGE RANGE____

SCHULLER TALENT • NEW YORK KIDS
(212) 532-6005

Above: 1986 head shot of Domenick John Sportelli, who was cast as Billy without an audition. (courtesy of Michael Gornick)

effects," says Marich. "It floated on the lake and it was connected with hoses to vacuum pumps. And that was hooked up to a keyboard, basically like a small synthesizer keyboard, and you could play it and the bladders would inflate and deflate."

Now, concerning the aforementioned heated incident, at the time of said visit the bladder machine was not working properly, but French had Walker bring it over anyway so he could explain its capabilities to the group, in particular Michael Gornick. After waiting for hours for the group's arrival French eventually sent Walker home with the machine. And it's important to note that French's loft/studio was just that – besides being his work studio, it also doubled as his home. French was married and had an infant son, so when the group finally arrived around 9 o'clock in the evening things got off terribly when Ball began shouting at French. This led to a confrontation between Ball and French's wife – documented in an epic eleven-page December 8, 1986 letter from French to Richard Rubinstein – when she decided to intervene. "That meeting in New York was really traumatic. Because Ed was not ready for us and he wanted to postpone production. There was a fight with David Ball and Ed's wife, you know, about, 'Don't treat my husband like that'...I mean, I was just overwhelmed at the tension, it was a serious misunderstanding about what

Above: Pittsburgh mime artist Dan Kamin would deliver more than just a "stiff" performance as Chief Woodn'head. (courtesy of Taso Stavrakis)

Above: Young New York actor Holt McCallany would be cast as Sam Whitemoon, delivering an intense and memorable performance in *Old Chief Wood'nhead*. (courtesy of Holt McCallany)

had to be done. And probably Ed, since he's a makeup effects guy, probably thought that he shouldn't be doing it anyway," recalls Bruce Miller. "I remember I exited and went down and stayed on the street while they finished the discussion and it was tough."

Unfortunately, other than the prepared statement which was referenced earlier in this chapter, French declined multiple requests to be formally interviewed about his experience working on the film.

And quickly before moving on I would be remiss if I didn't mention the contributions, small as they may be, of a few other effects artists who were apparently subcontracted by French during the prep work for the film, specifically for *The Raft* segment, performing mostly lab type work for the blob effect. Scott Coulter (who also served as a production assistant during the beach filming for *Something to Tide You Over* on the original *Creepshow*), Tom Lauten, Gary Yee, George Higham, and Dan Frye – most of whom had previously worked on Roy Frumkes' *Street Trash* – were all peripherally involved very early on. One of them actually suffered for his efforts, a sort of omen for how principal photography would unfold. "I was making parts of the creature that lay in the water; I am not sure if they actually used the foam latex pieces that I ran for them. I just ran foam and spread the foam into these stone plate molds that were around 18x24 inches and they had different sculpted details in them from half-digested body parts and bits of junk like cans and stuff like that in them. I also tried to make these nurnies made of hot melt vinyl," recalls Gary Yee. "I was instructed to melt this vinyl to around 400

degrees and then slowly pour the material into a bucket of cold water to make these tendrils of webby stuff for *The Raft* vignette in the film. When I poured the vinyl into the water it sort of floated on the top of the water. I thought the material had cooled off on the surface of the water, so I tried to push the vinyl to the bottom of the bucket with my hand so I could pour more material on top of it. To my surprise the material was still molten hot inside and the tendrils of vinyl wrapped around my hand and burned my hand and fingers giving me what felt like an electric shock up my arm. I screamed bloody murder! I think the words 'Jesus Christ!' leapt out of my mouth when the pain leapt through my arm. My friend George Higham who was also working with us ran into the room to see if I was okay; I had burned my hand with second degree burns. It looked like I was attacked by a jelly fish."

Meanwhile, pre-production was continuing in plenty of other areas. Laurel-CST, Inc. was making arrangements with Willie Fonfe of Willies Wheels in the United Kingdom to purchase multiple Mercedes Benz vehicles to be utilized during *The Hitchhiker* segment. "My friend David Ball, who was part of the production team, asked me to locate a left hand drive S class Mercedes; unusual in the U.K. as we drive on the left and steering wheels here are on the right," Fonfe explains. "Its previous owner was a unit driver who used it to ferry around cast and crew on a number of British productions; unfortunately he is no longer with us but it is safe to assume that 'A' list stars of the early 1980s had been chauffeured in it." And 'A' list they indeed were as

Above: Don Harvey, having just come off appearing in Brian DePalma's *The Untouchables*, would land the role of "Rich Boy" in *Old Chief Wood'nhead*. (courtesy of Don Harvey)

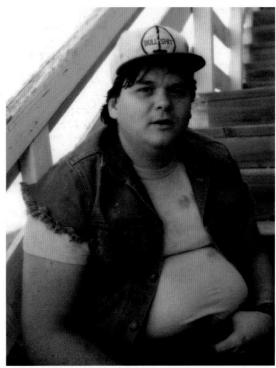

Above: David Holbrook, son of the legendary Hal Holbrook, was cast as "Fatso" Gribbens in *Old Chief Wood'nhead*. (courtesy of Michael Felsher)

Fonfe believes such legendary actors as Robert Mitchum and Kirk Douglas were probably chauffeured in one of the two stunt vehicles procured by the production.

The contract with Rick Catizone to handle the film's animated sequences was also now officially signed, which was an exciting time for the veteran animator. "You know, we did the animation on *Creepshow* and that was fun, but there was not a lot of character animation in that," Catizone says. "It was kind of thrilling – well it was more than kind of, it was really thrilling – to be doing a lot of animation for a major film again; and to do that much of it and be able to create the characters and control it." Much more will be covered regarding the enormous contributions from Catizone and his team once we arrive to Chapter 4.

The need for a stunt coordinator was also being addressed during this time with the production contacting another Laurel veteran, Taso Stavrakis, to handle those duties. Stavrakis' relationship with the production company dated back to the late 1970's while he was attending Carnegie Mellon University. It was there that he would form a life-long friendship with Tom Savini, who approached Stavrakis about helping out on stunts and makeup effects for *Dawn of the Dead* which was being filmed locally at the Monroeville Mall. This opportunity would lead to both acting and stunt work on other Laurel features such as 1981's *Knightriders* and 1985's *Day of the Dead*.

Born July 12, 1957 Taso Stavrakis originally entered the world at Timken Mercy Hospital in Canton, Ohio as

Andrew Nicholas Stavrakis. "I was born Anastasios, which is my Mother's Father's name. My older brother has my Father's Father's name, so I had my Mother's Father's name," he explains. "But back then, in the 50's, you had to translate – you got a Greek name and you got an American name, because we wanted to be Americans. So, they were arguing, up until the minute I was born, what American name to put on the birth certificate." Years later while in high school Stavrakis would have his name legally changed to Taso.

At a very young age Stavrakis would move to Pittsburgh with his family when his father, who was a Greek Orthodox Priest, took over a large church in the area. And much like Michael Gornick, Stavrakis cites the influence of the church as a possible seed to his entertainment career path. "It's not really that far of a leap when you see your father up there in a costume in front of the audience, you know, chanting and singing and preaching, talking to people," he says.

But it wasn't just the church which had an influence on the young thrill-seeker and his future in film. It was also, of course, television, which would help to hone a skill he would one day perfect in the zombie films of George Romero – dying! "I used to love to die. I watched the old movies on TV and so I would die, I'd fall off the couch and I'd perish in multiple ways. I'd get shot with arrows, guns and fall, hit the couch, roll off on to the floor," says Stavrakis. "And then I built a ski jump in the backyard – that was good, because I saw the guys in the Olympics doing that. I thought, 'That's great. I want to fly like that!' I built a ski jump, built a jump for my bike, same thing."

Above: Hollywood icon Dorothy Lamour with Bing Crosby and Bob Hope in *Road to Bali*. The screen legend would star as Martha Spruce in *Old Chief Wood'nhead*, her first film role in more than a decade. (copyright 1952, Paramount Pictures)

As mentioned, it was at Carnegie Mellon University that Stavrakis would cross paths with a soon to be famous makeup effects artist named Tom Savini, a kindred spirit for the future dashing stuntman. "Tom just got back from Vietnam, so he had traded makeup classes for acting classes. He wanted to go to Carnegie Mellon – the G.I. Bill wouldn't pay the whole way, so he said, 'I can teach makeup,'" Stavrakis explains. "Because by then he had already instructed himself just by watching Lon Chaney movies and studying all that; and Dick Smith, he started contacting Dick Smith and he started getting all the makeup information. Then he taught us makeup and then he was in our acting classes, so we were just school mates and we instantly hooked up. 'Swords? Yeah, you bet! Fighting? Sure! Jumping! Leaping! Swinging!' You know, we'd walk down the halls of Carnegie Mellon just arguing and screaming at each other: 'Fuck you'...'Fuck you!' And he'd pull out a gun and shoot me in the head and I'd have the blood pack. You know somebody's just walking by and 'Ahhh!!!' Can you imagine doing that now? Back then we just thought it was funny – 'Hahahaha! We scared you!' Now, it's like people would be calling the S.W.A.T. on us."

The friendship with Savini would lead to an opportunity

for Stavrakis to work on George A. Romero's sequel to his 1968 classic *Night of the Living Dead*. On *Dawn of the Dead* Stavrakis would act, assist with makeup effects, perform stunts, and do what he had always loved to do since childhood: pretend to die! Yes, whether it was as a zombie who's shot in the eye while being dragged from the back of a VW or as an unfortunate biker who's disemboweled by a horde of the living dead, Stavrakis would die and have a great time doing so. But it was performing stunts that would allow him to really showcase his talents, one in particular which came at the request of the film's creator, George Romero. "He said he wanted some Errol Flynn, because by then he figured we could do anything," Stavrakis says about the swashbuckling stunt from *Dawn* in which he swings from the mall's upper level railing. "You know, I'm stuck up on the balcony, everybody's trying to escape, it's not going well for the bikers and he wanted me to swing down on the rope string, it was a gag that he wanted. And me and 'Auggie' (Carl) Augenstein (*Dawn's* lighting director), I think, a couple of guys, who had actually repelled and done some climbing, had the harness. Okay, so I clipped into the harness and then we just couldn't get up above the balcony, there was nowhere to tie the pick, is what it's called, the high point to swing from. And so in the end, you know, we ran out of time and so I tied the rope to the same railing that I jumped from (laughs). What happened? I went underneath the thing and smashed into the balcony, like a pendulum. It's amazing, it's only twenty feet? By the time I got to the bottom it pulled this 10,000 pound rope so much that my feet skimmed the floor, I hit the floor and then I came back up and hit the bottom of the balcony – because that's physics (laughs)."

After the success of *Dawn of the Dead,* Stavrakis would assist Savini again on the horror smash *Friday the 13th.* Perhaps more importantly during this period Stavrakis would become one of the founding members of the Hanlon-Lees Action Theater, a theatrical jousting company, which would lead to a life-long passion for jousting in Renaissance fairs all across the country. Following his stint on *Friday the 13th* Stavrakis would make a move east where he would eventually start his own stunt company, The New York City Stunt League. "Went to New York after *Friday the 13th* – I didn't want to go to L.A., I wanted to go to New York and act," explains Stavrakis. "I called a couple of guys that I knew – Kent (Shelton), my jousting partner, and those guys – and I said, 'There's all these movies, there's room for more stunt guys, why don't we do some stunts?' So, we started doing fight choreography and stunt stuff and there wasn't anybody doing horse stuff and that's what I thought would be our 'niche', horse stunts. But, it didn't last long. We had a couple of small jobs and then I let it go."

Before letting the company go however Stavrakis would accept the position of stunt coordinator on *Creepshow 2.* And upon accepting said position he would immediately purchase nearly $2000 worth of scuba and diving equipment, which would be needed for *The Raft* segment. He also would make a key recommendation to Laurel as to who might be a good choice to play the hitchhiker – actor/stuntman Tom Wright. "You know who got me on to Tom Wright was Vic Magnotta. He was one of the most famous stuntmen in New York City, old time...Vic Magnotta," recalls

Stavrakis. "And right after that he died driving a car into the Hudson (River)."

I suppose the mentioning of actor Tom Wright is as good a place as any to begin discussing one of the most important processes of any production: casting the acting talent.

Creepshow 2's casting director, Leonard Finger, came to New York City via Houston, Texas with the hope of one day becoming a theatrical producer. Like so many who come to New York he learned how difficult the path to success can be, dealing with personal setbacks and in his case being cheated by business acquaintances. However, a favor he'd done for a gentleman several years prior would end up paying off in an enormous way. "I had worked in theatrical production and I'd had some moments of success and others of difficulties," Finger says. "And I had done casting on various shows with which I'd been associated. An old acquaintance, a person whom I'd assisted in getting an investment in a business which failed, contacted me and said, 'Look, would you like to do casting for a television show that I'm working on?'" That man was Laurel Entertainment's David Vogel and the TV show was *Tales from the Darkside*.

Finger would work with Laurel on the entire series run of the show and would also handle casting duties on their follow-up series, *Monsters*, years later. His approach to casting was really based on the parameters set by Laurel's head honcho, Richard Rubinstein. "Well, we were working on productions with very limited budgets. There was not much room for prima donna behavior from anybody, certainly not from actors or from people in the production. And it was all about efficiency and quality. That was one thing about Richard, I think that he always had a sense of...he knew what quality should be. And he also knew at times that he would have to make accommodations, but he always wanted a certain level of individuality and class about anything he did," says Finger. "This was not a highfalutin artistic enterprise. Nor was it a schlock production. It was really just getting the work done."

Unlike today with the internet and the use of technology aiding in the casting process, Finger would use his wits and resourcefulness to find the right fit for what Laurel was seeking. Often he'd use an industry standard such as *Breakdown Services*, which was a newsletter used by agents and managers to get their clients work. Other times he'd turn to unconventional methods such as visiting community centers or contacting acting teachers, thus becoming exposed to a rather wide spectrum of talent. "When I was working I was catching them on the way up and on the way down," says Finger. "And that was what the success of those ventures that I worked with for Laurel was – that we were able to find very good young people, some of whom went on to very big careers, and certainly they all went on to very stable, very respectable careers to this day, some of them in secondary or tertiary parts. But also we were catching people who had fallen out of favor or who were forgotten. Now with the explosion of television over the last several years...when we were working, working on television was considered a come down. There were people who refused to do television. And it was ironically, considering where things are today,

Above: Oscar winning actor George Kennedy, seen here as host of the short lived 1982 TV series *Counterattack: Crime in America*, would land the role of Ray Spruce in *Old Chief Wood'nhead*. (copyright 1982, ABC Television Network)

Bill Cosby who was the person that broke that because he was considered something of a movie star and a person of a very high level in television. And when he wound up owning part of his show – just as Desilu had done, Lucy (Lucille Ball) and Desi (Desi Arnaz) – he wound up becoming immensely rich by returning to television. And so it gave permission to a lot of other people to go to television. Well, that television success was part of the power that Richard (Rubinstein) was wielding. He had movie success. He had television success. And everybody knew that with *Creepshow 2* it was a property that would wind up having another life on television."

Now when it comes to knowing exactly how the casting process went, meaning who was cast first and in what particular order, there's no way to know for sure. Unfortunately, I wasn't privy to any such files. So, I think the easiest and most practical way to approach this would be to break the casting down by segment as seen in order in the film: opening prologue with Billy and the Creep, *Old Chief Wood'nhead*, *The Raft*, and *The Hitchhiker*.

Regarding the voice talent for the animated sequences

we'll discuss them once we get to Chapter 4, which will cover the post-production.

Wraparound Segment (live action)

As mentioned before, originally the role of the Creep was to be played by makeup effects artist, Ed French. However, issues concerning him would eventually prevent that. So, in need of a replacement for the role, Laurel would turn to an old and trusted friend. "It was *Creepshow 2*," Tom Savini explained in Arrow Video's 2016 Blu-ray featurette *Tales from the Creep*. "My friends were working on it, you know, 'Hey, you wanna play this part?' Oh, and they paid me a lot of money; yeah." **(6)**

"Ed French was to be the Creep at one point – never in my mind. I think I avoided every conversation that Ed would ever bring up about that. It was always in my mind to be Savini," Michael Gornick frankly confesses. "Yeah, this goes back to a pack that we had many years earlier because we had worked on a number of films together and we would always joke, 'Tom, when you make your film I'll shoot it. Tom, when I make my film you'll do the special effects.' So, it was kind of a nod to him, it was a promise that we made. I mean, I never was able to fulfill it for him, but at that point in time he could fulfill it for me. He was gonna assist in my film. And he assisted in many ways, I mean, most of the crew that wound up working with me in terms of makeup special effects were part of 'Savini University', you know, they were born of his stable."

This brings us to Billy Hopkins (eagle-eyed viewers will spot his last name in the original film's finale), the same Billy who used a voodoo doll on his stern father for throwing out his *Creepshow* comic book. "His dad had to be rushed to the hospital," Romero's *Creepshow 2* script reads. "All-night surgery saved his life but he still can't talk right." **(7)**

Stephen King's son, Joe, portrayed the character in the first film, but for the sequel the production would turn to 11-year-old Domenick John Sportelli to portray the horror comic obsessed "Billy". Sportelli, credited as Domenick John in the film, grew up in northern New Jersey, where his parents introduced him to acting and modeling at a very young age. He often spent his days in Manhattan going on casting calls after school and would spend summers in Los Angeles doing the same. He had appeared in television advertisements for companies like Parker Brothers and Canon, as well as appearing in a small role on the soap opera *Another World*. And as it turns out, landing the role of Billy would come about rather easily. "You know, this was unique in the sense that there was no casting process that I was aware of," says Sportelli. "And I'll explain that. Now, I started acting when I was eight years old and I was used to 'cattle calls', all these multiple castings, sort of like set ups, where you'd go talk in front of the camera and you'd meet the (producers) and all that. But when it came to *Creepshow 2* and getting that part there was no official casting. I was told specifically from my agency at the time, Schuller Talent – New York Kids, that the casting was strictly from the production seeing my head shots and reviewing previous work."

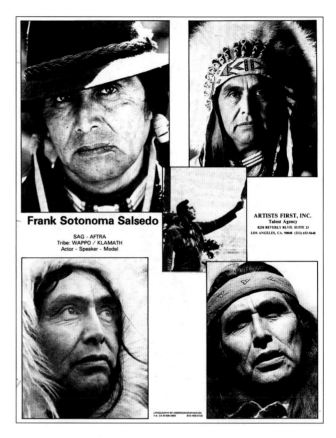

Frank Sotonoma Salsedo

SAG - AFTRA
Tribe: WAPPO / KLAMATH
Actor - Speaker - Model

ARTISTS FIRST, INC.
Talent Agency
8230 BEVERLY BLVD. SUITE 23
LOS ANGELES, CA. 90048 (213) 653-5640

Above: Head shot for Native American actor Frank Salsedo who was cast as Benjamin Whitemoon in *Old Chief Wood'nhead*. (courtesy of Rebecca Mayo)

"It was strictly visual," confirms Leonard Finger. "It was because of his look."

Old Chief Wood'nhead

Why not begin with the role that this nasty little bone-cracker is named after, shall we? The man who would be responsible for bringing to life the character of the avenging cigar store Indian, Chief Wood'nhead, would be Pittsburgh mime and performance artist Dan Kamin. It was while growing up in Miami, Florida that Kamin would discover his love of the arts and entertainment. "I was good at art, I was always able to draw things," Kamin says. "But, when I was a kid a movie about the magician Houdini came out with Tony Curtis. And I was so blown away by that movie that I became a magician, I became a boy magician. And the first way that I could find to make a living, to make money as a teenager, was I was doing magic shows, I started doing magic shows. I had business cards printed by the time I was 14. And I was doing magic shows for kid's birthday parties or Cub Scout troops or whatever I could get someone to hire me for. But I did not think of myself as a performer because I was going to go to college and be something to do with the arts probably."

Kamin's pursuit for a career in the arts would bring

him to Pittsburgh to attend Carnegie Mellon University. Unsure at first of what he wanted to do, he began studying industrial graphic design until a film series caught his eye at school. "On my campus they started off every year with silent movies and then they worked chronologically up to the really hip movies that were then coming out of Europe and blowing everybody away," Kamin says. "And midway through they showed a Charlie Chaplin movie and I'd never seen one because Charlie Chaplin had been pretty much erased from the America of my childhood because of the McCarthy era and things that say more about what was happening in America than about *him*. He was never erased from the rest of the world. And it blew me away and I just wanted to somehow be part of that world. But, I thought of it the same way I thought of magic, 'Oh, this is a hobby. I just want to know more about how he's making jokes, they're funny, but he's not talking. How can you make people laugh without talking?' And there just happened to be, on my campus, a great mime artist; because silent movies weren't being made anymore, but people still liked mime entertainment, non-verbal entertainment – visual comedy. And he happened to be a world class mime artist who had just been hired to teach in the famous drama department at Carnegie Mellon. And I saw him do a show and essentially I glommed onto him, I attached myself like a leech."

Little did Kamin know that this new and quirky fascination would wind up becoming the path he'd follow for the rest of his life. "I saw this man, Jewel Walker, on my campus and I discovered what I already knew from childhood: a great teacher is powerless before the enthusiasm of a student," says Kamin. "I would stop him in the middle of campus – you were not allowed to take classes in the drama department unless you were in the drama department – so I would just stop him outside the student union and say, 'How are you doing this thing where you make a wall or lean?' And he would just take five minutes and show me a couple of things and eventually he said, 'Just come over to class. Don't say anything to anybody, just come on.' And I started studying with him. Again, thinking I just wanted to learn the secrets of the magic tricks, but as my last years of college continued and drew to their end I realized I was spending more time thinking about this and I was starting to get some of my own ideas about how I could do creative story in mime; create a character, a story, do one of these illusions. But you just can't do an illusion you have to have some kind of story to go with it. So, I started arranging little shows for Cub Scout troops and coffee houses and before I knew it I never ended up working in the field of industry design or graphic design. I became a mime artist. I had to find out what there was...after I'd learned to speak that language I had to say things in it."

By the time *Creepshow 2* came about Kamin was working around Pittsburgh doing public shows in theaters and performing at events like the Three Rivers Arts Festival and that's when his work was noticed by Laurel. "They wanted somebody for the Indian part who was fairly thin so they could build the costume around because, of course, the costume was made of, basically, foam, painted foam," Kamin recalls. "And they wanted somebody relatively slim that could move well and so they approached me about that part."

"Well, Dan I knew through Pittsburgh connections.

Above: Daniel Beer would win the lead role of Randy in *The Raft*. (courtesy of Michael Felsher)

I'd seen some of his work as a mime and just knew he'd be absolutely perfect," recalls Michael Gornick. "In my personal relationship with him in terms of visiting at the office and meeting him under other circumstances in terms of film productions, he tends to put you at ease. He has an incredible aura about him and so I thought, 'Wow, this is the right kind of a guy to have with me. It's a positive force.'"

After now being cast in the role, Kamin would next travel to New York City where he would endure a different type of casting process. The makeup effects team would need to make a life cast of his entire body so a suit could be constructed for Kamin to wear during filming as the wooden Indian, a suit he would truly bring to life. "The idea of a statue coming to life had great appeal to me, since I had spent years learning to control my body for the purpose of doing convincing mime illusions, which are, of course, special effects created solely through movement," he says. "Playing an inanimate thing that comes to life was right up my alley, and it was fun to become the golem-like creature."

With the role of Chief Wood'nhead now carved out, we'll set our sights on his prey in the story.

For the pivotal role of Sam Whitemoon, Laurel would cast one of several young and unknown actors featured in the film, Holt McCallany. Though he may have been unknown at the time McCallany already exuded a presence of strength and charisma, along with some striking features to go along with that forceful persona. In fact, it's those features – his facial bone structure to be specific – that he believes helped him land the role. "You know, one of the stories that have stuck in my mind over all these years is that when I went in for my audition – Leonard Finger was the casting director – and I had originally auditioned to play a frat boy; I think the role that Paul Satterfield eventually played in the second sequence, 'The Blob'? Is it called 'The Blob'?," asks McCallany. "*The Raft*! Right, so I auditioned to play the frat boy and I remember I think it was Leonard saying, 'We'd like to see you play the Indian.' And I was

Above: The stunning Jeremy Green, seen here during principal photography, would land the part of Laverne in *The Raft*. (courtesy of Michael Felsher)

Above: Page Hannah, seen here in a 1984 press photo as Adair McCleary in the NBC soap opera *Search for Tomorrow*, was cast as Rachel in *The Raft*. (copyright 1984, NBC Television Network)

like, 'A Navajo Indian?' And Richard Rubinstein was in the room, too. And I said, 'I'm an Irish guy. I'm a white Irish guy.' And they said, 'Yeah, but you have good bones. And we could give you some makeup and a dark wig and stuff. You know, Burt Lancaster did it and he was excellent. You could do it!' And I remember – and ask Michael (Gornick) if he remembers this line, because I certainly remember it, and I think it was him that said it to me – I said, 'But I have blue eyes', and Michael said, 'We'll make you a half-breed.' Will you ask him for me if he remembers saying that? Because it has stuck in my mind for thirty years and I'm thinking about making it the title of my memoir: 'We'll Make You A Half-Breed'; because it was such an introduction to Hollywood. You know what I mean?"

"No," says Michael Gornick as he thinks it over. "It was Leonard."

"I said it," confirms Leonard Finger. "Not politically correct but I said it with humor." Indeed, Leonard Finger could never be confused with being bigoted or insensitive in any way, shape, or manner. He's a respected professional, with an impeccable reputation, who also happens to be quick witted and very funny. And to be clear McCallany in no way took offense to the quip, it just stood out in his mind because of how new he was to the casting process.

"I liked Leonard very much," says McCallany. "I'm very

grateful to him because it was really Leonard who was the guy...don't get me wrong, Michael cast me. But he cast me, I think, very much on Leonard's recommendation. So, if it hadn't been for Leonard I don't think I would have gotten the part."

"Holt, somehow when I saw him, was correct instantly. I knew he was right; even though we had to do so-called makeup alterations to make him look more ethnic in terms of his Indian background. But I knew," says Michael Gornick. "And I've got to tell you, a lot of what I do when I cast is almost like developing casting for a radio show – I listen. I listened. And I think physically he was right. I knew he had talent, I could see that in terms of the reading, but I loved the voice. You know, I knew there was kind of a tone, okay, a kind of atmosphere in an audio sense that was just absolutely perfect."

Gornick's observation here is astute as McCallany possesses a commanding voice, with a very distinct cadence, something he would use to great effect in the film.

So, McCallany was the choice for Sam Whitemoon, Laurel had their man. And it was actually a prior friendship that Leonard Finger had with McCallany's late mother that planted a seed in the mind of Laurel's clever casting director. "She was a wonderful human being, a woman called Julie Wilson. Julie was one of the most gorgeous

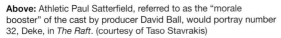

PAUL SATTERFIELD

Above: Athletic Paul Satterfield, referred to as the "morale booster" of the cast by producer David Ball, would portray number 32, Deke, in *The Raft*. (courtesy of Taso Stavrakis)

Above: Model/Actress Lois Chiles, seen here in a publicity photo with Roger Moore from the James Bond film *Moonraker* in 1979, would step in at the eleventh hour to play Annie Lansing in *The Hitchhiker*. (copyright 1979, United Artists)

women you've ever seen in your life when she was very young," says Finger. "She had been a showgirl at a night club called Latin Quarter and she was just one of the warmest, kindest people. And I knew her because in those very sad days I was involved with a charity for people with AIDS. And she was one of the main people doing benefits and contributing. And she told me, 'You've got to meet my son!' And Holt, at that point, was using her name, Holt Wilson, but his father, with whom the mother had been divorced, was dying and he changed his name back to his father's, his birth name, Holt McAloney. Anyway, he was such a talented actor, and still is, and he was extremely good-looking and really unique."

"She was everything that he just said," McCallany proudly confirms. "She was a fabulous entertainer. She was a gorgeous woman who had a long career on Broadway. She made films in Hollywood, she made twenty-one albums; she was a Broadway star. You know, she did everything."

Speaking with Holt McCallany the first time was not what I expected, to be honest. It's always a very pleasant surprise when the subject you're interviewing, someone who is still a busy professional, takes the time to really engage you. I'm not *The Hollywood Reporter* or *Variety*, mind you; I'm just a guy, a working stiff, in Pittsburgh. But McCallany was enthusiastic and happy to talk with me about the role that got him started in the film industry. When we began our interview the first thing he did was ask

about Michael Gornick and Laurel Entertainment, which I gladly obliged and filled him in with a "where are they now" status update. "Wow, man. You're really taking me back, I gotta tell you. A stroll down memory lane for me," says McCallany fondly. "So, what can I tell you, Lee?" And that's what Holt McCallany is like when you meet him: warm, sincere, and welcoming – regardless of who you are.

Holt Quinn McAloney was born in New York City on September 3, 1963. And despite the fact that he was American born, he and his younger brother would be sent to Dublin, Ireland to attend school and live with family friends abroad. And you might have noticed the change in spelling of his last name – I'll let Holt address that a little later.

McCallany came from a talented lineage as not only was his mother in the entertainment industry, but his father was as well. His father, Michael McAloney, was an Irish actor, producer, and director who won a Tony award for *Borstal Boy* in 1970. "My father was a very heavy drinker – a very charismatic guy with a lot of talent – but just like a lot of Irishmen of his generation, a very heavy drinker," reveals McCallany. "You know, my mom was a very strong and in some ways very independent woman – not a feminist. And definitely the kind of woman that wanted to make her marriage work. But ultimately my dad's alcoholism made it

Above: Actor/Stuntman Tom Wright, seen here in a 1983 press photo as Detective John "Colt" Colton in the NBC soap opera *Search for Tomorrow*, would secure the role for which his episode was named after, *The Hitchhiker*. (copyright 1983, NBC Television Network)

impossible for her to continue. But the problem was that in those days – my brother Michael and I were living in Ireland and going to school – and in the 60's in Ireland you couldn't get a divorce; it was literally illegal. The priest would tell you to go work it out. So she flew to Mexico and divorced my father. And the great story is that he was sitting in an Irish bar on Eighth Avenue in New York called Downey's, which used to be the actor's bar of New York, and somebody walked up and said, 'Hey, Mike. You made *Variety*.' And he looked in the personal section and it said, 'singer/actress Julie Wilson divorced legit producer Michael McAloney in Mexico City. They have two sons.' And that's how he found out that he was divorced."

After the divorce McCallany's mother brought Holt and his younger brother, Michael, back to the U.S. putting them in school in Summit, New Jersey. Later she would move them to her hometown of Omaha, Nebraska where Holt would become a self-described "juvenile delinquent", getting kicked out of school, and running away to Los Angeles in hopes of becoming an actor. "And my parents tracked me down and sent me back to Ireland to the same school that my father had attended forty years earlier, Newbridge College in County Kildare," he says.

When the time came to consider college McCallany assumed he'd follow in the footsteps of his father and step-grandfather who both had attended Dartmouth. But that assumption would lead to even further adventures in the aspiring actor's young life. "I just assumed that because I was going to be the third generation that I too would go to Dartmouth College in New Hampshire," McCallany says. "I applied to one school and when they didn't take me I was kind of stunned because I thought, you know, good old American nepotism will get me in, even with my lousy grades. And it didn't work. So, left without a place to go, I was up in the school library one day and I came across a brochure for a small fine arts school in Paris called The Paris American Academy where you could go and learn French and study art history and things like that. And so I went over there in part because I had read an interview once where Rod Stewart said that Paris was the best place in the world to hide. And I just wanted to be alone, be off the grid, and have a new experience. This was in the days long before the internet, long before cell phones, and it's on another continent, and they speak a different language. And you know what – the CIA can't find you over there, not in those days. So, I went over there and I spent a year at that school that I mentioned and then I quickly changed over to theater school because I knew I wanted to be an actor by the time I was six years old. And so I went to L'École Marceau and later to L'École Jacques Lecoq, which is still there, which is a very famous school. And I even did a few months at L'École de Cirque, which is like circus school. So, I did a lot of stuff like that, you know, just anything I could do that I felt would later help me when I became a performer. And those years in Paris turned out to be some of the best years of my life and I made some very important friendships there that have remained to this day."

While in Paris McCallany learned of some intensive Shakespeare seminars being offered during the summer at Oxford University. He applied and was accepted, spending one summer there. Afterwards he would perform with a theater group in Scotland at the Edinburgh Festival in a production of *Twelfth Night* portraying the character of Sir Toby Belch, complete with a large fake beard and stomach, a part he says he was not right for whatsoever. But he was determined to gain experience regardless of the role, remembering the words of his parents who had told him that every stage is a learning experience.

Upon returning to the States McCallany landed a job as an unpaid apprentice actor at the Great Lakes Shakespeare Festival in Cleveland, Ohio – the former stomping grounds of a young Tom Hanks. "I only did one season there; I think Tom Hanks actually did three seasons, which is amazing," McCallany recalls. "And then I came to New York and I got cast as an understudy in the Broadway production of *Biloxi Blues*, I replaced Woody Harrelson. And I was standing by in *Biloxi Blues* when I got a call from my agent saying there's an appointment for Leonard Finger for a film called *Creepshow 2*. So, we're talking about something that's *really* at the beginning of my career. Not only my first film, but one of my first experiences on film! And since then I've been in many films and I've done many television shows and I've got a lot of experience but that was definitely the first one and for that reason it will always be a very memorable one for me."

Oh yeah, before I forget, let's return to the issue regarding the spelling of his last name. "My middle name is Quinn. And Quinn is actually my father's real last name.

But he took McAloney because when he became a young actor in New York there's a law, a rule, in Actor's Equity that you can't take the same name as another actor who is already registered with the union, and there was already a Michael Quinn. And so out of respect for his step-father who had been very kind to him, a man named Holt McAloney, he became Michael Quinn McAloney. And so when I decided to become an actor I said, 'Well, I'm going to be Holt Quinn', because it's just simpler, it's easier to say. And the reason that my father objected to that was because before my mother married my father she had a long and very highly publicized romance with the actor Anthony Quinn. Now, nobody remembers that except my dad. But they were a couple for a number of years and often written about in the newspapers and gossip columns. They ended up not getting married and she later married my dad. But my father felt that if I became Holt Quinn that there would be confusion in certain people's minds as to whom my actual father was. So, I decided that the best thing to do was just to take my mother's maiden name of Wilson," McCallany explains. "Well, what happened there was that my dad didn't like that solution any more than me taking Quinn. Do you see what I'm trying to say? He was like, 'You're my son!' So, I decided to go with Holt McAloney. The trouble was that nobody could say it. It's just a very tough name, the way that it's spelled. We always pronounced it 'Muh-Cali-nee', but people would say 'Mac-alone-e', people would say different things. So, after long deliberation, I decided that I would keep my dad's name but I would change the spelling of it to make it more phonetic. And I don't know if I really solved the problem. (laughs) People still mispronounce it. But I am, I think, at the end of the day, happy that I have an unusual name, rather than a kind of average, every day name because it makes it more interesting for an actor."

Next up amongst Chief Wood'nhead's prey is the character of Andy Cavenaugh, a.k.a. "Rich Boy", played by the very jocular Don Harvey.

Born on May 31, 1960 in Saint Claire Shores, Michigan Donald Patrick Harvey was the sixth of eight children. Harvey would begin his journey into acting in high school performing in a handful of shows while attending Lake Shore high school. After graduation Harvey enrolled at the University of Michigan where he wasn't too sure of the path he should choose. "I don't know, I figured doctor, lawyer; teacher, what else is there? I didn't know what to do," says Harvey. "I didn't even know what to major in. I was gonna be pre-med when I went there, I was like, 'I'll be a doctor.' I did a week of work in chemistry and just dropped out, I said, "I can't do that. I don't even know what the hell they're talking about.' And then I started studying English and economics, just because I thought maybe that would be good for law."

After a couple of years there he found himself playing guitar, something he's enjoyed since childhood, in the orchestra pit for the musical *Sweet Charity*. He would receive some prodding from actor and friend Greg Jbara, who was also attending Michigan at the time, to join the other actors on stage. Harvey decided to give acting another shot, after he'd initially put it in the past. After his junior year he went to the American Conservatory Theater where he would expand his knowledge of the craft and upon returning for his senior year he began auditioning for plays, but still with the plan to pursue a career in law. "And there was a point there where I was supposed to take my LSAT test, I was in my senior year, and I was auditioning for a play. It was called *The Time of Your Life* by William Saroyan and my acting teacher was directing it," recalls Harvey. "And I went to the audition and he goes, 'Okay, the call backs are on Saturday morning. And I want you to come back – I'm calling you back for the play.' And I said, 'Well, Saturday morning I have my LSAT test. I paid like a couple of hundred dollars for a course to prepare to take this test and I need to take it because I'm filling out applications for law school and I gotta take this test in order to be considered.' He goes, 'Okay, well I guess you can't come to the call back.' I said, 'Yeah, okay.' And he goes, 'So, you can't be in the play then.' And I was like, 'Well, can't I just do the call back later?' He goes, 'Oh, I couldn't do that. You need to come to the call back with all the other actors.' And I was like, 'So, you want me to miss my LSAT test?' He goes, 'Well, I don't know. It depends on how dedicated you are. If you're really dedicated you'll come to the call back.' I was like, 'What the fuck are you talking about?'(laughs) I said, 'Well, okay. Do you think that if I come to the call back I will get in the play?' And he was like, 'I really can't say, Don. I really can't say at all. It depends on what happens at the call back.' And this girl that I was going out with in high school, who was now going to the University of Michigan, she was going to the call back. And I really wanted to get in this play so I could be in the play with this girl that I was in love with. So, I went to the call back, blew off the LSAT test. And I did not get into the play – the guy did not cast me in the play. What a dick!"

In 1982, after graduating from Michigan, Harvey decided to make a serious push towards acting as a possible career. During his senior year he was picked to be part of a small group of students, only ten in fact, to participate in a study of how to audition for graduate schools. This would provide him with a wealth of great monologues, helping to prepare him for what was to come next. "It was weird because I auditioned for all these other schools, you know, Juilliard, New York University, Temple, Southern Methodist, ACT, all these other great schools," he says. "Then I went to this league audition where there were about four hundred schools from all over the country that were there, you know, auditioning to get in. And I didn't get in to any schools; I just kept getting rejection letters saying, 'No, thank you. We appreciate your audition but unfortunately we don't have room for you.' So, I figured that was it, I was ready to go to law school. And then like the very last letter I got, two or three months after – I hadn't got any other letters from any other schools for about a month or two – I get a letter out of the blue. I open it up and it's from Yale, 'We are pleased to tell you that you've been accepted into our program.' It was the only school I got into – it was the best! It was the best of all, it was the number one. So, from the moment I walked into that school I considered myself a professional actor."

Graduating from Yale would give Harvey the confidence and the credibility to make the move to New York City and throw his hat into the ring for feature film roles. "And I was in New York for about a year when I auditioned for

Creepshow 2. That was about a year after I graduated," he says. "I'd just finished doing *The Untouchables* – that was my first movie, *The Untouchables*. And, I don't know, just being in New York, it was pretty amazing for a kid from Michigan to be walking around the streets of New York and auditioning for movies."

Simultaneous to landing the role of "Rich Boy" in *Creepshow 2* Harvey would also receive an offer to perform in the play *Progress* at the Long Wharf Theatre in New Haven, Connecticut. But it would require some assistance from his agent to secure both opportunities for the young actor. "And it was pretty much I got offered the movie maybe a day or two before," he says. "So, my agent, Michael Braun at Abrams Artists, just told the people at the Long Wharf Theatre that if they wanted me to do this role they had to let me go to Arizona to do *Creepshow 2* for two weeks. And it's very rare to be able to get out of rehearsals for a play for two weeks, that's really rare. But my role was not a huge role and there were not a lot of scenes they could work on so they let me out. But it was different. I'm working on a play for a week or so then I left to do *Creepshow 2*. It was pretty amazing."

This brings us to the last of Chief Wood'nhead's targets, the slobbish character of Steve "Fatso" Gribbens, played by David Holbrook.

The oldest of the three young actors picked to play the group of murderous punks – he was 31 at the time – David Holbrook wouldn't be the first member of his family to appear in a *Creepshow* movie. His father, Hal Holbrook, the Emmy and Tony award winning actor, had appeared in the original film as Henry Northrup from *The Crate* segment: "Ooh, just tell it to call you Billie." Perhaps that familial link would play a part in him getting the opportunity to audition and land the role? Well, that depends on who you ask. "Oh, I'm sure it mattered to them," laughs Holbrook. "Probably it's why I got the audition, I assume. I don't know how much it influenced the casting exactly, I imagine it might have influenced it somewhat, although I assumed they liked my audition and stuff like that. So, I assume they probably wouldn't have cast me if they didn't like that. But who knows what was in their mind?"

"It did. I mean, in all honesty it was kind of a goof," admits Michael Gornick. "It was, you know, somewhat of a minor role and he certainly had enough talent to pull it off. But I guess you do these things to entertain yourself sometimes, to just say, 'Wow, had a great time with Hal Holbrook on *Creepshow*. And, yeah, his son's perfectly talented, let's bring him on.'"

"You know something, I brought him in and I never mentioned it to Richard (Rubinstein)," says Leonard Finger. "I mean, of course, he loved Hal, but it was never even part of the mix. I just brought him in and he happened to get the job. It was not any kind of nepotism of any kind."

Holbrook was working in New York City at the time. Several years prior he had appeared in the low budget slasher film, *Girls Nite Out*, which also starred his father, Hal. And like many aspiring actors he performed whatever jobs were necessary to make a living, everything from working as a motion picture production assistant to delivering singing telegrams dressed as Buddha.

When *Creepshow 2* came around Holbrook decided he would go a bit further with the opportunity and make a visual impression at his audition as well. "Well, I knew I was auditioning for this character Fatso Gribbens and so I decided to go in there as sort of broad as possible and sort of dress as the character," he says. "So, I wore clothes that were too small for me, and shorts, and tried to make myself look as bad as possible. And I got a Tootsie Roll Pop and put it in my mouth like a cigar. I think I messed up my hair and made it look stupid and they laughed, the director was there and seemed to like it."

Above: After scouting other lakes in the region, including the much larger Lynx Lake, the production decided on Granite Basin Lake as the shooting location for *The Raft*. (courtesy of Michael Felsher and Bruce Miller)

When it came to finding the right pair of actors for the roles of Ray and Martha Spruce, the elderly couple victimized in their general store, the road to their casting would find one to be fairly easy to discover, while the other was a little trickier. So, in this case, we'll begin ladies first.

Dorothy Lamour was born December 10, 1914 in New

Above: An empty building on Main Street in Humboldt, Arizona owned by the Hinshaw family would serve as the interior for the Spruce's General Store in *Old Chief Wood'nhead*. (courtesy of Michael Felsher)

Orleans, Louisiana with the name Mary Leta Dorothy Slaton. Her parents' marriage was brief and they divorced when Dorothy was very young. Her mother would later remarry a gentleman named Lambour and Dorothy would take his last name as her own, dropping the "b" when she eventually created her stage name.

At the age of 16 she was crowned "Miss New Orleans"; soon after she would move to Chicago with dreams of becoming a singer, where she worked as an elevator operator in a department store. Eventually she was discovered in a Chicago talent show by big band leader Herbie Kay, who she eventually married. Kay would recommend her to Rudy Vallee, a very popular singer and actor at the time, and she performed with him at some of New York's grandest hotels and on his radio show. Around this time she would also become friends with Bob Hope, who introduced her to Louis B. Mayer, studio head of MGM, who offered Lamour the chance for a screen test. Lamour, however, didn't take the offer very seriously and passed on the opportunity. She went on to have her own radio program on NBC, *The Dreamer of Songs,* which eventually took her to Hollywood when the network moved the show to the west coast. It was there that Lamour would receive another offer for a screen test, this time from Paramount. She wouldn't refuse

the opportunity this go-round and was offered a contract by the movie studio. And from there a star was born as Lamour would go on to appear in films like *The Jungle Princess*, where she would wear the famous sarong that would become a trademark of her career. But it was in 1940 that she starred in the first of a series of comedy musicals that she would be best remembered for when she appeared in *Road to Singapore* with Bob Hope and Bing Crosby. She would go on to star in six more *Road to* films with Hope and Crosby making her a beloved figure to moviegoers, with a career that would span nearly 55 years. But it wasn't just entertainment where Lamour would leave a lasting impact, as during World War II she sold war bonds. In fact, because she sold so many, over 300 million, by the end of the war she was nicknamed the "Bond Bombshell".

In 1986 when *Creepshow 2* came around Lamour hadn't appeared in a feature film in a decade, with her work consisting of strictly television appearances. Leonard Finger briefly considered some others for the role, before suggesting the intriguing idea of Lamour. "I really don't remember the other people I spoke to," he says. "I know that I spoke to people about people like Esther Williams, who was never a great actress, none of them were great actors. But basically I went through a whole list of actors. I knew the grandson of Marlene Dietrich; I probably called him about her."

"Leonard and I didn't have any material that she had done recently," recalls Michael Gornick. "But I knew she'd be a joy to work with and I knew she was the right type and she brought this 'star value' to the film."

As for Lamour she viewed the opportunity in the most practical of terms. "But everybody talked me into it," she told the *Los Angeles Daily News* in 1987. "Who's everybody? Well, my kids, my secretary Donna, my friends – oh, and my agent." **(8)**

For the role of Ray Spruce the production would turn to reliable character actor and Oscar winner George Kennedy. Amazingly, as solid and believable as Kennedy was in his performance, he actually wasn't the casting director's preferred choice at the outset. "I can tell you about George Kennedy. That was actually something that I was pressured to...we were pressured to go to him," says Leonard Finger. "George Kennedy was a terrific actor. The only problem with George Kennedy was he was too young at that point to play opposite Dorothy Lamour, who was such an interesting idea to use according to Richard (Rubinstein) and other people when I suggested her because she was somebody who'd been a major star who still held a huge amount of allure for a lot of people and who had not been working in many, many, many years. So, there was something that had publicity value to it and also just the interest of seeing a movie with Dorothy Lamour. But to do that properly you have to have somebody opposite her who is appropriate and that was where the rub was and there were arguments about it. And unfortunately it wound up going to George Kennedy, who was a superb actor as a character man, but not as right for that as...my choice would have been a man called Leon Ames."

Leon Ames was a respected actor having appeared in such classic films as *Meet Me in St. Louis*, *The Postman Always Rings Twice*, *Peyton Place,* and *Peggy Sue Got Married;* as well as appearing on TV shows such as *Father of the Bride* and *Mister Ed*. As Finger alluded to Ames was older than Lamour, nearly 13 years her senior, while Kennedy was a little over 10 years younger.

Another noted actor that Laurel was definitely interested in for the role of Ray Spruce was Buddy Ebsen, of *The Beverly Hillbillies* and *Barnaby Jones* fame, but Ebsen was a little out of their price range. "He wanted money – that was the problem. Buddy Ebsen would have been perfect, but the thing is Buddy Ebsen was out of the picture completely," says Leonard Finger. "This is the thing I learned to do working with Laurel. My instinct, the way I was operating with other (producers) when I could, I would have gone to the very top of the top. But the thing is if I know they're not going to pay you for it, why waste everybody's time? And Buddy Ebsen was somebody who truly...first thing is he was an extremely rich man. He was an extremely *difficult* man. And he made very clear to me

when I first asked that he wanted a certain figure and he wouldn't work cheap."

"And Buddy I thought, I know Leonard and I had this conversation...you know, it's hard to shake some images that actors have," says Michael Gornick. "And we know what Buddy's image is and I'm not sure...I find that a kind of distraction. Whereas George Kennedy has done so many roles that he feels fresh to an audience when he arrives in a new role – I think, personally. And that's part of his talent too because, I mean, he wasn't ever typecast and he had variety in his roles – and an Oscar winner, my god. So, what I'm saying is, I think Buddy had sort of a kind of baggage that would have hurt the film, in my mind. So, I was most pleased that George was in contention and accepted the role."

George Harris Kennedy, Jr. was born February 18, 1925 in New York City. His parents were both involved in the arts as his father, who passed away when Kennedy was only 4, was a musician and bandleader and his mother was a ballet dancer. Kennedy would make his stage debut at age 2 when he traveled and performed in a production of *Bringing up Father*. Later he would work in radio performing voice work for children's shows.

After graduating high school Kennedy would enlist in the U.S. Army where he hoped to eventually become a pilot. His large frame would prove to be a hindrance to that dream however and he ended up serving in the infantry. Kennedy would serve 16 years in the military, fighting in World War II, and eventually earning the rank of captain. He would earn 2 Bronze Stars and numerous combat and service ribbons during his distinguished military career. And perhaps most interestingly he would serve under the command of General George S. Patton, who he would later portray on the silver screen in 1978's *Brass Target*. During his time in the Army Kennedy worked in Armed Forces Radio and Television where he opened the Army's first office of technical assistance for TV and movies. It was then that he got the chance to become a technical advisor for *The Phil Silvers Show*, also referred to as *Sgt. Bilko*. It was this experience that would lead Kennedy to move to Hollywood and pursue acting where he started off working in television. He would make numerous appearances on shows such as *Gunsmoke*, *Route 66* (yes, the same *Route 66* Stephen King mentions in *The Raft*), *The Untouchables*, *Bonanza*, *The Fugitive*, and *Rawhide* typically playing ruffians, outlaws, or cowboys.

It was Kennedy's performance in 1967's *Cool Hand Luke* though that would earn him respect in the Hollywood community. In the film Kennedy portrays the role of "Dragline", friend and fellow prisoner to Paul Newman's "Luke" character. He would win the Academy Award for Best Supporting Actor for his efforts in the role. Kennedy would enjoy a long and active career as a character actor appearing in such films as *The Dirty Dozen*, the *Airport* series, *Earthquake*, and *The Delta Force*. Always steady and always professional, Kennedy was a pro's pro. "George Kennedy: very quiet, unassuming. His wife was with him most of the time," remembers David Ball. "I think he might have been a bit of a hell raiser in the earlier years. You know, George, big heavy drinker with all the clan, the Lee Marvins of this world. But he was lovely and he was fine."

Above: School teacher Rebecca Mayo(right), seen here with soundman Felipe Borrero and assistant auditor Priscilla Dougherty, would serve as the production secretary in Arizona and prove to be an invaluable member of the team. (courtesy of Rebecca Mayo)
Below: Arizona location manager Michael Morgan would come to the production with prior experience on films like *Billy Jack* and *Junior Bonner*. (courtesy of Garry Greer)

For the elder tribesman, Benjamin Whitemoon, the role would go to the late veteran character actor Frank Fernando Sotonoma "Grey Wolf" Salsedo. "Frank Sotonoma Salsedo, what a nice guy he was," Holt McCallany fondly recalls.

Frank Salsedo was born May 20, 1929 in Santa Rosa, California. Salsedo came from a large family, as he was one of twelve children. He graduated from the Sherman Institute, an all Native American school in California, and upon graduation would enlist in the U.S. Navy. Later, after being discharged from the military, he would become a certified public accountant. He would go on to become the president of Jay Silverheel's acting school (Silverheel was "Tonto" in *The Lone Ranger* TV series) in Los Angeles where he would realize his dream of becoming an actor. He appeared in numerous film and television roles that featured Native American characters such as *I Will Fight No More Forever, Centennial*, and *The Legend of Walks Far Woman*. Salsedo even appeared in the popular "Gumfighter" advertisements which ran during the early 1980's for Hubba Bubba bubble gum.

"I found him in Los Angeles. I didn't know anything about him before; I just thought he was fabulous. But I brought in a number of real people, real Native Americans," says Leonard Finger. "There was an association at that point, and it probably still exists, but an association of Native American actors. And I went to them before I brought in anybody. I had them send people and then I called specific agents. That's how I did it."

Salsedo was quite popular among his fellow cast and crew and made a good impression during his time in Prescott. "And let me just also say one final thing about Frank who, obviously, was Native American, and I was not. But he couldn't have been more kind to me and a nicer guy," says Holt McCallany. "I had an opportunity to work with him again many, many years later and I really liked him. One of the real gentleman, one of the real class acts in the movie business."

"Listen, you're going to win the $64,000 grand prize if you can tell me whatever became of a guy named Maltbie Napoleon," asks Holt McCallany. "I'll never forget his name because who could forget that name?"

"That's funny because Holt, my grandfather, where I get my name from, his name was Matlbie Holt," says that man with the unforgettable name, Maltbie Napoleon. "Holt is a big English name. The Holt's were a big family here (Hawaii)."

Napoleon is featured in the *Old Chief Wood'nhead* segment as one of the young Native Americans who chauffeur around Frank Salsedo's character Benjamin Whitemoon. It's a non-speaking role, but Napoleon is listed in the film's ending credits as "Indian 1".

Born October 19, 1951 Maltbie Kameeiamoku Napoleon is a native of Hawaii, born on the island of Oahu, nicknamed "The Gathering Place". His ancestors, as he mentioned above, immigrated to Hawaii from England in the late 1800's. "But, you know, like most of us we're all 'chop suey'," he says. "That's English, French, East German, Dutch Irish, Italiano, so a little of everything."

Napoleon would grow up in northern California after his family moved to the Bay area, later enlisting in the U.S. Navy. By the late 70's, after spending a couple of years in Southern California, Napoleon decided he would move back to his native home of Hawaii. Since the age of 14 he had been returning each summer and helping his uncles with their surf board and canoe rental business, which he would make a full time gig upon returning home.

Several years after moving back to Hawaii, Napoleon would have the opportunity of a lifetime present itself on the beautiful sun-soaked beaches of Waikiki when famed photographer Bruce Weber showed an interest in him as a subject. The photos taken of Napoleon by Weber would be featured in fragrance ads for Calvin Klein and would become quite the sensation, which would come as a big surprise to Napoleon, who was still living his normal everyday life. "Now, I didn't realize what all these fashion magazines were. I mean, I'd heard of *Vogue* and a couple of others, but I didn't realize that these pictures are in every fashion magazine that I started picking up," he says. "My friends are saying, 'Wow, you're in this, you're in that, you're in *GQ*', I go, 'What?' And, I don't know, I didn't know what to really make of it. So, I just kind of continued my life living on the beach and everything was good."

Taking advice from a friend Napoleon would turn to a modeling agency to help land him work, which would lead to more lucrative photos for Calvin Klein. Following some encouraging from his agency, Napoleon would make the move to New York City, where upon arriving he would receive quite the surprise while taking a taxi ride through one of the Big Apple's most iconic spots. "I look outside and there's this big billboard in Times Square and I'm on it, from one of the pictures that Calvin (Klein)...and, well, it caught my breath. I go, 'Whoah!,'" he recalls. "So, I got out of the car and it's not only one, there are two of them. Across the street there's another big billboard and it's one of the other pictures, and I'm just stunned."

During his time in New York the desire to try his hand at acting would bite and that's when his opportunity for *Creepshow 2* came about. "And so I took a couple of classes here and there, I went with a couple of friends of mine. They said, 'Oh, come to this guy's class', and we'd go and I'd go once or twice; and I'd only been to acting classes like once or twice before the movie came out, so I wasn't real good, but I was just getting my feet wet at the time," Napoleon says. "But because I had shown some interest in the acting, my agency said, 'Hey, we want you to read for this part.' I said, 'Okay, sure', I was up for anything. And it was for *Creepshow 2*, and so I did a reading for them. They said they liked me but, you know, they could tell how inexperienced I was – and I was. So, I didn't have any problem with that. So, they said, 'Well, maybe we could use him for a small non-speaking part.'"

For the second Native American, "Indian 2", the part was filled by a Prescott local named Tyrone Tonto. I'm not 100% sure on the spelling of the last name since in production paperwork it's listed as "Tanto", with an A, instead of an O. Not much is known about him other than his contact information was care of a gentleman named Earl Lister, who is now deceased.

The part of "Curly", the gas station attendant, is oddly credited to a Philip Doré, but the individual playing the part was actually transportation coordinator Peter Levy (P.D. Levy), who handled the same duties on prior Laurel productions like *Tales from the Darkside, Day of the Dead, Creepshow,* and *Knightriders.* "I have to mention Peter Levy, the transpo coordinator because he was on everything Laurel ever did," laughs David Ball. "He didn't have a clue about transportation. I think he was the Laurel supplier of *extracurricular* things. I think that's basically what his claim to fame was. So, he had the job as transpo coordinator. But, you know, over the years he got the hang of it, he wouldn't take any shit from anybody, and he was fiercely loyal, too. I love Peter Levy to pieces."

Rounding out the *Old Chief Wood'nhead* segment brings us to the parents of Andy "Rich Boy" Cavenaugh, played by Shirley Sonderegger and Deane Smith, both of whom were Bangor locals.

At the time, Sonderegger was a personal assistant to Stephen King, mainly answering fan mail, and the time she spent working for the world famous author is something she looks back on with great fondness. "We got to be wonderful buddies and wonderful friends," Sonderegger says. "So, I never felt like I really had a boss. It was just that we were friends, you know, enjoying each other's company. So, he was a terrific guy to work for."

That friendship would lead to King one day approaching Sonderegger about the film, apparently for no reason in particular. "He just picked me out," she says. "I was working in the office and he said, 'I want you to be in *Creepshow 2.*' And I said, 'Really?'"

As for her fellow cast member, Deane Smith, he landed the part due to a connection with a colleague. "There was somebody in the production crew that was in the Air National Guard and I was in the Air National Guard. And she gave me a call and she said, 'We're looking for someone that's kind of grey, looking kind of old,'" laughs Smith. "And I guess I was in the middle of that description and so I went in and met them somewhere – can't remember exactly where I met them, I met them somewhere – and they said, 'Oh, yeah. You're perfect. What size pants do you wear and shirt?'"

Even though only seen from the back and from a distance, with no lines of dialogue as well, the pair is credited in the film's closing reel. "But, you know, not everybody's got a movie credit with George Kennedy," chuckles Smith.

And according to Sonderegger her and Smith's time together filming was apparently "on the house"! "We ended up...we never did get paid for that. That was just fun," she says. "I saw him another time and he said, 'Did you ever get paid for that?' And I said, 'No, did you?', and he said, 'Nope.'"

The Raft

We'll begin with the last victim from this bubbly bon-bon of a splintering tale – the man who thought he had beaten the blob, "Randy", played by Daniel Beer.

Although he grew up in the upstate New York village of Honeoye Falls, Christian Daniel Beer was actually born in Germany, where he spent the first two years of his life in the village of Peising, not far from Bad Abbach and Regensburg. He is the great-great-great grand-nephew of Friedrich Ebert, who served as Chancellor of Germany and was elected the first president of the country in 1919. Beer comes from a pedigree entrenched in the arts: his grandmother designed and created gowns for the Nuremberg Opera and his great, great grand uncle was the famous dancer and choreographer Helge Peters Pawlinin, who was hunted by the Nazis. "The whole German thing and the Nazi thing, you're kind of raised to kind of be quiet about it," Beer says. "Germany has kind of taken a real turn in a positive way and I just said, 'You know, I'm really going to take pride in my lineage', because it's a really rich lineage."

After graduating high school, Beer, the oldest of three children, moved to Manhattan to pursue a career in acting. His first month in the Big Apple he landed a small role in the low budget slasher flick, *Hell High*. Not long after the opportunity for *Creepshow 2* came along. "I was told that they went to Los Angeles and New York to find my role and they couldn't find what they were looking for," remembers Beer. "And my agent, Michael Kingman, at the time, who passed away from AIDS in the early 90's, walked me down to Leonard Finger's office because they didn't want to see me. And we walked in the office and I was, I don't know, eighteen or nineteen years old, and I said, 'I don't know, Michael', and he said, 'No, no. Come on', because Leonard Finger's office was in the same building. And he basically said, 'Well, we're not leaving until you'll see Daniel for one of the roles.' So, that's how I got the audition for the role. And I remember in the audition room – as an actor you remember all the auditions that you book the job for – so, I just remember I had to read the scene about the blob coming and I'm sitting in a chair and I remember Michael Gornick there, I think a producer, and Leonard Finger. And I remember after I did it they said, 'You know, it's this big blob and it's this and this', and I remember saying, 'Well, it's not in the room so I can't really respond to that. I have to come up with something else.'(laughs) I studied acting for six, seven years in New York and I'm a trained method actor and I still remember I was using – it's called an over-all – I was using being in a sauna for too long because that was one of the exercises we worked on since I was still just beginning in my studies. And when I'm in a sauna too long I start to get a little pensive and frightened and I want to get out of there. And that's what I used sitting in that chair, I used an over-all, and the lines come out of there. And I booked it."

"He had a kind of pensive way about him, but still full of energy. And he seemed to be able to read past the pages he had, which we give as sides for the actor's to prepare with," says Michael Gornick. "So, I gotta tell you that he was, if not my first, maybe one of my second reads on the role and I knew pretty instantly that he was absolutely perfect for that role. Perfect for the role; had a pure understanding. He was physically exactly what I wanted. And I think in terms of – I don't recall now – but in terms of Steve's (King) description of the young man, he was it. So, came pretty early to the conclusion that Danny was right for the role."

Our next unfortunate victim of the blob, "Laverne", is Jeremy Beth Green. Growing up in Long Island, New York, Green was an ice skater appearing a couple of years prior to *Creepshow 2* in a Wrigley's Doublemint chewing gum commercial with her identical twin sister, Pamela. "That was how I cast her. I cast her from the Doublemint gum commercial," says Leonard Finger. "Somebody involved in the production had seen it and said, 'Oh, that girl's cute!' I said, 'Well, look, let me find her', and I found her and called her agent and got her to come in. And she loved the idea of doing a movie and that was that."

One of the principal reasons why Green was cast in the role, according to someone who preferred not to go on the record, was the fact that she was amenable to performing nudity in the film – a requirement for the role – and not necessarily because of talent (which is ironic because her performance in the film is quite good and believable). Now, Romero's script does describe the character as looking like "a knockout straight from the pages of *Playboy's* 'The Girls of Horlicks' spread" and also as being a "sex-kitten", as well as mentioning her breasts being exposed in the scene with Randy. But that role requirement, more than anything, was apparently based on economics and executive producer Richard Rubinstein's desire to market the film overseas.

"The fact is this: Richard wanted somebody to be in a topless scene for whatever it was, for the marketing of the movie, I'm sure," says Leonard Finger. "The thing is again, do I care? Not particularly. So, I was not there with a tape measure, but I was trying to find somebody who was willing to and was also not going to be disappointing to the populace."

"Look, the story is these kids go out on the raft, they're smoking dope. They're out there for a reason, aren't they? And what's the first thing you see in that type of situation is a pair of tits, right? So it's exploitive, but the film is exploitive," says David Ball. "I don't think it's a moral issue, I think it's an issue of Richard being exploitive about what he wanted to see on the screen, to the point of titillating the audience."

"Richard felt that the nudity would enhance its foreign value," says Mitchell Galin. "It was not exactly something that we saw eye to eye on. I didn't think it made a material difference, but he did. And you know what? At a certain point he's gotta sell the foreign and make that deal, so it's kind of his call."

"I mean, she looked perfect for the role; didn't know until I read her that she would be appropriate also. And it wasn't just her good looks, she seemed to have a kind of perception and understanding of the role," says Michael Gornick. "I knew she didn't have much in the way of a background, per se, but she read so well for me that I thought that she would work. And so, you know, whenever you're doing these sort of things you don't want everything to be a given, you'd like to be able to work with some people. And she certainly had the looks, the temperament; she was very physical in nature. I could tell that in terms of her athletic abilities, so I figured she'd be perfect for this role. And I'm glad I chose her, I really am."

This now brings us to the first of our story's four doomed

victims, "Rachel", played by Page Hannah.

Born April 13, 1964 in Chicago, Illinois Hannah is the younger sister of actress Daryl Hannah, of *Blade Runner* and *Splash* fame. Upon deciding to pursue a career in acting she would move to New York where she attended NYU and Circle in the Square with the Tisch School of the Arts. "I went to school full time for the first two years and then in my third year I got on a soap opera called *Search for Tomorrow*," says Hannah. "I did that and then went out and did the TV series *Fame*, my senior year, in L.A. And so from then on I was back and forth doing different TV and films and things like that."

When the chance to appear in *Creepshow 2* came about Hannah was more than just a little intrigued. She had grown up a fan of Stephen King, so the opportunity to appear in a film with his name attached was an absolute thrill. "Loved Stephen King; loved...huge fan of Stephen King," she says. "And also just to do a horror film or something like that was just so different and just really exciting."

The connection Hannah had, being the sibling of a popular and well known actress, would definitely factor in when deciding to cast the role, but her talent also caught the eye of Laurel. "She was a lovely girl, she was talented, but she got out of the business – but she was Daryl's sister and it was really more because she was somebody that we thought that kind of had some possibilities," recalls Leonard Finger. "And she was a lovely person, she was cute."

"She is a diamond girl, let me tell you. She's a diamond girl," says David Ball. "She was lovely. She was young and she wasn't affected at all about her big sis, she wasn't in anyway affected. She was a nice kid. Nice kid, Page; very level, very straight, very feet on the ground. Good girl."

Above: Director of Photography Tom Hurwitz(w/camera) candidly admits he was probably not the right choice for the job considering his style is much more naturalistic. He would end up leaving the production early. (courtesy of Michael Felsher)

"She's pretty stunning and she read so very, very well. I'm a fan of soap operas and I actually had a few years prior seen her in a TV series called *Search for Tomorrow* and she was very, very good," says Michael Gornick. "And, yeah, she was actually appropriate from the very beginning. And again she read perfectly in the readings we had, so she was almost a no-brainer. She arrived and she had a certain kind of charisma as she walked in the room that you knew that she'd probably be exactly right."

"Page Hannah and I, we became close," says Daniel Beer. "I have a great story: Paul (Satterfield) was from California and Jeremy and Page and myself were flown out of New York. And we were at the airport, I had twenty dollars to my name, and I'm sitting there with Page and she said, 'Do you have any money? I want to buy some snacks and stuff.' I said, 'Sure', so I gave her my last twenty dollars. And when it wrapped (the filming) and I came back, she was wrapped before me, I was the last one, obviously, and I came back and I called her up and I said, 'I don't have any money, all of my checks haven't come through yet. I don't have any money. So, I can't really hang out.' She goes, 'Don't worry, I got you. I'll feed you.' I really didn't have any money, so she like fed me for a few days." That act of generosity from Hannah is something that has stayed with Beer all these years later. "So, I bumped into her like a few years ago in Malibu and I just told her the story that I told you, because I never told her at the time," he says. "I never told her that I gave her my last twenty, because she probably wouldn't have taken it. And she just couldn't believe it and she goes, 'Well, there you go, Daniel, karma.'"

And last, but not least, is our football hero, number 32, Deke, played by Paul Parsons Satterfield, Jr.

Born in Nashville, Tennessee on August 19, 1960 Satterfield is yet another member of the production with a family lineage steeped in the arts & entertainment industry. While his late father was a firefighter, his late mother was singer Priscilla Coolidge. But besides his mother's own music, his aunt Rita Coolidge produced hit songs like *(Your Love Has Lifted Me) Higher and Higher* and *All Time High*, of which the latter was featured in the 1983 James Bond 007 film *Octopussy*. And depending on whose story you believe she's actually an uncredited co-author of the magnificent piano coda from the classic Derek and the Dominos song *Layla*. From 1973 to 1980 Satterfield would also be able to call Kris Kristofferson his uncle when the popular singer/actor was married to his talented aunt.

"He was the morale booster in the cast on *The Raft*. He was terrific, Paul Satterfield. I had a lot of respect for Paul," says David Ball. "He was the most outgoing...he had a great torso on him, he was tall, he was big, he had a good body. And he was really, really...what we would say, 'Jack the Lad'. Really outgoing personality, lots going for him, lots of confidence, bags of confidence."

"He hated being in the yellow banana hammock Speedos. I said, 'Satterfield, don't worry about it,'" remembers Daniel Beer. "He's a good-time Southern boy, that's what he was. And his family, you know...he could sing; he's musical."

"I don't have access anymore to, you know, who all I looked at, at that point, but he was physically stunning, from just a visual standpoint. I knew he'd be perfect and he'd be a good compliment to Danny Beer. He was very, very charming. You know, some people when they come to these casting sessions just charm the hell out of you and he's one of those kind of guys that was charming as hell," remembers Michael Gornick. "And it was between him and another individual, who I don't recall, like I say. But Paul was very strong; I thought he had a great background. He understood his role, his interaction with the outdoors. He was a very physical guy – he was kind of a basketball, football star. And I thought he was right."

"He was a pretty young guy. That was why he was hired," says Leonard Finger about Satterfield. "And Daniel Beer was somebody who really had something going. He was good looking, but he was also a much more interesting actor. But see, this is something where I probably had very little input with any of that because it was just who they happened to like, whom they liked as a combination and it was really that. First of all, their interest was in the girls – then the boys were just sort of who would complement the particular girls who were hired."

Satterfield was part of a casting call that Laurel would hold in Los Angeles. Most of the principals, particularly the younger actors, were cast out of New York City, but L.A. provided the production with a different pool of talent than they were used to. "Part of what was happening in New York is we used Leonard Finger, who was quite competent, wonderful to work with," says Michael Gornick. "He was, at the same time though, feeding this weekly series called *Tales from the Darkside*. So, we were eating up a lot of moderately priced talented actors in New York. So, while we were doing lots of calls, lots of examination of talent, a lot of it was going in another direction or being siphoned off by *Tales from the Darkside* because they were very concerned about some sort of 'TVQ' for the series and tried to place in each episode an actor of note, which they did quite successfully. But, none the less, it took away from the pool of talent. So, while we were able to cast to some degree in New York, it seemed logical to go to L.A. And I think the film benefitted ultimately because it kind of expanded our horizons and we were able to both in terms of just physical look find some very attractive, talented people out there. And that became the L.A. experience. And that's probably thanks to David Ball; I think given our own devices Laurel Entertainment probably would have tried to slog it out in New York and just try to find all the talent and it wasn't happening. So, to David Ball's credit he convinced Richard to do an L.A. casting call and we did."

Part of that "L.A. experience" would involve seeing an old friend of the Laurel family help out with the casting sessions. "It's funny, you know, I had this memory release," recalls *Day of the Dead* actor, the late Joe Pilato. "I speak with Lee Karr often and I'm a huge fan of his, but he's probably not going to put this in because he's going to say, 'I can't do that', or some bullshit like that. But I have this wonderful memory of – that I completely had buried – being the reader (script sides) out here in Los Angeles for the actors and actresses in *Creepshow 2*. I believe – no I don't believe, I know – that David Ball and I believe Mike Gornick, but I'm not sure, there was somebody else in the room; but my fondest memories, I got to spend three days with David Ball."

"He did," confirms Michael Gornick. "He was, again, like an old friend of the family and he helped in regard, in terms, of just handing out sides and so forth before we would actually read people. So, yeah, he was quite helpful."

For Pilato being able to reunite with David Ball, as he stated, was special for the actor as the two had gotten along quite well during the production of *Day of the Dead*. It also meant being able to regale Ball, and anyone else in earshot for that matter, with his comical British accent. "He had this, it looked like something out of a World War II movie, I can't remember the year, but it was the first cell phone kind of thing, it was a big black box and it looked like it was out of World War II. He had to pump it up, wind up the battery," remembers Pilato as he suddenly bursts into a British tone impersonating Ball. "'Oh, I need to call the office; I need to speak to Richard. It's a wonderful invention, Joe.'"

"I remember the scenario well," says an amused Ball. "Problem was his British accent was so affected it made me roar with laughter which, in turn, made us all laugh."

And other than a vivid recollection of veteran actor Claude Akins coming in briefly – "'Claude's coming in, we're just gonna meet and greet him. Okay? We're not going to read him. Okay, Joe?,'" says Pilato as he once again channels his inner David Ball – Pilato's lasting memory of the casting experience is as follows: "I just remember the young chicks," he says. "A lot of young chicks and muscular guys."

The Hitchhiker

When it comes to the casting for this morbid masterpiece I think we'll start with the man that the segment is named after: the hitchhiker himself, Tom Wright.

Harold Thomas Wright was born November 29, 1952 in Englewood, New Jersey. Growing up he was an enormous fan of the genre and receiving the offer to appear in a horror film – very much like *The Raft*'s Page Hannah – was an exciting opportunity for the actor/stuntman. "I was always into horror. As a kid I used to subscribe to *Famous Monsters*," Wright fondly recalls. "Oh yeah, I watched all of the *Frankenstein* movies, including *Frankenstein's Daughter;* everything from *The Wolfman* and, of course, all of the iterations of *Dracula*. Monster movies were always a real big thing for me when I was kid. In New York City they had – I grew up in New Jersey – and in New York on channel 9 WOR they had a show called *Chiller Theatre*, maybe it was WPIX, it was probably channel 11(it was), but it was called *Chiller Theatre* and every Saturday night they showed a horror film and most kids of my generation and age were glued to their sets every Saturday night watching *Chiller Theatre*. So, when I got this I thought, 'Oh great, I get to actually work in a horror film!'"

But this wasn't just any horror film, no. It was one with an association to a certain iconic film-maker, and in particular his legendary first film, which Wright admired deeply. "Every teenager in the 60's got screwed up by that movie, you know. So, I was a big *Night of the Living Dead* fan and a big George Romero fan," Wright says. "So, I felt like I was continuing a certain tradition with African American males in George Romero related horror films." As an interesting aside Wright's name was submitted just a couple of years prior to Laurel Entertainment by his agency at the time, Abrams Artists & Associates, for the role of helicopter pilot John in George A. Romero's *Day of the Dead*.

In college Wright was an athlete, he played football at West Chester State near Philadelphia. After a couple of years at school though he would leave and sort of drifted for a bit, unsure of what he wanted to do. That is until someone close stepped in and helped show him the path he should take. "And a friend of mine dragged me into a theater and told me that I was going to be an actor, but I just didn't know it yet. And he said, 'I'll prove it to you', and he cast me in this play at Cheyney State University and once I got on stage I loved it so much I turned to him and I said, 'You're absolutely right,'" remembers Wright. "I then joined a theater company, People's Light Theatre Company, outside of Philadelphia, and I did fifteen plays in two years without ever taking an acting lesson. Everyone would take their scripts home at night and they'd come back and their performances would be markedly better and all I could do was take mine home and put it on the table and look at it. I had no idea how to break down a script and create a character; I was just going on instinct. So, I moved to New York with $150 in

Above: Scouting photos of downtown Dexter, Maine which would be featured in the film's opening scene. (courtesy of Michael Gornick)

Above: Director Michael Gornick with the "hero" tree picked out in Maine during the summer which was supposed to be used as the tree the hitchhiker is rammed into. Upon returning in the late fall the foliage had changed and they could not locate the tree again. (courtesy of Bruce Miller). See Chapter 3.

who's now not so young because he's got to be in his late fifties, that played the part of the hitchhiker, and that was Tom Wright. He was just such a terrific actor," says Leonard Finger. "He was somebody who really could kind of do everything. He was very versatile and just very, very fine. And I thought he'd have a big career."

"Leonard was the casting director and he knew my work as an actor and he sort of knew my work as a stuntman," says Wright. "But because the role had so many action sequences I mentioned to Leonard – when I went in to meet him – that I was actually a certified stuntman and that helped save the day."

It's important to note here, as a reminder, that Wright's name was suggested to the production by stunt coordinator Taso Stavrakis. In a letter from late July 1986 Stavrakis – before he was actually officially signed on to the production – discussed the subject with producer David Ball and production manager Charles Carroll. "I'm glad Tom Wright worked out, his name came to me with very good recommendations, and I'm looking forward to working with him," Stavrakis wrote. "Together, he and I should be able to pull off the entire *Hitchhiker* shoot." **(9)**

Unfortunately, circumstances in Maine would alter those best laid plans.

Now we arrive to the adulterous character of Mrs. Annie Lansing, played by Lois Chiles. Without a doubt this would be the role that would prove to be the most difficult to cast. In fact, it might go down as one of the most difficult roles to cast in film history. The path it took to eventually landing with Lois Chiles is so involved and so messy that I've decided to spread the story of it out as the book goes along. It's the best way to properly convey the story and make it clear just how maddening it must have been for the production. "I spent days and days and days and days with Leonard trying to cast this role. Reject, reject, reject, reject, million dollars, two million dollars, half a million dollars, no nudity, no, no, no, won't work with this guy, don't like it... you know, we almost never made that segment. We almost never had a leading lady," says David Ball. "And New World was pummeling my head daily because they had approval. But you can't...if something's not going to happen you can't make it happen! It was a nightmare, absolute nightmare. Mike Gornick and I used to laugh about it. I'm just trying to get number thirty seven! (laughs) And he said, 'I don't believe it!' I said, 'Mike, it's all I do! All I do is cast this bloody role. It's all I do.'"

"I think Lois Chiles did a very nice job," says Leonard Finger. "That was a last minute replacement and, of course, she had a little bit of pizzazz because of the James Bond picture."

Lois Cleveland Chiles was born April 15, 1947 in Houston, Texas. She was one of three children, with two brothers, and grew up in the small southern Texas town of Alice. She would attend the University of Texas at Austin before deciding to move to New York City to study at Finch College, a liberal arts school. And it was there that she would unexpectedly discover her career path to becoming a model and an actress. "It all happened, pretty much, simultaneously. I started modeling because when I arrived at Finch I saw that I'd been at this big school (Texas) and

my pocket, I didn't know anybody, and I started taking classes at HB Studio and I went through there. It took me a while to find the place that actually worked for me and that turned out to be the Neighborhood Playhouse and I studied with them."

Wright would have early success appearing in the 1981 Tony award nominated Broadway production of *A Taste of Honey.* Following that he would land roles on daytime soaps like *Search for Tomorrow* and *All My Children*, all the while landing stunt gigs on feature films like *Exterminator 2* and *Splash*.

Michael Gornick had remembered Wright from his part in the 1983 NBC television mini-series *Kennedy*, but it was another film that Gornick really appreciated that stuck out in his mind even more. "But also more importantly he was in *The Brother from Another Planet*," Gornick says. "Yeah, it was one of my favorite films, I loved that film."

"There was a wonderful actor, a wonderful young actor,

now a very small school (Finch) and I thought, 'Uh oh, I've made a terrible mistake.' I wanted to be in New York City, that's why I transferred to Finch. And then when I got there and it was small I thought, 'Oh, no. This is like being in a small school where everybody knows your business,'" admits Chiles. "So, I went down to the snack bar to have a Coke and *Glamour* magazine was down there looking for girls for their college issue. And they ended up choosing me. One of the girls at school was putting herself through school modeling – she had an agent already. So, one day we were on a *Glamour* shoot and we went up town and stopped at her agency and one of her agents came out while I was waiting for her in the waiting room and it happened to be Bernadette Peters' sister, Donna, and asked me if I wanted to model. I said, 'I don't really think I look right for modeling', and she said, 'No, you look like someone that they've had previously', and, 'Why don't you come back on Monday?' And so I started modeling and a boyfriend of mine said, 'You know what, you really should be an actress. You're really not exactly a model because every photograph looks like a different person.' So, he took me to Sandy Meisner's acting class and so I was studying acting at the same time as modeling. And being in acting class was amazing because it was the first time I...it was just a very amazing experience, being able to express myself in that way."

And while she enjoyed the modeling and would go on to be very successful at it, appearing on the cover of magazines like *Cosmopolitan* and *Bazaar*, it was with acting that Chiles found a real connection. "In a class when you're young and you're able to express yourself for the first time artistically, all of these feelings and pain and everything that's been running around inside of you, suddenly you have an outlet for. It was a revelation to me and I loved it," she says. "There's more to learn. You can grow and learn so much about other people inhabiting different characters. I'd say that it opens up your humanity."

Chiles' career was filled with notable roles as she appeared in *The Way We Were*, *The Great Gatsby*, *Coma*, *Death on the Nile* (with fellow *Creepshow 2* alum George Kennedy), and *Sweet Liberty*. Her role as Dr. Holly Goodhead in the 007 James Bond film *Moonraker* would bring her major notoriety though by appearing in an iconic film franchise.

When it came to *Creepshow 2* trying her hand at horror was something new so she was intrigued. "I didn't think of it as a horror film exactly," Chiles explains. "I mean, I know that it is in that genre. I thought the character was kind of interesting to explore; this woman talking to herself in her car. And I think that it's really important to do all genres. I think that, certainly, the actors of today are proving that – they're all doing all genres. And I actually had a lot of fun doing it. It was unexpectedly fun to do horror."

For the role of Chiles' husband, Mr. George Lansing, Esquire, Laurel would turn to Richard Parks, who was known more as a literary agent than as an actor. In fact, Parks' background was quite a diverse one. "I was a college professor and a scenic designer before I moved to New York and became a literary agent," responds Parks to a letter I sent him for this book.

As for the other man in Mrs. Lansing's life, her gigolo lover, Laurel brought David Beecroft on board. Hailing from the lone star state of Texas, Beecroft was one of five kids with quite the athletic background, as he was a former Golden Gloves boxer. Beecroft's older brother, Greg, had made a name for himself in the daytime world of soap operas as "Tony Reardon" on the long running *Guiding Light* on CBS. Following in his sibling's footsteps Beecroft would make the move to New York where he too would find work in soaps on ABC's *Loving* and *One Life to Live*. "That was a reading in New York – a strong recommendation by Leonard," says Michael Gornick. "We didn't read many for that role, he thought it would be absolutely appropriate and he liked his background. So, I kind of gave Leonard the nod on that one."

Also featured in this segment is stunt-woman/actress Chere Bryson, who plays the inquisitive woman at the accident scene. Bryson would come to the production with a diverse background as before entering the world of feature films she was a famed Playboy Bunny at the Playboy Club on Sunset Boulevard in Hollywood during the 1960's. By the time she worked on *Creepshow 2* she had accumulated an impressive resume having performed stunts on well-known productions such as *National Lampoon's Vacation*, *Scarface*, and *Fright Night*.

Rounding out our cast and making a noteworthy cameo appearance in this segment is none other than the story's creator himself, Stephen King. Playing the goofy truck driver who stops at the scene of the hitchhiker's demise wasn't much of a stretch for King who had already built up a resume of buffoonish characters in films such as George Romero's *Knightriders* (Hoagie Man) and *Creepshow* (Jordy Verrill), as well as the man who's insulted by an ATM machine during the opening of his very own directorial debut, *Maximum Overdrive* – "Honey, come on over here, sugar-buns. This machine just called me an asshole!" Apparently, for whatever reason, King was comfortable with portraying a bumpkin on the big screen and that would continue in *Creepshow 2*. "I played a part – a truck driver. My usual nerd," King said to Paul Gagne. "You'll know me when you see me. The guy who looks like he doesn't quite know what gravity is." **(10)**

By the start of August the production was finalizing the first of numerous shooting schedules, a practice not uncommon in film production due to unforeseen circumstances. And *Creepshow 2* would certainly have its fair share of those, and then some.

Unlike the script and the finished film itself production would begin first on *The Raft*, with *Old Chief Wood'nhead* following right behind. Obviously it would make sense to start first with *The Raft*, a segment shot exclusively outdoors, with the production now starting the last week of summer, with fall looming which meant cooler temps and shorter days were near. And the person whose job it was to sit down and figure out all the details for that shooting schedule was production manager, Charles S. Carroll. "I always look for story and emotional continuity. You try to group scenes that make sense for the actors to do, one after another, and that makes it easier for a director to know where he is. And then things are location dependent. They are set dependent, meaning if you have to build sets then you have to put those in the back of your schedule to do that. And then they're also dependent on light, and day and night. So, those are the four...and actor availability," he says. "Those are some of the broad strokes. I mean, those are the obvious things. It's an art. It's an art to do it well."

Carroll was another Laurel veteran having worked as an auditor on *Day of the Dead* and an accountant on *Tales from the Darkside*. So, when the chance to work on *Creepshow 2* came along he would take another step up the production ladder. "Charles was one of the most self-confident animals I'd worked with at the time," says David Ball. "And when we did *Day of the Dead*, I guess it would be fair to say that I taught him quite a lot about irregularity and how you do the accounting: A to suit yourself and B to suit others. We became very, very firm friends, Charles and I. So, I called him up, I said, 'Hey, Charlie. I'm doing *Creepshow 2*, you fancy it?' And he said, 'Hey, man! Yeah, I'll fucking do it. But I ain't doing the accounting.' I said, 'Well, what do you want to do?' He said, 'I want to do production manager.' I said, 'You think you can?' He said, 'Of course I can!' I said, 'Alright, come and see me.'"

"If I could say I had any kind of mentor in my career it would be David Ball," says Carroll. "You know, first of all, David was a huge amount of fun. I thought he was a great producer because I thought he so enjoyed the process and he made the people around him enjoy the process and when they did that I think they did their jobs better. And he was able to sort of sit back, look at situations, get people to do their best, and he always understood the absurdity of film-making. I don't know, we hit it off, we were kind of kindred spirits."

Meanwhile the search for someone to portray Annie Lansing from *The Hitchhiker* continued as actress Julie Christie was approached about the role. Landing a talent such as Christie would have been quite a coup for Laurel as the actress had a very impressive resume. In 1966 she won both the Oscar and the BAFTA for Best Actress for her highly acclaimed performance in *Darling*. She also had another Oscar nomination for her role in *McCabe & Mrs. Miller*, numerous BAFTA nominations including *Doctor Zhivago*, *Fahrenheit 451*, and *Don't Look Now*, and a couple of Golden Globe nominations including one for *Shampoo*. She was highly decorated, to say the least.

"Julie Christie, it was a back-and-forth thing," recalls Leonard Finger. "She was at a point in her career, as I recall, when she was sort of in limbo, which happens to older actors. And unfortunately, even though this is now thirty years ago, it was the same as it is today. You know, there's a moment when people wake up and they look in the mirror and they realize that in the eyes of the people who are buying talent, they're too old. Everyone outlives their fame, that's the human condition. Because everyone is interested in what's new, bright, and shiny. And there's a certain amount of reverence which is attached to people with great talent or who have had great fame, but even that, when all is said and done, it comes back to the newness. And I think that Julie Christie was somebody whose career

had been so astonishing, who had such amazing triumphs, and that was also one of the most beautiful women in the world, but there was a moment when she needed a job and we were talking seriously about it."

Charles Carroll was busy staffing up the production with key personnel and inking contracts on locations. Carroll was also following a fee calculation sheet that allowed for a maximum of 25 crew members between August 14 and September 8, which expanded to 50 from September 8 through October 8.

There was back-and-forth coordination between Bruce Miller's art department, Ed Fountain's mechanical engineering & construction department, and Ed French's special makeup effects department regarding the blob creature for *The Raft*, which was a key concern. A lot had to be done with the effect, including testing it on the lake surface to see how it would work in a natural environment. And originally that natural environment would not be Granite Basin Lake, where the film segment was shot, but rather another lake located in the Prescott National Forest, Lynx Lake. Literally more than ten times the size of Granite Basin Lake, at 55 acres, Lynx Lake was an entirely different animal. Aesthetically it was quite different with a beautiful ponderosa pine forest surrounding the area, giving it a more Western Pennsylvania look as opposed to the mountain lake perspective of Granite Basin Lake – and remember King's original short story took place in Western Pennsylvania. However, issues over the lake's depth being too great – coupled with some other practical concerns – would lead to a change of location. At only 5 acres in size and with striking views of Granite Mountain, Granite Basin Lake would prove to be a more appealing option for the production.

"I never liked Lynx Lake, no. I thought it was a little common, it didn't seem to have any kind of vista to me," says Michael Gornick. "When I saw the lake we used I thought, 'Wow, dramatically it's perfect; absolutely perfect.'"

"Granite Basin Lake was just kind of a no-brainer because it was the most photographic lake and small enough and shallow enough for them to do what they needed to with the blob," recalls Arizona location manager Michael Morgan. "At Lynx Lake there are not very many points of entry. Like, you know, there was a nice sandy beach at Granite Basin Lake where you could kind of just walk out into the lake."

Some of the other location contracts wrapping up at this point were for a former auto body garage, which was to be utilized for studio space, which came to be referred to as "The Big House" by the crew. Rented for 2 months, the spot cost the production $1600.

Another location inked was for an old store front on the main drag of Humboldt, Arizona which would serve as the shooting interiors for the Spruce's General Store in *Old Chief Wood'nhead* – the exterior shots were located a mile or so away at the Iron King Mine. Again, rented for 2 months the spot would only cost the production $600. "At one time it was like a drug store with rooms upstairs, like a little motel, with the drug store on the bottom," says Kathy Hinshaw whose late father, Ray, owned the unoccupied building at the time. In fact after Mr. Hinshaw purchased the building in the early 1970's the property remained empty

until Laurel came to town in 1986 and rented it for the filming, according to Rex Hinshaw, Kathy's brother. "It was just vacant the whole time, nobody used it for anything," he says. "It was just an empty building below and our storage up above, the family's storage up above."

It's worth mentioning that there is a behind-the-scenes photo which was taken during production with the word "CABINETS" written in large letters across the top of the front of the building. Apparently at one point, briefly perhaps, there was a cabinetry business located there as well; or it could be that was before Mr. Hinshaw purchased the property.

Above: The former Iron King Mine in Dewey-Humboldt, Arizona was chosen as the location for the town of Dead River in *Old Chief Wood'nhead*. Convincing building facades were constructed on the site including the general store and service station. (courtesy of Eileen Garrigan and Bruce Miller)

Crew members were also getting settled into their temporary new home in Prescott. The majority of the production would stay at the Prescottonian Motel, while a handful would stay a couple of blocks down at the smaller American Motel. Welcome packets were distributed by Rusty Warren and Priscilla Dougherty from the accounting

THE PRESCOTTONIAN MOTEL

CORDIALLY INVITES YOU

TO AN AFTERNOON PARTY

WELCOMING ALL THE "CREEPSHOW II" CREW TO PRESCOTT!!

WHEN: SUNDAY, SEPTEMBER 7th

WHERE: 4735 BOWIE DRIVE SOUTH
LONGVIEW ESTATES
(see map on reverse side)

TIME: 3:00 P.M.

MEMBERS OF THE GOVERNOR'S COMMISSION ON FILM IN ARIZONA WILL BE IN ATTENDANCE

OUR MENU WILL INCLUDE:

SCALLOPS
STEAKS
SHRIMP
COWBOY BEANS
GARLIC BREAD
SALAD
DESSERT
BEVERAGES

HOPE YOU WILL BE ABLE TO ATTEND AND ENJOY OUR BEAUTIFUL END OF SUMMER WEATHER!

R.S.V.P. to BECCA

Above: A week before principal photography would begin the production team was welcomed to Prescott by the Prescottonian Motel and the Arizona Governor's Commission on Film with a large party. Assistant to the production designer Steve Arnold takes it easy enjoying the party's atmosphere. (courtesy of Rebecca Mayo and Father William Kosco)

and auditing department letting everyone know about paydays, per diems, and petty cash procedures. A "Nitelife & Necessities" guide was also included letting crew members know where they could find bars, restaurants, bowling alleys, movie theaters, laundry services, medical care, taxis...even horse racing. Contact and crew lists were also included letting everyone know who was who and what their jobs were. Two of the key people in that crew/contact list were locals of the area: Arizona production secretary Rebecca Mayo and Arizona location manager Michael Morgan.

Creepshow 2 would be the only feature film in Rebecca Mayo's career; but not because she failed in pursuing a career in the business or because she wanted to choose a different career path. No, Mayo's profession was already in the field of education and the opportunity to work on a motion picture was a fun and inviting lark for the dedicated teacher. "Years ago when I was living in Prescott, Arizona I applied to be the first teacher in space," Mayo remembers. "And we know that Christa McAuliffe won that title, won that position, and went on to the Challenger and we know what happened on that fateful day. After that time, in the midst of my teaching career, I decided that I wanted to know what else was there to do besides teaching. Because I was a teacher for thirty years and I thought – and this is half way through my career – I thought, 'What else? What else could I do?' And so for a short period of time I thought, 'Well, maybe I'll work on a cruise ship', so I worked on a Princess Cruise Line as an assistant children's cruise director, like an assistant to 'Julie McCoy' (*The Love Boat*), and did that. And then I had a phone call from Bill McCallum, he was on the Arizona Film Commission Board, and he or his associate, Sharon, called me and asked me if I would be interested in working on a movie that was coming to Prescott. And I thought, 'Why not? I've never done it before.'(laughs) So, I said, 'Sure, I'd be happy to.'"

Mayo would take a leave of absence from teaching to accept the job and was involved nearly from the get go assisting with ordering telephones for the production office and booking rooms for the crew. And it would be her discipline and organizational skills, gathered from teaching, which would help her along the way. "In preproduction I was learning an awful lot since I had never had any movie experience in my life. I had to learn as I went day by day. There were thirteen department heads that I was responsible for," she says. "It was a lot of secretarial work, it was a lot of typing, phone answering, and being responsible for whatever they needed: if camera said, 'I need a dolly sent from Houston', I had to get a dolly there – an extra dolly or an extra camera. If they needed a Zeiss prism lens ordered I had to find a Zeiss prism lens and get it there for cameras. If costuming needed something special I had to go find it and get it to Prescott. So, whatever they needed came through me."

"In Arizona we had a girl called Rebecca Mayo and she was like our 'make everything happen in Arizona girl'," says David Ball. "And I just want to place on record what a wonderful person she was, and how helpful she was, and how great she was to all the crew. She was like a young Mum to the whole crew."

When it comes to Michael Morgan, as opposed to

Rebecca Mayo, he came to the production with prior motion picture experience. "The first film I did was *Billy Jack*," recalls Morgan. "And there were a lot of films being shot in Prescott and I worked a little bit on *Junior Bonner* and *Bless the Beasts and the Children*. But I worked extensively on *Billy Jack*."

Morgan had an interesting and varied background having not only worked on feature films, but also experience in the world of country music, photography, and reporting as well. His duties on *Creepshow 2*, much like his background, would vary wildly depending on the circumstances. Whether it was finding an area to portray the town of Dead River in *Old Chief Wood'nhead*, handling issues of loose bulls near filming locations, scheduling electrical work to be done for the wardrobe/costume department's work space, coordinating with the local school district to route school buses so they didn't interrupt filming, or filling in for Dan Kamin to play Chief Wood'nhead's shadow on a garage wall, Morgan handled it.

"Mike Morgan was great, says Charles Carroll. "He was fantastic."

"He reminded me of that actor with the mustache," adds first assistant director Katarina "Kato" Wittich. "He was like an old cowboy type."

"Sam Elliott," Carroll clarifies.

"I mean, the days were endless, they were like 16-hour days, every day," recalls Morgan. "The very first thing I would do was in the morning, if the call sheet wasn't available the previous night, sometimes it wasn't, I would get in there really early and look at the call sheet and see, 'Do we need cars? Do we need food? Do we need security? Does the art department need stuff? What needs to be where and when?', because sometimes you would move two or three different locations in one day. So, then I would get with Peter (Levy) and make sure that he was squared away with what he needed to do so that everybody else had what they needed to do: what we needed for craft services that day, what we needed for meals, stuff like that. Then I would get the petty cash from, I'm trying to remember the accountant's name – Rusty (Warren). So, I would get the petty cash for each department – and I can't remember how many departments there was on the film – like seven, eight, nine, something like that. I think each one of them got five or six thousand dollars in petty cash every day. So, I would get that and I would dole it out to all the departments as they came into the office before we started the day shooting. Then I would go out on set and just make sure that everything was there and running smoothly or whatever and be there in case somebody needed something or there was a change or a problem or whatever. And then at the end of the day I would go back to the office and I would collect everybody's petty cash receipts and I would go through it all and make sure it was all accounted for. And then I would give those packets to Rusty and she would sign off on them – it was like that evening because she worked nights mostly. And then, you know, start all over the next day."

By the end of August the production had eyed the small town of Drake, Arizona to fill in for Dead River in *Old Chief Wood'nhead*. Drake was a tiny community along

the Santa Fe Southern Pacific Corporation railroad, approximately 45 minutes to an hour from Laurel's base of operations in Prescott. Michael Morgan drafted a letter, along with several pages from the screenplay, to the head of the railroad's public relations department outlining the production's needs and plans for the site. With the area containing rail-bed, crossings, and train equipment it was of the utmost importance for Laurel to guarantee they would not perform any special effects or stunts on anything controlled by Santa Fe Southern Pacific. What's strange about Laurel considering Drake is the cost it would have incurred for the production. Santa Fe Southern Pacific had informed Laurel that a fee of $5,000 per day, for a minimum of three weeks, would be required to film in the area. There was mention of potentially adjusting that fee since Laurel would not be utilizing the railroad itself, but nothing promised. That amount of money would have been quite a chunk of change for a low budget feature such as this one. Interestingly enough, on the same day that Morgan would draft his letter to the railroad, Charles Carroll would produce his own letter to Morgan and David Ball objecting to the use of Drake as a filming spot, noting that just the extra time alone in travel for crew would jeopardize the budget. "There is no way to put a dollar cost on the transportation, communication, security, and logistical headaches from being this far away from home base but it is sizeable," Carroll wrote. **(11)**

As it turned out, despite the aesthetic merits of the area, Drake was abandoned as a filming spot for the production. "Yes, I remember Drake. Drake was beautiful," says Michael Gornick. "Much more development in terms of just architecturally it felt a little more like a western city. So, I mean, it was less to have to dress, less angles to have to contrive so that you kept the feel that you were within a western town – both interior and exterior. I mean, it's a headache when you have to move pieces about to give the suggestion that there is something across the way, you know, through a store window for instance. Whereas Drake didn't have that problem, you could just dress reality."

Rounding out the month of August, location agreements were inked for the exterior of Sam Whitemoon's home off of Old Black Canyon Highway in Humboldt (which is never actually seen in the film) and for Fatso's exterior trailer off of Highway 69 in nearby Dewey. The trailer, owned by Jim and Charlotte Goodwin, was located directly behind a convenience market, off the main highway. "I know they said they drove all around looking for a spot that would work perfect for what they were doing and they found us," laughs Mrs. Goodwin. "We weren't doing anything anyways, so yeah go ahead and use it, you know."

With the calendar now turning the page to September the production was just two weeks away from the start of principal photography and the man chosen to capture that photography would be Tom Hurwitz. As was briefly mentioned before Hurwitz was not the original choice for director of photography, Jon Fauer was. But according to Michael Gornick there was another D.P. from the *Tales from the Darkside* family he was interested in who has since gone on to a very successful directing career in Hollywood. "I had developed, as brief as it was during my stay at *Tales from the Darkside*, a relationship with Ernie Dickerson," says Gornick. "Ernie shot one of my episodes, early episode, from *Tales from the Darkside*, and he was a joy to work with. There were varying points when I was given the nod to do *Creepshow 2* that he and I communicated and it seemed like a natural event. I was not allowed to take him away from *Tales from the Darkside*. So, again, my choices were limited."

Born in 1947 Tom Hurwitz grew up in New York City, the son of the late Leo Hurwitz, the famous documentary film-maker who was blacklisted in the 1950's. It was after attending Columbia University that Hurwitz would start the path toward his calling. "I spent a few years doing various kinds of social work and still photography. And then I decided to do what I really wanted to do, which was to become a cameraman," Hurwitz says. "So, that took several years of apprenticeship and working in various different things, and also working at certain very different skills. So, I was an assistant cameraman, but I did other things as well because I also wanted to learn other crafts because I knew that as a cameraman I would have to kind of be in command of everything that went on. So, I was also a gaffer and I even did sound for about nine months. I always loved documentaries, but I kind of pursued the standard trajectory of camera men – which is you do various industrial projects and documentaries and stuff like that. And then you move into commercials, and then you begin doing television and then you begin doing features; so I was well into that piece of my trajectory."

Coming into *Creepshow 2* Hurwitz had a lot of experience under his belt as a cinematographer, but the problem was the majority of that experience was on documentary films and not as much on features. And despite having done some work on Larry Cohen's 1982 monster flick *Q*, which was released by Salah Hassanein's United Film Distribution Company incidentally, Hurwitz wasn't necessarily a fan of the genre or the heritage of George Romero for that matter. "It was an odd production. It was run from Pittsburgh, these guys had produced a couple or three films before," he says. "I wasn't a fan really of the *Living Dead* films, so at one level I wasn't the best choice for this material. I wasn't a horror film specialist, by any means, although I'm pleased with the job we did. Anyway, it was just a professional challenge for me. I wasn't an effects film or a horror film devotee and I wasn't a follower of the George Romero world."

A fascinating sidebar regarding the hiring of Hurwitz was the prior connection he in fact shared with Laurel and that world of George Romero. As Hurwitz hinted at he had spent some time recording production sound while working for Don Lenzer, the famed documentary film-maker, who shot footage for 1970's *Woodstock*, as well episodes of Laurel's *The Winners*, such as Mario Andretti and Reggie Jackson. In fact for the Jackson episode both Hurwitz and Michael Gornick share screen credit for the episode's sound! Amazingly neither one was aware of that shared link when *Creepshow 2* came around. "No we were not aware. I never heard Mike's name before *Creepshow 2*. (*The Winners*) was produced out of Pittsburgh but I was never near the production office or the cutting room. Production sound hardly ever was in those days. The tape got shipped off with the exposed film and that was that,"

Hurwitz says. "I knew that Laurel was Romero's company and Rubinstein talked about *Night of the Living Dead* from time to time."

"You know, Hurwitz...I don't know why Tom was hired in the first place, I think that happened early on. I'm not sure Tom was the right person for this," Charles Carroll confides. "Tom, you know, has this incredible reputation as a documentary film-maker and he's done some interesting stuff. It was a kind of 'down and dirty' show; Tom brought a sort of New York 'artiste' kind of attitude and he made some unfortunate choices. This is always hard talking about this; I mean, I could say, 'Look, artistic differences.' You know, he was a wrong fit for the show in a way. I'm gonna say that – he was just the wrong fit."

"I'm not sure they made the right choice in working with me," admits Hurwitz. "My feature films were very...my style has always been very naturalistic. I wasn't an effects specialist at all. Now, I think I took the challenge and I did it well and I was happy to do it. But it wasn't anything I was particularly interested in. So, we weren't cut from the same cloth to begin with, right? I mean, if you take a look at my work – and I'm tremendously proud of it – but its work that involves people, emotions, the social world, the arts (laughs). And I don't make science fiction and I don't make horror films. I'm just not particularly interested in those problems, not even those design problems. I mean, I took this on with a whole heart. But I was a different kind of breed than the rest of these guys, who had kind of come up doing this kind of stuff. So, that's fine."

Hurwitz's eventual departure midway through filming was just one of many issues that would plague the production and will be covered more in-depth in the following chapter.

Up to this point the vast majority of pre-production was happening in Prescott, Arizona. But there was another city where work was being done as well, a city nearly 3,000 miles away, and that city just happened to be the home of Stephen King.

To handle the location duties for Bangor, Maine Laurel would rely on Henry Nevison. A graduate of Temple University, Nevison came to Maine in the late 1970's for work on a film project about white water rafting. He would decide to stay in the area and went into business producing local television commercials. Around 1980 Nevison went to work for the University of Maine in their public relations office spreading the word about how the school improved the quality of life for residents of the state. It was during this period that Nevison would first meet Stephen King for a half hour interview special for local television in the Bangor and Portland markets. The 1982 *UMO Magazine* special hosted by Nevison – *Stephen King: I Sleep with the Lights On* – was an entertaining and revealing look into the author's life, work, and education. The special would spark a friendship between Nevison and King which eventually led to *Creepshow 2*. "So, we met because of this project and then we just stayed in touch and we exchanged music.

Right: Gary Hartle's storyboards and concept art helped realize what director Michael Gornick was searching for in each story. (courtesy of Michael Gornick)

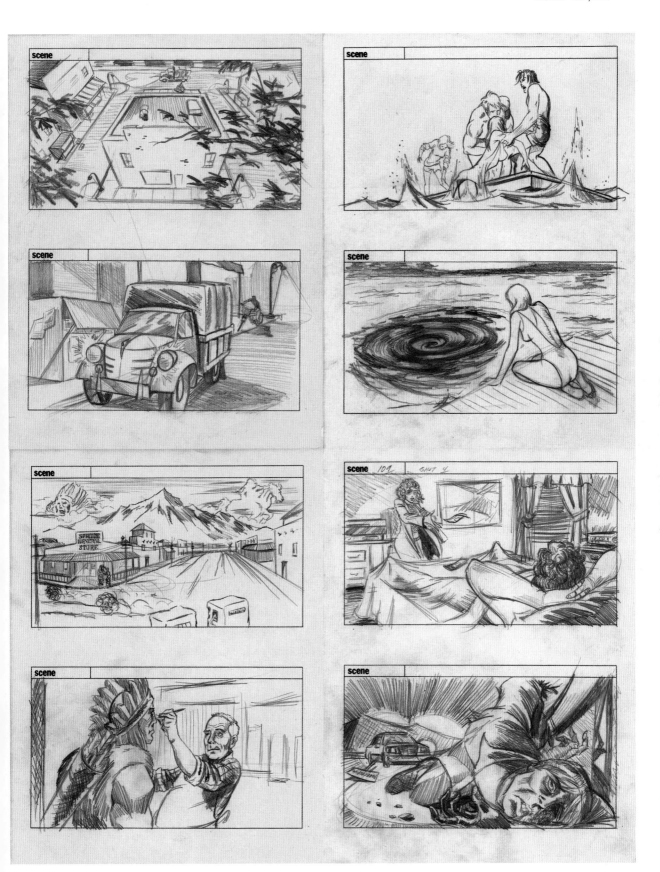

I'd go over there and give him records and we'd listen to some music and suddenly we got a good relationship going," Nevison says. "But what happened was he said, 'Hey, I've got a film coming up that we're gonna be doing. Would you like to get involved?' I said, 'Yeah. I'll call the folks at Laurel Entertainment', and so forth. So, I'm not quite...you know, I think it may be that I was doing some sort of preliminary scouting for *Pet Sematary*, but the real reason why I got involved with *Creepshow 2* was because of my prior relationship with Stephen King."

Nevison's connections with the community and its leaders would serve him well during his prep helping secure locations – including shutting down Main Street in Dexter, Maine for part of the day – and quickly finding local crew to work on the picture once the production arrived in town. But it was that Stephen King factor which Nevison believes helped secure people's cooperation. "And every time I said to someone, 'Hey, this is a film for Stephen King', or that it was a film based on a Stephen King book, 'Oh, yeah! I'd love to help Stephen King,'" he says. "I think part of it is that there was a great deal of admiration for him as a person and also because they felt like, 'Oh, that's cool. Gonna have a film crew come into Bangor, Maine? That doesn't happen every day.'"

And as far as his duties were concerned, just like Michael Morgan in Prescott, they were any and every thing you could think of. "Part of the location manager's job is to make sure that every need that they have from security guards to accommodations to enough space...like, the camera department had to have its own space," Nevison recalls. "The special effects people had to have their own space – there was a lot of makeup to be done. And then you needed offices for the producer and the director. And then I had to have a house, I rented a house, that was a screening room, where you could watch dailies, the producer and the director could come to the house on a regular basis, it was located not far from our shoot location, and they could come and watch dailies. So, I mean, there was just a multitude of things that had to be done way in advance. Probably a month I worked on that film before they even arrived on set, on location. It was just all the little details so they could just come in and do what they had to do."

Getting back to Stephen King for a moment... *Creepshow 2* would mark the first time that a feature film based on the writings of King would be shot in Maine, an interesting footnote in the author's canon as apparently it was something he had desired for quite some time.

"He, at the time, and rightfully so, was like one of the sole industries in Maine," explains Michael Gornick. "I mean, there was no more logging and lumbering per se to any large degree. It was kind of a depressed area. And he was a major manufacturer of entertainment material, meaning novels, and he saw the possibility of maybe even a film industry in Maine – that's never come to fruition, unfortunately. But I think he saw that he could supply the material, the thoughts, and perhaps there could be production that would occur in Maine, if not on

a formal basis, a frequent basis through, you know, a film commission. Which I gather Henry Nevison was also a party to, I think Henry was trying to set up a commission at the time. Yeah, so I think he said, 'This is my material, I would really, sincerely, want you to come and shoot at least an episode.'"

"Yeah, the Maine Film Commission, that's a very good point," says Henry Nevison. "I was hoping that there would be an opportunity because there's money to be made when a crew comes to town. I don't know, I can't really answer that as far as whether that really pushed more film-making in Maine. But, the thing is, I always felt that when you do something...look, what could you build from it?"

For his part, whether it was modesty or what have you, King denied his insistence to have part of the film shot in Bangor, instead saying it was a decision made by Laurel and Richard Rubinstein. "Well, first of all I didn't have anything to do with Richard's decision to shoot *Creepshow 2* here, it was entirely his own," King told Paul Gagne. "Most of the people here who need to put a meal on the table just love it. My brother-in-law is just scrambling right now. He used to be a crane operator. He worked on the *Creepshow 2* production, and he thinks Richard Rubinstein is God come down to earth. And for coming up here, I do too. I think it was a hell of a thing for him to do. They made a lot of friends up here." **(12)**

Back in Arizona the prep was continuing at a fevered pace. One of the projects engineered during this time was a platform system utilizing scaffolding for use in the lake during filming of *The Raft*. The challenges of filming the segment on the water would prove to be a formidable one for numerous reasons, which we'll discuss in the following chapter, but the idea would provide some sort of plan of action for tackling the difficult assignment. "What they wound up doing, technically, is the grips went in there and built scaffolding in the water," explains assistant cameraman Eric Swanek. "So, they put in scaffolding and topped it about two feet below the surface of the water. So, if you looked straight down from the raft, off to the side, you would see the pipes that were at the top, about two feet down, it was the top of the scaffolding. So, what that meant is in the morning you'd put the scaffolding on the west side of the dock and you'd shoot back light to the east side. And then if you needed to put lights or you wanted to have any support gear besides boats you could build a small section of scaffold on that whole side so that there was room for more than just the camera and the...I can't remember if we had a dolly out there, but we probably did. So, you have the top of the scaffold which is only, like, three feet by six feet. I don't remember how much scaffolding they laid. They might have made two sections so you could put a camera there, a dolly there, have a couple of bags for (film) magazines, and all that kind of stuff, so you weren't working out of boats. And then at lunch time the grips would stay on the job and they would move the scaffolding tops from the west side of the dock to the east side of the dock, so that in the afternoon you'd be shooting still that way. Looking back it probably would have been just as effective to do some shots like that, but basically just bring the dock to near the shore and shoot from the shore. It would have worked just as well. But, you know, logistically I don't know how it worked out. Nobody had a clue how to do it except for Tom (Hurwitz). So, Tom did it the way that he and, I guess, the key grip decided to do it."

"We were in the middle of the lake, they built a scaffolding platform and just below the water level you could walk around this thing," recalls soundman Felipe Borrero. "It looked like, you know, you were Jesus Christ or something walking around. And then in the middle was a platform and we shot everything there, so it was really difficult."

Pre-production schedules were beginning to be formally put together around this time, with the first scheduled for Saturday, September 6. The day would begin with camera tests at the soon to be new location chosen for Dead River in the Dewey-Humboldt region, one that had been surveyed just the day before in fact. With the site being closer to Laurel's base of operations, and also just a mile or two from the store property where the interiors would be shot, the former Iron King Mine would now stand in for the town that was "finally living up to its name". Under Bruce Miller's supervision the production would utilize some of the already existing structures on site, as well as building several facades to create the illusion of this small decaying western town.

Regarding the mine itself, beginning operations in the late 1890's the Iron King Mine would be active until the late 1960's where it mined various metals such as gold, silver, and copper. However, the mining work conducted on the property would unfortunately lead to the soil becoming contaminated with arsenic and lead. "We built all of that stuff, because we could not find that town," recalls assistant to the production designer, Steve Arnold. "We actually built it – I'm still alive so it must not have been too bad – but we built it on top of a very large area of mine tailings; I'm sure toxic beyond belief. We built these building facades and I think I probably designed the signage and all the rest of that."

The camera tests would be followed up later in the day with location scouting for the house that would stand in for "Rich Boy" Cavenaugh's home, which conveniently enough was located right down the road from Granite Basin Lake on Angus Drive. Later in the afternoon tests for the blob would take place, followed up with a special effects meeting to close out the day.

The next day, Sunday, September 7, would provide an opportunity for the crew to take a break from prepping and get to formally know one another at a welcoming party put on by the owners of the production hotel. "It was a ball, it was really nice," remembers Rebecca Mayo. "We had it catered and the Motion Picture Board of Arizona funded it. It was at the home where I was living and staying. The home belonged to the owners of the Prescottonian Motel – Neil and Jeanne Hurt. Their son, Allen Hurt, and the father, Neil, they owned the Prescottonian Motel where the cast was staying, the crew, and where the production office was. It was at their home and I was living there. So, we decided to have a cordial welcome to Prescott and let's all relax, take a breath, and have a very successful movie and just relax a little bit. So, I believe it was on a Sunday afternoon and

they came out to the 'Big House' – we called it the 'Big House' out there (not to be confused with the studio space which was also referred to by the same nickname). And there was a pond stocked with fish, a little lake area, and they could fish. And we had it catered for barbecue; it was an Arizona barbecue type menu. And it was lovely and we had a fire pit out there. We just all kind of got to know each other and talk and they got to know about Prescott and Arizona and hear some of the history."

On Monday, September 8 the pre-production schedule was slated to resume, this time at the lake location with a series of tests for the blob. Everything from its movement through the water to how it would nuzzle against the corners of the raft was scheduled to be covered. "Oh my god, we never figured that out. The design, if you watch it, is like embarrassing. It was horrible," says Charles Carroll. "You know, now we can go in and we can fix everything we do. And we do it all the time. And there's stuff we can't do, we make up and nobody knows. You know, back then we couldn't, which is why the blob in the lake is so awful."

The day would conclude at the "EFXACO", the special makeup effects lab, which was a former Texaco service station in front of the production hotel which had been re-purposed by Laurel to serve as Ed French's workspace.

Tuesday, September 9 would see crew returning to the "EFXACO" for continued tests regarding Page Hannah's character, Rachel, and the blob attack. Following that a trip back to the lake was scheduled to execute more tests of the blob and to perform camera tests to figure out some of the better angles to utilize when filming its attack on Hannah's character. "You know, this all was generated out of a comic book, kind of. You know, that's the whole idea, was interfacing with a comic," says Tom Hurwitz. "So, the screen compositions and the way the shots were built referred to that kind of graphic. And that was fun to work that way. And Michael (Gornick) was very well prepared as far as that went; he was very clear about what he wanted."

As Hurwitz states Gornick was indeed prepared. He had his shot list ready to go, his director's notes complete with diagrams of the raft and the action which would take place in and around it on the lake, as well as storyboard artwork from a member of the animation department – Gary Hartle, who we'll discuss further once we arrive to the post-production. But one can never be *too* prepared, so Gornick would also receive an assist from makeup effects lead Ed French, who contributed some of his own storyboard art. "In particular when we talked about some of the possible difficulties in terms of *The Raft,* for instance, of how some of those effects might happen to transpire I had to rely on him heavily because I only had so much particular knowledge in terms of applications and devices, potentially, and products that he would use to create the slime. And we knew in certain cases what he could do, what he couldn't do, whether we'd have to do some in

Right: A prime example of director Michael Gornick's preparation for the film: his director's notes. For scene 89 – 91 from *The Raft* he lays out what he hopes to accomplish with the sequence in great detail. (courtesy of Michael Gornick) See Chapter 3.

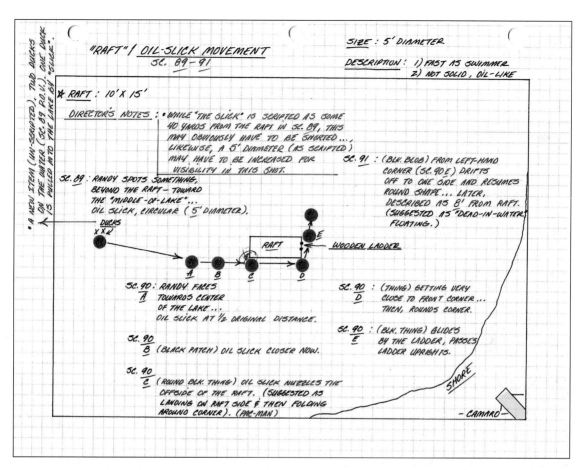

"RAFT" / OIL-SLICK MOVEMENT
SC. 89-91

SIZE : 5' DIAMETER

DESCRIPTION : 1) FAST AS SWIMMER
2) NOT SOLID, OIL-LIKE

* A NEW ITEM (UN-SCRIPTED), TWO DUCKS ON THE WATER (SC. 89 P.O.V.) ONE DUCK IS PULLED INTO THE LAKE BY "SLICK".

RAFT : 10' X 15'

DIRECTOR'S NOTES : • WHILE "THE SLICK" IS SCRIPTED AS SOME 40 YARDS FROM THE RAFT IN SC. 89, THIS MAY OBVIOUSLY HAVE TO BE SHORTED... LIKEWISE, A 5' DIAMETER (AS SCRIPTED) MAY HAVE TO BE INCREASED FOR VISIBILITY IN THIS SHOT.

SC. 89 : RANDY SPOTS SOMETHING, BEYOND THE RAFT — TOWARD THE "MIDDLE-OF-LAKE"... OIL SLICK, CIRCULAR (5' DIAMETER).

DUCKS
X X L

SC. 91 : (BLK. BLOB) FROM LEFT-HAND CORNER (SC. 90E) DRIFTS OFF TO ONE SIDE AND RESUMES ROUND SHAPE... LATER, DESCRIBED AS 8' FROM RAFT. (SUGGESTED AS "DEAD-IN-WATER" FLOATING.)

RAFT
WOODEN LADDER

A B C D

SC. 90 : RANDY FACES
A TOWARDS CENTER OF THE LAKE... OIL SLICK AT 1/2 ORIGINAL DISTANCE.

SC. 90 : (THING) GETTING VERY
D CLOSE TO FRONT CORNER... THEN, ROUNDS CORNER.

SC. 90 : (BLACK PATCH) OIL SLICK CLOSER NOW.
B

SC. 90 : (BLK. THING) GLIDES
E BY THE LADDER, PASSES LADDER UPRIGHTS.

SC. 90 : (ROUND BLK. THING) OIL SLICK NUZZLES THE
C OFFSIDE OF THE RAFT. (SUGGESTED AS LANDING ON RAFT SIDE & THEN FOLDING AROUND CORNER). (PAC-MAN)

SHORE

— CAMARO —

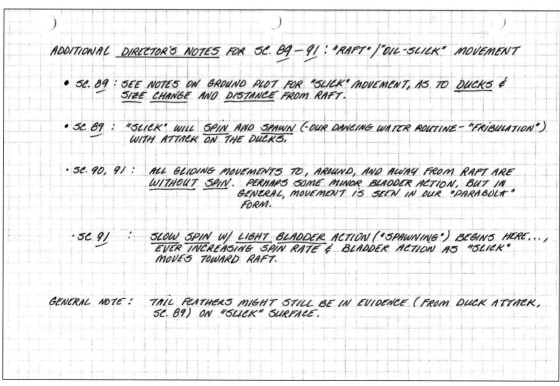

ADDITIONAL DIRECTOR'S NOTES FOR SC. 89-91 : "RAFT" / "OIL-SLICK" MOVEMENT

• SC. 89 : SEE NOTES ON GROUND PLOT FOR "SLICK" MOVEMENT, AS TO DUCKS & SIZE CHANGE AND DISTANCE FROM RAFT.

• SC. 89 : "SLICK" WILL SPIN AND SPAWN (-OUR DANCING WATER ROUTINE — "FRIBULATION") WITH ATTACK ON THE DUCKS.

• SC. 90, 91 : ALL GLIDING MOVEMENTS TO, AROUND, AND AWAY FROM RAFT ARE WITHOUT SPIN. PERHAPS SOME MINOR BLADDER ACTION, BUT IN GENERAL, MOVEMENT IS SEEN IN OUR "PARABOLA" FORM.

• SC. 91 : SLOW SPIN W/ LIGHT BLADDER ACTION ("SPAWNING") BEGINS HERE..., EVER INCREASING SPIN RATE & BLADDER ACTION AS "SLICK" MOVES TOWARD RAFT.

GENERAL NOTE : TAIL FEATHERS MIGHT STILL BE IN EVIDENCE (FROM DUCK ATTACK, SC. 89) ON "SLICK" SURFACE.

```
GENERAL PROP NEEDS: "CREEPSHOW 2"

"OLD WOOD'NHEAD" (NOTE: MOST PROP SIGNS / "INSIGNIAS" FOR PRODUCTS
   1. GASOLINE MANUFACTURER        SHOULD HAVE AN ANTIQUE-PERIOD
      a. GASOLINE PUMP USE              FLAVOR).
      b. MOTOR OIL DISPLAY & SIGNS
          * PENNZOIL, KENDALL, GULF, SKELLY, ATLANTIC *
            QUAKER STATE

   2. TIRE MANUFACTURER
          * KELLY-SPRINGFIELD, FIRESTONE, B.F. GOODRICH, GOODYEAR.

   3. OIL REFINERY (SEE ABOVE)

   4. AUTO PARTS
      a. SPARK PLUGS · CHAMPION, A.C.
      b. FAN BELTS · GATES.
      c. WIPER BLADES                       MUFFLERS?
      d. AIR, OIL FILTERS
      e. GASKETS
      f. HEADLAMPS!

   5. AUTO SERVICES
      a. WHEEL ALIGNMENT · BEAR.
      b. EXHAUST
      c. ENGINE TUNE-UP.

   6. AUTOMOBILES
      a. STUDEBAKER SCRIPTED (CHIEF)
      b. FIREBIRD (ANDY)
      c. EXPENSIVE AUTO (CAVANAUGH FAMILY)
          · CHEVY CAPRICE, IMPERIAL, CADILLAC.
      d. STREET-SIDE DEAD RIVER · OLD "DUSTY" AUTOS, PICK-UPS.

   7. BEER
          · LONE STAR, IRON CITY, BUD, SCHLITZ, NATIONAL BOHEMIAN.

   8. SODA BEVERAGES
          · COKE, NE-HI, MISSION, PEPSI, DR. PEPPER, VIRGINIA DARE.

   9. BEVERAGES
          · MILK, SPRING WATER, HERBAL DRINKS?.

  10. CAFFINE BEVERAGES
       a. COFFEE
          · MAXWELL HOUSE, HILLS BROTHERS, EIGHT O'CLOCK.
       b. TEA
          · LIPTON, SALADA, TETLEY.

  11. MEDICINES / PHARMACY RELATED
```

Above: Another example of Michael Gornick's preparation, a list of items he felt were needed for the general store featured in *Old Chief Wood'nhead*. (courtesy of Michael Gornick)

camera photography tricks to create the movement of the slime," Gornick explains. "But, yeah, I had to rely on him on occasion to at least produce some storyboards that I could play off of that would give me some background in a technical sense of what he could do; post Gary (Hartle)."

Taso Stavrakis would also draft a memo for all crew on the safety precautions of working on the water, complete with nine rules for everyone to know and follow. Whether it was ensuring that you had a "buddy" at all times or making it clear that horseplay wouldn't be tolerated, the memo was thorough. But like Stavrakis himself, it was also lighthearted and playful. "So let's not die just yet, shall we?," his memo read. "Let's live and have some fun. Remember when on the water be cautious and courteous." **(13)**

More contracts were being inked as well on this day. An agreement with the Bagby family would allow Laurel access to the Iron King Mine property to begin construction of Dead River. At a rate of $600 a week, which would be bumped up to $1000 for the final week of filming on the property, Laurel was saving considerable money compared to the $5,000 a day location in Drake.

And lastly a rental property on Ruth Street in Prescott for Eileen Sieff-Stroup to do her costume work was also acquired as well. "So, my workshop in Prescott was a little house they rented for me that was so cute," she says. "It was like a little two bedroom house with a picket fence in

the front and washers and dryers – because that was my requirement – and tables, because that's what I needed."

Sieff-Stroup's requirement for a washer and dryer was due to the amount of aging and dying needed for the film's costumes. But on *Creepshow 2* even that could lead to disaster! "So, I'd get to the place and I'd be like, 'Okay, I need a washer and dryer', and they'd be like, 'Oh, okay. We'll set one up for you. There's no hookup so we're just gonna put the drain pipe in the sink for the washer,'" she recalls. "And I'd be like, 'You can't do that', they're like, 'Oh yeah! It'll just drain.' I'm like, 'Have you ever seen how water comes out of a washing machine?' So, we'd flood the kitchen and then they'd have to come, get a plumber to put a standpipe in."

For Wednesday, September 10 the day was spent conducting location surveys. Most major locations would be visited beginning with the lake, then later Fatso's trailer in the Dewey area, and closing in Humboldt at the store rental property and in Dewey-Humboldt at the Iron King Mine.

Other tasks completed on this day included filing an application for a permit to film on White Spar Road/ Highway 89, the stretch of road that would be used the first day of filming for the opening shots from *The Raft* of the yellow Camaro speeding through the canyon on its way to the lake. Speaking of that Camaro it was one of several cars, including a Pontiac Firebird, acquired by the production for use in the film. "Well, those were all local cars," says Michael Morgan. "I mean, this is a car town; there are tons of hot-rodders and car collectors here and stuff, it's just always been that way. So, they were pretty much readily available."

And a revised shooting schedule was drafted on this day as well, with planning through the first 17 days of filming, basically covering *The Raft* segment.

Thursday, September 11 would be the first day the production would utilize call sheets, even though principal photography was still four days away. The beginning of the day would involve more camera tests at the Dead River locations: the Iron King Mine and the Humboldt store property. Later in the day special effects tests would again be conducted out at the lake including the shot of the duck being attacked by the blob and more of Rachel's demise.

This is also the day that the young quartet of actors featured in *The Raft* would finally arrive in Prescott.

Friday, September 12 would be another busy and productive day for the film's prep. Taso Stavrakis was busy at the Prescott Racquet Club swimming pool working and training with fellow crew members on their underwater swimming abilities and the use of scuba equipment. Wardrobe fittings with Eileen Sieff-Stroup were also conducted. A test of the character Deke's leg breaking through the raft would be executed as well at the studio space called "The Big House". And finally the editing department had their headquarters by this point on North Marina Street in downtown Prescott.

Saturday, September 13 would mark the final day of pre-production work. On tap for the day were further camera

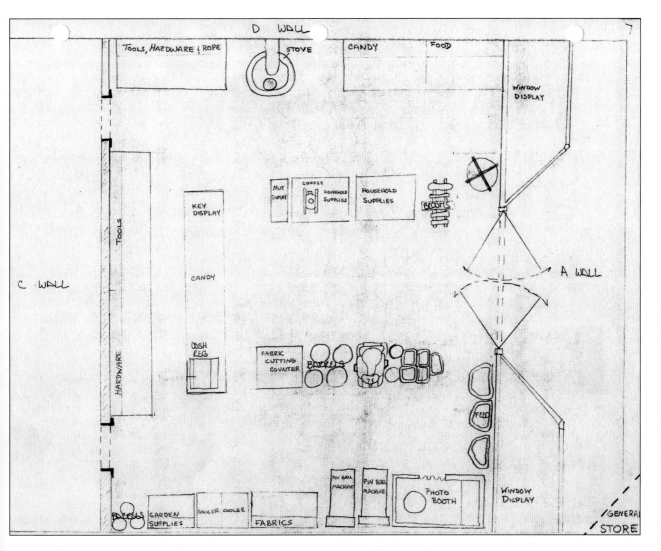

Above: Art department diagram for the interior layout of the Spruce's General Store from *Old Chief Wood'nhead*. (courtesy of Michael Gornick)

tests in the Dewey-Humboldt area at both the store property and Iron King Mine. Back at the production hotel makeup tests on the young cast of actors would be performed, along with a final production meeting. Out at Granite Basin Lake further makeup effects tests would be conducted, as well as a cast rehearsal.

And with that the pre-production and planning would come to a close – at least as far as *The Raft* was concerned.

With Sunday, September 14 being a day off before the start of the show a pre-shoot "get together" was scheduled by David Ball and Michael Gornick that evening in the production hotel conference center. It would be one last chance for the cast and crew to relax and enjoy each other's company before the stresses of principal photography would commence. The calm before the storm, you might say.

"Well, I'm not exactly sure how you're couching your whole book, your whole storyline or what stories you have heard, but *Creepshow 2* has to go down in the annals as one of those movies where if it could go wrong – anything could go wrong – it did go wrong. There were so many, you know, just things that for no conceivable reason just went wrong," says Steve Arnold. "It was my first feature film and I have always – to this day – said, you know, I could never get on a project worse than that."

"It was, like, cursed," laughs Bruce Miller. "It was a cursed movie."

Chapter 3 Jolting Tales Of Horror

This chapter will focus on the principal photography beginning Monday, September 15, 1986 in Arizona's Mountain Standard Time Zone and ending Sunday, November 23, 1986 in Maine's Eastern Standard Time Zone – a 58 day production all together. As with my previous book about the making of George A. Romero's *Day of the Dead* this chapter will basically serve as a diary of the production, detailing what was shot each day.

The information contained in this chapter comes from countless hours of interviews with cast and crew, as well as from the daily production call sheets. I've made every effort to maintain accuracy, but there's certainly the possibility – frankly, the likelihood – of the occasional error sneaking its way through. Honestly there were times when I was forced to make an educated guess based on what a call sheet provided, compared to a photograph or someone's memory. It's not easy and for a perfectionist it's quite maddening! But you do the absolute best

you can, nonetheless. Regarding that possibility I've made notations whenever necessary pointing out these potential discrepancies. It would have been fantastic if someone had kept a journal of what was shot each day, but that was not the case. When you're dealing with events that took place thirty plus years prior, which you weren't witness to, you have to rely on the recollections of others, recollections that often contradict one another. Memories are actually a fascinating subject because they can vary wildly at times and are usually colored by one's own personal experiences or perceptions. Thankfully some of the crew kept their production files, which were very helpful in writing this book.

Below: The four young stars of *The Raft* – Daniel Beer, Page Hannah, Jeremy Green, and Paul Satterfield - bonded during their time in Arizona, seen here at the Grand Canyon. (courtesy of Daniel Beer)

Above: Rigging the camera to the outside of the Camaro for interior shots of the four actors as they make their way to the lake. (courtesy of Bruce Miller) **Middle:** Director Michael Gornick discusses the arrival scene at Cascade Beach(Granite Basin Lake) with Daniel Beer(left) and Paul Satterfield(right). (courtesy of Michael Felsher) **Below:** Filming the kids exiting the Camaro to swim out to the raft. (courtesy of Michael Felsher)

And as Bruce Miller and Steve Arnold warned at the close of Chapter 2, you will see that the production would be fraught with difficult issues which would not only create havoc with the filming schedule, but with the crew's sanity as well.

Monday, September 15, 1986 – Day 1

The production would kick off with *The Raft* and this first day of principal photography was spent shooting the segment's opening moments of the four kids driving in the Camaro out to the lake and their interaction amongst one another: scenes 83L, 84, and 85. Filming would take place along White Spar Road/Highway 89 in Prescott, between mile posts 300 and 309, roughly 10 to 15 miles south of where the rest of the story would be shot at Granite Basin Lake. "The story structure is great. In that car, when we're in the back of the car, the characters are established without any dialogue – the relationships – in the first thirty seconds. Do you know how hard that it is to do? I touch Jeremy's hand. Page sees it. Satterfield's clueless to it. So, you get this triangle going on. You know what I mean? And that's established through a gesture. And you watch that thing, you watch the other episodes, there's a lot of that in there," explains Daniel Beer. "What I just described to you, describing in the car, and how they establish their relationships, I guarantee you everybody in the audience sees that and knows it and they figure it out. They're not

told that's their relationship – it's shown. It's saying, 'You, the audience, I think you're smart, you'll pick this up. I don't need to explain this.'"

An additional scene, number 86, was also scheduled if time permitted out at Granite Basin Lake of the Camaro pulling up to the lake and the kids exiting it; more than likely though this scene would wait until the following day.

83

One final note of importance for this first day of filming was that no rainfall occurred. The weather, as you will eventually see, would play a major role during the making of *The Raft*.

Above: Executive producer Richard P. Rubinstein pays a visit to Granite Basin Lake, seen here with actress Jeremy Green and producer David Ball. (courtesy of Michael Felsher)

Tuesday, September 16, 1986 – Day 2

Day two of filming would concentrate on scenes 86, 87, and 88. These scenes would consist of the Camaro roaring up to the lake in the sand – featuring a great crane shot of the approaching car that turns to reveal a beautiful vista of the lake and mountain background – followed up with the interaction between the four friends on shore as they disrobe into their swim suits and prepare to swim out to the raft.

"So, developing the costumes...again, the *Creepshow* theme, comic book theme, so everything needs to be really graphic looking...blocks of color, that whole look was what I wanted to maintain through the movie," says Eileen Sieff-Stroup. "I do remember getting my bathing suits at some showrooms in New York. And we talked about, again, color blocks. So, we wanted the white one piece (Page Hannah), we wanted the bikini bottoms with the Horlicks t-shirt on the other gal (Jeremy Green). So, we designed that t-shirt up and it was a combo between me and my roommate in New York at the time who was an artist and he helped with it a little bit, you know, uncredited, of course."

The mention of Horlicks is another endearing aspect to Stephen King's brilliant writing. King has created little worlds in his stories, the town of Castle Rock being at the forefront, where people and places share the same

"universe", so to speak. In this particular case Horlicks is a fictional university in Pittsburgh that not only is the school that the four kids in *The Raft* attend, but it's also the college that Hal Holbrook's and Fritz Weaver's characters taught at in *The Crate* from the original *Creepshow*, as well as playing a part in King's novel of *Christine*, also set in Pittsburgh. And as she touched upon, it would be Sieff-Stroup who would be charged with visualizing the fictional school's emblem that would adorn Jeremy Green's shirt in the film. "We needed something that was a Horlicks (design)," Sieff-Stroup recalls. "They'd given me the name and so – I'm not a graphic designer myself – so I went to a friend of mine who is pretty 'graphically' involved. And, you know, remember this is days before computers and so I think that was all drawn out. And we used, I believe, the University of Rochester – hope we won't get in trouble – my sister had gone there. So, we used that as inspiration for the medallion in the center of it and then set the lettering around it. And we had, I think, we had a couple of dozen of those silk screened in some different sizes so that we could fit it on Jeremy the way we wanted to. You know, we talked about, 'What's she going to wear under it?' And obviously this is a sexy thing so she's not going to wear anything under it. She's just gonna...you know."

For dealing with the male characters, Deke for example, Sieff-Stroup would receive an assist from her father regarding the San Diego Chargers jersey worn by actor Paul Satterfield, a jersey which would help play into the theme of bold colors she was after. "My dad worked at a shoe company in the 80's and I would get a lot of athletic wear, like, through my dad," she recalls. "And then I'd go and I'd search things out. It was blue and yellow, right? So, that was very primary colored. You know, that section of the movie is all crisply colored; there's the blue water, there's the green trees, blue sky – red, blue, yellow. So, we were looking for those crisp colors; where in the other episodes we get very de-saturated, in the painted Indian section. So, when you see things like the red paint that he uses that really stands out. I mean, design wise there's a lot of really good things for a little cheesy horror movie – although you shouldn't say that (laughs). But, you know, design wise we worked really hard. We were taking our jobs really seriously."

This morning Michael Gornick would receive an encouraging Western Union Telegram from New York courtesy of Bill Teitler, producer on Laurel's television series *Tales from the Darkside*. "Michael, good luck from everyone at *Darkside*" **(1)**, the message read, a simple but meaningful gesture to let Gornick know that back in the "Big Apple" the people at Laurel were thinking of him. "Well, he was just a total pleasure, really nice guy, always well organized and very...you know, he was a professional," Teitler says about Gornick. "He was part of the Laurel team. And I always loved working with him and he just could not have been a nicer guy."

And finally, the day was free from rain.

Above: Paul Satterfield jokes about the coldness of the lake as Jeremy Green laughs on shore. (courtesy of Michael Felsher)

Wednesday, September 17, 1986 – Day 3

The third day of filming was scheduled to pick up with scene 88, completing whatever was left of it from the previous day's shooting. The remainder of the day would be spent working on scenes 90, 91, 92, and 93 – scenes that would be rather involved so it's surprising that so much was scheduled for one day, even with it being noted on the call sheet that only part of each scene would be filmed. In fact these scenes would end up being scheduled all the way through the following week for a variety of reasons. The scenes would encompass the four kids arriving to the raft and climbing on it, Randy noticing the blob as a potential threat, the interaction between them all on the raft about what the blob might be, and finally the blob's attack of Rachel.

What's interesting is that scene 89, the shot of the ducks becoming ensnared in the blob, was not scheduled. In fact scene 89 would never be scheduled on any call sheets except for being listed at the bottom as part of the advance schedule with Friday, September 19 being the last time it would appear. The scene would be handled by Taso Stavrakis and one of his divers as they pulled the ducks down from below. "I don't remember who it was, the diver, that actually pulled the duck under, but I do remember the first few takes it just didn't work 'cause when whoever it was underneath would grab the duck's legs and start to

pull, the duck's neck would just sort of go forward and it would make this little, 'Blahhhh', noise," says production assistant Dex Craig. "And then it didn't struggle and they wanted it flapping its wings and struggling and I remember the diver saying something to the effect of, 'You don't want to know how I got the duck to flap its wings.'"

Not to worry, kiddies, as the mallards were just fine, with Stavrakis and his colleague posing for a photo afterwards with the waterfowl to prove they were unharmed. In his own personal shot list Michael Gornick made a notation regarding this scene stating that it would be saved for times when the crew was waiting on long makeups. However, there is a caveat here because some second unit photography did take place about four weeks later at the lake, so there's always the possibility it was done at that time.

The actual shooting script for *Creepshow 2* was quite colorful, with all the revisions it went through during the pre-production phase in the summer of 1986. The initial script printed on standard white paper would receive a polish on July 8, followed by a pink-page revision on July 25. After that, two separate blue page revisions would happen on August 7 and August 13. By September it was a yellow-page revision on the 8th, followed by a green-page revision on the 10th. Regarding *The Raft* the revisions were the August 13 blue pages and the September 8 yellow pages. These changes can occur for a number of reasons during a

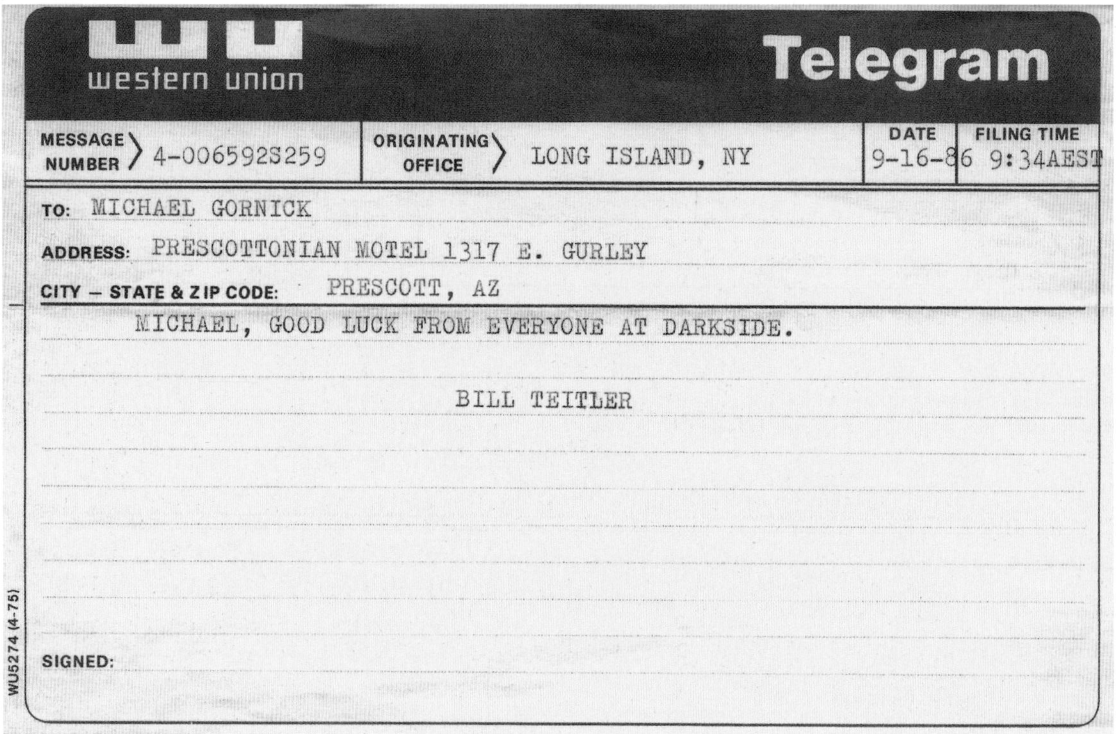

western union

Telegram

| MESSAGE NUMBER | 4-0065923259 | ORIGINATING OFFICE | LONG ISLAND, NY | DATE 9-16-86 | FILING TIME 9:34AEST |

TO: MICHAEL GORNICK

ADDRESS: PRESCOTTONIAN MOTEL 1317 E. GURLEY

CITY — STATE & ZIP CODE: PRESCOTT, AZ

MICHAEL, GOOD LUCK FROM EVERYONE AT DARKSIDE.

BILL TEITLER

SIGNED:

WU5274 (4-75)

film production and for the most part are typically standard procedure, with the different colors helping to make sure that everyone involved has the proper corrections. "Steve (King) would give us the story. George (Romero) would give us the screenplay. And we'd turn up in Arizona and it don't work per the screenplay," explains David Ball. "So, you have to adapt to the locations, you have to adapt to the cast, you have to adapt to the weather, you have to adapt to the daylight hours. So, sometimes a night exterior might work better as a night interior or vice versa. So, the script is never finished until the film is in the can."

In this case Ball would huddle up with his director and take care of any last minute changes. "George did a bunch of revisions and then we just did...Mike (Gornick) and I, we just talked it through," Ball says. "No material changed to the stories. More tweaks, if you like; tweaks. But that's part of the process of making movies." A perfect example of this tweaking process which Ball references is a line of dialogue from scene 91: in Romero's original drafts, dating all the way back to early 1984, when Deke asks Randy if he's ever seen an oil slick before, Randy responds that he had seen one on the cape four years prior and that the people he was with had pulled birds from the surf to clean them up. In the August 13 revision – the one that's in the film – Randy's line about seeing one on the cape is now Rachel's line, followed up by Randy mentioning the birds in the surf.

While most of the crew had their hands full working on *The Raft* some were quietly organizing things for the eventual move to Bangor, Maine. Henry Nevison had Laurel's production offices set up in a Bangor warehouse, just a little over a mile from where their hotel accommodations would

Above: Western Union Telegram from *Tales from the Darkside* producer Bill Teitler in New York sending well-wishes to Michael Gornick on location in Arizona. (courtesy of Michael Gornick)

be at the Holiday Inn. And Charles Carroll released a memo to all department heads requesting a list of everything each department would need for the eventual move to Maine: from the sound department's boom cases, to wardrobe's sewing machines, to the art department's fake newsstand to be used for the opening sequence with Billy and the Creep, it had to be inventoried and listed.

And once again the day was without rain.

Thursday, September 18, 1986 – Day 4

Day four would continue with work on scenes 90, 91, and 92. However, scene 93 of the blob attacking Rachel would not be scheduled. The reason for this could have been a lack of time, considering the challenges of working on and in the water, something we'll discuss shortly. Another reason could have been the major incident involving the head of the makeup effects department, Ed French. This issue is something we'll cover in as much detail as possible in Day 6 as the exact date is unknown, other than definitely occurring during the first week. As I mentioned in my preface, a lack of input from the members of the makeup effects team, including French himself to a large degree, clouds the details a bit.

Speaking of clouds, a cloud cover set was also listed for this day just in case it would be needed with scenes 98 and 99 – the night scenes of Randy and Laverne stuck on the raft and taking turns keeping watch – originally listed.

Above: Filming Daniel Beer swimming out to the raft. (courtesy of Michael Felsher)

Those, however, were instead crossed out for scene 100 of Randy taking advantage of a sleeping Laverne. It's highly doubtful anything was accomplished with these scenes as they would be listed again, multiple times, on future call sheets.

Working on and in the water comes with an assortment of challenges for any film production – just ask Steven Spielberg about filming *Jaws* on Martha's Vineyard – and *Creepshow 2* would be no different. One of the crew members who had a particularly tricky job was the soundman, Felipe Borrero. "The lower the budget, the more important my job becomes because I've got to get good, clean tracks. Good, clean tracks meaning good, clean voice tracks – everything else is secondary," explains Borrero. "And these were the days when wireless didn't have the range that we have now, so I had to be on a boat floating by this raft and circling around and my boom operator had to be on another raft where it would position him so he could get the sound."

"Sound crew, by the way, speaking of Felipe...I mean, champion work, difficult work and I thought did an incredible job," says Michael Gornick. "You know, sound always gets second shrift anyhow. They don't get positioned typically; they don't get consideration about their problems. And they just adapted constantly to every situation."

"Shooting on water in the middle of a lake is a significant production – we did some amazing production work to do that job," says Tom Hurwitz. "And we built an extraordinary rig to do it, with two lights on rafts and an underwater catwalk around the raft to put a dolly on and to put the camera on. We could build up the catwalk on one side and do dolly shots – it was really pretty amazing – and move the lights around as we needed to."

"Hair and Makeup had to have a boat. Wardrobe had a boat. Camera had a boat. Sound had a boat. So, you had this flotilla of boats that were going out into the middle of the lake. You understand what I'm saying? It's logistics. And it takes very little to throw a wrench into that," says first assistant cameraman Eric Swanek. "You go out on the dock, every time anybody...'Oh, I have to go pee!' Okay, put them in a boat – bring the boat to the shore. I don't know where the women peed; the guys would pee in the woods. I don't remember ever getting to leave to go to the bathroom because the camera department didn't have the ability, so we wouldn't get to pee until lunch. People never used to think about that. Well, why don't you just pee off the dock? It's like – we have divers in the water. And that was the other thing, because of the scaffolding, any one that was going to be out there on the dock had to take introduction to scuba lessons which were required for safety because if you fell off the dock into the water, the odds are you'd get entangled in the scaffolding."

Of course, before getting into the water to film you've got to ensure that you have one of the most vital requirements any film crew needs: power. "They had to figure out how to put lights out there; so, they had to figure out power out there," Swanek explains. "The electric truck had a generator built into it and the genny operator realized that you could then DC power out there and because it's fresh water if you got a short...DC power into water wouldn't harm anybody. If it was AC you could electrify people. So, he figured out that if they ran all the lights on DC they wouldn't have any

Above: Daniel Beer, Page Hannah, and Paul Satterfield stand around on the raft during a break in filming. Note divers Dex Craig (foreground) and Patty Tallman as well. (courtesy of Michael Felsher) **Below:** Page Hannah takes it easy during a shooting break. (courtesy of Michael Felsher)

problems. So, even the guy, the Teamster, that drove the truck, the electric truck, was pitching in on ideas. So, they basically had, like, milk containers that were buoying up the power cable that went out there, because they had lights out there, too."

"It wasn't deep (the lake), but it was completely zero visibility; because it's spring fed from underneath, so the minute you go underwater everything was by feel. So, the boys had been there like two weeks ahead of time, the crew, and they built an underwater scaffold in the shape of a horseshoe, and so you could walk knee deep in the water and you couldn't see it. So, you didn't have to be in the water, you could just walk around and pull the boat with the camera crew and sound stuff," recalls Taso Stavrakis. "And all the lights and electric went in and these gigantic electric cables went in to power them up. And I made... what's his name? I can't remember the electrician, the head electrician, (Tom Feldman was the gaffer on the film) I said, 'Before any of my guys get in, you put your hand in the water. Power up the lights, you put your hand in'; because I'm terrified of electricity. And, so, 'Poof', up come the lights and he was okay (laughs). And it's like, 'Alright, everybody in the water.'"

"I think we started with the water one, I think. And that was slow, any time you're working in the water it's slow," says key grip Nick Mastandrea. "But we didn't have things like spud barges or anything – it was really up to us to lay the scaffolding in the water, which is not fast."

Nick Mastandrea was a long time veteran of Laurel Entertainment, in fact his involvement with George Romero went as far back as Michael Gornick's, all the way to The Latent Image days in the Steel City. "I love the fact that I grew up in Pittsburgh, I still think it's one of the best towns in the world," Mastandrea fondly recalls. "I actually met George through my sister who was working for Nancy, his first wife, or his second wife? I don't know, I think his second wife. And he said, 'Look, man, I don't have any money to pay anybody that knows what they're doing. But if you want to come down and carry shit I'll teach you.' And basically that's what I did. And, you know, he taught me how to load a mag (film magazine), and run the Nagra, and sync film – we were still using rewinds then. And he could do rewinds faster than anybody could – he used a flatbed, I think, at the time. So, I knew all that stuff. So, then when The Latent Image was sort of going down I would go over to WQED and work in their film department, because none of those guys were 'film guys'. And I wasn't a very good assistant cameraman; I wasn't a very good key grip either, or a sound man, but I did them all and I knew how to do it and I knew what a good one was."

"Nick was like the on-set captain, if you like. He'd been through those early days, he'd grown up with George and Laurel and Mike as a boy. All of these Pittsburgh crew were pretty much self-educated and so they did it their way, they were pretty much self-educated," says David Ball about the man he refers to as his "brother". "But Nick was just a fantastic grip and had so much positivity, shall we call it, and nothing was too much trouble."

Mastandrea was brought in pretty early to the production, according to him, by Richard Rubinstein, even before Tom Hurwitz was hired. But when Hurwitz was

Above: Alternate angle of a well-known publicity shot of Daniel Beer, Jeremy Green, and Paul Satterfield. (courtesy of Michael Felsher)

brought on board he brought his own key grip, Denis Hann, along. With that being the case Mastandrea was initially slated as the dolly grip, but that would all change after Hann's dismissal. "They fired the key grip that I brought onto the job because he didn't rig cars fast enough," claims Hurwitz. "You can't rig cars fast. They brought in another guy who'd only worked in Pittsburgh (Mastandrea), which was not the capitol of sophisticated film-making at the time. So, my crew was kind of taken out from under me. I mean, key grip on a job like this was very, very important."

As far as ancillary activities were concerned Charles Carroll released a memo letting cast and crew know that the viewing of dailies would be limited to just department heads due to a lack of space at the editing facility in town.

And speaking of the editing facility, it would be the domain of the late Peter Weatherley – the film's editor, of course. Prior to meeting Weatherley for the first time Michael Gornick decided he would introduce his quirky sense of humor to the worldly editor. "David Ball had told me about Peter and given me some of his background, I was quite impressed by the work he had done," Gornick recalls. "He mentioned to me that, 'Peter was most curious though because you had done some beautiful films and why you didn't continue on as a director of photography?' He said, 'I had no explanation for Peter. He wants to become a director, I guess.' So, I thought, 'Okay', being kind of a jokester I thought, 'When I first meet Peter I'll do this – I'll give him a reason to maybe understand why I don't shoot anymore.' So, I went out to a Goodwill store, got the thickest pair of glasses I could find, Coke bottle glasses. So, the first time I met Peter in Arizona, before I went into the room, I said, 'David, play along with me.' I put the glasses on and stumbled into the room and David Ball

said, 'Peter, here is Michael Gornick.' And I used it to its full effect; I looked about the room trying to find Peter and said, 'Oh, Peter, there you are!' And I remember he was totally shocked at that. And I'm sure what raced through his mind was, 'Oh, the poor dear, he's blind!'"

And this day would also see no rain.

Friday, September 19, 1986 – Day 5

The fifth day of principal photography would once again see scenes 90, 91, 92, and if time permitted 93, on its schedule. Again, how much of each scene was shot is frankly anyone's guess due to the call sheets not listing specific details.

As was just discussed – and will be again – working on the water can be a challenge technically, creating difficulties for the sound, electrical, and camera departments. But besides presenting adverse situations from a technical standpoint it can also affect the health of those who are physically in the water.

And one of the most prominent examples of this would be star Daniel Beer. "That lake was freezing," he says. "And I remember at lunch people coming up to me – I don't know if it was five days into the shoot, I have no idea, but it was soon as I hit the water basically – and they said, 'You're green and you don't look good', and they went and got Michael Gornick and Michael just looked kind of horrified. And they stopped everything and then they said, 'I think we gotta get you to a hospital', and I was like, 'No, I'm okay.'"

Well, Beer wasn't okay and would indeed be taken to the hospital where hypothermia was diagnosed. "They said, 'He can't work. His entire body has hypothermia. He could go into shock and die.' And the producers, I don't know which one of them it was, I just know the producers said, 'We have to work him', and Michael Gornick simply said, 'If you work Daniel Beer I will walk off the set.' And for a kid who didn't have any family support in the middle of Arizona and only had his agent for support that meant the world to me. And it still means the world to me. That's why I think so highly of Michael Gornick and I just love that man. So, they shut it down. And we all had hypothermia; I was the most extreme."

"I went out there one morning, probably day two or day three or day four, I got stung right on my vein by a bee," recalls David Ball. "And I said, 'Oh fuck! Blimey, I've just been stung by a bee!' I thought no more of it and I went back to the office. Then all of a sudden I started to throw up and get woozy. So, I called the driver, I said, 'Can you take me to the hospital? I need a shot or something.' It was really weird this bee sting. So, they gave me a couple of shots and I went out for an hour and when I woke up it wasn't Daniel Beer, it was all four of them! And I woke up and I said, 'Blimey, what are you all doing here?' And they said, 'Hypothermia', and I said, 'Oh fuck. I need that, don't I?'"

"This was a big break for them and they were very grateful to be there, you know. And they were put in a horrible situation, it was a horrible predicament," says assistant hair and makeup artist Angela Nogaro. "It was

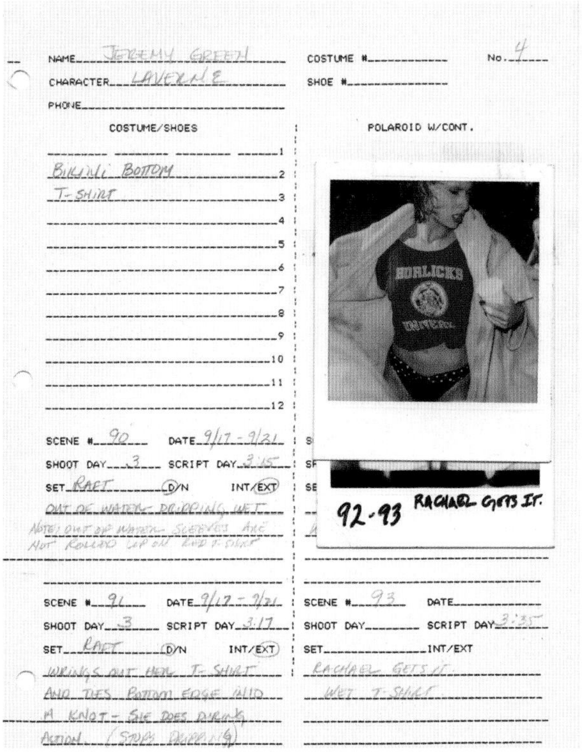
NAME JEREMY GREEN — COSTUME # — No. 4
CHARACTER LAVERNE — SHOE #
PHONE
COSTUME/SHOES — POLAROID W/CONT.
1
2 BIKINI BOTTOM
3 T-SHIRT
4
5
6
7
8
9
10
11
12

SCENE # 90 DATE 9/17 - 9/21
SHOOT DAY 3 SCRIPT DAY 3:15
SET RAFT D/N INT/EXT
OUT OF WATER - DRIPPING WET
NOTE: OUT OF WATER SLEEVES ARE NOT ROLLED UP ON ... T-SHIRT

92-93 RACHAEL GETS IT.

SCENE # 91 DATE 9/17 - 9/21
SHOOT DAY 3 SCRIPT DAY 3:17
SET RAFT D/N INT/EXT
WRINGS OUT HER T-SHIRT AND TIES BOTTOM EDGE INTO A KNOT - SHE DOES DURING ACTION (STOPS DRIPPING)

SCENE # 93 DATE
SHOOT DAY SCRIPT DAY 3:35
SET INT/EXT
RACHAEL GETS IT. WET T-SHIRT

Left: Jeremy Green and Paul Satterfield during filming on the raft, shortly before the attack on Page Hannah's character. (courtesy of Michael Felsher) **Right:** Eileen Sieff-Stroup's costume continuity page of Jeremy Green for scenes 90, 91, 92, and 93. (courtesy of Eileen Sieff-Stroup)

freezing cold, they had to get in to this water every day, you know. Then we had to get them back and get them into warmer temps so that they didn't get hypothermia. And they bucked up and they carried on through. I mean, granted, that's their job description, but...you know, actors make a lot of money because sometimes they're asked to really put themselves in situations that none of us would wanna have to. I wouldn't have wanted to have to get into that lake every day."

Of course hypothermia wasn't just a concern for the actors as the divers, despite their wetsuits, were also subject to the dangers of the cold water. "I wasn't ready. They said, 'You're going to the desert in Arizona to do this scene', and I thought 'Desert in Arizona, it's probably going to be boiling hot.' We got there in Prescott, we were up in the mountains, and we had to break the ice to get into the water – that's how cold it was. It was frozen. And, so, I had scuba gear and had I known I would have got together a dry suit, which doesn't get you wet. Scuba gear you get wet and then your body temperature raises the water temperature," says Taso Stavrakis, who recalls the system the production devised to counteract the conditions in the water. "We all took 15 minute shifts – you know, one of us 'on the clock' – you're out and onto the beach where they were boiling water and pouring it into our wetsuits to keep from hypothermia. 15 minutes, that's it, you're done, next guy in."

"One of my favorite memories, honestly, working on the film was after being in the water in that wetsuit... climbing out of the lake and there were several production assistants, they had lukewarm water on a camp stove and they would come up and pour that water into my wetsuit to warm me up and oh my god that was such an amazing feeling," recalls P.A. Dex Craig, who spent more than his fair share of time in the chilly lake. "A lot of those production folk would...it was almost like they were fighting to be the person who got to pour the water in the wetsuit of the people who were in the lake because they liked looking at the faces; we were just like, 'Ahhhhh.'"

And if it wasn't the water's temperature, the cast and crew would have to worry about what was living in the lake as well. "There was a parasite in the water," remembers stunt woman Patricia Tallman. "Just the lake itself was very...there was a lot of peat in the water, you know, sediment, and so it was impossible visibility wise. We had a really hard time as scuba divers trying to keep an eye on our actors because we couldn't see through the water at all. And, also, because of that – the water having such a high content of organic material – there was also some sort of bug. And we got really sick. I mean fevers and just crazy shit. It was nuts. It was nuts!"

Quickly, getting back to David Ball's bee sting, it wasn't only the producer who would fall victim to such a thing

Top, middle left and left: Working on the water was a massive undertaking which required coordination, manpower, and patience. (courtesy of Michael Felsher and Nick Mastandrea) **Above:** Original makeup effects lead Ed French(in black), seen here with Howard Berger, would be dismissed during the first week of filming in Arizona. (courtesy of Father William Kosco)

while on location at the lake as director of photography Tom Hurwitz would also be stung and had a very unique way of dealing with the effects. "Okay, so, Tom, back in the day, used to do a lot of documentaries and so he spent a lot of time in third world countries or whatever. So, he's got some sort of survival knowledge," recalls Angela Nogaro. "And he picked up a can of Coca-Cola – we were all on the beach shooting – and he picked up a can of Coca-Cola that apparently he had sat down. And a bee flew into it and he took a sip and the bee went into his mouth and stung him in the mouth. And whether he was allergic or whatever, but apparently he knew that ammonia is one of the things to get rid of the immediate reaction to a bee (sting). So, he ran off into the woods and peed into his hand (laughs), which needless to say didn't go over well with the crew who were not 'survivalists', and washed his mouth out with the his own urine to get rid of the bee sting. And I'm sure somebody can verify."

"Yeah, we were all pretty appalled, but I guess it worked. And he just kept going, so I guess it was fine," confirms lead hair and makeup artist Joanna Robinson. "I'd never seen anyone do that before...or since."

"The lake location was infested by yellow jackets. I had put down a Coke can and one crawled in, then it got me in the lip while taking a drink," recalls Hurwitz. "As one can imagine, it hurt like hell. I peed on a piece of paper towel or napkin and pressed it to my lip – a trick I knew from working in the outdoors. The ammonia in urine counteracts the venom in the bee sting. It worked and I went back to the raft. Healthy urine is sterile, I hasten to add."

But the dangers of working at Granite Basin Lake weren't limited to the water or yellow jackets as one of the desert's deadliest predators was also on hand and took an unknown production assistant hostage for a stretch of time during filming. "I remember because of the weather being poor they needed sun and it would look weird, of course, in a movie if all the sudden there's clouds, then shade, so they had to wait for these sun breaks," production assistant Billy Kosco recalls about his fellow P.A. "So, they finally said, 'Someone go up there on that mountain and we'll walkie-talkie and when you see the sun opening up and stuff, just let us know, tell us.' So, he was always like (in a walkie-talkie voice), 'I'd say about a minute out, you're gonna have some sun'...'Okay, let's get this ready! Let's get this ready, everybody ready? You pull the car in and you guys run to the beach, okay? Alright, let's get 'er ready!' And then, okay, he goes, 'Here it comes, here it comes!' And they're going, 'We've got the sun!' And so it would be racing like that with all the different shots, waiting for that sun. But with one shot they were like (again, in a walkie-talkie voice), 'Okay, how is it? Hey, can you hear us?' And they're like, 'Holy crap! Hey, looks like there's sun, is that gonna last? Where is that dude?' And somebody said, 'Does somebody else want to walk up there?', and it's like, 'I don't know, it's gonna take a while to get up there.' And there was a bunch of boulders and such and there was a boulder thing there that overlooked the lake a bit, too. Finally he gets on, 'Hey, guys', and we're like, 'Where the hell have you been?' Somebody's yelling at him, he's like, 'Hey, man. I was just moving around, sat down, and there was a rattlesnake right

here next to me.' And they're like, 'Oh, god. Are you okay?' He's like, 'Yeah, I killed it!' They're like, 'With what?' (laughs) Anyway, and they're like, 'So you're okay?'...'Yeah!'... (dramatic pause)'Is the sun coming out?'"

Of interest on this day was a special note on the call sheet from the film's producer to all cast and crew: "During the next 2 weeks we have an extremely difficult schedule of effects filming. There are to be no visitors without the express written permission of the Prod. Mgr. From now until the end of 'The Raft' segment this is a 'CLOSED SET'. Please save Joe Winogradoff(original 1st A.D.) the embarrassment of turning people away. Thank you. – David Ball" **(2)**

And this would be another day without rainfall.

Saturday, September 20, 1986 – Day 6

Day six was to originally see work on scenes 100 and 101 of Randy exploring Laverne's body as she lay sleeping on the raft and the ensuing blob attack of her. However, a revised call sheet would be distributed that would scrap those plans in favor of continued work on scene 93, the blob's attack of Rachel. It also had a hold on the actors report times to set that day, so whether they were. ever utilized is unknown.

The night before, after eight o'clock, a hand written letter from second assistant director Gina Randazzo was delivered to Patricia Tallman letting her and Taso Stavrakis know that Tallman would be used as a double for Page Hannah's character, Rachel, for makeup effects shots in the water and for the two of them to be ready by 6AM. These shots of the blob completely covering a terrified Rachel as she screams, "Help, it hurts. It hurts", have become iconic to the film. And under all of that slime, goo, and prosthetics was Tallman. "That was pretty horrible. It was horrible. Yeah, there was a lot of effects stuff glued all over me and then being in the water, it was a little scary," Tallman explains about the effects appliances which covered one of her eyes. "I had that white bathing suit that Page wore, I had one, and it had glue all over it where they glued that appliance to the bathing suit into me. It was nasty."

Here's where things get interesting though. In the behind-the-scenes featurette, *Nightmares in Foam Rubber*, Greg Nicotero states that Patricia Tallman was under all of those prosthetics and slime in the lake. And as you just read Tallman herself confirms that she performed the scene. However, there are numerous behind-the-scenes photos that clearly show Page Hannah in the makeup both on shore and in the lake itself. "Yes, that's me; yeah, it's not a stunt double," says Hannah. "Yeah, I definitely did it. I mean, maybe they...I know they made the mold to me and I remember being in the water and shooting it and scuba divers around, so maybe there are some shots that are me and some shots that are her? I'm not sure."

"The way that it was filmed I was just off camera standing on the underwater scaffolding and she was on the underwater scaffolding. And she had foam latex on her face and as I recall a little bit down on her chest, her body,"

explains Dex Craig, who remembers the scene being shot with Page Hannah. "And she would go underwater and then come up to deliver her line, 'It hurts'; and they covered her with Ultra-slime, so there was all this gooey stuff. And then she would go back underwater and hold as long as she could, but by that point the foam latex had absorbed the water and became really heavy. And so as soon as they would call, 'Cut', I would step in and pull her up, stand her up, so that she wouldn't drown."

So, what's the deal? Perhaps they shot the scene initially on this day with Tallman and then later due to whatever circumstances with Hannah? Or was it vice versa?

It should be pointed out that scene 93 would be listed several times on future call sheets over the next week to week and a half, due to the fact that it incorporated over a dozen shots in Michael Gornick's shot list log. Howard Berger is even on record in the *Nightmares in Foam Rubber* documentary stating that the makeup effects crew rebuilt most of the work to be utilized for *The Raft* over this first weekend. If that is accurate then who was on set from the makeup effects team to handle these shots on this day of filming? Which in turn raises the question of whether these shots were actually even filmed on this day at all? Maybe Berger was using a little hyperbole there or could it have been that they were on set for a portion of the day and then spent the rest of the day and all day Sunday working on the re-engineered effects for the remainder of the segment? Honestly, I just can't say.

Regarding the fact that Berger mentioned having to re-work the effects over the weekend, that's where the issue of effects leader Ed French comes back into play. As mentioned previously, things came to a head with French during this first week of filming and according to French the first day of filming was his last day on the production. However, the first day was spent filming the opening scenes of the Camaro on its way to the lake, so that couldn't be accurate because no effects work was needed that day. Perhaps he meant *his* first day of filming? Again, people's memories can often vary and be rather sketchy. For example, both David Ball and Tom Hurwitz were positive that it rained constantly during this first week, but in reality the rain wouldn't arrive until the second week of production. Like most of the things I inquired about to French he only officially responded once and rather vaguely in a one-page letter, but without a doubt he would be gone from the production during this first week.

"The narrative for why and how that came to be is complicated, convoluted and even after all these years, somewhat speculative," French wrote in his letter. "I won't comment on the quality of the finished film itself other than to say that many of the ideas and makeup effects I visualized are on the screen, albeit without my participation on set. That is why my name appears in the opening credits."

The following information regarding French's departure is taken from an eleven-page letter, which I obtained from

Left: Patty Tallman, Page Hannah, Jeremy Green, and Taso Stavrakis at the Yavapai County Fair demolition derby; Eileen Garrigan paints the *Creepshow 2* demolition derby vehicle. (courtesy of Taso Stavrakis and Eileen Garrigan)

Michael Gornick, that French sent to Richard Rubinstein in December 1986 explaining his side of the events which led to his termination, as well as seeking proper screen credit along with monies he felt were due him from Laurel. Much like Romero's 1983 letter about who would be the best choice to helm the film, French's letter about his firing is frank, thorough, and quite fascinating. He discusses in detail the pre-production incident in his Brooklyn loft with David Ball, the subject of his character being maligned by the production over issues with the effects themselves, and his eventual dismissal from the production. His breakdown of events and how they all unfolded and built upon one another is exhaustive in detail and one can find themselves feeling empathy towards his situation. From French's viewpoint it was David Ball and Charles Carroll who were most responsible for his departure.

"Standing on the raft in the middle of the lake, my two assistants and an actress prepared for a special effect," French wrote to Rubinstein. "I stood on shore, waiting to be ferried to the raft where I would oversee the shot. At first, Mr. Carroll lied and told me a boat would come back to take me out. After a few minutes, I asked again for a boat and was told that there 'were too many people on the raft already.' I asked for a walkie-talkie to talk with the director and was ignored and finally an ugly scene ensued where I shouted out over the water that 'I need to see how this will be shot!' I was physically restrained by Mr. Carroll when I tried to take a canoe that was on shore and only when I was finally given a walkie-talkie and spoke to Michael Gornick did I give up trying to do my job. He had to be the one to finally tell me that the producer did not want me on the set, even though Mr. Ball was standing on the raft and had undoubtedly seen me on location before this unfortunate incident." **(3)**

French would find out later that day he was suspended from the film and the locks to the effects workshop, the "EFXACO", had been changed due to concerns he would seek revenge by sabotaging the effects prep and molds contained inside the workspace.

"When we were out shooting on the raft and Ed French was on shore screaming, 'Those are my effects! Stop shooting! Stop shooting!' – I mean, it was kind of sad," remembers Michael Gornick. "Whose fault was that? It could have been my fault in selecting him initially. It could be my fault in not giving him enough information. It could be my fault for not giving him the right crew to work with him. But, he was part of the process early and it all seemed to be a good match, you know. But, it didn't work."

"You know, I actually remember Ed sort of fondly. I think Ed was a great guy," says Charles Carroll. "I mean, Ed was doing *Tales from the Darkside*, right? And he was basically a one man show – you know what I'm saying? And I think this was much bigger and I just think he...you know, he got put in a tough situation. Because 'Ballie' (David Ball) comes in and Laurel says, 'Okay, we'll let you use our people. He's great. He'll do this.' But it was much bigger; it was a much bigger task than a *Tales from the Darkside*. He wasn't quite equipped for it. He was falling behind, he had problems. And that's what happened to him. So, it's not that he wasn't skilled enough, he just wasn't experienced enough and the show was too big for what he was used to. And he didn't

have a support system. You know, you do these things and you say, 'Okay, yeah, we can do this. We've got these people', and then you get there and the demands of the script, the demands of the director, the demands of making a movie – as opposed to a little TV show – are greater, and you kind of go, 'Oh, shit. These people don't have the skill to do that', you know, and that's what happens. So, I think, that's what happened to poor Ed."

"I'm only going to say if you can't cut it you have to go," David Ball asserts. "It was very important to Mike (Gornick) that the standard in *Creep 2* was as high as the standard in *Creep 1*. And all I can say is if some of Ed French's effects were not deemed up to standard he would have been gone and I would have sent him packing and I would not have had any problem with that. So, that's all I can think."

One of French's assistants, Howard Berger, would now take over as the makeup effects lead. Three and half years prior, as a high school senior, Berger had been featured in an *L.A. Times* photograph making up someone as a witch for a Shakespeare Festival, and now, with just a handful of credits to his name, he was the top man of the makeup effects department for a major motion picture. "But it should have been myself and Greg Nicotero," Berger told Anchor Bay Entertainment. "Because Greg and I did the same amount of work, I felt." **(4)**

"Around the time I first started at *Fangoria* the former editor, Bob Martin, gave me good advice. Well, you know, *Fangoria* was sort of like the bible of the makeup effects business, so he said, 'When you go on set always hang out with the makeup guys because they love *Fangoria* and they'll give you all the dirt on what's going on behind the scenes,'" says the former editor of *Fangoria* magazine Tony Timpone, who wouldn't visit the set until the production moved to Maine for *The Hitchhiker*. "So, anyway, the way Howard and Greg told the story was that Ed just didn't know what he was doing, he was in over his head, he was used to doing these small episodes of *Tales from the Darkside* and not stuff that was really overly complex like *The Raft*. So, that kind of got him bounced off the movie. Now, after I ran my article Ed French contacted me to say that – because in the article we said that Ed left the movie for artistic differences or something to that effect, Ed told me that was not true – he alleged that his assistants on the movie, Nicotero and Berger, badmouthed him and got him fired. So, that was Ed's version of the story. Maybe the truth is somewhere in between. I don't know if someone else has told you what went on, but that's basically what I was told at the time."

Besides the issue with Ed French, David Ball was also dealing with the continued headache involving the search for an actress to portray the Annie Lansing role from *The Hitchhiker*. On this day he would send a terse one-page memo to New World executive Jeff Schechtman regarding the status of a potential candidate for the role, a candidate famous for her role as "Hot Lips Houlihan" from the long

Above right: Property master Jim Feng tends to the "blob".
Below right: The man behind the "blob", mechanical engineer and construction coordinator Ed Fountain; (courtesy of Bruce Miller and Rebecca Mayo)

running television series *M*A*S*H*. "It is conceivable that many decisions by New World take an allotted period of time to filter through to me. What is inconceivable and impractical is that the very important matter of casting 'Annie' is left unanswered," Ball wrote. "Loretta Swit must give four weeks clear notice before she would be available for work in Maine – I need her in four weeks and three days." **(5)**

And finally, you guessed it, there would be no rain on this day.

Monday, September 22, 1986 – Day 7

Before we delve into the details of the production's seventh day I want to backtrack for a moment to the previous day on the calendar – Sunday, September 21. Sundays would be the production's lone day off each week and would give the cast and crew an opportunity to take it easy or check out some of the local fun available in Prescott. It just so happened that during this time the annual Yavapai County Fair was in town and wouldn't you know it Laurel-CST, Inc. would find a way to publicize their arrival to the area in as strange a way as possible. "They had a derby, a demolition derby, and one of the guys, old hippies, you know, kind of hanging out in that town, they got an old, what was that? It was a station wagon," says head carpenter Logan Berkshire. "We put that thing in the demolition derby and it did alright. It won the beauty contest because they had painted *Creepshow 2* on it and all this stuff."

"They found this crappy station wagon, which is the wrong car for a demo derby to begin with because the drive train's way too long; one hit on the side and that drive train's done. And it may have been a Nissan station wagon, too, so it's made out of crappy metal," says Billy Kosco, who remembers the crew wanting to have a little fun while in town. "And it was also sort of a way of maybe advertising to the hometown crowd, you know, 'Hey, your Hollywood movie people, too, are going to participate in your thing.' You know, 'We're here, watch our movie when it comes out.'"

The seventh day of shooting would once again deal with scenes 90, 91, 92, and 93 – familiar territory by this point for the production. This day would be noteworthy because it would be the first day of filming that would fall victim to the spectre of precipitation as .30 to .35 inches of rain would fall. Bear with me – I promise we'll get back to that subject in just a bit – but first...

One aspect of a film production that is often taken for granted, yet always greatly appreciated by the crew, is craft services. Providing refreshments, snacks, and treats can be quite a comfort to have on hand for crew members who are slogging through a 12 to 14 hour day. And there's an important distinction to point out about the difference between craft services and catering. Caterers typically provide the hot meals which feed the cast and crew, usually twice a day – in the case of Prescott it was Cinema Edibles. Whereas craft services makes sure that crew members have plenty of items to keep them energized throughout the day: fruit, candy, water, soft drinks, and the industry standard, coffee. The man who would handle

this during the making of *Creepshow 2* would be an out of work software engineer, who was in between jobs at the time, Garry Greer. "It was basically be there first and go home last," laughs Greer. "But it was basically just, you know, putting together different kinds of food and drinks and snacks and whatnot, whatever the cast and crew wanted. Sometimes it would be like, 'Get me a breakfast burrito!', or at the end of the day, 'Get me a beer.' But it was all day long because everybody was doing things at different times."

Setting up at the start of the day would require, as Greer mentioned, having things ready to go in intervals. For example, at 5:15AM on this particular day he would need to have enough coffee prepared for 10 crew members. However by 6:45AM that number would balloon to 60!

Now, back to the topic of rain...as was touched upon in Day 6, the memories people have can often be betrayed by the actual facts. The first week of shooting was rain free but some remember it raining every day during that time. And I have a possible theory on that which I'll throw out momentarily.

"Day one of principal photography we probably got forty seconds of screen time because the weather was *shit*! It was shit for eight, nine days," recalls David Ball. "And everybody would be saying – on their asses – New World, Rubinstein, 'Why aren't you shooting?' Well, because of the rain! It was a hundred percent exterior segment and we hadn't had the opportunity or the time or the money to have the *Wood'nhead* set ready. So, we were stuck! We had no weather cover. We had canvases over the cameras, canvases over the kids on the raft; we threw bodies at...anything we could do to shoot. But we could not shoot! Mike (Gornick) was tearing his hair out. I said, 'Mike, listen, man. There's a knockout effect here. It's a financial implication of being four days behind after five, but let's just push on. Let's get what we can when we can.' I told him, 'Don't worry about it. Don't worry about it. Let's just press on.' We were at the mercy of the weather and it was despicable, the weather. And then the sun came out enough and we cooked it. We really cooked. We were shooting five, six, seven minutes a day to get it going."

"First of all, it was getting colder by the minute. Actually the color of the leaves changed during the making of the sequence during our three to four weeks on that lake," Tom Hurwitz remembers. "The worst part of it was that it rained for the whole, like, first ten days that we were supposed to be shooting there. So, we were in the soup to begin with. And there was nothing we could do, we didn't have any cover, we couldn't go to cover; we just had to wait it out. And the reason why we were in Prescott, Arizona is it didn't rain (laughs)."

Now, why is it that both Ball and Hurwitz recall that it seemed to rain during the entire first week of shooting? One potential theory is the hypothermia issue some of the actors dealt with could factor into that as Daniel Beer recalled filming being shut down because of it. Perhaps that's where the discrepancy in memory comes from? It's tough to say for sure though. In any event the information on the weather and rainfall during production was culled from multiple sources including *The Courier*, a local newspaper that covered the

Above and right: Cast and crew in a production trailer wait during some of the crippling rain which plagued filming of *The Raft*; Page Hannah, in special effects makeup, hoping for the opportunity to film at some point. (courtesy of Taso Stavrakis)

Prescott area, the National Weather Service website, and the Weather Underground website. Strangely, the precipitation totals varied from source to source, so I'll make note of that when necessary. But it would be *The Courier*, in my opinion, which contained the most accurate weather details.

"The dynamics of that weather, we paid the price," Michael Gornick laments. "God bless Accuweather, out of Penn State, my alma mater, they were pretty much insistent that we would be weather free, even into the fall there in Arizona. What occurred there was a torrential storm that came up through the Baja, which is so rare, it happens every twenty to twenty-five years or whatever, at best, and that's what happened."

One last note concerning this day: on the call sheet, listed under "Locations", it states that the production campers would be warm and ready which tells us issues with hypothermia amongst the cast had already occurred and was being dealt with by the production.

Tuesday, September 23, 1986 – Day 8

Day eight would see a potentially busy schedule with continued work on scenes 90, 91, 92, and 93 planned. There was a cloud cover contingent as well with scenes 102 and 103E, along with 103F (which isn't in the film's shooting script, but is described in Mike Gornick's shot list)

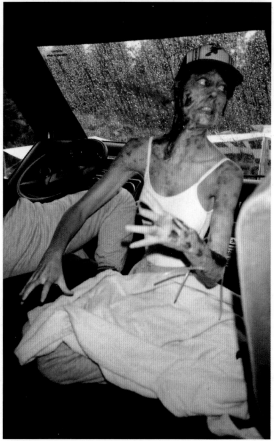

which comprises Randy swimming for his life after Laverne is attacked.

And for good measure a shot from *Old Chief Wood'nhead* was also scheduled of scene 25, an establishing shot of Andy "Rich Boy" Cavenaugh's house at night which would be filmed on the Rubel family property on Angus Drive, not far from Granite Basin Lake.

Now, I use the word "potentially" regarding the schedule because this day would see a significant amount of precipitation as anywhere from 2/3 of an inch to little over an inch of rain would fall in the Prescott area, depending on which source you go by. The National Weather Service recorded 0.67 inches of rain, Weather Underground listed 0.76 inches of rain, and *The Courier* reported that 1.08 inches of rain fell on this day. How much work could have been accomplished on a day like that? In anticipation of such inclement weather the second of two call sheets prepared for this day would list "W/N" (Will Notify) next to the actors names.

"I just remember we were sitting out on the shore waiting to see if there was ever gonna be a break in the rain that we could get a shot or two in," says first assistant director Joe Winogradoff. "All of us either in campers or out in tents just sort of looking, waiting, hoping that there would be something of a break long enough for us to get a shot or two in."

"I remember days when it just poured rain and we sat in Page Hannah's trailer playing Monopoly for hours and hours at a time because there was literally nothing to do," Greg Nicotero recalled talking to Anchor Bay Entertainment. **(6)**

In case of such weather members of the electric and grip departments were notified to work on prepping the store location in Humboldt for *Old Chief Wood'nhead*.

A significant note for this day would revolve around the continued casting ordeal for the Annie Lansing role from *The Hitchhiker*. David Ball would send a Western Union Mailgram to Jeff Schechtman at New World which read, "Regarding *Creepshow* casting: Unless I hear from you by the end of today, I shall make firm offers and hopefully book either (Loretta)Swit or (Britt)Ekland for the role of Annie subject to financial negotiations." **(7)**

Swit we already discussed, but Ekland was an interesting choice because like the actress who would eventually author the role, Lois Chiles, Ekland too was a "Bond girl" having appeared as "Mary Goodnight" in 1974's *The Man with the Golden Gun* alongside Roger Moore.

Wednesday, September 24, 1986 – Day 9

The ninth day of production would bring with it more rain and, depending on the source, it would be anywhere from a tenth of an inch to 0.38 inches to 0.68 inches. Concerning those differences I consulted with respected meteorologist Todd Gutner of NBC News Center Maine in the greater Portland area and he informed me there could be a couple of possibilities for the discrepancies. One that the measurements were taken from different locations in the Prescott area, while the other could be that the 24-hour tracking period might be different for each source.

The schedule though would be full with several options for the crew to choose from. If conditions were sunny scenes 90, 91, 92, and 93 would once again be on the menu. However, if it was cloudy then scenes 100, 101, plus a new one, scene 103, which is actually broken down into multiple separate scene listings of A through F – Laverne's body being "digested" by the blob and Randy racing for the shore as the blob begins to chase him – would be on tap.

And for good measure scene 25 from *Old Chief Wood'nhead* would once again be listed as a possibility.

With the rain creating major havoc on filming, and the location being a bit remote, the production would be forced to get creative with their downtime and figure out something – anything – that could be accomplished. "Hotel was too distant in most cases. So, we would hang out in production vehicles, you know, makeup trailers and so forth," says Michael Gornick. "Good time to rehearse and get prepared for future shoots. And we also devised many of the scenes that are on the raft and are relatively tight and don't exhibit any kind of background, per se, and have a little higher angle in terms of shot; we shot under tents while it was raining. A sound headache, you know, we had to put additional blankets on the top just to reduce on the pitter-patter of the rain."

Thursday, September 25, 1986 – Day 10

Day ten would once again fall victim to rain as anywhere from 0.06 inches to 0.23 inches of rain would fall in the Prescott area.

As for the schedule it would be another full one, with continued work on scenes 90, 91, 92, and 93. A cloud cover alternative was also listed for the possibility of scenes 100 and 103 – as well as for scene 104 of Randy desperately making his way onto the shore after being chased by the blob – if needed.

And speaking of said blob now is probably as good as any to discuss its creation in more detail.

"I built the blob," says construction coordinator and mechanical engineer Ed Fountain. "It was a tough thing to shoot, but it was just a tough idea. The blob was just a big, like, twenty-something foot diameter circle of latex. It was made by brushing out latex on a concrete floor, rolling out with a paint roller and just adding layer, and layer, and layer, and putting in junk in the layers so that there was garbage basically in the blob itself. And then we would peel it up and they'd have a big blob."

"There were no conceptual drawings," Greg Nicotero told Anchor Bay. **(8)**

"The blob was really complicated and it was way over our heads, I think, at the time and maybe over the heads of even our bosses of how to solve it. And it was a constant problem; it was painful for all concerned, myself included," admits Bruce Miller. "You know, it had to float; it had to go towards people. We would pull it under the water very carefully and then the top would flip up over itself. Or it would start to sink; it would go under the water. It was a constant difficult thing to do (laughs)."

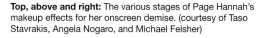

Top, above and right: The various stages of Page Hannah's makeup effects for her onscreen demise. (courtesy of Taso Stavrakis, Angela Nogaro, and Michael Felsher)

"We were looking for random things to put into it to make it look like it was garbage, but also the 'blobbey' blob thing," explains Dex Craig who worked closely with prop master Jim Feng. "Poured a bunch of latex out on to the floor in this garage, cut up a couple of mini figurines from Bob's Big Boy, the hamburger restaurant, so there were little Bob's Big Boy figures in there. So, we took to calling the blob 'Bob'. And then we made a second blob which we called 'Bob's baby brother Bo'. And then there was a third blob that was shaped in a parabola shape, so when we were filming it floating through the water and trying to look like it was moving fast it had a more paraboloid shape to it.

Above: Stunt coordinator Taso Stavrakis and his dive team would find working in the water a challenge at times. (courtesy of Michael Felsher)

And we called that blob the 'Parabolob'."

"'Bob the blob' ended up being mostly a black, plastic tarp and we would paint black latex out on the cement in front of this gas station, which is pretty funny, and then just peel it off and then we would go in and glue it on top of the plastic tarp. It was literally, pretty much, a plastic tarp," recalls Arizona makeup effects assistant Matt Marich. "I think they just pulled it with wires through the water and that kind of thing. But some of the earlier stuff with it moving and undulating might still be in the film from Ed French's little contraption that he had made; which I thought was very cool, very innovative with what he did."

The sophisticated mechanism devised by Ed French and his associate, Ken Walker, would be abandoned for a more simple and practical approach. As Marich says the blob itself basically just floated on the lake, pulled along at times by scuba divers, members of Taso Stavrakis' team. There

was a device "MacGyvered" by Ed Fountain made out of PVC pipes and small jets, powered by the lake water itself, which allowed the blob to rotate for some shots, however.

One of the most indelible "character traits" of the blob was its tremendous slime factor, one that both cast and crew would fall victim to. "The effects makeup guys had this stuff called Ultra-slime. I don't know, are you familiar with that? It's this methyl-cellulose (Methocel) stuff and it's usually for like slime on aliens' mouths and that kind of stuff, whatever. It was just slimy junk. And they used so much of it on the blob that – this lake we shot it in was not very big, it was a mountain lake – and there was so much slime, there was like this layer of slime on the surface. So, it rained and the entire surface of the lake was covered by tiny bubbles," laughs Ed Fountain.

"Methocel, basically it's just a thick goopy liquid like K-Y jelly," says Matt Marich. "Ultra-slime is a stringy...best to describe it as a very runny, snotty kind of thing. It's much like snot. It's rubbery and adhesive and it makes those long, stringy strands."

"What was interesting is they didn't bring the blob out of the lake at night and they used some sort of gelatinous material to put on the people as they got slimed, so to speak," recalls Arizona production still photographer Stan Obcamp-Fikel. "And what would happen is the ducks liked it – and there was always some of this stuff left on the blob when they put it back in the lake, and the ducks liked it – and they ate it and when you'd get back in the morning there would be ducks on the blob and there would be feathers left everywhere, so it just added a more realistic image to the blob. And then you could see the fish underneath the blob touching up to the top surface and so it looked like the blob was actually alive."

That "gelatinous material" that Obcamp-Fikel refers to, the slime, would fall under the purview of Matt Marich, who would be charged with the chore of concocting it daily. The methyl-cellulose portion of said concoction is a compound found in numerous consumer products – everything from ice cream to laxatives – while the other, Ultra-slime, is made for one thing only and that's to make movie monsters look slimy and gross. "One of my tasks was to make the Methocel and the Ultra-slime, dye it black every day, and send five, ten, fifteen gallon buckets out to set every day for Greg (Nicotero) and Howard (Berger) to work with out on the set out there," says Marich. "They brought in the raw powder for it. So, we would have to get water really hot in order to get that dissolved down, the raw Methocel. But we also had the Ultra-slime, I think that was pre-made. But I remember you had to dilute bleach half way with water in order to get that stuff off of you, because it just will not let go. You touch one thing, and then another thing, and now it's on another thing, now it's on another thing."

"I do remember us putting the tinting color in the slime and kneading it with our hands to try and get it all mixed up. Because, you know, everybody just had to pitch in and do whatever they could. So, I remember kneading slime," laughs art director Beth Kuhn. "So, I do remember the slime. It was cool stuff! You know, two people could stick their hands in it and they could walk away and there would be this long string between them."

As mentioned before it wasn't just the cast that was

victimized by the slime, one of the makeup effects crew members would also feel its wrath as well: Greg Nicotero. "So, Greg calls from the set, he goes, 'We're out of slime. Mix it now, I'm on my way back,'" recalls Matt Marich. "So, Everett (Burrell) and I and Mike Trcic are in the shop and we mix two big batches of it, get it dyed. Greg comes flying up in the rental car and we put it in the back seat and Greg takes off. And like five minutes later Greg comes back and parks the car and we see him and he's walking out kind of away from the EFXACO towards the street and we go, 'What's going on?', and he goes, 'Look in the fucking car.' All ten gallons of that stuff had spilled in the car. The entire floor board of the car was full of black slime."

"I'm driving down the road at 50 miles an hour and I make a turn and I hear this weird sound and then I look down and this wave of black slime comes up underneath my feet," Nicotero recalled while talking to Anchor Bay. "My feet were sliding off of the brake and off the gas because it was slime. So, both 5 gallon buckets spilled." **(9)**

"We grabbed the shop vac, cleaned it out; sucked it out with the shop vac, if I remember correctly. And then they sent it to a car detailer," says Marich. "But it was kind of a bad situation because we were running low on the actual product at that point, you know, having to get it out of Los Angeles – methyl cellulose and so forth."

"I had to go to production and say, 'Umm, I think I ruined one of the production vehicles'," Nicotero laughed while revisiting the incident with Anchor Bay. **(10)**

Meanwhile, on this particular day of production, other tasks were getting accomplished all the way across the country in Dexter, Maine as multiple releases were signed for store front properties along Main Street, the location to be used for the film's opening shots of Billy and the Creep. And all for the bargain basement price of $1 each!

Friday, September 26, 1986 – Day 11

The eleventh day of filming was basically free of rain with only the National Weather Service recording 0.02 inches of rainfall in the Prescott region.

The day's schedule would be a mixture of old and new, as once again scenes 90, 91, 92, and 93 would be on tap. By the end of the week, though, the majority of those scenes would finally be in the rearview mirror. As for the new scenes scheduled, they would include number 94 of Randy, Deke, and Laverne reacting after Rachel is devoured by the blob, beginning with Randy vomiting and ending with his humorous line, "But if it still wants chow..."

Another new scene on the ledger was 103B, a shot of the blob digesting Laverne. Now, in the film this is quickly achieved with a skeletal figure of Laverne bobbing up out of the water and then slowly sinking back down. The way originally described in Romero's script though her body would be "twisted, distorted, and stretched like taffy", truly gruesome and disturbing imagery. However, the restraints of the budget, now coupled with the weather delays, prevented that from being properly visualized. "Weather wise we kind of got screwed. But, part of it was just not

Above: Director Michael Gornick would be tested more than anyone during the shooting of *Creepshow 2*. (courtesy of Michael Felsher)

Above: An elevated Tom Hurwitz shoots Paul Satterfield's death scene on the raft. (courtesy of Michael Felsher)

today'…'Right, that's when we shoot. We shoot one hour and we shoot the shit out of it.' But the pressure that it put on everybody meant that we probably delivered ninety percent of what we wanted to deliver."

"Really the thing that happened with *Creepshow 2* was that there was no budget, there weren't enough resources to support the scope of the film. And so, that was it," laments screen-writer George Romero. "And I thought that it should have been. Not that it was lacking *millions*… probably another five, six hundred grand – another million would have done it. But *bada bing*, it didn't happen."

"Thank you, thank you. He's absolutely right," agrees Michael Gornick with Romero's assessment. "He's absolutely right. Another half million would have made life comfortable."

Briefly touched upon by David Ball was the bondsman, in this particular case Ted Kurdyla from Film Finances, who eventually would play a significant role in the production life of *Creepshow 2*. "Ted was a decent guy, but it was difficult," says assistant production manager Debra Tanklow. "I think they used to call him 'Ted the Fed', you know, because he was…I think it's just demoralizing for a lot of people (when a bondsman steps in)." We'll discuss Kurdyla and his impact on the production a little later once the production moves to Bangor, Maine.

Finally, scene 105 would be listed as a cloud cover option. What's interesting is that in the shooting script there is no scene 105, but a scene 105L instead. Scene 105L, as described in the script, consists of the shot of Randy being attacked by the blob wave in stunned terror. However, in Michael Gornick's shot list that imagery would be part of scene 104E instead. So, scene 105L would consist of the blob pulling Randy's now covered body back into the lake as the camera pans across the Camaro towards some reeds to reveal, in classic E.C. style, a "No Swimming" warning sign.

Saturday, September 27, 1986 – Day 12

Day twelve would be another day free from precipitation as the production was scheduled to wrap up scenes 90, 91, and 92. Scene 93 was nearing its finish line, too, with it being scheduled just once more after today. Also, scenes 94 and 103B would be listed as well.

By Tuesday, September 30, Page Hannah would be slated for Travel, meaning her time on the production was coming to an end. "I felt like I was supposed to be there for eleven days and there were all these delays and things that happened. I can't remember what they were, but I ended up being there for thirty-one days," says Hannah. "I guess it was raining and stuff. So, it was a lot longer. You also plan on being there for one period of time and then you kind of let go after a couple of delays. That sounds like there would be a lot of tension because of that but I think it ended up being just everybody said, 'Alright, well, we're here to get this done!', and it was a really fun experience."

Part of the fun experience that Hannah refers to is a connection that formed between cast members, one in which they would do more than just hang out in their hotel

having enough money to realize a script that was pretty ambitious back then," says Charles Carroll. "We just didn't have enough money. I don't think I even knew that then. You know, now I'd go, 'Are you fucking kidding me? Come on.' But it probably seemed like a huge amount of money for Laurel at the time. I mean, Laurel was bargain basement and they did great stuff for, you know, very little. I mean, that was their kind of stock-in-trade, if you will."

"The thing is, given our severe problems with the weather on the first segment on *Creep 2*, we were slightly under the hammer to move a lot quicker than we were moving," explains David Ball. "Not only have you got New World on your ass, you've got the bondsman on your ass as well. You know? And they're saying, 'Why aren't you shooting?', and I said, 'I can't shoot! You think I'm doing this for fun? I'm getting up at six every morning to go out there. I've got weather people talking to me every half an hour'…'Yes, you're going to get one hour without rain

rooms when not on set. "Yeah, you tend to bond when you're out there, especially when you're young. Yeah, we went to the Grand Canyon together and some Fred

Above: Makeup effects artist Everett Burrell holding Paul Satterfield's prop leg; Satterfield gets into his "can-can" position. (courtesy of Angela Nogaro and Michael Gornick)

Flintstone place that was out there that I thought was just dynamite! We were driving out there to the Grand Canyon and there's Fred Flintstone's house and everything," recalls Daniel Beer. "So, yeah, we all became close. Everybody was cool. Paul and I were like brothers for a while. When I finally moved from New York, and I was going back and forth from New York and Los Angeles, I was staying with him."

Another issue touched upon by Hannah was the length of time she was on location stemming from the much-discussed issues with the weather. Those issues would create tremendous pressure on the film-makers to make up for lost time.

Now, look, pressure on a film director is as old as the craft itself. When you're the captain of the ship you're going to face adversity, whether it's with a modestly sized crew on a low budget exploitation flick or with an enormous crew on a big budget blockbuster – it just comes with the territory. It's how you treat your cast and crew during those patches of rough waters that define you as a leader. In the case of Michael Gornick he made quite an impression on some of the young cast. "Michael Gornick...what a champion, just a champion; I mean, under pressure, not a moment of anxiety came through him. I mean, what a leader," praises Daniel Beer about his director. "And the way he handled it, just incredible. (He) didn't misdirect anything upon any of us or anybody that I saw. And he just fought his way through it. And quick on his feet, fought his way through it, and made the adjustments."

"Yeah, I can't even imagine what kind of pressure he was under," echoes Page Hannah. "You know, I don't remember feeling that tension from him. And I felt like he was extremely efficient. When the window came to be able to film and do what we needed to do that he got it done really well. And it was tricky; I mean, water and scuba people and special effects. But these weren't special effects done after, they were done right there!"

"He was certainly under a lot of pressure and there were a lot of problems on the set," says Holt McCallany, who would soon join the production and begin work on *Old Chief Wood'nhead*. "I'm sure he's told you more about this than I can share with you; because it was his first film and he had primarily been known as a director of photography, the producers and so forth, there was a lot of second guessing of Michael going on. And a lot of which I felt was very unfair. Do you know what I mean? He was obviously an experienced and competent guy, but whenever it's your first movie you've got people looking over your shoulder. And they were really doing that with Michael and creating a lot of unnecessary anxiety."

"Yeah, it's funny because I heard that; but I wasn't really aware. You know, at that time in my life I wasn't...I was kind of wide-eyed and I didn't really ask a lot of questions. So, I wasn't really aware of the specifics of what was going on with the movie, but I just had this feeling that there was something, that there were problems, like, just artistically with the movie," reiterates McCallany's co-star from *Old Chief Wood'nhead*, Don Harvey. "But the thing is I thought he was a wonderful director, really was very personable and he really made me feel like he was very happy that I

was there and that he was very confident that I was going to be able to do exactly what he wanted after every take. He was very positive and would tell me it was great, and he'd give me some really interesting directions to work on."

"I think the director did a pretty decent job with this movie," says fellow *Old Chief Wood'nhead* actor, David Holbrook. "And I always remember my dad saying to me, he said, 'When you see something that everybody is good in, that's the director. That's not an accident, that's not just luck of casting. When everybody in a movie is good, that's the director.' And he was a nice guy and I think the actors were probably pretty comfortable around him."

Of course, like most human beings there are two sides to the same coin. And while the cast and the majority of the crew raved about Michael Gornick, which I will discuss further in just a bit, there were a handful of contributors who recalled a different side to their director.

"Memories of Mike were that he was a hothead and you wanted to fly as under the radar as much as possible, because he was a bit of a screaming lunatic. And I don't know if it was because of the producers that he had with him or his inability to get what he wanted done," says hair and makeup assistant Angela Nogaro. "You know, there are people that are suited to do that (directing) because they can lead 70 people, 80 people with constant questions and constant 'What do you wants' and you have to have answers. I mean, that's really just the job of the director. And if you're not good at dealing with that amount of people and really articulating what you want and having a game plan, well you're sort of setting yourself up to fail, you know. And there are people that fail graciously and there are people that fail with a temper and he was sort of a lunatic, you know, he didn't fail graciously and just didn't manage his frustration well."

"He was fine with me, although he did...we used to talk about that he was a little Dr. Jekyll and Mr. Hyde – one minute he was like your best friend, the next minute he was really disappointed in you," says Bruce Miller. "That could just be the pressure that was on him or the pressure that was on me and misinterpreting his comments and things. He was never mean, but he was definitely focused and probably nervous as hell."

"This is a funny story. He would sometimes blow up when he couldn't get what he wanted the way he wanted it. You know, he'd say, 'I want this here...', and it wasn't working, 'Rahhh!' He'd get into this rage, you couldn't talk to him. But the people in Pittsburgh who knew him they would have this instant thing to get him out of a bad mood: they would say, 'How 'bout those Steelers?' And his demeanor would change completely. He was like, 'Oh yeah. You know if we would change this guy and change that guy that would be...' So, that's how they'd...they would know," recalls soundman Felipe Borrero. "I think I remember he was a smoker. So, he had to go out sometimes and smoke and when he'd come back if it wasn't the way he wanted it... it was sort of like, 'What if we do this?'...'Don't tell me what to do! Rahhh!' He would get really angry. Other than that, he was the nicest man you could be with. I mean, we got along. But when he got in that mood...'How's those Steelers?'"

The individual that Borrero references regarding the comment on the Steelers was longtime Laurel veteran, Nick Mastandrea. For Mastandrea, who had known Gornick for

Above and right: Michael Gornick directing the scene where the blob oozes up through the raft's boards trying to get to Daniel Beer and Jeremy Green. (courtesy of Michael Felsher)

more than a dozen years to that point, it was unsettling to see perceived changes in his longtime colleague. "Yeah, I think Mike was really detached from everybody. And I don't wanna slam Mike or anything, but he was detached. But that started as of *Day of the Dead*. He was a different sort of animal," admits Mastandrea. "Look, me and Mike we were together every day for years there for a while in my early days at The Latent Image. You know, we just, I don't know, we just never even talked after that, I don't think. But we never talked during it. It's not like we ever went out with everybody and had a beer. We never hung out. Never had meetings and said, 'Here's what I want to do', you know."

Nearly twenty years after *Creepshow 2,* Mastandrea would have the opportunity to direct his own film, *The Breed*, after having served as first A.D. under Wes Craven on numerous films. It was then that he was able to understand the strain of having to live up to the standard set by a legend of the genre and what Gornick must have been going through, but in looking back he still was surprised by what he saw from his longtime comrade during *Creepshow 2*. "I know when I did my film, you know, you've got a lot of pressure on you; I had to live up to Wes. It's a lot," he says. "But I think he should have embraced people more than alienate because it just made it worse. I mean, I remember days him swinging his story boards and shot lists in the air and it was just weird to see because we had all been such good friends."

Above: One of the "day for night" shots from *The Raft* – as you can see it was quite sunny the day it was filmed. (courtesy of Lakeshore Entertainment and Daniel Beer)

Now, approaching Michael Gornick with some of these comments was a delicate subject. I say that because Mike is a close friend. Over the last two decades I've gotten to know him as a person, not just as a fan. We've spent time working together and traveling to conventions, going to Pirates ball games and Steelers training camp practices, watching his grandson's hockey practices, dining together with our respective loved ones, and engaging in countless conversations about his career, politics, and just life in general. Full disclosure, he's someone I look up to and admire greatly and I really can't stress enough what a decent and kind human being the man is, not to mention a very talented one as well. He's been a father figure, an older brother, and a best friend all rolled into one for me and I'm eternally grateful for that. So, having to ask him for his reaction and thoughts on critical remarks wasn't easy. In fact, after doing so in our second interview for this book I received a phone call from him in which he expressed his feelings about hearing such things. It was unsettling and even made him doubt whether to continue participating in this project. "Maybe we're just dredging up comments from people that, you know, are best just left alone," he told me. Those feelings I understood and empathized with completely. In getting to know one another you discover similar character traits and I definitely feel a kinship with Mike in that regard. I mention these things, again in full disclosure, because while I'm not out to create a fluff piece about the making of the film, I certainly wanted to handle the comments with great care because I *know* Michael Gornick and respect him immensely. And even if I had wanted to create an "airbrushed" version of the production Mike wouldn't allow me to anyway, which speaks to his level of integrity. So, in laying that all out, we'll begin with his reaction to the comments from his long-time colleague on the production, Nick Mastandrea.

"It's a whole different vibe. I mean, doing those early productions it was a little more of a goof, I guess? But the responsibilities were different, too, at that point," says Gornick in response to the critical observations. "I mean... but, even then...I think that vaguely, I'm a different kind of personality than I think he believes I was in the early days, perhaps, versus the contrast of *Creepshow 2*. I'm not a very social guy and I am pretty stoic; If I could go back in

time I'd probably be happiest working in German cinema – it was very strict and exacting, you know. And I didn't ever enjoy his clowning and goofing off, he and the grips...the grip initiations. I mean, it's just not part of my character. I don't despise him for doing it, but I just never got it, didn't like it, you know. So, I think I've always been kind of aloof, but maybe he wasn't aware of it because I had a different dynamic when I became a director. Where, as opposed if I'm the D.P on set, you know, I feel like I'm one of them, I'm part of them."

Next we discussed the remarks from Bruce Miller, another trusted Laurel veteran. "I mean, Jekyll and Hyde, I suppose? But, I think what happens is that a good 70% of my time I'm engaging, at least, with somebody. But when it comes to the business at hand I take it very seriously," Gornick says. "So, did he fail me or did we just fail, you know; whatever situation he might refer to in his mind in terms of about something on set. *We* failed, I'm not saying that he failed necessarily, but he's part of that failure. And, yeah, would I exhibit that disgust? Yeah, sure."

And finally we touched on the comments from Angela Nogaro. "And she may be right, I don't know. I mean, I can't play back every last minute on set, but did I express disappointment? Absolutely," he admits. "But, that's what I'm saying in terms of my style also; I mean, while I can be friendly, when it comes to the task itself, it becomes very, very clinical. And so if you're looking for a pal at that point, I can't be a pal because we have failed, this is wrong, and so I will state it as such, you know. But, I don't remember interacting that much with her to begin with."

Now on the other hand there were plenty of behind-the-scenes crew and production personnel whom just like the young cast members had a very favorable view of their director and the effort he brought to the film. "A gentleman and a scholar; Michael was extremely professional. He was the kind of man that I did not get to see that often because he was always on location and I was always in the production office, but when I did get to see him and be around him I thought what a gentleman he was, very

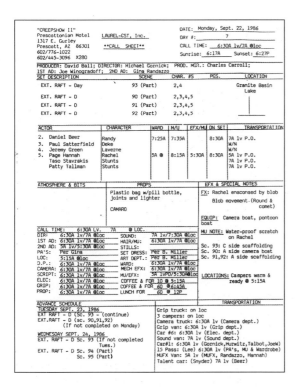

professional," Rebecca Mayo fondly recalls. "I remember him being rather soft spoken and very intent on creating a good piece of film, wanting it to be very successful, and wanting to do a good job. So, I just remember him as gentlemanly and hard-working and very, very friendly."

"Mike thinks about other people. He respects other people. He's aware of what makes 'em buzz, what doesn't make 'em buzz. He respects people, as he deserves respect himself," says David Ball. "His feet were on the ground. He was a religious man with a lovely family, a firm discipline, and a gentleman to boot. Always a gentleman, always well mannered, always ahead of the game, did his homework, knew what he wanted."

"He was very nice. I don't have any bad memories of him and I just know we had a really nice time, you know. I mean, obviously, the director is very, very busy and they don't have time to socialize; when they're not working they're doing their own prep work," says script supervisor Jeanne Talbot. "But I remember Michael was very, very, very prepared – knew what he was doing. And, you know, to this day – well, this is why you're interested in his work – I mean, he was a master at it. He was really good at it; he knew what he was doing."

"He and I…he was very lovely for me. I mean, I think that our relationship was probably one of the easiest ones he had," remembers Eileen Sieff-Stroup. "Because we'd have a discussion, 'Do you like this?'…'Yes. No.'…'Okay, I'll go do it.' So, I think that it was easy for me. Michael, he's always like a nice uncle to me."

"My experiences with Michael Gornick were nothing but great," said Greg Nicotero to Anchor Bay. "And I think that he did a really good job with the cards that he was dealt." **(11)**

"You know, I think any director is under a lot of pressure; any director. It's just a grueling job. You're trying to be an artist and you have your vision and then you've got the pressures of all the practicalities of shooting and then you've got all the emotional components…it's like running a small city. You know, you're like mayor! You get blamed for everything," says Patricia Tallman. "Mike is a doll, just the greatest guy. So kind, so fun to work with, because he's just so kind and decent; you know, just a really good person. And, yeah, I wish I'd had the great, good pleasure to work with him again; never really happened."

"He's a really sweet man, you know. And he was a really talented guy," says Charles Carroll. "That movie was…I mean the script was difficult to do, to sort of realize it in a visual manner. The thing was thrown together pretty quickly, we didn't have enough money; I don't think there was quite enough planning. And I think there was a lot of pressure on him – not just from Laurel – but I think he put a lot of pressure on himself. That's the kind of guy he is."

As for Gornick himself he views it all in his typically collected fashion. "If one was to live their life over, I would most like to emulate a director that I once worked with, Andrei Konchalovsky – *Maria's Lovers,* and he did *Runaway Train.* I'm of that kind of same Slavic origin which is high emotion, bubbling over sometimes, what you see is what you get. But also very, very exacting," he says in looking back at his shot at directing a major motion picture. "And I often imagined that what the old UFA German studios were like when you had a director who was kind of like a king, a monarch, and had complete control. That's why UFA shot indoors, they wanted no weather problems, and everything was to complete scale. It was complete control.

And that's, I guess, in my mind what I would enjoy having, is that kind of control, that kind of manipulation. And that's what I saw when I witnessed Andrei Konchalovsky, that he had high emotion, you could see good take/bad take in his very demeanor, and it was quite simple. I enjoyed that. That's the style I like."

Regarding other production related activities David Ball would notify Charles Carroll that Dorothy Lamour, who was soon to be in town to begin her portion of the filming, was going to have a higher cast cover deductible with the insurance company – $35,000 instead of the standard $10,000 – due to slightly high blood pressure and arthritis. He would close out his memo in classic David Ball style with, "I believe it goes without saying that we should treat Dorothy as we would any other septuagenarian." **(12)**

Ball would also send out memos to various department heads to thank them for their positive attitude in facing the inclement weather and for getting as much done as possible in such adverse conditions.

Monday, September 29, 1986 – Day 13

The thirteenth day of filming would most likely be one free from rain. One source, *The Courier*, reported no rain, however the National Weather Service reported 0.15 inches of rain. The day prior *The Courier* would report .09 inches of rain, while the National Weather Service reported none, so perhaps it was a case of some overnight rain that wouldn't have impacted the shooting? Regardless, with such low totals it's probably safe to assume precipitation wasn't much of a factor.

The day's ledger would see scene 93 make its final appearance on the schedule, with Patricia Tallman around for any potential shots involving Page Hannah's character Rachel being attacked by the blob. Also on tap again was scene 94 of Deke, Laverne, and Randy reacting to Rachel's demise and 103B of Laverne being digested by the blob.

A new scene would also debut on this day, 95, involving the character of Deke telling Randy and Laverne that he's going to swim for it while the blob is under the raft and suddenly reacting in agony as the blob attacks him from below through the raft's boards.

Other points of interest for the day included Michael Morgan sending out a thank you letter to John and Nora Rubel for the use of their house exterior as the home of Andy "Rich Boy" Cavenaugh for the *Old Chief Wood'nhead* segment. "Thank you so much for your cooperation and use of your home for the 'Dead River' segment of 'Creepshow 2'," Morgan wrote in his letter. "Here's hoping your film industry experience was a pleasant one." **(13)**

An updated shooting schedule would also be circulated with filming slated to end in Arizona on Saturday, October 18. However, that too wouldn't hold up.

Left: Production assistant Billy Kosco(w/red hair) takes center stage with Ed Fountain's "wave blob rig", used for the most iconic moment in the segment. (courtesy of Father William Kosco)

Tuesday, September 30, 1986 – Day 14

Day fourteen of the production would be rain free as the schedule completed work on scenes 94 and 95.

With a film production constantly jumping from sequence to sequence and only partially completing scenes over a period of several days, one of the most vital members of a film crew, someone who helps to keep all of this organized chaos knit together, is the script supervisor. And for *Creepshow 2*, that person would be Jeanne Talbot.

"To be a script supervisor you have to multi-task, you have to juggle three balls in the air. You always have to keep thinking what happened? What's happening now? And what's going to happen?," says Talbot. "So, you have to keep all of those things in your head when you're reading the script. So, what you do when you get hired is you read the script and you do a breakdown. And the breakdown consists of the scene number, the time of day. So, as the script supervisor you have to do the continuity to make sure that the film is gonna cut."

One of the key elements in that multi-tasking process is creating a time plot, which basically details when the events of the story are happening – what day, what time of day, and how many days overall the story takes place. In the case of *Creepshow 2* all three stories each take place within 24 hours. "My time plot would be approved by the director and it would be shared with the A.D. and we would make sure that my time plot and his or hers – most of the time they were men – that we were both on the same page, that we were both in sync," explains Talbot. "Because they have to do the call sheets, so that call sheet gives information to the other departments and that's kind of like the Bible, you know. Because a lot of departments have to prep, like wardrobe and sets and the art department, so they need to know."

Another vital aspect to the job of a script supervisor is observing and taking notes, which will later play an invaluable role during the picture's editing. "So, you would take all the notes for the editor: the camera roll, the sound roll, the scene that you're shooting and what camera roll and what sound roll they're on, because the editor has to find them. You write down the scene, the lens, and you write down if it's a print or not. And there's a section in the forms that you have of what happened during the scene: Was it good? Was it not? Why did it work? Why didn't it work? And you write a brief description of what the shot is – like, it's a long shot," Talbot says. "And at the end of the day you have to go through your notes and do what they call a 'Print Log' and take all the prints, and you have to go to the camera department and they have to circle their prints, and you have to do it to the sound because they're going to the lab. And then after the lab they go to the editor and the editor syncs them up."

Doing this requires a kind of system and for Talbot part of that system would be lining her script, which was a method of keeping track of what was shot and how exactly. "So, you get these colored pencils and each shot would have a color. Like, if it was a wide shot it would be red, if it was a close-up it would be blue, if it was a medium shot it would be green, if it was a two shot...you know, you have a coloring system," she explains. "And what you do

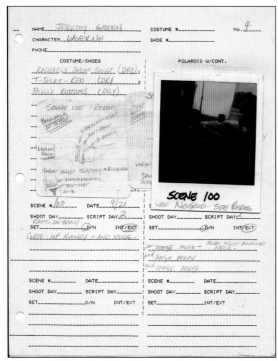

Above: Director Michael Gornick confers with director of photography Tom Hurwitz during shooting at Granite Basin Lake. (courtesy of Angela Nogaro) **Below:** Costume Designer Eileen Sieff Stroup's continuity page for scene 100: Randy taking advantage of a sleeping Laverne. (courtesy of Eileen Sieff-Stroup)

is you take the script when you're shooting the scenes, you draw a line down from when the shot starts to where it ends, right. And then you do that and you write at the bottom how many takes there were or whatever, and if it

was a sound take, if it was what they call MOS, which is without sound; 'mit out sound'; is where it came from – German. So, MOS, in other words, there's only picture, but no sound, you let the editor know. There's really like a code. So, when the editor gets the script at the end of the day, they'll get the pages, too."

And lastly, two other critical aspects of filming that fall under the purview of a script supervisor are continuity and screen direction. With so much going on, with scenes not typically being shot in order, these two facets can easily be overlooked. "When you're on the set you were in charge of the screen direction, which way the actor looks. Like, when there are two people talking to each other, it gets complicated, three, four, five people, they all have to look in the right direction so that when they're having a conversation they look like they're talking to that person. And the eye line has to be correct and that's also the script supervisor's job, to make sure that's right," says Talbot. "Your job, ultimately, is to pay attention, because the director's not thinking about it. You're on the set with 30 people and sometimes you think, 'Oh, 30 people, 40 people. Somebody would see if there was a mistake.' They don't! They're not paying attention to that stuff."

Speaking of people paying attention to their job, Michael Gornick certainly did that. One of the most fundamental aspects of film-making, besides being talented and good at what you do, of course, is preparation; knowing what you want to see on the screen *really* matters. If you've got only X amount of time to chop that tree down, you better spend some of that time sharpening your axe!

During my research I was granted access to Gornick's personal production files from *Creepshow 2* – his homework, so to speak. It was amazing the level of planning and attention to detail Gornick put into the pre-production phase. On stacks of grid paper Gornick would lay out a host of things needed for the film such as recommended grocery props for the general store in *Old Chief Wood'nhead*. He would diagram in explicit detail, almost like an architect, sequences for *The Raft*: how they should be shot, complete with measurement diameters. And on yellow legal paper he would handwrite his detailed shot list, which would eventually be re-typed for principal photography.

"You've gotta prep! I mean, you've gotta walk on the set and you have to have done your homework," exclaims Jeanne Talbot. "Steven Spielberg, people have told me he's there before anybody. You know, he's not rolling up in his Jag or his Mercedes with everything set and he's ready to yell, 'Action!' He's there before everybody; and Michael was like that, too. And you have to be. You've worked so hard to get this puppy on its feet you don't wanna blow it by partying (laughs). What happens is the crew loses respect for you because they don't want to stand around while you're deciding what to do. You should have done that last night."

"I've always been prepared on set, as best I can be. Even when I shot I would try to read ahead," says Gornick. "I had a brilliant assistant camera person (on prior films), Tom Dubensky, who would also leap ahead in terms of the script and we would have ideas at least prepared in terms of visual circumstance for the film, long before we

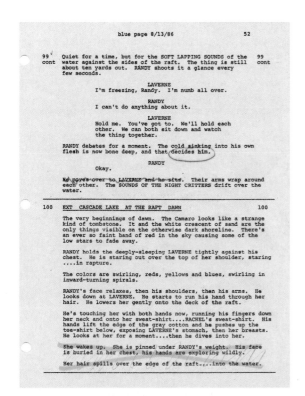

```
                    blue page 8/13/86              52

99    Quiet for a time, but for the SOFT LAPPING SOUNDS of the    99
cont  water against the sides of the raft.  The thing is still    cont
      about ten yards out.  RANDY shoots it a glance every
      few seconds.

                        LAVERNE
                I'm freezing, Randy.  I'm numb all over.

                        RANDY
                I can't do anything about it.

                        LAVERNE
                Hold me.  You've got to.  We'll hold each
                other.  We can both sit down and watch
                the thing together.

      RANDY debates for a moment.  The cold sinking into his own
      flesh is now bone deep, and that decides him.

                        RANDY
                Okay.

      He moves over to LAVERNE and he sits.  Their arms wrap around
      each other.  The SOUNDS OF THE NIGHT CRITTERS drift over the
      water.

100   EXT  CASCADE LAKE  AT THE RAFT  DAWN                       100
      The very beginnings of dawn.  The Camaro looks like a strange
      kind of tombstone.  It and the white crescent of sand are the
      only things visible on the otherwise dark shoreline.  There's
      an ever so faint band of red in the sky causing some of the
      low stars to fade away.

      RANDY holds the deeply-sleeping LAVERNE tightly against his
      chest.  He is staring out over the top of her shoulder, staring
      ....in rapture.

      The colors are swirling, reds, yellows and blues, swirling in
      inward-turning spirals.

      RANDY's face relaxes, then his shoulders, then his arms.  He
      looks down at LAVERNE.  He starts to run his hand through her
      hair.  He lowers her gently onto the deck of the raft.

      He's touching her with both hands now, running his fingers down
      her neck and onto her sweat-shirt....RACHEL's sweat-shirt.  His
      hands lift the edge of the gray cotton and he pushes up the
      tee-shirt below, exposing LAVERNE's stomach, then her breasts.
      He looks at her for a moment....then he dives into her.

      She wakes up.  She is pinned under RANDY's weight.  His face
      is buried in her chest, his hands are exploring wildly.

      Her hair spills over the edge of the raft....into the water.
```

```
                    Revised 9/8/86
                                                    52

99    Quiet for a time, but for the SOFT LAPPING SOUNDS of the    99
cont  water against the sides of the raft.  The thing is still    cont
      about ten yards out.  RANDY shoots it a glance every
      few seconds.

                        LAVERNE
                I'm freezing, Randy.  I'm numb all over.

                        RANDY
                I can't do anything about it.

                        LAVERNE
                Hold me.  You've got to.  We'll hold each
                other.  We can both sit down and watch
                the thing together.

      RANDY debates for a moment.  The cold sinking into his own
      flesh is now bone deep.

                        RANDY
                Okay.

      Their arms wrap around each other.  The SOUNDS OF THE NIGHT
      CRITTERS drift over the water.

100   EXT  CASCADE LAKE  AT THE RAFT  DAWN                       100
      The very beginnings of dawn.  The Camaro looks like a strange
      kind of tombstone.  It and the white crescent of sand are the
      only things visible on the otherwise dark shoreline.  There's
      an ever so faint band of red in the sky causing some of the
      low stars to fade away.

      RANDY holds the deeply-sleeping LAVERNE tightly against his
      chest.  He is staring out over the top of her shoulder, staring
      .....in rapture.

      The colors are swirling, reds, yellows and blues, swirling in
      inward-turning spirals.

      RANDY's face relaxes, then his shoulders, then his arms.  He
      looks down at LAVERNE.  He starts to run his hand through her
      hair.  He lowers her gently onto the deck of the raft.

      He's touching her with both hands now, running his fingers down
      her neck and onto her sweat-shirt....RACHEL's sweat-shirt.  His
      hands lift the edge of the gray cotton and he pushes up the
      tee-shirt below, exposing LAVERNE's stomach, then her breasts.
      He looks at her for a moment....then he dives into her.
```

got to set. I think that's of the upmost importance because I think time on the set, while sometimes protracted, is also distracting because there's so much else to be considered that if you don't walk in with a vision at least...and you must be flexible because the situation will alter as, you know, an actor brings something to the game or the environment brings something, a level of change."

As for official production related issues a meeting between David Ball and one of New World's top tier executives, Steve White, would be held on this day, the details of which we'll soon discuss.

Wednesday, October 1, 1986 – Day 15

With the calendar now turning over to October, the fifteenth day of filming would see another rain-free day as work on scene 98, a day for night shot of Randy and Laverne deciding who would keep watch during the night, was once again scheduled.

A new scene made its debut on this day as work on scene 96, Deke's demise, would begin. This scene, one that would last no more than 90 seconds on screen, would be quite extensive as it appears on the call sheet for the next six days of filming. It's a horrific scene as Paul Satterfield convincingly reacts in agony as the blob comes up through the bottom of the raft's boards and attaches itself to his leg, pulling him down with enough power to break the boards, snapping his leg in the process. "I cast that leg out of an old stock mold they had," recalls Matt Marich. "And the hair work was actually put on by Tom Savini when he came in to have his life cast done; Tom's marvelous with hair. And

Above: Revised script pages for scene 100: note the bottom of the pages where particular language was crossed out and later removed per Michael Gornick's request. (courtesy of Michael Gornick)

I'm trying to remember, it might have been Everett (Burrell) or somebody shaved their arm, if I remember right, shaved their arm hair to put it on and then Tom transferred the hair on there, he meticulously did it."

Marich's mentioning of Tom Savini coming to town to have his life cast executed refers to the Creep character, which would be sculpted by Everett Burrell. Unlike the cast and most of the main crew the special effects makeup team would stay a couple of blocks down the street from the Prescottonian at the American Motel, which Marich recalls as "divey", and it would be at that location that Savini's Creep character would be born. "The Creep was sculpted in that little 'divey' hotel, Tom Savini's makeup," Marich says. "Tom Savini came in, we did his full life cast; I did his ears and hands – helped Everett do ears and hands – and they did a full life cast. Then made a bust on it, did an Alcote on it. Everett took it to the hotel room with his girlfriend and disappeared for a week sculpting this thing and brought it back, floated it off, and they broke down all the molds for that."

As for the previously mentioned meeting from the day prior between David Ball and New World's Steve White, it would be in regards to the casting issue involving the Annie character for *The Hitchhiker* segment. The clock was continuing to tick down on the production with filming on the segment scheduled to start before the end of the month, and a memo from Ball to White on this day would enforce that urgency. "This becomes of the utmost priority bearing in mind current availabilities and the fact that 'Annie' should appear on camera in about three weeks' time," ended Ball's memo. **(14)**

For New World it broke down into groups of desirable names for the part. List A would consist of Julie Christie, Faye Dunaway, Jacqueline Bisset, and Catherine Deneuve (who was apparently uninterested, regardless of the financial offer). There was one backup name for that initial group, which would be Barbara Eden. List B would consist of Anita Morris, Catherine Bach, Sheree North, Morgan Brittany, Elizabeth Montgomery, and Catherine Harrold. List C would be Loretta Swit and list D would be Britt Ekland, both of whom Leonard Finger was apparently no longer interested in pursuing.

Thursday, October 2, 1986 – Day 16

Day sixteen was more than likely a day free from the pest of precipitation, despite Prescott's *The Courier* newspaper reporting trace amounts of rain for the day (the National Weather Service reported none). Oddly enough the next day would be the exact opposite.

On tap were scenes 98 and 99 of Randy and Laverne on the raft taking turns keeping guard during the night. These "day for night" shots are something we'll discuss further in the coming days ahead.

Work would also, of course, continue on scene 96, Deke's terrible demise on the raft. The effect where the raft's boards break and take Deke's leg underneath was handled by construction coordinator and mechanical engineer and longtime Laurel veteran Ed Fountain.

Hailing originally from Westchester County, New York, Fountain would find work in Upstate New York – Syracuse to be precise – as a school bus mechanic shortly after graduating. As fate would have it there was a theater located across the street from Fountain's place of employment that happened to be in need of a carpenter. He would go on to become the head carpenter for the Syracuse Stage Theater where he would stay for a couple of years until moving to Pittsburgh when he was hired by Bruce Miller with the Pittsburgh Public Theater. "Did a couple of seasons there and in the summer between seasons one year I was asked to build a houseboat for *Once Upon A Classic* for WQED which was called *Leatherstocking Tales*," recalls Fountain. "I built an eighteenth century houseboat, delivered it to the lake, and was hired to run it. So, I met the film crew and it turned out to be George Romero's film crew."

Fountain would go on to work on Romero's *Knightriders* and *Creepshow*, as well as other low budget horror/exploitation titles such as *C.H.U.D.* and *Sleepaway Camp*. When *Creepshow 2* came around he found himself once again doing what he excelled at: solving problems. "Well, the way I looked at it I was hired to build the scenery and also to take care of whatever mechanical effects the special effects people, which was the special effects makeup people, were not going to handle," Fountain says. "So, you know, there's always stuff that comes up which it's nobody's responsibility, so those are the things I took on."

Case in point: the raft's boards breaking and pulling down Deke's leg. "I had a hydraulic rig under there that made that whole scene work," Fountain recalls. "It basically broke the boards and pulled the thing down, the fake leg down. I forget exactly how it worked, but I built something that did all that."

Another memorable aspect of this scene, as well as the upcoming scene 97 with Randy and Laverne, involved the blob manipulating itself up through the boards of the raft. Since these shots were tight close-ups the crew was able to engineer a simple and safe solution on shore, rather than in the middle of the lake. "We started experimenting with taking the raft, putting it up on blocks, and then building troughs filled with black Methocel," Greg Nicotero told Anchor Bay. "And that way we were able to squeeze the troughs underneath the raft and the black stuff would ooze up and then ooze back down and then ooze up and ooze back down. So, we were making gallon after gallon after gallon of black Methocel and gallon after gallon after gallon of black Ultra-slime." **(15)**

Another interesting facet to this scene, one that perhaps you wouldn't necessarily think of immediately, is the pill bottle which Deke drops as he's being attacked. Inside the container were supposed to be marijuana joints that the character has brought along for the foursome to smoke while they're out on the raft. The task of handling that would fall to someone who admittedly had little experience with illicit drugs. "I had actually never smoked pot or anything, I never took up cigarettes. But I wound up having to roll about eighty joints," says Dex Craig. "It was all just an herbal tobacco but, boy; I learned how to roll joints super well!"

Craig would also have the opportunity to realize the shot of the pill bottle exploding as it makes contact with the blob itself, which turned out to be slightly more difficult to achieve than initially planned. "We tried casting a pill bottle out of foam latex, we tried all sorts of ways of making the pill bottle so that it would melt and collapse on command and we really couldn't. So, we instead pre-cracked one of the prop pill bottles – several of them actually because we wound up doing about fifteen takes of this – and we had basically string through the floorboards of a small section of the raft, it wasn't the full raft, this was shot on shore," he explains. "We pulled the string and it sort of like exploded, just like little pieces of plastic going, 'Pewww!', everywhere; and then it went through and they used the shot."

The last portion of filming for this day was second unit work in Dewey, Arizona for *Old Chief Wood'nhead*, scene A23. The scene, an exterior shot, would involve David Holbrook's character "Fatso" Gribbens standing in the doorway of his trailer, moments before he's dispatched by the now come to life wooden Indian, letting out an audible belch after crushing a beer can. "I liked it because it was comic, my role was a comic role," says Holbrook. "So, that sort of dis-inhibits you as an actor. You don't have to worry about being *real* or whatever. You just ham it up and that was so much fun."

Apparently things didn't go completely smooth at this location as the owners of the trailer, Jim and Charlotte Goodwin, were paid over two hundred dollars by the

Above and right: Filming Jeremy Green's death scene: hair & makeup assistant Angela Nogaro preps Green's hair; makeup effects artist Greg Nicotero monitors the oozing of the blob as it attacks Green. (courtesy of Michael Felsher)

production for burn damages to their carpet. "Well, they had like extension cords and stuff and they said it probably pulled too much juice or something? And where the chord was lying it just made a round hole in our carpet," recalls Mrs. Goodwin.

And despite the minor issue with the carpet it was still an interesting opportunity for the Goodwin family to watch a motion picture being filmed, on their own property no less, even if it ended up being a late night for everyone. "We were there quite a bit and in the evening and stuff we just got in the van, had the kids get in the van, and just kind of sat there and watched them filming it," says Mrs. Goodwin. "And then, you know, we had it all cleaned up, all around it, and they bring in all these junk chairs and garbage and made it a mess! (laughs) But they did clean it up."

Friday, October 3, 1986 – Day 17

The seventeenth day would see possible trace amounts of rain according to the National Weather Service website, despite Prescott's *The Courier* reporting none at all. There were scenes listed on the call sheet under "cloud cover", so apparently the production anticipated potential issues for this day.

Once again the filming of Deke's death, scene 96, was on the schedule. A new scene, 97, in which Randy attempts to straddle the cracks of the raft's boards trying desperately to avoid touching the blob, while at the same time holding a terrified Laverne in his arms, was also listed. "I remember my acting teacher, he saw it and he said, 'You played it the right way,'" recalls Daniel Beer. "He said, 'It's like being trapped in a nightmare and that's the way you have to play those types of movies.'"

As for those potential cloud cover scenes they would consist of scene 100, Randy taking advantage of a sleeping Laverne, and scene 101, the blob's attack of Laverne before Randy jumps into the lake. The two scenes would be divided on the call sheet though because some of the shots for 100 would be executed on the beach, utilizing close-ups, while the shots for 101 would be filmed on the raft in the lake itself. Sandwiched in between those two scenes on the call sheet was scene 105(remember there's only a 105L in the script) of Randy being engulfed in the blob and his body being dragged back into the lake.

Even though the majority of the crew were busy filming *The Raft*, some were prepping things for the film's next segment, *Old Chief Wood'nhead,* and one of those crew members was Matt Marich.

Marich joined the production shortly after the dismissal of Ed French, receiving a solid endorsement from the late John Vulich, who had gotten to know Marich over the phone for a project they were both attached to years prior. Vulich, who at the time was just coming off of *The Texas Chainsaw Massacre Part 2,* contacted Marich to see if he was still in the Phoenix area. "He said, 'I'm just exhausted, I don't wanna go on to another film right now. But some friends of mine are in Prescott and they're looking for somebody local that can help run molds and do some painting and that kind of stuff,'" recalls Marich. "He said, 'I recommended you for it. Why don't you go up and talk to them?'"

With that recommendation in hand, Marich traveled to Prescott to meet up with the entire gang of up-and-coming makeup effects artists in their office, the abandoned Texaco gas station, the "EFXACO". "So, I went in there and I was introduced to Mike Trcic – and he and I, of course, got along immediately because we're both Croatian – and then Everett Burrell and then to Howard Berger and Greg Nicotero," Marich remembers. "I could see right out that Greg was phenomenally talented and he was the more business end – at that point in their careers – he was more of the business end; I felt this, I don't know that it was true or not. And Howard was the wacky, plucky sidekick. You know, to quote *Galaxy Quest*, 'He's the plucky sidekick.' But both (are) amazingly talented."

At the interview it wouldn't be just his artistry skills, but his voice talents as well, which would help push Marich over the top for the job. "I was very much in the infancy of my career and they just needed somebody. So, that was great that they gave me the opportunity and I think they

Left: Stunt woman Patty Tallman doubles Jeremy Green for the shot of her being pulled into the water by the blob. (courtesy of Angela Nogaro and Michael Felsher)

were appreciative because I worked as hard as I possibly could," says Marich. "But I remember Howard said, 'Okay, you can have the job if you can do a cartoon voice', he said, 'It's the only way you're getting the job.' So, I did Marvin the Martian for him. I did, 'It made me very, very angry', you know, that one."

And even though he would assist with *The Raft*, creating batches of Ultra-slime for example, Marich's main duties were to assist Mike Trcic on *Old Chief Wood'nhead* with the creation of the wooden Indian suits; more on that later.

Saturday, October 4, 1986 – Day 18

Day eighteen would be a rain-free one as some familiar scenes would fill the day's ledger: 96, 97, 100, 101, and 105 would all once again appear on the call sheet. Finally, hand written on the call sheet is the day for night scene of Randy and Laverne discussing who would keep watch during the night, scene 98.

Shooting day for night is an old film technique that Michael Gornick chose to employ in this situation more than likely because of how cool it got at night in the desert at the lake location. And with his actors having already dealt with hypothermia, shooting in the daylight simply made more sense. "So, you want to shoot on a day... typically it's most successful when there's high contrast, you have a lot of shadows, so you're trying to simulate the sun as the moon," he explains. "And so you're gonna pray and hope or create contrast through lighting as best you can, in terms of creating this contrast of light to dark and shadow work. And then later in the laboratory – you can also do it on set, if you're shooting outside and you pull your 85 Wratten filter when you're shooting motion picture film, you'll get a bluish look to the film, which I believe we opted to do – and then further in laboratory use you can create that kind of emotional blue/cyan look of night. Yeah, a cool look. And you can often times, again, through timing drop the scene even more in terms of luminance so that it looks more 'night like'. It was a cinch in the old black and white days because you basically didn't have to work with saturated colors; often times what defeats you is the saturation of colors when you do day for night."

The most important subject regarding this particular day is the fact that it apparently marked the end of employment for the two assistant directors: 1st A.D. Joe Winogradoff and 2nd A.D. Gina Randazzo. Even though they were still slotted in place on the daily call sheet, the daily production report had their names scratched out, replaced by "Carol" and "Morgan". "Carol" is most likely just a misspelling of Charles Carroll's last name and "Morgan" refers to Michael Morgan. When filming would resume on Monday morning Katarina "Kato" Wittich and Grace Prinzi would assume those A.D. roles respectively. So, why did Winogradoff and Randazzo face the chopping block? "Winogradoff would probably have made a better location manager or unit manager," claims David Ball. "It's about chemistry, isn't it? When the chips are down, and let me tell you the chips were down because the weather was so bad, sometimes you need to increase the size of your balls. And you need to weather the storm

115

Above: P.A. Dex Craig and prop master Jim Feng work on the blob covered skeletal dummy of Laverne. (courtesy of Angela Nogaro)

and once again if you can't weather the storm you've gotta go. There were certain un-pleasantries with Winogradoff's character with Mike Gornick. And Mike's number one, Winogradoff's number two. A lot of the frustrations stemmed from we weren't able to make the schedule because of the weather and we had nowhere else to go."

"As far as Joe and Gina...you know, I think what happens when there are problems very often you fire the D.P or you fire A.D.'s. I don't know that they were doing such a terrible job at all, I think it's just that...you know, I honestly don't know," says Debra Tanklow. "But, I mean, the fact that the water was so cold, there's nothing an A.D. can do about that if you can't have the kids in the water for more than fifteen minutes at a time."

"It was a terrible production, I mean, frankly. Look, I don't want to speak badly of anybody – it's a long, long time. But there was...we had a very, very nice and skillful assistant

director who they fired. And then they brought somebody else on who was...there was an entirely different feeling on the set, which didn't make me particularly happy," says Tom Hurwitz. "I don't know where David Ball is now. I don't know who he is or where he went after this – I should know those things – but I'm sure you've talked to him, right? Well, he and I got along fine. But the mood on a set tends to roll down from the top, it always does. That's kind of one of the rules of film-making, probably every job. But in film-making the feeling of the work, the feeling on the set itself, is kind of the responsibility...it comes from above. And I've been on sets where the feeling is tremendously positive and everybody's involved in making something wonderful. And then I've been on jobs where everybody kind of dreads coming to work every day. And these guys did a lot of firing early on."

"Here's, I think, what it came down to – and I may be wrong for all I know," Joe Winogradoff theorizes about his dismissal. "One of the things I had asked when we were in pre-production of David Ball was, 'Listen, we're shooting a sequence that has everything outside and we're in Arizona and if there's any kind of rain storm we're sunk.' I asked him about getting weather insurance and he said, 'No, it's Arizona and it costs too much and there's a 99% chance of sun.' And, of course, we got socked with three days of not being able to shoot, which obviously sets back your schedule. So, we were behind schedule. The other side of it is that shooting on water is a problem: crews have to be in small boats maneuvering around; water needs to be still otherwise the camera's bobbing up and down the whole time. And the other side of it was that it was freezing cold, the pond was really cold. Guys were in wetsuits; the actors, you know, we would grease them down to try to protect them, but you couldn't be in the water for terribly long before their lips would turn blue and everything else. And one of the actors in particular, Danny Beer, really was shivering – I mean, seriously shivering – and went to see a doctor who said, 'You've gotta stay out of the water for at least a day or so.' And that became a problem also because we were already behind schedule. And I know several people kept trying to call up that doctor to get him to change his prognosis or diagnosis or remedy. And there came a point when I said, 'I am not comfortable if you are pressuring a doctor to change his recommendation for what happens to this kid. The doctor said he shouldn't go in the water, you've got the doctor, perhaps, to change his mind and we put the kid in the water and something happens; that's just bad news and I don't want to be a part of that.' And so we didn't shoot for a day, which also put us behind schedule further. And so, you know, people came in, we had a discussion. Mike wanted to shoot what he wanted to shoot and he and I had some discussions about trying to lose some shots, if possible, to try and make up some time. And I think then it just all sort of came to a head and the easy thing to do is to let go of the first A.D."

Winogradoff's remark about asking to drop some shots with Michael Gornick really stood out to me and so I asked Winogradoff if he could expand on that, plus his working relationship with Gornick in general. "I thought it was fine, I thought it was good. We talked about shots, planned them out," he says. "You know, an A.D. is in slightly a weird position every now and again, depending on circumstances, especially on low budget films, where if you start running into scheduling issues and before bondsmen start coming in and forcing cuts with shots and things...so at times I would discuss with Mike, you know, 'We're behind schedule, are there some cuts that you could make in some shots?' And my asking him that, I think, may have already started, 'He's not on my side.' And I think ultimately that was part of Mike's thing because the producers came in – Rubinstein and David Ball were there – and they were saying, 'We're behind schedule', and at one point I think they may have asked me, 'Does Mike have too many shots?' And I went, 'Mike wants to get what he wants to get. We're behind schedule though.' And he may have taken that as not supporting him."

"I think in no way was I instrumental – no one ever came to me and said, 'Do you want to get rid of this guy? Is he a pain in the ass?,'" responds Michael Gornick. "I think there are just naturally conflicts on set between a director – and other members of the crew, also – and with the first A.D. And the first A.D. is always there to drive the project, to protect schedule, to protect the monies of the producer and so forth, and get things done, and answer to the needs of the director and the creative team. But, honestly, you know, he or she is a very strict scheduler and that's their function. It's a happy marriage where they can do both, where they can keep schedule, keep the creative forces happy. But they are restricted, typically, by what the producer allows them to offer in terms of latitude. But, no, I was never integral in saying, 'I want this guy out of here, he's a pain in the ass.' Was he a pain in the ass? Yeah, but A.D.'s always are pains in the ass. I mean, I experienced that with my *Monsters* shoots in New York and *Tales from the Darkside* shoots, you know. But, again, I understood that they had a task and that was their task. Beyond that, I think given the situation of the loss of days and the rain and losing schedule and the subsequent costs to the budget of the film that something had to give, there had to be certain scapegoats. And I think not by my design, but more by the immediate producer David Ball; they look to some sort of dramatic solutions that they thought they could take to almost as a kind of stage play for the bonding company and say, 'We've made these corrections. The film wasn't being driven properly by the A.D.'s in particular, so let's make these changes.' So, I think that's very typical that happens; those kinds of people are expendable, in essence, because you can make these simple and dramatic changes without affecting the overall shoot. That's what happened. I mean, you know, I certainly could never wield the kind of power that would get people fired."

Unfortunately Gina Randazzo never returned numerous attempts for an interview, so her view of events remains unknown. However, Winogradoff did share his feelings on her dismissal as well. "When I started assistant directing – I knew that Katarina was one – but there weren't very many female A.D.'s around and I just thought, you know, people deserved a shot. So, I knew Gina from some other things and offered her the opportunity to have a second A.D. shot," Winogradoff says. "I felt really badly for her when we were let go just because, you know, first shot and the first shot you have is getting canned. I mean, obviously they weren't gonna

Above: The second unit crew works on shots of the blob at Granite Basin Lake. (courtesy of Wolf Forrest) **Below:** Taso Stavrakis and a member of his dive team pose with a pair of ducks used for the scene of the blob devouring the waterfowl. (courtesy of Taso Stavrakis)

keep the second on if the first goes. The first A.D. should have the choice of who he or she is going to work with."

Monday, October 6, 1986 – Day 19

The nineteenth day of filming was another one where it's difficult to know how much precipitation actually fell, if any at all. According to the National Weather Service 0.21 inches of rain fell in the Prescott area while the local newspaper, *The Courier*, listed only trace amounts of rain in the region. Whatever rain there was it wouldn't prevent filming from going on, however.

Once again scenes 96 and 97, plus scenes 100 and 101,

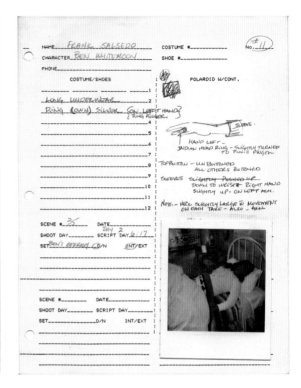

Above: Day 24 call sheet where you can see the two segments, *The Raft* and *Old Chief Wood'nhead,* overlapping with one another. (courtesy of Michael Gornick)

Above: Continuity costume page for scene 35 where Frank Saldeso's character Benjamin Whitemoon wakes to find the pouch of tribal treasures. (courtesy of Eileen Sieff-Stroup)

would all be listed. A funny side note regarding scene 96 is the description on the call sheet for Deke's demise: "Deke does can-can and is sucked thru raft." For days the call sheets would list under the "EFX & Special Notes" section the words "can-can leg". The can-can is a dance maneuver where the dancer kicks their leg high in the air above their head – think The Rockettes for example. This, of course, is a humorous reference to Deke's leg going completely vertical in the opposite direction when he dies on the raft.

And one more note regarding scene 96 is this would be the last day that Deke's ring would appear on the call sheets under Props. So, chances are this would be the day that striking image of Deke's fingers sliding below the raft as his class ring stays stuck in place between the raft's boards was shot.

These scenes weren't the only ones on the day's ledger though as perhaps the most iconic shot from the segment would be captured on this day. We'll return to that in just a bit.

Today would mark the first day on the job for the production's new first assistant director Katarina "Kato" Wittich and new second assistant director Grace Prinzi. Attached to the day's call sheet was a brief note from the producer in which he formally announced the news. "The first few days are bound to be a little difficult for them and I would ask all the crew to give the girls as much help as possible in order that the transition is smooth and productive," wrote David Ball. **(16)**

Wittich coming on board was an easy one considering her history with Laurel Entertainment: on *Day of the Dead*

she served as second A.D. and on *Tales from the Darkside* she served as an A.D. on numerous episodes of the syndicated TV show, including two of Michael Gornick's directorial efforts. She understood how Laurel worked and knew how to get things done in an efficient manner. "In essence, Kato coming in off of that *Tales from the Darkside* situation understood the need for speed," says Gornick.

For Wittich though she viewed the chance to work on *Creepshow 2* as more of an obligation, a quid pro quo scenario, truth told. "It was a little bit of an odd one for me because I had been first ADing on *Tales from the Darkside* for a while and I had just proposed a story idea that they had accepted, they hired a writer. And I had just literally left from finishing directing an episode of *Tales from the Darkside* to go out to *Creepshow 2*," she recalls. "And it was one of those things where it's like, you know, I'm sort of in the middle of prep, about to shoot my first official directing (gig), and they sort of come and say, 'Okay, so we gave you this great thing' – which is what was wonderful about Laurel, that they really bring people up – 'We gave you this great thing, and in return you have to go A.D. *Creepshow 2*.' And I don't think I really particularly wanted to – in particular because it meant I had to skip all the editing on my episode and that was quite important to me. So, I actually had to do it all from a distance during that first month of first ADing. So, it was an awful lot to juggle. It wasn't necessarily what I wanted to do, but I also had a lot of connection with and cared for a lot of people who were working on it and I was very grateful to Laurel for supporting me, so that was the deal."

One of those people that Wittich cared for and shared a connection with was Charles Carroll. The two were seeing one another and deeply in love (still are to this day as a matter of fact). Wittich and Carroll had initially met a couple of years prior while working on a toothpaste commercial, but it was when their paths crossed again on *Day of the Dead* that the romance truly blossomed. Under normal circumstances this wouldn't be an issue – movie set romances are quite common – but in this case it was more complicated. When things took off between the two on *Day of the Dead* Carroll was married and had just become a father. Wittich was seeing someone who just happened to be a close friend of Carroll's wife. This situation was frowned upon by some of the crew on *Day of the Dead* and was touched on briefly in my book on the making of that film. In mentioning the situation I didn't want to dwell on it, but I also didn't want to ignore it either; it was part of the history of that production and that was how I saw it. However, what I didn't take into consideration was how both Wittich and Carroll would view that. After the book was released Kato contacted me and let me know that she and Charles were not happy about the way their relationship was framed in the book. She was in no way nasty about it though and in fact helped to open my eyes to being more sensitive to personal matters such as these

because, after all, these are real people with real feelings. And to their extraordinary credit they agreed to speak with me again for this book project.

"I think we both love all the things we've shared in our lives and that includes all the production experiences we've had, regardless of whether they were difficult or not. The fact of sharing them with your life partner is kind of great. You know, we can trade these stories now and we know exactly what we're talking about; we have such marvelous interweaving of our lives. But, I think, for me, as it showed in your other book, to a lot of people, I was the 'bad guy' that broke up the marriage. You know, guys get away with a lot. Women get blamed," explains a heartfelt Wittich. "Put it this way: there was a lot of screwing around on all of those sets. But very few of the people were actually finding the love of their lives. But, there was a lot of judgement of us getting together because of Charles being married and his wife having a new baby. It was a very difficult situation for everyone, but particularly for her. And it was not an easy thing for people to understand. Because anyone from the outside thinks, 'Okay, it's just an

Below: Eileen Sieff-Stroup displayed the qualities of a veteran costumer designer as she made some wise, yet inspired, decisions for the film's characters. (courtesy of Michael Felsher)

affair. No big deal', and doesn't understand. I mean, we fell in love the second we met."

"You know, and this is so true, in all aspects of life, judgement is so easy; everyone judges," echoes Carroll. "Understanding takes work. And work takes time."

As for replacing Joe Winogradoff on set, despite her history with Laurel, it would still be a tricky situation for Wittich for a number of reasons. "I'm a real prepper, I love to prep; I love to be really on top of what I'm doing. And so I was coming in to something that I hadn't had any time to adequately prep. And it probably had some awkwardness for me, too, because Charles was the production manager and I knew that a number of the crew had some difficulties with us, you know, years earlier starting our relationship. So, I didn't know what I was walking in to in terms of people's attitudes," says Wittich. "And I also want to raise something that may or may not have been mentioned to you by others, but when I was first 1st ADing, there weren't other first woman A.D.'s. There was Yudi Bennett, there were, like, two or three others. But I was really among the very first female 1st A.D.'s to be working regularly and it was a 'boys club'. And Joe Winogradoff is very much a 'boy'. But I was already accustomed to running into, a great deal, where you would walk into crews and they were really resistant to having a female first. Often, by the end of the day, I'd have them eating out of my hands." (laughs)

One of the first changes with Wittich now on board was something I personally noticed just from doing my research and that involved the call sheets. Typically a call sheet will list which scenes will be filming that day, along with a brief synopsis of the details: "Deke does can-can and is sucked thru raft. Laverne grabs Randy" is a perfect example of this. Before Wittich's arrival the call sheet would list only the scene number, along with it being an exterior shot on the raft during the day (EXT. RAFT – DAY – SCENE 96), for example. With Wittich now in place as the first A.D. all of that information would still be on the call sheet, but the description of what specifically was attempted that day would be as well.

"Almost no one memorizes scene numbers to such a degree that they would know at a glance which scene you are talking about on a call sheet, so it is standard process to have a brief description on it. Some people do more or less, and you want to be as un-wordy as possible, but it's also really helpful to note down any specifics that are out of the ordinary so people are reminded," explains Wittich. "One of the reasons my predecessor was let go, and that I was brought in, was that communications on the set were poor, and one of the things I was known for was good and thorough communications, and a call sheet is a big part of that since it is the thing everyone has in their pocket and pulls out to look at every once in a while."

Now, back to that iconic shot I mentioned – Randy's surprise demise: scene 104, which had been previously scheduled on September 25, would be broken down into multiple shots for this day. In Romero's shooting script the well-known shot of the blob leaping out of the lake and engulfing a screaming Randy was actually part of scene 105L, but Michael Gornick had incorporated it into his shot list selection for scene 104 instead. Gornick had the sequence broken down into six different shots, but only three of those would be scheduled and filmed on this day. Scenes 104B and 104C of Randy scampering out of the water onto the shore and telling the blob he had beaten it and scene 104E, our famous money shot, of the blob rising out of the water to snatch Randy would roll before the cameras on this day.

Perhaps the easiest way to explain the effect of the blob coming up to envelop Randy was that it was similar to a convertible top on an automobile. "There was a big rig at the end when he's on the beach and the blob comes and goes over him. That was a giant rig that I made that basically you pulled a rope and the blob basically reared up and went over him. It was pretty good actually," says Ed Fountain, who designed the "wave blob rig", as it was named on the call sheet. "I don't remember how far we took it. But I know that it was easy to re-set it, so we couldn't have taken it too far."

"That was done on pulleys. That thing goes up and I had to time it and I had to look like I was running. It kind of looks like you're stuck in place, but it works because it's so quick. And they brought these pulleys up and that's how it came up," explains Daniel Beer. "And I remember Michael saying, like, 'Okay, you've gotta time this.' I think I got that on the first take, got that all down on the first take actually."

One person who proved to be instrumental in helping the blob leap out of the lake would be production assistant, Billy Kosco. A native of Prescott, Kosco had recently returned to the area after graduating from college with a degree in Communications Arts, with an emphasis in film-making, and was one of the first local hires for the film. "I was hoping, since I was one of the first guys there...because the production manager, real tall guy, he was doing all the hiring, Charles (Carroll), so for a while I'm helping, I'm working with Charles – I'm working with everybody, I'm 'Mr. Gopher', really is what I was, local boy gopher. So, I knew where the food was and I knew where this was, and if they said, 'Where's a fun place to hang out?' you know," Kosco remembers. "So, I was helping him with his interviews and stuff and I kept sort of saying, 'Hey, look, I've got a degree in film-making. I mean, put me somewhere where I can really make movies!' He's like, 'No, you're doing great where you're at', and stuff. I'm like, 'Crap, man. You're hiring people...I want to be an editor, cameraman, something big here, script supervisor', 'No, we've got that.' But, anyway, they fill up the crew and stuff and they said, 'Yeah, you're just gonna help us with managing the set and security things and helping us ascertain actual places where we're gonna create things.'"

For the shot Kosco was one of the crew members attempting to pull the blob up to engulf Daniel Beer, but as they were doing so an issue developed with the rig. That's where Kosco stepped in with a helpful suggestion. "They made the plastic little blob out of whatever they made it out of and stuff and then the idea was they physically wanted it to jump out of the water, so they just made a thing like it was a chin up bar, a real long one, like an Olympic chin up bar thing, on some scaffolding and, like, a little pulley system," Kosco explains. "So, they just laid it down right on the edge of the lake and then there were just two wires and so they made it wide enough so the camera could get

a good shot without seeing the wires. But the wider they made the thing the heavier it was...it took up more space. And they had to put a little bit of water on it, so they didn't use it until he's on the shore in that scene. And they had him crouch down and they just said, 'And, action!' and made it look like he just came out of the water, you can't see it there, but the shot shows the lake, you know, because it's low enough and he's blocking it, but it's right behind him. And then on three, when he thinks he's made it, we'd drop these sand bags and it would pop out just enough and

Above: The interior sets for "Fatso" Gribbens' and Sam Whitemoon's homes, seen here in Arizona, were packed up and trucked to Maine where they were rebuilt and used for filming there. (courtesy of Father William Kosco and Bruce Miller)

then, 'boing, boing, boing'. And it worked fine inside of the little place where they made it, the garage, and it worked fine inside the workshop. But then when they actually put it in the water, water got on top of it, it didn't float on the water – and plus if it floated on the water dry, it would pop up looking dry; and even though they poured a lot of slime on it so that it had a glistening look, they did want a little bit of water on it. But it made it weighty, so we just couldn't get it up and it was like, 'And action!' (mimics struggling to lift/pull something too heavy) It's like, 'No!'...boom!, you know, 'Pop it up, pop it up!' And I think we were even like, 'Okay, this time two of us will jump'...'One, two, three, action!' And it just, (makes sound of something collapsing down). He's (director Michael Gornick) like, 'That's not gonna do it guys. I've gotta have this fill the frame here, quick.' So, they were just like, 'I don't know what to do.' And I said, 'Well, I don't know, I'm not an engineer or anything but it seems to me that physics would say if you could break it into pieces… you know, all you've got to do is take the side board, cut it and hinge it, cut it and hinge it, cut it and hinge it.' I said, 'I don't want to tell you guys what to do, you guys have made movies', but they were like, 'Let's do it. But if we cut that board and it doesn't work, I'm gonna have to take this back and re-frame the whole thing.' So, they did it and they just put door hinges on it or something. And we tried it, I said, 'I think this is gonna work because all we've got to do is lift this much of it...Voooom! And now we're out of the water and now the water is falling down and it will work.' And sure enough it worked; Yay!"

This day would also see Margaret Rogers from New World's Music Affairs department draft a two-page letter to David Ball regarding the monetary details of Les Reed's and Rick Wakeman's contract for the film's score. $45,000 would be paid to the composers as part of a package deal. However, unlike the typical work-for-hire scenario where New World would retain complete copyright and publishing interests, they decided that based on the relatively low figure of the score's composition and the respected status of both artists, they would be willing to split the profits 50/50 with whatever label Reed and Wakeman decided to use.

"David Ball was particularly keen that I wrote for the major part of the project," says Les Reed. "And we decided that I would score for the first of the three films, *Wood'nhead*, and the last film of the project, *The Hitchhiker*. This left the middle film, *The Raft*, which Rick was very happy to score. Apart from the three integrated films within *Creepshow 2* we also needed further sections of which we both worked on together."

"Because the post was being done in London I decided to look around for a composer and I thought, 'I'm gonna give Les Reed a call! He's done so many fantastic songs,'" recalls David Ball. "So, I called him up and I said, 'Les, we're coming over to London, near Pinewood, and we're talking about maybe doing the music', and we met with Gornick, and he said, 'I'd love to do this!' I said, 'Well, I've only got a limited budget', I think I had fifty grand or something for all the music. And he gave a bit of money to Rick and he got a bit himself, I think, too. He certainly didn't get rich out of it. And they worked their socks off!"

Lastly a contract pertaining to the upcoming filming for *Old Chief Wood'nhead* was officially inked on this day. The owners of a small Humbodlt feed store property on Main Street, which was adjacent to the building where interior filming for Ray and Martha Spruce's store would take place, agreed to let the production use their space and parking area for the bargain basement price of $100. The building would be used by the makeup, wardrobe, and special makeup effects departments to prep each day for the duration of the segment's filming.

Tuesday, October 7, 1986 – Day 20

Day twenty would be free from rain as some recognizable scenes would again be on tap. Work on scenes 96 and 97, along with scenes 100 and 101, were once again scheduled.

The segment's wonderful last shot, the classic E.C. style reveal of the "No Swimming" sign, scene 105L, would also be scheduled for today. However, most likely it would be captured on film the following day.

Another early departure from the production was looming on the horizon with director of photography, Tom Hurwitz. About three weeks before filming would end in Arizona Hurwitz, tired of the negative atmosphere surrounding the production, plus seeing the handwriting on the wall regarding Maine, let the producer know he wasn't making the trip to Bangor with the rest of the crew, but he would fulfill his obligations in Arizona on the two segments there. "Listen, the only thing with Tom was – he was masterful, he had a great eye, very impressive reel, communicated well, understood instantly in terms of shot design, as you might have saw from my notes, I had pretty copious notes in terms of how I wanted to handle a scene and what kind of angle I wanted to give things, he understood instantly, so he was very, very supportive – he just had a certain kind of pace," explains Michael Gornick. "And given the stresses of Arizona at that point there was no way that Tom Hurwitz could have survived the need to move quickly, you know. And that was the major criticism of him; that he couldn't move quickly in terms of getting a shot in, setting up for the next event."

"Tom Hurwitz had a problem keeping up with Gornick's schedule," confirms David Ball bluntly. "End of story."

"I don't want it to get ad hominem. Let me just say that the feeling on the set did not make it fun to go to work every day. And I was looking at another month in the incredibly cold wilds of Maine, with just a continually unpleasant set," Hurwtiz explains. "There was finger pointing, but the pointing didn't go to me. But they fired the A.D. and they fired the grip. But that added to a kind of bad feeling on the set. I had worked in Los Angeles and, you know, these guys obviously didn't feel any particular allegiance to me. The finger pointing went on and on and on. And I'm sure Michael felt that the finger was pointed at him as well. And it just led to just kind of a bad atmosphere. Life is too short as far as I'm concerned (laughs)."

Hurwitz's mentioning of having worked in Los Angeles was a reference to the fact that *Creepshow 2* was a Laurel production and Laurel productions were known for their Pittsburgh based crews, despite the fact that this particular production featured a healthy dose of crew members from the "Big Apple". "You know, mostly it's the Laurel/Pittsburgh DNA," says Charles Carroll. "With some New Yorkers thrown in."

"That whole Pittsburgh crew is so great. There's so much kindness and lovingness between them all and connection

and everybody's sort of on board for everybody else," Kato Wittich fondly recalls. "And so, you know, there were days that were incredibly fun even when they were difficult."

"I'll tell you, as far as I'm concerned, this was a Romero factory production. My job was to light it and get it shot," Hurwitz follows up. "It was two kinds of a problem. It was a logistical problem to get the film shot and it was a kind of personal struggle to get it shot under the conditions that were really unpleasant; very, very unpleasant working conditions. Now, this might have been the way the Pittsburgh guys worked all the time – I have no idea. That unit might have just worked with that level of incivility all the time. That's not the way I worked, I never worked that way in my entire career on big and small films."

Speaking of incivility, during my research and interviews I came across one rumor that really blew me away – because it's so far afield from the person I know – and that story is in regards to a physical altercation involving Michael Gornick and Tom Hurwitz. "I don't have the best memory, I have to tell you. It's not one of my greatest qualities," admits set decorator Andrew Bernard. "But, some of the things I do remember from the film were, one, the first D.P. did not get along with the director. Tom Hurwitz, who I worked with after on a documentary called *Down and Out in America*, it actually won an Academy Award, and I worked...or did I work on that before? Maybe I worked on that before. Yeah, I worked on that before *Creepshow 2*. So, I had worked with Tom. And I remember those two going at it to the point where, I wasn't on set, but I had heard that Michael Gornick had choked Tom Hurwitz (laughs). And I don't know if that's true or not, I just remember that."

"Michael never did anything of the kind," Hurwitz refutes. "Nor did we have anything more than the normal minor disagreement in the course of work."

"I don't remember that, honestly. And Tom was kind of a 'Gentle Ben' character. I mean, you would never imagine, like, grabbing him for any reason," says Gornick. "It sounds like one of those stories that David Ball would later tell, that he would say, 'If I was Michael I would have grabbed his neck and thrown him on the ground.'"

This story was another topic that came up during my second interview with Gornick and along with the comments made from his old colleagues at Laurel, Nick Mastandrea and Bruce Miller, it touched a nerve that would prompt that follow-up call I mentioned in the Day 12 section. "The silly rumor about squeezing someone's neck, I mean, you know, no matter how stressed I would get I would never squeeze somebody's neck physically," he says. "That's such an odd rumor to be perpetuated."

Wednesday, October 8, 1986 – Day 21

The twenty-first day of shooting saw very light rainfall, .06 inches according to Prescott's *The Courier*. Nothing that would alter the day's plans though.

Left: The interior set for the Spruce's General Store was a fantastic achievement by Bruce Miller's art department, led by set decorator Andrew Bernard. (courtesy of Bruce Miller and Steve Arnold)

Kicking off the day's schedule was scene 105L of the camera panning away from the blob dragging Randy's body into the lake, past the Camaro, and towards the reeds to reveal the sign, "No Swimming". Careful inspection of the scene reveals a layer of mist hovering above the lake which would indicate this was probably shot fairly early in the day.

As mentioned in the prior day's section the reveal of the "No Swimming" sign is a classic E.C. style trope, no doubt an ironic and fitting denouement to the story. Incredibly it was never part of King's story or Romero's screenplay, but instead the idea would come from the director himself. "That was my design from day one to create something in the way of a bit of irony, that the group who had arrived earlier had missed this damn sign because it was kind of buried by foliage," says Michael Gornick. "Early, when I read that episode, I thought, 'Gee, it would be perfect irony', if after this final attack that we as an audience got a peek of something that they should have seen possibly had they been paying attention, if they weren't high on drugs! They *were* smoking marijuana. Don't do drugs. And no swimming either."

And speaking of said E.C. style, *Creepshow 2* would abandon a technique used to great effect in the original film, borrowed from the comics, which was the use of splashy colorful lighting and backgrounds, used to heighten the horrific moments in the film. The decision, one I assumed would have fallen under budgetary concerns, was actually the preference of Michael Gornick, who had helped to design the ones featured in the original film. "I never really enjoyed those in *Creepshow*, no. I didn't want to use them," he explains. "It's just that, I guess, when you're part and parcel to the actual setup and the creation of those things that they always become transparent, you can see right through it, it feels phony. It's difficult to preserve that illusion for yourself. So, I mean, from a technical standpoint I just found that they were weak."

With it now being the third day with Kato Wittich as first A.D. some of the crew were beginning to notice a more rigorous tone to the pace, one born out of necessity due to the issues from the weather. And it was a hard-nosed approach from Wittich, not one she necessarily wanted to employ, which was the cause of that feeling. "All the sudden I had a flash to, I think Katarina came in as an A.D.? And she was really cracking the whip," recalls Eric Swanek. "And I remember – I didn't have words with her – but she was like, 'Quick, get the camera on the dock! Get the camera on the dock!' And there's the goop that they used for the slime, I think it's called Methocel, which they told me it was something like you find in a Twinkie, it's often used on the *Alien*'s jaw, so it's ridiculously slippery. She's like, 'Just get the camera on the dock!', and I'm in a boat stepping onto a dock that's floating with Methocel on it and I'm holding, you know, an $80,000 camera and lens set up – I'm not going to be running to do that. I remember turning to her, 'I'm sorry; I'm not that stupid to do something like that.' You know, because you can crack the whip all you want, but you have to be smart. So, that's their job, is to crack the whip, and I understand that and in retrospect she was right to an extent. But I'm not gonna risk myself and/or the camera

Above: The creation of Dead River was another amazing achievement for Bruce Miller's hard working and talented team, led by his assistant Steve Arnold and head carpenters Gary Kosko and Logan Berkshire. The Spruce's General Store would be the center piece of that hard work. (courtesy of Bruce Miller, Steve Arnold, and Michael Felsher)

on doing something stupid like jumping onto a dock that's covered with stuff that you could just slip and fall."

"You know, one of the things that were definitely true on this show is that we had to work in a lot of dangerous and physically difficult circumstances," Wittich says. "But we were always caring...neither Michael (Gornick) nor any of us were the kind of people who put people's lives at risk or pushed past where we should have. So, either with the hypothermia or with the car issues (the filming in Maine, which we'll eventually get to), with any of those things, they weren't things where people were being forced into doing unsafe things, it was just that the circumstances were so difficult."

Another scene on this day's schedule would be the completion of number 96, Deke being pulled through the raft by the blob. And with the completion of said scene it would mark the end of Paul Satterfield's work on the production. And unlike the character description in Romero's screenplay – "Deke's thick neck tells us he's Varsity Football. His perpetually wrinkled forehead and his down-turned eyebrow imitation of Matt Dillon tell us he's kind of an asshole" **(17)** – Satterfield made a favorable impression among his cast-mates and crew. Sure, he was definitely an athlete, but when it came to personality he was anything but an "asshole".

"He's a very entertaining guy, he's a Southern guy. I mean, he was funny; really, really funny," Daniel Beer fondly recalls about his co-star. "And I think he does a great job in that role. A lot of that stuff he comes up with, we improvised some stuff in the car, a lot of that, and Michael just let it happen. And he improvised some stuff; I think he's dynamite in it."

"Paul, I got to be kind of friends with him," says craft services' Garry Greer. "An interesting note with him was the first week he was bored to death and he was a pretty big guy and he said, 'You know what, I really need a set of weights. You know anybody that's got any weights that I can borrow and just take to my room?' And I said, 'Well, I got some!' I had a set and I had about 150 pounds of barbells and stuff and I brought it to him and then the next day he said, 'You got anything heavier?' And I said, 'No, that's it' (laughs)."

"Paul Satterfield, to me, was a gentleman and a scholar," Rebecca Mayo says. "He knew I was a teacher and let me tell you what he did in that rainy weather in Prescott. When it rained and would pour down rain in the evening and it was time for me to go home – he drove my car around in the parking lot. He would go get it, put it under the portico where it was dry, and he drove it around for me to get in to so I didn't have to get wet when I left the production office at night."

Other work scheduled for the day were scenes 100 and 101(cloud cover options), as well as extensive work for scene 97.

Thursday, October 9, 1986 – Day 22

Day twenty-two would be another one challenged by

Above: The fabrication of Curly's Service Station at the Dead River location was just as impressive, if not more, than the general store. (courtesy of Bruce Miller, Eileen Garrigan, and Steve Arnold)

precipitation as *The Courier* would report 0.44 inches of rainfall in the Prescott area. And as an FYI, at this point in my writing I've come to rely more on data provided by *The Courier.*

Today would see the end of work on scene 100, Randy exploring Laverne's body as she lies sleeping on the raft.

Filming sex scenes can be awkward, especially for lesser experienced actors and in this case both Daniel Beer and Jeremy Green were just that. But with Green she was the one who would be more vulnerable seeing that her part required nudity. Perhaps that could have led to some apprehension or nerves? Not so according to her co-star, Beer. "To me there's nothing sexual about it. There's a crew around you. It's very kind of technical," he explains. "That scene Michael goes, 'Okay, you're gonna start here. Kiss her hip. Kiss here. And then after the second kiss lift her shirt up a little bit. Now look over here at the blob.' It's very technical. It's literally connecting dots, you know, and then trying to make it look like it's not technical. So, no, Jeremy was not nervous. She was fine. I'm not some skeevy guy that was getting a cheap thrill, you know."

But according to the director and the producer there were some jitters for Green when it came time to do the nude scene. "You must understand at that point in time in her career that she had done few performances, let's say inexperienced," says Michael Gornick. "Although we discussed this early in the casting process too; I always liked to talk about these things after you become serious about somebody and you've eliminated your choices down to two or three people, you've gotta discuss these sort of things, that there is a nudity factor in this or partial nudity, if they're uncomfortable. And she wasn't at that point in time. But I think later, why not? I mean, you suddenly realize that you're gonna be on set with a number of, you know, set people with gawking eyes and so forth and it's uncomfortable. So, we had subsequent conversations all the way on to set, between myself and her, about the attempt to keep it as private as possible and the need for it in the scene. So, yeah, there were ongoing conversations and was she hesitant? Of course; I must say also, aside from her, Danny Beer likewise as a male, although he had gotten into performance, also had reservations about the whole thing, too."

"I remember that there was a very beautiful young actress in *The Raft* section and I remember that they had some kind of an issue with her, right? I'm trying to think of what it was. Maybe she'd agreed to do a topless scene and then didn't want to do it when the time came or something like that," recalls *Old Chief Wood'nhead* star, Holt McCallany. "I think it was just something that I heard around the set and, you know, it didn't seem to me like the producers were totally understanding of her position. But I stayed out of it, I mean, it didn't involve me."

"But then she didn't want it, did she?," laughs David Ball. "Afterwards, you know, she didn't want to, no. 'Hey, lady, you signed the contract, you read the script, you knew

Left: Sadly, the Dead River Bank wouldn't find its way into the finished film. The work, however, was just as impressive as the general store or service station facades. (courtesy of Eileen Garrigan)

126

what was in it', so she was a little bit nervous about it. But we said, 'Okay, guys, this is a closed set'...I mean, we're in the middle of a lake on a raft. You can't say it's a closed set, but you try, 'It's a closed set or look the other way because Jeremy's gonna get her tits out.' You know? There's not much you can really do. You couldn't put a curtain around her, could you? Not many people saw anything of her because the weather was so bad! We had tarpaulins over the camera, we had everything. It was unbelievable, man."

Ball mentioning the weather again couldn't be more on the money. Indeed the sequence was finally caught on film and done so in the rain. And according to Eric Swanek it was the new 1st A.D., Kato Wittich, who really took charge in rallying the crew to get the scene completed. "I still remember it was raining and everyone's sitting around, like moping around in rain, she said, 'Why can't we just tent this and shoot like that?,'" Swanek recalls. "And it was probably the ill will with the A.D.'s being fired and the key grip being fired and everyone being mad at Tom (Hurwitz) because they thought he made a bad decision about the scaffolding in the water, where nobody else had a plan. So, she was still able to think clearly enough to say, 'How about we do this?'"

As for getting the shot accomplished, what exactly does Swanek mean when he references tenting the scene? "Tenting out, in this case, just meant hanging a silk over the top of where we were filming. The sides were not necessarily covered. But, you wouldn't have crew hanging out there, they'd be off to the side under umbrellas and stuff, they wouldn't be standing next to her when that's happening," he explains. "They had another dock that was on the shore that we did that on. We weren't out in the water."

Having nudity featured in this new film was a bit of a departure from the original, which contained no nudity or sex at all. As mentioned in Chapter 2, when introducing Jeremy Green as part of the cast, the requirement of nudity was based on the executive producer's desire to hopefully boost the film's sales overseas, an assertion made by both Michael Gornick and Mitchell Galin, and confirmed to me by the executive producer himself, Richard Rubinstein. "Sounds right," he acknowledges.

But when it came to shooting the scene and making it tasteful, yet still fulfilling the executive producer's mandate, that's when it fell squarely on the shoulders of the director. "I don't have the script in front of me and I'd still argue the point that things like the nudity and the fondling of breasts and so forth were not explicit to that script. And I never felt that the comics ever offered that. So, I didn't find it as necessary. I found things to be necessarily sensual, inviting, highly sexual – but not overt. Okay? And that's when I had a major disagreement with Richard Rubinstein. He wanted things to be overt, direct; blatant. He was on set a number of times asking for more visibility for breasts, for overall nudity and groping and etcetera, etcetera. Now, Richard's point is and he may have a good point – I never heard from Steve King – but he claimed I was violating the spirit of the script by not shooting it in a fashion that was blatantly sexual. So, I disagreed and I *think* I got my way," laughs Gornick as he explains how he viewed approaching the subject matter. "If you remember what I did in that shot is that the breasts are exposed, but they're not blatantly flopping, you know.

Richard wanted some full titillation, some oral satisfaction, I mean that sort of thing. And the point that he argued was for alternate versions, foreign versions. You know, Richard, you're talking to the wrong guy."

During research for a book on film productions you're bound to hear anecdotes that are a little crazy, often quite funny, and at times totally off the wall. A perfect example of this is a story I learned from hair and makeup assistant Angela Nogaro and it concerned our star of scene 100, Jeremy Green. "Jeremy, she ultimately got...she had a moment where she got engaged to one of our special effects makeup artists. They continued a relationship after the show, which they then, I think, broke up before they ever got married," says Nogaro. "But we had crazy things with her because our producer – I don't know if you're ever gonna want to put this in your book (laughs) – in the sex sells mentality, when she was topless on the raft, that the blob was going to attack her on, we were asked to make her nipples darker because they didn't feel that she was presenting this arousal thing as much as she needed to be. Which was the strangest request I think I've ever had in my entire career (laughs)."

"I remember that, yes," confirms Michael Gornick. In fact, Gornick even recalls another suggestion from a member of the production for the use of ice to help out with the situation even further. "It was all in trying to justify, seriously, just the form and the moment," he explains. "It had nothing to do with being lecherous, I didn't think."

"The ice was then suggested to help make them erect," Nogaro follows up. "It all of a sudden became a movie all about her nipples!"

"Her nipple on *The Raft,* that was erect because it was fucking cold!," laughs Mitchell Galin. "It shrunk my testicles, it inflated her nipples."

As for the producer who made the actual request to darken the nipples? Let's just say that it was NOT David Ball. And the makeup effects artist who allegedly got engaged to Jeremy Green? Even though he didn't want to participate in this book he did get back to me through a mutual friend and denied that he and Green were ever engaged – something Angela Nogaro begs to differ on. "Yes, they hooked up for a while," laughs Nogaro. "He's married now, but he was quite the 'Ladies man'. We used to tease him that he had, basically, a drawer full of engagement rings that he used to hand out."

Now, the idea of Randy taking advantage of an exhausted and sleeping Laverne seems rather unsavory, especially in the day and age we currently live in, with the "#MeToo" movement. In King's original short story though Randy does more than just fondle and explore Laverne's body as he actually is engaged in intercourse with her, even though Laverne is slightly delirious and not in her right state of mind. A key line contained in Romero's original screenplay, one that was in the shooting script as recent as August 1986, would be removed in a yellow page revision dated 9/8/86. The line would follow a detailed description of Randy pushing up Laverne's shirt, exposing her stomach and breasts, and then the words "then he dives into her". Following that was, "She wakes up. She is pinned under Randy's weight. His face is buried in her chest, his hands are exploring wildly." **(18)** The removal of this line attempts to soften, just a bit, the situation – and the individual most responsible for this alteration was Michael Gornick. "This was part of the ongoing controversy with Mr. Rubinstein and as he categorized it, it was a violation of Steve's intentions and George's screenplay for me to eliminate this kind of action," he says. "And my point to him was that as cast and as performed and as directed I didn't feel that Randy would have done this, nor did I feel it advanced the situation. And I thought it was far better seeing him confronted by a teenage innocence and opportunity, for the first time perhaps, than making him like a pseudo rapist in essence. So, that's why I wanted it gone. And, you know, everyone supported me, obviously, on set – even David Ball."

And although Randy's actions are not as exploitive as what is described in King's short story, even Romero's original script for that matter, it still requires punishment from the horror gods. "It's funny, that scene, they call it all kinds of stuff, but at that time you had to put a sex scene in a horror movie; basically that was like standard issue to help it get distributed. Then people ask me about the scene, 'Why did you do that? Why did you do that?' And I'm like, 'Because it said so in the script. We're actors! There's a script!,'" laughs Daniel Beer. "If I didn't do that then I couldn't die at the end. All teenage horror movies are about morality, right? And the reason we're all dying is we're all smoking pot, but my reason is I'm trying to take advantage of her, right? So, I have to die. If I was heroic and didn't do that and got her off that thing and then we died, the audience would be like, 'That doesn't make sense.'"

Also on this day scene 97 was slated for more work of Randy and Laverne terrified as the blob oozes and pulsates through the boards of the raft.

Scene 101 of Laverne being "blobbed" on the raft was also on the ledger for this day. The makeups for Jeremy Green's character of Laverne were broken down into three stages, the first two of which Green would be forced to endure herself. "We did this thing where the tentacles, like, go up into her face and all that stuff. We sculpted appliances that we put onto Jeremy," Howard Berger said to Anchor Bay. "We put 'goo' tubes in, and we put all these hot melt vinyl tentacles into her face, just weaved them in and out." **(19)**

The third stage however would be handled by Patty Tallman, who would take the plunge into the lake covered again in prosthetics and slime. "That was me getting pulled into the water," she says. "Anytime that we were covered by the blob they really didn't want to have the actors doing that. So, you know, getting stuck under...the risk of not being able to resurface easily."

And finally a new, updated shooting schedule would be distributed to the crew which would cover the production up through the move to Maine.

Friday, October 10, 1986 – Day 23

The twenty-third day would see light precipitation as .06

inches of rain was reported by *The Courier*.

Today should have been the last day for work on *The Raft*, but as it turns out there would still be additional photography needed – mostly second unit – stretching into the middle of the following week, which we'll cover in due course. Today would be the final day of filming for Daniel Beer; however Jeremy Green wouldn't be as fortunate.

One final shot for scene 97 was scheduled on this day for late in the afternoon, the shot of the blob moving away from the raft as Randy and Laverne nervously look on.

Also, scene 103 of Laverne being "digested" by the blob, an effect which wouldn't be quite realized as scripted, was on the schedule for late afternoon. As discussed in the Day 11 section the shot of Laverne being digested by the blob in the water was to be rather spectacular as it twisted and stretched her body like taffy, after having separated her at the waist for good measure. Instead a brief shot of a skeletal, blob covered figure would rise up out of the water and then sink below the surface; again, a simple case of the budget, plus weather issues, altering things for the low budget production.

The majority of the day's scheduled work was for scene 101 – basically every shot for the scene – which encompassed at least six individual shots: Laverne getting "blobbed" on the raft as Randy looks on in shock, Randy jumping into the water, etc.

Meanwhile, with filming for *Old Chief Wood'nhead* rapidly approaching today would be a travel day for two of its cast members, Holt McCallany and Don Harvey. And it would be quite memorable for each as they would meet not only their fellow co-star, but as it turns out a lifelong friend as well. "I remember I got to the airport to check in to my flight to go to Arizona. I saw this guy, he looked at me and I looked at him, and the first thing I thought was, 'Oh, I know that guy. Who is that? That's a very...', then I was like, 'Maybe I don't know him.' And he was looking at me and I was looking at him and we were just like thinking...and then he just walked up to me and he said, 'Rich boy?'," laughs Don Harvey. "I was like, 'Holy Shit', and said hi to him, and I was like, 'Oh my god, Sam Whitemoon!' I was picturing someone a little different, you know what I mean? The guy's like an Irish kid with short blonde hair, so he didn't really look like an Indian. But I was like, 'Really? Okay.' So we started to go sit in the first class cabin of our flight and get totally wasted on our way to Arizona."

"That's true. Yeah, it is. And I think that's where Don and I met for the first time," Holt McCallany recalls. "We were both in there getting on the plane and he just had this look about him. I don't know why, I just knew. And that began a thirty year friendship that still exists today. And he

Above right: The talented carpenters and painters who brought Dead River to life, from left to right: top row - Jan Pascale(who left very early), Eileen Garrigan, Aaron Newton, Logan Berkshire, Gary Kosco(standing) / bottom row – Bob Turpin, Danny Watson, Dave Whittlesey, unknown, but possibly Peter Cahn, and Eileen Winterkorn. (courtesy of Eileen Garrigan) **Below right:** Helping Dan Kamin into his Chief Wood'nhead suit: Howard Berger and Matt Marich(right) apply the arms, while Mike Trcic does touch up work on those arms. (courtesy of Wolf Forrest and Eileen Garrigan)

Above: Dan Kamin does a little reading before getting into character. (courtesy of Garry Greer)

is, was, and continues to be one of my favorite guys in the business; and a very underrated actor. Don Harvey's a really, really good actor who hasn't always had the roles he deserves; but he's really, really good."

Saturday, October 11, 1986 – Day 24

Day twenty-four would be the first day of principal photography that didn't include scheduled filming at Granite Basin Lake, but that didn't mean *The Raft* was over just yet. Much like the blob itself filming for the segment just wouldn't go away. A last minute re-shoot for scene 101 of Laverne getting initially covered by the blob would force itself onto the day's call sheet. "For the shot where Jeremy Green gets engulfed by the blob we literally tilted the raft sideways and we were pumping the black sludge over her

head," Greg Nicotero told Anchor Bay. "So, she turns and then she looks at camera, the illusion is that the stuff has come up over her face." **(20)**

The reasons for the reshoot aren't known, but according to the daily call sheet, this time it would take place not at Granite Basin Lake, but at the rented studio space, a former automobile body shop, referred to as "The Big House", which was less than two miles away from the production hotel.

Once again rain would attempt to be a nemesis to the production with a reported 0.44 inches falling in the area, according to *The Courier*. But with the schedule now moving a large portion of the filming indoors, wouldn't you know it, rain was on the way out making its final appearance for the duration of filming in Prescott over this very weekend. Beginning Monday not a single drop of rain would fall in the Prescott area while the production remained in town. "After *The Raft*, which was an unmitigated disaster due to weather, we were behind schedule so the budget was threatened and we really had to crack on. Mike (Gornick) would work as hard as he could, we all worked as hard as we could," says David Ball. "We had this little place called Humboldt that we went to and dressed it up a bit and fortunately the weather turned in our favor and we were able to kick on quite well and get ourselves, not completely back on schedule, but a long ways towards being back on schedule. But that was testimony to the professional crew and the cast, they were all great. You couldn't have asked anymore from any of them, really."

The day would begin with a scheduled morning meeting to discuss the plan of attack for *Old Chief Wood'nhead*. Michael Gornick, Tom Hurwitz, Charles Carroll, Kato Wittich, Howard Berger, Eileen Sieff-Stroup, Taso Stavrakis, and Jeanne Talbot would all be present to make sure everyone was on the same page. As David Ball just touched upon this was a critical phase for the production, one that was desperately trying to make up for lost time due to the weather delays incurred during *The Raft* which had put the production a full week behind schedule. For a low budget production with a first time director this could have been a worst case scenario, being that the bonding company was keeping a watchful eye on things. And according to Michael Gornick Film Finances did in fact make their presence known in Arizona, but it wouldn't be until the production moved to Maine that a little more pressure would be applied. All one can do in that situation is give their best effort and "crack on", as Ball said.

"You know, it's all bullshit. They come in, they kind of go, 'Well, what are you guys gonna do? What's your plan?'," says Charles Carroll. "And you say, 'Look, if we make this schedule...' I think (David) 'Bally' said, 'Look, I can post this thing in London, I can do it over there much cheaper. I've got friends I can call in favors, I can get back some money and we'll do it.'"

Right: Working on the different aspects of Chief Wood'nhead's costume: Matt Marich paints the arrows for his quiver, while Mike Trcic touches up his feathered headdress and face(note the small motors on the top of the head used for facial expressions). (courtesy of Michael Felsher and Wolf Forrest)

As for the rest of the day's scheduled scenes they would concentrate on *Old Chief Wood'nhead*, the first of which would be scene 35 of Frank Salsedo's character, Benjamin Whitemoon, waking to find the returned pouch of his tribe's treasures, or "rock candy" as young Sam Whitemoon refers to them. Looking back on decorating that bedroom set brings about some humorous feelings for set decorator Andrew Bernard as he sees what he would probably do differently with the knowledge and experience he has today. "It's funny because after that I did decorate a few westerns. I did *Young Guns II*, I did *Return to Lonesome Dove*, and some other TV movies, and learning more about Native American culture. And since then I have several Native American friends who grew up on the reservation and I have to say decorating that room, his bedroom, was pretty cliche. It definitely was an exaggerated, comic book, white man's version of an Indian's bedroom," laughs Bernard. "I'm sure when I was doing it I didn't know what tribe he was supposed to represent, you know; and I probably had three different tribe iconography in there. I would have tried to have been more true to the character and I think it would have felt a little more like a real person's bedroom rather that the way it turned out."

Completing the scheduled work for today were scenes 23 and 24 of Fatso at his trailer watching TV and getting skewered by our vengeful wooden Indian statue come to life. Now, scene A23 had already been completed on October 2 by a second unit crew, which established the outside of the character's trailer. Scene 23 in Romero's script was slightly different than what's in the film though,

which is just a brief shot of David Holbrook looking outside his trailer door, presumably after hearing Wood'nhead's howling war cry, drinking a beer, and then retreating back inside. As scripted Romero begins the scene with an overstuffed suitcase landing on the floor next to the refrigerator, as Fatso is packed and ready to leave for "Hollywood, U.S.A." He's now sporting a Hawaiian shirt, as well as a Greek fisherman's hat. Once again, perhaps losing these small touches was a budgetary consideration because anytime you're dealing with wardrobe you've got to have multiples in case something were to happen; after a while the numbers can begin to pile up. "And then everything there's six of," explains Eileen Sieff-Stroup. "Like David Holbrook's t-shirt that has food all over it? That's not food, that's paint, because you had to be able to wash it, because he wore it, you know. And then the arrow pops out of it, so you have to have six of them."

And with a preliminary wardrobe budget of $38,000 – which included her salary – Sieff-Stroup had to stretch every dollar. "I think my budget was only like $12,000," she says. "Something like that." That $12,000 figure would become a slight issue in the coming weeks once the Annie casting ordeal with *The Hitchhiker* was finally settled, however.

As for other little touches concerning Fatso's costume Sieff-Stroup would turn to a well-known and diverse commercial section of New York City where *Dawn of the*

Dead's costume designer Josie Caruso had shopped nearly a decade prior for the SWAT uniforms seen in that film. "I think I bought that hat, the 'Bullshit' hat, I think I bought that in New York on the street or something. I did a lot of shopping on Canal Street for that," Sieff-Stroup says. "It's all different now, but in the 80's Canal Street was very, like, kind of junk stores and Army surplus. I did a lot of Army surplus shopping on that show."

The interiors for Fatso's trailer were shot in a stage/warehouse setting – but as it turns out not today. In fact those shots of Fatso going to the fridge and grabbing some food, then sitting down in his chair to watch *The Cisco Kid* before he's eventually dispatched by Wood'nhead's arrows wouldn't be "in the can" until well over a month later when the production made their move to Bangor, Maine. "The trailer set was shipped up to Bangor because we were unable to finish that scene when the Holbrook kid, David Holbrook, got killed by the arrows coming through the trailer," says Ed Fountain. "The effects makeup guys had all these tubes going to David Holbrook's body, which were filled with this fake blood. And it took so long to light it for whatever reason, I'm sure they were good reasons, but by the time they got around to shooting it they called, 'Action!', my arrow stuff all worked okay because it's simple, but the blood things were all stuck in the tubes because there's a lot of sugar in it, so no blood came out. So, that's why they moved it all to Bangor."

One of the tell-tale signs that the footage was shot later is the placement of Fatso's hat, which inside the trailer is slightly cocked to the side on his head. The rest of the film it sits squarely on his head for every scene. It's a very minor continuity error, but it's definitely noticeable. And it's something which conceivably could have easily been missed five weeks later, which apparently was the case here. Now, there's always the chance that some of the footage in the final print was from this day, but it's impossible to know for certain because it's unknown how much of the scene, if any, was completed before they gave up and decided to finish it in Maine. We'll dive further into the filming of this scene in Bangor in the mid November section.

Also of note for this day was a makeup test for Holt McCallany, with lead hair & makeup artist Joanna Robinson, followed by a photo session for the young actor with still photographer Stan Obcamp-Fikel.

With McCallany and co-star Don Harvey arriving just the day before, the pair was beginning to adapt to their new environment in Arizona. "By the time we got there we checked into our hotel and then we immediately went...I probably went up to Holt's room and just started watching baseball with the Mets playing the Houston Astros, I think, in the '86 NLCS (National League Championship Series)," Harvey fondly recalls. "And then we met 'Fatstuff', David Holbrook, and all the sudden me and Holt and David Holbrook, we were like inseparable for the next two weeks. It was just hilarious; we stayed up all night playing cards every night, gambling our per diem and watching baseball and just getting really wasted. So, it's like by the time we got on the set I think we were kind of like, I don't know, we were a force of nature (laughs). I think Michael (Gornick) really appreciated that."

Monday, October 13, 1986 – Day 25

The twenty-fifth day, while rain free, wouldn't be able to escape the effects of the weather, unfortunately. After substantial rainfall blanketed the area over the weekend the dirt and landscape at the Iron King Mine, aka the town of Dead River, was just a little too muddy to shoot.

Originally several outside scenes from *Old Chief Wood'nhead* were on the schedule for today: scene 10 of Ray Spruce touching up Chief Wood'nhead's war paint as his wife Martha Spruce comes outside with a glass of lemonade / scene 12 of Ray and Martha sitting on the porch as Martha lectures Ray about his charity and kindness to the townsfolk / scene 14 of Benjamin Whitemoon arriving at the store and greeting the Spruces / and scene 16 of Benjamin Whitemoon departing the store and saluting Chief Wood'nhead before driving off. All of these scenes would find themselves back on the schedule over the next several days.

With the store exterior location at the Iron King Mine in Dewey-Humboldt out of the picture for the day the production would shift about a mile or so down the road to the store interior location on Main Street in Humboldt. Here they would work on scene 15, which would entail Benjamin Whitemoon's discussion inside the store with Ray Spruce about leaving his tribe's treasures as collateral for their debt.

With filming on *The Raft* encountering numerous delays it had afforded Bruce Miller's art department additional time to prep the interior general store set. Their work was simply astonishing, as you were hard pressed to believe this wasn't a real, authentic, old time general store. In fact it was so impressive that Tom Hurwitz took notice of a little set dressing work that was of personal and sentimental value to him and his wife. "As we were lighting the store set for the wooden Indian segment, I was browsing about the cashier's counter while some lights were adjusted," he recalls. "I noticed a bunch of old postcards, bought by the prop department at some junk store, and pinned to the counter as if they were souvenirs sent by family and friends from all over — and sprayed down with diluted paint as if they were covered in dust. There among them was a postcard from the Sandy Shores Motel on North Collins Avenue in Miami Beach. When I was shooting the feature *Hard Choices* the crew stayed at the Sandy Shores Motel. It had been very romantic because by that time Margaret (Klenck), the star of the film, and I were together."

"Yeah, it was an actual location and we dressed it up to make into like a hardware store and general store, sort of thing, as you would have in those old forgotten days out west, as it were," says David Ball. "They did really well with that, Bruce and his team. It looked very good, I thought."

One of the people from Miller's art department unit who really helped to bring that general store to life was set decorator Andrew Bernard. And what made his effort even more impressive was the fact that he was a rookie, one determined to take full advantage of the opportunity given to him by Miller. "I can tell you that *Creepshow 2* was the first set decorating job I ever got and I definitely was very humbled and grateful that Bruce Miller gave me the job. Because I had credits, a few credits, mostly as production assistant and as set dresser and I had never even interviewed for a set decorating job until *Creepshow 2*," Bernard recalls. "I worked on *9 ½ Weeks*, I worked on *Wise Guys*, I worked on a few bigger film productions as the production assistant in the art department, which is a great way to sort of move up in the business. And I think one of the art directors had given my name to Bruce as a possibility. So, anyway, when I went to the interview… you know, I didn't even know what to bring with me other than my resume, I didn't have a portfolio or anything. So, I remember bringing like some of my black and white conceptual art photos to the meeting. And looking back on it, I was like thinking, 'Wow, if somebody had brought those in, if I was hiring a set decorator and they came in with their portfolio of conceptual black and white art photography photos…', which some of my photos were way out there (laughs). And he still hired me! So, he must have seen something in me that he liked."

Tackling a job like this one for Bernard would require plenty of extra help, people who wouldn't just be gofers, mind you, but people who knew how to quickly find what was needed and appropriate. "And what I did was I hired a lot of local people from around the Prescott area – some people had never worked on films before. And after doing my research on the general store of a small sort of western town…and remember it wasn't period. We weren't talking about a western general store from the turn of the century. But, you know, you wanted to have that flavor of being a general store from the turn of the century with the modern flourishes of the time period," he explains. "Rather than bringing people in from Los Angeles or film people from New York or close by, I hired people from town. My lead man, his name was Nigel Clinker and he looked like Rod Stewart and everybody always posed with him to take pictures. And he had worked on a couple of films, so he was my lead man. The assistant to him was this guy Tal Schneider who was a drummer, a heavy metal drummer, who had never worked on films before. And he was just a genius at going out…like, you could tell him to go out and find something and he would just go out and find it in town. And we just went into town and we made friends with antique stores and people. And *Creepshow 2* didn't have such a big budget so we would just beg, borrow, and steal everywhere and just try to make deals: 'Look, we'll rent your tools'…'If you just lend us your can food for a day.' So, we just went everywhere. And it was just a great area to pull for all the sort of flavors of trying to make that sort of exaggerated general store that the George Kennedy and Dorothy Lamour characters would have had in this depressed sort of one-horse town."

With ample time, Bernard's assistants would hit countless businesses like Skull Valley General Store, Allen's Nu-Way Market, Chapman's Trading Post, Granite Dells Rock Shop, Arizona General Hardware, Whiskey Row Emporium, countless antique shops, and even private collectors to breathe life into Spruce's General Store. Whether it was a Williams *Aztec* pinball machine or a Sonic *Super Straight* pinball machine, an antique cash register, a gumball machine, a horoscope & weight machine, a photo booth machine, rakes, brooms, tools, fabric, bags of grain, canned foods, snacks, drinks, sombreros, you name it –

nothing was overlooked. "It did look real, I have to admit," says Bruce Miller. "It looked very real."

"I remember spending a couple of days replacing labels on Butterfinger bars and things like that so that we didn't have trademark issues," recalls Dex Craig. "And I also remember suggesting to Jim Feng (prop master) that we get the original *Creepshow* comic book cover from the first movie to put in a magazine rack because someone in the set dressing department had found a magazine rack to go into the general store. So, he was like, 'Well, what do we put in here?' And so it seemed obvious to me to put the *Creepshow* comic in there. And I remember Jim saying, 'Oh, that's a great idea!' And then I didn't hear anything about it until maybe a week later, a shipment came in from Laurel, out east somewhere, with a few or maybe ten or fifteen printed copies of the comic book, so we put it in there."

As for the exterior of the general store, we'll cover its creation and the attention to detail it received in tomorrow's section.

This day would also see the "return of the blob" as second unit work at Granite Basin Lake was scheduled as well; in fact the next two days would feature second unit work on the call sheets.

Tuesday, October 14, 1986 – Day 26

Day twenty-six would start off at the general store interior location on Main Street by completing work on scene 15. In case of continued issues with mud at the Iron King Mine partial work on scene 19 was also scheduled of the gang ambushing Ray and Martha Spruce in their store. Scene 19 is easily the longest in the script covering nearly nine pages, but any work related to it most likely wouldn't start until Saturday the 18th.

From here the production would move about a mile down the road to the exterior location of the Spruce's General Store, as well as Curly's Service Station, to start work on scenes 10, 12, 14, and 16.

The town of Dead River would come to life, so to speak, on the grounds of the old Iron King Mine in Dewey-Humboldt. Bruce Miller, along with Ed Fountain, would have to make the most out of very little, but they would do so in typical Laurel Entertainment ingenuity, much to the relief of Michael Gornick. "I mean, there wasn't much in the way of a town, per se. I mean, what we wound up using was a few rudimentary buildings that were pretty much stuck in the high desert," he recalls. "And so at some point I thought, in conjunction with Bruce Miller, I asked, 'Could we use this site and develop it?'; because in terms of a vista, and a background beyond the set, it was perfect."

"We built the store. We found this little mining encampment outside of Prescott that had some buildings in it," says Bruce Miller. "There were a couple of buildings that were on a little dirt road. So, we built the store and we built the gas station across the street."

Erecting the facades for the store and the service station would initially prove to be tough due to the fact

that the ground at the Iron King Mine was basically granite and rock. And without the budget to rent heavy machinery to dig into the ground head carpenters Gary Kosko and Logan Berkshire had to think of a plausible alternative to solve the problem. "They couldn't get the ground to hold anything up so Gary had come up with using fifty gallon drums and then filling them with water and banding things to them. And that's how we held all the facades up," Berkshire explains. "I mean, it's all rock there and we were like, 'Oh my god.' And we thought and thought and then Gary said, 'Well, you know, a drum is like 400 pounds' (filled with water), we're like, 'Ah hah!' So, we got banding and we did that and it worked."

From there people such as head scenic artist Eileen Garrigan would take over and begin adding that weathered, worn down look. "That was a big job and I do have pretty keen memories of all of that," she remembers. "It was a big adventure to be in Arizona and it was a big job in terms of what I had done so far. Everything was built from scratch; it was just a completely empty desert, no vegetation or anything when I got there. And they just started cranking up these building fronts and sculpting the roads and the passage ways and how the different buildings would be connected to make it look like the roads were worn to those areas. They put up all the raw wood – we kind of pre-painted some of the wood as they put it up and then other buildings just went up raw – and then we started working on ladders and scaffolding and getting it all painted and aged."

Above: Some days required only the upper portion of Wood'nhead for filming, allowing the performer Dan Kamin to dress a little more casual, you might say. (courtesy of Bruce Miller and Garry Greer)

The set dressing team would continue their fantastic work by populating the exterior of the general store with details such as a horse post and water trough, a vintage Pepsi ice chest with soda pop bottle crates, and old-timey wooden benches. The gas station would receive just as much care as once again you'd be hard pressed to believe that what you were looking at wasn't a real, authentic service station. A pair of old gas pumps rented from Jeff's Automotive and a Texaco sign from Elbo's Antiques, along with old license plates, hubcaps, tires, and oil barrels helped to bring the illusion to life – even if it was only glimpsed ever so briefly on screen.

While the store and gas station were just facades, along with a bank which is not even seen in the film, some of the existing buildings at the mine would be converted into other businesses for the fictional town such as the Dead River Bar and Feng's Laundry, a humorous nod to propmaster Jim Feng.

Also of note for the day was the fact that second unit work was still going on. However, I'm not sure if it was for *The Raft* or for some shots meant to be used for *Old Chief Wood'nhead*. The reason I say this is because it doesn't specify on the call sheet where the second unit work was being conducted. But Wolf Forrest, a freelance writer from

Cinefantastique, mentioned that he was present when the second unit was working in Sedona, which is roughly about an hour northeast of Prescott. "No actors, just background shots of the beautiful rust-red hills," he says. "I can't recall if this footage actually made it past the editing and into the finished film."

Unfortunately no such footage made it into the completed film, which is a shame. Sedona features incredibly breathtaking vistas and eye-popping scenery which would have added some wonderful texture to the landscape surrounding Dead River. Or perhaps this would have been footage meant to lead up to the Camaro driving through the mountains at the beginning of *The Raft*? I wish I could tell you.

Wednesday, October 15, 1986 – Day 27

The twenty-seventh day would continue work at the general store exterior location at the Iron King Mine with some familiar scenes on tap: 10, 12, 14, and 16.

Before we delve into the creation of our title character, Chief Wood'nhead, perhaps we should briefly touch on the history of cigar store Indians. Illiteracy was a major issue centuries ago so symbols were used as a way to advertise businesses to citizens: a red, white, and blue pole meant a barber, while three gold balls represented a pawn shop, and so on. The use of carved wooden Indian statues to advertise tobacco dates all the way back to England during the 1600's when ships returning from America would come back carrying tobacco, retrieved from Native Americans. Many of the artisans who would carve the wooden Indian statues of the time were experienced in shipbuilding where they had carved figureheads for numerous vessels.

By the mid 1800's, cigar store Indians exploded in popularity after the ship industry changed from wooden ships to iron, freeing up many of the artisans to showcase their skills for retail businesses instead; this was when the statues began popping up on the streets of America. During this time the statues would receive nicknames from local townsfolk, giving the piece of art a personality, so to speak. Names such as "Old Eagle Eye" in Reading, Pennsylvania and "Chief Semloh" in San Francisco, California are a couple of well-known examples. But by the early 1900's the popularity of the Indian statues began to fade as new laws were passed requiring two feet of open space in front of each business, thus limiting room for them; plus more people had learned how to read by this point. The vast majority of the statues were sadly thrown out. Today, authentic wooden cigar store Indians are extremely valuable and considered museum worthy.

Regarding the creation of our title character Michael Gornick recalls Ed French dedicating himself to the task of creating as authentic a character as possible. "Ed

Left: Mike Trcic(sporting a red *Day of the Dead* crew t-shirt) and Howard Berger flank the amazing statue version of Chief Wood'nhead. (courtesy of Michael Gornick) **Right:** Aging the prop statue of Chief Wood'nhead: head scenic Eileen Garrigan begins the process of weathering him, while painter Joel Griffith applies some finishing touches on set. (courtesy of Eileen Garrigan)

was so wonderfully studious about his work in terms of organizing his thoughts by doing research work, graphic research work. And long before we got to even a final rendering of the cigar store Indian he provided me with research materials," Gornick says. "He would spend hours and hours at the New York City Public Library researching looks and went into great detail about the history of the cigar store Indian and its carving techniques and so forth."

During my research for this project I came across a couple of black and white Xeroxed reference book pages in Gornick's production files of cigar store Indians, showcasing different examples of sculptures. Someone, I don't know who, made notations on the pages taking different characteristics from various statues. The face and headdress would come from one example, while the tomahawk and knife would come from another. In the notes the name "Gary" is referenced, so I can only assume they mean Gary Hartle who would create the majority of the story-board art for the film.

Now, our title character from the tale of *Old Chief Wood'nhead* would be both a performer in a suit, Dan Kamin, and a prop statue, both of which were created by the special makeup effects team. Most of the shots contained in scenes 10, 12, 14, 16, as well as 18, which we'll eventually get to, are of the statue – only a total of five shots during these scenes feature Kamin in his suit. "We knew that we had to create two things for Chief Wood'nhead," said Howard Berger to Anchor Bay. "We needed to create a full statue of him that would be used as a prop and then we had to produce a suit. But we could only do one sculpture." **(21)**

The process for creating Chief Wood'nhead began in New York at Ed French's Brooklyn studio/loft. Dan Kamin came in and his body was cast producing a fiber glass positive mold. "And the casting process was fairly grueling because they essentially packed plaster around me and they had me standing up, which they shouldn't have done, it was a mistake. And when it hardened it added something like forty pounds to my body and I had to stand there while it dried. And there was no reason for me to be standing up during that and I actually had some physical problems because of it," recalls Kamin about the ordeal. "The face casting was done in the usual way where I was lying down and they essentially poured a liquid/gel kind of thing over your face and you're breathing through holes, through straws in your nose, and that was like a living burial experience. And I had been through that before, so I was sort of ready for that."

Following the casting process Ed French and Mike Trcic would tackle the job of sculpting the Indian, with French handling the head and Trcic the body. "I spent about a month and a half with my makeup lab assistants working in my Brooklyn loft sculpting, molding and fabricating many of the prosthetics, the *Old Chief Wood'nhead* character costume (my favorite effect), as

Above: The beautiful Pontiac Fleetleader, loaned to the production by a local elderly lady, sits in front of the general store facade. (courtesy of Eileen Garrigan) **Below:** Frank Salsedo, production assistant Bud Paine, Tyrone Tanto, and Maltbie Napoleon take a break during filming at the Dead River location, which once was the Iron King Mine. (courtesy of Rebecca Mayo)

well as blood rigs and mechanical effects," French wrote in his prepared statement.

As for the detail contained in Trcic's body work for Wood'nhead it impressed his colleagues thoroughly – Howard Berger has referred to it as "beautiful". And it made an enormous impression on Matt Marich (whose participation in this book project was a godsend for information regarding some of the makeup effects) when he studied it up close as well. "I remember just being marveled at the way he sculpted the wood grain. I mean, it looked like wood," Marich says. "In this instance it's an example of seeing something in person that is far better than it ever is on film; that's how good."

From there, perhaps simply due to a time crunch, the effects team would turn to an outside vendor to assist with some of the work needed for the suit. "Then we found these two Italian guys, artisans from the old country," Howard Berger explained to Anchor Bay. "And they produced fiber glass molds of all this stuff – feet, hands, everything. Everything we needed." **(22)**

And if Dan Kamin thought enduring the procedure to create the suit was demanding he was in store for a double whammy when it came to wearing it. "The suit provided challenges too because, essentially, I was glued into the suit; it had a front and back section," Kamin explains. "And the first day on the set I was put into the suit and I was in it for about 15 hours and they didn't end up shooting actually with me, but I was just kind of kept on a stand-by basis. And when they pulled the suit off, the arms had been glued along the inner arm, the inside of my arm, and whether it was because of the seam, I had huge blisters that were like an inch high running all up and down my arm (laughs). And we had a quick trip to the emergency room and I was not made to sit in the suit for 15 hours after that. So, I think, we were all young at the time and I think there were some mistakes made just because people weren't as experienced as one might hope."

"Dan Kamin, who played the wooden Indian, he was a mime and a wonderfully nice guy," says Matt Marich. "We would glue...basically put on the foam latex arms, which by the way were cast in GI-1000 silicone molds. And everybody said, 'You can't cast foam latex in silicone, there's no way; that's not gonna happen.' From my understanding we were one of the first people to do that, or they (Berger, Trcic, Nicotero, and Burrell) were. And they came out great and they popped right out of there. So, anyway, we would glue these arms on him and they would come up to about mid bicep and we were using the old 355 adhesive. And then he would put on the suit, which was slit up the back, and that overlapped where they were glued. Well, what we didn't know, the first couple of days that was rubbing and rubbing and rubbing. So, one night when we were helping to remove the arms we're looking at this jelly – this is kind of disgusting, I'll just warn you – he had blistered all the way around his arm, because he had such soft skin. The rubbing had created literally blisters like you would get on a foot with a bad pair of shoes. I don't remember what the solution was, but I think we ended up having to put bandages or something around it, I don't remember. And not glue them; just let them go at that point."

"The suit was also a challenge because it was essentially

like getting into a giant condom – it was a sealed rubber thing," continues Kamin on his Indian disguise. "The eyes were mechanical; I could not control the movement of the mouth and the eyes because it was like wearing a helmet and there were motors in them. So, I couldn't see out of the eyes. I'm not sure if I could see anything or just a blur; and I couldn't hear. So, to breath they ran an air tube from an aqua lung in. So, effectively I was blind and deaf – I couldn't see and I couldn't hear. Michael Gornick, there was a microphone strung into it, in my ear, so I could hear him talking to me. But I was effectively blind and deaf standing on a tree trunk that was about two feet high, which was sitting on the edge of a porch which was about two feet high. So, I was four feet off the ground, blind and deaf."

"Dan, who was in the suit, was really, really great. He was a mime and he knew how to emote out of the suit," Howard Berger said to Anchor Bay. "When you're wearing suits you have to overcompensate for your movements because it's almost like half the movement outside the costume. And he did a really great job being this wooden Indian." **(23)**

As for the suit itself and what it was made of? Well, let's allow Matt Marich to explain some of the more technical details of that subject. "The arms on the wooden Indian were foam latex, and the head. The entire body was Polyfoam and SC 89, which is a BJB product; it's a urethane that you can make paint out of. So, we would spray that in the molds – and it forms a skin – and then put in the Polyfoam," he says. "Now, the first three suits we made all collapsed and we couldn't figure out why. And what it was, we were using BJB SC 89 and we were using Polytek? Can't remember the name of the company at the time, but we were using their Polyfoam and they weren't compatible. So, it was causing the Polyfoam to collapse. And I remember I was getting really discouraged

and Howard and Greg came in that night from the set and Howard saw that. And they're just such wonderful guys, Howard walks up to me and he goes, 'What's wrong?', and I said, 'I just want it to work', I remember saying, 'I just want this to work for you guys.' And he goes, 'Don't worry about it. We're going to find out what's going wrong with it. Don't worry about it.' So, we finally figured out that issue and started making them. I think we had two suits, but we had to keep foam latex arms and one for the mechanical head also. So, we ran several of those."

And what's really fascinating, and also evidence of the resourcefulness of the young makeup effects crew, was the makeshift oven they used to bake the prosthetic appliances used for the film. "The oven was, oh, approximately four feet by three feet by three feet and it was, of course, a wooden box that just used a space heater in it," Marich says. "Yeah, that's all it was, a fan forced space heater."

So, with the suit now covered, that finally brings us to the amazing prop statue. "Then we had to produce the prop piece. Mike (Trcic) and I laid it in liquid latex and burlap; that was the skin. Then we blew foam into it and then armature wire so we could position the statue and all that stuff," Howard Berger explained to Anchor Bay. "The statue was painted with acrylic paints. Mike hand painted it because we wanted to get that very worn distressed look." **(24)**

And finally, with the "distressing" of the statue the makeup effects guys would receive an assist from head

Above: Director of photography Tom Hurwitz would leave once filming in Arizona was complete, citing a general unpleasantness around the production. (courtesy of Wolf Forrest and Angela Nogaro)

scenic Eileen Garrigan, whose specialty was just that. "Yeah, we got to work on the statue, or I did," she says. "They sculpted it, you know, they get total credit for the creation. And when it came to me it was already in its color, so I think what they did was colored their latex, the rubber latex, and put it into kind of primary colors. So, he was a brightly colored Indian when he came to me. And I have a good picture of me working on him outside in front of the steps getting him to look aged, to make him blend in with the environment. So, I did the aging on top of all that. It was beautifully textured, you know, all the feathers and his skin, and so what I was putting on laid into the texture of what they created and so then I blended it around to make it look aged and dusty."

Speaking of distressing, it wasn't just Chief Wood'nhead whose character required work. Eileen Sieff-Stroup would labor just as hard to provide George Kennedy's wardrobe – which wasn't easy acquiring to begin with – that authentic, worn look. "You know, when you go buy stuff, you'll go and buy things, and you'll get a size range and return what doesn't work. There was not very much slush. And we had situations like George Kennedy...he is huge! You don't find overalls easily for someone like that. So, I had to order them from some place. And then when they came in they were like standup, dark blue, brand new starched overalls that had to really be worked. I mean, that was lot of work to get his clothes into that condition," she says. "I think I had them stone washed to start and then I sanded them and over dyed them."

Above: First assistant cameraman Eric Swanek(striped shirt), seen here with second A.C. Todd Liebler, decided to follow his D.P., Tom Hurwitz, when he decided to leave the production. (courtesy of Garry Greer)

Above: Location manager Michael Morgan takes a break with good friend Garry Greer(right), who served as the craft services P.A. on the film. (courtesy of Garry Greer)

"She was sandpapering them and one day she goes, 'Yeah, help me sandpaper these things, I gotta make them look rundown.' I said, 'Why don't we just tie them up and drag them behind my car or something,'" laughs Billy Kosco. "I think we did that, too; just anything to make them look like they were worn out and stuff."

Other work scheduled on the day's ledger included scenes 11, 13, 17, and 18. These are fairly brief and would entail shots of Benjamin Whitemoon having his green early 1950's Pontiac Fleetleader serviced at Curly's and then pulling up to the general store as the car spews steam from the engine / that same Pontiac backing up and driving off from the store / Ray promising Wood'nhead he'll finish his paint touch-up the next day / and finally Ray and Martha heading back inside the store.

The mentioning of the Pontiac Fleetleader, originally scripted as a Studebaker by George Romero, brings us back to Bruce Miller's assistant, Steve Arnold, who was in charge of locating most of the vehicles – other than the Mercedes from *The Hitchhiker* – seen in the film. "My grandfather had one of these and it had the Pontiac Indian Head hood ornament on it which I thought was appropriate for the story," he says. "It was owned by a little old local lady who did not know me from Adam and I remember sitting in her living room explaining how I would pay her $50 to borrow it on the day we needed it – and her going

along with it completely. On the day I went to her house I gave her the money and drove away with her car – she was a trusting soul."

That trusting soul's generosity is something that made quite an impression on Michael Gornick, who just like Steve Arnold, had a sentimental attachment to that particular car. "You know, unfortunately I never met her directly I only heard through others about how charming she was and how sweet," he explains. "She provided the Pontiac that was used in that particular episode, *Old Chief Wood'nhead*, and I fell in love with it only because it was like instant recall of my youth, when I was growing up. My family never had an automobile when I was growing up until much later in life when my sister finally learned to drive at age 17, so we were without an automobile. And we would often be transported – we went on distant travels – we would be transported by a friend or neighbor and one of our neighbor friends had a Pontiac, which I idolized."

When filming with the car was completed it was returned to the owner who learned of Gornick's affection for the car. And it was then that she made an even more heart-warming gesture. "She offered to give it to me. Amazing, I know. And to this day I wished I could have found some way to transport it back," Gornick fondly recalls. "And I wish that I'd had the time, if nothing else, even though I couldn't take the car, I was touched by her offer, I would have loved to have stopped by and say, 'Thank you so much for the

Above: Producer David Ball huddles up with 1st A.D. Kato Wittich during the filming of *Old Chief Wood'nhead*. (courtesy of Rebecca Mayo)

car, it meant so much to me and it was an inspiration on set. Thank you,' you know. But as always with film shoots there's time for little else and we were moving on to Bangor, Maine swiftly after that, after shooting in Arizona."

Today would also be the final one for second unit work at Granite Basin Lake. A visitor to the set during this time was the previously mentioned Wolf Forrest who was in town to write a piece for *Cinefantastique* magazine, a topic we'll delve deeper into once we reach Chapter 5. Forrest was able to witness some of the second unit filming during these bonus days at the lake and recalls just how difficult it was for the crew to work with the "Thing", which the blob was known as during early shooting schedules. "I remember how much trouble the crew had getting that weird pancake monster to move properly at Granite Basin Lake – despite the lack of wind that day, the divers who operated the thing from underneath were struggling to keep it from sinking," recalls Forrest. "It was supposed to rotate slowly, menacingly, and I think that's why the shots of it are very short cut-aways as you see in the finished film."

Once the second unit crew was completed with their work at the lake the plan was for them to make their way to the Iron King Mine for planned work on scenes 20 and 22. These scenes would encompass the gang of thugs leaving the store and shooting up the store front, plus Wood'nhead coming to life and adding his war paint before unleashing his war cry. Both scenes would also find their way on to the following day's call sheet, so how much work, if any, was completed on this day is unknown.

One final bit of housekeeping before we close out the day involves the ongoing search for an actress to portray Annie Lansing for *The Hitchhiker*. David Ball would draft a memo to be sent to New World's Jeff Schechtman regarding the options Laurel was currently looking at. At this point Ball was approaching Barbara Eden, from *I Dream of Jeannie* and *Harper Valley P.T.A.* fame, for the role – but as a contingency he listed Anita Morris, Catherine Bach, and Morgan Brittany as potential options should Eden decline their offer of $75,000.

One final name I should mention from Ball's list was Sheree North, who had officially expressed interest in playing the role. Make note and remember that name. "I will 'sign up' the first one of these that we can reach terms with and I will hope that this final principal casting matter will be over within a week," wrote Ball, before signing off with a polite, "Thank you". **(25)**

Thursday, October 16, 1986 – Day 28

Day twenty-eight would again cover familiar territory with work at the Iron King Mine on scenes 10, 14, 16, and 18. Again, how much was done isn't precisely known because next to a lot of the scenes are notations such as "complete if necessary", which was quite common. Perhaps work was wrapped up the day before on some

of these scenes, who knows? However, one shot most likely completed on this day was the opening crane shot of the segment, from scene 10, the one which transitions from animation to George Kennedy in front of his general store as the pickup truck drives by. The truck was driven by William "Bud" Paine, listed as a production assistant in the credits, but according to the crew list Paine was the on-set medic, as well. Paine also could be our mystery P.A. who encountered the rattlesnake while filming *The Raft*, but I digress. And the 1950 dark blue Chevy pickup truck that also passes by as Dorothy Lamour laments about Dead River was driven by Garry Greer from craft services, which was his own personal vehicle.

Speaking of scene 10, in Michael Gornick's shot list log the sequence is broken down into eleven separate shots and for one of those shots Gornick would receive a welcomed assist from his lead actor, George Kennedy, by way of the classic folk song *Jimmy Crack Corn*, which Kennedy's character sings to his beloved wooden Indian. "That's George Kennedy, absolutely. That was his original thought," says Gornick. "It's one of those things that if you honestly work with an actor and don't make them self-conscious about things they need, you know, be it hand props, be it some other method to get through their performance, that it becomes such a contribution if you just give them that freedom to speak about it."

A new scene would make its debut on the call sheets with number 36L which is Frank Salsedo's character, Benjamin Whitemoon, pulling up to the general store and finding the bloody scalp of his nephew, Sam Whitemoon, dangling from the hand of Chief Wood'nhead. It would also appear

on the following day's call sheet so again I'm not sure how much, if any, was accomplished with it. As for the actor in the scene, Frank Salsedo, despite his serious demeanor on screen, members from the production remember a jovial and fun spirited man away from the set. "A good sense of humor; liked to party, liked the women," laughs Rebecca Mayo. "Good time Charlie, you know, wanted to have a good time while he was there filming. He was smiling every time I saw him. He was very polite to me, very good. But he always wondered why I didn't go to party with them afterwards. They would go to a lot of after-hours parties that they would have either in their rooms or downtown somewhere. I never went to those. And so he kept inviting me, 'Please come. Please come. I really want you to come.' But I never did."

"Just a really nice guy, you know, and an authentic Native American actor who had been around Hollywood for decades and had worked with everybody. And who might have been expected, I don't know, to be a little bit perplexed as to why this white guy was playing his nephew," says co-star Holt McCallany. "But he was very gracious about it and we had a very cordial relationship. And I remember that he liked to play cards. So, we would play kind of quarter/dollar poker together sometimes at night after we'd wrapped with Don (Harvey) and some of the guys. I liked Frank very much."

Others who were around Salsedo though remembered

Above: Director Michael Gornick works with star George Kennedy on a scene as D.P. Tom Hurwitz(left) looks on. (courtesy of Rebecca Mayo)

a more focused individual while on set. "You know, we didn't talk much," laughs Maltbie Napoleon, who played Salsedo's chauffeur in the film, "Indian 1". "There was me and another fellow that was also in the car. And he didn't really talk to us; he was kind of focused on what he was shooting. And I didn't feel like I wanted to disrupt that, so I never really said anything. We saw each other on the set and just before they started shooting, we both kind of said hello to each other and that was about it."

Napoleon's comment about Salsedo concentrating while preparing to shoot was of interest and made a lot of sense after hearing remarks from Michael Gornick, who found working with Salsedo to be a bit of a chore in terms of performance execution. "(He was) classically untrained as an actor, so probably my most difficult direction. Whether he was unfamiliar or maybe inexperienced or un-attentive to his craft he had to be coached a lot in terms of the moment where his attention needed to be in terms of performance against somebody else," says Gornick. "But in the final analysis he did deliver and was always very cooperative, always very, very kind – and took criticism very well. But in terms of a performance it was one that I had to struggle with so that it emerged on film."

As Rebecca Mayo touched on just a minute ago, getting together and socializing is usually a favorite past time of film crews. Putting in long hours, typically 12 or more, usually leads to a desire to blow off some steam, have a good time, enjoy a couple of drinks, and share a few laughs. And *Creepshow 2* would be no different. What would be different though – and remember the film's own production designer accused it of being cursed – was that

on this production getting together to socialize could very well cost you your life.

One evening in Prescott a gaggle of crew members were enjoying themselves at dinner when soundman Felipe Borrero, who was known to be a prankster, began having some trouble. "We're at a steakhouse, there's a whole row of people eating steak," remembers Eileen Sieff-Stroup. "He chokes, he's choking. And everybody's laughing; they think he's fooling around."

"Well, the problem is because Felipe was *always* joking," says Joanna Robinson. "You know, we thought he was just joking because he was always doing that."

Well, this time Borrero wasn't joking. In college he believes he damaged his esophagus, actually stretching it, while working as a paste up artist. During that work he had a habit of pressing his nose up against the glass and breathing in fumes from the formula – one he had altered to speed up his output – through his mouth causing the issue with his esophagus. "So, what happened was I didn't have the muscles that push the food down, so any little thing – a mushroom piece, a piece of steak – I would choke," Borrero explains. "And it was on that film that I discovered that I had that problem."

So, now he's experiencing the problem, but what can he do? Everyone thinks he's playing around – everyone except Angela Nogaro that is. "No one caught it! He was foaming at the mouth and everyone thought that he was kidding around," she says. "I saw the look of *terror* in his

Above: Stars Dorothy Lamour and George Kennedy were very popular with the *Creepshow 2* crew, who were honored to be working with such Hollywood royalty. (courtesy of Michael Felsher and Rebecca Mayo)

eyes. I jumped up and ran around the table and gave him the Heimlich maneuver."

"So, she jumped up and just grabbed me, because she's a powerful girl, and popped it out. And if it wasn't for that, that would have been the end of my story," says Borrero. "'Oh, I remember Felipe! He died on *Creepshow 2*, didn't he?' Well, she saved my life." Borrero has since, within the last decade actually, had a procedure to correct this issue.

Finally, work on scene 20, which would finish up the following day, and 22 was once again scheduled.

Scene 22, where Chief Wood'nhead finally comes to life and smears war-paint on his face, is one of my personal favorites from the entire film. Everything about it is so well executed: from Dan Kamin's performance (notice how his abdomen breaths in and out as the camera pans up), to Mike Trcic's amazing sculpture work on Wood'nhead himself, to Michael Gornick's shot design, to Les Reed's pitch perfect score. It's just a wonderful scene. But for the man who played the character there's one aspect of the shot that still bugs him to this day. "The only shot I actually regret in the movie though is – I couldn't tell it was happening because my hands, my fingers, it was like wearing a pair of mittens – I had to scoop the paint up and smear it on my cheek. And I could not tell that the fingers were actually bending backwards, so it's very evident that they're soft foam. I wish that somebody had let me know that and re-shot it," says Kamin. "But, the overall effect, once I'm up and moving around, of course, those things are irrelevant because the issue becomes, you know, you're imagining what a golem, essentially a wooden creature, would be like if it was animated. Obviously, it's gonna be a little stiff (laughs)."

Other notes of interest for this day included a full-page article about the production running in Prescott's local newspaper, *The Courier*, in the Yavapai County section of the paper, with writer Robert C. Holquist apparently having visited the set the same day as *Cinefantastique* writer Wolf Forrest. The article features quotes from David Ball detailing the production's progress along with a couple of great behind-the-scenes photographs.

Also, following up on the heels of David Ball's memo from the day before, Richard Rubinstein would draft his own memo, this time for New World's Steve White, stressing the importance of wrapping up the Annie Lansing casting situation. He informed New World that Laurel Entertainment was waiting to hear back from Barbara Eden regarding their offer and anticipated a response by Friday, October 17. In case that offer would be rejected, he requested New World immediately name their preference from the list of actresses sent the prior day by Ball, this time including Loretta Swit in the mix. "I would also point out that I feel the strongest foreign value name is Loretta Swit as a result of her role in *M*A*S*H*," wrote Rubinstein. "It's not a strong foreign name but I suspect by degree it's better than the others. I look forward to our meeting personally under less pressured circumstances." **(26)**

Wheels were beginning to turn concerning the production's big move to Bangor, Maine as well. Charles Carroll and Debra Tanklow sent out memos to department heads and crew with pertinent information regarding the moving truck and flight and baggage information. We'll delve a little deeper into this subject once the actual move takes place the following week.

And as the production was prepping in Prescott, Arizona for the move back east, Maine location manager Henry Nevison was in Bangor continuing to get things ready there. More location contracts were being addressed with businesses along Main Street in Dexter, Maine for the opening shot of the film, including Reny's department store, where the Creep pulls up in his delivery truck, a popular Maine business still in the same spot today as it was in 1986.

Friday, October 17, 1986 – Day 29

The twenty-ninth day of production would be the first one to see a PM call time – the previous days had all morning starts, anywhere from 5:30AM to 10AM – and tomorrow would follow suit with an even later PM call time. Afternoon

Above: Dorothy Lamour takes a smoke break at the Iron King Mine; Lamour, who wasn't happy getting her picture taken sans makeup, heads to the interior location for the general store on Humboldt's Main Street, with director Michael Gornick not far behind. (courtesy of Eileen Garrigan and Garry Greer)

and evening call times, however, would become the norm once filming began in Maine.

The day would begin around 1PM with Tom Hurwitz and the electric crew pre-lighting the interior of the general store location for filming of scene 19 which, beginning tomorrow, would occupy the vast majority of the next four days of filming. The plan called for Hurwitz to depart from there by 2PM, leaving the crew to continue pre-lighting, and head back to the Iron King Mine for scheduled work outside the general store.

As mentioned before Hurwitz's time on the production was rapidly drawing to a close, which was just fine by him. "I've been on lots of films with a lot of financial pressure and the sets have still been extraordinarily pleasant places to work; even if we were under the time gun or under a lot of push, you're still working and friendly. And this was absolutely not that way; this was people making paper trails on each other," he says. "I had other work, I was a busy guy. I really didn't need to follow this very unpleasant working situation to Maine."

Hurwitz wouldn't be alone though as his first assistant cameraman would follow his lead. "When the D.P. said he wasn't gonna go up to Maine, I was like, 'Yeah, I've been working with this guy awhile,'" says Eric Swanek. "But also the way the production is being run, you're gonna go up to Maine, it's winter time at night in November, it's gonna be cold there and if this A.D. is pushing like this, what's it

gonna be in a situation where we have cars driving on the road at night where there could be icy conditions and all the rest of that?"

At the general store exterior work began by finishing up scene 36L, the final one of the segment, of Benjamin Whitemoon pulling up to the store and finding the bloody scalp of Sam Whitemoon held by Chief Wood'nhead. Of particular interest with this scene is the dialogue from Frank Salsedo because in Romero's screenplay Benjamin Whitemoon gets out of his vehicle and says, "Adigash, Adigash", which is Navajo for Witchcraft. However – and more than likely suggested by Salsedo – Whitemoon instead says his goodbye to Chief Wood'nhead like this, "Now, may your spirit rest, old warrior. Hágoónee'. Hágoónee'." Little touches like this was something Michael Gornick encouraged from his actors, whenever he could find the time to do so that is. "Much of my joy in working on set and probably much to the chagrin of the writers, be they screenplay writers or the original story material writers, is that what I enjoyed about working on set with actors is you could make changes, okay. And not always legit, I'm sure if you're up against the Writer's Guild they'd be very upset with you, but in my career I did it quite often with the actors, where they'd make an adjustment and they could justify it," he explains. "I mean we had so little prep with the actors, fly them in and you're shooting the next day. But you grab those moments in time where you can discuss things in seriousness with them: what they needed, what they didn't like about the script and so forth."

Another interesting topic concerning scene 36L was the use of a split diopter lens. If you've ever seen a Brian DePalma film then you know how effective a split diopter can be as it adds a slight bit of strangeness to a scene. Michael Gornick had used it to great effect in the original *Creepshow* when he served as D.P. during *The Lonesome Death of Jordy Verrill* segment in the doctor's office scene as the quack M.D., brandishing a meat cleaver, tells Stephen King's character, "This is going to be extremely painful, Mr. Verrill." Bingo O'Malley, in the foreground as the crazed looking doctor, and Stephen King, in the background as the petrified Jordy Verrill, are each in focus giving the shot an off-kilter feel. "It's probably the most closely aligned device or adaptation you can make in terms of a film part or photography that can relate to comic book art," says Gornick. "It amounts to the fact that you have in comic book art endless depth of field – what's in the foreground is in focus, what's in the background is in focus. And so it's very difficult to achieve on set because then your F-stop or your depth of field has to be *incredible* in terms of lighting on the set. Whereas with a split field diopter you can literally create a line, which is semi difficult to find, but you can literally create a line on the shot where the item in foreground is in focus and the item in background also is in focus, so you have two focal lengths."

Unfortunately, the split diopter was not used much during filming due mainly to the constraints of time – especially after the delays with the weather. It's something that takes a bit of time to prepare and time was precious at this point. "It's very difficult to set up only because you have to observe that center line where if you move what's in foreground to the right or left, depending on how you set up your diopter, it becomes out of focus so you've lost the effect," Gornick explains. "So, it becomes kind of a cosmetic setup, but it does work. It's a lot of fun."

The shot in which you can clearly notice the use of the split diopter is during 36L and it's very brief, only about a second long. As Benjamin Whitemoon races back to the Spruce's General Store his Pontiac Fleetleader screeches to a halt with its iconic Indian Head hood ornament in frame along with the bloody scalp of Sam Whitemoon dangling from the hand of Chief Wood'nhead. The shot is slightly imperfect as part of the hood ornament briefly crosses the center line becoming obscured for a moment. "We specifically planned for the hood ornament shot and ordered the diopter, because it was in Michael's story-board. We put the line of the split in the right hand doorframe," explains Tom Hurwitz. "I didn't like the way the car bounced when it hit the sandbag stop. The A.D. – new after the first one was fired – was yelling for us to move on. And the new grip from Pittsburgh – my original key having been fired for not rigging a car mount fast enough – was not up to a quick solution."

Also on the day's agenda was scene 21 of Sam Whitemoon, "Rich Boy" Cavenaugh, and "Fatso" Gribbens driving in the Firebird discussing their plans to leave town immediately. The scene would be accomplished using a tow bar hooked to a pickup truck with the camera mounted directly onto the hood of the Firebird.

As for that "Fuckin' Firebird", that "hot-shit Firebird" as Romero phrases it in his screenplay, it would again fall on the shoulders of Steve Arnold to locate one suitable for the film. According to Arnold the production actually bought the Firebird, rather than renting it. This is obviously due to the amount of damage that would be done to it, per the requirements of the story. In Romero's screenplay the vehicle is described as being bright red, but the one Arnold found was gold – and this wouldn't be the only difference with the vehicle either.

"Michael Gornick was adamant that he wanted a car with a T-top, something he felt was very cool. This was of course before the internet and I must have found it in the newspaper want ads in Prescott where we were shooting," says Arnold. "The guy I bought it from was a young kid, maybe 20 years old, and it was in pretty rough shape. Those T-tops had a history of leaking so all the carpeting and upholstery was shot with mold and rust and what not; this kid was obviously not the original owner and although it was Arizona I don't think the car was ever put under cover. I could tell right away the kid was a bit of a scam artist, said he didn't have the pink slip – told me maybe his brother had it and kept sliding around on the price, etc. But it was the only T-top I could find so I gritted my teeth and bought it. I actually had to force him to take me with him to the DMV or the courthouse – I can't quite remember which – to get the pink slip signed and transfer the title. Not quite sure if my memory is correct but I think I paid $700 for the car."

And after purchasing the car Arnold and the entire production would be hit with quite the surprise. "The first night I had the car parked at our art department office it was broken into," Arnold says. "The next morning we reported it to the police – the stereo system had been torn out and there were loose wires on the seats and floorboards, etc. The police immediately tracked down the stolen goods at the house of the guy we had bought the car from. Seems he told them he had sold the car, but not the stereo. Not sure whatever happened to him."

From there work would wrap up for scene 20 – in particular Holt McCallany's character, Sam Whitemoon, shooting up the front of the store, followed by the murderous trio of punks tearing out in the Firebird, and ending with the brief, but beautiful, dolly around Wood'nhead himself; a shot which perfectly leads into scene 22 in the finished film of Wood'nhead coming to life, wonderfully edited by Peter Weatherley. And when it comes to scene 20 our theme of problems plaguing principal photography would once again raise its ugly head. "I remember they gave me this old shotgun that I would have to shoot in the movie and one of the things that I remember was *every time* I went to shoot the gun it jammed and we'd have to cut," recalls Holt McCallany. "And there was this moron who was our gun expert who had brought the famous gun and he would have to come out and un-jam it. It was just a nightmare."

Above: George Kennedy with actor Holt McCallany (Sam Whitemoon); Kennedy with stuntwoman Patty Tallman and key grip Nick Mastandrea. (courtesy of Garry Greer and Nick Mastandrea)

"I do remember that. But, see, that's so damn typical with those guns," says Michael Gornick. "I'm sure given time having worked in the industry he realized that it's not an exacting art, you know, it really isn't. But as a young actor I'm sure it would piss you off eventually. And also, here's something else that actors are not immune to, and the set in general, is the pressures of time and money and, 'Let's get this shot!' And I can imagine that steeped along with the fact that an actor's trying to deliver a performance that he has this mechanical thing that won't work, that's got to be *incredibly* frustrating."

"I must say that it was quite nerve-wracking to be blasted by a shotgun," Dan Kamin says. "I knew the gun wouldn't have live ammunition, of course, but Tom Savini had put explosive squibs in the costume, and a plate glass window behind me was set to shatter at the same moment. I know Tom Savini, and he's a madman; a very nice madman, but a madman nonetheless. So, I was relieved when that shot was completed with my real body – which is, after all, the tormented inner soul of that Indian – intact."

Yes, you read that correctly, Kamin did say Tom Savini. If you'll recall, Savini had come to Arizona to have his life-cast done for the Creep sculpture which Everett Burrell would create for the Bangor leg of filming.

And as for the shattering of the window mentioned by Kamin, well, that's where the real fun begins. "Ed Fountain had this idea that he would use these wrist rockets with ball bearings to break the windows, it would be fairly safe and wouldn't require a pyrotechnical apparatus and all the rest of that," says Steve Arnold. "But unfortunately when we built the set we had used plate glass and so instead of exploding into a million pieces when the ball bearings hit the glass they just went through and made a little round hole. So, they were flailing away with all kinds of things."

"But they finally had to put, I don't know, dynamite or something in the window," Bruce Miller recalls. "And the problem is when the dynamite goes off there's a flash, which is what they didn't want, because that's not how a window breaks when you fire a bullet at it. And in the computer world today they could take the flame out and

gotten rid of it. But if you look real closely there is a little flash of fire when they finally blew that window."

"We went to go blow up the front of this store, when Holt comes in and he shoots...or the Indian...somebody shot the front of the store, I couldn't remember who," laughs Angela Nogaro as she rewinds the events in her mind. "It's Holt, right. And he shoots the front of the store and so he shoots it and our special effects, they have the whole thing rigged and, you know, nothing happens. And he shoots it again and nothing happens. And then they re-rig and now everybody is screaming, 'Bigger! Larger! It's gotta be threatening!', and blah blah blah. So, they go in and they do their thing and they load it up again and then he shoots it and the two windows burst out in flames. It all of the sudden becomes *The Towering Inferno* and you're like, 'No, no, no. It was somewhere in between. It was supposed to just get shot out.' Once again, it was truly if it could go wrong on that movie it kind of did."

Lastly, another location contract was inked for the scheduled shoot in Dexter, Maine as the owners of the old Rexall drugstore on Main Street agreed to let their building be featured in the opening of the film. Any Rexall drugstore signage isn't visible however, so the art department would create their own business signs.

Saturday, October 18, 1986 – Day 30

Day thirty would see filming move back to the general store interior on Main Street in Humboldt for work on scene 19. The scene begins with Ray and Martha Spruce walking back into their store after having said goodbye to Benjamin Whitemoon only to be ambushed by the gang of punks led by Whitemoon's nephew, Sam, and ending with the murders of both Ray and Martha. As I mentioned before this scene

THE MAKING OF CREEPSHOW 2

is the longest in the *Creepshow 2* screenplay – not just *Old Chief Wood'nhead*, but the entire script. Covering nearly 9 pages in Romero's screenplay, and with 34 separate shots in Michael Gornick's shot list, it was a substantial sequence to film. What's of particular interest is the pre-planning for this scene with the shooting schedules. During August and September the plan was for this entire scene to be tackled in one day – close to nine full pages in a single day! That's amazing when you begin to unpack that and consider there would be elderly actors squibbed with blood effects, numerous camera angles and setups, not to mention the amount of dialogue required – it's astonishing really. By early October it would change to two scheduled days for filming. In the end it would require four days to complete, which would have a domino effect on other major scenes in the segment – Don Harvey's and Holt McCallany's death scenes – shifting their filming instead to Maine.

One of the legendary stars of *Old Chief Wood'nhead* is, of course, Dorothy Lamour, or "Dottie", as she preferred to be called. Speaking with numerous crew members it became abundantly clear that her presence was easily one of the most memorable aspects of the production as Lamour made quite an impression with her unique, charming, and often demanding, personality. "Dottie, Dorothy Lamour, she asked me to call her Dottie, every evening she would call the production office before I left and she would say, 'Becca, instead of putting my call sheet under my door would you mind bringing it to me personally and we could sit and chat for a while?'," Rebecca Mayo fondly recalls. "So, at the end of the day I took the call sheet to Dottie's room. She would have her glass of white wine, a cigarette, and the *National Enquirer* on her bed and she would launch into stories of *Road to* movies with Bob Hope and Bing Crosby."

"What I remember from that specific episode is Dorothy Lamour was *very* concerned about her hair because, you know, that's what she was known for," says Joanna Robinson. "And she was really very unhappy that they wanted us to put grey in her hair because she was so known for this beautiful truss of hair from the *Road to* movies, like the *Bali* one especially."

"Dorothy Lamour only wanted to be photographed from her left side and came up to me and said that she likes her left side photographed and if I could do all the photography on her left side she'd be happy," remembers Stan Obcamp-Fikel. "Well, sometimes the photography required me to obviously photograph on her right side and this is while they were in the process of takes. And every now and then she'd catch me out of the corner of her eye and raise her finger up and wave at me, you know, like to scold me, saying 'Now, you're not supposed to be on that side.'"

"So, Dorothy Lamour, we would make her up – and she was this lovely little grandma who was in this shop, who was this little store keeper – and we would make her up and she would look sweet and then she would go in her trailer and she would put on her red lipstick," Angela Nogaro laughs. "And we were like, 'Dorothy, this is not *Road to*', you have to stop with the red lipstick. This is not a Bing Crosby movie. You're not the young ingenue anymore, you're a grandma.'"

"I got to work with Dorothy Lamour – that was so exciting. I said, 'Oh, wow. Dorothy Lamour's going to be on the set.' So, I look and there's this little old lady in the corner and she comes up to me and she does that old, 'Hi, so what are you doing here?'," laughs Felipe Borrero. "She was like 80, still flirting! It was wonderful."

"I'd take her shopping three or four times a week and she'd say, 'Okay, well, I fancy eating this now', and I'd say, 'Dorothy, I've gotta get up in the morning'…'Yeah, well, don't worry about it.' So, she insisted that we go have dinner nearly every night. But she sort of adopted me and we stayed friends for many years," says David Ball. "You know, she was remarkably nervous because she hadn't done anything for a considerable time and so she needed something to cling on to and I became her adopted son. Which is great, that will be in my memoirs as one of the happy parts of my life."

The appreciation the crew felt for an icon such as Lamour wasn't exclusive to her alone though, as having an Oscar-winning actor in George Kennedy around the production was as equally impressive. And he was just as popular for his quiet and unassuming nature. "George Kennedy was impeccable; a gentleman, low-key," says Rebecca Mayo about the respected actor. "His wife was with him most of the time – she traveled with him – and they were absolutely the most wonderful, sweet couple that you'd ever want to meet; easy to talk to, extremely low-key. Just like someone's grandma and grandpa, they were just lovely."

"He was one of the nicest people I've ever met in my life. When he wasn't on camera doing something we talked all the time about his ranch in Spain and all the cool things he was doing back there and what he'd done in his life," Garry Greer warmly recalls. "He was just a great guy, really enjoyed talking with him."

"George Kennedy, we were shooting, he wasn't on the set at that particular moment, but he was behind the cameras, he was giving us play by play of a ball game that was taking place when we cut," remembers Stan Obcamp-Fikel. "I do remember him wearing a pair of earphones and a radio of some sort and then when they'd yell cut he would give out the scores or the plays that had happened during filming."

"Every morning I'd go down there and behind the EFXACO was this huge hotel that everybody stayed in," says Matt Marich. "And every morning George would come down, go to this little restaurant, get breakfast, come over, get a newspaper – which there was a little newspaper stand, you know, where you put the money in and pull the newspaper out – George Kennedy would come down, grab his newspaper and come over and say good morning to us and talk to us – a wonderful, wonderful guy."

But it was one of the most important people on the production, director Michael Gornick, who would be most affected by the presence of someone such as Kennedy. His professionalism and confidence would help to alleviate any potential doubts or apprehension that Gornick might have felt as a first time feature film director. "It's only frightening in the regard that you wonder if you are up to actually giving him some sort of guidance or some sort of travel on set that you would recommend to him. So, there's a little bit of a worry in terms of the so-called super stars, okay, and

he was one of those in my mind. As was Dorothy," confides Gornick. "So, it developed a kind of concern in your mind, but at the same time a kind of relief because you somehow suspicioned, and it proved to be true, that given his history and his abilities and his time in the industry that it would be a breeze working with those kinds of people. Because they could perceive instantly, they weren't prima donnas, they had no preconceived conceptions about what they'd be doing on set; how they should look, and so forth. They were free. They had a kind of freedom because of their own past, their own abilities; their talents. They weren't frightened by any portion of the process; they weren't insecure about it, more importantly. So, I mean, the short of it is what began as a concern, and not necessarily a fear, but a questioning in my mind of whether I was up to the task, it was relieved by the fact that you soon understood that they had their own kind of security and talent that would get you through it, that would sweep you along, in essence."

And for others in the production just having the combination of two legendary actors to work with brought about a sense of pride and excitement for the project. "Two classy people; I didn't realize how fortunate I was back then to be working with such class," says Eric Swanek. "And they don't make 'em like that anymore."

"That's one thing that when I got the job, you know, that I was going to do a job with George Kennedy and Dorothy Lamour. And I was psyched because I loved George Kennedy. And Dorothy Lamour was such a huge star of so many movies, of older films," says Andrew Bernard. "So, that was something that was really special to me and I was in awe of."

"The thing that my dad really was excited about was George Kennedy and Dorothy Lamour. I mean, he flipped

Above: Assistant hair & makeup artist Angela Nogaro works on turning Don Harvey into "Rich Boy", while lead hair & makeup artist Joanna Robinson transforms Holt McCallany into Sam Whitemoon. (courtesy of Garry Greer) **Below:** David Holbrook("Fatso" Gribbens), Holt McCallany(Sam Whitemoon), and Don Harvey("Rich Boy" Cavenaugh) outside the building which housed the interior set for the Spruce's General Store. (courtesy of Garry Greer)

out! He couldn't believe it," recalls Don Harvey. "I took a picture of myself with those guys, George Kennedy and Dorothy Lamour, and he was just beside himself because he was just a huge, huge movie guy."

Of course, beloved legends such as Kennedy and Lamour are still human beings and with that can come some amusing anecdotes as well. "George Kennedy, when we were dressing the set for the store, he was being fitted for his costume and whatnot and I remember him walking into the location and he was having trouble with the jeans that they had given him," recalls Dex Craig. "And I remember the costume person saying, 'Well, what's wrong with them?' And he just pulled his hands away and his pants fall to the floor."

"So that's quite a trip to think that I worked on a movie with Dorothy Lamour. Unbelievable, huh?," Eileen Garrigan says. "I have one of my best stories I can tell you and I'm not sure whether I ever really told anybody that this happened because it was so embarrassing and horrible. Yeah, I was doing some standby work when they were filming in the front of the store, the general store, and Dorothy Lamour was, in between takes, behind a screen door, in the dark behind a screen door, and I was outside at the store front and they called for a dust down on the glass; which was kind of a continual thing, trying to get the glass to look the right level of dustiness, to help mask the reflections, and to look natural. And I had a concoction in a Hudson Sprayer of water and a little bit of raw umber kind of coloring and I would mist that across the windows when they called for it and I misted Dorothy Lamour through the screen door (laughs). And I didn't know she was in there, I heard this little, 'Oohh', and I'm like, 'Oh my god, somebody's in there', and she said, 'Don't worry, honey, I've had a lot of worse things happen.'"

Perhaps one of the funniest memories I learned regarding the film icons came from an unexpected source who recalled having dinner one evening with Michael Gornick and the pair of Hollywood royalty. "I particularly remember George Kennedy being annoyed that the locals in the restaurant became more excited about seeing Dorothy Lamour over George," says Richard Rubinstein.

Above: Laurel's Mary Ann Volvonas, assistant to producer David Ball, sits behind the wheel of Rich Boy's "fuckin' Firebird". (courtesy of Garry Greer)

Monday, October 20, 1986 – Day 31

The thirty-first day would continue work on scene 19 as the call time returned to an early AM start.

One of the more unpleasant aspects of a horror story like *Old Chief Wood'nhead* – a classic E.C. cautionary tale on morality if ever there was one, as is *The Hitchhiker* for that matter – is that innocent people have to suffer before the scales of justice can be balanced. "I've tried to suggest throughout this book that the horror story, beneath its fangs and fright wig, is really as conservative as an Illinois Republican in a three-piece pinstriped suit; that its main purpose is to reaffirm the virtues of the norm by showing us what awful things happen to people who venture into taboo lands. Within the framework of most horror tales we find a moral code so strong it would make a Puritan smile," wrote Stephen King in his 1981 book *Danse Macabre*. "Modern horror stories are not much different from the morality plays of the fifteenth, sixteenth, and seventeenth centuries, when we get right down to it. The horror story most generally not only stands foursquare for the Ten Commandments, it blows them up to tabloid size. We have the comforting knowledge when the lights go down in the theater or when we open the book that the evildoers will almost certainly be punished, and measure will be returned for measure." **(27)**

In the case of this particular story it would be the murders of elderly couple Ray and Martha Spruce which would, of course, trigger the inevitable vengeance to come. But while as awful as it may be to witness loveable and sympathetic characters terrorized and mistreated on screen, for those behind the scenes it can be quite different, even humorous. "Well, you know what, it was actually fun because Holt was doing more of the terrorizing than I was. I was cringing the whole time because, I mean, Dorothy Lamour was like, I don't know, what seventy, eighty years old? And Holt was kind of man-handling her," laughs Don Harvey. "And her face was just like...she looked like – she's a great actress – so she looked like she was really in pain. I was just like watching, 'Oh my god!' Fortunately I didn't have to do too much to terrorize those guys. But George Kennedy, he's a really big dude, and he was just telling me, 'Do whatever you want. Just grab me, throw me around, whatever...'"

"And then Dorothy Lamour, as much as I liked her, was a handful. She was a handful, you know? She was already an elderly lady," says Holt McCallany on the scene where he guns down Lamour's character. "By the time she got on to our set in the 80's she was frail and she didn't have a lot of energy. And to be honest with you she hadn't really done the kind of acting that we were doing in that...it wasn't a genre that she was familiar with. I remember like when I shoot her with the shotgun at point blank range she does this like elaborate sort of swan-type death. Do you know what I mean? Which, of course, is not what would happen at all – the thing would rip you in half and you would drop like a sack of hammers. So it was tough, but that just wasn't the school of acting that she came from."

"She wouldn't allow them to squib her," laughs Angela Nogaro. "So, when we had to shoot her with this shotgun that she gets shot with, they had this blood pump and thirty years ago...I mean, it's not great now, these things still cause problems, but when you have to do blood in a pump – because blood is really thick and sticky – it sticks. So, it's not an easy thing, you know what I mean? We've gotten better with it, but there are still complications with doing it. So, here she is and she gets shot with this shotgun and rather than there being this explosion, like 'Bam!' and the blood comes out, it seeps. It was a whole seeping thing. And blood's sticky and there were so many problems with this that by the time all was said and done, she was basically glued into her pantyhose from the sticky blood, that they had to put her into the shower with all of her clothes on to try and loosen everything up so that she was able to get it all off."

"Dorothy Lamour was wonderful," says Matt Marich. "I remember they were putting the blood all over her and I remember her saying, 'My, my, my; Hollywood has changed since my days.' You know, because she's got this shotgun wound in her or whatever; it's like, 'Yeah, honey, this ain't Hope and Crosby.'"

Of course when it comes to putting blood on the actors, among other things, that's where the special make-up effects team comes in to play. With Creepshow 2 who knew at the time that this group of young, wild and crazy guys would one day go on to accomplish big things, start their own effects companies, and win prestigious industry awards. Before Berger and Nicotero would begin KNB EFX with Bob Kurtzman, before Burrell would start Optic Nerve with John Vulich, and before Trcic would land a key position with the Stan Winston Studio they were all one team making magic happen with little to no money and only their talent and ingenuity to get them through. "The effects

on Creepshow 2, for the technology that was around at the time and the budget and the time that we had, they did an amazing job," says Andrew Bernard.

"They were like fraternity brothers, frat brothers. That's what they were like," Rebecca Mayo warmly recalls about the up-and-coming group of young artists. "I loved them. They had the quirkiest sense of humor. One afternoon at the production office they needed a body and I was that warm body. And I had to go down to the EFXACO, the special effects workshop, because they needed a warm body to sit in a chair because they wanted to see what it looked like when the blood came out in Old Chief Wood'nhead when they were shot, what the blood looked like when it came out on their head, and how it ran down the face and the lighting – they wanted to get the lighting as the blood was coming down. Did the blood look too thick? Did it look too thin? Was the coloring right?"

"They were so, so awesome. And I had so much fun with them because they were ridiculous people," laughs Patricia Tallman. "You know, we were all ridiculous together."

"I mean, you know, what happens on a motion picture set is there's a sudden collision, a society is formed suddenly of all these people who are foreigners to each other. And who do you trust? Who do you know?," says Michael Gornick about the comfort he felt with his young makeup effects technicians. "It's only human to grasp for that, to try to find some sort of satisfaction in people that you know and can trust, and you bring along old friends. I always considered Howard and Greg – those kinds of people – they are of a comfort to you."

Other goings-on scheduled for this day included a tractor trailer or some type of large truck which would be moving as much as was needed to Maine for the shoot there, including sets for scenes which were unable to be completed from Old Chief Wood'nhead. All kinds of equipment and gear, including sets for David Holbrook's and Don Harvey's characters would all be shipped, along with the Firebird, to Maine via truck. Those scenes would be completed in November in a rented warehouse space in Bangor.

But even when it came to simply moving stuff there would be issues, which would continue to add worries to an already stressed out production designer in Bruce Miller. "I felt so bad for him because, you know, living in Cletus' (Anderson) shadow and then having to work with a troubled production," says Nick Mastandrea. "I think he just...it was a bad...yeah, he was totally traumatized."

"There was a point in time when we were in Arizona and we had packed all the sets and the cars that we kept in a big moving van or several moving vans, I can't remember – probably one moving van. And we sent it off to Maine," says Steve Arnold. "And about an hour or an hour and a half later we get a call from somebody and it's like, 'Oh, the videotapes! The videotapes that we need to look at from the dailies...' or whatever it was. Some videotape, I can't remember what it was. And Bruce was just frantic and he's like, 'They must be here. They must be here!' Finally we think, 'Oh, they must be in that truck, that moving van that just left.' So, we literally sent a P.A. after this truck to try to catch this truck. And I remember Bruce being almost sick, almost physically sick because he was just so distraught about, 'Oh my god! How could this happen?' And then about that time we found the videotapes."

By the way, for those interested in such details, the missing videotapes which caused Bruce Miller so much anxiety were 3/4" video tapes of *The Cisco Kid*, which would be of great importance to the segment. At the end of production a humorous fake call sheet would reference this incident.

Also, regarding the subject of moving, Debra Tanklow sent out a memo to all crew members traveling to Maine informing them about their upcoming flight on Eastern Airlines, what time the bus would be leaving from the Prescottonian Motel for the Phoenix airport, and weight limits on luggage. We'll hear from her on Wednesday, right before the big move east.

Rounding out the details for this day was a letter drafted by composer Les Reed to David Ball in response to the offer from New World Pictures from two weeks back regarding the contract for the film's score and soundtrack. Reed felt the two sides were pretty close to finalizing a deal, but suggested a few proposals which he felt made more sense from their vantage point. One of those proposals involved bringing in rock musician Denny Laine, formerly of Paul McCartney's band Wings, and singer Maggie Bell – in addition to Rick Wakeman. "I initially wanted Denny and Maggie to sing and perform the opening music to the film, but David Ball was not keen to start the film off with singers," says Reed. "A shame because both artists are extremely good and rate very highly in my own opinion." And if you think that sounds a little "unusual", pardon the Tom Jones pun, wait until we get to some of the songs suggested for the Camaro in *The Raft*; more on that in the post-production section.

Before sending his kindest regards Reed left Ball with this: "In finishing, I would like to say that both Rick and I are very excited about this project and, providing all the wrinkles are ironed out, we could be at your disposal from November onwards. I would like to thank you for negotiating on our behalf and will return the favour by giving you an 'Oscar-winning score' and a number one album!" **(28)**

Tuesday, October 21, 1986 – Day 32

Day thirty-two would again see scheduled work for scene 19 at the general store interior location. Of interest here is that no call time appeared for any of the actors on the day's call sheet, only "W/N", meaning "Will Notify", was printed.

Also of note is the fact that at some point this day the plan was to move to the "The Big House" warehouse space to film the death scene for Holt McCallany's character Sam Whitemoon – scenes 31, 32, and 33. Whether or not that happened, I'm not 100% sure. It's, of course, listed on the call sheet, but the scene would actually be shot once the crew got to Bangor. Could they have accomplished some of the scene in Prescott and then finished it later in Maine or did they get nothing done in Arizona? It's highly doubtful they did, especially considering that the large truck which left the night before more than likely contained the Sam Whitemoon set. "Boy, I do remember shooting that scene

in Maine," says McCallany. "But the specific details about the schedule are very murky after all this time."

"I just remember that in looking at the sequence of events of things we had to accomplish in Arizona, before we pulled stakes and moved out, that we were getting such pressure from Film Finances to get out of there, they just wanted us out of Arizona. And rightfully so, they understood as we did that the impending winter season was coming in Maine," laughs Michael Gornick. "We just simply ran out of time, I mean, that's basically what it was."

So, with that, we'll tackle the filming of this sequence in-depth once we're situated in Bangor.

Speaking of Sam Whitemoon I suppose now is a good time to discuss that role and the actor whose process brought it to life, Holt McCallany.

As scripted and portrayed Sam Whitemoon is a bitter, angry young man who's grown tired of living a destitute life and feels stuck in a dying region that provides no hope, no way out. While in Arizona, McCallany actually took the time to dig a little deeper into the psychology of such a character by seeing first-hand how Native Americans lived. "Listen, I went to visit the Navajo Indian Reservation in Arizona while we were making the movie, just to get a sense of... just to meet some real Navajos and get a sense of what that culture is all about. Let me tell you: the poverty, the isolation, and the lack of opportunity – I mean, it's palpable, man; palpable," he shares. "They got a bad deal, bro. And a few casinos don't make up for that. So, in a sense, you know, I could relate to a young man with a lot of anger. And he wants to go to Hollywood, and he wants to be a star. And that was me, too. So, I probably had more in common with Sam Whitemoon than I'd like to admit."

As for portraying a Native American on screen it was a different day and age in the mid 1980's. Today, with political correctness in all aspects of society, particularly in the entertainment industry, it wouldn't be accepted. At the time though McCallany was green and simply looking for a role, any role, which would help him attain his dream of making a career in "Hollywood, U.S.A." It just happens to be that role was as a Native American. "To be honest with you, all the way back in 1986...first of all I was very young. And number two I was not as politically astute, not as politically aware, as I later became. And so those kinds of considerations just simply did not occur to me," he says earnestly. "But I guess what I would say to you is that when you're a young actor trying to break into the movie business there was probably no part in that movie that they could have offered me that I would have refused. And the other part of it is that Sam Whitemoon was a good role. So I did it for better or for worse, yet I'm aware there are people who disagree with my choice to have accepted the role and I understand and I respect their position. They're not wrong. But I just put it down to youth and just my desire to be in the movies."

Despite his young age it was very apparent that McCallany took his craft seriously, even if it was for a low-budget horror film. One of the things he did to help mold his character was to seek out the assistance of a dialect coach who could add a bit of legitimacy to the sound of his performance. "So, I worked with a dialect coach named

Above: Holt McCallany with grip Jim Walsh. **Below:** Holt McCallany, in full Sam Whitemoon costume and makeup, with Joanna Robinson and Taso Stavrakis. (courtesy of Angela Nogaro)

Timothy Monich, who is considered probably the best dialect coach in the entertainment business. He still works today and has worked with all the big stars and Timothy is a brilliant guy," says McCallany. "The Navajos were based, if memory serves, in New Mexico and in parts of Arizona. So, it was an attempt to try to adopt more of a Southwestern dialect. You know, it has hard *Rs*: 'You want some wate*rr*? I need some wate*rr* for my truck si*rr*'. You know what I mean, this kind of a thing. And then incorporate with that a few phrases in actual Navajo. So, we visited the reservation and I spoke and met with some real Navajo Indians. They seemed a little bemused by my questions, but they were very nice and that was a wonderful experience; and so, again, just hoping to bring some degree of authenticity to the character."

"Well, even in terms of the casting process I remember Holt offered that as a need," says Michael Gornick. "We were getting close and I said, 'I love what you're doing', and he promised that he would work on his dialect and his delivery. I just loved the tone of his voice, number one. I knew he could probably, even if he had to struggle on set, he could eliminate some of the seeming references to the east coast that he possessed, and they were minor. But he offered that himself, that he would work on those. And he did. I've gotta be honest with you, I didn't know that he worked with a coach and so forth. That's great."

Another thing that McCallany did while innocently attempting to create his character was met with a little less enthusiasm however. "Holt McCallany playing the chief baddie, Sam Whitemoon; he was good," says David Ball. "You know what he did? He put some ladies special non-removable makeup on his face to make him look like an

Above: Holt McCallany terrorizes Dorothy Lamour on set as stunt coordinator Taso Stavrakis hides off camera as a safety backup for the elderly Lamour should she fall. (courtesy of Michael Felsher)

Indian. And he walked in and he hadn't thought for one moment about continuity, he'd just done this. And it was like burning his face and it took them hours and hours to scrape this shit off of his face and get him back to normal. He was in some degree of pain. A real dumb thing to do, but that was Holt for you."

"Well, gee," McCallany laughs after hearing Ball's telling of the incident. "Look, you know, I'm grateful to David, first of all, for his 'charitable' description of the incident. I guess what I would say to you is that I don't remember doing that, but I wouldn't dispute David's version of it – for this reason: one of my chief concerns from the moment I accepted the role was the fact that my ancestry is Irish and Swedish, primarily. And, you know, to play a Native American was always going to be a real challenge. Frankly, if they offered me the role at this juncture in my life I wouldn't accept it because just politically and socially we've all moved on. And there are a great number of very talented Native American actors in Hollywood who would be far better suited than me. But at that time in the 1980's, you know, I guess the producers and casting felt like they didn't have a Native American because they came to me. But, look, I don't remember, it's a very long time ago, like over thirty years ago. So, if that's what David says happened then maybe that's what happened."

"We had to even him out or take care of the fact that he was darker and it was muddy and it wasn't a good color. These are the problems we still face with actors that still go off and do something on their own and you're like, 'Oh, really? Geez,'" laughs Angela Nogaro, who didn't recall it being something they had to remove from McCallany's skin, rather something they had to basically cover up. "You just put more makeup on and you hope that it all blends in together. I mean, he didn't make himself 'blackface'; he just had one of those shitty self-tanning tan things that doesn't necessarily...is not even and it gets splotchy and blotchy and unfortunately it's darker than they wanted, so then you have to do what you do: you just put more makeup to compensate."

"That sounds more reasonable," says McCallany. "But look, what can I tell you? It certainly wasn't anything I did maliciously, it was just my enthusiasm and my desire to try to be as authentic as I could, which at the end of the day was never gonna be very authentic".

Another aspect of the authenticity factor would come from his hair, in this case a wig, of course. And the story behind Sam Whitemoon's hair/wig, which supposedly originated in Canada, is a very interesting, yet slightly puzzling one. "I just remember the wig was made for somebody in another movie, who was a really big guy, he was like two-hundred and something pounds and we had to, like, stick the wig on him (McCallany). I don't think it fit very well," says Joanna Robinson. "It was from *Powwow Highway*, both Angela and I had worked on *Powwow Highway*. And it was for Gary (Farmer)."

"Yes, I do remember that the wig was made for Gary Farmer and for the life of me I can't seem to remember the timing on that. I could have sworn that *Creepshow 2* was my first location shoot out of New York, but that wouldn't make sense," confirms Angela Nogaro. "But, yes, the wig wasn't originally made for Holt and needed to be 'jimmy rigged' in order for it to fit him."

Above: Assistant production manager Debra Tanklow would handle the massive task of booking transportation to move the entire production crew across country from Arizona to Maine. (courtesy of Father William Kosco)

Now, here's where those pesky issues I've mentioned concerning memories comes back into play. *Powwow Highway* was released in 1989. Now, that alone doesn't make the story any less accurate – Daniel Beer filmed *Hell High* before *Creepshow 2*, yet *Hell High* wouldn't be released until 1989 as well. Situations like that occurred quite often back in the 1980's with low budget independent films seeking distribution. The situation with *Powwow Highway* is different though and Nogaro's remark about remembering *Creepshow 2* being her first film away from New York is part of that. I decided to check the U.S. copyright office and the earliest information I could find regarding *Powwow Highway* was a screenplay dated 11/20/1986; everything else in the database is 1987 or later concerning the film adaptation. I even contacted the film's director, Professor Jonathan Wacks, who informed me his recollection of shooting the film was in the winter of 1987-1988. All of this, of course, places it after *Creepshow 2*. So, what's the deal? Could they be remembering the story in reverse: the wig was for Holt McCallany and then later used on Gary Farmer? Was *Powwow Highway* in pre-planning in 1986 and they started work on it and then there was a delay? At this point, I've got to let it go because this book is about the making of *Creepshow 2*, not *Powwow Highway*. Regardless, it's an interesting sidebar.

"You know, I did not know that. They may have kept that from me, you know what I mean," says McCallany. "The actor is very often the last to know where these things are concerned."

Despite the issues concerning the skin and the wig, for my money, you can't tell. It took me years, in fact longer than I'd care to admit, before I realized Sam Whitemoon was played by a Caucasian actor. "I've got a picture of him

with his Levi's jacket on and his shirt off, but he's in full makeup," says Garry Greer. "And, I mean, he looks like a bad-ass Indian."

Precisely, the illusion worked! The makeup and hair artists, Robinson and Nogaro, did a fantastic job on McCallany's appearance and should be commended for their hard work. But it was McCallany, looking very much like rock star Ian Astbury of The Cult, and the confidence he exuded in his performance which really sells it – especially for the film's director. "I mean, those were his props in essence. He had a comfort with them," says Michael Gornick. "You know, if you don't feel comfortable in your own skin – and in his skin, it was the prop – it's not gonna work. But he adopted it. Even the way he fondled the hair and so forth, I mean, it's his. It's *all* his."

As for the way McCallany grades his performance of that angry young man it's typical of him in general: diplomatic and forgiving, yet very honest about the things he perceives as possible missteps. "I felt like I really went for it. I guess I'll put it this way: I give myself an A for effort and an A for enthusiasm. I really kind of attacked the part. And for that reason I think it's memorable," he says. "I've learned a lot since then about film-making. I was really a babe in the woods in those days and now I'm a guy with a lot of experience. But given the limited experience that I had I tried to really trust Michael and just go for it and try to do the best job I could. But there are some moments there where I'm overacting. There are some moments where I've

LAUREL-CST INC.

928 Broadway, New York, NY 10010
(212) 674-3800

October 25, 1986

Ms. Rebecca Mayo
c/o Prescottonian Motel
1317 East Gurly Street
Prescott, Arizona 86301

Dear Becca,

Although always an inevitable part of filmmaking, there was a certain
sadness at the point of leaving Prescott and we shall all have fond
memories of our time spent there.

By nature, I am not given to singling out personnel for their contributions but in your case I feel worthy of making an exception. Everybody
on the production team has left Arizona deeply gratified by your constant
devotion to duty and pleasant working nature and we were all saddened
that the restrictions imposed by our budget did not allow for you to come
to Maine.

However, it is the intention of this letter to be treated as the highest
possible recommendation on your behalf and you may feel free to use its
contents in the furtherance of your career.

Once again, my sincere thanks for a job extremely well done and it is
my fervent hope that we shall have the opportunity of working together
again sometime in the future.

Kindest personal regards.

Yours Sincerely,

David *X.*

David Ball
Producer
Creepshow 2

DB/mav

Above: Letter of recommendation from producer David Ball for Rebecca Mayo, expressing his sincere gratitude for her diligent, hard work on behalf of Laurel-CST, Inc in Arizona. (courtesy of Rebecca Mayo)

got a lot of tension in my face that isn't necessary, and there's some grimacing and stuff like this, as I recall."

Today was slated as a "Travel" day for Don Harvey, so his time on the production was now completed – in Arizona that is.

And finishing off the day's topics of interest Howard Berger sent out a memo to Charles Carroll, David Ball, Kato Wittich, and Michael Gornick making them aware that the makeup effects team had concerns regarding the number of makeup appliances needed for Tom Wright for *The Hitchhiker* due to the shooting schedule not yet being posted. "We are running as many sets as possible in the time given, but it would be very helpful if we knew exactly how many times each make-up played," Berger wrote. "Due to lack of equipment in Maine, we will only be able to provide a certain number of sets once on location." **(29)**

Wednesday, October 22, 1986 – Day 33

The thirty-third day of principal photography would be the final one in Prescott as the production was ramping up towards its move to Bangor.

The day's schedule was fairly light with work finishing up on scene 19, specifically for shots 15, 27, and 29. These shots would feature only George Kennedy and David Holbrook and would mostly cover Kennedy reacting to seeing his character's wife manhandled and threatened,

David Holbrook attempting to grab the pouch of tribal jewels away from George Kennedy, and finally Kennedy's character being shot and killed.

More cast were on their way out on this day as well. Both Dorothy Lamour and Dan Kamin were scheduled for "Travel" and Holt McCallany, while not gone just yet, was listed as "W/N" on the call sheet.

When writing a book like this you will inadvertently find yourself unearthing controversial topics now and then and I'm not really sure why this is. There's always drama when you're dealing with human beings is as good an answer as any, I suppose.

"All of us were kind of starting out then, so every buck we made was real important to us. And they...I don't know if I should tell you this," laughs David Holbrook as he decides whether or not to spill the beans. "I don't know. Have you interviewed the production manager?"

Now, right there he's grabbed my attention. What on earth could this be in regards to Charles Carroll? Stories like this almost always come about unexpectedly when you ask a simple question: what memories/stories come to mind for you when you look back on the experience? Now, I was warned ahead of time by one of the special makeup effects guys – the same one responsible for the rest of the makeup effects unit deciding not to participate in the writing of this book – that *Creepshow 2* had even more issues and controversies than *Day of the Dead*. And this is certainly true.

"There are rules – SAG rules – about how many hours they can work you. You're supposed to have...I think it's a twelve hour turnaround from when you stop shooting and stuff. And they were trying to save money, so when they had us on the set they kind of just kept us there a certain amount. When they paid us, they kind of ignored the fact that they'd actually broken some of the rules and really owed us for a lot of double time and stuff like that. You know, I'm sure they were careful with that with George Kennedy and Dorothy Lamour," laughs David Holbrook as he further explains what allegedly took place. "But in theory they're supposed to give you twelve hours to rest and stuff between when you finish one day and start the next morning. And they weren't really doing that with me and Holt and Don. I had calculated – we had a lot of time sitting at our hotel room – and I'd calculated how much money I should get paid, when we finally did get paid. And we wound up getting paid a lot less. They just paid us the standard rate as if there had been no overtime, like they had followed all the rules and stuff. So, I checked with Don and Holt and they were cool with this – and I think Holt actually went and collected with me after the movie – we went down to SAG and we said, 'Hey look...'"

"I remember this guy coming to me saying like, 'Listen, man, about all these meal penalties...if you don't mind we'd like to not pay the actors the meal penalties because we're hurting in other areas.' You know, sometimes when you're talking to a first time actor in his first movie, you can get away with things like that," says Holt McCallany, who backs up Holbrook's version of events. "And I remember going to George Kennedy and saying, 'George, what should I do?', and he said, 'Holt, you take the money that's

"CREEPSHOW II" LAUREL - CST, INC. DATE: MONDAY OCT. 27, 1986
Prescottonian Motel
1317 E. Gurley   ***CALL SHEET***   DAY #: 3A
Prescott, AZ 86301   CALL TIME: Company lv from office 2P
602/776-1022
602/445-3096 X280   Sunrise: Tues.6:12 Sunset:Mon.4:40pm

PRODUCER: David Ball; DIRECTOR: Michael Gornick; PRODUCTION MANAGER: Charles Carroll;
1ST ASSISTANT DIRECTOR: Katarina Wittich; 2ND ASSISTANT DIRECTOR: Grace Prinzi

SET DESCRIPTION	SCENE #	CHARACTER #	PGS.	LOCATION
EXT. INTERSTATE RAMP - N Annie drives up the onramp	116	Taso as Annie (stunt double)	1/8	ONRAMP - 395 PARKWAY SOUTH
EXT. MERCEDES - N Front tire runs off burm, car swerves and hits guardrail	118 - 120,shots 2 & 3	Taso as Annie (stunt driver)	2/8pt.	PARKWAY SOUTH

ACTOR	CHARACTER	WARD	M/U	EFX/MU	ON SET	TRANSPORTATION
Taso Stavrakis	Stunt driver	3:30p			4:30p	LV from office @ 3:15P

ATMOSPHERE & BITS	PROPS	EFX/SPECIAL NOTES/Stunts
	116 - Onramp sign, Mercedes 6 cylinder. 118-120 - 8 cylinder Mercedes, guardrail and reflectors, road dressing for hitcher hit. area	116-Double wardrobe and wig. 118-120-Double wardrobe and wig. Stunt: Mercedes glances off guardrail. NOTE* Make up and wardrobe should meet w/ B. Eden Stunt Double btwn 1P and 2P.

CALL TIME: 2:00P LV.From Office
DIR.:	3:30 lv for loc.	SOUND:	4P lv
1ST AD:	2P lv	HAIR/MU:	2P lv
2ND AD:	2P lv	STILLS:	- -
PA'S:	2P lv	SET DRESS:	Per B. Miller
LOC:	2P lv	ART DEPT:	Per B. Miller
D.P.:	2P lv	WARD:	2P lv
CAMERA:	2P lv	MECH FX:	- -
SCRIPT:	2P lv	MUFX:	- -
ELEC:	2P lv		
GRIP:	2P lv	COFFEE & FOR 55 @ 1:30P	
PROP:	2P lv	LUNCH FOR 55 @ 8P	

TRANSPORTATION
*** All personel w/ own or designated vehicles leave from production office 2P. All others: Transportation to office will leave from hotel lobby at 1:45 P SHARP.

ADVANCE   SCHEDULE
T.B.D.

SEQUENTIAL SHOT LIST - "HITCHHIKER"   Page 1 of 1

Scene 118 - EXT. THE MERCEDES - NIGHT
120

1. M.S.: (Side car mount) Tire commercial special as front tire runs off road onto burm of road.

*2. W.S.: (Low-level road position) Mercedes moves past camera and away toward edge of road and guard rail. Mercedes driver's side glances rail and recovers onto road and curve.

*3. W.S.: (Camera at head lamp level) Mercedes moves right toward burm and guard rail. Mercedes glances rail on driver's side and quickly moves back onto curve and roadway. End of shot finds Mercedes' blinding headlamps streaking toward camera.

* Two camera road stunt.

Above: October 27, 1986 call sheet - the first night of shooting in Bangor which featured scene 118-120 - and Michael Gornick's shot list page for that same scene. Stunt coordinator Taso Stavrakis would take center stage on this night. (courtesy of Michael Gornick)

---

owed to you because if it doesn't go into your pocket it will go into theirs. And I'll believe that til the day I go to hell.' They did try to short us, not that we were getting paid much to begin with. David, of all the people there, was very conscientious about keeping track of exactly what we were owed; whether it's overtime, whether it's meal penalties. He would be the guy who knows the answer to that because that's one thing I remember very clearly about that movie. So, if David Holbrook told you we went to SAG to collect additional money that we were owed, you can take that to the bank."

"For them to say they've been cheated by Charles Carroll, I would say, is nothing less than slanderous really," David Ball passionately fires back after hearing the story. "You need a bit of give and take, alright? You need a bit of give and take. For someone to complain about not getting their turnaround when nobody's getting their turnaround? If any of the cast felt for one minute that they were treated any worse than any member of the crew – they certainly were not! The crew suffered far more than the cast. You don't call the cast at five o'clock in the morning if you ain't gonna use them til nine. So, yeah, there might have been a slight abuse of their turnaround time, but listen at this level you've just gotta get on with it! Charles is one of the straightest guys I've ever met in my life. And I don't even need to say any more than that. I'd trust my life to Charles Carroll. We haven't spoken for twenty years, but when you love someone you love someone. And Charles is a good, honest technician and he knows what he's doing."

"Actually, I've worked with Holt since then – *Criminal Minds*. So, no, I actually never heard that. And, you know, I don't know how to answer that. Cast payroll is usually handled separately through payroll, which I obviously would have overseen. But, no, I can't say anything about it. I know nothing about it. It's absolutely possible, happens all the time. There are always disputes about that kind of stuff," says Charles Carroll in response to the assertion. "So, let me explain turnaround. SAG mandates that actors get 12 hour turnarounds and you can violate that turnaround, but you have to ask an actor if they will do it, and then you can violate that turnaround up to 2 hours. So, let's say you can bring them back after 10 hours; then you have to pay them a certain amount of money. I can't...I mean, it's certainly something I would never do now or I would never counsel the people who work for me to do. Look, you can ask someone if you can force their turnaround, but you always have to ask them and you can only force them so much. I mean there are times when an actor says, 'No, I don't want to be turned around', and I will go to them and say, 'Look, I need your help here. I need to force your turn around, here are the reasons...' You know, I've never had an actor once I've sat down and said, 'Look, these are the reasons', refuse it. Could I have gone to them back then, in those days, when we didn't have any money and say, 'Hey, we need to force you, man, but please don't put in for it'? You know, I may have. I honestly can't remember. But, it would have been done in a, 'It's your choice', kind of way. It wasn't like, 'Hey, you have to', because we have no power to do that. He could just say, 'Hey, fuck you. It says in the SAG contract if you force my turnaround you

Above: Hilarious costume continuity page for Taso Stavrakis as the double for the Annie Lansing character in *The Hitchhiker* segment. (courtesy of Eileen Sieff-Stroup)

gotta pay me.' It was probably $700 or $500 back then. So, could I have asked him? Yeah. But to be honest, I certainly don't remember.

"I mean, the one thing I will say in answer to that is this was an incredibly difficult shoot – physically – in many, many ways. It was not an easy film. And it would have been impossible to not sometimes go into things like meal penalties or forced turnarounds and things," says Kato Wittich. "We were really, really conscious around the well-being of the actors on the shoot. Partially because we were in such difficult physical circumstances all the time, but also because both Charles and I really love actors. Some production people treat actors like they're a necessary evil (laughs) to get things done, but neither of us are like that. We're very much aware that they have a job to do that requires that they be well in themselves. And so we really pay attention, both of us, through our whole careers, to taking care of actors."

"George Kennedy reminded me of this because I talked to him about it. I said, 'Yeah, they're not paying us right and I'm going to report them and stuff.' He was like, 'Yeah, go for it,'" reiterates David Holbrook as he wraps up his memories of the ordeal. "So, it was like a big deal to me because I made a total of like $27,000 on *Creepshow 2*, with all the over-time and the other stuff. And for me at the time, I was however old I was, I mean, that was enough to live on for a year! And I got unemployment and stuff like that, so it was a big deal to me. Never got hired by them (Laurel) again (laughs); probably a bad judgement on my part."

Putting this subject to bed I made an attempt to contact SAG-AFTRA, the Screen Actors Guild & American Federation of Television and Radio Artists, to see if they could shine a little light on this situation but was informed that they have "a longstanding policy to not comment on or provide information about individual performers or claims".

And while we're discussing David Holbrook now seems like a good time to discuss a particular moment from the filming of scene 19 that has stuck out in his mind all these years – the moment immediately after Dorothy Lamour and George Kennedy are gunned down in the story. "I throw up and then I say something like, 'I didn't expect that to happen!' or something like that. And it's a story I tell a lot of people because, just in terms of acting, it was an interesting story," he explains. "Michael (Gornick) gave me an extra take, another take. I spent the whole day before doing that shot, it was sort of a close-up on me and all that kind of thing, trying to kind of get myself in the mood of somebody who is very upset and freaked out. So, I was kind of trying, in a sense, a method acting thing of trying to think the whole day about things that might have upset me in my life and stuff like that. And then I did the take and I didn't like it. I thought it looked really...it felt clearly contrived, which sometimes, in my opinion, when you're trying to make it 'real' it just winds up looking very self-conscious when you act, especially on screen. So Michael, I don't recall him reacting in any particular way, but he just said, 'Would you like to do another take?' And I said, 'Yes, can we?' So, when I did the second take, and you know you're really on the spot, it's not like you're going to get a lot of takes on a low budget movie or anything like that; I had done very little screen acting, so you're really on the spot and everybody's watching you. I decided I was gonna just completely fake it! The nice thing about this part is that it's a cartoon character basically and you can paint it with really broad strokes and that was fun. It's fun, it's sort of dis-inhibiting as an actor to just know that you don't have to make it 'real', this is like a cartoonish, goofy character. So, I just really, really faked it and I found that when I did that and sort of committed to faking it, it actually came across as more real (laughs)."

As mentioned before, today was the last day of shooting in Prescott as the big move to Bangor would begin for the crew tomorrow. But before leaving Prescott on Thursday Charles Carroll would leave a thorough memo for Michael Morgan addressing important details which needed attention regarding wrapping up the Arizona portion of the production. It detailed everything from the set dressing at the Iron King Mine being removed, to the scaffolding at Granite Basin Lake being returned, to the production office at the Prescottonian Motel being cleared out by the end of the month. Within just a couple of days though Morgan would find himself unexpectedly traveling to Maine to assist there, which would end up being quite memorable to say the least, so other Arizona personnel such as Billy Kosco, who we'll hear from again by the end of the month, and Rebecca Mayo would handle the dirty work of tidying up the place.

"I had to make sure that everything from all thirteen department heads was returned that they had rented,"

LAUREL-CST INC.

928 Broadway, New York, NY 10010
(212) 674-3800

MEMO: *10/29/86   *This memo is a typed version
                                             of a handwritten memo RPR
TO: Bob Rehme   delivered to RR by hand in
                                             Milan.
FROM: Richard P. Rubinstein

RE: Creepshow II Casting

CC: Steve White (verbal via Bob)

I've been informed that Barbara Eden's mother became
very ill and Barbara is on her way back to California
and can't do the picture.

We are coordinating with Jeff & hoping to sign Sheree
North immediately.

I suspect there are costs associated with the situation
which we will need to discuss. I would hope all concerned
would agree that these costs should not impact the picture's
contingency nor Laurel's financial status in the venture.

I'm leaving for N.Y. in the a.m. and will stay in touch
with Jeff upon my return. I would appreciate if you could
let Steve know about the above as I can't make copies at
the moment.

Above: *I Dream of Jeannie* star Barbara Eden would originally be cast as Annie Lansing before dropping out due to the health of her mother; memo from Laurel's Richard P. Rubinstein to New World's Bob Rehme addressing the situation regarding Eden. (photo copyright 1965 NBC Television Network / memo courtesy of David Ball)

says Mayo. "All of the equipment: dollies, lights, everything that was on the set had to be returned to where it came from. So, everything had to be returned to Lee Lighting, big dollies had to be returned to Houston, Texas. So, all the major equipment from all the department heads had to be returned. I had to make sure that all the bills were paid and settled in Arizona; that Rusty Warren, our accountant, had either taken care of them or that they would be taken care of. I had to close out the telephone lines. I had to include forwarding addresses for the people who had worked on the movie so that mail would be sent to them in Maine. Make sure that everything was settled, paid, sent back, cleaned up – everything had to be cleaned up."

Leaving Mayo behind in Arizona was met with a bit of sadness on the part of David Ball who took the time to pen a letter of recommendation for Mayo, someone he came to rely on heavily. "By nature, I am not given to singling out personnel for their contributions but in your case I feel worthy of making an exception," Ball wrote. "Everybody on the production team has left Arizona deeply gratified by your constant devotion to duty and pleasant working nature and we were all saddened that the restrictions imposed by our budget did not allow for you to come to Maine." **(30)**

As for that long trip back east to Maine the person who was in charge of making that happen was Debra Tanklow. She would send out an updated memo on this day to let everyone know the schedule for tomorrow's planned mass exodus. The vast majority would be traveling via Eastern Airlines connecting in Boston for their flight to Bangor, while a handful of others, including Holt McCallany and David Holbrook, would be leaving on America West headed for LAX.

Handling the challenge of a move of this size - for

someone who was relatively new to the job at the time - is something Tanklow looks back on with great fondness. "This is something I'm really proud of," she says. "I mean, it was quite a job to get the crew from Arizona to Maine. I don't remember, I think with the help of a travel agent we figured out that the best thing to do – and this is quite an operation – we got...okay, because we had equipment too, because a lot of, I think, the grips had some of their own equipment and the camera equipment wasn't out of a rental house or anything. So, I hired a bus and a truck and we put all the equipment and the luggage on a truck, like everybody had to bring their luggage to the office and then we put everybody on the bus (laughs) and we rode to Phoenix and put everybody and all the equipment on an Eastern Airlines flight to Boston, where we had a chartered flight; I chartered a plane to take us to Bangor. And it was kind of cool because it was during the Mets/Red Sox World Series, so I remember being in the Boston airport and watching that. So, yeah, that was fun having our own chartered plane; guys were getting up and pretending they were stewardesses and that sort of thing."

Other notifications for the crew included their room placements for the Holiday Inn in Bangor as well as helpful information about the Bangor area regarding restaurants, shopping centers, movie theaters, museums, and nightlife; maps and location addresses would also be included.

And while some in the production viewed the move to Maine as a welcome relief and a potential new start, having

NEW WORLD PICTURES

JEFFREY SCHECHTMAN
SENIOR VICE PRESIDENT
PRODUCTION

31 October 1986

Mr. Richard Rubinstein
LAUREL ENTERTAINMENT
928 Broadway
New York, NY 10010

Dear Richard:

This will confirm that NEW WORLD is hereby withdrawing its approval
right with respect to the role of "Annie" in the hitchhiker scene, and that
you should cast the first available actress, other than Sheree North.

It is my understanding from David Ball, which he has just reconfirmed,
that Sheree was to begin shooting on Tuesday, November 4. I trust that we
will be able to find a new actress who will also be able to begin on Tuesday,
thus preventing any further delays or costs beyond those which have already
been incurred due to the departure of Barbara Eden.

Sincerely,

Jeff Schectman

CC: Kurt Woolner
    Film Finance

1440 SOUTH SEPULVEDA BOULEVARD LOS ANGELES CALIFORNIA 90025
TELEPHONE (213) 444-8324 TELEX 664913 NWUSA FAX (213) 444-8101

Left and above: Laurel would follow-up the unfortunate casting issue with Barbara Eden by offering the Annie Lansing role to Sheree North. New World Pictures would step in and block her participation in the film, setting off even further complications for the production. (photo copyright 1974 CBS Television Network / memo courtesy of David Ball)

dealt with so many unexpected obstacles in Arizona, a large number viewed their adventure out west as great fun, filled with pleasant memories, funny stories, romance, and even close calls with the local authorities.

"Prescott was beautiful. I learned how to two-step," says Daniel Beer. "I don't remember, but I learned how to two-step."

"Prescott at that time was a Mecca for collectible shops at a time when collectible shops were exploding all across the country," remembers Dan Kamin. "And I'm really into old stuff, like, old postcards, various old artifacts; of course, souvenirs of the silent movie days. So, I was just haunting these shops and it was very cool."

"It was deer season, right, and Prescott has this big square, this big town square, and there's this one street that's called Whiskey Row and it's just bars all up it, all up the street. And all the cowboys come in on the weekends and drink there, but it was a weekday. And these guys came driving through town with a guy strapped to the hood with, like, blood hanging out of his mouth, and he was strapped to the hood, and they had deer outfits on. And they were driving around like they were the deer and they shot the guy. It stopped traffic and everybody was like, 'Oh my god, look at this!' Now, that's funny," laughs Logan Berkshire uncontrollably as he flashes back. "That's one of the things I remember about Prescott, that moment. And it was like, 'Oh

my god, you've gotta love this place. They've got a sense of humor.' And they were in a convertible, so the antlers; you could see their whole heads. God, I mean, it was a Gary Larson cartoon come alive, it was absolutely brilliant."

"I hooked up with Patty (Tallman) on that show and that was great. So, I had a great time," says Nick Mastandrea. "Yeah, we were together then for about a year and a half after that, I think."

"Like a couple of years. It was a very serious relationship for me, yeah," says Patricia Tallman about her romance with Mastandrea born from the experience out west. "A couple of the fun dates that we had were there in Arizona. We drove to the Grand Canyon one day and did some road trips and kind of explored that beautiful, beautiful area."

"So, Taso, like two or three o'clock in the morning, he decides to race down Gurley Street in Prescott. You gotta realize Prescott, at that time, maybe the population was 20,000 people maybe?," recalls Matt Marich.

"I was gonna get to this. Now, go ahead, let me hear the story," an amused Taso Stavrakis responds as he prepares to relive a wild moment from his past.

"But the famous story is he's driving as fast as he can down the street, he's drag racing. But there's nobody else on the street – it's three o'clock in the morning in Prescott," Marich continues. "And he gets pulled over and he's got his little Sony 8-millimeter camcorder going – he showed

NEW WORLD PICTURES

November 3, 1986

RECEIVED
NOV 07 1986
RECEIVED

Mr. Richard Rubinstein
Laurel Entertainment
928 Broadway
New York, NY 10010

RE: CREEPSHOW II

Dear Richard:

This will confirm that New World will not hold Laurel-CST responsible for any and all outstanding monies which may be due Sheree North as a result of New World's decision not to employ her services for the role of "Annie". I understand that it is currently expected that the amount due to Sheree North is $60,000. New World agrees to pay directly to Ms. North any sums ultimately agreed to be paid to her, provided that New World shall have the right to negotiate a settlement with her on whatever terms New World deems satisfactory in its sole discretion.

New World's agreement to pay Ms. North is in no manner to imply that New World will pay any additional costs which may be claimed or inferred by Laurel-CST, Film Finances or any third party as a result of New World's decision to replace Sheree North.

It is our belief that the production costs incurred as a result of the substitution of Lois Chiles for Sheree North are minimal and should be borne as a normal production contingency expense.

Sincerely,

Jeff Schechtman
Senior Vice-President, Motion Picture Production

cc: Bob Barry
    Amy Rabins
    Lee Rosenbaum
    Kurt Woolner
    Steve White

1440 SOUTH SEPULVEDA BOULEVARD LOS ANGELES CALIFORNIA 90025
TELEPHONE (213) 444-8100 TELEX 664347 NWLSA FAX (213) 444-8101

LAUREL-CST INC.

928 Broadway, New York, NY 10010
(212) 674-3800

MEMO

DATE: November 4, 1986

TO: Jeff Schechtman

FROM: Richard P. Rubinstein

RE: Creep II/Casting Delays

CC: R. Rehme, S. White, K. Woolner, D. Ball, M. Galin

Further to our conversation yesterday I want to state that I believe that it is appropriate for N.W. to reimburse the contingency for costs incurred as a result of N.W.'s failure to approve principal cast on a timely basis. (This reimbursement should be in addition to the $60,000 which may be due Sheree North for which N.W. has already assumed responsibility.) I also believe it appropriate for an adjustment to be made in the delivery date and any other dates effected by the delays in getting cast approval and the arrival/departure of Barbara Eden (who along with Sheree North was a N.W. initiated & approved hiring). I also note it is self-evident from the enclosed correspondence that more than adequate notice was given to N.W. about the need to resolve casting on a timely basis.

Another impact of the casting delays is that the $50,000 of fees which Laurel agreed with Film Finance to make available as additional contingency has been exposed to additional risk.

As you are aware Film Finance has put substantial pressure on the production to complete the picture given costs to date. I believe it important for N.W. to relieve some of this pressure immediately!! Frankly I think that if N.W. is willing to absorb 60K as a result of a breakdown in its corporate communications (Sheree North). I would hope that N.W. would be just as supportive of the movie itself.

Please note that I am well aware of other problems for which the production is responsible but I do view these to be mostly normal contingency items (with the exception of the highly abnormal weather conditions in Arizona and a production auditor who can't seem to keep the computer running to get a cost report out on a regular basis).

In closing I would note that despite the problems Mike Gornick still feels confident that we are making the picture we intended to make. My comments as above are intended to continue to support Mike within reasonable cost parameters.

Above: New World's Jeff Schechtman and Laurel's Richard P. Rubinstein would exchange memos regarding the Annie Lansing casting fiasco and the financial implications of it. (courtesy of David Ball)

us the video of it – and it was the cops had pulled him over. They said, 'What are you doing?' He goes, 'Oh, I'm the stunt coordinator on *Creepshow 2* and we're going to be doing a really big drag race scene down here in about a week and I was told I could test out the road to see how it's going to be (laughs).'"

"That's exactly right! Me and Greg Nicotero were drunk and we were out in Prescott driving; and I don't know if we were looking for something or we were just hootin' and hollerin'," says Stavrakis as he revisits the tale. "Greg is sitting there and he has his new little camcorder; and it was a company car, we had the board on the front that said *Creepshow 2*. And then underneath it said Stunt Coordinator, my department car, can't remember what it was, an old Ford 500 or something, it was fast. And we're driving around Prescott like a nut and sure enough, 'woo, woo, woo, woo', one cop pulled us over and he saw the board, he said, 'You guys with the movie?' And Greg, of course, has the camera in his lap and he's got his thumb over the little red light and shooting across me up to the policeman. I said, 'Yeah, I'm sorry I didn't alert you ahead of time. We're gonna do a chase scene and I'm looking for good locations.' And the cop went, 'I got the perfect place!' He told us it was about a mile up the road, it was an old shopping mall, it was kind of abandoned. And he said, 'That's where I take my kids and we go driving up in there.'(laughs) I was like, 'Really? Okay'; completely got off."

And while most of the crew who happened to be from Pittsburgh viewed their time in Prescott with great fondness, their presence in Arizona was actually appreciated just as much by some of the locals who worked on the film; none more so than carpenter Aaron Newton, who could not have

been more impressed. "I did enjoy the Pittsburgh people. I was fascinated by their stories of working for Mister Rogers; that made them almost gods to me. I was just sort of taken back by the whole thing, you know, them coming to Prescott, Arizona," he says. "One day Ed Fountain was looking at me and I was kind of nervous in what I was doing, Ed was standing over me, he said, 'Enjoy it; just relax, this is going to be fun. This is fun, so relax and do your job, do what you do well.' And that chilled me, you know, right away."

Finally, as the crew were flying across the country on Thursday the wheels of the production were still busy turning with more location contracts being inked in Maine, including the spot featured at the end of the film when the Creep tosses out comics as his delivery truck drives away.

Monday, October 27, 1986 – Day 34

Day thirty-four of principal photography would begin in Bangor, after a four-day intermission, allowing the production to get situated following their move from Prescott, where they would now turn their attention to *The Hitchhiker*.

Bangor, Maine – incorporated in 1791 – would earn its namesake from the Reverend Seth Noble. The legend goes that while waiting in Boston, Massachusetts to petition for

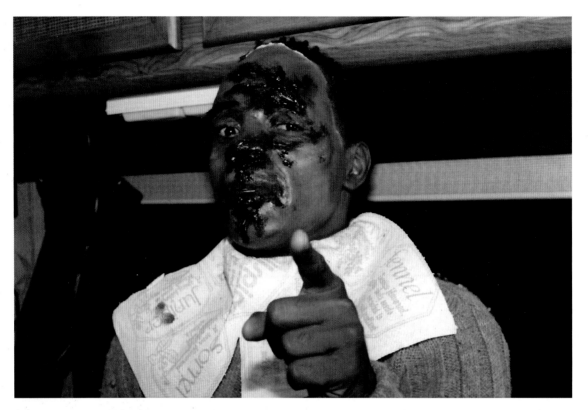

the small Maine town to be named Sunbury, Noble began to whistle an Irish hymn called *Bangor*. When asked by an official of the court what the name of the town should be, Noble inexplicably replied, "Bangor", rather than Sunbury, and so it was.

By the mid 1800's Bangor was known as the "Lumber Capital of the World" with the Penobscot River so full of logs that one could walk across the river shore to shore. Bangor and central Maine's dominance in the logging industry would supposedly even give birth to the legend of Paul Bunyan, the mythical lumberjack, of which a giant statue exists to this day in Maine's "Queen City". But by the 1980's Bangor's claim to fame would rest with the writing talents of Stephen King, the master of horror.

As hinted at previously there were some in the production who welcomed leaving Prescott with open arms – not because they disliked the area, you understand, but because of the adversities suffered while shooting there.

"We couldn't wait to get out of Arizona at that point," says Angela Nogaro. "And we all knew that we were going to go to Maine...you know, because we had faced so many trials and tribulations in Arizona, we were waiting for the end of that."

"It was one of those camaraderie...you know, you suffer in a war and we were in a war and were making it together," explains Kato Wittich.

"By the time we got to Maine, we were sort of battle hardened," adds Charles Carroll.

That sense of being battle hardened would come in quite handy for the crew while in Maine because the continued challenges of making a motion picture on a low

budget, under the pressure of a short schedule and being punished by Mother Nature once again, would push the envelope for those involved. "I was away so long, I would send my summer clothes away and they would send me my winter clothes because I never got to go home," says Felipe Borrero. "You know, we went from Arizona sitting on top of a restaurant drinking Corona beers – that's the first time I had Corona beer with a lemon inside – to sitting in Bangor, Maine in the freezing cold, trying to stay warm by hugging each other."

After struggling for weeks to find the right actress, Laurel had finally landed the services of Barbara Eden, of *I Dream of Jeannie* fame, for the role of Annie Lansing, the adulterous wife at the center of our tale, *The Hitchhiker*. Eden's involvement with the production, much like Dorothy Lamour's and George Kennedy's, brought an air of respectability to the film, since she brought with her a familiar and endearing persona. "She was always a very good actress," says Leonard Finger. "And also she was good for these, what I had mentioned to you before, these sorts of subsidiary possibilities for *Creepshow 2* for TV; because Barbara Eden was somebody who was much beloved."

"So, originally they cast Barbara Eden to be the woman in *The Hitchhiker*. So, I went to Los Angeles and fit her in clothes," recalls Eileen Sieff-Stroup. "I went for like three days, we did fittings, I went to her house – I think she drove when we went to Beverly Hills to go shopping – but I was sitting in her living room and there's the Jeannie Bottle sitting there. You know, I sat in the same room with the Jeannie Bottle! She was lovely, lovely, lovely."

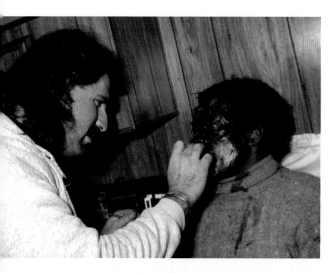

Left, above and right: The various stages of the hitchhiker's deterioration at the hands of Annie Lansing. Tom Wright's gruesome makeup would be handled by Howard Berger. (courtesy of Michael Gornick and Michael Felsher)

However, as was now becoming par for the course with *Creepshow 2*, unfortunate circumstances – this time news of a family crisis back home for Eden – would become yet another obstacle for Laurel-CST, Inc. to overcome. "Barbara Eden did come to Maine. Barbara Eden did come to do the picture. But her mother was taken ill," says David Ball. "And she phoned me and she said, 'David, its Barbara.' I said, 'Hello, Barbara. What's up, darling?' She said, 'David, I've gotta go.' I said, 'I'll come to your room.' I went to her room and I said, 'What's the problem?' And she was crying and she said to me, 'My Mom's really sick, I've gotta go. I can't stay here, I've gotta go. I'm very, very sorry to let you down, but I've gotta go.' I said, 'Listen, Barbara, I understand, these things happen.' Now, whether that was a good bit of acting on her behalf, I don't know. But I took her at her word and I respected her word, she was a respectable lady. And she went, simple as that."

"I wanted to do it very, very much. In fact I was there," Eden told me during an open Q&A session at the April 2016 Steel City Con in Pittsburgh. "And my brother-in-law called me and said my mother was dying and that's why I had to leave. But I really wanted to do it."

"She bailed right after costume fittings in Maine," Michael Gornick sadly recalls. "Never even a read-through on the script."

Sadly, two weeks after returning to Los Angeles Eden's mother, Alice Mary Huffman, would pass away after battling cancer.

With Barbara Eden now gone from the production, before she even had the chance to start, this meant David Ball would have to pick up the pieces and resume his search for Annie Lansing.

Before we get started on this first night of all-night shoots for *The Hitchhiker*, I want to quickly mention something you might notice about the scene numbers which will be listed during the filming of this segment, something that

was unique to it in particular. The scene numbers listed on the daily call sheets for *The Hitchhiker* were all lifted directly from Michael Gornick's shot list, just as they were with *The Raft* and *Old Chief Wood'nhead*, but with one noticeable difference. Take for example scene 118-120, which we're about to discuss, you might assume that would be scenes 118, 119, and 120 – right? Well, it's not; in fact its scenes 118 *and* 120. Gornick combined these shots in his sequential shot list and that's how they are listed each day on the call sheets, but there was a definite method to his madness. "Pure efficiency at that point," the director explains. "I wanted to be as speedy as possible because we were down to the wire."

And some days the scene might be listed as 118-120, while another day it will be listed as 118/120. It's still the same scene, just typed differently that particular day, for whatever reason; this would happen repeatedly throughout the filming of the segment.

Now, as for the filming that took place this evening you could say things started with a bang as the production "crashed head on" into the schedule. On tap were scenes 116 and 118-120, both of which entailed the Annie Lansing character driving her Mercedes erratically onto the I-395 on-ramp, driving off the road, and bouncing off the guard rail. And the star of the night would be stunt coordinator, Taso Stavrakis.

But before we delve into the events of the evening, let's talk a little about the other star of said evening, the Mercedes Benz. And I'd like to point out the slightly different versions of the same story you're about to hear. Again, memories are fascinating because accurate details get lost to time or they're augmented based on what someone focuses on during an experience. You'll basically hear the same story, but with crucial details varying a bit.

"I was working on that project for about a month before the crew even showed up," recalls Henry Nevison. "One of the most interesting things I had to do was in that scene where she keeps crashing into that hitchhiker we purchased two Mercedes Benz from Germany and so they came on a flatbed and they weren't street legal because they were picture cars. So, you had to have them delivered on a flatbed and they were European Mercedes' and they were different colors. And, so, what I had to do was I had to actually replicate the color of the first Mercedes to the picture cars that we were using for the actress to drive by in, the actual one that was actually drivable. And we had to change the headlights because the headlights were European headlights."

"Well, first of all we were trying to figure out how we could afford two Mercedes Benz and (David) 'Bally' came up with the idea of, 'We'll buy them in Europe, we'll ship them over, it will be much cheaper' – which we did," recalls Charles Carroll. "And then, of course, we proceeded to wreck both of them the first night of shooting. And then we went to a local Mercedes Benz dealer and talked them into giving us a Mercedes Benz, which we proceeded to beat the living shit out of over the course of the show. So, at the end, I think he may have sued Laurel because of the damage we did to the Mercedes Benz."

"David Ball had them brought over from, I think, England or something. He had somebody who he knew who was, I guess, a used car dealer or maybe a Mercedes dealer, I don't know. But these were second-handers when they came over," says mechanic George Dreisch, someone who would prove to be invaluable during the filming of the segment. "And I believe they had to post a bond on them because they were Euro-spec, they weren't federalized or anything, the two. And then the other one they had, I guess, leased off of somebody local."

"We needed several identical (Mercedes) which we could not afford or get so we got three that had been imported from Europe and could not be registered for regular use here, so we got a deal on them. I think around $4,000 each," says Steve Arnold. "The interiors did not match, so we had to dye the fabrics to try to make them match. One of these cars was damaged on the first night of stunt driving so that's when Henry Nevison, the locations guy, came up with renting a matching but better model of Mercedes with leather seats from the local Maine dentist. Ultimately at the conclusion of filming the dentist ended up suing the company for $50,000 for damages to the car and $50,000 for emotional distress. Not sure how that all ended."

"Steve is right, at the lower level – I believe one was $4000 and the other $5000ish," David Ball says. "We took photos of the doctor's car which we sent to Willie (Fonfe) to match. He found a couple in Germany and shipped them over; one had to be re-sprayed to match. They were not identical to the doctor's but the same basic body shape which was okay for wide shots and, of course, by auto suggestion once we'd established the hero vehicle we were able to cheat. The double vehicles were used for ultra-wide or extreme close-up shots of short duration – and clever cutting – but the trained eye could have spotted the difference; they were both much older than the hero vehicle. The camera never lies, eh!"

Now, as you can see, there are various discrepancies amongst the memories of those closely involved with the production. There were three Mercedes Benz vehicles: two were European imports, brokered through Willie Fonfe's U.K. film and television services company Willies Wheels, which were intended for use as stunt vehicles – the other was a U.S. model that was obtained locally in Bangor, as David Ball accurately recalls. However, the local one was not obtained from a dealership or a doctor or even a dentist. In fact, it's a little funny, most of the film crew thought the car belonged to either a doctor or a dentist and that assumption even appeared on a humorous – and fake – call sheet at the end of the production, which I'll detail when the time comes. No, the hero Mercedes of our tale actually belonged to a local insurance agent in the Bangor area, Gerry Roy. And what would happen to his pride and joy 1985 Mercedes Benz during the making of *The Hitchhiker* is something that still angers him to this day. "I would have said no for them using the car had I known what they were gonna put it through. So, that's really where I'm at," explains a still very disgusted Roy. "It was not a pleasant experience."

Don't worry, we'll get to those details soon enough.

The production was making use of a stretch of new unopened road on Interstate 395 in the Bangor area with the on-ramp to the Parkway South in Brewer, Maine – exit 5 today – being the exact location where filming would take place for the evening. The new $55 million construction project had been several years in the making as it also involved construction

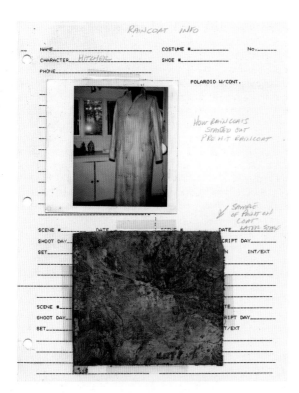

Above, top and bottom right: The majority of the blood on Tom Wright's yellow raincoat was actually red paint supplied by costume designer Eileen Sieff-Stroup. (courtesy of Eileen Sieff-Stroup)

of a new bridge over the Penobscot River.

To say that the roads were freshly paved would be quite the understatement as art director Beth Kuhn can attest to. "I think about being out on that highway in the winter," she laughs. "It was a stretch of highway that hadn't been opened yet, so there were no lines painted on it, and we weren't allowed to paint lines, so we had to buy stick-on lines. And then I remember we had to wet down the highway and so, you know, I don't even remember who got the water truck, but it came without any kind of a hose hooked up or anything. So, we were trying and we didn't have the right size hose for the truck, so when we would try to water down the highway the lines would start floating away and we'd have to put them back down."

You might have taken note of Charles Carroll's earlier comment regarding the Mercedes being wrecked on the first night and indeed one of the stunt import models was heavily smashed up right off the bat. The man behind the wheel when this happened was Taso Stavrakis, dressed up to double Barbara Eden, complete with bad blonde wig and all. For Stavrakis it was a situation of trying to please two masters, a tough situation for any professional. "It was a really difficult, almost impossible, stunt. And I choreographed it, I re-choreographed it," says Stavrakis. "What Mike (Gornick) wanted and what David Ball wanted were completely opposite. Mike is standing there on the set and said, 'I want to see damage', and this is after like the third time. So, I'm in the car, with the wig, down low – I'm supposed to be Barbara Eden. I don't even know if

we'd chosen Lois Chiles yet? We started shooting before we realized that we didn't have Barbara Eden anymore, I had this curly blonde wig on. And the car is supposed to be going fast around the entrance ramp or exit ramp, can't remember which, and Mike wanted contact with the guardrail. And so I said several things: I said we could use

Above left and right: Good fortune would finally smile on *Creepshow 2* when Lois Chiles accepted the role of Annie Lansing at the last minute. (courtesy of Michael Felsher and Michael Gornick)

strips of titanium and get sparks, we could...and it had been raining, so there was mud and it was very slippery. But not slippery enough, so they were putting Ultra-slime on the road. But you're going around a curve and you're hitting a guardrail, so you have to do it just right or it will go with you. Because that's not what they're meant for, they're meant to stop you. And that's, of course, what happened. I skidded and I skidded and I skidded, like three times, and Mike said, 'You have to go faster; you have to really hit it. I want to see damage.' And David Ball said, 'Don't fuck up that car.' That was the third of three Mercedes', none of them were really alike. The picture car, the beauty car, was a really expensive Mercedes that she drove, Lois Chiles drove. But we had two more, one was older, that was my stunt car. And David Ball wanted to take that car home, that's what I found out later. So, he said, 'Don't fuck up that car', and then Michael saying, 'I gotta see damage.' And I went, 'Bam!' – slammed into the guardrail, and just came to a complete stop. I mean, you know, I hit so hard the radio went on! (laughs) Yeah, that's how hard I hit. And I mean I crumpled the fender; that car had to be dragged off and the whole thing had to be redone."

"When I told Taso not to fuck up the car it was because it was the rented hero car," David Ball responds. "What possible good would a left-hand drive trashed Mercedes

be to me in England? We're right-hand drive! So, he has these facts hopelessly wrong."

"Taso's account is absolutely correct, except for his belief that he was dressed as Barbara Eden," laughs Michael Gornick. "David absolutely wanted no damage to any of the vehicles; I with Taso wanted it to be realistic. The first night's shoot with all its adverse weather and dangerous road conditions made for a very hairy situation. Taso was a champion however, and performed a beautiful stunt. How fortunate I was to have a performer like Taso!"

Again you can see the fog from the passage of time creating differences in the recollections of those who were intimate to the situation: Michael Gornick had forgotten that Taso Stavrakis was indeed dressed as Barbara Eden. And David Ball's version of what car not to damage differs from that of Gornick and Stavrakis. Also, according to Maine unit still photographer Richard Greene, Stavrakis lost control of the Mercedes during the shot not because of Ultra-slime, but for another reason entirely. "Now keep in mind it's colder than hell outside, they wanted the pavement to look really black, really slick black, which it was already pretty darn black because it was brand new pavement. But they had a water truck that wet the whole damn thing down and, of course, one of the scenes or one of the takes, I should say, is when the car comes around the corner it totally lost control because, I mean, it's speeding on ice!," laughs Greene as he thinks back on that night.

The one issue there however is that the low temperature according to the National Weather Service was in the mid 40's, which would make the ice story unlikely. So, you can see once again how shaky memories can be.

Tuesday, October 28, 1986 – Day 35

The thirty-fifth day of shooting would go on as scheduled despite the departure of Barbara Eden and the mangled stunt Mercedes. And with Eden gone, that meant her scheduled scenes would be scrapped for the evening: scene 117/119 of the Annie character dropping cigarette ashes inside the Mercedes and yelling to herself, "That's real leather, Mrs. Lansing! That'll cost you seventeen-hundred and forty-two dollars and ninety-two cents!"; as well as her reacting in terror as she loses control of the vehicle. However, POV shots from the Mercedes during these scenes were scheduled and most likely captured of the car running off the road, clipping the reflectors, and the view of Tom Wright's Hitchhiker character just before he's hit.

Scene 118/120 was also listed again and for the final time. Just how much was shot tonight I'm not exactly sure; the scene was obviously incomplete due to the wreck from the night before and according to the Bangor Daily News the backup stunt Mercedes was towed onto the site for filming use. However, in the editing room things can be manipulated and cleverly pieced together. Watch the scene carefully and the film cuts just before the Mercedes driven by Taso Stavrakis crashes into the guardrail, then the follow-up shot is of the Mercedes making a glancing blow, from a slightly different camera angle, with minimal damage. Could that have been an earlier attempt from the previous evening that Stavrakis mentioned taking place before the big wreck? Or did they play it safe this night with the backup vehicle and do a softer hit on the guardrail? It's tough to say.

More than likely born out of the first night's Mercedes carnage, coupled with the production already being extremely under the gun, uneasiness between Stavrakis and David Ball began to form. "Actually I saw the tension, if you would, begin the night we were shooting...I believe it was almost the first night when they piled up the Mercedes into the guardrail," says George Dreisch. "Well, anyway, I had made an observation that, I guess, was received and kind of respected or whatever, kind of my own little technical analysis of what happened, and that'd be the angle of incidence with the guardrail being way too steep, meaning it should have been way more glancing than it ended up being. Anyway, that seemed to have been well received. And I don't know that I was even talking to anybody (laughs), to be honest. I think it was just over heard by David Ball and Mike Gornick and a couple of the

others and, you know, I guess without anybody saying anything they concurred, so I think that kind of earned me some brownie points. Anyway, with that incident with the guardrail not going down the way it was supposed to, I kind of perceived some tension right there; maybe a question of Taso's experience or something?"

"Taso's a great guy. I don't know if he's a great stunt driver, but he was a really good stunt man and he was part of the Laurel 'community'," says Charles Carroll. "He was a great stuntman if you wanted to do fights or action kind of stuff like that – or what they call parkour, now – he'd be great. I'm not sure he was a great stunt driver; I mean he knew basics."

This begs the question then: exactly how skilled was Stavrakis as a stunt driver? Was this his first ever experience? "It was," he candidly admits. "I, you know, like to drive and I drive fast and I could do a lot of that stuff. I thought, 'Why not? I can do it.'"

Additional scenes scheduled for the evening included 121/122 of the hitchhiker being struck by the Mercedes, as well as scenes 123-135A of the aftermath of the hit and the Mercedes doing a 180-degree spin, including the elevated shot of the Mercedes getting the hell out of Dodge to avoid being seen by an oncoming vehicle. These scenes would be revisited multiple times over the next two weeks so just how much progress, if any, was made is unknown. For sure the shot of the Mercedes performing a 180-degree spin would be an issue down the road, something we'll delve into when the time comes.

Another issue that arose from filming scenes like these was the fact that the car itself was a Mercedes, a vehicle revered for its engineering and safety. Usually this would be a great problem to have, but not in the case of The Hitchhiker. "First of all, I told David and I told Michael, I said, 'Why don't we use a Cadillac?' I told them the day they showed me the script in the office, 'Let's use a Cadillac, a Lincoln, something really nice. But not a Mercedes,'" Taso Stavrakis explains. "Mercedes' – even then – were built with anti-lock brakes so you can't make them spin out. Unless you disable the anti-lock brakes, which I had George (Dreisch) do. You can't make them go out of control, understand, because they had all the modern stuff, these anti-lock brakes: stop-stop-stop-stop-stop. I said, 'You just fucked me. How am I supposed to wreck this car?' So, that was hard. After that, with that Mercedes, I beat the fuck out of it."

Wednesday, October 29, 1986 – Day 36

Day thirty-six would push on despite the lack of a leading lady for the role of Annie Lansing. Fortunately for the production there were scenes available that didn't involve the Annie character, so the production would continue to spend the next two days on the I-395 on ramp to the Parkway South concentrating on those. A sizeable number of scenes would be scheduled for the evening, more than half of which would feature Tom Wright as the dead hitchhiker. But undoubtedly the star of tonight's filming would be the undisputed master of horror himself, Stephen

King, appearing as a truck driver, one who hilariously sports a "King of the Road" trucker hat.

Before we get started discussing King's cameo there's a couple of interesting side notes from the daily call sheet I should quickly mention concerning his appearance. One is that it lists his character for scenes 143 and 146, which is noteworthy because in neither George Romero's screenplay nor Michael Gornick's shot list does the truck driver appear in scene 143. However he is indeed in scene 146, but instead is listed as "Man #2".

The other interesting aspect is that his character, listed as "Trucker", is labeled as TBD (To Be Determined). I found this to be a little curious, so I asked the producer to see if he could clarify. "It was because we wanted to avoid publicity, we wanted to avoid people coming up and stopping us shooting and being nosey and rubber necking," explains David Ball. "So, we didn't announce it because it was in the days of paper, and call sheets were flying all over Bangor, Maine. So, it would have been to protect us from the public and to protect Steve from the same thing, really. He was always going to do it because when we were in pre-production he said, 'You got a role for me?' I said, 'Yeah, we've got a role for you. Don't worry about it.'"

"One of the really funny evenings was the night Stephen King showed up to do a cameo," says Tom Wright. "We shared my camper, you know, because it's a low budget film and Stephen King came in and he brought a case of Schaefer beer, I think it was, and we sat there and he drank the entire case. And we laughed and talked and I asked him about *The Shining*, about different movies. I mean, it was great."

Now, Wright mentioning King and the case of beer is a subject that touches upon personal demons – something each and every one of us deals with in some form or fashion – for the world renowned author. As it just so happens *Creepshow 2*'s production was during quite a lengthy period of King's life when the prolific writer struggled heavily with substance abuse, alcohol and cocaine to be exact, a subject he's openly discussed in his writing and in interviews. He's a man that has admitted to being drunk when he gave his mother's eulogy at her funeral, to being asked to leave his son's Little League game because he was drinking in the stands, and to stuffing cotton swabs up his nose to prevent blood from dripping out, induced from heavy cocaine use. This is a man who drank mouthwash to get his alcohol fix and barely remembers writing the book *Cujo* because he was so high on drugs. I mention these things not as criticism or in judgement, mind you, but to show the depth of his addiction and the honesty he's displayed in confronting it since then, something not easily done. In his 2000 book *On Writing* King dove headfirst into his years of drug and drink and said he employed "the Hemingway defense" when it came to his long journey with substance abuse. "As a writer, I am a very sensitive fellow, but I am also a man, and real men don't give in to their sensitivities. Only *sissy*-men do that," King explained. "Therefore I drink. How else can I face the existential horror of it all and continue to work? Besides, come on, I can handle it. A real man always can." **(31)**

So, on this chilly late October night King's struggles with addiction would play out in full view of the cast and crew of *Creepshow 2*. "You know, someone with a drinking problem showed up and showed you that, at the time, they had a problem," says a crew member who requested his identity remain off the record. "As a man in his mid-fifties it's not nearly as funny as it was when it first happened."

"Listen, he was into his second six-pack by the time we got around to it at about 3:30 in the morning," says David Ball. "He was well gone, it's true. He was shit-faced!"

"Yes, he was," adds Richard Parks, who portrays George Lansing in the segment.

"Stephen King did show up, for whatever reason – he was supposed to come out, say his lines, and light a flare – but the lines were hard enough, the flare was impossible," remembers production assistant Andy Sands. "I think he went through every flare in the state of Maine until they could get it. But he was determined to do it and Mike (Gornick) had the patience, he said, 'I'm gonna get this scene the way that Steve wants it to be shown in this movie. So, if I have to go through every single fucking flare in Maine until he says the line right and lights it, one right after another, then that's what we're gonna do because it's gonna make Stephen King happy. He's not asking for a lot here.'"

"Are you going to ask me if he was inebriated? Look, it was very, very late in the evening...yeah, I think he was. But I forgive him and I wish I had some to drink that night," laughs Michael Gornick. "Yeah, I think he had some, you know, motor problems in terms of things that might have assisted him in terms of getting through that day or ending that day. And I don't know what his choice was at that point in time; I actually never saw Steve drink or smoking anything, so whatever it was he arrived happy."

"Everyone knows that Steve used to walk around with a six-pack of beer and drink it. Everyone knows that; he's been sober for I don't know how many years. He showed up absolutely drunk and had a six pack of beer and he had to sort of drive up as a trucker, step down, light a flare, and go, 'Oh, shit!', right? When we were doing this it was late, it was like the last scene of the night. We did something like 30 takes," recalls another crew member who requested their identity also remain off the record. "Because he would come out of the cab, he would drop the flare. Then he would come out of the cab, the flare wouldn't work. Then he would do it and the flare would break. Then he would do it and he would fall out of the cab. Then he would do it and he would forget his lines. And it went over and over and over. And then he would ad lib something that you couldn't put in the movie. I was laughing so hard that you couldn't even be, like, upset. And everyone's on overtime and everyone was freezing. And it was who he was."

"Later on, I'm sitting in my truck half nodding off and we had rigged up – back then it was still cassette players, just so we had tunes – and I was sitting there having a toddy. Well, guess who comes bee-bopping by?," recalls George Dreisch about his encounter with the inebriated master of horror. "He heard the tunes cranking and he knocks on the window. So, I roll the window down and he's like, 'What's up?', and I'm like, 'Just chillin'. He ended up getting in and, I don't know, we probably drank a few too many sitting right there."

As mentioned previously, King's cameo consisted of scenes 143 and 146. In Romero's original screenplay

Above and right: Setting up a POV camera angle on the unopened stretch of I-395 in Bangor. (courtesy of Michael Gornick)

scene 143 was simply a one sentence description of the hitchhiker's travel sign drifting in the wind near his body and George Lansing's vehicle – a Continental, before being changed to a BMW in the film. In Gornick's shot list it's a low-level angle with the hitchhiker's body in the foreground as the George Lansing character, standing in front of his vehicle, moves in to take a look at the hitchhiker. Gornick simply moved part of the action from scene 146 into scene 143, which would be King's trucker character pulling up at this moment. Scene 146, nearly a full page in the script, is basically the rest of the sequence where Lansing and the trucker talk as the other onlookers pull over to see what's going on. And it's also worth noting that basically all of King's lines are ad-libbed here; in fact some of his lines are re-worked dialogue originally scripted for the George Lansing character, such as seeing a car but not being able to make out the license plate or what kind of car it was exactly. Another interesting tidbit regarding this scene with King is that the woman who pulls up and gets out of her car in the film and says, "Hey, what's happening?", is stunt-woman/actress Chere Bryson who would double Lois Chiles during a lot of the stunt driving sequences.

And one for the road concerning King's cameo involves the truck he's in when his character pulls up to the accident scene. "I was told they wanted a really nice truck for him to drive and I found this gorgeous semi," remembers Michael Morgan. "The guy took the time off and he drove in and got to the set and they said, 'Oh, my god! No, this is wrong. We can't use that; it's supposed to be an old decrepit truck.' And I went, 'Crap. Now you want me to find that right now?' You know, because it was the night of the shoot." Luckily for Morgan a local contractor, Vaughn Thibodeau, would come to the rescue and loan one of his trucks to the production.

The other scenes listed for the evening would all make their way back onto the following day's call sheet, so just how much was accomplished with these is unknown. Scenes 137, 137-139, 141, and 144 of Richard Parks, as George Lansing, pulling up in his BMW to the accident scene were on tap. And once again, another noteworthy mention is that early on in the script the George Lansing character is simply listed as "Man", and then "Man #1" once the truck driver character shows up. This, of course, is intended to conceal the surprise at the end when we learn he's Annie's husband.

Also scheduled were scenes 140, 142, and 145 of Tom Wright lying on the ground after Annie has sped away and her husband pulls up to the scene of the crime.

One last bit of news for this day involved, you might have guessed, the search for an actress to play Annie Lansing. Richard Rubinstein would send a memo to New World Pictures head honcho, Robert Rehme, a memo he apparently hand delivered personally to the head of the studio while in Milan, more than likely at the MIFED film market, regarding the issue of casting for the role. Laurel

Above, left and right: The Creep's Comet News truck was another triumph for Bruce Miller's art department, particularly art director Beth Kuhn and head scenic Eileen Garrigan. (courtesy of Eileen Garrigan, Steve Arnold, and Beth Kuhn)

of Laurel. We'll return to this in a couple of days because offering the role to Sheree North would end up being a $40,000 debacle for the production.

Thursday, October 30, 1986 – Day 37

The thirty-seventh day of filming would see most of the previous day's scheduled scenes on tap once again.

Scenes 140, 142, and 145 involving the dead hitchhiker lying on the side of the road would go in front of the camera tonight. Tom Wright would be in what was called his stage 1 makeup, the character would have six stages all together, and the man behind those six stages of makeup would be Howard Berger. "I life-cast him and then made, you know, six busts of him and then sculpted all the makeups," Berger said in an Anchor Bay interview. **(33)**

For Berger, the opportunity to work on Wright's makeup would be an invaluable lesson for working with African-American performers as he learned some of the differences in skin pigment and how to properly match a black actor's flesh tones. "That was actually the first time I had done a makeup on an African-American actor and it was really hard," said Berger in that same Anchor Bay interview. "They have a tremendous amount of red in their skin and it was difficult to finally figure out how much red I had to put into that makeup to match Tom's skin tone, but yet not over red it. Foam is a very dense material and when light hits it, it doesn't look realistic like flesh. It just, like, absorbs the light and stops there and it can be really grey. So, it was interesting to find the right colors to use." **(34)**

With Wright having to spend so much time in makeup

was intending to offer the role – in fact *would* offer the role – to actress Sheree North. The memo also touched upon some of the financial implications of Barbara Eden's departure and the price therein of finding an actress at the last minute. "I suspect there are costs associated with the situation which we will need to discuss," Rubinstein wrote in the memo. "I would hope all concerned would agree that these costs should not impact the picture's contingency nor Laurel's financial status in the venture." **(32)**

These concerns, of course, all revolved around not going over the film's agreed to budget, which was very tight to start with, as any overages could be laid at the feet

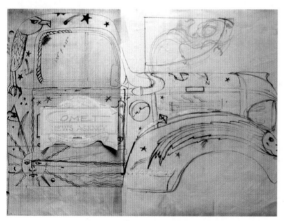

discovering the body of the hitchhiker. And yes, you are reading that correctly, scenes 137 and 137-139 are separate from each other in Michael Gornick's sequential shot list log. And I should also mention that scene 138 would apparently not be filmed. The scene would have been an establishing shot from inside Mr. Lansing's BMW of Annie's Mercedes fish-tailing up the ramp away from the accident scene.

Speaking of that BMW the vehicle was loaned to the production from Edward O. Darling and Down East BMW, a local auto dealership in Brewer, Maine. According to Darling the dealership received no compensation as they lent the vehicle to the film simply out of respect for Stephen King. "Of course, we're always intrigued with what Stephen King does," Darling says. "So, we not only let them use a car, we let them use an empty showroom that they used as a staging area for some of their activities."

"They had me drive the BMW to the set every day," laughs Beth Kuhn. "Yes, because they figured I was a really cautious driver, I guess; because normally the art director doesn't drive a picture car to the set. On a big movie it would come on a flatbed and it would be carefully taken off and there would be a whole team of people. But, you know..."

"I know they had borrowed the, I'm trying to remember the model, it was the husband's car, BMW, I think, it was like an M7, which is like a 735 with all the high performance shit in it at the time. And, anyway, I guess it had ended up out on that 395 a couple of different times. Somebody wailed the shit out of it and the tires were all flat spotted from sliding it and stuff," laughs a very droll George Dreisch as he insinuates having had a little fun with the expensive car. "But, no, that never happened."

And one final shot, 191A, of the Mercedes speedometer at 90mph, would find itself on the call sheet again in about two weeks' time, so either they didn't have time to do it this evening or there was an issue which required that it be re-shot later.

Friday, October 31, 1986 – Day 38

Day thirty-eight of production, All Hallows' Eve, would feature no principal photography; in fact, three of the next four days (including today) would have no scheduled filming. This was mainly due to the lingering problem of Barbara Eden's sudden departure, which Laurel thought they had solved with the $60,000 signing of the late Sheree North for the Annie Lansing role.

At the time Sheree North, born Dawn Shirley Crang, was a thirty-five year veteran of the entertainment industry having appeared alongside such legends as Elvis Presley in *The Trouble with Girls*, Burt Lancaster in *Lawman*, and John Wayne in *The Shootist*. North was also a talented dancer and had a prolific television resume guest starring on such well-known shows as *The Mary Tyler Moore Show*, *Fantasy Island,* and *Magnum P.I.* In 1955 she appeared on the cover of *Life* magazine when 20th Century Fox was planning to groom her as the next Marilyn Monroe. It seemed that the "blonde bombshell" was an inspired choice for the role of Annie Lansing, but more importantly

prosthetics naturally he would spend a great deal of time around the technicians responsible. The young makeup effects crew – Berger, Nicotero, Burrell, and Trcic – took to him immediately enjoying their time with the actor/stuntman and the feeling was definitely mutual. "Well, those guys are probably the reason why I have the fondest memories of the film, along with Michael (Gornick)," says Wright. "I was in that makeup trailer six hours a day. They were complete pleasures to work with and I never had an ill feeling or a cross word or any tension or stress, none of that passed between us. They were really, really delightful to work for. They were really good at what they did, they really cared a lot about their craft, and they put 100% of themselves into their work."

Also on the ledger again were scenes 137, 137-139, and 144 of the George Lansing character pulling up and

the money was right and she wanted to do it. However, of course, nothing works out that easily for Laurel-CST, Inc., right kiddies? And remember my mentioning at the close of Day 36 that this would end up being a $40,000 boondoggle for the production? Well, you're about to hear why.

"Barbara Eden was the 42nd actress that we attempted to get for that role. Sheree North, when she went, Sheree North was the 43rd", says an exasperated David Ball as he revisits the ridiculous scenario. "Yes she would do it. And then someone, either Bob Rehme or someone high up at New World, said, 'Over my dead body.'"

Indeed on this day New World Pictures sent out a memo from their senior vice president of production, Jeff Schechtman, in which he informed Laurel of New World's insistence on not casting Sheree North in the role of Annie Lansing. "This will confirm that New World is hereby withdrawing its approval right with respect to the role of 'Annie' in the hitchhiker scene, and that you should cast the first available actress, other than Sheree North," wrote Schechtman. **(35)**

"So, I said, 'Well, I'm not fucking paying for it. I've got $40 short of four million for this film and I'm not paying for it,'" David Ball says regarding his response to New World. "And they said, 'You have to pay for it.' I said, 'Well, you're going to fuck my budget and I'm gonna have trouble with the bondsman. And I have an allegiance to the bondsman because I worked for them between working for you. I take over pictures in trouble; I have a very good job with them. And so I'm not going to fuck myself for you guys for sixty grand.' That's a lot of money when you haven't got any spare."

And why would New World demand that Sheree North not be a part of the film? Ball would never receive a reason, leaving him only to speculate as to what it might have been. "Yeah, they just said, 'No, she ain't doing it. She's not doing it,'" he says. "Yeah, I think someone upstairs was probably giving her one and it all fell rotten or something or whatever, I don't know. Well, nowadays, with everything being revealed, you know, something along those lines could have been the case."

Even the man who wrote the memo himself couldn't really recall for sure what the reason might have been for New World's stern position. "I can't, except to say that Sheree North had been in another New World picture that hadn't done very well," claims Jeff Schechtman. "Yeah, I think she was in another New World picture. I can't remember which one, but I think that was part of the reason."

Now, in my research I could not find a film or television show which North appeared in for New World, at least during the Robert Rehme regime, which began in 1984. In 1978 North did have a small role in the Joan Rivers' directed film *Rabbit Test*, released by AVCO Embassy, which Rehme ran at the time. That's about all I could find as far as any sort of link.

Regardless, Sheree North was now out as quickly as she had come in – with Laurel having just printed updated schedules with North penciled in as the "new Annie" for Tuesday, November 4! But just like that, chaos concerning the role was back again and it was due to an executive(s) thousands of miles away with little to no regard for what the *Creepshow 2* production was dealing with on the ground. This, you can imagine, didn't sit well with David

Ball. "Jeff Schechtman was my point of contact at New World and I didn't get on very well with him because I didn't think he knew anything about film production. So, I didn't respect him because he was not sympathetic to our cause at any single time," says Ball. "I am not a baker, a butcher, or a candle stick maker. I do movies and I speak movie language to movie professionals, I work with professionals. And when you have all these executives who know fuck all about film-making and the process of film-making and the chemistry and the very important things that put this jigsaw together..."

Ultimately, the brash studio would relent and grudgingly do what was right by Laurel. "New World Pictures were amateur and not helpful at all. $40,000 added to our cost was a lot of dough at the time...1% pissed away due to their inertia," says Ball. "New World said to cost it in the budget which I did, knowing Film Finances would kick it out, based on a clause which said the producer must cast to budget. New World weren't happy but had to swallow it internally."

And swallow it they would because just a few days later, November 3, Laurel would receive another memo from Jeff Schechtman notifying them that New World would not hold Laurel responsible for the monies owed to North. "New World agrees to pay directly to Ms. North any sums ultimately agreed to be paid to her, provided that New World shall have the right to negotiate a settlement with her on whatever terms New World deems satisfactory in its sole discretion," Schechtman wrote. **(36)**

In the end New World would settle with North's representatives with the $40,000 sum mentioned by Ball.

Meanwhile Laurel had no choice but to pick themselves up, dust themselves off, and start looking again for a leading lady – immediately. And this time good fortune would finally smile on *Creepshow 2*'s search in the form of Lois Chiles. "It was Halloween and suddenly my agent called and said, 'We have a script and you have to make up your mind in 24 hours' – or it may have even been less than 24 hours – 'You have to be on a plane tomorrow,'" recalls Chiles about the offer for the part. "And so I had already had a busy day and I had a lot of things I had to do so my friend, Kate Ginsburg, who happened to be Michelle Pfeiffer's producing partner, and I were supposed to do some things together and I didn't have time to do it all so she read the script to me while we drove around and did things. And so then we decided I'm gonna go for it – she agreed, 'Go for it!' So, I got on a plane and it was so fast."

"When you reach her kind of a category, you know, there's no reading, per se. You have to pretty much rely on people like Leonard Finger, but also your own instincts," says Michael Gornick. "God bless her, she was willing to take on the role immediately."

Today would mostly be a day of scheduled meetings and preliminary work involving the Sam Whitemoon set at the makeshift studio Laurel had acquired in Bangor. Taking over space in the recently closed Viner Brothers shoe factory on Farm Road, Laurel was able to reconstruct sets from *Old Chief Wood'nhead* which were not completed in Arizona, as well as utilizing it for a handful of shots for *The Hitchhiker*.

Above and right: Tom Savini in full Creep makeup and wardrobe in downtown Dexter, Maine for the opening shots of the film. (courtesy of Rick Catizone and Michael Felsher)

The day would get started at 10AM with a walk through of the Sam Whitemoon set with only a handful of key personnel present including Michael Gornick, Bruce Miller, Dick Hart (the film's new D.P.), Kato Wittich, and Howard Berger. At 10:30AM there was a crew call at the production offices located on Perry Road, about half a mile away, followed by the crew leaving at 11AM for the studio space in which they would begin rigging and pre-lighting the Sam Whitemoon set. At noon a meeting involving department heads and key personnel was also scheduled at the production office.

As mentioned before a brief schedule for the following handful of days was printed and circulated amongst the crew, featuring the debut of Sheree North on Tuesday, November 4. However, with North now gone from the mix that schedule would change – but only partially so and not nearly as disruptive as it could have been. Filming for Sam Whitemoon's interior scenes would move from Monday to Tuesday and Lois Chiles' debut as Annie Lansing would take place on Wednesday. So, the upheaval was fairly limited.

More important news for the day involved some script revisions as scenes 110 through 114 were deleted. These scenes took place immediately after Annie leaves her gigolo's condo and involve her backing into a street lamp pole as she's attempting to quickly get on the road. After taking off in her vehicle, which is now noticeably damaged, she flies through town, running through red lights, and

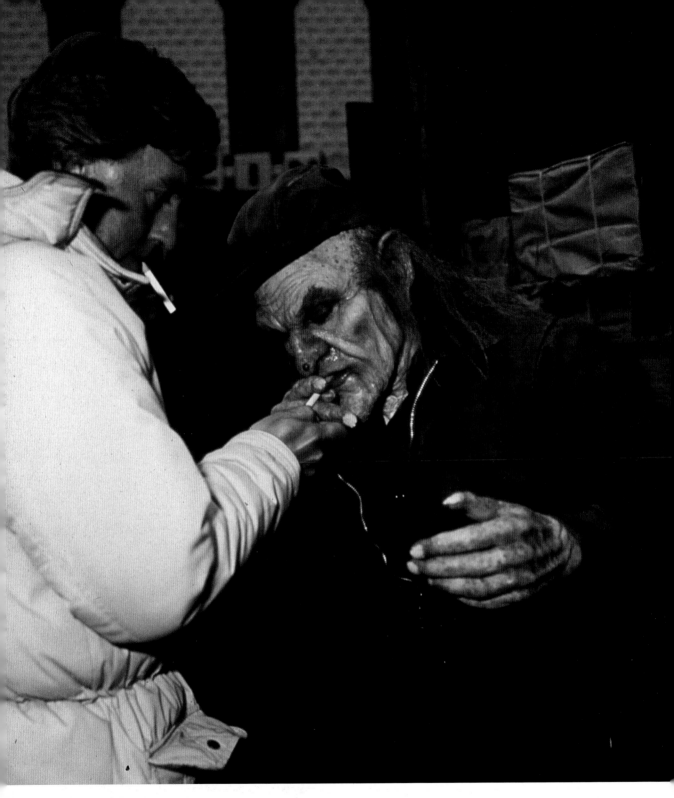

nearly causing multiple car wrecks. Frankly, losing these scenes doesn't hinder the story at all and taking into account the problems the production had faced up until this point, it made sense to remove them seeing it would help save money on the budget. But even though these scenes were now officially gone from the schedule, some of it would survive and make it into the completed film anyway. Annie's monologue to herself from scene 114 about being the winner of the hundred yard dash and joking about telling her husband that she went to get laid would indeed be filmed, as well as her leaving her gigolo's condo, plus some shots of the Mercedes driving through a quiet and deserted downtown.

By this time Michael Morgan, the location manager in Arizona, was now situated in Maine. "Kato and Charles were both big fans of mine because I worked my ass off, you know, they always had what they needed," Morgan says. "And so they called me up one day and said, 'Hey, this guy's not working out. You've gotta come here.' So, they sent me a plane ticket and off I went."

The guy Morgan references is Henry Nevison. We'll delve a little deeper concerning this subject in the coming days ahead as there were issues with Nevison's experience in the position, as well as his disdain for the perceived disrespectful tone some of the crew members had toward locals.

For now though, Michael Morgan's to-do list for the day included traveling about forty-five minutes to an hour northwest to the small town of Dexter to check out the location for the film's opening sequence of the Creep pulling up in his truck, which would be shot on Sunday. "We had done a downtown renovation project and spent a lot of money on it, from our point of view, so we were really proud of the way the little village looked," says David Holt, who was the Dexter town manager at the time. "We thought vainly, because that's how we viewed the world I think is a little bit vainly, that we had done such a beautiful job that they wanted to come because it was beautiful. In reality I think we looked a little bit like a Stephen King village, so that's why they wanted to come (laughs)."

With Michael Morgan busy in Maine, a lot of the final cleanup in Prescott was being handled by people like Rebecca Mayo, as well as production assistant Billy Kosco who sent a full page letter/checklist to Morgan letting him know that things in Prescott had been handled as instructed: from utilities being shut off, to signs at Granite Basin Lake being placed back into the ground, to the Humboldt store property's condition receiving a thumbs up from the Hinshaw family – "Kathy Hinshaw is a very happy landlord, Humboldt store A-O.K." **(37)** – no stone was left unturned. "You literally have to clean this up and get it, you know, presentable back to the people; there are items that have to be taken...there's a mad rush of everybody packing," recalls Kosco. "If we borrowed stuff from a pawn shop, or wherever we got stuff, it was just like, 'Pack it up.'"

As for Rebecca Mayo she too would have an invitation to travel to Maine, but unlike Michael Morgan she would decline the offer not wanting to step on anyone's toes, so to speak. "They asked me if I would come to Maine. And David (Ball) even called me from Maine, from Bangor, and he said, 'Please, please, please get on a plane and come out here and help us. We need you. Please, please, please.' And I said, 'David, I was only signed up for the two Arizona segments, not the third segment.' And I said, 'You have hired a production secretary in Maine,'" Mayo recalls. "Well, my phone rang off the hook from David: 'Please, please come to Maine. She's not you! We've got to have you.' They were all calling and begging me to come to Maine; all of them, Charles, all of them: 'Please come to Maine because she's not you!' And I said to them 'I'm not going to do that to her. You have already hired this woman. I'm not going to come to Maine and act like a know-it-all or show her up, you know, show her what her job's supposed to

Above: Domenick John Sportelli as Billy waits for direction by the prop newsstand. (courtesy of Michael Gornick)

be when I was a greenhorn when I started with you guys."

And with that the school teacher's trial by fire in the film business came to an end. "For me I was the novice, brand new, didn't know what I was doing. And so I had to learn as I went, but it was an incredible experience. Thank god for a teaching career because it kept things organized and on track," Mayo says looking back on the opportunity to work on a motion picture. "Halloween day was the final day that I left the production office and it was empty when I left, completely empty and cleaned."

Saturday, November 1, 1986 – Day 39

The thirty-ninth day of production, All Saints' Day, would see the calendar flip to November and another consecutive day without filming. However, this was definitely not a day off for the crew of *Creepshow 2*.

The day would start at 11:30AM with a gathering at the Viner Brothers shoe factory, Laurel's makeshift studio space, to test the height of the Creep truck for tomorrow's shoot. Among others at this test was the Creep himself, Tom Savini. Eileen Sieff-Stroup was also on hand with Savini's wardrobe, as well as Michael Gornick, Bruce Miller and his art department crew, Kato Wittich, and D.P. Dick Hart.

With his mentioning I suppose now is a good time to introduce the new director of photography for the film, Richard Hart – Dick as he was known to the crew. "Well, they had a New York cinematographer (Hurwitz) and I don't exactly remember how he was removed from the show, I don't know," Hart begins. "But the insurance company (Film Finances), the guys that insured different shows, I had worked with on a couple of other movies and out of the clear blue sky they called me and asked if I was available and would I like to shoot this movie."

As a young man Hart worked for Charles and Ray Eames, the famous architect and furniture design couple. Later he would marry the daughter of the head of the electrical department at MGM Studios where he would work for years becoming a best boy. Eventually his path would cross with John A. Alonzo's, a well-known cinematographer, and he would get the chance to work on 1971's *Vanishing Point*. He would go on to work on such notables films as *Harold and Maude, Thief,* and *Romancing the Stone*.

But it was an early 1980's film that Hart worked on, alongside director of photography Jordan Cronenweth, which he's asked about more than any other title – Ridley Scott's 1982 epic masterpiece *Blade Runner*. "I mean, it was just...it wasn't the normal go in, punch the card, and go home," says Hart. "It was an amazing experience."

It was during the early stages of *Blade Runner* that Hart would receive the inspiration for his future career path and it would come from the film's director. "'I want shafts of light', and he would put his arms up in the air, 'I want shafts of light,'" recalls Hart in his best British impersonation of Ridley Scott as he flashes back on the director's vision for *Blade Runner*. "Well, we started doing tests of all kinds of different studio lighting, bottle spotlights, and everything else. And nothing really worked and I knew it wouldn't – and so did Jordan. But the whole thing...we were still not even in prep yet. Well, the prop master came up to me and said that he had seen these flashlights that were amazing and they were just shafts of light, they didn't spread. He said, 'I think I can get you the number of the company that makes them.' Well, it wasn't the company that makes them, but it was the company that was helping the people that were making them. And so I called, and at that time it was called Skytracker, and they were 1 kilowatt xenon lights and I asked if they could bring a couple of them to the studio, 'Because we might want to rent them from you. Do you rent?' He said, 'Oh, sure.' So, they brought over two, went into a stage, the same stage that we were doing all the other testing, and the first time we lit the light Ridley was so excited I couldn't believe it, 'That's what I want! That's what I want!'"

From there Hart would begin working with his own engineers to create larger, more powerful xenon lights that his own company would produce. So, in 1986, not long before accepting the gig to work on *Creepshow 2*, Hart would launch Xenotech, which specialized in high intensity lighting equipment for use in aerospace, entertainment, promotional advertising, and security lighting. "Well, all of that came out of *Blade Runner*; it was all xenons. There are

a little over sixty kilowatt xenon fixtures in Florida for the space launchings – of course, we don't do them anymore there. But those, we built them. And they used to use 20K and 25K xenons, liquid cooled. And ours were air cooled," Hart explains. "You've been to Las Vegas? The Pyramid (Luxor Hotel & Casino) with the beam coming out of the top, that's my equipment."

And as far as the crew was concerned Hart was welcomed with open arms and viewed in a different light, pardon the pun, from his predecessor, Tom Hurwitz. "I just remember watching the crew watch him do stuff because he wasn't utilizing them. You know, he's a crew leader and he should be delegating," remembers second assistant cameraman Todd Liebler about Hurwitz. "Dick was great; he knew how to use his crew. I mean, they both were nice. Dick definitely seemed more in line just with working with a big crew, you know, more easygoing I'd say."

"He was incredibly professional," remembers Richard Greene. "I don't know if you know what pulling focus is or measuring a shot and all that kind of stuff where the actor or actress has to hit a mark...you know, they were shooting virtually wide open on the lens which gives you a very, very narrow depth of focus. You've got to be spot on or it will go soft on the screen. And he'd do retakes because he wasn't happy, he knew ahead of time, even before the film was processed, that he didn't have what he knew they wanted; yeah, extremely professional."

"He was a great guy and to come in under those circumstances was pretty tough," says additional camera operator Henry Lynk. "He was an ex-gaffer and a cameraman, so he had very good experience and his personality was super nice, so he was a great guy. And he got along well with Gornick."

"Ah, it was a joy. A joy," Michael Gornick says about working with his new director of photography. "And he was accustomed to that kind of pacing because he'd worked both on motion pictures and a lot of TV material, so he knew how to move on quickly, he knew how to save time, he knew how to talk in advance to his grip crew and so forth so they could start prepping down the road, you know, which is the key. And, in terms of talent, I think they're both equally talented. I think it's just that Tom was in a situation that was novel to him, in terms of the need to pick up the pace. And given a perfect situation in Arizona and no bad weather, per se, Tom probably would have survived."

After the test for the Creep truck was completed another meeting for key personnel was scheduled at 12 noon at the production offices. Following that there was a 1PM crew call and by 1:30PM the crew would depart for Dexter in which they would begin setting up for tomorrow's filming, the first of two Sunday shoots for the weary production. "I know in Dexter, Maine where the opening shot got filmed was really interesting because we had to get that street completely cleared," says Henry Nevison. "Now, that's a main street – you know, a small town, but an active town – and I had, like, several P.A.'s going door to door and saying you can't park your car in the street this morning, or this night, because we're going to shoot the first scene of that truck coming down the street. And we had to have the street watered down, so I had to have trucks standing by with water so it could make that effect where there's a glistening street for the truck to come down. And so that was huge!"

"You know, many of these little towns have been through a tremendous change – their mills have closed and jobs have been lost overseas," says David Holt, Dexter's former town manager. "So, when somebody says, you know, we want to come to your town and spend some money the town is more than willing to do whatever it takes. So, anything they wanted to do I tried to make it possible for them to make it happen."

Sunday, November 2, 1986 – Day 40

Day forty would see the quaint Maine town of Dexter become Stephen King's and George Romero's Elmville for the day. Funny, Billy's hometown was Centerville in the original film, so apparently the Hopkins family moved after Stan's brush with death via Billy's voodoo doll.

Today's shooting would cover the opening and closing scenes from the film – scenes 1, 2, 3, 4, 5, 6, 7, and 230 – the wraparound segment featuring the Creep and Billy. It would be the earliest call time of the production with most of the crew having to be ready by 3:30AM. However, the makeup effects team would have to be ready even earlier with a 12:30AM call to start the makeup work on Tom Savini as the Creep. The makeup design by Everett Burrell would be applied by Howard Berger, along with Burrell, and they would begin the application process in their hotel room in the wee hours of the morning. "There were hand appliances. And then we bald capped him. There was a back of the head piece; there was a neck, forehead, nose, cheeks, chin, and upper lip. And we glued all that down and Everett pre-painted it and all – it was really beautiful," explained Howard Berger to Anchor Bay. "We applied it once; it was a six-hour makeup. We started at midnight – it was ready at six in the morning." **(38)**

"We went back, at that point, all the way to *Martin*," says Michael Gornick about his Creep performer, Tom Savini. "And I had both seen him in a number of roles and understood that he was a film-maker, you know, he knew how to project and deliver in front of the camera, in many ways – both as an actor and also as a technician providing materials for the camera."

"You know, the one thing about Tom is he really...he's so theatrical that he really knows how to bring a makeup to life," Greg Nicotero said to Anchor Bay. "I mean, it's really about performance and Tom really brought that character to life." **(39)**

Nicotero's comment here is one hundred percent correct. Indeed, Savini most assuredly breathed life into the Creep with his theatricality; his love of the great Lon Chaney shining through in the role, despite the limited screen time he was afforded.

I should mention that while filming the scene of the Creep Tom Savini was lip syncing to pre-recorded dialogue of actor Joe Silver, something Savini has described as being a bit of a challenge. "Yeah, that was tough," Savini said in the

Above and below: Director Michael Gornick rehearses the opening scene of Billy waiting on the Creep; Tom Savini as the Creep preparing to toss the bundle of comics from the Comet News truck. (courtesy of Rick Catizone and Michael Felsher)

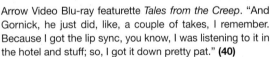

Arrow Video Blu-ray featurette *Tales from the Creep*. "And Gornick, he just did, like, a couple of takes, I remember. Because I got the lip sync, you know, I was listening to it in the hotel and stuff; so, I got it down pretty pat." **(40)**

And while it was a comfort to have someone like Tom Savini on set and being supportive of his effort there was still one person in particular that Gornick longed to have around, to lean on for support or advice, who was no longer there – George Romero. "Yeah, I mean, I knew it probably would be strained after what happened on *Day of the Dead* and that whole dynamic of prepping the script and so forth," Gornick says. "We had one brief conversation before we went into production where I discussed the script with him, just some minor changes that I wanted to make, and it was a very similar discussion that we typically had, even with *Day of the Dead*, where it would be long periods of silence when I would pose something to him on the phone and he would finally say, 'Sure, go ahead.' And for efficiency's sake we just moved on. I didn't say, 'George, you seem troubled. I really want to make that decision, how do you really feel about it?' You just knew there was no conversation to be had. So, aside from those early discussions about a few minor script changes, that was it."

Of course, Tom Savini's Creep wasn't the only star of today's filming. No, our hero of the story, young Billy, would also feature quite prominently. Domenick John Sportelli recalls how exciting it was as a young horror fan to be part of a Stephen King production. "I remember getting up super early, as a matter of fact it was 3AM and a young girl who was part of the crew picked us up, and it was dark and all

Above left and right: Tom Savini as the Creep proudly poses with his group of young protégés: (left to right) Greg Nicotero, Howard Berger, Everett Burrell, and Mike Trcic; Savini's Creep goes Norman Bates on Greg Nicotero! (courtesy of Michael Felsher)

that fun stuff, and drove us to the set," says Sportelli. "So, as we're driving to the set in the dark it was sort of like this discussion about Stephen King and how he gets his ideas; just really cool stuff. So, that was a really cool set up for me, you know, to get me into like that cool kind of mood. And then getting there, I remember vividly, getting to the scene and seeing that beautiful, like, just idyllic town, that center of town, with the hill. And they were spraying down the whole town with fire hoses to make it look like fresh rain. And as a kid I'd never been exposed to anything like that, so it was just so cool to see such a big production."

As for being on set Sportelli doesn't recall much prep or rehearsal, just simply showing up and following the directions from Michael Gornick, who made a favorable impression on the young man. "I never felt intimidated, I never felt as though this guy disliked kids or was hard on me or anything. He was just pleasant and funny and happy and gave direction really well; never seemed frustrated with me when a take didn't go well. I never had that impression of being anxious or nervous," says Sportelli. "He was just so calming and calling me by my first name, 'Domenick, so this is what I want you to say and do and look; you're so surprised and, wow, you just wanna get your hands on this comic book and it's the greatest thing you've ever seen and you can't wait to get it, it's the first one, it's hot off the presses', you know, this kind of thing; very interactive and happy and friendly."

As for his co-star in the film, Tom Savini, even though his time was limited, Sportelli has nothing but positive memories of the horror legend. "Super, super cool; it's funny, because as a child, growing up with family that watched horror movies he was a known name with horror movies and makeup effects and stuff like that," he says. "You know, I never really had the opportunity to speak with him directly or spend time with him on the set, aside from the actual shot, but vividly remember him across from me with that makeup on and seeing it for the first time and being like, 'Wow!'; him being very lighthearted and kind of silly with me to make me more comfortable as well."

Next, we'll discuss one of the more interesting facets of the day's filming – for me, at least – which would be the Creep's ride, the Comet News Agency delivery truck. And one quick side note, if I may, regarding the name of the Creep's truck is that it was born out of nostalgia for Michael Gornick, such as the filming of George A. Romero's *Martin* which was shot ten years prior in the little town of Braddock, PA. "I named it Comet News because my favorite store in Braddock, Pennsylvania was Comet News right on Braddock Ave," he fondly recalls.

"The Dodge truck that the Creep drives up in, in the opening of the movie, I rented from some guy in Maine who was in the process of restoring it," says Steve Arnold. "He had not quite finished his restoration when I found it but he agreed to let us choose the final midnight blue paint color and we had it professionally painted for him – seems like that cost about $700."

The Creep's truck was a 1947 Dodge, one-ton flatbed, with a stake body, and the story of how it was located by the production is quite an entertaining and serendipitous one. "I was living in Orrington, which is adjacent to Bangor, was taking a load of garbage to the Brewer town dump and a crew was out in the field trying to set up shots for this movie, saw me driving by, chased me down the road, stopped me or flagged me down, and then told me they wanted my truck for the movie," says the truck's owner Patrick Reid. "My truck had some body damage to it from decades before; somebody had hit a telephone pole and damaged one of the fenders. They showed me an artist's drawing, one of the sketches, of what the perceived truck in the movie is supposed to be and it looked a heck of a lot like my truck, which is why they were so excited and chased me down the road and stopped me. And then they offered to go ahead and do the body work, you know, in exchange for using the truck."

The production would indeed deliver on their promise and have the truck's body work repairs completed and have it painted for Reid. Someone in either the production art department or the auto body repair shop did a little research and found out one of the original colors that the truck was manufactured in and had it painted to that specification. They would also have the windows temporarily tinted to conceal the driver.

And to lend a little personality to the vehicle, to make it the "Comet News Agency" truck, they would add a bevy of artwork and graphics to it as well. But they'd have to get creative to pull that off. "We couldn't really get the approval, I guess, to paint all of this graphic stuff on this truck. And so we were like, 'Well, what are we going to do? How are we going to do this?' And we ended up doing all those graphics on paper that we glued on to that truck with rubber cement," says Steve Arnold. "And we took photographs of the truck and we made measurements and then we laid out patterns and all that kind of stuff."

"What we did was, they generated vinyl, we didn't hand paint the stuff on the truck," Eileen Garrigan explains. "The art department, Steve Arnold, I think, and Bruce (Miller), came up with all the drawings and had them made in vinyl so that we could do it quickly when it was time, you know, when we had the truck. I think they had to paint the truck to like a midnight blue maybe, I think is what I remember. Yeah, midnight blue. And then we put all the...you know, we were thinking of them more like decals. We wanted it to look like it was a hand-painted truck and we did our best to get it all smoothed on there."

To design those graphics Steve Arnold and Bruce Miller would turn to Beth Kuhn, who had come in late to the production out in Arizona as a sort of fill in for whatever Steve Arnold couldn't take care of at the time, but for all intents and purposes serving as art director. Kuhn would rely on her artistic instincts and design an array of dragons, demons, and celestial imagery to adorn the antique Dodge. "You know, I think I talked with Bruce (Miller) about the kind of things he wanted on it and I just started drawing and did it in such a way that we could use this low-tech stick-on stuff," Kuhn explains. "But I just did research on monsters – that's my natural drawing style, the style of those creatures and things on the truck."

Another important aspect to the design of the Creep's truck was the canopy that covers the flatbed, which was a large canvas top made rigid with conduit tubing. And once more the scenic artists in the art department made it come to life, so to speak. "I think we also had to dye down the canvas tent cover, or whatever you want to call it, that's on the truck," Eileen Garrigan explains. "Yeah, I think they had to have that made, so it was like a white canvas, and we toned that down with coffee or something; I think we dyed it down with coffee and made it look dusty."

As for driving the truck during the scene it would be the owner, Patrick Reid, who would handle the duties rather than stunt coordinator Taso Stavrakis, who would ride shotgun relaying directions from Michael Gornick via radio communication. "I think originally they weren't going to have me drive the truck at all, but the truck was a very difficult truck to drive. And that's why they decided to ask me to do it and Taso to be inside taking the communications over walkie-talkie from the director," says Reid. "The reason why they couldn't drive it was that it popped out of first gear on occasion; and also had pretty poor steering."

"They do that with antiques a lot – antique and custom cars, classic cars – when you're doing something like that you just let the owner drive," says Taso Stavrakis. "You know, I'm not gonna grind your old clutch on your '47 Chevy truck, whatever it is. You wanna drive it, I'll just sit here."

"They just had to caution me, because I was used to driving the truck, on how to slow it down so that the boy on the bicycle could catch up to me," follows up Reid about shooting the opening scene. "Because the first few times we ran through it I just drove it, you know, and I didn't realize there was a little boy on a bicycle chasing after me."

Much like they did with the Creep's Comet News truck when it came to dressing Main Street in Dexter the art department would once again take center stage. Some of the signs and storefronts along the street would be transformed such as the old Berry's Rexall pharmacy becoming an antique & toy store and the former Sears lighted sign being re-dressed. Even the Webber Oil building down the street would have prop gas pumps placed in front, along with a wrecker truck. Unfortunately most of these details are lost to the viewer because they're simply too far off in the distance to be clearly picked up.

However, something not too far off from the eye of the camera is the prop newsstand that Billy stops at while in pursuit of the Creep's delivery truck. The newsstand, which was built in Arizona, would be painted by Eileen Garrigan. "It was a dark green, in fact I remember it was Benjamin Moore Park Green was the actual paint color," she says. "That was one of my go-to colors. It was one of Benjamin Moore's standard colors, Park Green. It was just a ubiquitous color."

And although it's difficult to spot on film the newsstand was littered with initials from various crew members; a makeshift "curtain call", if you will. Some of the names include "GN '81" for Greg Nicotero - who graduated high school in 1981 in Pittsburgh - and "LRB" for Logan Roy Berkshire, among numerous others. I should mention that the detail of the newsstand is lovingly replicated in the film's animation with one of the initials featured on it, "TAL", possibly for Tal Schneider - an art department production assistant in Arizona - clearly visible.

As for the locals in Dexter it was an unusual – and at times monotonous – but highly educational way to spend the morning as they got a chance to see how a motion picture is filmed right on their very own Main Street, U.S.A. "They drove this old truck delivering newspapers from the top of the hill, at the top of the street, to the end of the street and it stopped, I think, once. And they shot that two or three times and to me it looked like the same thing each time," says then Dexter town manager David Holt. "But who am I to criticize? You know, I'm not a film-maker. So, I guess they were happiest with the last shot."

By lunchtime Laurel had everything they needed for the film's opening sequence to go ahead and move on, and so they did.

The production would drive about 5 miles southwest out of Dexter to an area called Ripley at State Route 154 and Fire Road 95 (which today is named Neals Drive). Here they would film the closing shot of the Creep in the back of his truck throwing out copies of the *Creepshow* comic book.

For the scene, Savini's Creep character would sport quite a different look than he had earlier where he wore a simple workman-style uniform, which he'd utilized his own personal socks and shoes for. For the closing scene he would don a more elaborate costume which would feature an ascot, vest and chain, and a flowing cape. "I'm sure we made some of that," says Eileen Sieff-Stroup. "We probably rented it from CMU, rented some bits and pieces."

As it appears in the completed film the animation

transitions back to live action as the camera pans away from the field, where Billy's Venus flytraps have just devoured the bullies, over to Tom Savini's Creep standing in the back of the Comet News truck. As the camera pans over you can see some prop cyclone fencing in the foreground which brought about a humorous, yet highly appropriate, memory for Beth Kuhn regarding the preparation for the scene. "We needed chain-link fence for part of a shot and so we figured out how much we needed, bought some, and we set it up. And then it was towards the end of the day and everybody decided we needed more chain-link fence. And it was shooting in the morning, but there were no more stores open with chain-link fence. And the art department's driver was Stephen King's brother-in-law (Tom Spruce). He goes, 'Oh, well, Stephen has some chain-link fence in his basement!' And I said, 'Oh, would he let us use it?'...'Oh, sure!' So, we get a truck and drive over to Stephen King's house and go in his basement and he's got bats living in his basement," laughs Kuhn. "Bats living in the basement! And we have to go in and get this chain-link fence out of there at like, I don't know, seven o'clock at night in the winter time. And I just thought it was cool because, you know, he had that iron fence around his house and on each corner post there was a bat on the rod iron."

Unfortunately there would be some slightly negative news for the day as David Ball notified all crew members that the bonding company, Film Finances, had appointed Ted Kurdyla to the film in an executive capacity. Kurdyla would now have approval on all production matters which meant, of course, he was now closely monitoring the production's purse strings. "It was something that Film Finances was doing on its own," says New World Pictures' Jeff Schechtman. "Because the deal that was made with New World was really for a very specific price and it was like, 'You have to deliver this film and Film Finances is bonding it and we're not responsible for anything a penny over X', whatever X was at the time. And there was real pressure on Film Finances to make sure this got done."

"What happens normally if the bondsman thinks that the production is threatening to claim on them they will send in somebody like me," David Ball explains. "And that's what I've done for them many, many times. So, they send this guy that's basically their accountant, Ted Kurdyla, who's going to look in and see the threat to Film Finances; fine. But he wasn't running the production, he's a bean counter. He wasn't a particularly nice person, but he didn't have a particularly nice job. You know? And I sympathized with the job because I've done it many times. To walk on set and say, 'Hi, guys. I'm the new unit asshole.' Well it's true. Isn't it? Nobody wants *them* coming in to the set. Nobody wants *them*, the bondsman, on the set."

"Look, he (Kurdyla) had a responsibility and they are the insurer in essence and so while initially you see them as the boogeyman you realize later in time that they're a necessary evil. They, just like me, are reacting to the situation and it's no one's fault, they're protecting money, and I needed the money to make the film. So, I mean, at some point I had to respect where it was coming from," says Michael Gornick. "So, it was a new process for me to go through. I never witnessed George (Romero) having those kind of problems or at least they weren't visible to me. But, he never had a bonding company, per se. But, we're talking about major monies now; we're talking about millions as opposed to hundreds of thousands that we typically would make motion pictures on. *Dawn* was made for basically $400,000, you know, that's still a nice hunk of change, but once you get into millions you involve banks and investors and that's why you have bonding companies, to protect their money, and so I understood. It was tough in many cases and there were decisions made based upon the fact that you had to crunch the schedule to satisfy the bonding company. But they were always gentlemen, it was never like a strong-arm, it was never somebody coming on set and saying, 'Come with me'. They were very, very considerate."

Tuesday, November 4, 1986 – Day 41

The forty-first day of production would begin after the first and only scheduled off day for a Monday – November 3 – which also just happened to be the 40th birthday for one Tom Savini who celebrated in Bangor with his young makeup effects protégés.

However, while the cast and crew were taking it easy there was some news to report from the previous day involving a letter from Richard Rubinstein to David Ball requesting that he prepare an estimate of the costs incurred after New World failed to approve Loretta Swit for the Annie Lansing role, which dated all the way back to late September. This was intended to help alleviate a little more financial stress on Laurel considering that New World had ample opportunity to prevent such a fiasco from occurring early on.

Also, a short memo addressed to Charles Carroll from Taso Stavrakis was drafted on Monday in which Stavrakis let it be known that he was concerned about non-stunt persons performing tasks that could be considered a stunt. "Inexperienced people pose a higher degree of risk and danger to themselves and others on the set," Stavrakis wrote to Carroll. "This risk can be somewhat alleviated with time, time for rehearsal or practice. This 'time' however seems to be an illusive commodity." **(41)**

Just who Stavrakis is referring to I'm not completely certain of, but it's a safe bet that it was the actor who would feature prominently on this day of filming – Holt McCallany.

Filming for today would take place at the former Viner Brothers shoe factory on Laurel's makeshift sound stage. "I remember there were, like, shoe molds all over the place," says Bruce Miller. "It was wet and it was dark and cold."

The day's schedule would encompass scenes from *Old Chief Wood'nhead* – 31A, 32, 32A, and 33 – which you might know better as the death sequence of Sam Whitemoon. With time having had run out in Prescott Holt McCallany was flown into Bangor for the day to finish up his character's doomed storyline. "I remember that it was a challenging scene because I'm pulled through the wall," says McCallany. "Right, I'm pulled through a wall and then scalped. Isn't that what happens? Yeah, and so it was a little bit of a challenging scene physically, you know, because I had to kind of be able to support my weight. You

Above and below: Stunt coordinator Taso Stavrakis stands alongside the Comet News truck in Ripley, Maine preparing for the final shot of the film; Michael Gornick shares a laugh with Tom Savini before filming begins. (courtesy of Bruce Miller and Michael Gornick)

know, I was in good shape in those days, I used to do a lot of sit-ups and it helped me on that day, do you know what I mean, because I needed to support my weight on the other side of that wall."

As McCallany describes, it was indeed a physically challenging scene to perform because it was in fact a stunt; being grabbed by the hair and pulled through a wall is something typically reserved for the stunt department. However, with this being McCallany's first feature and him being young and gung-ho – something he still retains to this day in his work ethic – he decided he wanted to perform the gag himself. "From an actor's standpoint, I mean, I know exactly why they want to do their own stunts," says Michael Gornick. "I mean, how do you leave your character to someone else? You want to continue; the continuity, you want to make sure it's there."

"I've always tried to do all my own stunts in all my films. The only times that I haven't done it is when producers have forbidden me to do something, you know, a driving thing is usually what it is," McCallany explains. "And what they don't always understand is that the audience likes to see the actor try to do it himself, you know. And certainly in a scene like that where, I mean, it's almost a close-up, right? I mean, if I remember the shot correctly. So, there are certain times when you just can't use a stunt double."

Of course in doing your own stunt work one of the potential risks could very well be inexperience, as Taso Stavrakis cited in his memo. Another, however, could be something that the performer, whether it's a certified stuntman or the actor himself, has zero control over and that would be the craftsmanship in the scene, in this case the wall. "Now, we had built like three of the walls where he was gonna pull him through so if something went wrong we could put another wall in there and it would have the opening so he could reach through and pop him through there," says Logan Berkshire. "And we were watching from up above and they said, 'Okay, now we're gonna pull him through there.' And I remembered at that point that we had nailed, we had not screwed them, we nailed through that portal where he was gonna pull through and there were nails sticking in there and I thought, 'Oh my god, he's gonna pull him through and he's gonna get impaled on those nails', and we had to stop everything; right when they were ready to shoot – 'No, no, no!'"

"Well, when you speak to Logan next, thank him for me," laughs an appreciative McCallany.

"So, we went down there and we quickly took the drywall off and the director said, 'Oh my god! Those were sitting in there?' And I was like, 'Yeah, I'm sorry, man. We just remembered it.' He said, 'Well, thank god you remembered it,'" Berkshire recalls. "And Gornick, you know, he was such a great guy about it. It was great, you know, I expected like, 'Get the hell out of here, you dummy!'"

But the breakaway wall wasn't the only misadventure on set today. Who would have thought that simply breaking a mirror with a television set would be anything other than easy? You must remember that we're dealing with a production where if it can go wrong it most certainly will. "Alright, this is a great one, you'll love this," Charles Carroll begins the story. "You remember in the story about the wooden Indian when, I think, he comes into kill Holt and Holt's, like, looking in the mirror and admiring himself and his hair and all of the sudden a TV flies over his shoulder and hits the mirror? When we first tried to do that, we couldn't break the mirror. So, we'd throw it at it. Then we put it on a cable and we'd try to do it. Then we would try to do it, there was someone on the other side of the wall with a sledgehammer trying to time it so they hit the back of the wall at the same time the TV got there to break the mirror. It was absolutely hilarious! These are things you learn: if you want to break a mirror against the wall, you just put little spacers between it and then it breaks real easy. We didn't, the mirror was right against the wall. It took us, like, twenty takes to break a freaking mirror on a wall – on a set that we completely controlled."

One tidbit about this scene that echoes throughout the finale of the segment is all three of the young thugs are watching *The Cisco Kid* when Chief Wood'nhead shows up for retribution, whereas in Romero's original screenplay the soon-to-be-dead trio all have John Ford's *Rio Grande* playing on their televisions. The production would find it much more budget friendly instead to use a property like *The Cisco Kid*, plus it was a clever nod to *The Raft* where Randy and Deke called one another Pancho and Cisco.

During filming of these scenes a 3/4-inch video playback machine was used and production assistant Andy Sands was placed in charge of running it, which as it turns out was a terrifying task for the young man. "They had to film a bunch of *Wood'nhead* in Maine. And I remember that the video playback when they were watching *The Cisco Kid* stuff – they actually put me on the tape recorder to do the video playback – and I was like living in fear every time they called me, 'I'm gonna hit the wrong switch on this thing and hit the wrong button and it's all gonna be over,'" Sands remembers. "It was adjusted to film speed, so they would be able to film it into the scene because video moves at a different speed than film; had they just played a normal videotape the line would have shown up, the registration, but they're running all at the same speed. But it wasn't running constantly, they needed someone, 'Alright, you have to turn this on, run it back to this spot, and play it again.' And they said, 'Alright, Andy, you go do that.' And I'm like, 'I've never touched one of these devices before!'"

During the filming of this sequence Michael Gornick had the opportunity to add just a little extra flair to the proceedings with the use of Dutch angles, in particular the shot of Sam Whitemoon backing into the hallway shocked as Chief Wood'nhead stands in the doorway, the camera angle slightly askew, giving it that classic comic book feel. It's a technique he would have enjoyed using more if time had been more of a luxury. "I think Dutch angles were probably lost depending who was the D.P. at the time, because we went through a transition at some point," he explains. "But, I mean, it's part of a director's duty, I think, to visually set up the circumstance. I would initially have to walk through them, but once we established the fact that I wanted to use Dutch they would come back at me sometimes and say, 'Do you want to place it here? Do you want to do it again?' So, it became a kind of device that they understood quickly. But, yeah, it was born out of the comic books. I think it was also born out of my TV viewing habits as a kid; that, you know, the TV set was high, I was typically low, lying, or whatever and that's how I viewed the world, like, from a Dutch angle."

As for other production-related news, Richard Rubinstein would draft a full-page memo to Jeff Schechtman stating Laurel's view of the whole casting fiasco regarding the Annie Lansing role and demanding that New World, in addition to paying off Sheree North, reimburse Laurel for the additional costs encountered by the delays because of New World's failure to approve an actress in a timely fashion. "As you are aware Film Finances has put substantial pressure on the production to complete the picture given costs to date," Rubinstein asserted. "I believe it important for New World to relieve some of this pressure immediately!!" **(42)**

"I mean, he was not the easiest guy in the world to get

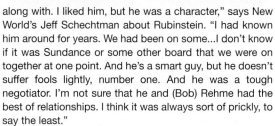

Above left and right: Savini's Creep poses for photos with Maine location manager Henry Nevison and stunt coordinator Taso Stavrakis. (courtesy of Michael Felsher)

along with. I liked him, but he was a character," says New World's Jeff Schechtman about Rubinstein. "I had known him around for years. We had been on some...I don't know if it was Sundance or some other board that we were on together at one point. And he's a smart guy, but he doesn't suffer fools lightly, number one. And he was a tough negotiator. I'm not sure that he and (Bob) Rehme had the best of relationships. I think it was always sort of prickly, to say the least."

Another important memo sent out today was from Charles Carroll letting all crew members know that company expenditures were now going to be much stricter and that anything over $50 would need written approval. Again, this was due to the presence of Film Finances now being on location for the duration of filming.

Wednesday, November 5, 1986 – Day 42

Day forty-two would be noteworthy because finally – yes, it was for real this time – Laurel had their Annie Lansing with the debut of Lois Chiles.

Now, we've already discussed most of the headaches and budget issues regarding the casting of the role, but there's one topic you might not have thought about that was just as important and that would be her wardrobe for the film. Remember, time and money had been spent with Barbara Eden selecting a particular look which would now, of course, have to be adjusted to suit our new lead actress, Lois Chiles. And that task would fall on the shoulders of Eileen Sieff-Stroup. "In both cases, with both Barbara and Lois, I wanted to use a sweater because: very limited budget, I knew the stunt people driving the car were not all

going to be women, so I was going to have to fit whatever I got over whoever they gave me. So, I thought sweaters, the twin set, fashionable at the time, beautiful cashmere, that's going to help the look, you know, that soft look," she explains. "Well, so they cast Barbara, we did her clothes and then her mother became ill and she dropped out; so, then they cast Lois. So, they're like, 'Well, can't you use Barbara's clothes on Lois?' And I'm like, 'Well, she's a foot taller. You know, she might be about the same size around but, no, you can't use anything.' So then I flew to New York and shopped with Lois."

Sieff-Stroup would strive for a similar style for her new Annie, but she would receive an assist from Chiles who definitely had ideas of her own as to what the character should dress like. "I might have used the same jewelry – (that) might have been the only thing that I transferred," Sieff-Stroup explains. "Barbara had, like, a taupey wool skirt that was really pretty. But with Lois we talked about it and she was like, 'I think...' – you know, she had this cute Southern accent – 'I think she should be in a leather skirt.' So, we went and we shopped these beautiful taupey-colored leather skirts and that's what Lois wears, she wears a leather skirt."

As for what was scheduled tonight on the still unopened I-395 on-ramp for the Parkway South, it was a mixture of old and new, you could say.

For the old, scene 117-119 would once again make its way onto the schedule of Annie dropping cigarette ashes inside her vehicle and then reacting in terror as she runs off the road. Scenes 121-122 and 121A-122 of the hitchhiker being hit by Annie's car and scene 123-135A of the aftermath of the hit, including the 180-degree spin of the Mercedes would also be on the day's ledger. All of these would be listed on upcoming call sheets, so just how much was accomplished I really can't say. However, a major mechanical issue with the Mercedes would prevent the 180-degree spin from being performed this evening, which would in turn cause some friction between Taso Stavrakis and Charles Carroll. I'll discuss that in tomorrow's section.

As for our new material this evening, those would include scene 130-132, scene 127/129, and scene 124, 126, 129, 130, 131A, and 132. And just to be clear, yes, 124, 126, 129, 130, 131A, and 132 are all part of the same scene in the sequential shot list. Now, while this all sounds like a great deal of action taking place, it would just entail Lois Chiles sitting in her Mercedes immediately following her striking Tom Wright, observing the Dover sign blowing around in the wind near the hitchhiker's lifeless body, and momentarily opening her car door to get out and then promptly getting back inside the car. And with the exception of 127/129 the remainder of these would not find their way back onto the schedule, so we know they were most likely completed on this night.

And since we're on the subject of Michael Gornick's sequential shot list perhaps now is the perfect time for him to describe the process in preparing such a list and how soon it got started. "It began the moment I was given a kind of green light from Richard Rubinstein to become the director," the meticulous Gornick explains. "I remember going home that very weekend and I would immerse myself in just a kind of relaxed mental situation where I would almost meditate on the entire film. So, I would read it and then bring up individual pages and try to conceptualize visually because at that point I probably had a stronger history in terms of being a director of photography, so I needed to see things visually first before I could imagine any kind of a direction that I might give it – or guidance... you know, direction is probably a misnomer, how much can you direct a script, per se? It basically gives you an outline, a format. But visually I had to see it, so I would spend hour upon hour looking at individual pages and visualizing a movement, camera angles, coverage, inserts."

And while Gornick was always thorough and prepared as best as possible, he never was so rigid that suggestions from cast or crew would be disregarded. "Working with Michael was actually a real godsend because he's a real kind human being," says Tom Wright. "He was very generous, he had his ideas, but he was open to collaboration and if I had an idea that he felt was better than his he would go with it. He just wanted to make the best film possible and whenever a director has that as their primary function or primary goal you're going to have a good work experience."

"Yeah, he was pretty cool. You know, he was kind of dry, pretty much all business and all that," remembers George Dreisch. "He was real good to work with, especially setting up stunts and things like that. You know, he was always, like, right there listening. And that was the biggest thing, he was always listening. He'd accept valid input from anybody."

As for production office-related work, David Ball would

Above: Tom Savini as the Creep rehearsing the final scene of the film shot in Ripley, Maine. (courtesy of Eileen Sieff Stroup)

draft a letter to Dexter town manager David Holt, thanking him on behalf of Laurel-CST, Inc. for the town's cooperation and hospitality.

Thursday, November 6, 1986 – Day 43

The forty-third day of production would fall victim to Mother Nature as inclement weather once again decided to wreak havoc on *Creepshow 2*. It started with 1.7 inches of snowfall that blanketed the Bangor area in the morning hours, which was then followed up by an additional 0.18 inches of rain. So, with all of that to contend with, filming would be moved from the I-395/Parkway South location to the Viner Brothers studio cover. "You think we had bad

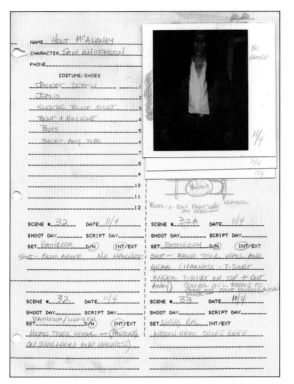

Above: Holt McCallany's wardrobe continuity page for his death scene, which he flew into Bangor to shoot after the production ran out of time in Prescott. (courtesy of Eileen Sieff-Stroup)

weather in Arizona, in Prescott? Forget it! We had dreadful weather in Maine," says David Ball.

All of the scenes originally scheduled for today would appear again on future call sheets and it's doubtful much of anything from them was accomplished, but for the sake of it we'll include the scheduled scenes here anyway. Familiar territory would once again be on tap with scenes 117-119, 121-122, and 121A-122 finding their way back on the day's ledger.

New scenes would also be featured with scene 136 being scheduled of Annie looking into her rear-view mirror, as Stephen King's character's truck blows by, immediately after leaving the scene of the accident. This scene would be scheduled tomorrow as well, but most likely was completed the following week. Also new to the schedule were scenes 147, 148, and 149 of Annie driving moments after she's initially hit the hitchhiker. In these scenes you see her cleaning the blood off her windshield with her wipers and then talking to herself about whether she can live with what she's done. Scene 147 – which is an establishing shot of the Mercedes passing by the camera – would be listed again on future call sheets.

Now, writing a book like this can be an immense challenge when you're striving for complete accuracy and thoroughness. I'm a perfectionist at heart and when I can't achieve the accuracy I'm striving for it bothers me. But despite that feeling you do your best and make educated guesses based off the material you have available. It's very

much like detective work where you're searching for clues in an attempt to piece together a mystery. In this particular case it was thanks to the November 5 call sheet and Eileen Sieff-Stroup's costume continuity binder which came to my rescue for this day.

At the bottom of the November 5 call sheet, under the advance schedule, scene 183 would be listed as a cover set option. Well, that's exactly what would happen as the production would indeed work on tackling most of scene 183 on this evening, which would encompass Annie sitting in her car moments after the hitchhiker has just been knocked off the roof of her vehicle by a downed tree, followed by the hitchhiker opening the passenger side door and being shot by a terror stricken Annie. Numerous continuity Polaroids of both Tom Wright in his stage 3 makeup and Lois Chiles in her stage 2 "dirty" wardrobe were in Sieff-Stroup's binder dated 11/6. Scene 183 would also be revisited five days later as it consisted of nine separate shots all together (183 through 183H). Tom Savini, who was still in town, would handle the squib hits on Tom Wright being that Berger, Nicotero, Burrell, and Trcic weren't licensed for such work.

What's really of interest here is the fact that for these scenes of Chiles blasting Wright with the pistol inside the Mercedes the production chose to not use one of the stunt cars, but instead used the "hero" car, the film's picture car, which belonged to insurance agent Gerry Roy. This was supposed to be the car used solely for glamour shots of Chiles driving, not for scenes requiring special effects. You have to remember that Tom Wright was wearing multiple squibs and as he told *Fangoria* magazine during their visit to the set Tom Savini didn't hold back in the blood department. "Savini's bloodbags are like water balloons," Wright told reporter Tony Timpone. "When the shoulder squib went off, the blood showered the crew on the other side of the stage!" **(43)**

"The biggest problem with the stunt cars is that they were good for pass-by and wider shots, but once you got into detailed work like interiors and so forth they fell apart," Michael Gornick explains. "Because they were imported and a lot of times the coloration didn't match; the continuity was bad, they were missing parts. Looking inside, in terms of what car we had available for us at that point, it wouldn't have played – it would have looked dreadful; there were imperfections with the glass and so forth."

It's also important to note that on the upcoming November 10 call sheet towards the bottom portion of the section where set descriptions and scene numbers are listed it states "INT MERCEDES/N – Complete unfinished Scs: 181, 183, 182, 177". So, that tells us besides scene 183, the other scenes listed on that call sheet possibly had work attempted on them during tonight's filming, as well.

One final note regarding this night involves a story I was told from George Dreisch about an issue regarding blanks for the gun used to shoot the hitchhiker. Before I go into the details of the story I want to clarify that this incident could have happened on another night, which would be November 11. But based on certain details of the story I felt it was safer to assume it would be this night, especially considering the plan originally wasn't to film at the studio space.

For the scene where Tom Wright opens the car door to

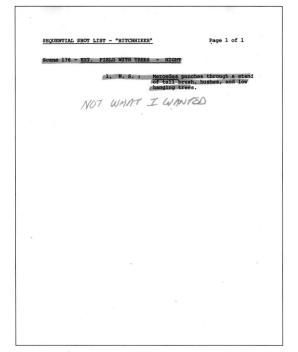

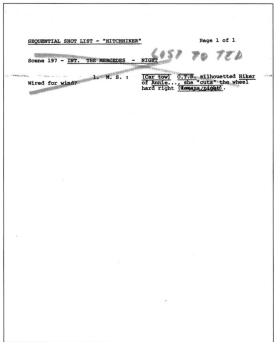

reach for Lois Chiles, Dreisch was in the midst of preparing to raise the height of the Mercedes so that it was easier for Tom Wright, who's on the ground basically, to reach inside the vehicle to accomplish the shot. "In the course of me working on the car is when I guess it came to the forefront that they didn't have ammunition, blank ammunition, for the gun, which as I remember was a .38 Special snub-nose. So, once again, I threw myself in there and volunteered that I knew somebody where we could probably get a couple dozen prime cases on relatively short notice – like about 30 minutes," Dresich says. "But, there was still the stress of, at least from what I saw, and again this was kind of happening on the periphery and behind me, there was, I guess, a question as to who had actually dropped the ball. And I'm not certain, it might have been – Jim Feng (property master) might have been involved. I'm pretty sure Bruce Miller was, as was Taso, and David (Ball), and I don't know, there might have been some others. And, you know, it got fairly heated as I remember. And that was semi-prior to me volunteering that I knew where we could get some prime cases. Anyway, the exchange going on looked like it was kind of an accusation/counter accusation deal as to who had dropped it and stuff. And that's when I kind of turned around and said I could make it happen by getting these primes cases, which I guess is not necessarily as satisfactory as having regular theatrical blanks, but anyway, they went for it. So, Taso and I beat feet over to the Bangor police station and I spoke to a sergeant I knew who did reloading and that and he hooked us up with some prime cases. So, we were back in probably 30 to 40 minutes time and things could move forward again. But, through that exchange there was definitely perceptible tension – you know, almost to the degree of I think it was probably almost on the verge of going unprofessional (between Stavrakis and Ball)."

Okay, regarding the 180-degree spin for scene 123-135A – which was originally scheduled again for today – and the mechanical issues involved with it that I touched on in yesterday's section, here's what happened. Charles Carroll drafted what could be considered a rather stern memo to Taso Stavrakis and his Mercedes mechanical team, which included George Dreisch, about "collective responsibility" and the fact that the Mercedes vehicle to be used on November 5 apparently had no rear brakes. "Not only was work time lost, but we had a potentially dangerous situation on our hands," wrote Carroll. "I cannot tolerate this kind of over-sightedness on *Creepshow 2* again." **(44)**

This would instigate an even more stern response from Stavrakis about that "collective responsibility". In his letter Stavrakis explained that the Mercedes had indeed been inspected and tested just mere hours prior and that no problems were observed. Apparently an accidental loss of brake fluid was the culprit and Stavrakis paid compliment to his mechanic, Dreisch, for discovering the issue before the vehicle was utilized and for the quick remedy provided by his team. "Fortunately for you, I was prepared for a difficult water shoot in Arizona when few others were, and I took up a great deal of the slack then. Now, I'm under the gun and I need all the help I can get. A slap on the wrist for another piece of bad luck is not a great boost for morale," Stavrakis stated. "I have tolerated your oversights from the beginning of this picture, sir, please be kind enough to tolerate mine." **(45)**

And lastly a memo from David Ball was given out to crew

notifying them that there was some unfortunate news regarding the payroll. "The ongoing saga continues and you've heard producers' excuses before, but would you believe that we received the paychecks for a film entitled *Destiny*?," Ball wrote tongue in cheek. "And the destiny of our checks is at present unknown." **(46)**

Friday, November 7, 1986 – Day 44

Day forty-four would receive a rare break from Mother Nature as temperatures rose into the low 50's which, coupled with the previous day's light rainfall, helped to quickly melt the 1.7 inches of snow that had fallen on Thursday.

With that being the case the production would return to the I-395 Parkway South location where work would wrap up on scene 123-135A, meaning that pesky 180-degree spin would finally be in the can. And unlike the shot of Annie's character fish-tailing away from the accident scene, which upon careful Blu-ray inspection reveals it to be Taso Stavrakis, the shot of Annie spinning 180-degrees after immediately hitting the hitchhiker would be performed by stunt woman Chere Bryson. Now, why certain scenes were handled by Bryson, while others were performed by Stavrakis, I couldn't tell you. I was unable to reach Bryson for an interview for this project and, frankly, Stavrakis had such a negative experience on the production, particularly once it moved to Maine, that he admittedly blocked a lot of it out of his mind.

As for Chere Bryson, she was brought in by Stavrakis when it was decided that a more experienced stunt woman would be needed for the rigorous requirements of the segment – this was when Barbara Eden was still attached. Before finally deciding on Bryson, however, Stavrakis looked at several potential stunt women for the gig including Christine Baur (*Silver Bullet*, *Maximum Overdrive*) and Laurie Creach (*Motel Hell*, *Reform School Girls*). One of the more interesting candidates he considered was Sandra Gimpel, who had worked as a stunt coordinator on *Harper Valley P.T.A* with Barbara Eden, where she had also doubled her on the show. Gimpel had a wealth of production experience under her belt having worked on classic television series' like *Star Trek* and *Lost in Space,* as well as numerous feature films such as *Escape from New York*, *The Goonies*, and the recent *Evil Dead 2*. In the end though, it would be Bryson's job.

"I called Barbara Eden at her home, I called her, and I asked her if she had a double that she uses – a lot of stars do. I figured, you know, I'll give that person work. You get work, they get work – most of them come with them," Stavrakis explains. "And she was mad that I had called her at home. Now I see why, I hate it when people call me, 'How did you find my number?' I said, 'I'm sorry. I'm the stunt coordinator, I just wanted to know if you had a stunt double for you that you want me to hire?'...'No.' Okay, so I find Chere."

"The driving they were talking about I was not comfortable with," says Patty Tallman. "It was snowing and sleeting and ice on the roads and that was not my expertise at all. So, we were very happy to have Chere on board."

Work would also be completed on scene 127/129 – the immediate aftermath of Annie hitting the hitchhiker, his lifeless body on the ground – and scenes 121-122 and 121A-122 of Annie actually hitting the hitchhiker. Also scheduled for the evening were scenes 117/119, 136, and 149. Each one of these would be scheduled for next week, so we're assuming not much was accomplished with these. And scene 147 would once again be featured on the day's ledger – however it too would be listed again on a future call sheet, but instead as second unit.

Saturday, November 8, 1986 – Day 45

The forty-fifth day of production would see a change in venue as the crew would travel roughly a mile west on I-395 to what is today exit 4, the main exit ramp for Brewer, Maine, featured as the Hampden exit in the film, which would be home for the next two days of shooting.

As for what was scheduled this evening it would be scenes 150, 151, 152, 154, 155, 156-158, 159-161, 161A, and 162. These scenes are all part of the sequence where Annie has her second encounter with the hitchhiker. As Annie turns off on to the Hampden exit she notices the hitchhiker walking along the side of the road and screeches her Mercedes to a halt. The hitchhiker – in his stage 2 makeup – takes Annie by surprise by suddenly appearing at her driver-side window and for the first time utters his classic line, "Thanks for the ride".

I should also mention that scene 157 from Romero's screenplay would not be incorporated into Michael Gornick's shot list for this sequence. The scene contains a line of dialogue from Annie when she first notices the hitchhiker as she exits off the highway: "Sorry, pal. I'm not stoppin' to pick you u..."

As previously mentioned in the Day 38 section there were some questions about the Bangor location manager, Henry Nevison, and his experience, or lack thereof, with film productions which began to surface. "Henry, I think this was his first time doing locations," Andy Sands explains. "He was really trying to make sure everything was okay."

"That was something that Stephen King wanted," says Michael Morgan. "He wanted as many people from Maine hired as possible."

"Yeah, I mean, Henry, god bless him, he just...I don't think had a production sense," an apologetic Michael Gornick says. "Very nice guy; loved Henry."

"All I can say is that I had a taste of doing that and I would never do it again; because as a location manager you can do 99 things right and the thing you don't do right, that's all they talk about," says Nevison as he looks back on the experience. "It got frustrating for me because I busted my ass on that project. I mean, I just did so much to make that happen. It's not that you want people to pat you on the back, but you want a little bit of acknowledgment of what you did to make things happen. And I think Stephen King saw that, and Mike Gornick, but it was everybody else who were..."

And while some on the production had concerns about

Nevison and his capabilities, at the same time Nevison had concerns with how some of the out-of-town crew members were treating locals in Bangor. For Nevison he sensed an attitude amongst certain crew members that the locals were just bumpkins not worthy of respect, which bothered him a great deal. "And that was kind of an attitude that I was trying to kind of be a buffer zone with because it was a little bit off-putting," he says. "You know, they'd come in here and just, 'Oh, whatever we want we're gonna get because we're a film crew and we're working with Stephen King.' So, it was the attitude that they brought with them when they arrived that was kind of disconcerting."

"Absolutely; it was sad, it was very sad," agrees Michael Gornick about Nevison's perceptions. "And even producorially speaking, you know, to the very top, there was a distaste for people in Maine, and joking."

And one of the prime targets for members of the production, according to Nevison, was the local caterer. "They gave the caterer such a hard time," he says. "It was always something they had to complain about: 'Well, there's not enough vegetarian entrees and there's not enough...' You know, it was just this prevailing attitude that got very, very uncomfortable for me and the way they treated the local people."

"Shooting nights, especially outdoors in the winter, lunch is like a huge thing because it's the one chance to warm up. You know, get comfortable again," says Ed Fountain. "(The caterer) would make dinner or lunch, whatever it was, and she always had a vegetarian dish. And one day one of the vegetarians said, 'There's pepperoni in here', and she said, 'So what? Pepperoni's not meat, Pepperoni's a spice.'"

Monday, November 10, 1986 – Day 46

Day forty-six would resume shooting the sequence of Annie's second encounter with the hitchhiker on the Hampden exit. Scenes 151, 152, and 156/158 would again be scheduled, along with a gaggle of new ones such as 160, 162, 163, 163B, 163C, 164, and 166. These scenes consisted of the hitchhiker attempting to reach through the sunroof, after Annie has sped away from the exit off-ramp, and getting his arm stuck inside the vehicle.

Additionally, as a cover set option, scenes 177, 181, 182, and 183 would be listed as well. It's of interest to note that scenes 181 and 182 of Annie closing her sunroof as leaves fall inside her car would not appear again on any future call sheets, so apparently the work was completed by this evening.

Much like its predecessor in some respects you could say that Creepshow 2 was a bit of a family affair for some members of the production and none more so than production assistant Tom Spruce. "Now, Tom Spruce is Stephen King's brother-in-law. He's a local guy, he's Maine born and bred. So, he'd be taking me around and we hit it off really well," remembers David Ball. "I'll give you a couple examples of Tom Spruce, his pot was always half full. He'd say, 'Hey, David, look at this.' I'd say, 'Yeah, I'm looking.' He'd say, 'See that radio station?' I said, 'Yeah', he said, 'So, Steve calls up and says, 'Hey, what are you playing

all this shit music for? Put some Doobie Brothers on.' And they said, 'Fuck off. Who are you?' And he said, 'My name is Stephen King.' And they said, 'Oh, sorry. It's not in our program.' He said, 'Oh, fuck it', so he bought the radio station. That's a gem that you wouldn't even know unless you were sitting in the car with Tom Spruce. And then I'd say to him, 'Tom, this is such a beautiful place. What do you do up here?' And he said, 'Well, in the summer we hunt and we fish and we fuck.' And I said, 'What do you do in the winter?' He said, 'We don't fish' (laughs)."

Besides immediate family there were, of course, couples as well: you had production manager Charles Carroll and first A.D. Kato Wittich; you had makeup effects artist Mike Trcic and his wife Christine, who worked in the wardrobe department; and there was best boy Kurt Rimmel and second A.D. Grace Prinzi. All of these couples are still going strong today, as of this writing.

But perhaps the most unusual family ties would belong to Henry Nevison. "At the time I was still married, but my wife (Edith) and I had separated and kind of were estranged, I guess, is the word. And she needed work and we got along even though we knew our marriage wasn't going in the right direction. I said, 'Would you like to work as my assistant, as a P.A.?' And she said, 'Sure.' So, what happened was the producer one day he's talking to me and he says, 'Henry, I noticed that this woman has your same last name. Is she a relative?' I said, 'Well, actually, she's my wife, but we're probably gonna get a divorce.' And he looks at me, he says, 'Wait, wait, I don't understand. You hired your estranged wife to work as your assistant?' I said, 'Yeah.' And you know what, I didn't even think about it before I said it, I said, 'Well, I needed to hire someone I could trust that wouldn't screw me,'" Nevison laughs. "And then, as it turns out, she hooked up with the genny operator (Tom Colston) and they went off and they actually got married. So, as a result of me hiring my estranged wife to work with me on Creepshow 2 she found her next husband."

Tuesday, November 11, 1986 – Day 47

The forty-seventh day of production would once again see filming shift to the makeshift studio at the former Viner Brothers shoe factory. With the weather forecast calling for a mixture of snow, sleet, and rain – which is exactly what the Bangor area received – the production decided wisely to play it safe and plan ahead this time.

Tonight's schedule was another mixture of old and new. Familiar territory such as scene 117-119, Annie clumsily dropping her cigarette in the car, would once again make its way onto the call sheet. As would scene 163 of Annie in her car moments after the hitchhiker surprises her on the Hampden exit ramp. Scene 177, a close-up of Annie

Right: Ed Fountain(right) and Don Hedenburg, who was in town to see his future wife Eileen Garrigan but ended up helping out the production, spread dirt inside the makeshift studio space Laurel rented to replicate a dirt road used in The Hitchhiker(note the set in the background used for the death scene of "Fatso" Gribbens); the fake birch tree limb that Tom Wright bounces off of, which head scenic Eileen Garrigan worked on. (courtesy of Eileen Garrigan)

yelling, "You bastard!", as she drives through the woods and branches smack across the windshield was also revisited. And the completion of scene 183 was on tap mainly consisting of insert shots of Annie fumbling for her revolver and firing it at the hitchhiker, plus a shot of her through the windshield driving the car away. Finally, an insert shot, 191A, of the Mercedes speedometer at 90mph was once again scheduled.

As for our new scenes those would include 171, 173A, and 188C, which were simply insert shots of Annie's foot hitting the brake and gas pedals of the Mercedes. Scene 178A of Annie's point of view as branches slap against the windshield as she wildly drives through the woods was also on tap. Scenes 201, 203, 204, and 205 were also scheduled which were close-ups of Annie's face as she rams the hitchhiker into the tree eventually knocking herself out on the steering wheel. All of these scenes, including 191A, would eventually be re-listed towards the end of production – most as second unit insert shots – so either they weren't shot this evening or there were problems with what was shot and they had to be re-done; chances are they simply never got to them. Another new scene on the night's menu is 200 which according to the call sheet is a shot of Annie while the hitchhiker is on the hood of her car. And lastly scene 189 of Annie smiling as she drives over the hitchhiker as he's down in the middle of the dirt road was also scheduled. And even though the line is actually from scene 187 in Romero's script it was on this night of shooting that Chiles would utter her classic vengeful line, "I got you. I got yooooouuuuu!!!!", just before she runs over the hitchhiker's body.

Tonight's filming would see a visitor to the set in the person of Tony Timpone from *Fangoria* magazine, his first of two nights with the production. In fact the next three days would see press visits from the likes of CNN, *Entertainment Tonight*, and local Bangor media outlets. Timpone's visit, however, was different because *Fangoria* was the horror buff's first option when it came to news about the genre. "I remember when we heard they were shooting in Bangor, Maine we were having a hard time finding a writer in Bangor who could visit the set for us at the time and the editor of *Fangoria* at the time, the interim editor, David McDonnell, suggested, 'Well, why don't you go, Tony?' And I said, 'Sure, that would be fun. I'd love to do it.' You know, I'd been on sets before, but this was a really cool opportunity, so I jumped at it," Timpone recalls. "And I flew into Bangor – it was one of these small propeller planes, it was like a six-seater, because it was a pretty short flight – and Richard Rubinstein was on the same flight, funny enough. And I'd met Rubinstein previously at a horror convention and waiting on line to see *Hannah and Her Sisters,* of all things. Or, wait, maybe it wasn't *Hannah*? It was a Woody Allen movie. I remember I was on line at a movie theater in Manhattan a few months before that and I

Left top, middle and bottom: Annie pays a visit to her gigolo lover to open the story; set photos show the work Steve Arnold did to create the gigolo's condo set which was actually filmed inside the Franklin Place Condominiums. (courtesy of Michael Felsher and Steve Arnold)

ran into Rubinstein. And there he was on the plane, again. So, we couldn't escape each other."

As for his interview subjects while in Bangor he came away most impressed with the actors from the segment. "They were filming scenes of the hitchhiker menacing the woman, played by Lois Chiles. They had a Mercedes inside the stage and they had crew people shaking the car back and forth to create some suspense, of course. They couldn't get the reactions they wanted. I met the actors. I met Lois, she was very sweet," he recalls. "And the coolest actor that day was Tom Wright, who played the hitchhiker; he was a stuntman/actor. I remember he was looking at this as a big break for him because he always dreamed of being a horror star."

One of the more memorable angles Timpone took away from the set visit was just how low budget the *Creepshow 2* production really was, after having had spent time on the set of David Cronenberg's remake of *The Fly* for 20th Century Fox where money wasn't a concern. "As I recall *Fangoria* wound up paying for my flight and hotel, the production wasn't even willing to kick in anything," he says. "That's how cheap the film was being made; I had to pay my own way to get there. Well, not me, but the company had to pay. Back then, you know, the flight wasn't that expensive. It was only an hour and half flight or whatever and the hotels were nothing in this little town. Maybe they paid for the hotel and we just had to pay for the flight? But I have a feeling we wound up paying for everything."

Wednesday, November 12, 1986 – Day 48

Day forty-eight would get started with an early afternoon production meeting with some key personnel in attendance including Michael Gornick, David Ball, Ted Kurdyla, Charles Carroll, Kato Wittich, Eileen Sieff-Stroup, Bruce Miller, and Taso Stavrakis, among others.

One person who was not required to be part of this meeting, or meetings like this, was mechanic George Dreisch, but he wasn't about to let that stop him from joining in. "I put myself there, I basically planted myself there to be able to put in a little feedback," he says. "And for having a little insight into what the day's – or usually the next day's – shooting was gonna involve, you know, it gave me a real leg up. It allowed me to pre-position things and come up with a script of our own as to how we were gonna do it and what sequence and what we had to bring along versus what we didn't have to drag along. You know, whether we were gonna make last call or not."

Filming would shift back to the I-395 Parkway South location to wrap up work on scene 117-119 of Annie dropping her cigarette in the car, 121A-122 of Annie's reaction upon first hitting the hitchhiker, 136 of Annie checking her rearview mirror as the semi-truck passes by her, and 149 where Annie attempts to calm herself down and asks herself whether she can live with what she's just done.

Additional scenes, 167 and 167A, were also scheduled this evening of Tom Wright shifting along the top of the car, peering in through the sunroof, as Lois Chiles desperately tries to knock him off. These scenes were shot not on

I-395, but on the parkway road that runs between I-395 and Wilson Street in Brewer, near the local high school.

It was during filming on this night that yet another incident would occur involving a Mercedes Benz. However, this time it wouldn't be stunt coordinator Taso Stavrakis to blame, but rather the star of the segment, Lois Chiles, who would be behind the wheel. And it wasn't the stunt model suffering damage this go around, but instead insurance agent Gerry Roy's "hero" car. "It was pretty much almost new. I can't remember the model; I think they were 380 SEL's or something like that. Does that sound right?," says George Dreisch. "Yeah, well, anyway, that car that they leased off this doctor was...it was nice. It was damn near showroom. Well, what ended up happening was they had set it up on a tow bar behind a truck that was set up for filming and they were shooting points of view, I guess, through the windshield of Lois Chiles. And what ended up happening was I guess they wanted her to feign putting in steering wheel inputs by sliding her hands over the wheel or something. But, anyway, what she ended up doing was actually jackknifing the whole thing (laughs) and so it staved up the nose pretty good. I'm not so sure the frame wasn't actually bent, the front portion of it."

"People were thrown, especially on the camera rig. I don't think anyone was hurt, maybe bruised. But I remember Mike (Gornick) just falling off that thing, like air born, and then he just gets up and looks around and says, 'That's a wrap,'" laughs Andy Sands.

"So, yeah, we were out and about on the streets of Bangor, Maine and how do you blame an actor once they get into a role and she's in a point of panic in her belief in terms of as an actress? So, you know, she turned the wheel and I guess it did some sort of counter move against the rig itself which is being towed by a truck; and not just me, but a whole group of us were tossed about. And luckily the driver of the truck stopped suddenly before we got out of control; I can imagine if we would have been like a rig out of control where the trailer itself is meandering and liable to tip over. He stopped suddenly, but due to that, yeah, I fell off the truck," Michael Gornick recalls about the close call. "I know Lois, though, was very upset. I mean, she was very concerned that, you know, she had harmed somebody."

Now, somewhere around this time, unfortunately I'm not certain of the exact date, Gerry Roy decided to pay a visit to the set to check in and see how things were going with his vehicle. And that's when he would receive quite an unsettling surprise. "I had someone from the Holiday Inn (the production hotel) stop in and said they had seen my car at the site of the filming and everything was fine," he says. "I was a little bit puzzled by why someone would mention that to me, so I decided to go on site and when I walked into a large building my car was sitting there with the front bumper off. And I could tell that they had used suction cups on the side of the car that would likely be to take inside pictures. And there were a few minor pits on the paint itself. So, I was quite upset because my car was supposed to be used only for close-ups. They were going to use two used taxi cabs from Germany to do the so-called rough stuff with, okay. I left there, called my attorney, and my attorney said, 'Why don't you go take pictures?', which I did. And then they ended up buying the car. Of course, my car was not for sale in the first place. So, was it a pleasant experience? Certainly it was not. I felt a little bit deceived."

That feeling of deception Roy mentions is in regards to Henry Nevison who was Roy's point of contact on the film. But Nevison was even more shocked than Roy when he discovered what had happened to the Mercedes. "That's a six-figure car, that's a very expensive car, and I convinced him, 'Hey, look, we're doing this film with Stephen King...,'" explains Nevison. "And, so, the guy was very receptive to me, he said, 'Yeah, sure.' So, I think I rented it for a $1,000 a month. And I said, 'I'll take care of your car. I promise you nothing will happen to it. It's just a picture car, which means the actress will sit in the car, and we'll use that as the drive by vehicle. The other vehicles we're gonna use to smash up and drive on dirt roads and so forth and so on.' And so I convinced him. And, you know, I had a good reputation in the area, too, because I was sort of like a television personality, I had a television show, people knew who I was. And, you know, I had a good reputation and I think that was very helpful because I could make things happen in the area there. Anyway, so the famous words that I gave him were, 'Nothing will happen to your car.' Well, what wound up happening was, I think, it was the first day of shooting, one of the cars that I had converted for the purposes of smashing up and all that, the stunt driver had some sort of an accident with it and it became unusable. And I arrive on the set, as I always did, because as location manager you're the first one that arrives and you're the last one that leaves. So, basically from 6AM to 2AM, six days a week, was basically my schedule. And so I got on set and I see this vehicle on set and I say to myself, 'Wait a minute. That's not one of the German Mercedes. Oh, my god. That's the car!' So, they decided unilaterally, that, well, they had no choice. So, they took apart his car. They put a camera mount on the roof with these big suction cups, they took the passenger door off, they took the seat out; they had fake blood inside the car. And I'm saying, 'Holy Shit!' I said, 'You've gotta be kidding me.' I said, 'This is not one of those cars!'...'Well, we had to do it. The other car got messed up in one of the scenes and we had to do this.'"

For Nevison it developed into a worst-case scenario as he was present when Roy decided to drop in at the most inopportune time possible. "I always said to him, 'You know what, you can come anytime you want. You know, come on set. Just look me up.' Because I felt, you know, the guy was letting his car go for a month and I thought that the least I could do was say to him, 'Hey, you wanna check out what's going on? No problem,'" Nevison says. "Well the day he decides to show up is the day that they took his car apart. So, he came on set and he was...and the interesting thing about it...you know, he just started saying, 'This is insane. This is insane. I can't believe this. This is insane.' And the first thing I thought he was gonna, like, rip into me, rip me another asshole because of the fact that I guaranteed him nothing was gonna happen to his car. But he was really a great guy, you know, he said, 'Henry, I'm sure this had nothing to do with you. I'm sure this was not your decision.'"

"I arrived one day and George, who was the mechanic, the car guy, had taken the door off of this gentleman's car,

which required cutting wires, because there's mechanisms in the door and everything, it's all sealed up and everything. Somebody gets in the car – its leather upholstery – with a screwdriver that's sticking out of their pocket, you know, and makes a hole in the upholstery. The guy's car was not destroyed, but was very badly handled," explains Steve Arnold. "And near the end of the project, as I recall, I don't know if it was Charles (Carroll) or who it was, was at their motel room when they were served papers by the lawyer or whatever for this guy. It was like $50,000 in damages and $50,000 of mental anxiety or something to that effect."

"There were a few scratches on the doctor's Mercedes, on the hero Mercedes," says David Ball. "I'd say, 'George, clean up that fucking car! We're in dreadful trouble with this doctor; he's going to kill us! Clean it up', right? So, at the end of the shoot when we finished we had these two smashed Mercedes, which we sent to the scrap yard, and we had him cleaning up the doctor's rental Mercedes. And he said to me, 'Dave, I've got a problem here.' You know the badge, the badge that goes on the grill, on the top, the Mercedes badge, the logo basically? It was missing. And I said, 'George, he's going to kill us! Where's that bloody badge gone?' He said, 'I don't know, I don't know. Someone stole it overnight.' I said, 'I can't believe the trouble we're having with this.' And the guy did sue us, I think. A couple of hours later I was leaving for the airport and I swung by the warehouse and he was out there, I said, 'George, I'm off to London. I'm finished, I'm done here. Thank you very much; give us a hug.' And he gave me a little box and he said, 'This is for you, from the lads, D.B. Hope you have a safe journey, it was wonderful working with you.' So, I put the box in my suitcase and I thought no more of it and I came home and I unpacked and there was this box. I opened the box and what was in it? The fucking Mercedes logo! Put on a plinth with the words 'Thanks for the ride!'"

"Well, David returned to England, the whole thing with the Mercedes was still up in the air. So, for a couple of months I actually had the thing hidden in my garage and was communicating back and forth with David Ball before we actually ended up giving the thing back to the doctor. There was some, kind of, tense moments related to that because there were threats of stolen automobiles and things of that nature," remembers George Dreisch. "I'm thinking back to when I had that car in my garage, I think for about three months afterwards I was still getting checks from *Creepshow 2*, Laurel-CST, because I was charging them storage for it. But, the deal was...you know, it was kind of an under-the-table deal I had going with David, 'Keep that fucking thing out of sight and don't give it back to him until I tell you to.'"

In the end, after receiving the run around from Laurel regarding the car, Gerry Roy was left with basically no other option. According to the Bangor Daily News on Monday, November 24, 1986, the day after principal photography on *Creepshow 2* ended in Bangor, Roy would file suit in the Penobscot County Superior Court for $100,000, plus the cost of the Mercedes, which was valued between $40,000 and $50,000. In the suit Laurel was accused of dismantling, denting, scratching, and defacing the car as well as failing to pay the agreed upon rental fee for it. Eventually Laurel would settle with Roy for an undisclosed amount.

"My husband's probably one of the nicest men in the world. He doesn't like conflict, he doesn't like controversy," says Gerry Roy's wife, Renee. "This was a terrible, terrible blow to him. You know, what they put him through was quite unbelievable."

As for other production-related news a cover set option was listed for today just in case it was needed which was for scenes 108L and 109 of Annie visiting her gigolo.

Thursday, November 13, 1986 – Day 49

The forty-ninth day of production would get started at the production hotel, the Holiday Inn, at 1:30PM with an informal press conference for some of the local Bangor media, followed up by a brief 2:15PM interview session with *Entertainment Tonight*. Shortly afterwards a small contingent of key personnel would leave the hotel for a rehearsal/walkthrough of the gigolo bedroom set located at the Franklin Place Condominiums in the heart of Bangor.

Filming for the evening would take place at 112 Franklin Street, along the Kenduskeag Stream, at the aforementioned Franklin Place Condominiums. The task of filling the condo/apartment set with furniture would fall on the shoulders of Bruce Miller's assistant, Steve Arnold, who rented as much furniture as he could from shops in the area. "The building that was chosen as the location was in Bangor and as I remember was quite nice having been recently built or refurbished," he recalls. "What I remember most is the building manager was super protective of the building and very concerned about any damage we might do to it. He was particularly obsessed with the wall covering in the hallway which was a woven grass cloth type with a very open fiber quality. I assured him we would take extra precautions to protect his precious hallway wall covering."

Now, hearing that might immediately conjure up visions of catastrophes in your mind – especially considering the headaches this production has already incurred – and, of course, you'd be correct. "Before I start this I have to explain two things that might not be clear to those who don't work in the film business. First is something known as Streaks 'N Tips. It is basically an aerosol spray-on temporary hair coloring product that comes in various hair colors: brown, black, red, and blond. It is sometimes used in film-making when something needs to be darkened or colored for the camera department that you might ordinarily paint but don't want to damage permanently. On most smooth, hard surfaces Streaks 'N Tips can be washed off," Arnold explains. "The next is a piece of equipment called a camera dolly which the actual camera is mounted on and used to hold it steady and allow it to be wheeled smoothly around a set, and in addition it has a scissor-shaped hydraulic arm allowing the camera to be smoothly raised and lowered."

Okay, at this point you might see the inklings of a

Above and below: Patty Tallman, Tom Wright, stuntwoman Chere Bryson, and Taso Stavrakis before things went south between Wright and Stavrakis; Chere Bryson and Taso Stavrakis share a moment between takes. (courtesy of Taso Stavrakis)

Above left and right: Michael Gornick, Lois Chiles, and Tom Wright at a Bangor Chamber of Commerce party celebrating *Creepshow 2* coming to town to film; Stephen King and Richard Rubinstein at the same party. (courtesy of Michael Felsher)

disastrous image starting to form here, right? We'll let Steve Arnold go ahead and complete that image for us. "Since it was not a full day's worth of filming the plan was to start late in the afternoon to shoot the interior scene in the apartment and then the company would move on to some exterior night driving scenes on some nearby streets and highways," he says. "My plan was to stay behind since I had the keys to the apartment and after the last crew members had wrapped up their gear and left I would be locking up, thus safeguarding all the furniture rentals. I remember the last two people out were an electrician coiling up cables, and pulling them in through the window, and a very tall, young grip trying to muscle a very large camera dolly out the door by himself. He was obviously unfamiliar with the finer points of how best to steer and maneuver the large piece of equipment. I was holding the door to the hallway open for him as he started to yank and pull on the handle that you steer it with, and that also raises and lowers the scissor arm. I did not notice that the scissor arm had not been lowered to its closed position as it should have been before moving it and just as the first set of wheels bumped over the threshold of the door a can of dark brown Streaks 'N Tips that had been left sitting somewhere on the dolly started to fall while simultaneously the scissor arm began to close to its lower position. The aerosol can fell squarely into the closing scissor arm and was sliced in half – its contents exploding in all directions. It sprayed on the walls, the door, the ceiling, the furniture and the carpeting both inside the room and out into the hallway. The grip ran off to try to get medical attention having been sprayed in the face. I rushed inside the apartment because I knew where the cleaning supplies were kept hoping to get it cleaned up while it was still wet and before anyone saw it, but

when I opened the cupboard it was empty. Jim Feng, the prop-master, had taken all the cleaning stuff with him out to the highway shoot; I didn't even have any paper towels. Just as I went back out into the hallway to assess the damage the building manager came around the corner...I thought he was going to have an aneurysm he was so livid. 'How could this happen?', etc. I just stood there and took it for a minute or two and finally assured him it would be cleaned up although I was the only one there. I remember how the pigment from the hair dye was deeply imbedded in the fibers of the wallpaper, I had to go back in with small brushes to try to dislodge it and scrub it to try to get it out and I think we later sent a whole cleaning crew back to try to restore things."

As for the scenes scheduled for this evening at the condo they were 108L and 109 involving Annie hurriedly getting dressed to leave so she can beat her husband back home, after having overslept at the condo of her gigolo, played by David Beecroft. "He was good, he was very good," says Michael Gornick about Beecroft. "It's a brief moment that he has, or moments, but I think he does a very credible job."

In the scene there is brief nudity performed by Lois Chiles, something that begs the question, would Barbara Eden have performed a nude scene? With Sheree North it wouldn't have been an issue considering she had appeared nude on screen before, but such was not the case with Eden who had never done so prior, something she continued throughout the duration of her career. What's important to note is that in Romero's script there is a description which would leave you to believe that nudity would be a factor in the scene: "Suddenly she realizes the implication of the constantly blinking 12:00. Her eyes pop with alarm and she sits up like a jumping-jack, the sheets falling away from breasts (equally as well cared-for as her face)." **(47)**

Of course, there are a variety of ways to shoot a scene like that without actually exposing someone's body, but the question was one I found interesting considering the actress's history. And I got two different responses from the director and producer on this topic. "I think so much of this is a matter of trust," Michael Gornick explains. "You can have adult discussions about this, clinical discussions, in terms of what the script requires, or even producorially what is required in terms of performance, and she was very adult and said, you know, 'I trust you.' And see that's the importance, I think, if you enter into a discussion and a conversation and you have an inter-play with your actor/actress and they can trust you or you can identify that early, 'Will they trust you?' It's very, very clinical; it becomes part of the art of what you're doing. So, yeah, I think she would have."

"I don't think it would have been written specifically as nude. But once again, she's paying a gigolo to give her 'a good seeing to'; it's a bedroom scene, you can't do it with pajamas on, can you? Come on, you've got to take a little bit of license here and you've gotta say, 'What would really happen?'," says David Ball. "Barbara Eden would not have done a nude scene."

As for star Lois Chiles she never really gave it much thought and just jumped in to the part head first. "Because when you come in that fast like I did, I mean, you're either all in or you're all out. You know, so, whatever was in the script I suppose I knew was going to be there, so I just did it," she says. "But it's always a little strange to be naked walking around with people."

One last note regarding this sequence involves the shot of Lois Chiles coming out of the condo then walking across the street and driving away in her Mercedes. Remember, on Halloween it was decided that scenes 110 through 114 would be deleted, but several shots and even dialogue would wind up being filmed anyway; the scene in question of Annie exiting the condo for her Mercedes would have been part of scene 110. As it turns out, a second unit crew would grab this quick shot, along with several others on Monday the 17th.

Regarding scene 110 I found it interesting to learn that in Michael Gornick's original sequential shot list log he had inserted an optional shot potentially for Bangor's most famous resident to appear in. As I discussed in the Day 38 section after leaving her gigolo's condo Annie damages her vehicle by backing into a street light pole and in Gornick's shot list there is a description of a man walking his dog as this occurs, which he had noted as a potential cameo for Stephen King.

And while we're on the subject of Stephen King we might as well discuss the sort of brief cameo he has in the gigolo's condo – or his books cameo, that is. Eagle-eyed viewers will notice on the headboard shelf a few King titles sitting above Annie and her hired lover: *Different Seasons*,

Firestarter, and *Danse Macabre*. But one title in particular really jumps off the screen, which would be *It*. And the decision to include the book in the scene as a tip of the cap to King came from Michael Gornick after he had apparently spent some time in Maine – this would have been prior to the development of *Creepshow 2* – scouting locations for *Pet Sematary*, along with David Ball, which was then set to be directed by George Romero. "Steve was writing *It* at the house when I stopped by. I was scouting most of Maine and at one point I stopped in to see him just to give him a progress report, you know, what I had found for locations for *Pet Sematary*...but when I dropped in on him he was literally in his study, which is enormous, listening to rock music and writing *It*. And at that point it was already voluminous, I mean, it was thousands of pages that he'd already written," laughs Gornick. "But, yeah, that was just kind of an in-joke thing. And I think he knew about it, I got a copy at a local book store and asked if he would mind if I put it in."

And, finally, scene 148 of Annie driving immediately after she's hit the hitchhiker, washing the blood off her windshield with the wipers, was scheduled if time permitted. As Steve Arnold stated earlier the crew did leave from the condominium set for continued filming on the highway, plus the scene would not appear again on future call sheets, so it was most likely completed on this night.

This night would also see the first of ten 15 minute production meetings schedule at the wrap of each night of filming with Michael Gornick, Dick Hart, Kato Wittich, all department heads, and the bond company representative, Ted Kurdyla, basically to ensure everyone was still on the same page and keeping up with the schedule.

Friday, November 14, 1986 – Day 50

Day fifty would see the production spend the evening in Stephen King's former stomping grounds, the University of Maine, where scenes 191/193/195, 192A/193/195, 192, 194, and 196 would be shot near the university's bike trails and a former civil defense bunker. These scenes would consist of Annie driving and screaming about how much the car will cost to be repaired – "Four thousand, Mrs. Lansing, and the car will look like you just drove it out of the showroom. What happened, Mrs. Lansing? I ran over some guy...and over, and over, and over!" – as well as the hitchhiker suddenly appearing on the front of her car with his sign now reading "You Killed Me!!!"

Also, scene 168 of Annie turning off the main road on to a dirt road attempting to throw the hitchhiker from her roof was scheduled. Tom Wright, who by now was in his stage 4 makeup, would keep the makeup as is with the shot being an elevated one, plus fairly dark as well, making it next to impossible to notice any difference in continuity.

As just mentioned Tom Wright was in his stage 4 makeup, which by this point had become pretty grisly, and just the sight of him was a bit challenging for some on the production to stomach. "It was a little disconcerting as Tom got more and more injured by Annie," says Lois Chiles. "It was kind of hard to have dinner with him because he had so many…you know, he was just tough to look at after he'd been mashed up by Annie."

"I remember Joanna (Robinson) and I, we'd go and we'd hang out with Tom and he was in full makeup, right. By this time, I remember this one night, he'd been hit by the car. And I don't have to tell you how brilliant Howard (Berger) and his crew were. I mean, it was really disgusting to look at him, it was so realistic. His face is falling off, there's blood everywhere; his eye's coming out of his socket. I remember saying to him, 'Tom, you know, I really love you. But, ohhh, eating dinner with you is not such a pleasant experience. Can you put a bag over your head?'," laughs Jeanne Talbot. "It was so gross."

Have you ever wondered what a production assistant does? Well, the position is as un-glamorous as any job in film production – ground zero basically. Whatever menial task you can think of, that's usually the job of a production assistant: help an extra fill out their paperwork, grab some coffee for a crew member or actor/actress, crowd control, driving someone to set, etc. "Nobody does something else and then they go back to being a production assistant. That's the starting position," says Andy Sands.

The story of Andy Sands becoming a P.A. on *Creepshow 2* is quite a unique one, and it was all thanks to the extraordinary kindness of Michael Gornick. While in high school in Pittsburgh, Sands worked for *Questar* magazine, a science-fiction and horror periodical, whose offices just happened to be in the same building as Laurel Entertainment. Through working at *Questar,* Sands got to know a lot of important people associated with Laurel, including Gornick. "Mike really took me under his wing," Sands says. "And while I was still at the magazine, still in high school, they were doing post-production on *Knightriders* and Mike would have me come up, because I was honestly interested, and sit in the editing room while they were cutting it."

Several years later Sands would move to Los Angeles looking to make it in the film industry. After having limited success working as a carpenter on some Olivia Newton-John music videos and as a production coordinator on *Surf Nazis Must Die* Sands returned to Pittsburgh when the opportunity to work on *Creepshow 2* came around. "Mike Gornick takes me out to lunch – because I'm in the movie business now, I've worked on stuff out in L.A. – and he tells me, 'We're doing *Creepshow 2*, you're on it. I'm gonna get you on this,'" Sands warmly recalls. "So, as *Creepshow 2* is coming together – and they're not filming it in Pittsburgh at all, none of it – finally he says, 'Andy, I've got some bad news for you,' he says, 'We're filming the first half of it in Arizona and then we promised Stephen King we would finish the movie, all the rest of it, in Maine. They're not letting me take you. They're not gonna fly this kid out to Arizona.' And I'm crushed. That's it, it's over."

But was it actually over? Not really, as fate would step in and change events for Sands. "And then one day out of the clear blue sky I get a call from Mike Gornick and he said, 'Don't ask; I'm sending you a plane ticket. You're gonna come out to Maine with us for the rest of the movie. Don't ask.' And I'm like, 'Okay, I'm back in the movie business!'"

This, of course, brings us full circle as to the kind of work production assistants deal with. Some might say it's just "shitty" work that can "piss" you off at times, while others might simply tell you it's a "waste" of time. In Sands' case, you could say it was a combination of all the above. "There was something that we were gonna film where it was looking like the porta potties weren't going to be where they were supposed to be when they were supposed to be. And Henry (Nevison) said, 'This isn't going to be all that bad. I think we can move them.' He said, 'Come on, come with me. We're gonna move the porta potties,'" Sands laughs as he recalls the story. "And a porta potty is bigger and heavier than you probably think it is. So, we were like, 'We can't physically move these ourselves', you know. It seemed like maybe we could, but we can't. But we've got his truck and we'll put a line around it and then maybe we'll slip some cardboard under it and we'll just be able to get it to where it really should be. And somehow or another we're moving this porta potty where I'm on one end of it to make sure it doesn't tip over while this truck is trying to pull it – and the porta potty starts to tip over. And it's so unbelievably cold and somehow it tips just enough and I'm holding it up and it's like those stories about the grandmothers that flip over cars to save their grandkid, I'm getting this strength to hold up this slowly falling porta potty – because that's not how I want to die, I don't want to go out this way – to keep this from falling and crushing me. But it's tipped just enough that the semi liquid content in the porta potty has, like, run up to the over flow valve, and I'm holding this, and I'm slowly realizing that my feet and legs are warmer than the rest of me and there's steam starting to rise up. And this porta potty is just like spilling over on to me and I'm thinking, 'Alright, I'm going down. If he doesn't stop this car I'm going down for the count.' And luckily – he sees this in the rear view mirror, how it's not gonna end well – he stops the car so the thing starts to right itself. As the porta potty is slowly righting itself and that 'glug, glug, glug' sound is stopping the thing that is flashing through my head is, 'Hey, I'm in the movie business for real! I'm working on a movie here!'"

Saturday, November 15, 1986 – Day 51

The fifty-first day of filming would see another change in location as the production moved to the Dyer estate in nearby Hampden, Maine. The near fifty acre site, which overlooked the Penobscot River, was home to the Edythe L. Dyer Library and to the Dyer family mansion, whose exterior is seen at the end of the segment as the Lansing home (the interior of the Lansing garage would be shot elsewhere). The property was also home to a large wooded area, filled with trails, which would serve as the production's "set" for six of the remaining eight days of filming.

The property was filled with history in regards to the story of Hampden and Bangor and featured breath taking views of the area. "(It's) the highest point on the river, a river that's more than…something like a hundred and fifty miles long. I'd have to check that number, but it's an extremely long river in New England," says Jack Dyer, the owner of the property at the time and whose parents, Ralph and Edythe, built the mansion featured in the film during the 1930's.

"Quite gorgeous, absolutely gorgeous at that highest point on the turn there at what was called the narrows in the river; had a downward view of where the ships gathered for the Battle of Hampden during the War of 1812. It was also the location of the gathering place and camping grounds, so forth, for the Red Paint People – which was a prehistoric Indian tribe from thousands of years ago."

According to Dyer there were only two stipulations expected of Laurel-CST, Inc. for use of the property and allegedly neither one was honored. "I was asked how much I would charge for them doing it and the response I had to them was, 'I have only two requests. One, that you pay as much to the Edythe L. Dyer Library as you would have reluctantly been willing to pay to me; you don't have to pay me anything, but I appreciate you paying to the library what you would have been willing to pay to me,'" he says. "The other request I had was that the actress who appeared in that movie, that my daughter would be able to meet her. And those are the only two requests I had. But, I don't have reason to believe that either of those two things occurred."

Unlike Gerry Roy, the owner of the "hero" Mercedes, Dyer never pursued the issue, as deflating as it turned out to be, even though he was an acquaintance of Stephen King. "It was extremely disappointing, it was," Dyer says. "I passed on entering into a contract with them on the theory that there was no financial gain involved so there was no need for a contract, at least on our end. I trusted that they would benefit the library and allow for my daughter to meet the actress whom she was interested to observe and watch during those days on the production and forward."

As for tonight's filming it would include scenes 172-174 and 172A of Annie sharply turning the Mercedes at a 90-degree angle and looking towards the field of trees which she decides to drive through. Scene 176 would also be scheduled of Annie plowing into the field of trees with the hitchhiker clinging to the roof of the Mercedes. In his sequential shot list log Michael Gornick left an interesting note regarding scene 176 and what he was apparently forced to accept regarding its composition: "Not What I Wanted", Gornick wrote with a highlighter underneath the scene description.

These scenes would be performed by stunt driver Chere Bryson, who as it turns out would be spending her final night with the production as her services would no longer be required because of the addition of another stunt driver, this time a male one. We'll discuss this topic, and the consequences it had on another important member of the stunt unit, once we get to the Tuesday, November 18 section.

Also on tap for the evening were scenes 169, 173, 175, and 175A which consisted of interior shots of the Mercedes as Annie drives while fighting off the clutches of the hitchhiker who is attempting to grab her through the open sunroof.

Another point of interest for the day included a scheduled test at lunch of the articulated hitchhiker dummy which would be used for scene 188 on Tuesday the 18th. "So, we made a fully jointed dummy that actually had stops on it so that it wouldn't like bend both ways," Greg Nicotero said to Anchor Bay. **(48)**

Above top and bottom: Like Holt McCallany, Don Harvey and David Holbrook would also fly to Bangor to film their death scenes which the production was unable to finish while in Prescott. (courtesy of Eileen Sieff-Stroup and Michael Felsher)

Tomorrow, Sunday the 16th, the production's scheduled day off, cast and crew would participate in a party at the Maine Center for the Arts on the campus of the University of Maine sponsored by the Bangor Chamber of Commerce with Stephen and Tabitha King in attendance. For David Holbroook, who was in Bangor to finish up his death scene as "Fatso" Gribbens from *Old Chief Wood'nhead* on Monday, it was an opportunity to meet the famous author, despite the fact that he wasn't much of a fan. "Didn't really know anything about Stephen King; I did meet him when they had to do some re-shoots with me up in Maine and there was some kind of...I think there was a wrap party or something up there where Stephen King was there and so we met. And I think I might have gone up to him and introduced myself or something and he said, 'Oh, you don't really look the part!'," Holbrook laughs. "I mean, he was nice about it and all that, he wasn't mean or anything, but he said something like, 'You don't really look scary enough', or something like that."

At the party Richard Rubinstein would be presented with an honorary statuette of Paul Bunyan from the Chamber of Commerce's executive director as a show of appreciation for the production coming to Bangor, the first Stephen King production to do so. This is something that would be pushed by members of the production in the local press, which covered the event, as a great reason to strengthen the presence of a film commission in Maine, which King described at the time as "a phone...in an empty office." **(49)**

Above: Stunt driver Jery Hewitt, seen here in 1979's *The Warriors* as the leader of the Baseball Furies, was brought in at the request of Tom Wright, which would lead to Taso Stavrakis abruptly leaving the production early. (copyright 1979 Paramount Pictures)

Speaking of Paul Bunyan the statuette given to Rubinstein was a small replica of the giant 31 foot tall, 3700-pound statue of the legendary lumberjack that stands in downtown Bangor which was created to commemorate the 125th anniversary of the city in 1959. Legend has it that the mythical Bunyan was a native of the area and represented Bangor's early days as the lumber capitol of the world. Of course with a target that large, and with film productions full of pranksters, it becomes too tempting at times to pass on a little fun amongst the crew. "I'm sure somebody told you about the statue of the forty-foot lumberjack that's in the middle of Bangor, Maine?," laughs Angela Nogaro. "I remember some of the guys climbed up onto that lumberjack and they put one of the grip's phone number across the lumberjack and they were like, 'For a good time call...' – forty feet up in the air."

"That was Nick (Mastandrea) and 'Pinky' (grip Kurt Rimmel) doing that on, god...was it Nicotero?," asks an unsure Logan Berkshire regarding the lumberjack prank. "I think they did it on Greg Nicotero, yeah."

"Pretty sure it was Greg," confirms Nick Mastandrea. "Had help from SFX crew, I think."

Before moving on, and since we're on the topic of Sundays, I should quickly mention how members of the crew were able to spend part of their Sundays or down time in Bangor courtesy of Laurel-CST, Inc. "Every Sunday there was this incredible old inn outside of town on a lake and the entire crew would go there for Sunday brunch," recalls Charles Carroll. "And then we would move into a back room that had this huge fireplace and we would just take it over and everyone would be in there just drinking. And then they would go back to the hotel and sleep all through the next day because they didn't have to go to work until it was dark. And I just remember how much fun we all...I mean, you know, there was a huge amount of booze consumed."

"There was a certain kind of rambunctious energy connected with film-making on location in the '70's and the '80's. Most films could sort of chalk their reputations up to being sort of drug fueled, you know, but not *Creepshow 2*. There weren't drugs on the show at all," says Tom Wright. "But in the '80's people partied as hard as they worked and this was a hard working crew, so it was also a hard partying crew. And I remember a couple of incidents. I wouldn't have recommended anyone buying stock in the Holiday Inn right around that time because we did do a little damage to the hotel. I remember, one of my favorites, was Howard (Berger) and I were bombed and we were pushing each other in the laundry cart as fast as possible down the hotel corridors just letting it rip, letting it go, and bouncing off the walls. I remember diving out of a window into the snow on the ground floor; when someone opened the window I just dove through it just for the hell of it. It was the last of, for me, it was the last wild ride I've had on a movie since."

"The hotel bar became, like, the center of everything. And they would actually keep it open, I think, a little bit for the crew when they closed it to everybody else. Not everyone, but a bunch of the crew would spend hours and hours in this bar, just hanging out and decompressing and burning off steam," says Andy Sands. "I would doodle these little cartoons on bar napkins and everyone would look at them and pass them around and all this. One of the guys, I think it was one of the camera assistants, says, 'I want these cartoons.' I gave him all the cartoons and they wound up printing them up like a yearbook. And at the wrap party everyone got handed a book of these cartoons – I did a cover for it."

Monday, November 17, 1986 – Day 52

Day fifty-two would see the return of Don Harvey and David Holbrook who flew into Bangor to wrap up work on their death scenes from *Old Chief Wood'nhead* which were not completed in Prescott. These scenes, just like the ones with Holt McCallany, would be shot at Laurel's makeshift studio space at the former Viner Brothers shoe factory.

With Harvey scenes 26, 27, 28, 29, and 30 would all be taken care of tonight, which covered his character, Andy, sneaking down the hallway while his parents watch television, him finding his Firebird destroyed in the garage and then suddenly being attacked by Chief Wood'nhead, ending with his bloody corpse laying on the hood of his car as the garage door closes.

It's noteworthy that for the silhouetted shots of Chief Wood'nhead on the garage wall and garage door it wouldn't be Dan Kamin, who did return for the Holt McCallany scenes, but rather Michael Morgan performing in the suit. "It was fun. The actor was busy on another project and wasn't available," Morgan recalls. "The suit was damaged somehow during transit or last use, I don't recall which. In any event, they used super glue to repair it after I got it on and the tears were significant enough and they used so much glue it leaked onto my skin and glued me into it. Don't recall how we got it off. Don't recall who made the decision to use me; I think it was because I was closest in size and height."

Harvey, who had been allowed to leave the play *Progress* in New Haven, Connecticut when he was cast in *Creepshow 2*, would return to the Long Wharf Theatre to pick up where he had left off. "It's funny, we finished shooting and I went back to do the play," he recalls. "And then, I guess, I'm not sure if the play ended or what happened...I think I was still doing the play actually and I believe on my day off – I had a couple of days off – I had to fly up to Maine, which was wild because I guess they had to do re-shoots. And I wasn't really familiar with the whole film process at that point. I'd only done that one film (*The Untouchables*) and some TV, so I was like, 'What do you mean re-shoots? What is that?' And apparently they just rebuilt the whole set and brought us up there and we did all sorts of stuff. I think we may have done that one scene in the garage where I get hit with the tomahawk; I think that might have been the one scene I had to do up there. And it was funny because the whole city that we went to, I guess it was Bangor, and then we drove up to some tiny little city, and everyone in the city was related to Stephen King. Just walk down the street and you'll see Stephen King's second cousin, you know, a great aunt, a nephew; everybody knew Stephen. He was like the favorite son, but not only that – not only the favorite son – but related to everybody. It was incredible. It was an amazing little town and it was quite an experience. I mean, I looked around at all these huge pine trees and mountains and all this snow and all this weird shit and I was like, 'Okay, so this is where the greatest American writer comes from.'"

"He is high energy, I tell ya," co-star Deane Smith says about Harvey. "He had a great sense of humor."

Smith would play Harvey's father in the film, seen only from behind watching *The Cisco Kid* on television, along with Shirley Sonderegger as the mother. He recalls how fascinating it was to watch Harvey's death scene being filmed. "They'd actually taken an axe and chopped holes in that Trans-Am," he says. "They have someone down that's just out of camera range when the hatchet comes down and hits him on the head, this blood splatters on the wall and how they do that is kind of neat."

As for the process of participating in a feature film, something completely foreign to his everyday life, Smith remembers it rather fondly. "It was kind of fun for the night. It was mostly...in there about, oh, seven or eight o'clock – got out about two or three in the morning," he recalls. "I don't think they did one or two takes to get the whole thing. What they wanted to do...someone said, 'Well, you ought to have us say something like, Andy, is that you?' And they said, 'No, because it's a non-speaking part', because they'd have to pay extra money for that."

As for Sonderegger her main take away from the experience was the fuss regarding her wardrobe for the part. "They decided that I needed an outfit to wear and it wasn't to be anything fancy. I said, 'Can't I just bring something from home, like an old skirt and something like that?'…'Oh, no, no, no.' So, we spent a whole afternoon – the people from the costume department with the film company – we spent the whole afternoon going from the Goodwill store to the Salvation Army store to a resale shop. And, you know, I could have brought something just as equally tacky from the back of my closet," she laughs.

David Holbrook, of course, was also on hand to finish up his death sequence, scene 24. And for him, despite the challenges of working with makeup and mechanical effects, it's an interesting memory to revisit. "I shot this thing where I get shot by the Indian so they built a device, two devices for that," he explains. "One was I'm wearing a baseball cap and they put a device in the cap and the camera was to my right so they're shooting from the side. And they built another device; they built a false belly for me and a false arm. My left arm is a false arm – my real arm is behind my back in the chair. Which I had to sit there like, I don't know, ten hours or something with my real arm behind me – that was fun. And they built out with rice… they built out a false belly on top of my real belly. And so then they had this hand with a beer can in it and they built a device there that was embedded in the rice that made this arrow come out through the can and then you see the can squirt and stuff like that when the arrow goes through – same thing with my head. But I thought it was kind of cool just the way they do that. The camera's off to my right, so they didn't have room in the hat for an arrow to actually come straight out. So, the way they rigged it is that the arrow is in a device in my hat and before it goes off the arrow is actually pointing to my left and then it just goes straight! So it comes out like a mouse trap, sort of, in reverse and the arrow is pointed straight in front of me. But because the camera is to the right, from that angle, it looks like the arrow is coming straight out of my head. I think with the belly one they didn't have to do that because they were able to build this container for the real little arrowhead to come out and through the can and stuff like that. They had to do it a couple of times because they had, like, blood come down my face and they weren't happy with that so they had to clean me up, do it a few times."

In the course of writing this book I heard countless insane stories of "If it could go wrong, it did" and as Bruce Miller and Steve Arnold warned at the end of Chapter 2 it was simply a cursed production. The next story, which is born out of scene 24, is a perfect illustration – and it's not even the most extreme example, that's still to come – of how unforeseen things can cause colossal headaches and near nervous breakdowns. "Poor Jim Feng…we got to Maine, we were doing the re-shoots and the 'Fatso' character was supposed to be eating tater tots or something, french fries or tater tots or something, and had a little paper dish that you get from a fast food restaurant," recalls Steve Arnold. "So, we're up there, we've been

up there working on all these sets, and we're ready to shoot this. It's late at night, it's probably like ten o'clock at night, and we can't find the little paper dishes that we were supposed to have. Jim Feng was the prop master, he's looking around for them: 'We thought they were in the truck', and, 'What happened?', and, 'Where are they?' So, we call the local fast food place, which is not very local, it's like forty minutes away or something and they're about ready to close for the night and we can't send somebody fast enough to get them and get them back. Someone remembers, 'Hmm, I thought somebody had that for lunch a couple of days ago…' Poor Jim Feng dumpster dives in a forty foot dumpster for this paper dish and about an hour and a half later he comes out with the dish. You know, it was like that every single day."

While the main unit was handling the scenes with Harvey and Holbrook, a smaller second unit crew consisting of roughly a dozen people including Taso Stavrakis, Charles Carroll, Henry Nevison, Henry Lynk, Peter Levy, and Joanna Robinson would work on a list of seven separate shots. Most of these were of the Mercedes passing by the camera through downtown Bangor, including the shot of the bank clock reading 11:23PM, for example.

Also included among the night's tasks was the shot of Lois Chiles exiting the Franklin Street Condominiums, jumping into her Mercedes, and taking off. As well as scene 147, a shot of the Mercedes out on I-395, which would finally be completed, I assume. I say assume because by this point the unopened stretch of highway that the production had been utilizing was no longer so, as it was now officially open to the public. And wouldn't you know it, the very next day it would record its first auto accident when a 29-year-old woman would lose control of her vehicle on an exit ramp no more than two miles from where they shot the scenes of Tom Wright being struck by Lois Chiles. That didn't take long! Fortunately she was okay physically, despite the fact that her car left the pavement, clipping some reflector poles (sound familiar?), and would have to be towed away. Regarding the cause of the crash? It was excessive speed, of course. "Our concern with these ramps is that people slow down," said Brewer Police Captain Charles Shuman in the *Bangor Daily News* at the time. **(50)**

Other noteworthy subjects for the day included Eileen Sieff-Stroup drafting a memo for all crew letting them know that a production wardrobe sale was on-going, including plenty of ladies and men's swimsuits from *The Raft*.

Taso Stavrakis would also send out his own memo to Rusty Warren in the accounting department in regards to scuba equipment purchased for *The Raft* segment. Apparently there was a minor dispute about the equipment being part of a bonus package for Stavrakis in lieu of stunt adjustment and overtime pay he was due. This is interesting to note because issues regarding a potential bonus owed to Stavrakis would become a bone of contention after the conclusion of principal photography.

Tuesday, November 18, 1986 – Day 53

The fifty-third day of production would see filming return to the

Dyer estate in Hampden, specifically Library Road. Included in tonight's schedule were scenes 184, 185/187, 186, and 188 which consisted of the Mercedes driving away from the hitchhiker, after he's been shot, only to suddenly stop and then back up running him over, and then for good measure running him over once more! Other scenes scheduled included number 180 of the Mercedes bursting out of the woods, moments after Annie thinks she's lost the hitchhiker to a tree branch, and number 190 of Annie speeding away after she's run the hitchhiker over multiple times.

As was touched on in the Day 51 section a new stunt driver would join the production during this final week of filming in the person of the late Jery Hewitt. Now the reason why Hewitt was brought on board is a discussion best dealt with in tomorrow's section, as it pertains to a particular stunt performed that day. And we will do just that, hearing from all the important players involved in that situation. In the meantime, let's introduce our newest crew member...

Hewitt, a self-described "product of the boroughs of New York", originally went to school for Food Science. However, a love for comedy, of all things, and an interest in stunt work would lead him to a completely different career path in motion pictures. Hewitt would go on to coordinate and perform stunts on countless productions leading up to *Creepshow 2* – and even more since – including *Wolfen*, *Exterminator 2*, *F/X*, *Crocodile Dundee*, and *Legal Eagles*. Some of those films would also feature Tom Wright as a stuntman, so the working relationship between the two went back quite a few years. "What a good guy. I really loved him and I still do," laughs Hewitt about his longtime friend and colleague, Wright. "Just a good influence; he was so much fun to work with and to be around."

But despite having worked on a lot of high profile films, it was Hewitt's first feature that he is best known for to this day. In Walter Hill's 1979 classic New York City gang film, *The Warriors*, Hewitt would portray the iconic leader of

Above left: Lois Chiles lays her head on Taso Stavrakis' shoulder during a lighter moment in Maine. (courtesy of Taso Stavrakis)
Above right: Arizona location manager Michael Morgan(center) would fly to Bangor to assist with things in Maine. Here he is with two of his favorite people from the film, 1st A.D. Kato Wittich and production manager Charles Carroll. (courtesy of Michael Morgan)

the Baseball Furies gang, complete with baseball uniform, KISS inspired face paint, and baseball bat. "The story about me getting on that job...," begins Hewitt. "The stunt coordinator was from L.A., Craig Baxley, really a good guy, and I was just completely honest because I didn't know anything else but to be honest, and I helped him and he helped me a great deal. And I have a feeling that as I worked out with him and helped him with equipment and helped him in a lot of other ways that I could – I had some information because I'm kind of a technical guy – I think he saw some ability in me. And when it came to the part of that running guy, that leader, unbeknownst to me I think that he talked to Walter Hill and said that this guy's the best one we've got right here, so I got that part. And my knowledge of film-making was incredibly tiny and I did what they told me to do. So, they said, 'Okay, you've gotta run from there to there', and meanwhile I didn't know that there was a track that was a mile long and there was grips and everything; you could imagine trying to lead me and then follow me. I don't know how they did it as fast as they did because they told me to run flat out as fast as I could and I have no idea how they kept up."

Wednesday, November 19, 1986 – Day 54

Day fifty-four would continue work at the Dyer estate with scenes 178B, 178C, and 179 going in front of the cameras. These shots would cover the sequence where Annie knocks the hitchhiker off the top of her Mercedes by clipping him with a large fallen tree in the woods.

Creating things such as the tree which Tom Wright bounces off of lands in the lap of the art department, and at times to the set construction or scenery crew, and that's when these talented artisans step in and perform their movie magic. "So, we made a big rubber log that we made to look like a birch tree. So, that was a fun project, a lot of people were involved in that, making this big rubber log. And I was getting real pieces of birch bark from real trees and sort of wrapping it around in sections and then matching my paint to the real bark. And it ended up looking really good," says Eileen Garrigan. "It was built from a pipe of some kind. I just don't remember if it was PVC or a cardboard tube; probably just a cardboard tube."

"There wasn't any scenery per se but there were things like...there was some fake branches that were made of foam and stuff that the hitchhiker gets hit with while he's on top of the car, those kind of things," Ed Fountain says. "We were kind of at the mercy of the effects and the stunt guys to provide whatever they needed because the stunt guys come in and they need stuff for the shots and somebody has to provide it and that's what we do."

Another scene listed for the evening, in case it wasn't completed from the night before, was number 190 of Annie speeding away in her Mercedes after running the hitchhiker over on the country road. And listed at the bottom for the day's agenda was scene 201 of Annie ramming the hitchhiker into the tree. In fact just above that is a note reminding crew that they would be moving to another section of the wooded acreage on the Dyer estate to set up for scenes 201 through 214. How much, if any, was completed for 201 tonight is unknown. It would be listed again in the coming days so we'll discuss how it was accomplished at that time.

So, that brings us to our main story from tonight's filming: scene 198. This scene, by far, would be the most dangerous stunt performed in the segment – in the entire film for that matter. Scene 198 is when Annie drives the Mercedes through a fence post, with the hitchhiker clinging to the front of the vehicle, and plunges the car down a steep hill. This is why Jery Hewitt was brought on board, a decision which would lead to stunt coordinator Taso Stavrakis quitting the film, despite the fact that the production was nearing the finish line. "It was almost over, but it was just a shitty day," Stavrakis candidly admits. "Another one; another shitty day."

The steep hill which the Mercedes descends was part of a large gravel esker that was located on the Dyer property, which bordered a local construction company. "That drive, it wouldn't be right to say road, it was really just a path," explains Jack Dyer. "Imagine for example the car coming down the hill, on the right side of that car is the woods and then the Lane Construction Company. On the left side of the car coming down was a bit of a depression in the esker and some gravel had been taken there by my father during his lifetime."

Stavrakis had put a lot of thought into the stunt and had planned out the shot with Patricia Tallman, videotaping their tests multiple times. But when he learned that Tom Wright, someone he personally had a hand in bringing onto the picture, wanted someone else to take over the stunt it felt like a betrayal to the young coordinator. "It was a mine or a gravel pit or something...it was a big gravel hill. So, I wanted to see what would happen, so we drove the car over. I can't remember if I actually got up on the hood and let her drive it or not? I might have, but I definitely drove the car over the hill with us in the car videotaping to see how it would go. And then I had to rig a seat for Tom sitting on the front of the car. I wanted to make sure the car wasn't going to bog down and him get crushed or whether it would roll over and him get crushed. So, yeah, we videotaped it, the test drive," says Stavrakis. "And by then me and David (Ball) had all these arguments about the Mercedes and a bunch of other stuff leading up to that, so it had all been building. And it was Tom who went to David and said, 'I don't know this guy. I want somebody who I know driving the car' – Jery Hewitt, really good stunt guy from New York. So, it wasn't that I, you know, was mad at Jery for coming in. I was mad at Tom, 'I gave you a job and you just fucked me.' David just took control; David took control of the stunt department. So, I said, 'Okay, you design the stunts then,' that's when I left. 'This is on you. If something goes wrong now, it's on you. It's not on me.' Of course, nothing was gonna go wrong, both of these guys were professional stunt guys and they knew each other and that made them comfortable. So, I can't really blame them. But they just fucked me."

"I think I had probably something to do with that, unfortunately, but it's just the way things work out. I started doing stunts in 1978 in New York, so we're talking I had been doing it about eight years up to that point," Tom Wright explains. "So, I knew the stunt world pretty well and I was a member of an organization called Stunt Specialists, which was one of the preeminent stunt organizations in New York at the time. Taso was a young stunt man and young stunt coordinator and I honestly did not feel as safe with Taso driving the car as I would have with the person who actually wound up driving it, Jery Hewitt. And I sort of...I just...you have to go with your gut instinct when you're talking about your life being on the line. There's no such thing as being a nice guy. When it comes to your actual physical safety you have to make a judgement call based on all of the information that you have in front of you and I just didn't feel as though Taso had enough experience. It wasn't that I disliked Taso or that I thought he wasn't a good stunt man or anything like that. It was purely the fact that I knew how much experience Jery had and I knew how much experience I had and he did not have as much as experience as either of us. So, I sort of insisted that Jery be the one who'd drive the car."

"There was a stunt coordinator, but I don't think he (Wright) had faith in the guy. The little bit that they had done he got really nervous about who was driving the car and who was rigging the car, because the gentleman did not have a great deal of experience," recalls Jery Hewitt. "He (Stavrakis) treated me kindly and I did him. I did not exclude him from anything, I felt. As much as he was there I tried to make him feel like he was...you know, I kept my place."

"We didn't do it until Tom Wright was happy. But Taso had thrown a wobbly and he said, 'I'm the stunt coordinator, I say how it's done.' And Tom said, 'No, I'm the hitcher and I'm on this and I'm saying how it's done.' And so there was a disagreement and we had to bend in favor of Tom because he was going to be the potential victim. So, his safety could only be prejudged by himself," David Ball says. "We did the right thing; that was the right thing to do. We weren't gonna do it until Tom was happy. Well, when Tom said, 'Let's do it', we had, I think, we had three cameras and we rolled all the cameras and we did it and it worked great. And I said to Mike (Gornick), I said, 'Mike, there is no take two on this.' And he said, 'Well...', and I said, 'No, Mike, there's not. We're not here to threaten people's lives. And if Tom is happy we'll do it, but we're only gonna do it once.' And we did it once and I said, 'That is a wrap!' The minute Mike called cut, I said, 'It's a wrap. That's it, we're out of here.'"

It's interesting to note that in Michael Gornick's shot list he has an X crossed through the scene with a note saying "Down-Hill Plunge", as apparently he envisioned a grander shot from an elevated position or with a POV perspective.

As for pulling off that dangerous stunt, it involved a great deal of engineering, along with a dash of good old-fashioned cleverness. "It came time to start setting up for the gag going down over the hill and basically that amounted to Tom and I putting him on the front of the car and measuring it up and putting in some attachment points in the engine compartment and stuff and figuring out how he could best situate himself; just a lot of issues, well not issues, but coming up with solutions, I guess, would be the best way to put it, that made him comfortable," explains George Dreisch. "Also, you know, it's real easy for someone who's not a mechanic to say what they want, but have no idea what's realistically possible. You know what I'm saying? So, there's back-and-forth consultation and ideas and things like that. I think we came up with some real good solutions and later on when Jery Hewitt showed up and all that, he kind of went over the whole deal with us again, he seemed to be extremely comfortable with the whole thing. I think getting that secondary re-enforcement of confidence in what we had done or set up ended up making Tom more comfortable with the whole thing."

The stunt Mercedes that had been wrecked early on during the first night of shooting in Bangor would be utilized for this shot of the car coming down the hill. Since the vehicle's departure, the production had taken the time to improve it – not quite on the level of *The Six Million Dollar Man*, mind you – but close enough. "That first car that we piled into the guard rail that night, in the course of repairing it, we actually put some box steel into the front frame rails. And we made a seat that sat on the front of the thing at about, I guess it would have been bumper height, but it projected a couple of feet out in front and it was made out of, I think, three or four inch square tubing. So, it was very, very stout. And we then incorporated some attachment points with aircraft cable and stuff and eye bolts and all that to the front structure of the car. So, when Tom was on the front of the thing he was actually 'carabinered' into it with his harness and everything and actually had that seat that he ended up riding down over the hill there," Dreisch explains. "How that worked was, like I said, there was square tubing installed in the front... well, we actually sleeved it into the front frame rails and it

Above top, middle and bottom: The garage of Miles and Cindy Greenacre's home would fill in for the Lansing garage seen at the end of *The Hitchhiker*. Prop walls, shrubs, and leaves were brought in to help sell the illusion. (courtesy of Eileen Garrigan and Miles Greenacre)

let us be able to take the whole front bumper assembly off or slide it on. We also made a thing that would slide into the same receptacles that allowed the thing to be used as a tow bar so they could tow it behind a truck or whatever, if they wanted. Then there was the seat that slid in and, you know, it just worked out real well."

"We actually took out the radiator and put it in the trunk so that I could get my left leg, I think it was, into the engine and we cut a hole in the front grill. We also welded some eyelets so that I could be strapped in to the front bumper, to the front of the car. So, I stuck my left leg alongside the engine, my right leg was outside of the car on the bumper, and I wore a harness and was calibrated into a welded eyelet," says Wright. "It was a pretty gnarly gag to do, but it really went extremely successfully, so I was really proud of it."

"In the set up for that we sandbagged the front of the car to simulate his body weight and I actually drove the car down over the hill for the test shot there," Dreisch follows up. "It did two things: it gave us an opportunity to see what the dynamics of the car were bumping down that hill and all that, you know, whether he was in danger of getting thrown off or stuffing the nose or something. And in addition to that they wanted to play with the camera angles and stuff like that. It gave them an opportunity to verify what they wanted to do."

"I had never driven off that...you know, we didn't practice that kind of thing. I knew the car wasn't gonna flip, I knew the car wasn't gonna do anything crazy. I mean, we could tear the suspension up, perhaps, but I was confident the car was gonna behave itself. But, the first time you do it you don't know what you're gonna feel, what the impact is,

Above and right: The Greenacre's garage won the day since it wasn't finished, allowing for better camera angles. The garage at the Dyer estate, where the exterior of the Lansing home was shot, was not as accommodating. Note mechanic George Dreisch in the one photo wearing a black beanie cap and glasses. His mechanical skills and wizardry would be a life saver to the production. (courtesy of Miles Greenacre)

what it's gonna be. And when we left the ground – because the car did go slightly airborne for a very short time – but the nose, of course, is airborne for a long time and that's where Tom is, and his eyes got so huge!," laughs Hewitt recalling the stunt. "I remember his expression very well. But when we hit the downside then, you know, he was still wide eyed, but as soon as we hit he realized that everything was okay and then he really got into his acting. So, it was just a great shot from my view point, it was brilliant."

As you can see, George Dreisch played an enormous role in pulling this scene off – many scenes from the segment, in fact. He was an invaluable member of the production and that fact wasn't lost on those who witnessed his hard work, but also relied on it for their safety. "Now George, he was a mechanic. He didn't know about call sheets and getting up at five in the morning. It was his job to keep the cars going," says David Ball. "And when we were ramming them against the tree he'd be there with a great big hunk of metal and straightening out the dings so we could do take two or putting another wheel on so we could do take three. And George was a rock."

"Good guy," Taso Stsavrakis recalls. "And he kept saying, 'I can do this. I can do that. I need 15 minutes.' And I said, 'George, I don't have 15 minutes. You've

got 2. You've got 2 minutes. Can you do something in 2 minutes?'"

"There was a very, very talented mechanic that they had hired and he was from the local area in Maine and he had no information about film – a young man – but, man, he was really talented. And he designed stuff in this car, I should have dragged him back to New York and got him on the special effects department," says Jery Hewitt. "As a matter of fact, I was determined to destroy the car, in the three days of driving or whatever it was, and I could not! That car was...I'm sure that George got it back together and one of the producers probably drove it for a long time (laughs), I don't know. I don't know where that car went, but he did a remarkable job."

Thursday, November 20, 1986 – Day 55

The fifty-fifth day of production would see filming continue at the Dyer estate. Before we delve into the events of tonight's schedule though, I'd like to quickly revisit the issue of Taso Stavrakis and his departure from the production.

David Ball would draft a one-page letter to Stavrakis in which he discussed some of the issues that had occurred in Maine, such as the crash on the first night of filming and the impasse over scene 198 which eventually led to the stunt coordinator's premature departure. "You informed me in front of the director and production manager that you had 'quit' and with some reluctance I accept your decision," Ball wrote. "I am extremely sorry that all your hard work and devotion to this film should come to a seemingly sour end and I would like to record my sincere thanks for your more than considerable contribution to date." **(51)**

For Stavrakis, leaving the film early was something that bothered him in regards to his long time working relationship with Michael Gornick, who he was rooting for and wanted to see do well with the film. "The whole thing ended so badly that I just kind of put it all out of my mind and it's too bad. I feel bad because now I see Mike all the time (at conventions) and I really stabbed him in the back," says Stavrakis. "He took me to the side and said, 'Please don't leave me. Please don't leave me.' I'm like, 'I can't stay because these guys are putting me in this situation somehow.' That was the worst, right in the middle of a shoot day."

But for Gornick there were no hard feelings as he empathized with Stavrakis and the situation he found himself in, despite the fact that it did hurt him to watch his long-time collaborator abruptly leave. "I fully understand why he had to do that or why he wanted to do that. I mean, I think in a very personal sense he saw that as his domain, his expertise, and he was right," says Gornick. "To be shortchanged, many cases, both financially and also in terms of the stunt work, it was offensive."

"It was a dangerous stunt which required total precision driving rather than an all-rounder such as Taso. The crunch came and I went with Tom to allow him to feel comfortable with the stunt," says David Ball. "A producer has to make hard decisions sometimes but I made the correct one."

Gornick's mentioning of Stavrakis being shortchanged on not only the stunt work, but financially as well, is

something I'd be remiss in not discussing a little further here. In response to Ball's letter, Stavrakis would send his own on November 24, the day after principal photography ended in Bangor, and addressed some of the remarks in it. For the most part he simply defended himself and his department from what he felt were minor slights by Ball regarding the crash on the first night of filming, as well as the final straw with scene 198 and the replacement stunt driver. And in closing he made his best attempt to smooth things out between himself and Laurel. "This was a painful decision for me to make just three days before wrap. I appreciate your reference to my hard work and devotion which I hope helped make 'Creepshow 2' a better film," wrote Stavrakis. "Here I would like to offer my sincerest apologies to Mike Gornick for making a Herculean task even more unjustly arduous. And I hope we all have gained something from this experience." **(52)**

The back and forth between Ball and Stavrakis would continue via written correspondence all the way through December as questions about a bonus for Stavrakis would come to the forefront, serving only to increase the bitter tone between the two men, and in a December 6 letter Ball would directly address the issue. "With regard to your being excited to hear news concerning your bonus I can inform you that any bonus which may have been payable by your department being under budget was more than fully utilized by the selection of a specialist stunt person to perform activities beyond your experience," Ball wrote. "In fact, the stunt budget finished up considerably over." **(53)**

In response Stavrakis took the time to draft another letter to Ball on December 29 expressing his dismay at the way things had turned out. "I am truly sorry if the hurt and injustice I feel slipped out in my letters as sarcasm," wrote Stavrakis. "I am equally sorry, though not surprised, that you found a way to waste my hard-earned bonus. I suppose then, all those hours I put in as overtime were my free lesson in contract negotiations." **(54)**

Stavrakis would apparently never send that final letter though, as it remained in his personal files with the notation "Not Sent" written at the top. Frankly, revisiting the film wasn't the easiest thing in the world for Stavrakis to do, but he did so anyway because of his desire to help this book project. "You know, it was one of those really bad ones. It was a bad experience," he admits. "But all experiences are good in the end, but at the time it really hurt me. It hurt me emotionally and I'm sure it hurt me fiscally because I didn't work for a while after that."

As for the scheduled filming tonight – how much so Mother Nature would ultimately dictate – we'll begin with scene 201. This is the brilliant shot from Annie's point of view inside the Mercedes of the hitchhiker being rammed into the tree. To achieve the illusion of Tom Wright's body making impact with the tree once again a little engineering and cleverness would win the day.

"Well, that seat setup that we used going down over the hill was actually on the front of the car there. And, again, Tom was 'carabinered' in with a harness, and all that, with all those attachment points, but he was on that seat," George Dreisch explains. "Well, where that seat kind of a came

Above: Lois Chiles makes a friend in Miles and Cindy Greenacre's daughter, Kelci. Crew members wound up spending a lot of time inside the Greenacre home during their time there. (courtesy of Miles Greenacre)

into its own was I had set up a bunch of cable restraints to some attachment points I had installed in the back and bottom of the car and actually chained it back to, I don't know, half a dozen trees, I guess, that we daisy-chained between, and all that, to keep it from actually impacting the tree. And I think we ran it through and we did a couple of tests shots at it with nobody on and it worked out good, it was stopping about six inches short of the tree."

"So, I'm looking at it and I'm looking at his wardrobe (Wright's) and I said, 'Huh, what would happen if you put a limit on the car, so it cannot go any further, and we put a block of foam in your rain jacket that's tied to you? It will hit the tree pushing you forward as it compresses and you'll never hit the tree.' So, we tried it out and it worked so well and it was so simple," Jery Hewitt explains. "I bought a bunch of chains; we chained it down to another tree. I had two big chains, one was an absolute dead limit, the car could not go beyond that chain, when I hit that chain it was done. But then I had a shorter chain that was connected into double-used tires and the tires had to stretch, which you know is not easy to do, but with the weight of the car they will elongate. And so when I would pull forward the tires would give us a little bit of a cushion as I was coming to the tree and then it would come to the dead chain and it would rock the car at the same time that Tom's back was getting pushed by the tree on the foam. And to me, you know, to skin that cat and make it look that good? Man..."

For the scenes of Annie repeatedly ramming the hitchhiker into the tree, which includes scene 201, of course, the production had picked a particular tree on

the Dyer estate for filming. During pre-production location scouting, Michael Gornick and Bruce Miller picked a very distinct three-trunked crotched pine tree, labeled the "hero tree", and placed a red band around it so they could easily identify it upon returning. But like most things on the production, that didn't quite work out as planned. "I remember when we went back to Maine...we went there and scouted and picked the tree and we put that tape around it. And then, of course, three months later we go back and it's fall, the leaves are gone, and it's winter and it looked totally different," says Miller. "I know that Michael was a little miffed that we couldn't remember where the original tree was; as I remember, he was a little miffed. But it just looked totally different in the fall as opposed to the spring or summer when we were there the first time."

"Yeah, it was lovely. It was lovely," Gornick recalls. "We never found it again."

As for the rest of the night's schedule, it would consist of scenes 201A/202/203/204, 201B-203, 203A, 205A, 208, 206/207/210, and 210, all of which comprised Annie's rampage in the woods and ramming the hitchhiker against the tree over and over. Just how much was completed for these scenes is unknown because as I alluded to earlier in the section Mother Nature would have a say regarding the night's schedule. "They were shooting and then all of the sudden there was, like, a flash blizzard. I don't know how else to put it!," says Andy Sands. "The weather seemed nice until it was nothing but white snow, so they had to stop shooting."

"I'm sure you have information on the 'big freeze'. The 'big freeze' was awesome," recalls Eileen Sieff-Stroup. "And they had to shut down that night and we went into the bar and the bar had one of those glass roofs over it and we just sat in there and it snowed like two feet. And I'm not kidding it snowed two feet, it snowed multiple, like, feet of snow."

"And obviously we couldn't shoot because it was pouring, you know, the snow was coming down. So, we went and we rigged a sled, a couple of the crew people, we got some big piece of cardboard or something, we rigged a sled. So, it was me and Joanna (Robinson) and Lois Chiles, we were sled riding," laughs Jeanne Talbot. "It didn't turn into a big deal. I mean, it wasn't like one of these situations where we were shut down for a week, you know. I think that we figured it out and we were working the next day. But, I remember that night we all got a break because they had to figure out what to do."

And while there wasn't multiple feet of snowfall in the Bangor area – that much did fall in northern Maine, however, closer to the Canadian border – according to the National Weather Service it did snow close to four inches, causing a halt in filming for the night. "And Mike (Gornick) was gonna have this conference call – which even then seemed unbelievably high tech, how he was going to get this call from Richard (Rubinstein); this was the mid 80's, it seems perfectly mundane now, and they were going to have this conversation about what to do and how they were going to do it – he didn't have time to go back to the office, so they were going to do it in this van," remembers Andy Sands. "And I'm, like, locking up the set and all of this; the set is now under snow, nobody knows where the set is. He's gonna do this conference call – we know it's important, I mean, I heard that. And he's (Gornick) like, 'Andy, come into the van.' And I'm like, 'No, no. I gotta do this and you're having an important call with these people...'; it was Charles Carroll and David Ball and all of that. And he just looks at me like I'm insane and he says, '*Get* into the van'. So, they're having this really intense business conversation, you know, with the heater blasting and every window is all white. And it's Charles (Carroll), David Ball, Mike Gornick, and the voice of Richard Rubinstein – and me, in there. So, I have nothing to add to this conversation, I'm just sitting next to a heater. But it was an intense learning experience. And it made me appreciate all the more the grace with which Mike handled a very difficult situation for a first picture and how well he made it work."

And it wasn't just the snow – which would now be cleverly incorporated into the story – that the cast and crew would have to endure. As Eileen Sieff-Stroup hinted at, frigid temperatures would also be a nemesis. The low temperatures in Bangor were either at freezing, 32 degrees Fahrenheit, or below freezing for three of the four weeks that the production was in town filming, with some evenings going as low as 11 degrees Fahrenheit, such as the previous night for example.

"Literally, the crew would all laugh at me because I'm quite physically sensitive so I would wear three layers of long-johns and then this ski suit that made me look like the Michelin Man," says Kato Wittich. "And then we all had battery operated socks that we would wear because your feet would get just so incredibly cold in the middle of the night shooting. And I would literally schedule in, every two to three hours, we had to stop and change our batteries."

"When we shot the movie it was colder than the 'Holy Bejesus' out," Richard Greene recalls. "I remember the coiled chord that goes from my power pack that runs my flash on the camera was so stiff it wouldn't coil anymore; you'd extend it and it would just stay extended, it was that cold."

"We'd come in, in the mornings, and my makeup trailer was frozen," Howard Berger told Anchor Bay. "The water wasn't running. The toilet was frozen over, materials frozen

Left to right: The art department goes to battle against the frozen driveway at the Dyer estate, the location for the exterior of Annie Lansing's home. Even director Michael Gornick pitched in before the fire department showed up, saving the day and blasting the ice off the driveway. (courtesy of Eileen Garrigan)

over. It was like an ice cave." **(55)**

Working under these types of hostile conditions wasn't lost on the stars of the film who appreciated the efforts of everyone involved and enjoyed spending time in their company. "It was a brutal shoot, but the thing that made it really tolerable, more than tolerable, but fun, was the fact that the crew got along really well," Tom Wright fondly recalls.

"We really all enjoyed it, I think," says Lois Chiles. "We were a tight little group."

And that same level of appreciation was also deeply felt for those stars as both Lois Chiles' and Tom Wright's hard work was never taken for granted by the "higher ups" during those harsh conditions. "She was a trooper," says David Ball about Chiles. "You can imagine she's wearing a little cashmere top on that Mercedes that's being towed at three o'clock in the morning in effectively minus thirty degrees. Absolutely freezing! We've got six layers on and gloves and everything and she's wrapped up and then, 'Right, get in the car, Lois! Get in the car!', and she's like, 'Quick, hurry up! It's fucking freezing!' And it was freezing! It was absolutely, bitter cold. What a trooper. What a trooper, Lois."

"He was a real pro," Michael Gornick says about Wright. "Always a gentleman and I couldn't have done better, because it was one hell of a shoot. Aside from all the pains and difficulties he went through in preparation daily, you know, the weather was adverse, the conditions, again, were terrible because it was winter already in Maine. So, my hat will forever be off to Tom Wright."

Friday, November 21, 1986 – Day 56

Day fifty-six would see yet another change in venue – still in the Hampden area though – as filming would move about a mile and a half from the palatial Dyer estate to a more modest middle class dwelling on Papermill Road, home of Miles and Cindy Greenacre, where the interior Lansing garage scenes featured at the end of the segment would be shot. "Actually, the issue that they told me was the Dyer estate, the garage was completely finished inside, and what they needed was a garage where they could get the lights up higher," recalls Mr. Greenacre. "So, our garage had the same type of two-car garage door – one door, but two cars – but it wasn't finished, so they could put the lights up higher on the ceiling."

"They built a false facade in front of our garage and a little bit towards the left where the house was, to match the Dyer estate," Mrs. Greenacre adds. "They brought in trees and leaves."

The production had scouted the Greenacre's house in August during the pre-production phase and both Miles and Cindy remember how odd it was to have their home staked out at times by strangers. "Well, what I remember most was, actually, a car driving by slowly several times for days before they actually approached us," Mr. Greenacre says. "We didn't know what was going on. We didn't know if the house was getting cased or what? So, finally, I was out in the yard one day doing some yard work and they went by and I kind of waved them down and that's when we first found out that they were considering using our house."

"They said they'd get back to us soon, but it took weeks, and we figured they weren't going to use our property," says Mrs. Greenacre. "But, you know, eventually they did."

As for use of the garage Laurel-CST, Inc. would pay $500, according to the Greenacres, but like any wily outfit the production would find a way to squeeze a little more out of that deal. "Actually, the agreement was that they would just use the garage," says Mr. Greenacre. "Well, you know, the weather turned awful the night they were gonna do the filming. And so we told them they could set up downstairs, we had a playroom, down cellar. So, they set up a table down there and had some refreshments and food down there."

"They talked us into it, as I remember, Miles. We didn't offer. They *asked*," Mrs. Greenacre begs to differ. "It was November – November 21 thereabouts – and we had a few inches of snow and they didn't want to go back and forth to their trailers and stuff. So, they kind of took over everything, but our bedroom."

The day would start with a memo attached to all call sheets from David Ball informing the crew that unfortunately due to the snowfall from the previous day, filming would have to continue past Saturday. "Bearing in mind a general desire by you all to be home for the Thanksgiving festivities, it has been decided that shooting this coming Sunday would both complete the picture and allow you adequate wrap and travel time," Ball's memo read. "Should any of you have a serious objection to this proposal would you please discuss it with Charles or Kato. In the absence of any objections, I thank you for your continued support." **(56)**

Regarding tonight's filming scenes 218, 219, 220, 220B, 220C, 222A, and 223 would all go in front of the camera encompassing Annie pulling her battered Mercedes into the garage, then being attacked by the mangled remains of the hitchhiker, culminating with her husband finding her dead inside the car.

For the shot where the hitchhiker, now in his stage 6 makeup design, suddenly appears underneath the driver side door of the Mercedes, scene 220B, the makeup effects team would use a puppet, as the damage by this point to the character was so extreme it wasn't plausible to do so on Tom Wright: the eyes were pushed to the sides of the head, the mouth is torn open with the tongue dangling, he's just a bloody mess. "We called it the Admiral Ackbar head, from *Star Wars*," Howard Berger recalled in an Anchor Bay interview. **(57)**

And to achieve that shot of 220B, what seemed like a fairly simple shot, it would take more ingenuity and good old-fashioned elbow grease to capture the moment. "We were shooting the interiors of the garage over in Hampden – I think it was – at a house there. Well, we had one of the Mercedes over there; the one that originally got hit or went into the guard rail the first night, kind of ended up being the number one because it got all the work and all the modifications done to it in the course of the repairs. So, that ended up being almost our primary car. That, plus we removed the rear seat and stuff and had a roll bar in there they could take in and out and stuff for five point harness attachments and things like that," recalls George Dreisch. "But, where I was going with the Hampden garage thing was they were going to shoot doing the interior thing and the problem was they couldn't get the camera angle they wanted because of the...

if they tried to shoot through the door, the door was in the way or they couldn't get the angle or something. So, my solution for them was, 'Well, how about I cut the door post out and we can take off the whole back door and that leaves the whole side of the car open for you?'"

After a brief conference David Ball would give Dreisch the okay to go ahead with his plan, but only after hearing that Dreisch could put it all back together in 20 minutes! "Well, the problem was they needed it all back together or something for the next shot because I think they were shooting from the other side of the car," Dreisch explains. "So, I had some vice grips that – they're meant for gripping panels – but, anyway, for having the doors still attached to the door posts. I had put some marks as like tell-tales or legend lines before I had cut it, it was just a matter of clamping it in. And at that time I had just bought myself a Snap-on MIG welder that ran on 110 volts, so I actually had that in the garage there and at least tacked it in, and all that, and welded it back in fully later on. But, I had the door back in, I think it was something like twelve minutes, and David's like, 'You know, you've still got time' (laughs), you know, because he was actually timing me. I guess he was gonna bust my balls or hold me to the twenty minutes, but I beat it considerably, so he was pretty ecstatic at that."

Now, regarding that aforementioned hitchhiker puppet featured during this scene, Andy Sands recalls some of the last-minute challenges to bring it to life once the camera began to roll. "They had put together the effects they had, but to get the stuff on the schedule, in particular the animatronic zombie hitchhiker...you know, with most special effects, unless you're on the very highest level, you're shooting your prototype – certainly on a movie like *Creepshow 2*, you're shooting your prototype. And they had this great, very simple pulley animatronics of the zombie hitchhiker; that was great. But by the time they got ready to actually shoot the scene they had been using it and demonstrating it and all that, the animatronics to get it to move, they weren't working as well as they should. Had they used it when it was fresh it would have been brilliant, but it got played with and demonstrated a little too much and it wasn't performing for Mike (Gornick) the way that he wanted," Sands explains. "And so Greg Nicotero, who solved the problem, got under the car and started to sort of hand puppet the thing – I think he got some rods and shoved it in and basically he was gonna get this shot for Mike; they weren't gonna be able to rebuild the animatronics because they were gonna shoot it now and he was gonna make it work. So, they were doing it, his articulation was great, but Mike's only getting what he needs from half the body, they need to move the rest of the puppet. Well, Howard Berger, or Everett Burrell, or Mike Trcic, they're all like seven feet tall – I mean they're linebackers, they cannot get under this car comfortably, if at all. But 'shrimpy' me, you could literally just like toss me

Right: Head scenic Eileen Garrigan, with her trusty Radio Flyer wagon, would do battle, along with the rest of the art department, against the snow at the Dyer estate. With bags of mulch and cans of paint the crew would create the illusion that the snow never happened. (courtesy of Eileen Garrigan)

from one end of the bottom of the car to the other and I would slide through, I tell you. So, I climb underneath the car with Greg Nicotero and shove my hand in and they give me some stick or something to move the other half of the puppet for this thing."

Quickly, a very interesting side note regarding the hitchhiker puppet comes from *Fangoria* magazine's set visit by Tony Timpone. In his original 1987 magazine article in issue #64, and then again during my interview for this book, Timpone mentions being told by the makeup effects crew that the animatronics for the hitchhiker puppet were created by David Kindlon, who is not credited on the film. An exceptionally talented and brilliant artist Kindlon worked with the *Creepshow 2* makeup effects team on the previous Laurel production, George A. Romero's *Day of the Dead*, just two years prior handling the mechanical duties for Tom Savini. Unfortunately, interview requests for Kindlon were not returned.

And wrapping up the details for today, another second unit crew would be scheduled to work simultaneously picking up insert shots of 171, 173A, 188C, and 220A which were shots of Annie's foot on either the gas pedal or brake pedal, depending on the scene number. Other scenes scheduled were 178A of Annie's point of view through the windshield as she drives through the woods and 191A of the speedometer at 90 miles per hour. All of these scenes would be scheduled again on Sunday, the last day of production, so it's probably safe to assume that they simply never got around to working on them this evening. Now, if you've seen the film, and I have no doubt you have, you'll know that none of these shots are in the finished film. That's right, not a single one. So, either they never got around to completing them before production ended, or there was an issue with what was filmed, or they just didn't work somehow during the final edit. Who knows?

Saturday, November 22, 1986 – Day 57

The fifty-seventh day of production would return back to the Dyer estate where it would remain for the last two nights of filming.

Included on tonight's schedule were scenes 216, 221, and 222, exterior shots of the Lansing home and garage. "I remember quite distinctly because my daughter and I, she was just a child at the time, were actually in the window of the garage watching all of the events with the lights turned off in the room," remembers Jack Dyer. "I was always a little concerned that we might show up in the movie and spoil the movie, but we didn't. But, we were able to kind of carefully and surreptitiously watch the events as the car went into the garage below us."

These shots of Annie in her Mercedes, and then later her husband in his BMW, pulling up to the garage of their home would end up becoming far more arduous to achieve than anyone could have possibly anticipated. But, remember, this is *Creepshow 2*.

"So, the very last scene in the movie is Lois Chiles gets back to her palatial estate and drives up the drive way and goes into the garage and then gets asphyxiated," recalls Steve Arnold. "And what happened was it had been a sunny day and water had melted and then had re-frozen on this fairly steep, curving, concrete driveway."

"Well, you know, in Maine once the water freezes it's black, you can't even...so everybody's going, 'Whoops', and falling down and you can't get up," says Logan Berkshire. "So, we all took axes and hoses and spent like three hours de-icing this entire driveway."

"And we're literally there with shovels and tools to remove ice because it's like an inch and a half of ice on this driveway and it's all the way up to the garage. And we're beating away on this ice and it's not gonna get cleared off. It would take fifty people a day to do it," Steve Arnold explains further. "We're chipping and chipping and Michael Gornick arrives and he's like, 'Oh, I'll show you how to solve this.' He goes into...there's like a little house or guest house or something that's right there at the front of the driveway. He gets a garden hose and he hooks it up to the hot water in the kitchen sink and he's run it out and I'll never forget Ed Fountain, who was our construction coordinator and special effects guy, he was like, 'This is crazy! This isn't gonna work.'"

"Mike, he was in the middle of it, you know. He was in the middle of it, 'Let's go! Let's go!' We're like, 'Okay, let's go! Let's go! C'mon, Mike!' You know, you're not gonna stop him, he's a force of nature, man," Berkshire warmly recalls about the energetic director. "He was the commander, I mean, just totally. Not only was he about to direct the film in three hours, he was directing everybody... you know, 'There's ice right there! Get that over there! I've got the hose, you guys...'"

"But it was kind of therapeutic," Michael Gornick says. "I think we were all so frustrated by events, you know, arriving in Maine, no snow – suddenly snow, cold weather, freezing weather, that it was almost therapy to beat the shit out of the ice."

The exhaustive work proved to be futile though, so plan B was called in. "As it got dark and we were all trying to figure out, 'How the hell are we going to get this car to go up this driveway?', finally something right happened," says Steve Arnold. "Henry, the locations guy, he had somehow enlisted the help of a local volunteer fire department and this enormous sort of chartreuse colored truck, tanker truck, drives up and all it says on the side is H2O, in huge letters. And it had been parked inside, it was full of water, it had been parked inside somewhere so the water was room temperature. And they basically got out and fire hosed it and just blasted the ice off of this driveway so we could get the shot."

As for the other scheduled scenes this evening they would include 206/207/210, 207, 209, 210, 211, 212, 213, and 214, all of which would encompass the aftermath of Annie crashing her Mercedes into the tree repeatedly: coming to after knocking herself out on the steering wheel, gathering herself, and then slowly driving away out of the woods. Additional scenes were also scheduled, if time permitted, of 203/201/204 and 205, which were Mercedes interior shots of Lois Chiles selling the impact of the Mercedes slamming into the tree over and over. Several of these scenes would be re-listed tomorrow, so their completion would have to wait.

With the snow having blanketed the area, which led

to the decision to incorporate it into the story, that meant completing some of these shots would become a bit of a challenge in terms of the continuity of the actual snow. Naturally, with countless crew members shuffling about through the woods, tracks would be left from both people and equipment. How would that issue be addressed? "So, very quickly the powers that be decide, 'Okay, well, we're going to use this towards our advantage,'" says Steve Arnold. "'So, we'll shoot the part where Lois Chiles knocks herself out and she wakes up and it's snowing or has snowed...' So, there's snow everywhere, but there's not very much snow. It's like an inch and a half of snow. And so the crew comes in, it's around the car, there are foot-steps, there's all this stuff that has to be...so, we're literally taking wheel barrows of snow from the surrounding area to dress it all in and cover all the foot-steps and all the crew stuff and everything else and make snow look like, okay, there was a snowfall."

Just wait until tomorrow when you'll learn the absolutely insane, yet ingenious, way in which Laurel-CST, Inc. managed to basically erase all of that work to keep continuity for scenes that had not been completed prior to the snowfall.

Sunday, November 23, 1986 – Day 58

Day fifty-eight, the last day of production, had mercifully arrived at the Dyer estate location for the cast and crew of *Creepshow 2* – the proverbial light at the end of the tunnel.

The main course for tonight would be completing scenes 201 through 205, Annie ramming the hitchhiker into the tree. "When we were shooting at the Dyer estate there, and doing the woods, there's a part where they show Lois Chiles' head is supposed to be bouncing off the steering wheel, then I think there was a POV shot from inside the car. I was actually lying on the floor behind the seat and wailing on the back of the seat to drive her forward into the steering wheel. And on the first take, I guess, I did bounce her off the steering wheel," laughs George Dreisch. "At the same time they also had it hooked up with...you know the chrome water fire extinguishers, like they have in schools and stuff? Well, they had one of them rigged up with fog fluid in it and they had lines running out to the front of the car or at least under the hood, and all that. So, that's how we were generating the illusion of the thing actually overheating, we were spraying fog fluid from this fire extinguisher on to the exhaust manifold."

For Dreisch the time spent at the Dyer estate working on this portion of the segment was one filled with fun memories, such as the time producer David Ball approached him regarding damage needed for the Mercedes. "David comes up to me one night and he's like, 'Okay, we need to distress this car', and on and on and on. I'm like, 'Okay, hop in,'" laughs Dreisch. "So, we went out on the trail there and we preceded to freaking bounce the thing off trees; we beat the shit out of it. Between impacts he'd get out and look at it and he's like, 'Yep, that's good.' So, that was like an interesting, probably, 45 minutes."

Above: A sample of the comical cartoon drawings done by production assistant Andy Sands while in Bangor. (courtesy of Andy Sands)

During my research for this project I encountered one of those slightly uncomfortable scenarios where an individual claims credit for work accomplished after you, the writer, have already been informed that another individual was responsible for the effort. Case in point would be the Mercedes procured for the film by Willie Fonfe's company Willies Wheels. "The vehicle had to crash into a tree head on and the problem was that they could only afford one of a kind. This meant that after the initial crash the damage would immobilize it. The problem was that only one crash could be staged," explains Fonfe. "We therefore removed the radiator from the front and placed it in the boot with all the necessary piping. We then placed a steel plate in the space normally occupied by the radiator. Thus multiple crashes could be filmed without immobilizing the vehicle."

"Well, you know, he didn't do that," replies George Dreisch. "As far as the mods on that Mercedes go that all happened in Maine."

"But the thing that was really interesting is that a friend of mine (Dreisch) – who's a guy who's a real talented car mechanic – one of the special effects people had talked to him and said, 'You know, we've got to find a way to protect the engine radiator of the car because we're gonna crash it into trees and things like that,'" recalls Henry Nevison. "So, we actually found a way – this guy, who's a genius – he was able to put the radiator for the car in the trunk, with tubes going underneath through the middle of the car, and then re-enforced metal in the grill so it would protect the engine."

"So, I took the car and the guy who was working with/for me there, Dean (Wiseman), was acquainted with some guys down in Hampden – Hampden or Winterport, I'm not sure – anyway, down around (Route) 1A, that had just opened a body shop and I knew somewhat of them and they were pretty handy on fabrication and all that," Dreisch explains further. "So, for the combination of the body work (due to the crash during the first night's filming) and what I wanted to have done with the car for mods we went and spoke to them and they took it on and that's where the moving radiator into the trunk and then the modification of the front end, like, the provisions for the seat in front of the bumper and the metal screen...it was expanded metal screen that we put in front of the, like, accessory drive stuff, you know, in front of the belts and all that, so that Tom (Wright) wouldn't have to...basically to keep Tom's legs from ending up in the belts and stuff. And that's when those modifications happened."

As to the confusion with who was responsible, once again, we're talking about people's memories. Perhaps this is something that Fonfe recommended the production do? Perhaps he heard later that's what had been done to the car once it was in Maine and over time remembered that his company had performed the work? Over the years details can easily become blurred and mixed together.

The issue of continuity would be the largest factor tonight because the action takes place before the snowfall, which was now part of the story of Annie coming to and discovering that it had snowed while she was unconscious. Scenes 201 through 205 were obviously prior to this in the story, so how could the production tackle this enormous continuity issue? Of course, in 1986/1987 CGI wasn't an option, there was simply no way to digitally erase the snow and fix the problem in post-production as you could easily do today. But like the old saying goes, where there's a will there's a way – and regardless of how crazy it might have sounded at the time the route Laurel-CST, Inc. took to hurdle this enormous obstacle was sheer brilliance. "The last day, okay, we'd been shooting all this stuff in the woods and we had to do the last bit, which was Lois Chiles killing the hitchhiker, ramming him against this tree," says Charles Carroll. "So, I go to Bruce (Miller) and say, 'Bruce, what are we going to do?' And Bruce is like, 'I don't know! Oh, my god! We can't do anything!' And I can remember going to Ed Fountain, because Ed was such a mensch, and going, 'Ed, come on.' And we went to, like, I don't know, they didn't have Home Depots, so we went to the local nursery or hardware store and we bought every bag of peat moss we could and we bought brown paint. And we got all the set dressers and all the art department people you could and we went out there and we sprayed, like, an acre

LAUREL-CST INC.

928 Broadway, New York, NY 10010
(212) 674-3800

December 6, 1986

Re: George Dreisch

To Whom It May Concern,

George Dreisch was originally employed by this company as a mechanic in charge of the three Mercedes used for the production of "Creepshow 2." In reality he was asked to do much more than be a mechanic in that the vehicles suffering constant heavy stunt damage needed to be kept running.

To meet this challenge George often had to work twenty hours a day and was constantly required for welding, cutting, mechanical work and interior re-arrangement. Had it not been for George's total dedication to his work the production would have undoubtedly lost time on it's considerably tight shooting schedule.

In addition to George's mechanical wizardry I have first hand evidence of his driving ability. Any person who is able to drive a large Mercedes in reverse, round a tight bend at speeds exceeding 70MPH must be a candidate for consideration as a specialized stunt driver and I have no hesitation in recommending that, should the opportunity or necessity arise, you use George's abilities to their fullest extent.

Thank You,

David Ball
Producer
"Creepshow 2"

DB/mav

Above: Letter of recommendation from producer David Ball for George Dreisch, extolling the young mechanic's abilities and key contributions during the making of *Creepshow 2*. (courtesy of George Dreisch)

or two of woods brown. And then we spread peat moss all around this tree where the car had to drive up and ram into the thing and kill this guy, you know. So, by the time the crew showed up it looked like a normal forest."

"We had all of our equipment – of course, it was freezing cold!," Eileen Garrigan remembers. "Everything was breaking, these Hudson Sprayers that I mentioned before, you know, that I used to spray Dorothy Lamour, we were out there now spraying raw umber color on all the snow and it was just too cold for this water based paint and the hoses were breaking. And the hose would then be under pressure and just 'slap, slap, whap, whap' the brown paint all over, I was soaking wet with raw umber paint out there in my snow suit, and I'm all wet with this mud-colored paint. People were waking up the local help that we had saying, 'What kind of sprayers do you have?' They got me a big generator and an airless sprayer and we were waking up paint vendors, 'Just sell us whatever paint you have', and just throwing all kind of colors into giant buckets and mixing it up to be whatever kind of mud color we could get."

"And that was a classic, a classic moment," says Steve Arnold. "I'm sure environmentally very bad, you name it, we did everything wrong. But there you go."

"Yeah, unbelievable," says Bruce Miller. "Then it warmed up and it started drizzling and so all the paint started washing out of the snow, so the ground got whiter and whiter as the night went on. People were really tired trying to finish the sequence."

JOLTING TALES OF HORROR

"But we did it, you know, we did it," says Carroll as he wraps up the story. "But it was like, 'Holy Christ! I need another career. I want to do something else with my life, this is gonna kill me.'"

As mentioned at the end of the November 21 section second unit inserts would also be scheduled today for scenes 171, 173A, 178A, 188C, 191A, and 220A. However, as I previously discussed, none of these shots would ever appear in the completed film.

Scheduled as well were scenes 211 and 213 which were supposed to be interior shots from the Mercedes of Annie smoking another cigarette and continuing to talk to herself as she drives away from the tree she's just smashed into. These shots would have been accomplished by utilizing a car mount on the driver side of the Mercedes, but issues with the wooded area would create havoc in doing so. "We're doing the very last day, the very last night. We're doing a shot that we have to get, we have to get this shot," recalls Steve Arnold. "And they start to drive with the rig and all of a sudden someone yells, 'Stop!', because the camera was going to hit a tree, it was sticking out too far of the car and the little road that they were on you could not deviate. And basically they never got the shot because the sun came up and that was the last day."

"I remember when we wrapped, it was like pre-dawn, dawn was just breaking and Charles (Carroll) and I were standing in a muddy field with champagne in the rain and so glad it was over," says Michael Morgan as he sums up the feeling of reaching the finish line. "I mean, that was a moment I'll never forget, you know, him and I standing there in the rain with champagne and going, 'God, it's over!'"

It wasn't quite over just yet, however. Scenes 211 and 213, as well as 214, required dialogue and since the interior shots of Lois Chiles were not completed, as we just heard from Steve Arnold, Chiles' narration during these scenes would need to be recorded. According to Bruce Miller that too would end up being a near catastrophe. "And then we didn't even finish and we found out that Michael Gornick thought the crew was so angry at him, that they were making cars backfire at the base camp. But we found out it was the first day of hunting season, so people started hunting around us, so guns were going off," he says. "And so they packed up and they went and, I believe, they broke into a closed gas station to try to do the final sound stuff, the dialogue, and it was right under the flight path for Bangor airport. So, the minute 7 o'clock came along airplanes started taking off. And so, god knows, Michael must have just been beside himself; that the gods were against him."

"I don't remember that at all. Wow, that's bizarre," Michael Gornick responds. "I remember doing the sound work, we caught it where we could, you know, to find a quiet moment. But I don't recall the feeling that it was the crew trying to subvert our efforts."

And with that principal photography for *Creepshow 2* would come to a close; the end of the insanity for a beleaguered production, one that suffered through enormous obstacles, constant misfortune, and mind bending pressures that took a toll on the people involved. "I do know that there was one incident where...in Bangor our offices were kind of like a railroad car a little bit, so I had to go through Charles' (Carroll) offices to get to my office in this big warehouse," recalls Bruce Miller. "And one day where everything seemed to be falling apart I walked through and Charles had his back to me where I would walk through and he had a 'movie' gun in his hand and he was pointing it at himself and clicking the trigger. And I don't know, I think I said something like, 'It's just a movie', and I may have even taken the gun out of his hand. But I remember thinking that Charles is under just as much as stress as all of us. And that was a sobering moment, I guess; also kind of a humorous moment."

"I have to admit, I don't recall it," Carroll responds. "Of course, the gun was unloaded."

Indeed, everyone would endure and make it out alive from the grueling experience. That endurance, along with some applause worthy ingenuity, is one to be admired and respected. But it was also a harsh learning experience for so many involved, one that prepared them for careers in a very demanding industry. "I learned how to go with the flow and that things don't always work out the way you want them to," says Steve Arnold. "But I guess the thing I learned the most was probably just perseverance and sticking to the project. It's probably not the most brilliantly designed movie out there, but for what we had to work with, the limited amount of money and time, you know, it's a genre kind of movie. And that's my take on it."

Out of the 100+ interviews I conducted for this project though perhaps no one encapsulated things better than art director Beth Kuhn when she explained in the simplest of terms why the production seemed to encounter so many of those continuous challenges. "I really feel like 90% of the problems were that they were trying to do, you know, a $25 million dollar picture on $4 million dollars," she perfectly summarizes.

Chapter 4 Hagoonee', U.S.A - Ya'at'eeh, U.K

The end of principal photography had mercifully come for the crew of *Creepshow 2*. They could head back home and enjoy the upcoming Thanksgiving holiday with family and friends, take a load off and finally just relax. "I'm not even sure I said goodbye to anybody," says Bruce Miller. "I had rented a truck, the company had rented a truck, to take stuff back to Pittsburgh, in case we needed it, and I ended up driving that truck to friends of mine outside of Plymouth, New Hampshire where I had college friends that were there. We were going to spend Thanksgiving in Plymouth, New Hampshire, I was going to spend Thanksgiving; but I remember sleeping almost the entire time I was there. So, I barely saw them."

Before clearing out of Bangor someone in the production office - I'm not sure who - decided it would be fun to create one final call sheet for the remaining crew to share a laugh over. The tongue-in-cheek call sheet - featuring the production title of "HOW I LEARNED TO STOP WORRYING AND LOVE THE BLOB" and listing the production day as #999,999,999 - was loaded with

Above: Early concept art by Gary Hartle for the Creep. (courtesy of Rick Catizone)

in-jokes aimed at certain production members such as "Special guest appearance by Tom Savini as God" listed under the "Atmosphere & Bits" section, "more flares for Mr. King please" listed under the "Props" section, and "EXT PRESCOTTONIAN - D: Truck pulls up with 'Cisco Kid' tape aboard, Bruce throws up quietly in the background" listed under "Set Description". It was a funny, playful way to say goodbye to a production that had tested, for the most part, everyone's sanity.

Under the "Advance Schedule", at the bottom of the call sheet, read the words "SOMETIME NEXT YEAR: Location scout for *Creepshow 3* in Beirut, Lebanon".

Among some of the post filming tidbits, David Ball would take the time to type a heartfelt letter of appreciation for mechanic George Dreisch to help him with future employment opportunities. "Had it not been for George's total dedication to his work the production would have undoubtedly lost time on its considerably tight shooting schedule," Ball's letter read. "In addition to George's mechanical wizardry I have first-hand evidence of his driving ability. Any person who is able to drive a large Mercedes in reverse, round a tight bend at speeds exceeding 70MPH must be a candidate for consideration as a specialized stunt driver and I have no hesitation in recommending that, should the opportunity or necessity arise, you use George's abilities to their fullest extent. Thank you, David Ball, Producer, *Creepshow 2*". **(1)**

"I got a letter from David Ball that he wrote for me when we got done and basically it's a letter of recommendation, but, you know, it's kind of interesting, I've always kind of enjoyed it and cherished it," says Dreisch. "I've carried that thing, as far as in the past, when I applied for jobs, and all that. Sometime after that I ended up working as a civilian technician on helicopters and when I got that job I actually had the letter in my package."

Another letter from around this same period which warrants mentioning would come from Richard Rubinstein. As was discussed in the Day 6 section of Chapter 3 makeup effects artist Ed French penned an 11-page letter to Rubinstein laying out his grievances in regards to his dismissal from the production and his claim of compensation due him from Laurel, along with proper screen credit. Rubinstein's response would be brief and to the point in which he told French that from his prerogative he was satisfied with the outcome decided on by David Ball, and closed with a warning for French should he take legal action. "With respect to further payments to you I told you in person that David's approach to computing money due you was justifiable and I would not override his position. If that means you wish to have the matter to go to attorneys that will be your decision," Rubinstein's response read. "Please be aware however that such an approach effectively leaves yourself and Laurel-CST irreconcilably on opposite sides of the fence on a long term basis. I would much prefer you look to the potential value in an on-going relationship as a source of recouping what appears to be a small amount of money in dispute." **(2)**

The final letter(s) worthy of mentioning would come from *Old Chief Wood'nhead* star, Dorothy Lamour. As we discussed in the previous chapter Lamour really made an impression on the crew of *Creepshow 2* and fostered many new friendships including Michael Gornick

Below: Animation rough of the Creep. (courtesy of Rick Catizone)

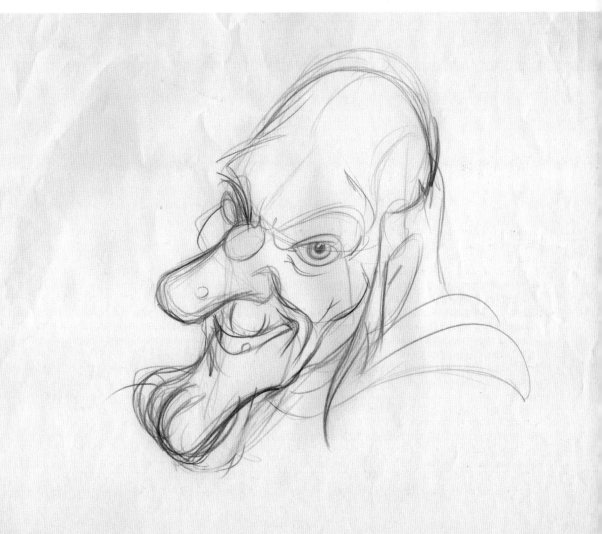

and Rebecca Mayo, who Lamour took the time to send personal holiday notes to. "<u>Love</u> is a gift that cannot be demanded, a blessing that comes from the heart, and all those who share it, find their thoughts turning heavenward, where love began," the screen legend's letter(s) read. "I wish you <u>Love</u>. Merry Christmas! Happy New Year! And Happy Holidays! Aloha! Until we meet again, Dorothy Lamour (and, Coco, of course!)". **(3)** Coco, by the way, was Lamour's beloved Scottish Terrier, who she included a stamp of his paw on the page next to her name. Over the next couple of years Lamour would stay in touch with Gornick and Mayo sending them both correspondences during the holidays, something I have no doubt she did with others from the production.

While the majority of the crew was now done with *Creepshow 2*, such was the not case for David Ball and Michael Gornick. A preliminary post-production schedule would be prepared by Ball spanning from the final week of November 1986, when Michael Gornick would be scheduled to return to Pittsburgh for meetings with animation supervisor Rick Catizone, all the way through to the end of March 1987 when the final cut of the film would be hand delivered to New World Pictures by Laurel.

In this chapter we'll attempt to cover in detail as much as possible about that schedule - from the animation, to the editing, to the score. And perhaps you took note of the chapter title, a playful nod to Benjamin Whitemoon's greetings to Chief Wood'nhead, which is in reference to the production saying goodbye to the United States and hello to the United Kingdom as post-production would be based out of Pinewood Studios just outside of London.

Perhaps the best place for us to begin is covering the most crucial aspect to this portion of the production - which was created in Pittsburgh, Pennsylvania - the film's animation. To handle this key element of *Creepshow 2* Laurel would turn to an old friend of the company: Rick Catizone.

Growing up in Pittsburgh Catizone enjoyed a passion for comics, as well as hand drawn animation. "Well, when I was really young, say seven or eight, I loved comic books; I really wanted to be a comic book artist. I loved (Jack) Kirby and (Joe) Kubert, as well as Alex Raymond's *Flash Gordon*, Harold Foster's *Prince Valiant*, and *The Phantom*," he fondly recalls. "I always did love animation, but I don't think I really was aware that it could be a career path until I was older. I loved watching the old Disney show, because they would do behind the scenes of the animators working on the different films. It was always magic to watch them flip their drawings and see them come to life."

As he got older an interest in stop-motion animation also began to develop for Catizone, which would turn out to be just as big a passion. "I'm pretty sure that while I was really aware of the different quality of *Mighty Joe Young*, I didn't really know how it had been created," Catizone says. "Then *Famous Monsters* did a three-part article on Ray Harryhausen and that pretty much cemented what I wanted to do."

By the mid 1960's, not long after graduating high school, Catizone would catch on with The Animators, a local Pittsburgh animation studio owned by a gentleman named Bob Wolcott, where he would work on a variety of projects including television commercials and corporate slide show presentations, as well as creating the end credit sequence for George Romero's 1968 masterpiece *Night of the Living Dead*. "I first met Bob when I took in my very crude animation sample reel. He was impressed that I had done stop-motion combined with rear projection on minimal home equipment. In fact, when he asked how I did some of the effects, and I explained what I did, he said, 'You can't do that on that type of equipment.' And I said, 'I know', and we laughed. Bob hired me about 3 months later, and told me that he was very impressed with what I was able to do on equipment that wasn't made to do it, that he knew I'd be able to do some impressive work with the professional animation stand," Catizone says. "He was someone who took a chance on this young kid one year out of high school; he helped make my dream a reality. A few years later, Lee Hartman, who was their main animator, decided to leave The Animators - I really wanted to step into that spot. I got a chance on a public service commercial, animating some hybrid racing cars with 'faces' all gearing up at the starting line. After that, I took over handling the character animation. It was actually a pretty intense learning curve, because I realized very quickly how much better I had to draw, and how much better I had to animate, to turn out the quality we were known for. So, for the most part, aside from a couple of questions about animation that I was able to ask Lee about, I was pretty much self-taught."

By 1980 Catizone would start his own animation company, Anivision, where one of his biggest projects would come along, 1982's *Creepshow*. He would handle the film's animated sequences, as well as assisting Tom Savini with the creature "Fluffy", from *The Crate* segment, sculpting its hands, feet, and chest. "*Creepshow* was unique for me because it would be the first time I would get to animate a character for a feature film. A bit like the witch in *The Wizard of Oz*, the Creep isn't on-screen very long, but you feel the presence through the film," Catizone says. "So, it was really exciting and it was a great opportunity. How many people get to have the chance to do animation on a feature film, let alone one by George Romero and Stephen King?"

By the time the opportunity to work on *Creepshow 2* came along Catizone had twenty years of professional experience under his belt, so his work didn't typically come cheap. However, this was a project directed by Michael Gornick, someone he had known and been friendly with since the early to mid 1970's when their respective offices were in the same building in downtown Pittsburgh. "I'm sure Mike was pushing for me because we'd worked together for ages and I respect Mike a lot and I think Mike respects me," says Catizone. "First of all, I think he felt comfortable with me and I think he also felt comfortable with the fact that we could talk to each other, we had good communication, I think, on things. And he also knew there wasn't going to be a ton of money for it."

"I was calling upon a lot of favors," Gornick confirms. "I mean, Rick and I grew up at 247 Fort Pitt Blvd, he was there from the first day I arrived. We worked extensively, he did a lot of commercial jobs; at the time we had a sound studio there so I became his sound mixer for a lot of his

CREEP
Head Model
Rick Catizone

Above: Creep model sheet for his different facial expressions. (courtesy of Rick Catizone)

spots, I did voices for him and so forth for his spots. We were close friends, so he felt some sort of obligation to support me. And he did, you know, he did."

During the production of the original *Creepshow* in 1981 Catizone was paid $35,000 for the animated sequences featured in the film, which was roughly four and a half minutes of screen time. *Creepshow 2* would require twice the amount of animation on a proposed budget of $80,000 - which would actually come in under $72,000 according to the Estimated Final Cost Report - all of which, of course, was in 1986 dollars. Not only that though, the animation in the sequel would be far more complex compared to the original due to the level of character animation required this go around. Catizone recalls discussions with the film's producers and the dubious acceptance of his offer to handle the sequel's animation at such a bargain basement price. "I think it was David (Ball), saying something like, 'Well, you know, I don't understand how you can do it for this price because R/Greenberg wants a quarter of a million dollars', or something," explains Catizone. "And I said, 'Well, one, I'd like the opportunity to do it; I worked on the first film and I'd like to see the continuity continue. I know there's not going to be a ton of money for this to begin with and I'd like to see it happen rather than not happen.' And I said, 'I've been friends with Mike and George for most of my career and I've worked on a number of films with them and I'd like to continue that. And I'd like to help if I can by

contributing in a way that gets you what you need without costing you something that you can't afford or maybe somebody decides to go a different direction.'"

As for Michael Gornick he couldn't have been more thankful for the financial sacrifice Catizone was willing to make for him and his film, even though he hated to see it happen. "Ahh, it was sinful. It was almost like they didn't want it to happen," Gornick says. "You know, I don't quite recall, but I think at points the producers in general, and I have to include David in this too, were not keen with the whole idea of animation. And certainly when I suggested the expanded animation they were saying, 'Oh, no, please. It's not a cartoon.' They thought less was better. So, I think they actually tried, through budget, to stymie the animation and Rick resisted and gave me more. So, to this day I owe a lot to Rick. I really do."

I should remind you that Catizone's hiring was prior to principal photography beginning, due to the large amount of leg work required for traditional cel animation. So, this would place us in the summer when work started on the character designs. And while I spoke with several key people from the animation unit - Phil Wilson, Gary Hartle, Jim Allan, Ron Frenz, and Lori Chontos - a large amount

221

of the information for this chapter was gleaned from the animation supervisor himself, Rick Catizone, via telephone interview and extensive email correspondence. Rick, much like Mike Gornick, displayed the patience of Job in dealing with my constant and numerous questions. Quite simply, I could not have written this chapter without his unwavering support and vast knowledge.

As for a general over-view of how animation is brought to life, Catizone describes the process for us. "Stages for animation once we have the script: design characters, create the story-board, and do full size layout drawings, create the Key animation drawings, then the Breakdown animation drawings, and finally the In-betweens," he explains. "Before animation keys are begun the animator will usually act out the scene, in his head or up and about, draw thumbnail ideas for poses that reflect the acting he envisions, and then begins full-size animation drawings. When animation for a scene is done, it is photographed, and if no changes are needed, it goes to be inked. The drawings are inked onto acetate, on the front. The cels are turned over and painted on the back, so the line-work doesn't get obscured. Once painted and dry, they are placed on a background and filmed, one frame at a time. There are 24 frames per second in film, so that's an incredible amount of drawings."

Now, most of those terms seem pretty easy to interpret, but for those of us who aren't necessarily up to speed on animation lingo, we'll have a brief crash course. Basically, a Key animation drawing would be the beginning and ending of some type of action - the hero swings from a rope across a crocodile infested river, for example - while a Breakdown animation drawing would consist of the action that gets you from point A to point B, a sort of middle section, for lack of a better term. But what about the In-Betweens, what are those? "Well, what the In-betweening is, is the animator does the Key drawings," explains Ron Frenz. "The primary animator will do this, this, and this. And the In-betweener will do whatever is needed to complete the motion in between. So, it is exactly what it sounds like. So, you have to be able to understand the mass and the shape of the thing."

An immensely talented and driven artist, Pittsburgh native Ron Frenz would win a half scholarship to the Art Institute of Pittsburgh while attending A.W. Beattie vocational technical school during his last two years of high school. It was at A.I.P. that he would come to know the head of Anivision, who would soon become his boss. "So, I did my two years at the Art Institute. As I was graduating there, you know, they have placement assistance and all this kind of stuff and I interviewed for a couple of jobs and ended up meeting Rick Catizone, showing him my portfolio, and he took me out to lunch. And he knew that my ambition was to work for Marvel Comics. I mean, from the time I was seven or eight years old, if you asked me what I wanted to do when I grew up it was work for Marvel Comics and draw *Spider-Man*," Frenz says. "And, anyway, had lunch with Rick Catizone - one of the things Rick brought up at lunch, he says, 'Ron, let me give you a scenario: I hire you and I take the time to train you and then Marvel calls and says, 'Ron, we'd like you to come and work for Marvel.' Do

you leave me in the lurch after I've taken the time to train you? How do you approach it?' And I went, 'Wow, I know what you want me to say. Umm, no, Rick, I will not leave you in the lurch.' And he said, 'Okay', and he hired me."

The way Catizone viewed it though he believes his own childhood desire to be a comic book artist had a significant influence in his taking a chance on Frenz. "I was mainly looking for somebody who had solid drawing skills, that could be my assistant; I believed I could teach him how to In-between my work," says Catizone. "Ron not only had the solid drawing ability that I was looking for, but he wanted to get into doing comic books. I interviewed a number of people, but few had the solid drawing ability and dynamics that Ron had in his portfolio."

Frenz would work on the original *Creepshow* as Catizone's animation assistant where, among other responsibilities, he was tasked in augmenting the comic book page panel intros that transition from animation to live action between segments. The main art was created by former E.C. artist Jack Kamen, but one crucial aspect was missing, and that's how Frenz would receive his "Spectre Art" title in the end credits. "Yeah, that was just a credit they pulled out of their ass," Frenz says. "The Spectre Art credit came from the fact that on those pages, in the first one that Kamen did, when you're panning across them and stuff, he didn't do the little introduction panels the way we really played them up in the second one, where there was a title and all that kind of stuff. He didn't do that. I drew the spectres for those pages and we pasted them back together. We composed the pages with Kamen's art and I did the host spectre stuff where he's like pointing at the titles and all that kind of stuff."

It was after *Creepshow* that the scenario Catizone pitched to Frenz when the two first met would actually unfold, leaving Frenz with a big decision to make. "I think even at the time I had met with Rick I think the reason the Marvel thing was even out there was because I had met with Jim Shooter, who was the Editor-in-Chief of Marvel at the time, he did a shop appearance locally, and I showed him some samples and he said, 'Okay, well, Xerox these and send them in and I think you and I will be talking', and I was very hopeful," he says. "But, after I'd been working at Anivision for a while, and I was still living at home with my folks out in the north hills (a Pittsburgh suburb) at the time, I came home one evening and had gotten a phone call from an editor at Marvel and they were interested in having me do some stuff. So, I was able to get back in touch with them and make some arrangements. But because of the promise I made to Rick I stayed at Anivision and was working 9-5, at least, for him, and then going home and doing any Marvel work I was getting at night. And I did that for, I'd say for a couple of years. I think I started...the cover date for my first stuff for Marvel would have been '83, so I think it was late in '82 that I started getting some work from them. So, I had been with Rick for a year and a half or more or something - I forget exactly when I started working for Rick - and I kept my promise as long as I could. I didn't leave Anivision until I was offered *Spider-Man*."

Above and below right: Paint guide for the Creep, juxtaposed with the finished cel from the film. (courtesy of Rick Catizone)

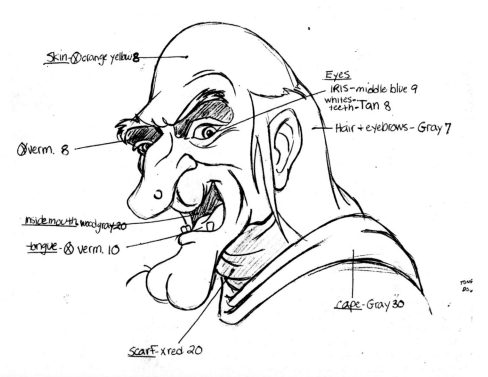

CREEP Normal Colors

Skin - ⊗ orange yellow 8

Eyes
IRIS - middle blue 9
whites--
teeth - Tan 8

Hair + eyebrows - Gray 7

⊗ verm. 8

inside mouth - wood gray 20

tongue - ⊗ verm. 10

cape - Gray 30

scarf - X red 20

TONG
DOU

Above: Early designs of facial poses for Billy by Gary Hartle. (courtesy of Rick Catizone)

"Ron is a great guy and a great artist. I'm glad he's done so well, he deserves it," says former Marvel Editor-in Chief, Jim Shooter. "I met Ron Frenz in a comic book shop on Pittsburgh's north side, I think. His samples were terrific. I got his information, and when back in the office, showed copies of his work to Al Milgrom, one of the dozen or so editors who worked for me. Al was very good at working with new artists. Al didn't have anything for Ron at the time, but Louise Simonson needed an artist, so Al showed her Ron's stuff, and she offered Ron some work. Louise was very good with new talent, too. Ron eventually wound up working with Tom DeFalco frequently. Tom was an editor, but also did a lot of writing. Working with Tom as writer, Ron drew the first appearance of Spider-Man's black costume in *Amazing Spider-Man #252*, which went on sale in January of 1984, I believe. Some people mistakenly believe he designed the costume, but actually Mike Zeck did many months earlier; no one needs to pad Ron's excellent resume. Ron and Tom developed the costume into the alien symbiote, which eventually became *Venom*."

Phil Wilson, another native of western Pennsylvania, would also graduate from the Art Institute of Pittsburgh in the late 1960's. After graduation he would find work with the county where he and friend/collaborator Jim Allan - another product of the Art Institute - would receive an opportunity to create something they both loved a great deal. "Jim and I worked at the county graphics department for Allegheny County doing brochure covers and maps and slide shows, you know, not the sexiest stuff in the world," Wilson explains. "We had always wanted to do animation so we were always experimenting on our own as a little bit of a sideline."

"Phil and I sat down one day and we were saying, 'What could we animate that might get on TV?' Well, back then everything was about pollution, there was a lot of water pollution, there was a lot of stuff about the rivers being polluted and everything," says Wilson's colleague, Jim Allan. "So, we said, 'Let's do a water pollution film. We'll tell the story with a drop of water doing the narrating and talking about it and describing what's going on with the pollution.' So, we started working on ideas for that."

"And there was a fellow who worked there (at the county) as an intern whose mother was the head of the Group Against Smog and Pollution, G.A.S.P., and it was about air pollution, things like that, water pollution," Wilson follows up. "And he asked us, he said, 'I was telling my mom about you guys playing around with animation and she was wondering if you'd want to do a public service announcement?' We said, 'Sure!' And we hadn't done squat up until then, just experimenting on our own, nothing on film."

Wilson and Allan would go on to create G.A.S.P.'s cartoon mascot, "Dirty Gertie, the Poor Polluted Birdie", which was part of a successful public service campaign to raise awareness about Pittsburgh's poor air quality due to pollution. By the late 1970's Wilson and Allan, tired of the grind at the county, decided to strike out on their own and create an animation company, aptly named Allan & Wilson Animation Studio, when they would receive an offer to create the animation for *Allison and the Magic Bubble* for HBO. "I told Phil, I said, 'This is really crazy!' I said, 'We've got about three minutes worth of animation under our belt and we're talking about a half-hour children's special for HBO?'," Allan laughs. "I said, 'This is insane!'"

Not long afterwards they decided to ask another local Pittsburgh animator if he might have an interest in sharing some office space with them - Rick Catizone. "When we started our studio, Jim Allan and myself, we had rented a building, the second floor of a warehouse building in Castle Shannon (a neighborhood in Pittsburgh), because we had to hire about twenty-five people," says Wilson. "So, when we had that building we knew Rick at that time anyway and we asked him - he was sort of stuck downtown in that little space that The Animators had - we said, 'Would you like to move out and join us? You'll be your separate company and we'll be ours but we'll share equipment, we'll share people, and so forth and work on each other's projects.' He said, 'Yeah, great.'"

And in 1981 that's exactly what happened when Catizone would help Wilson and Allan on their animated special *A Star for Jeremy*, while they would in turn assist Catizone on his project *Creepshow*. "Just very briefly; I just did some backgrounds, painted some background pieces for the animation on that one," Wilson recalls. "I think I did a curbside with the sewer when you see the comic getting thrown down, I did the background for that. And I'm not sure if I did anything behind the Creep (the spectre) when he comes to the window or not. That's a little foggy."

The next key member is, you guessed it, from the "Steel City" of Pittsburgh. Gary Hartle grew up loving to draw, creating his own illustrated children's stories and comics as a kid that he would use to entertain his siblings. It would be another family member who would eventually turn Hartle on to the art of animation, which struck a nerve with the young artist. "A cousin of mine showed me, he drew a stick figure at the bottom of a flipping notebook and then I began to get 3x5 cards and I would draw on the top and bottom of both sides; little stories and things like that," Hartle says. "When I went to art school I went

to the Ivy School of Professional Art, mainly because they had animation. So, I began to take classes in animation and I think things started moving more in the animation direction. After that I got out and I was gonna come to California right away, but I went to Mike Schwab's - his animation (company) was called Kensington Falls. So, I started doing animation over there and eventually I was his animator. We would do things like the Pittsburgh Penguins, and the Maulers (USFL football team), and local TV shows and all that. Then I went to Rick Catizone's animation."

During the pre-production of *Creepshow 2* Hartle would create story-board art for Michael Gornick, who remembers how easily the work came to the young man and how attuned he was to the story and what Gornick was looking for. "We'd spend day after day with a few scenes that were scripted, talk about them in terms of angle and so forth. His ability to interpret that, listen and create those was a mind boggle," Gornick says. "I don't remember many situations where I'd say, 'No, no, Gary, that's all wrong. This is the wrong angle, I wanted more of a god's POV and you don't quite have that.' So, his visual nature was amazing in terms of that translation to the pen, you know; talented guy, very talented guy."

Our last key member of the animation unit is Lori Chontos, another Pittsburgh native, who was the head of the ink and paint crew. Chontos grew up with a deep love of animation, particularly the works of Walt Disney. Like fellow artist Gary Hartle, Chontos would attend the Ivy School of Professional Art. Afterwards she would catch on with Allan & Wilson Animation Studio, impressing them with her inking skills. Having the opportunity to do something she felt such passion for was quite a thrill for the shy and private artist. "I fell in love with it and just doing animation - especially the ink and paint stuff - couldn't wait to get up in the morning and do it until I couldn't keep my eyes open any longer," she says. "Time just flew by, it was just a passion of mine; I loved doing it. It just made me very happy - just to be able to see your work come together was pretty amazing."

It was while working for Allan & Wilson that the dedicated work ethic Chontos displayed would catch the eye of Rick Catizone, who would utilize her for his company Anivision's commercial work, eventually leading to *Creepshow 2*. "I was a pretty fast painter and very detailed and neat about that," Chontos says. "And, I guess, he approached me, I don't remember, it's been so many years, to head up the ink and paint department and it kind of went from there."

"I used Lori on many of my projects and my decision to put her in charge of ink and paint on *Creepshow 2* was because she sincerely loved her work, was meticulous in her execution, was extremely precise, had a great personality, and *cared* about her contribution," Catizone states. "She understood its importance; she was indispensable in running that part of production. It left me free to deal with all the other demands of the film."

Without a doubt the most important character to animate for the film would be the host himself, the Creep, which supervisor Rick Catizone would handle personally. "I took all the Creep work for myself because first of all it was the main body of work and there was so much of it; you know, he would talk for twenty or thirty seconds and stuff in one burst. And while I knew I had other talented people in the studio, I didn't think we would get it in on budget on what we had to work with. Because I knew if I didn't do it, it would have taken a lot longer and so I tried to work in a methodology to it that I knew that we could get it all done," explains Catizone. "In reality, while I really wanted to do most of the Venus flytrap stuff, my first objective was to create the character and personality of the Creep and his acting so it would be consistent and that the dialogue and lip-sync would be accurate."

Of course, before you can begin with any of that you need to actually design the character first. Trying to find the perfect look for the Creep would take some time. Unlike the original film, where the Creep was more skeletal and spectral, this outing the Creep would be more flesh and blood. This is interesting because in Romero's screenplay the Creep's appearance is described much the same way he was in the original film. "The DELIVERY MAN turns to reveal a spectral face. It's hideous! Long dead! It has materialized out of the miasma, a mangled mummy made of maggots and mold and mucous and mud!" **(4)**

"Well, offhand, I can only say that when Mike (Gornick) said the Creep had huge hunks of dialogue I brought up the fact that the skeletal Creep had no lips and therefore mouth movement would look like a ventriloquist dummy, and that would look really bad," recalls Catizone. "It may have been that he suggested something more like the E.C. characters. Or I might have simply said whatever way we go I wanted the character to have flesh and lips to be able to do dialogue properly."

By augmenting the Creep's look for this new version though another challenge would come to the forefront when his appearance began to ape another well-known character from Warren Publishing's classic magazine, *Creepy*. This too would require addressing, but without taking away from what the character *needed* to be. "I think Gary took a shot at it, and maybe Ron as well...and I did some. I did the final one and then did a sculpture for reference and sent them photos of that. I may have sent my model sheet as well...but since they needed the design quickly, I don't think I had that done yet," says Catizone. "A lot of the takes on the Creep felt too close to Uncle Creepy. I rounded and exaggerated things to make him unique. We looked through all the E.C.'s, and they had three basic storytellers. And when you're designing a 'creepy' guy you can't deviate too much from certain devices or they aren't 'creepy' anymore."

After settling on the Creep's design, Catizone would also need to plan out the scenes for which he would be involved in, how his character would move, and so forth. The level of commitment this requires from the artist is actually quite demanding, but Catizone would receive a much appreciated assist from the actor who voiced the character, Joe Silver. "Once I had the tracks recorded I plotted out the scenes. And then once I decided which Creep scene I would start with I would play the track over and over, acting out what I felt would be an appropriate motion and attitude based on the phrasing and emotion in the track," explains Catizone. "Joe Silver gave a great performance."

Unfortunately, by the time Catizone had mastered his work with the Creep it was time to move on to something else, which can be both frustrating and exciting at the same time. "About the time we were maybe with one month left in terms of animation I'd done so much work with the Creep that it really wasn't hard to do because I understood the character really well by that point," he says. "And I was thinking, 'Gee, what a shame that I'll have to stop now that I really have a handle on this'; and that's the way it is with everything, of course. And at the same time it was nice to kind of wrap up and do some different things after that."

Some of the other different things that Catizone would tackle included designing and handling the animation of the postman, Mr Haig, which was trickier than you might initially think. "Mr. Haig took a while because as soon as you start getting characters that look a little bit older, or a lot older, you're dealing with...well, you're trying not to put too many lines in the face," says Catizone. "Because number one it's not only going to be difficult to track but it starts to make the character look ugly."

Besides Mr. Haig, one of the other tasks Catizone would tackle included the flying demons which morph into the *Creepshow 2* title font featured during the opening credits sequence.

The second character we should discuss, of course, is the hero of our wraparound story. And the person who would handle a large portion of that character's animation would be Phil Wilson. "Most of the character work that I did was of Billy," Wilson says. "I did him at the beginning where the comics come off the truck and he's there looking at the comics and I did some scenes where he's riding the bike later on in the film, I think that's about the time where he's going into the pit with the Venus fly traps."

And as it turns out one of the toughest issues in tackling Billy's animated character would be his clothing, specifically his shirt, something Michael Gornick wanted as a carry-over from the original film. "Billy's shirt had stripes in the first film; Mike wanted to keep that design. Of course, we didn't have to animate Billy in the first film, but there would be a lot of Billy in the second. Now, the problem for an animator is that all those lines have to be drawn in the correct place on every drawing, and they have to animate properly around the figure as it moves in space. So, essentially a lot more work. I tried to make that case to Mike, and he was sympathetic to our issues, but rightfully felt Billy should have his signature striped shirt. Mike, being the cool guy he is, suggested that Billy could have a jacket on for some of the early scenes, and that would at least save us some work," says Rick Catizone. "Now, for the ink and paint crew, it is an issue because getting the wrong stripe the wrong color would cause all the gray stripes to go red and the red stripes to go gray - 'popping' back and forth. And something like always starting from the top, or from the bottom, and making that stripe red wasn't going to work all the time either; because depending on the perspective as he moves, or if his head lowers, and you can't really know if that's the top stripe, or the bottom stripe, or not. So, the animators had to shade in the red stripes on their animation drawings or to save time simply make an 'X' in that stripe to denote it should be red; and make sure they tracked that in their animation. Then the painters would have to just match what was indicated on the animation drawings."

"Working on the Billy character was always tricky, as it is with any semi-realistic human character," confirms Phil Wilson. "Yes, as Rick said, his shirt stripes drove us all crazy! Keeping the same number of stripes consistent on all the drawings was tricky for us animators and it was also an issue for the cel painters to paint the red stripes red and the white stripes white and not the other way around. There were a few 'hiccups' along the way, as you can well imagine!"

I should quickly add that the mentioning of the ink and paint crew, the cel painters, is a topic we'll return to later because there's significant ground to cover there, including an unfortunate wrong which needs to be righted.

Phil Wilson wouldn't just deal with Billy though, as his main duties on the film were actually less character driven. "I would do maybe two or three backgrounds a day at times," Wilson recalls. "I don't know how many there were total; there was probably sixty, seventy - somewhere between there and a hundred backgrounds. I would do a whole slew of them in maybe one day and then the next day I would work on a scene; just whatever came across the board, there was really no rhyme or reason. I just remember doing a lot of twelve, thirteen hour days where you'd be sitting there at the drawing board and your lunch would be maybe a pretzel stick and a can of Pepsi while you were working at the (animation) disc. Some days you might be lucky enough to have a slice of pizza (laughs)."

"Phil Wilson single-handedly painted all the back-grounds," says Rick Catizone. "For the neighborhood, they sent us shots of homes that they wanted to emulate, and Phil used those as a guide."

Those homes that Catizone mentions were from the New England region of the U.S. and if you've got an eagle eye you just might notice, ever so briefly, a background shot of a maroon colored Victorian style house during the sequence of Billy riding his bike through the neighborhood just before the gang of bullies stops him. You could say the house looks an awful lot like the long-time Bangor, Maine abode of one Stephen King, even though Wilson doesn't quite remember. "Color Polaroid shots were provided to me by the production team, and I chose colors that would work well with the characters and not overpower them. I wanted the background to be somewhat subtle while still looking fairly realistic in nature," Wilson says. "As far as I know, there were no shots of Stephen King's home among the shots, but I don't know if I would have recognized it if there was! I did the backgrounds in watercolor using airbrush, and tried to maintain a feeling of late summer or early fall in the mood."

While we're on the subject of backgrounds, one change from the screenplay to the finished film concerns the Creep's introduction. In Romero's 1984 second draft of the script the Creep's intro - which was still intended to be live action - takes place at the newsstand...

CREEP

Welcome, kiddies...heh, heh, heh, heh...to another edition of *Creepshow*.

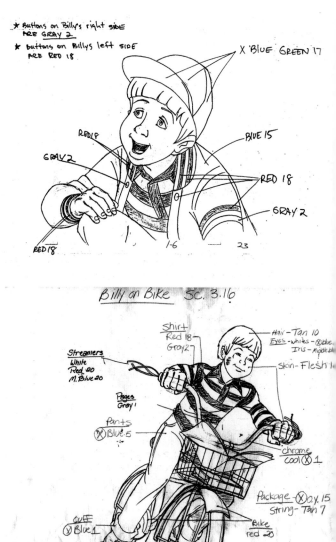

Above: Paint guides for Billy. (courtesy of Rick Catizone)

EXT. THE INTERSECTION - MORNING

The comic book lies open on the newsstand counter-top. Billy is leaning over it, reading with rapt eagerness. The VOICE continues and THE CAMERA PANS off Billy to find the real, live-and-in-person Creep lurking in the shadows behind the boy's back. The thing looks directly into the lens. It grins at us while it finishes its speech. Its words gurgle around in its rotten throat but we can understand them all.

CREEP

It's amazing that you bores and ghouls keep coming back for more. You must be gluttons for <u>pun</u>-ishment. Heh, heh, heh. **(5)**

This detail was eliminated for whatever reason in the script polish from July 1986, with no mention of where the Creep physically was when he begins to speak to the audience. With the animated Creep's introduction, immediately following the opening credits, the action would now take place in a dark and gloomy castle. I asked Catizone if he recalled what the inspiration for this change might have been. "I'm not sure. Ron did the story-board...I think Gary did the design for it," says Catizone. "If it's not in the script, it's possible Mike suggested it...but more likely something we came up with to give the Creep something to do, besides sit there and talk."

It's worth mentioning that in Catizone's timing suggestions for Michael Gornick, which was a multi-page handwritten breakdown of the script's animated segments, Catizone has a description for the Creep's intro: listed as scene 8F Catizone's note reads "CREEP walks 'through' book." So, that tells us at that early stage there was no thought just yet of the Creep in the castle. By the way, this topic, the Creep's introduction, is of particular interest regarding the animation budget. We'll return to that subject a bit later, though.

The lizard/dragon creature which lurks in the shadows of the Creep's castle was handled by Gary Hartle. "Some of the ones I really got into were the minor scenes like the lizard coming out and grabbing the meat and crawling back in," says Hartle. "Just because it was, you know, a monster and fun like that. It was fun to do the scene with the monsters eating the kids, too."

The monsters that eat the kids, which Hartle makes reference to, are the giant Venus flytraps which appear at the end of the film, devouring the gang of bullies that have pursued Billy throughout the wraparound segment. "A lot of the dramatics that are in the sequence with the plants and all this kind of stuff, when the plants finally take root and everything, come from Gary Hartle," says Ron Frenz. "He was a terrific craftsman and had an amazing sense of drama and action."

"We struggled for a day or two. We were trying to be faithful to the structure of the real plant, but these had to be lethal and I wanted to get a serpentine striking (aesthetic) as they attack," explains Rick Catizone. "Someone started playing around working with the 'jaws' on top and bottom and the stalk centrally in the middle; add exaggerated spikes which also act like fangs and there you go. I thought it worked great and was more important to look scary as opposed to being literal. After all, it is an abstracted reality."

And despite the fact that his hands were full with animating the Creep, Catizone would also pitch in for the Venus flytrap sequence, as his desire to help shape it - and as much of the animation as he could, for that matter - was just too great. "I did a few scenes at the end with the fight with the Venus flytraps because I actually wanted to do more on that sequence but there was just so much to do it was not possible," he says. "The one specific scene that I know that I did was the one where they grab the kid and they're fighting over him and I wanted that to be something like...you're always looking for something to make a shot have some meaning and interest. So, let's have 'em fight over the kid, but let's have the one be smarter than all the others and he's smart enough to release his hold so that he can actually go after it and wind up winning it."

Something I should also mention is the clever little tip of the hat to the film's director which the animation crew inserts into this sequence with the Venus flytraps. As Billy races past the gated entrance to the pit area you see a quick glimpse of a sign that reads: "KEEP OUT PRIVATE PROPERTY - BY ORDER OF GORNICK REALTY CO." Unfortunately, no one from the animation crew could remember whose idea it was to pay tribute to Michael Gornick as Rick Catizone thought it might have been Phil Wilson's suggestion, while Wilson himself couldn't remember at all.

As for the bullies, the unfortunate victims of Billy's Venus flytrap monsters, they would be a collaboration of Catizone and Gary Hartle with "Rhino", the big bruiser and only bully to actually receive a name in Romero's screenplay, at the forefront. And quickly, I would be remiss in not mentioning that "Rhino" was actually a holdover character name from an April 1974 synopsis George Romero wrote for *Dawn of the Dead*. "It's funny, not everybody draws everything the same, despite having model sheets and stuff sometimes... like I pictured him as a much bigger kid and sometimes maybe Gary didn't always keep that proportionally fat, where he wound up not so immense. And that stuff happens, but it all kind of works in the film," Catizone says. "Particularly for Rhino's face, he has that rounded sort of face and I wanted it to be pliable, but I wanted him to be mean and wanted that sort of egg like quality where the skull is a little bit smaller or a lot smaller than the rest of his face and head."

On early concept drawings of Rhino's character brief notes to describe what his personality should be like would be scribbled onto the paper by Catizone, something done for each of the bullies. "Every move is a show of strength to reinforce his 'superiority' in his own mind," Catizone's note reads. "He has his thoughts implanted by gang members because his own brain does not pick up on things quickly."[6]

For the bully "Snot", the short, freckled faced, spectacled sporting hood, Catizone's notes were a little more concise. "Little weasel, know-it-all, instigator," his note states. [7]

The next bully, "Spark", the red headed hood in the unbuttoned blue shirt, would receive a little more nuance: "A little crazy," Catizone's description reads. "'Brightest' of the gang in his ability to assess a situation; uses verbal digs to egg Rhino on." [8]

"Actually he kind of looked like Gary," says Catizone. "I think Gary designed himself in to that."

And our last bully, "Chris", the least stylized member of the gang, would have an interesting back story that resided close to home for Rick Catizone, you could say. Originally named "Cocky", with a completely different appearance all together, the character would end up being adapted by Catizone into one he was already quite familiar with - his own son. "He's the kid that's in the sort of gray sweatshirt or sweatsuit," says Catizone. "Chris had a real cockiness to him at that age and I thought he'd be perfect for one of

Right: Paint guides for the winged demons that appear at the beginning of the film and the Venus flytraps featured at the end. (courtesy of Rick Catizone)

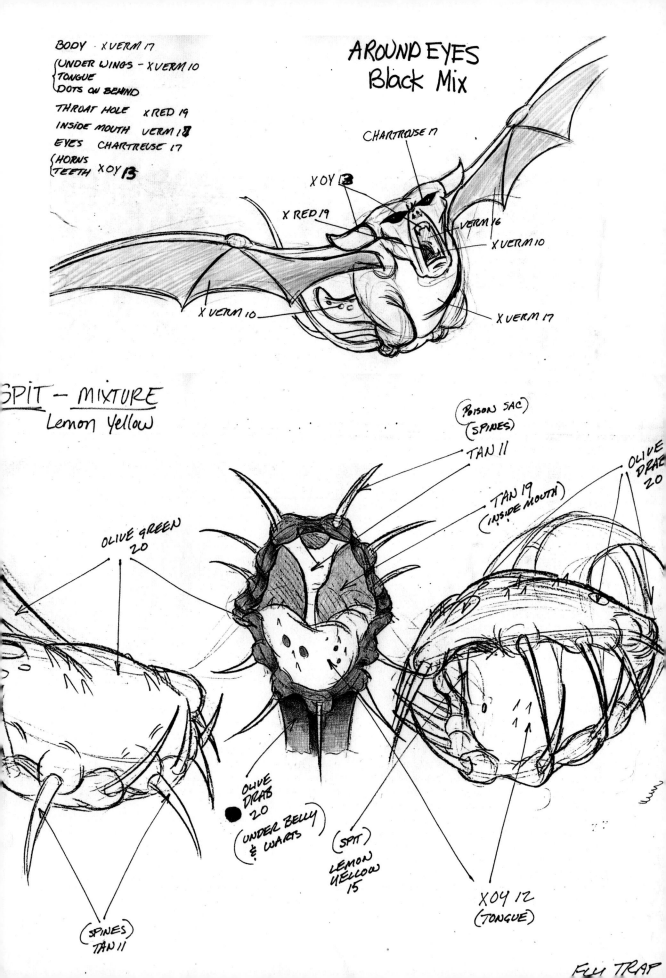

the gang members. It was fun to put one of your own kids in there, so I did a little sculpt of him, too, at the time."

The final design task for Catizone's animation department would be handled by Ron Frenz, which was creating the comic book transition pages from live action to animation, and vice versa. For the original *Creepshow* those panels were handled by Jack Kamen, the famed E.C. artist, with Frenz only assisting by adding the introduction panels of the Creep for each story. This time around, though, Kamen - for whatever reason - wouldn't perform these duties leaving the chore for Frenz to tackle. While he would end up being pleased with the results, there was a bit of frustration for Frenz because his own style was very unique and amplified, which wouldn't quite work for what was required. "I was a little sorry that it didn't look as... because what I liked about what Kamen did was that it was his own style. It still looked like a stylized comic, but it still matched up with the photos," Frenz admits. "And I wanted to be a little more stylized and they told me, 'Just make sure it matches the pictures.' So, I tried not to go too

far afield from being photo realistic. But it worked, I mean, I was happy with the way they finally came out. And we were doing them...I mean, I did them on regular board and then they were transferred to cels and they were painted like traditional cels. I'm not sure exactly who did the painting on the cels, but they did a terrific job with them."

For Catizone he was sympathetic to Frenz's predicament, but understood there was no way around it, the panels had to match the film's imagery, and there was no room for artistic embellishment. "I know that's not creative or anything for him but the reality is if you're going to match the dissolve that's the whole point of it," Catizone says. "Ron's always done very dynamic layouts and so you get to some of those and he can't really maybe go full-bore on them; it's got to be literally to trace off or it kind of defeats the idea."

As for Frenz's process in accomplishing these panels - before they were transferred onto animation cels - he would handle them much the same way as if it was a project for Marvel. "I did all of that stuff on 11x17 boards, just like a real comic book page. I just worked in black and white on

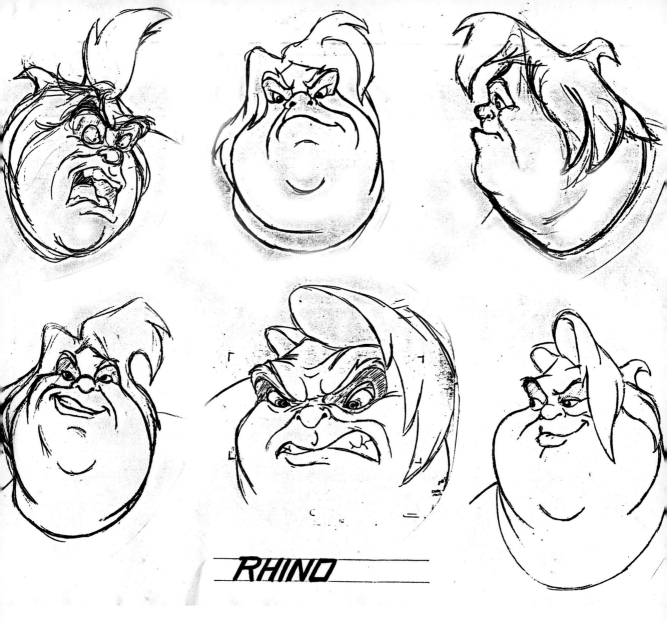

RHINO

Above left and right: Gary Hartle's early concepts for the gang of bullies who terrorize Billy; model sheet for Rhino, the leader of the bullies. (courtesy of Rick Catizone)

Bristol. I inked it myself with, you know, markers and felt tips and all that kind of stuff. Then they were Xeroxed onto cels and painted like cels," he explains. "Rick had a Xerox machine and I'm assuming that's one of the things we used it for. And he made sure that you could put cels through it and you could Xerox from regular paper onto cels, like they used to back in the old Hanna-Barbera days."

Handling this much volume with only a few animators could be quite a daunting task. You've got a limited amount of time, with a limited number of people, to pull off a substantial amount of work. "I think we had a total of about six months to deliver all the animation," says Rick Catizone. "I think we were figuring about two minutes per month, which is moving pretty fast, especially when they weren't funny, cute little characters that you could draw really quickly either. You had to maintain the integrity of a

fairly more realistic design and anatomy than you do on a three fingered, little nebbish kind of character that has no clothing and just a funny face."

"Well, I think, the thing about it was there was only three of us animating and so there was a lot, a lot of work. It was a night and day type of thing," Gary Hartle shares. "So, quite literally I had to take an animation board home. And I'd just put the TV on and have my dinner over there and be animating one of those scenes."

"I remember taking cels home and inking and painting cels at home in order to keep up," says Jim Allan. "It's a very tedious thing, you know. I used to tell people that if you like taking knots out of shoe laces, you'll love animation."

"It was hectic. It was long days. You'd be tired just sitting there at the drawing table," says Phil Wilson. "I'd get in the studio around eight thirty or quarter to nine. I'd be the first one to open up and I'd be the last one to leave. There were a few mornings that I would come in the morning and I would sit there and I would stare at that white paper on the drawing disc and I said, 'Ugghh', you know, knowing that I have a whole other day ahead of me like that. And then when Jim would come in I'd say 'Jim, I've just gotta go out. I'm going to walk around the block. I've gotta clear my head.' And I had to do that a few times just to shake it off, you know, the, I don't know what you'd call it, I don't want to use the word monotony because that's not really fair, but after a while you just have to do something that's not looking at a piece of paper!"

With that much work to complete it's necessary to have a system which allows you to keep up with what you've accomplished. Catizone wouldn't just have one for himself though as he made sure the entire team had something to go by, too. "While I had my own production charts to track the shots and progress of the film, I decided it would be really important to create some system for the crew. A way they could determine what needed done next, how much work had been done already, etc.," explains Catizone. "So, I thought about it and came up with what I thought would be an easy visual system. I had Ron's full-size story board panels reduced to around 50%, and then all those panels were cut out and pinned to large 4' x 8' homasote boards that had been painted white. They were pinned in case shots might be added or removed. So, that let the crew *see* what it was we were creating overall, as opposed to seeing one scene at a time. I then bought those little round colored dots at an office supply store; then we applied them to each story board panel as each phase of production was completed for that shot. So, at first, you just have the entire set of story board panels, with no dots. But when a scene was animated, we added a brown dot. After it was approved and inked, we added a black dot. When the scene had been painted and was ready for camera, we added a green dot. And when it was photographed and approved, we added a red dot. So, little by little, panels came to take on more and more dots of all colors, which allowed all of us to see progress on the work, which I felt would be really important on a long project."

Another vital aspect to the creation of the film's animation is the job of the sound reader. To handle this rather complex part of the process Jim Allan would step in and assume the role. "Well, you take the recording of the entire voice track. There's exposure sheets, that's what they call them, that breaks it up into 24 drawings per second and on that track you use the Moviola and you guide that through to listen to it. And you have to write down exactly where a word begins and where it ends. And if it's in syllables you have to pick up each syllable and make sure that the animator knows exactly where the character is going to say 'M' or 'O', because the lip movements are going to be totally different," explains Allan. "And then, of course, the exposure sheets are what's used to do the filming; so that when you go back to film, you go back to the exposure sheets, and it will tell me to take three pictures of number 2 or four pictures of number 5 or whatever. It's a very exacting science you have to follow, it's pretty rigid."

Again, it can't be understated how crucial this job is to the end result, as the soundtrack dictates not only what we hear, but what we see as well. "I'm one of the few people that probably did sound reading and putting it all together on exposure sheets and then handing the exposure sheets out to artists to animate that section.

Then I would be the one to do a test of it; sometimes we would run a test to see if it was going to work in pencil first, see if the movement was right, and then if it was, it went to the inkers and painters. It was a process, you had to keep track of all the stuff, what was going on and who was doing what," Allan laughs. "Because you could very easily skip over something and miss a scene or miss something out of it. So, the soundtrack was the main thing that controlled everything. You had to control everything from the soundtrack; if it wasn't on the soundtrack it didn't exist. Even if the soundtrack said, 'You're walking through the woods', you know, or something, you knew how long it was going to take to animate that section, even if somebody wasn't talking, you knew that somebody had to put in music or something when it was all finished. So, it's a very complicated process."

As you can see it's not just the animators themselves who serve a critical role in the creation of the work. Another team, the previously mentioned ink & paint crew, also help tremendously in bringing an animated vision to life. "For the main body of the ink and paint crew I think we called the local art schools and saw who was recently graduated that we could bring in and test out. And as simple as cel painting sounds, there are a lot of people that can't do it. And a lot of people didn't get hired and some people who were hired didn't stay," laughs Rick Catizone. "So, there's that. Rich Yanizeski, he had worked doing ink and paint for me on different jobs and stuff. It was pretty much...the main part was, the essence of it was, the people that I used on my commercial work when I needed help."

"A lot of our people we hired on to do the ink and paint and so forth, they'd never worked on an animated film before, so it was a little new to them; it was sort of on-the-job training," Phil Wilson says. "But with people that had never had any experience in animation before, obviously there's going to be glitches. That got to be a little frustrating some times."

"Again, painting cels, while it seems relatively simple, is an art and there are also some technical things you have to keep focused on. And one of them is there are color let downs, like one cel level difference for each color. So, there are basically twenty values of a single color. The difference between 'Flesh 19' and 'Flesh 18' is almost imperceptible to the eye, until you paint them and lay a cel over it and you see the difference," Catizone explains. "And so what happened in one shot was that the flesh was sometimes painted - and these aren't always painted in order, for speed you're painting by what's accessible - some faces were painted 'Flesh 19' and some faces were painted 'Flesh 18'. Again, imperceptible to the naked eye, but when you put them next to each other as they are filmed and you play that back it sort of flickers. So, unfortunately we had to have the scene re-inked and re-painted. And again it's not a big budget production and yeah there's a little bit of money for some overage or whatever for a mistake, but we pretty much had to jump on that right away and probably wasn't done as tactfully as I could have."

"Rick's a terrific guy, but he liked to delegate what he could, okay. And by that, that included even interacting with the ink and paint crew," says Ron Frenz. "I mean,

Above and right: Comic book splash pages by Ron Frenz which introduce each story in the film. (courtesy of Rick Catizone)

Lori Chontos had a lot of pressure put on her because Rick didn't like to...maybe he understood...he's not a really warm guy, he's not like a guy that you feel really comfortable around quickly. The first year I worked there it was just he and I so, I mean, we got to the point we got very comfortable with each other. But once he started bringing on crew he didn't really seem to enjoy interacting with the crew that much, so he would pick somebody. And in Lori's case, unfortunately, it was Lori (laughs). And he would put a lot of the pressure on her to interact with the crew and be his liaison. So, he would unload on her and then she was supposed to translate that to the crew. And I can remember, unfortunately for the poor woman, that she spent some time in the bathroom catching her breath, you know, because it got pretty crazy, deadline wise and stuff."

"I don't even remember it, no. So, it obviously wasn't that big of an impact on me. But I was young," Chontos says. "So, if that happened it's made me stronger now."

"Lori Chontos was my ink and paint supervisor, wonderful girl, amazingly dedicated, talented, and fastidious in terms of detail," Catizone says. "I said, 'What we have to do now is we have to make a major decision here.' And I had just watched a film with Richard Williams (famous animator) having a meeting with his studio over another small issue like that and it sort of stuck in my mind, I guess. I said, 'Okay, well here's the deal. You need to go through and you need to get this information through to them.' I said, 'Here's

Above: The late, great Joe Silver who provided the amazing and ghoulishly funny voice for the Creep. (copyright 1975 NBC Television Network)

a list of points, they need to completely focus on this. If they can't then we're not going to be able to use them.' And so they had a meeting, I don't think I was there, and we got that all straightened out. And, you know, that happens on a production, but with animation it's a costly thing."

But it wasn't just utilizing wrong flesh tones that could cause a disaster, painting cels on the wrong side was another issue that could - and sometimes did - happen during the project. "There's hundreds and hundreds of cels that have to be painted. It's unbelievable. When you watch it on the screen you don't realize...sometimes one cel can have as many as a dozen different colors on it," says Jim Allan. "So, you have to paint one color, and you start with the darkest ones first and go to the lightest in painting it. So, if you paint something that's white and you get a tiny bit of dark blue over the top of the white, it won't show through. So, you have to keep in mind that you have to keep working from the dark colors to the light colors. And like I said, there could be five, six, as many as a dozen colors on one cel. So, it's a tedious thing and it's very exacting. You have to watch them; we had people that did nothing but check them and make sure everything was alright with them."

"Rich Yanizeski was a real solid worker. He would sit his ass down and aside from a lunch break he was inking, you know. I mean, he really took his job seriously," Ron Frenz says. "He was the primary inker on the job and when he would get a stack (of cels) that was painted on the wrong side or something - he had to re-ink it - he had the ink and

paint room terrorized! They'd be terrified if they would hear his thudding step coming towards the ink and paint room because they knew somebody screwed up and there was going to be hell to pay."

Now, hearing such stories might give the impression that working on the animation portion could have been unpleasant or stressful. That would be a misrepresentation, however, because there were plenty of laughs and good times to be had. "I just want to make sure that it gets mentioned that it just was a whole lot of fun and we enjoyed the long hours," shares Lori Chontos.

"Well, I love all those guys. That's the thing, I think there was such a camaraderie we had," recalls Gary Hartle. "There was as much silliness going on around there - when we had to break down and get something done we did that - but we would do things like...I think there was a (toy)lizard somebody had and there was all these gals making paint, trying to knock things out. Me and Mike Trcic (yes, that Mike Trcic - we'll return to that later) and some of the other guys tied a string around this lizard and when we dragged it across the wooden floor it would make a high squeaky noise and we kind of made the string go through, I don't know, kind of like a gauntlet of things. And when this gal was coming back with cels in her hand we...first we talked to everybody saying, 'There are rats in this place. There are rats! Did you see the size of that rat?', just to kind of get that in their head. And then we'd drag this thing (laughs while making a squeaky noise) right in front of her, but she had a hand full of cels, and then Rick chewed us all out because it's like, you know, all that work all over the floor (laughs). Now I gotta do it all over again or check which ones are scratched or whatever, you know, because cels back then you had to be careful with them."

"Now, once in a while we just had to take a break," Phil Wilson recalls. "One thing that we did start to do as a rule of thumb was we took, at that time VHS tapes and Warner Brothers *Looney Tunes* cartoons, and we would just sit around and watch two or three of them while we were eating lunch during the day, just to break the mood a little bit. So, that was nice."

"We watched all these *Twilight Zone*'s all the time, almost every day we'd come in. And if it wasn't *The Twilight Zone* it was something else. Phil would be an arbiter of the cassette tapes at the time and he'd make sure we were all there, like a master of ceremonies, and then he'd plug it in and turn it on. And we pulled a practical joke, we put a train horn in a box and when he went to turn it on, the train horn went off and I think he almost crapped in his pants," laughs Hartle. "So, that's what I'm talking about - you didn't know what was coming at you each day when you were with those guys, you know."

One of those guys, which Hartle mentioned, was Mike Trcic, who as it turns out was a regular presence at Catizone's Anivision, long before he started work on Laurel's *Tales from the Darkside*, *Day of the Dead*, and *Creepshow 2*. "Mike came in one day and he had a cyclops puppet based on Ray Harryhausen's that was really good and another creature that he made. They were foam rubber, ball and socket and I thought, 'Wow! Where were you when I was 16 and needed a compatriot?'," Rick Catizone fondly remembers. "So, he had that and he had animation...

first of all he had puppets. Second of all they were foam rubber and had armatures in them. Third of all he'd shot animation footage. So, we hit it off right away and I tried to use him whenever I had commercials and whatever. He did a couple of different sculptures for some puppets for me on some commercials and he did ink and paint work for me until he found his break. He always was interested in doing makeup. First I think it was the whole full mask thing and stuff, he was always sculpting and was really into that. But, yeah, he started here and went on to have a great career. Heard he did something with a T-Rex once?"

"A lot of times it was just Mike and I working for Rick on some commercials or whatever, because you couldn't staff everybody," recalls Lori Chontos about working alongside the multi-talented Trcic. "I mean, I knew how talented he was when he was there, too."

And not only would Trcic work on *Creepshow 2*'s makeup effects team during principal photography, he would also lend a hand during the post-production with Catizone's ink and paint crew. "Yeah, Mike did. Mike did come out and he did paint cels," confirms Gary Hartle. "He and Yan (Rich Yanizeski) would go at each other, it was funny. They're both titanic guys and they were smashing (while play wrestling) a very thin hallway and the ceiling was coming down. You know, it's that kind of stuff. It's like being in a locker room all the time to be around those guys."

Our final topic concerning the ink and paint crew involves the subject I mentioned earlier about righting a very unfortunate wrong. If you were to believe the closing credits there was only a crew of six people who were responsible for the animation work you see in the film: Rick Catizone, Gary Hartle, Phil Wilson, Ron Frenz, Lori Chontos, and Jim Allan. That, however, wouldn't come close to the truth. "We had a bit of a disaster regarding credits for the film. Mike (Gornick) lobbied for me to have a head credit since the animation was such a significant element of the film, so I was credited as Animation Supervisor. That was something I very much appreciated. But as we neared the end of production I submitted our credit list, which had around 25 people on it. Now we didn't have a constant 25 man crew, but we had more painters because some came on at different stages and some people moved on. I think we had a 'constant' crew of about 8 to 10 painters. But I included everyone because I believe people should be credited," says Rick Catizone. "Well, without asking in advance, someone on the production decided that was just too many credits, and randomly selected some of them. I was very upset, and could not comprehend why they wouldn't ask me to pare the list down to what they would accept. It caused some hard feelings among the crew, and rightfully so; some who had worked full-time on it got no credit. It was unfair, but unfortunately nothing I could change at the point I was made aware of it."

"You find at certain times in the process you have no control, especially when it comes to credits," explains Michael Gornick. "It always flows back to the executive producer who alters, takes things out, puts names in, you know, special thanks to, and it's just outside of my ability to control. And certainly David Ball had no ability to control at that point; especially when it comes to end credits.

And Richard (Rubinstein) is an absolute stickler about end credits; I mean he'd steep over them for hours on end."

"It's a huge injustice that the ink and paint crew got no credit," says Ron Frenz. "The first one, I don't even remember us having all that big a crew. On the second one we had a big ink and paint crew because it was more animation, which was why everybody was so pissed off that ink and paint didn't get credit. Everybody loved the animation and the transitional stuff in the first one; it was arguably more so part of the movie in the second one because they had a whole story arc in the animation in the second one, so that's what made the movie unique, that's kind of what they were selling the movie on. And yet when the movie comes out and they're rolling the credits, ink and paint didn't get any credit. We're like, 'Son of a bitch!' I mean, good lord. And they were given some cock and bull story about there wasn't room."

"Yeah, it was very bittersweet because you're excited for yourself, but I still don't get it either. A few more names, what does it hurt?," Lori Chontos says. "I don't know whose call that was or why they had to make it that way, but you look at movie credits now they go on and on forever. It's just a shame."

Well, at least here those contributors, artists, and technicians will receive their due recognition. The following people were originally in the submitted list for the animation crew and should have received proper credit in 1987:

John Buynak: (In-betweens & Ink)
Alice Craig: (Paint)
Dan Kerekes: (Paint)
Jacqueline Lukus: (Paint)
Laura Miller: (In-betweens & Ink)
Jerry Minor: (Paint)
Michele Story Moehring: (Paint)
Kim Moore: (Paint)
James Murphy: (In-betweens & Ink)
Jim O'Connell: (In-betweens & Ink)
Pat Olliffe: (Paint)
Troy Retallack: (Paint)
Stacey Russell: (Paint)
Frank Urbaniak: (Paint)
Ed Urian: (In-betweens & Ink)
Bob Wolcott: (Camera)
Rich Yanizeski: (In-betweens & Ink)
Diane Yingling: (Paint)

As mentioned previously there were some issues which arose concerning the animation budget, according to Rick Catizone, which in turn would require some cuts to be made to the material. The introduction of the Creep following the opening credits, which could never be eliminated, would be at the forefront in all of this. "It's a little fuzzy, but it sounds like some of the initial Creep intro stuff was originally going to be part of the title sequence, and title sequences generally have their own budget. So, I 'assume' that the animation of the demons, Billy, and the Creep in the intro was originally going to be in a separate budget for the opening. Apparently that must have changed and I had to figure out what I might be able to cut that wouldn't be missed," explains Catizone. "So, I cut many of the 'simple' shots, ones that I really wanted for mood and effect. So, close-up shots of bike tires splashing through the mud, close-ups on spokes turning during the chase, and similar bits of business, were things I could lose and not harm the essence of the storytelling, but shots I felt added to the feel. And eliminating 'simple' shots meant that I had a bid based on knowing some shots would be very involved and difficult, some of medium difficulty, and some simpler in execution. When you cut the 'simple' shots, it means your budget is now producing more of the complex shots for less money, if that makes sense."

By doing this it would mean that Catizone would end up losing money on certain sequences, the Venus flytrap sequence being a prime example, due to the complexity of the animation required.

Now, back during the summer, long before we got to this point, Catizone had discussed with Laurel the length of the animation based on the script, all of which fell into his budget proposal. "Here was, what turned out to be at least when I did the first script count, they said, 'Oh, we have about ten minutes of animation,'" Catizone says. "I called them back and said, 'You have about twelve minutes of animation here, the way I lay it out.' And they wound up cutting it back to around eleven or something, whatever it finally wound up in the final film. Probably pretty close to that."

In Catizone's hand written timing suggestions, which was referenced earlier, there is an estimated running time of 10 minutes and 45.5 seconds - 9 minutes and 20.5 seconds without the opening credits animation. Contrast that to memos obtained from Michael Gornick from the summer of 1986 which have Laurel estimating the animation to be anywhere from just under 7 minutes to a full 9 minutes in length. And in a memo sent from David Ball to Catizone in January 1987 Ball calculates the animation clocking in at 8 minutes and 50 seconds, which if you've ever bothered to time it in the completed film is basically right on the nose. Once again, Ball's head for numbers showcases itself. "I mean, as a piece of work it sort of works okay, you know. But we were always restricted by not having…we never had enough money," says Ball about the animation for the film. "But on this occasion it was very tight indeed."

Another interesting aside from Ball's aforementioned January 1987 memo is he mentions to Catizone that he understands the reasons for some of the delays in the animation, which by that point apparently only 2 minutes and 47.5 seconds had been completed. So, with an answer print due in March the pressure to complete the animation on time was significant. As to the reasons for some of the delays, one centered on the fact that Catizone wouldn't receive photos of the newsstand and the Creep's truck until November, while another was because he didn't receive an approval on the makeup design of the Creep until mid-October! "We never received the Creep makeup design to match our character to. In fact very late in the game we were called and told to go ahead and design it ourselves," says Catizone. "The Creep screen time is one of the biggest tongues of this picture, and waiting really set us back. But we still met the deadline."

And meet the deadline they would, completing the animation in just the nick of time. By February 25, 1987 Catizone would deliver the last of the animation footage to

Michael Gornick who would hand carry it back to London for the post-production personally; additional elements which were needed would be finished on February 28, 1987 and hand carried to London by assistant sound editor John Bick. "It was pretty late; we had some scenes. I think Rick was working up until the very end," remembers Michael Gornick. "We would mix around, we would do dubbing in terms of the soundtrack work on the big stage at Pinewood, depending on what we had available to us in terms of the animation. So, we would skip around quite a bit on the reels and await something to arrive and then insert to make sure it worked."

According to Catizone he would end up contributing a full minute of animation to the film at no charge because there was simply no way to cut crucial story material. In the end though that didn't necessarily bother him because he understood that the work being accomplished would live on forever in a major motion picture, one directed by a close friend. "Mike Gornick, besides being a friend since he first came to work with George (Romero), is one of the most talented people I have ever worked with. His knowledge, taste, and skill-set in so many areas of production is amazing," Catizone proudly proclaims as he looks back on the experience. "And, really exhilarating moments where you realize, 'Hey, I'm working on a feature'…you can never underestimate the cool factor of that and knowing that long after I'm gone somebody's going to be watching it."

In this writer's opinion, Catizone couldn't be more on the money, pardon the pun. When it's all said and done you don't think of how much money you earned for the work you put into something that comes from the heart. Looking back on the work they created brings about an array of memories and feelings from the animators. I could tell it was something they all felt a sense of pride about, an appreciation for, that is still with them today. And it's even more rewarding for them to meet fans who have an affinity for the classic form of animation on display in the film.

"I think of the camaraderie of just everybody diving in and working. You know, there was no question about, 'I don't feel like working today.' Everybody was really excited," Jim Allan remembers. "We were very pleased with it, we thought it was excellent. They did an excellent job in putting it all together and fitting it into the stories and everything."

"I mean, looking back on it there's always things you wish you could change or wish you could have done better. But with the equipment we had and the experience we had at the time, I think we did a heck of a job," Phil Wilson says. "Of course, now everything's done digital with the computer, so it looks very dated from that standpoint, in a way. But we were happy with it, we were proud of it. It's a bit of a kick; I have to admit it's something I never thought I would experience. It's something you always dreamed of is going to a movie theater and seeing your work up on a seventy foot screen, seeing your name in the credit crawl. And that was a hoot, that's something I can say I've done."

"I never was experienced doing anything like this so to me it was beyond any expectations that I had; it was just stuff that I would watch and see on TV or at the movies, but to be able to do it myself was incredible," recalls Lori Chontos. "When I got to do some of the shading and stuff with grease pencils and putting some of the highlights on

Left: The late Gordon Connell who provided the voice for Mr. Haig, the postman. **Right:** Jason Late was one of four young boys who provided the voices of the bullies who pursue Billy. (copyrights 1962 ABC Television Network and 1986 NBC Television Network)

the characters, Rick let me do that. Even the plant spit for the Venus flytrap, you know, to create something like that. I mean, just stuff like that, it's like it's your work and you're doing it and there it is for everyone to see."

"It's definitely a product of its time," says Gary Hartle. "I look at it now and I can see some of the influences that were out during the time, like (Don) Bluth and whoever else, where you're almost over animating it. And I could have made more subtle choices, I think, in some cases. But I was young and dumb and just crazy and wanted to put as much into it as I could."

"This is an impressive animated sequence though, there's no doubt about it. Given the budget, the time element and everything, these guys did a hell of a job with this stuff," Ron Frenz remarks. "To this day, when I mention to people that I worked at an animation studio they'll say, 'Oh, really. What did you work on?' And I'll say, 'Mostly local and regional commercial stuff. But we worked on both the *Creepshow*s.' They'll say, 'Oh really!', you know that kind of thing. Everybody remembers the *Creepshow*s - more the animation to a large degree, more the whole transition from a comic book to reality and back, you know. So, that's always something that gets a rise out of people, so it's nice, even after all these years."

"When I was asked to appear at one of the *Famous Monsters* conventions a few years ago, I pulled out some of the animation drawings to show. It had probably been 25 years since I had actually looked at some of my drawings and animation," says Rick Catizone. "I found myself reflecting on the work I had personally done and thinking, 'You know, I really did some nice work in here.' That might sound odd, but I never really dwelled on the work I created. It was always about taking on the next animation challenge

and trying to make a living to support our family. And then when computers came in, that was another challenge, because I saw it as an additional playground to animate in. But it has been really rewarding when I am a guest at a convention and flip a 10 second scene, about 120 drawings, of the Creep, and see people amazed at the work, and hear how much they loved that type of animation."

With *Creepshow 2* employing far more animation than the original, featuring more animated characters as well, the use of voice-over artists would be required this go around, seven all together. Trying to pin down exactly when the recording sessions took place turned out to be one of the trickier subjects to cover. Michael Gornick was of the belief that they would have been well into the post-production phase before the sessions would have been recorded in New York City. "As I recall it was like an interim session; finished principal photography, I went over to Pinewood in early January just to say hello, establish myself there with Peter Weatherley in the shop at Pinewood. And then went back home and then had the sessions with the boys and brought back the material with me later in the month or early February to begin cutting," he says. "Which is probably a mistake, actually; voice assists animators so much that it probably would have been better to have done that early in the game and give Rick Catizone tracks to animate to."

However, Rick Catizone, who was also present at the recording sessions, remembered it being very warm when

Above and left: Legendary British musician, songwriter, and arranger Les Reed stepped in to compose the score for *Creepshow 2*, going in a different direction than John Harrison had with the original film five years prior; Reed's sheet music for *Old Chief Wood'nhead*. (courtesy of *The Telegraph* and Michael Gornick)

he flew to New York at the time to assist in them, which would rule out January or February. He was nice enough to dig through his files and found an old date keeper calendar that he used to jot down important dates from the production, discovering that by the first week of September he was already counting soundtracks and working on story-boards. "This verifies that we would have had to have recorded the voices in New York in August, probably two weeks prior so Mike had time to make all the selected takes and supervise the editing into the final tracks," Catizone says. "It also means that we would have been animating whatever scenes we could, except the Creep."

Once again the recurring subject of memories sometimes not being as accurate as we might believe raises its head. This is understandable though because a film production is a whirlwind of activity; especially in Gornick's case with him just coming off a challenging and at times frustrating shoot, after having been heavily involved with the pre-production, then culminating with travel overseas to the U.K. for the majority of the post-production.

For the most important animated character, the Creep, Laurel turned to the late veteran actor and voice-over talent, Joe Silver. "Joe Silver - always respected, loved his voice. That was so exciting to be able to cast him," says Michael Gornick. "One of my first casting notions was to have Joe do the voice."

Hailing from the Midwest, Joseph Silver was born in 1922. He began his career in show business in 1942 when he appeared on Broadway in *Tobacco Road*. In 1972 he would be nominated for a Tony Award for his performance in *Lenny*. From the 1950's through the 1980's he would find work in television appearing on countless shows including *Lights Out* (based off the popular radio serial), *Car 54, Where Are you?*, *Sanford and Son*, and *The Equalizer*. He performed voice-over work for cartoons including the Paramount Pictures "Go-Go Toon" series - *A Bridge Grows in Brooklyn* and *Keep the Cool, Baby*. And, of course, he provided the voice of The Greedy in *Raggedy Ann & Andy: A Musical Adventure*. Silver was no stranger to the horror genre as well, appearing in a pair of David Cronenberg films - *Shivers* and *Rabid*.

"I believe Mike had already given some direction of the kind of character he wanted, possibly before-hand as well, but certainly in the studio itself," says Rick Catizone. "At this moment, I can't recall for certain if Mike specifically asked me about my thoughts, but that would've been very much in keeping with the way Mike has always worked. He has a great vision, but also collaborates to get the best he can in any avenue. You should actually ask Mike about that to be sure, but I highly suspect that he explained the character and what he wanted. If he did indeed ask me, or perhaps Joe asked me if there was anything particular I wanted him to bring out of the performance, I probably said that voice variance in terms of highs and lows as well as attitude changes really gives the animator something to play with and helps generate ideas for motion and gestures so the character isn't just standing around, or looking like what he's doing is out of place for the dialogue. He had done some nice things with The Greedy's voice in *Raggedy Ann & Andy* and so I pointed to that, as well as the performance of Mr. Ages in *The Secret of Nimh* (voiced by Arthur Malet). Joe gave us great readings...every time. They were just wonderful, so much character. And I think Mike suggested for him to throw in anything else like breaths, chortles, inhales, etc.; and he threw in some great stuff."

"Incredible voice," Gornick reiterates. "I heard him doing commercials in New York, just knew of his work in general. And there was no doubt in my mind of in just an oral sense that he was the Creep. I mean, good lord, how fortunate I was at that time and place that he was still around and we had him. And he was absolutely perfect. And I would die to have a voice like that - beautiful, beautiful voice. God bless him, may he rest in peace."

For the voice of the postman, Mr. Haig, Laurel would employ the services of Gordon Connell. Born in 1923 in Northern California, William Gordon Connell would have a long and vibrant career on the stage and in television. After performing in San Francisco nightclubs with his wife, Jane,

Connell would move east to New York where he and Jane would have successful careers in theatre and television. Over the years Connell would appear on stage in well-known productions such as *Hello, Dolly*, playing the judge, and *Big River*, where he played Mark Twain. In television he appeared on popular shows like *Bewitched*, *The Six Million Dollar Man*, *The Love Boat*, and *The Incredible Hulk*. Connell was a talented musician as well - he played the piano - and was also no stranger to voice acting as he and his wife, Jane, had performed radio serials for NBC in the 1940's.

For the gang of bullies who pursue Billy we'll begin with the hulking leader of the group, Rhino, voiced by Marc Stephan Del Gatto. It was while in elementary school in the Bay Ridge section of Brooklyn that Del Gatto was first discovered. Asked by his music teacher to participate in a community event, he would be noticed by a talent agent in the audience. On his first audition he would score the lead for a national advertisement for Duncan Hines cookies. From there he would land a small role, and also become an understudy, in the 1984 Joseph Papp production of William Saroyan's play *The Human Comedy* at the Royale Theatre on Broadway, which coincidentally also starred Gordon Connell. "The majority of stuff I did leading up to *Creepshow 2* were musicals, you know, singing in cabarets in the city as a young kid in Manhattan," Del Gatto says. "Places like *Don't Tell Mama* and *Catch a Rising Star*."

After being cast to voice one of the bullies, Del Gatto recalls walking into the studio and naturally gravitating towards the character he'd end up voicing. "I'll never forget when I walked into - after I got the part - and we walked into the recording studios to do the voice-overs," he says. "I saw on the ledge, figurines - you know, probably made of clay, but really detailed. First time I ever saw anything like that, something you would see in a Toys R Us kind of thing. And there was a string of them, I'd say about maybe four or five characters. And there was one in the middle, a real big, fat, kind of bruiser, kind of character which I felt stood out from everybody else. And I walked directly up to that figurine, I'll never forget that, I walked through and I picked it up. And as it turned out that was the character that I was doing the voice-over for. Yeah, Rhino was the name."

Next up we'll deal with Rhino's fellow hoods and we'll begin with Jason Late. Growing up in New Jersey, Late would decide pretty early in life that acting was something he wanted to take a shot at. "Basically when I was about six just decided that I could act better than all the other kids on television. For no good reason, obviously, but for some reason just thought that," recalls Late. "And then after knowing my parents long enough they basically found some open calls that you could take your kids to in New York City and then I was able to get an agent after going to some of those open calls. And then basically after a couple of auditions started getting some roles, so it actually seemed to work out."

One of those roles was for director Ron Howard in his 1984 comedy *Splash*, starring Tom Hanks and Daryl Hannah. In the film, Late is featured in the opening scenes as the young version of John Candy, dropping coins on the deck of a boat so he can look up the skirts of unwitting females. "*Splash* was great," Late says. "A first experience and a really good one as well because you got to see how so many people come together and work on a big theme to really make something happen."

Up next for Late was a short lived sitcom for NBC, *Fathers and Sons,* starring Merlin Olsen. Not long after that show's cancellation the opportunity for *Creepshow 2* would come along. Unfortunately it's one of those cases of memories being lost to time. "I mean, at the time, I was doing a lot of auditions for a lot of different things and this one came up just like any other audition. I remember just going in for it and getting called back a couple of times and it was a pretty straight forward, standard process," Late says. "To be honest, I don't remember enough about it."

Another one of the hoods who attempts to bully our story's hero was voiced by Clark Utterback (who now goes by the name of Clark Everitt, his mother's maiden name) and his story is actually a fascinating one. Originally from Utah, Utterback took an early interest in singing on stage during his pre-school years appearing in productions of *A Christmas Carol*, *The Music Man*, and *The Sound of Music*. His incredible vocal abilities as a boy soprano would eventually lead him to Manhattan when a noted Italian-American composer, librettist, and stage director decided he would be perfect for his opera, *Amahl and the Night Visitors*. "I was invited because I'd performed that locally in Utah, first time in Provo, second time up in Salt Lake at a bigger opera house. And off of that performance up in Salt Lake they invited me to come to New York to audition for the New York production and Gian Carlo Menotti, the composer, would direct that production in New York City on Lincoln Center; it was at Avery Fisher Hall in Lincoln Center," says Utterback. "And then after that experience I was approached by a woman, her name was Ruth Melville, she was the head of the Metropolitan Opera and the New York City Opera Company's boys choir, I guess you could say, probably the best term. She invited me to come and be a part of her organization and perform at the Met, perform at the New York City Opera Company. And that's sort of when we sparked this conversation as a family and decided that summer we'd move out and pursue singing and performing. And that's what took us to New York."

Utterback would toil doing an array of different gigs in his young entertainment career besides his work for the opera, including one that even he would chalk up under the "strange" category. "I got booked to sing the songs of Rainbow Brite's voice in the *Rainbow Brite Birthday Party*," Utterback recalls. "I mean I could disguise my voice and do weird stuff with it. There's this Rainbow Brite birthday celebration thing and she's talking to all the kids and all the sudden she bursts into song and she's singing and everyone thinks it's this girl singing and it's actually me singing on behalf of Rainbow Brite. So, it took me a while to come to terms with that one."

One of the more fascinating jobs he would score was roughly around the same time as the *Creepshow 2* gig, related to the soundtrack for another genre picture which was a massive box office hit in the summer of 1987, *The Lost Boys*. "There's a song, kind of the theme song there, you hear, it sounds like a small boys choir, 'Cry little sister. Thou shall not fall, thou shall not kill...,'" says Utterback. "All of those verses, all of those choruses are me and it's myself dubbed over three or four times against myself; the one that always comes in and says, 'Thou shall not kill, thou shall not fall...' Yeah, that's me."

Now, with that last little tidbit of background information Utterback really grabbed my attention. Not only was he involved in *Creepshow 2*, but *The Lost Boys* as well? That film is another personal favorite of your humble author's youth as I spent much of August 1987 at the movie theater watching it repeatedly. My curiosity got the best of me and so I decided to get in touch with the gentleman most responsible for the song's creation, Gerard McMahon (aka G Tom Mac), to ask him about it. "I hired 12 young boys ages 9-12 to sing the choir part. I wrote and arranged to get the sound and articulation to what I wanted it to sound like and perfect its essence with my voice. Upon getting one live pass throughout the song I had them do another pass through the song to double what they already did so I could achieve a richer and full sound of 24 voices I envisioned," McMahon says. "So, to answer your question it was certainly NOT one voice looped over and over to make that choir. I did audition each boy to do a solo vocal of the choir so I could use in the film should I have needed, and I chose a voice of one of them in which we did use in the very opening of the film over the Warner Brothers logo. Sorry to say you were wrongly informed."

So, with that being said, I have no doubt that Utterback was involved with the song. Perhaps it's just not exactly as he remembers it, who knows? Still a great story nonetheless.

As for *Creepshow 2*, similar to Jason Late, it was just part of the cycle of auditions and gigs Utterback went through during that part of his life. "You know, it was just one of those things. I had an agent, I had a manager and I was in that circle of people doing jingles, doing voice-overs," he says. "I did a lot of jingles and voice work and this just happened to be one of those calls where I was invited to come out and audition to be one of the voices for those boys in the animated portion of it, and went out on the call, got booked. And I think it was just one day of work - one or two days of work maybe - and came in, did my thing, and moved on."

Our final two voice artists are P.J. Morrison and Brian Noodt. Unfortunately, I was unable to learn much about Morrison's background leading up to *Creepshow 2*. These days he's a television producer having worked on projects such as *Cash Cab* and *Impractical Jokers*. He would not respond to multiple efforts for an interview.

Brian Noodt, who wavered quite a bit on whether to speak with me, ultimately decided not to be interviewed. He did, however, inform me over the telephone that he was the voice of our story's hero, Billy. Learning this, yet not being able to interview him about it, was quite frustrating, as you can imagine.

Born in March 1973 in Freehold, New Jersey, Noodt's background was quite diverse including singing, dancing, and piano. He had done modeling work for Bamberger's, a New Jersey department store, appearing in one of their catalogs, as well as appearing in *Red Book* magazine. His work in regional theatre included productions of *Fiddler* on the Roof, South Pacific, and The Music Man. And on Broadway he appeared in a production of Oliver! Michael Gornick remembers how easy it was to work with Noodt during the recording sessions and how much he brought to the character. "It was a breeze. And that's seldom the case, especially with children, any kind of work like that," he says. "And he could interpret...maybe because he had a child's mind and enough imagination it worked easily enough for him in terms of delivery. But it was a cinch; I think we did maybe two takes."

As for Rick Catizone, while his memories of working with Joe Silver are more clear, he does recall being around for the kids sessions. "I think Mike and I joked about the people outside who might've been wondering what we were doing to these kids who were screaming at the top of their lungs when they were being devoured by the Venus fly trap plants," Catizone says.

As mentioned earlier in the chapter the post-production would move across the pond to England at the legendary Pinewood Studios. Tucked away in the village of Iver Heath, Buckinghamshire, roughly 45 minutes west of London, Pinewood Studios was home to some of the finest motion pictures in film history: from Richard Donner's Superman, to Ridley Scott's Alien, to James Cameron's Aliens, to countless James Bond films, the studio was steeped in classic productions. "That was a lot of fun. Actually, what convinced me is David Ball said, 'If you come to England, Mike, I'll pay you in pounds for your stay and you can convert that into dollars when you get back and you're ahead of the game.' I thought, 'Damn, he's right! What a genius.' Because at that point the pound was worth about $1.55 to the American dollar," recalls Michael Gornick. "And the glory of going to, like, a Pinewood Studios where Bond was shot, you know. Historically it's quite a place to work in. Working next door to Clive Barker; yeah, Clive and I went to have high tea together at three o'clock. Absolutely, here comes the cart!"

"Pinewood was like dead; we were like one of two productions there doing post. The other was Clive Barker, who was doing the first Hellraiser. So, that was kind of fun. I mean, it's a massive studio, but it was pretty dead. It was shocking to me; I expected, 'Hey, it's Pinewood Studios! Where's James Bond?'," laughs Mitchell Galin who came over to assist with the post now that things had wrapped up on the latest season of Tales from the Darkside. "Pinewood was not that busy at the time. They went through a period of time where they were really sucking wind in terms of production so we were able to make a pretty good deal over there and they had some really good post people and effects people that could handle what we were looking to do."

For Michael Gornick one of the biggest pluses in traveling to England would be the chance to spend more time with his editing staff. "I wanted to keep working with Peter Weatherley, who was my editor throughout the process. He was on set working in Arizona and later on in Maine, so that's a very important link," Gornick says. "Films, I'm convinced, have always been and always will be made in the editorial room, ultimately, either destroyed or enhanced. It's gotta be there, obviously, but it's a critical process."

RICK WAKEMAN

Above: Keyboard wizard and rock god Rick Wakeman would assist Les Reed with the score for Creepshow 2, supplying his trademark style to the keyboard sections of the film, particularly The Raft. (courtesy of rwcc.com)

Weatherley - nicknamed "Mother" because of his tendency to be "such a fucking nag", according to David Ball - was a twenty-five year veteran of the British film industry having a good deal of genre experience with credits such as Blood from the Mummy's Tomb, Alien, and the television series Hammer House of Horror under his belt. Ball first teamed up with Weatherley on the 1982 film Enigma, starring Martin Sheen, and it was during that experience that Ball came to appreciate Weatherley's precise work ethic. "'Mother' refers to him being finicky about exactly where to put the scissors in and he'd often stand his ground on four frames less or more - at 24 frames per second - but that's why I admired his work," explains Ball. "He would never go home without finishing a sequence and would always give an option, i.e. two versions. I've always held the belief there was no old school or new school, there was only the school and Peter was a graduate with honors. Quiet, unassuming and a great technician more suited to Mike's chemistry than most, a thinking man's pair of scissors which is why I chose him."

"David found him more of a nag than I did, actually. I've always learned to love and respect editors," says Gornick. "He was very exacting and very concerned about the conditions and the atmosphere of his editorial room being proper, but that's what an editor needs to be - very exacting."

But it wasn't just Weatherley who Gornick appreciated, as the veteran editor had a strong staff with him. "And Jimmy Shields, likewise. They did major contributions, I thought, to my motion picture," Gornick proudly states. "I had on a couple of occasions a very nice dinner with Jimmy and his wife and Peter Weatherley and his wife. They invited me over to dinner; it was a real nice family situation."

The late Jim Shields who Gornick references was a long time sound editor with quite an impressive resume featuring several James Bond pictures to his credit, as well as Ridley Scott's *Alien* and *Legend*. If you actually pay close attention to the sound effects in *Creepshow 2* you'll notice a unique quality to them, particularly during *The Raft* segment. "Jim, he'd have his own sound effects and he'd have the layering sound effects where he used many sounds to make one effect. I didn't really get his secrets. He would sort of, you know...like I'd ask him, 'How did you make the hoof sound for *Legend* when he ("Darkness") hit in the gravel?' He'd never tell me," laughs assistant sound editor John Bick.

By the time post began in the U.K. there was already an assembly of the picture, a rough cut, which was put together while the production was in Prescott and Bangor. "The only thing I remember from the editing is, I guess they were cutting the scene from the 'Wild West' thing or whatever (*Old Chief Wood'nhead*) and there was a line, 'One more step and blam!'," remembers an amused Debra Tanklow. "And they were constantly going like, 'One more step and blam!', like, they were just hearing it over and over and over again in the cutting room."

"Well, the film was shot, they'd send it to Technicolor, and then it's called dailies. So, every day you'd get a shipment of film from the previous day or the past two days; then you'd sync it up. Then at night the director and the D.P. and whoever, the producer, would watch the dailies," explains John Bick. "So, the film kept coming in and then after the dailies were shot, we'd organize the footage and scenes, then Peter would cut it right there on location."

Bick had worked under Pat Buba and Michael Gornick during the editing and post on Laurel's previous feature *Day of the Dead*. And after having the opportunity to work on films directed by George Romero and Michael Gornick it would give him an insight into the different technical styles of the two directors. "George Romero, he was basically an editor. I mean, he was an editor. Mike Gornick, he was a D.P. So, they had different approaches to directing," Bick explains. "See, George he would basically shoot the film in his head the way he wanted to cut it. I mean, if the scene was running...he wouldn't shoot masters really. He'd shoot, like, medium shots and close-ups and he knew exactly what he wanted. Now, Mike Gornick he would shoot your master scene and then he'd go in for the close-ups for the entire scene. And then he'd do all the dialogue, then Peter would cut it. George was different because he was basically an editor."

Some final tidbits concerning the editing phase involved the film's beginning and ending credits. During the film's opening animation sequence the featured cast and crew's cards would run an estimated four to six seconds. This is when Holt McCallany would inform the production that he preferred to have his name spelled "McCallany" rather than "McAloney"; while director of photography Dick Hart preferred being credited as Richard Hart. Also, Clearface Extra Bold Italic would win out over Helvetica Medium Italic for the film's closing credits font.

Of course spending time in England didn't mean everything had to be solely about work. While he was "in the neighborhood", so to speak, Michael Gornick decided it might be fun to journey to the place that was the namesake of his hometown in Western Pennsylvania. "He used to live in a place called Trafford," says David Ball. "So, when he came here, I said 'What are you doing this weekend, Mike?' He said, 'I'm gonna go to Manchester on the train or I'm renting a car because I wanna see Trafford', which old Trafford is the home of Manchester United football team. So, he went to pay homage to Trafford, PA, of course, to Trafford in Manchester."

"I had envisioned this 'American boy comes home to his namesake in England,'" laughs Gornick as he recalls the journey "home". "And so I drove up to Manchester, which is probably a two and half hour schlep, it's a pretty good drive. But, it was fun, it was on a weekend, went up there. Had the damnedest time finding a place called Trafford Park, which is what Trafford, Pennsylvania is named after. Finally found it and it's kind of like one minor block, one city block. Saw a cigarette shop, thought, 'I'll stop here', I was a smoker at that point and stopped to buy some cigarettes, walked into the cigarette shop and said, 'Hello!' Greeted with silence. I said, 'Hi! I'm from Trafford, Pennyslvania in the States.' More silence. 'I'm excited about being here in Trafford Park.' More silence. Finally the gentleman said, 'May I help you?' And I bought a pack of Marlboro straights and come back to my car and thought, 'Oh well.' He was not impressed whatsoever."

The next portion we'll cover is the score and soundtrack. As mentioned earlier in these pages John Harrison would not return - nor was he asked - to compose the score for *Creepshow 2*. In this writer's opinion, that was an enormous mistake. Harrison's score for *Creepshow* is one of the best horror film scores of all time, right up there with the finest works of Bernard Herrmann or John Carpenter. It's iconic. From the eerie main theme which bookends the film, to the melancholic feel that bridges the end of *Father's Day* with the beginning of *The Lonesome Death of Jordy Verrill,* to the flat-out intense and scary mixture of synth and piano from *The Crate,* Harrison captures the feel of what Romero and King were chasing perfectly. In fact, for those of you who love trivia, Harrison would be the first person to ever give voice to the Creep, who can be heard cackling throughout that main theme from 1982. "The Creep voices both at the beginning and the end of the film are me," Harrison says. "I recorded them on a Sony two track recorder with an old Electro-voice mic and a low-end reverb unit I'd had since the 60's. I mixed them in with the temp score, and George (Romero) loved 'em. So, we kept them – unchanged - in the final."

Instead legendary British composer and songwriter Les Reed would step in to fill Harrison's shoes on the sequel. "Even though John Harrison scored a very interesting score for the original *Creepshow*, I had the distinct feeling that he did not go far enough in his endeavors to create the 'fear of god' in people," Reed says. "Having said that, John is a very fine writer. My initial ideas were to lift some of the action - which I felt was not quite there - into a different dimension through my music. I think I achieved this in certain segments of the film."

In the hopes of persuading Michael Gornick with a particular sound for the film, Reed would send a cassette tape to Pinewood Studios in mid-January 1987 for Gornick to consider. The cassette, 1973's *The New World of Les Reed*, was full of classical music such as *Romeo and Juliet* and *Swan Lake*. Besides the orchestral material, Reed also sent some tunes such as *Here it Comes Again*, which he felt would be perfect for *The Raft* segment. "My motivation in this case was to get Michael to listen to the albums to see if indeed there was anything that may appeal musically to him for the film," says Reed. "Not a good idea as he totally rejected the genre of the kind of music I sent, I knew from that response that I really had to work in a different direction. Indeed, a nightmarish score, which was quite a new direction for me!"

Reed, always the consummate professional, wouldn't take Gornick's initial rejection personally. Instead he would focus on the material and do his best to craft something more appropriate. "I think the ultimate feelings were to write something relating to the action which was at times quite frightening," the music icon says. "And my brain entered into the devilish mode to compliment the director on his fine productions."

Of course, Reed wasn't alone in this endeavor as rock god and keyboard extraordinaire Rick Wakeman would also contribute significantly to the film's score. "Rick and I, from the 1960's were both session men - in fact I go back to 1958 - when I was pianist with the John Barry Seven and we made many recordings and in particular, many films, of which Rick, now and again, played keyboard on, we knew each other very well," Reed says. "I was always a fan of his musical expertise and suggested that Rick should be my partner in this venture."

In an October 1986 letter, which was referenced in the Day 31 section of Chapter 3, Reed would discuss Wakeman's involvement and how they envisioned it fitting in. "My last three films have included Rick Wakeman as soloist (keyboards) and <u>not</u> as composer and this has worked very successfully," Reed's two-page letter reads to David Ball. "I don't know Rick's strength as a composer and I know he would prefer to be credited as a guest performer than joint composer (Rick is contracted to Rondor as a writer and I think the mechanics could be confusing to say the least)." **(9)**

This would explain the "Additional Music by" credit that Wakeman receives during the opening credits sequence. Remember though, earlier in the book in the Day 19 section of Chapter 3, Reed mentioned that Wakeman did in fact score *The Raft*. And in his liner notes for Waxwork Records vinyl release of the *Creepshow 2* score, Reed reiterates this. However, David Ball remembers Reed coming to him to discuss either *The Raft* or *The Hitchhiker*, he was unsure of which one it was, and the fact that it was heavy on keyboards. What exactly does that mean? Could it be that Reed had already composed the score for *The Raft*, rather

Right top, middle and bottom: De Wolfe session musicians Eddie Jones (guitar), Tim Broughton (drums), and bassist John Hyde would collaborate to create the hard rocking *Driving to the Edge of Time* which bookends *The Raft*. (courtesy of Eddie Jones, Tim Broughton, and John Hyde)

than Wakeman? "He said, 'There's a lot of keyboards in there, Dave. Do you know Rick Wakeman?' I said, 'Yeah, I know of him', he said, 'He's the best keyboard player in the world. What if we get him in?' I said, 'Fine, okay.' We were waiting on the animation, we had a delivery date, and we were waiting on the animation to come in from the 'Burgh," says Ball. "So, we were like a week away from delivery of the film and we didn't have the final bit of animation, so we couldn't mix. So, when we got the animation my editor cut it immediately. The following day Rick Wakeman came into the dubbing studio, the mixing studio, him and Les composed, recorded, and mixed twelve minutes of music, including the end music, in one day and we left there at 11:30 at night. What a fantastic achievement. They made it up as they went along! Mike and I were sitting there in awe of these two guys."

I decided, of course, to ask Wakeman himself about all of this. Unfortunately, I was unable to secure an interview with the busy rock star, but he was kind enough to briefly respond via email through his website. "My involvement was extremely minimal; one afternoon at Pinewood Studios playing along live to the animation bits of film... in and out in an hour!," Wakeman wrote back to me. "I did play keyboards at the sessions for Les Reed, who is a great friend and talented composer, but that was the sum total of my involvement."

Those sessions with Reed which Wakeman references took place at Havoc House Studio in Berkshire, roughly an hour west of London. "Reckon I spent three whole days in Havoc House Studios. On the first day we performed on keyboards together to form the base of the scores. The second day was taken up by bringing my musicians in - strings, brass, woodwind, etc... - where we overlaid the full score onto the already recorded keyboard tracks. The third day was purely reducing and fitting everything together, to make up the complete score," Reed recalls.

As for Michael Gornick he remembers watching Reed and Wakeman work on the score and came away impressed by what he saw - in particular Wakeman. "I thought what they did for me - in many cases it was not necessarily complete, they did as much as they could - was very, very thorough and very theatrical. I thought it was right on, dead on. I mean, Les knows his stuff. And Rick was a blow away!," says Gornick. "It actually was the most amazing thing I've ever seen, to see someone absorb... there was a playback, as I remember, I was given a 3/4 inch tape of some segments to show him and his response was so instantaneous, in terms of, 'Let me show you this', and he would begin playing and I suddenly realized, 'How could anyone be so attuned with material so quickly?' We had a little bit of conversation here and there about where the material was born and what it came out of in terms of the genre itself before he even screened it, but he had this kind of understanding; which, later, when you examine his whole career and his whole body of work you realize that he is a genius and he does react almost instantaneously to a situation creatively."

"It was amazing. I remember meeting him because I was a big Yes fan growing up and he's a pretty big guy," recalls John Bick. "And he walked in and I said, 'Nice to meet you, Mr. Wakeman.' He goes, 'Call me, Rick.' And so,

I mean, everybody involved, they had no egos. You know, it was just a nice thing."

And as a show of appreciation for Reed agreeing to do the film's score for such a budget friendly fee - $45,000 - Richard Rubinstein would offer Reed a bonus of a percentage of the film's net profits, which Reed was pleased to accept.

The soundtrack wouldn't just feature original music from Reed and Wakeman though, as there would also be a need for music playing on car radios for both *The Raft* and *The Hitchhiker* segments. This is where the library of De Wolfe Music would come into play. Founded in London, England in 1909 by Meyer de Wolfe the company originally provided a library of sheet music for silent films, which was played live in theaters. Over time as technology improved De Wolfe began recording their music onto phonographs and 35mm nitrate film soundtracks. Besides providing music for motion pictures De Wolfe would also score newsreels, which played between showings in theaters. Following World War II they would expand into the United States, which also happened to coincide with the booming success of television, opening up an entirely new market for the company with commercial advertising. By the time the 1960's arrived De Wolfe was providing their music on vinyl records. They would also provide music for popular TV shows such as *Doctor Who* and *Monty Python's Flying Circus*, among others. And, of course, any self-respecting George A. Romero fan knows the vital role De Wolfe Music played in 1978's classic *Dawn of the Dead*; one listen to Herbert Chappell's *The Gonk* will tell you all you need to know.

With Michael Gornick having served as Romero's post-production supervisor on *Dawn of the Dead*, as well as the original *Creepshow*, which also featured library tracks, he was well versed in the world of De Wolfe and library music. For *Creepshow 2* he'd have the opportunity to spend time at the headquarters of De Wolfe, a company that had served Laurel so well over the years. "That was pretty exciting because years prior to that going back to The Latent Image days, when I first joined George, he principally had two libraries there - but the primary library was the Music de Wolfe library," says Gornick. "And that was licensed out of New York City, but the home office was London, so you knew that London was the birth of Music de Wolfe. So, that was our principal library for music at the old Latent Image, both for commercial work and even for many of George's features. Originally in *Night of the Living Dead* he used the Capitol Hi-Q library, but later in time that became kind of tired and they had nothing new in that library, so he moved to Music de Wolfe, prior to me joining. So, anyhow, that was the music library for years at The Latent Image and we would update it, there were a lot of updates to the library. And so when it came time to apply some music, aside from the material Les Reed and Rick Wakeman wrote for the motion picture, we had a lot of filler areas and transitional moments that we needed to use some music, so we elected to use the Music de Wolfe library, which I knew very well.

Originally an idea was floated for the filler material to be some of Les Reed's hit songs from the previous two decades. "The opening segment of 'The Raft' could feature an 'oldies' program on the radio," David Ball suggested in a letter to Les Reed in June 1986. "Which means that we might consider inserting some of your hits from the 60's and 70's." **(10)**

Now, initially, that sounds like a terrible idea. Why would college kids in the mid 1980's be listening to an oldies station? More than likely they would be jamming to some more current hard rock tunes, right? Of course, this is the path Gornick would choose and it was indeed the correct one. However, in Ball's defense, I'll remind you that in King's original short story he makes reference to Beach Boys oldies and in the *Skeleton Crew* version of *The Raft* Randy sings the lyrics of Gary U.S. Bonds' *School is Out*, which makes sense considering King claims to have originally penned the story in the late 1960's.

"David Ball has no taste," Gornick playfully jokes about his trusted producer. "If it was a period piece, I'd accept it. But to have Herman's Hermits playing out of the Camaro in a 1980's situation didn't quite work for me, you know. *Mrs. Brown You've Got a Lovely Daughter* would have been cute, but compound that with the rape on the raft, it never would have worked. And Les wasn't offended by that. I mean, you know, there probably would have been major negotiations to get some of that material anyhow. Because, I mean, there's so many layers in terms of music that has been published already. There's the publishing rights, the synchronization rights, the performance rights, and so it probably would have been so damn messy that it wouldn't have paid off anyhow, we probably couldn't have gotten the material."

And Gornick would be correct regarding this subject. In the aforementioned October 1986 letter which Les Reed sent to David Ball, Reed would touch on the issue of utilizing some of his older music and the costs involved. "Regarding the use of 1960's material that you mentioned - I have spoken to Kay O'Dwyer, of EMI Music, and she tells me that there is a statutory fee per 30 seconds of music used and it works out at £1,250 per 30 seconds for full use or £750 per 30 seconds for lesser exploitation," Reed explained. "Perhaps you can have a word with her sometime, as this is not really my territory." **(11)**

"We did put forward three of our hit songs: *It's Not Unusual*, *There's a Kind of Hush,* and *Delilah* for the car radio music, but I guess the director had his own favorites," Reed says.

The majority of Gornick's "favorites" from De Wolfe would be utilized during *The Raft*, some of which make quick cameos in *The Hitchhiker* as well if you're paying close attention.

We'll begin with the catchy tune that opens *The Raft* as Deke's speedy yellow Camaro races through the canyon: *Driving to the Edge of Time*. Written by drummer Tim Broughton and guitarist Eddie Jones the song originally appeared on the 1981 album *25 Years of Pop*, described by De Wolfe as "Forceful, Beaty, Heavy Metal". Broughton became associated with De Wolfe Music when he was sharing a house with Meyer de Wolfe's grand-daughter. Thanks to her father, James de Wolfe, Broughton was able to have his first ever recording session arranged at the legendary studios of De Wolfe. From there he would meet De Wolfe employees, John Hyde (aka John Saunders) and

Above: Christopher Blackwell's 1986 effort for De Wolfe - *See the Day* - would contribute two songs to *The Raft*: *Overdrive* and *Sacred Heart*. (copyright 1986 Music De Wolfe)

Colin Lloyd Tucker, who asked Broughton to join their band Plain Characters, eventually releasing their one and only album *Invisible Yearnings*, also released in 1981.

During his time at De Wolfe Broughton also met Eddie Jones, who when he was only 16 years old played the Cavern Club in Liverpool, made famous by The Beatles, where he was paid £1 for his efforts. Jones had been playing in garage bands since the age of 14 and was influenced by guitar god Jimi Hendrix, who he cites as his biggest musical inspiration. Prior to *25 Years of Pop*, which he and Broughton are credited with 3 songs on, he played guitar for the Dave Travis band, which was more of a rock-a-billy, 1950's style music.

As for the duo's *Driving to the Edge of Time*, which bookends *The Raft*, two versions of the song appear in the segment: the instrumental only version opens the story, while the version with lyrics closes it out. As it turns out - and fittingly so considering the tune blasts from Deke's Camaro - the arrangement was put together rather fast. "On *Driving* Tim is on drums, I am on guitar, and John Hyde is on bass," says Eddie Jones. "The song probably took us all of 10 minutes to create and was recorded mainly live, with vocals added later; I think there was just one guitar over-dub. The session was fun and I think we all broke sweat a few times!"

"We wrote it in Eddie's living room," Tim Broughton explains. "The brief was to write a heavy rock track. The title came first, the rest quickly followed."

The singer featured on the lyrical version of the song is Elfed Hayes, who was a member of the band Flint roughly around the same time. Hardcore George Romero afficionados will appreciate that Hayes once spent some time in vocal sessions with the band The Pretty Things, who sometimes went by the moniker of Electric Banana, who performed the memorable *Cause I'm a Man* featured

Musical Portrait

Above: *Festive Season 1* (or perhaps 2), which plays on Annie's car stereo in *The Hitchhiker*, was featured on side 2 of De Wolfe's 1985 vinyl release of Simon Park's *Musical Portrait*. In 1987 the album would be re-released on CD as *Classics One*. Park had a history with Laurel, with some of his music from 1977's *Sun High* appearing in George A. Romero's *Dawn of the Dead*. (copyright 1985 Music De Wolfe)

in *Dawn of the Dead*. "John Hyde and myself had played many gigs together and I sang on some of his recordings. I had played a gig or two with Eddie having been introduced to him in the 70's by Gary Thomas - a De Wolfe studio engineer and producer. Gary was producing Flint at the time - 1977," Hayes recalls. "During a spell in the 80's working as a sound engineer for De Wolfe, I was on hand for guitar and vocal sessions. I remember that Eddie was in for a week or so, recording a library album and he invited me to sing."

The next track we'll cover is *Forces of Evil*, which plays not long after Rachel's demise and just before Deke's. Written by the aforementioned John Hyde (a.k.a. John Saunders) and Steve Gare, *Forces of Evil*, also described as "Forceful, Beaty, Heavy Metal", appeared originally on the 1983 album *Chartbreakers*. Providing their clients with a much more economical alternative to well-known music, De Wolfe allowed film-makers the ability to enhance their features with original music and songs from their in-house library. Like a lot of the studio session music produced by De Wolfe there would be instrumental versions, as well as ones with lyrics - basically to give the client options for their project. In the case of *Forces of Evil* the instrumental version would be employed in *The Raft*, while interestingly enough the lyrical version would appear in another low budget shocker released by New World around the same time, *Slugs*.

Musician John Hyde had been with De Wolfe for quite a while and performed in a number of capacities with the company - from office work, to composing and recording his own original material, to working as a music consultant on films such as *Monty Python and the Holy*

Grail. Hyde would even serve at one point as an assistant to De Wolfe composer Simon Park, whose contributions to Laurel productions we'll soon get to. As for the song itself the origin of *Forces of Evil* ironically had a comedic background. "It was based on a heavy metal parody song we'd done at school," says Hyde, who played bass on the tune as well.

In regards to the other artists on the track initially Hyde was not completely sure who they were, but had his suspicions. "I wish I could remember! I got the album out and was amazed by how good the guitar playing is, but can't remember anything about it," he says. "I've thought about all the people I was in bands with at that time and nobody played like that - my only guess is that it was Eddie Jones who was a mate of the drummer Tim Broughton. I can hear it's me playing bass."

Now, I say Hyde was initially unsure because as luck would have it he would make a discovery from those days gone by at De Wolfe - over two years after our initial first interview - which enabled him to inform me of who those other artists were. "You won't believe this but a friend came round the other day and we were talking about old films and I said I had an EP of a soundtrack of a film he mentioned and all my singles fell off the shelf and my old diaries were behind them in a wall cavity," Hyde emailed to say. "So, I've been looking at 1983 and found the sessions that led to *Forces of Evil*. Tim Broughton played the drums, I played the bass. The guitars were played by a friend with whom I was in a band at the time — then he was known as Craig Whipsnade, although his real name is David Hubbard. The vocals were done by somebody called Larry Oliver — I've just looked him up and I think he was the guy who was in The New Seekers. Apparently he was very good at the sessions and I was very pleased with him!"

Forces of Evil wouldn't be Hyde's only contribution to *Creepshow 2* however as another track of his from that same 1983 album, *Chartbreakers*, can be heard very briefly during *The Raft*. After the four kids initially make it safely to the raft, Randy is spooked by the site of the blob and it dawns on him that no one knows they're out at the lake. As he glances back to the shore you can hear Hyde's *Anarchy* echoing from the Camaro parked on the beach. The song, described by De Wolfe as "Brash, Up-Tempo, Punk Rock", can also be heard for a second during *The Hitchhiker*, as well. After hitting Tom Wright's character, the hitchhiker, Annie, played by Lois Chiles, goes to turn on her car stereo looking for something to calm her nerves and the first snippet of music you hear is once again *Anarchy*. Moments after that you can quickly hear the lyrical version of Hyde's *Forces of Evil* as her car stereo scans for a powerful broadcast signal to lock onto. Again though, you have to pay careful attention to pick up on it.

In regards to *Anarchy*, and even *Forces of Evil*, Hyde was busy cranking out so much material besides participating on other songs and albums - *Driving to the Edge of Time*, for example - that memories about those songs are a bit fleeting. "I've done about 500 library albums," Hyde says. "So, I'm not very good at remembering."

The next two songs we'll discuss are also from *The Raft*, both of which are from the album *See the Day* by drummer Christopher Blackwell. Released in the mid 1980's - De

Wolfe lists 1986, while Blackwell seems to believe it was around 1984 - the opportunity for Blackwell to record the album at De Wolfe would come about from a classic case of serendipity. "I had just started to branch out into writing songs and one of the new singers I was writing for asked if I would like to meet her boyfriend, Warren, to talk about my doing some library tracks," recalls Blackwell. "Turns out that Warren was Warren de Wolfe (grandson of Meyer de Wolfe) and I ended up recording four albums for him!"

The first Blackwell track featured in the segment is *Sacred Heart*, described as "Heavy, Riffy Electric Guitar", which plays once the four doomed protagonists arrive at the lake and begin to enter the water. A fascinating side story regarding this track is that it also appears in the 1987 James Bond film *The Living Daylights* - during the "ghetto-blaster" scene - which was released just three months after *Creepshow 2* and was, of course, shot at Pinewood Studios.

The second track from Blackwell utilized in the story is *Overdrive*, described as "Laid-Back, Heavy Rock", which plays at first light after Randy and Laverne have slept overnight on the raft.

I asked Blackwell about his memories of creating these songs for that first De Wolfe record, which have become so memorable for fans of *Creepshow 2*. "Well it was such a long time ago now...I had taken some friends into the studio with me to make things quicker and, if I'm honest, for moral support," he says. "I had Doug Boyle on guitar, Phil Scragg on bass, and Chris Marshall on keyboards. Doug and Phil both went on with me to record *Now and Zen* for Robert Plant - Doug staying on and coming on the road with us."

A couple of things to unpack there: one being that Blackwell would go on to perform on the amazing *Now and Zen* album with former Led Zeppelin front man Robert Plant. How incredible is that! But the second issue is his comment about Phil Scragg and Chris Marshall. There is a YouTube video of the song *Sacred Heart* which was uploaded in April 2012 by "Ty Davies" - several years before I conducted my interview with Blackwell for this book - which is still online as of this writing, in which Blackwell posts in the comments section regarding the song. "Hi there, I wrote this track bloody ages ago and it's one of the first I did for De Wolfe," Blackwell commented. "That's me on drums, bass, guitars, keyboards, everything really apart from the lead guitar which is played by Doug Boyle. Thanks for taking an interest in the track guys, appreciate it!" **(12)** Now, why no mention of Scragg and Marshall? In my opinion most likely due to the theme that has run throughout this book - people's memories. When Blackwell posted that comment he was probably just forgetting, I suspect.

The last of our library tracks to cover, which was featured during *The Hitchhiker*, is from someone with a tangential, yet very significant, connection to the world of Laurel: composer, conductor, and arranger Simon Park. *Festive Season 1* or possibly *Festive Season 2* - they sound virtually identical, despite 1 being twice as long as 2 - is from the 1985 album *Musical Portrait*, later reissued on the 1987 CD *Classics One*. "It was all quite deliberately, pastiche classical styles, which was something that De Wolfe did specialize in," says Park. "Actually, for composers

such as myself, to be doing that kind of stuff was always wonderful because being essentially timeless, I mean, it's already pastiche, it doesn't date; unlike if you're asked to do an album of contemporary pop stuff - ten, twenty years later it just feels out of date, it's passe. This stuff doesn't date and it's still doing very well to this day."

Park, whose paternal grandmother was a professional musician and music teacher, developed a love of music very early while attending church with his grandparents, becoming captivated as he watched the organist play during services. He would eventually go on to graduate from Worcester College, Oxford with a B.A. in music during the 1960's. A few years after graduating he would find himself at De Wolfe where he would initially begin working in their offices. "I studied music at Oxford University; I studied with two very fine twentieth century composers, but whilst I was doing that I was also very much into rock - rhythm and blues particularly - Ray Charles was my great idol. So, I was playing with rock bands in the evening and studying Mozart operas during the day," Park says. "And when I came down with my degree...I loved both types of music equally and I didn't feel I had what it took to become a serious classical composer, but also I didn't want to lose touch with the 'lighter' sort of music as well. And it struck me that the best way to do this was to try to get involved with the film music world. So, I actually don't really remember now how I came to find De Wolfe, but I applied for a job with them - in fact, I think they were advertising for somebody, a trainee music consultant; yes they were, it was in *Melody Maker*, a musicians rag in those days. So, I applied for the job and went and had an interview and got the job. And I started as a trainee learning the library, which even then was a pretty big library!"

It wasn't long though before Park would bend the ear of the top brass regarding his true goal. "But I had immediately tried selling myself as a composer to James de Wolfe, who was then in charge, and he said, 'Yeah, yeah, we'll give you a try.' And he let me start to write some stuff for the library and gradually that built up as they seemed to think that I was pretty good at it," he says. "And it built up and built up to the point that by, say, the late 70's I was one of the two or three principal composers for the library."

As one of De Wolfe's principal composers Park would go on to produce countless pieces for them over the years, close to 1400 by his estimates. If you've ever watched any vintage NFL Films highlights from the 1970's and 1980's then you've heard his work: titles like *Gun Law* and *Blockbuster*, fantastic pieces that any Pittsburgh Steelers fan will know from Super Bowl X and XIV highlight films, respectively, the music is instantly recognizable.

But for George Romero fans they will recognize Park's sound from *Dawn of the Dead* where multiple tracks from his 1977 album *Sun High* are permanently ingrained in their mind. "The album was written and recorded in 1976, so that was a long time ago," Park recalls. "And I will put my hand up now and admit straight out that I was very much influenced by an album by Jan Hammer. You remember Jan Hammer? He was the keyboard player with Mahavishnu Orchestra and he was an early synthesizer 'geek', he used the Minimoog on stage before anybody else did, and then he went on to use the Fairlight. And about '74 or '75 he

Colliers

JULY 9, 1949
·15¢

NEW REBEL YELL IN DIXIE | **DEMOCRACY IN THESE...**

Collier's Editorials

MAC SHEPARD

The OLD FOLKS take it harder than JUNIOR

SOMETIMES IT SEEMS as if comic books are exciting parents more than they are supposed to excite youthful readers. At least there have been quite a number of irate elders and a few psychiatrists breaking into print lately with charges that the comics are totally bad, and that they are corrupting children's taste, degrading their morals and encouraging crime.

Excitable people frequently accuse certain books, magazines, movies and plays of doing the same thing to adults. The difference is that parents are inclined to fire a broadside of condemnation at the whole field of comic books rather than concentrate on individual offenders. This approach, we believe, is wrong on three counts.

It implies the need of censorship—a malignancy that can spread rapidly once it gets a start.

It complicates the job of coolheaded civic and parent groups and responsible publishers who are trying to promote the better comic books and discourage the reading of trashy ones.

It exaggerates the importance of comics as an evil force in the lives of American children.

Any kid needs some vicarious adventure in his life. The comics help fill that need, as the dime novels did before them. A youngster's taste in adventure stories runs to simple problems solved by simple means. Parents are often shocked when these solutions are achieved with the help of fists, knives and guns. But if a child is healthy and happy it isn't likely that he is going to absorb enough poison from blood-and-thunder cartoon books to steer him toward a career of crime.

The comics have been held responsible for juvenile murders. Perhaps the children involved thought that they got the inspiration to kill from a comic book. Maybe their parents and the authorities thought so, too. We don't.

A comic book might provide a suggestion, but not a motive. If a youngster shuts himself up in the unreal world of lurid comics to the point where they seem to dictate his actions, there must be something pretty bad in his real world that he is trying to run away from.

Juvenile delinquency is the product of pent-up frustrations, stored-up resentments and bottled-up fears. It is not the product of cartoons and captions. But the comics are a handy, obvious, uncomplicated scapegoat. If the adults who crusade against them would only get as steamed up over such basic causes of delinquency as parental ignorance, indifference and cruelty, they might discover that comic books are no more of a menace than *Treasure Island* or *Jack the Giant Killer*.

74

---

did an album called *The First Seven Days*, which was his musical exploration of 'The Creation' and it had a big influence on me. And, in fact, I suspect now if I listen back to *The First Seven Days* alongside *Sun High* I might go, 'Ouch!' I was a bit close with that one because there's an awful lot of Jan Hammer on that album. That's how it came about. And it was in the very early days of synthesizers and electronic keyboards; it was recorded in De Wolfe's own little studio in Wardour Street in Soho in central London. They had a Minimoog, which the company had bought, and we had an electric piano of some kind, there were all kinds of weird and wonderful things about in those days. And I know we spent a lot of time experimenting with sounds and putting things together and clever editing techniques, all kinds of stuff. It was a very exciting time and it was an exciting album to do. And I think they were a bit perplexed by it, De Wolfe. But then it was used in *Dawn of the Dead*, so I think that probably went some way towards getting their money back eventually. It was a fun time, a fun album to do."

As for *Creepshow 2, Festive Season 1* or possibly *Festive Season 2*, described by De Wolfe as "Lively, Mozart Style", can be heard when Lois Chiles turns on her car stereo and winds up listening to a classical station as she attempts to talk herself into living with what she's just done. As I say it's very difficult to tell the difference between the two recordings, even to the trained ear of the composer himself who admitted he wasn't really sure which version was featured in the film, but suspected it might have been the second one. The unusual idea of creating different versions of such pieces as *Festive Season 1* and 2 would actually come from De Wolfe's top man at the time. "I do remember James de Wolfe had this idea that he'd like to do all of the pieces or at least half of the pieces anyway in two versions: one with a full orchestra and one with a chamber orchestra," Park explains. "There's not a lot of difference. With benefit of hindsight I would say it really wasn't worth doing because the size of the sound, if I can put it that way, isn't dramatically different between the two versions. There is a harpsichord on the bigger version which I don't think is there on the smaller version. And it was just basically a matter of using fewer strings because basically they're just strings and continua, so that's really all."

So, with the film's music now covered, another topic worthy of dissection from the post-production is the quote which appears at the close of the end credits:

"Juvenile delinquency is the product of pent-up frustrations, stored-up resentments and bottled-up fears. It is not the product of cartoons and captions. But the comics are a handy, obvious, uncomplicated scapegoat. If the adults who crusade against them would only get as steamed up over such basic causes of delinquency as parental ignorance, indifference and

Above and below left: The closing paragraph from the editorial "The OLD FOLKS take it harder than JUNIOR", which appeared in the July 9, 1949 issue of *Collier's* magazine, would stick in director Michael Gornick's mind and was something he insisted on placing at the end of the film's closing credits. (copyright 1949 The Crowell-Collier Publishing Company)

cruelty, they might discover that comic books are no more of a menace than Treasure Island or Jack the Giant Killer."

The quote was from an editorial featured in the July 9, 1949 issue of *Collier's* magazine entitled "The OLD FOLKS take it harder than JUNIOR". In the column the topic of comic books and their so-called negative effect on the youths of America was put on full blast, dismantling that notion all together, even stating the hysteria surrounding it could imply a need for censorship. And you have to understand this was nearly five years before Dr. Fredric Wertham would publish his book *Seduction of the Innocent*. This subject had been a talking point for years prior to that book's publication along with the U.S. Senate hearings which it helped to inspire. "Any kid needs some vicarious adventure in his life. The comics help fill that need, as the dime novels did before them. A youngster's taste in adventure stories runs to simple problems solved by simple means," the *Collier's* column read. "Parents are often shocked when these solutions are achieved with the help of fists, knives and guns. But if a child is healthy and happy it isn't likely that he is going to absorb enough poison from blood-and-thunder cartoon books to steer him toward a career of crime." **(13)**

"That last scene, one of the things Mike wanted in the movie is he had read this comment from the '50's about how comics really weren't bad for you and it had always stuck with him. And he got them to agree - he said, 'I want this at the end of my movie,'" says Andy Sands about Michael Gornick's desire to have the quote close the film. "So, when they were in pre-production - again, god love Mike - he hired me to find the quote and get all the information so they could get the rights to it. So, I was the guy, I had to go down to the library and go through all the microfilm and actually had them pull out an old copy of, I think, *Collier's* and get all of that information."

"Yeah, I thought it was very important, again, to try to make some sort of allusion to the E.C. days and what transpired in that whole period," Gornick says. "And also in today's world I'm totally opposed to censorship, any kind of ratings and so forth. I'm kind of a Libertarian when it comes to that, in terms of my reading material and your reading material and what you view and how you view it and so forth. And I think that was a very critical age where erroneously, and even to this day, there are these weird associations between what you see and what you'll become. And that's insane; if you're not prepped, if you don't have any inner fortitude, if you can't make any sort of discernment, everything will influence you. Everything!"

Securing permission to utilize the quote for the end roller would turn out to be a rather simple task as Laurel would discover the copyright had not been renewed since its original date in July of 1949. Thus, *Creepshow 2* was free to use the language from the editorial just as Michael Gornick envisioned.

Around this same time Laurel would also receive official permission from Blair Entertainment for excerpts from *The Cisco Kid* for use in the *Old Chief Wood'nhead* segment. For $500 and proper screen credit Laurel could utilize 2 minutes of picture and 5 minutes of soundtrack from the

1950's syndicated television show in any and all forms of media, throughout the world, in perpetuity.

While at Pinewood some optical work was completed for the film by the late, great Roy Field of Optical Film Effects, Ltd. Field was already a legend in the effects industry having worked on numerous James Bond films, as well as the *Superman* film series. If you pay close attention during *The Raft* you'll notice some minor effects touch-ups such as little stars that sparkle on the blob right before it attacks Page Hannah. And apparently the death of Jeremy Green's character, Laverne, was to be punched up as well with some work by Field, but viewing the finished product it seems the work was never accomplished. David Ball would send a memo to Field in early January regarding the "Laverne death gag stage 2" effect letting him know that the production would need to know precisely what he had in mind for the shot, as well as the cost, before any approval would be given. "Roy was fiercely creative and pushed the boundaries in full knowledge that he had time, given the animation was running behind schedule. I have a feeling he was attempting to cavort Laverne's face or add layers of goop to it," remembers Ball. "My memo was purely a nudge that he not get carried away given our limited resources, because he had a tendency to."

Some other effects insert shots for *The Raft* were also being handled while in England, but rather than optically they would instead be captured in camera. "We needed close-ups of 'Bob the blob' so I called in another wizard, David Speed, one of the first to use stop frame photography and endoscopes. We melted black candle wax into a kiddie's paddling pool which set on contact, and stirred the water up with a stick. David used a star filter to create the effect of the sun glistening off the blob, absolutely simple, cost effective and with spectacular results. We used other close-ups without the filter to match the awful conditions we suffered when shooting *The Raft*," David Ball says. "'Speedy' was light-years ahead in his thinking and everything was based on simplicity."

As *Creepshow 2*'s post-production was nearing its end and all the other technical details like answer prints and inter-positives were being completed a sense of relief finally began to take hold for those who had been around since the very beginning - and none more so than for its producer. "The great thing for me was when we delivered that film it was like a weight off your mind. You know, let's go out and get absolutely *shit faced* because it's a weight off your mind! And there was as much pressure in post-production A) financially and B) timely because of the animation. So, there was pressure from June '86 to May '87 when we finally delivered it. But it's one that stands the test of time; it's not a bad movie," says David Ball. "And in the end, we finally got the film finished and the bondsman elected to return the fee. Once the film was in the can they said, 'Okay, we know you've all had a very difficult time; yeah, you're in post-production, let's say that this film was never bonded', which was a very, very remarkable assessment of the hard work that Mike and I put into that production."

Chapter 5 Second Issue Collector's Edition

With Laurel Entertainment now passing the baton to New World Pictures, the marketing and distribution of *Creepshow 2* would begin. In fact, New World were already hard at work promoting the upcoming release while post-production was still on-going as early as February 1987 at the ShoWest annual trade show (we'll return to that in a bit) and with a promotional ad in the weekly edition of *Variety*. The man who would play a vital role in seeing that Laurel's newest production would receive as much awareness as it possibly could get was New World's Rusty Citron.

"My exact title was senior vice president of worldwide promotion and publicity. And what that entailed was creating - in working with the advertisement department - the promotional and merchandising and in-theater visibility for the film in terms of how we were going to sell it; my job, basically, was to put 'tushies' in seats," Citron explains. "And the way that works is that the first weekend's performance of a picture is a function of its marketing. And everything after that is a function of its distribution. But if you can't get enough interest by consumers to go see a movie then the rest of it doesn't matter. So, you can only buy a certain amount of eyeballs with television and back in those days television was a very efficient way of selling movies, but for the young male, which is primarily our audience, reaching them required a little different nuance in terms of available media. I mean, emails didn't exist. There were three networks and so we were very, I would call it, static versus the kind of programs that exist today. But we were very static and it was like plowing the fields - it was, 'This is what you did and this is how you did it.' The point was to get promotion and publicity, which means we were in front of people without having to pay for it, in terms of media. Now, if you go to television, you need X amount of ratings points, it would cost you $10,000 for the spot and you produce the spot and you were there. But the rest of it, in terms of promotion work, was laying the ground work to make that final offer to the customer."

A perfect example of the kind of marketing strategy Citron refers to was implemented by New World just two years prior when a certain classic Japanese monster made his way back onto the silver screen. "It was all about making money. It was all about doing stuff that was fun. And we had a blast, because we were making movies that nobody else cared about in the industry," says Citron. "In '85 we released *Godzilla* and so we made up lifeguard vests and we gave them out to lifeguards and people on the beaches in California and New York. Because we knew that Godzilla was coming from the ocean and they became the watchdogs - the 'Have you seen Godzilla?' - walking the beaches to make sure Godzilla wasn't coming up on the shore. That's the kind of stuff that we were known for."

"Rusty and I had the best time in life because we were like, 'We're not just making t-shirts, we're making weird stuff.' So, we just would create the craziest promotional items for every movie," says Lori (Koonin) Schneider, who was manager of national promotion and field publicity at New World under Citron. "The only thing I remember about *Creepshow 2* was I found this slime bubble bath in Fred Segal on Melrose and I'm like, 'Wait, we can do this for *Creepshow*.' It was a big green hand coming out of the bottle, you know, a container and we changed the labeling to *Creepshow 2*. And I remember the guy on *Entertainment Tonight* picked it up and he said, 'But, the greatest thing I found at the Cannes Film Festival was this *Creepshow 2* slime bubble bath.' So, I was like, 'Oh, my thing made it to the screen!' I was so excited."

Among several approaches which a film studio can employ one of the most tried-and-true forms of publicity for any motion picture is the coming attractions trailer. "The way that it worked basically is there was a team at New World that was basically the advertising, trailer, and poster people and that was the extent of advertising," explains Rusty Citron. "And that really was a function of working with a lot of outside vendors and the way the process worked basically is that when a film came in and we were ready to set a release date, which was the first part of the process, you then had to pick and create a trailer. And in some cases - with *Creepshow 2* it was easy - with other cases, you know, it was a little more challenging; because *Creepshow 2* already had, to a certain degree, a built in audience. So, what we had to be able to do was figure out how to make it unique. But the first aspect is always to create the trailer, and to a certain degree that's true today. And the trailer and how you present the trailer really defines the rest of your marketing campaign because that's the first impression that people get."

To create their trailers for *Creepshow 2* New World would turn to Marshall Drazen, one of those outside vendors that Citron made reference to. Drazen, a graduate of NYU film school, came to California from the east coast to avoid getting "sidetracked", as he puts it, only to become just that, sidetracked, in the world of advertising, specifically writing copy for film trailers and posters. Some of the campaigns that Drazen lists on his resume include *The Hitcher*, *Raising Arizona*, *Jaws IV: The Revenge* (he claims to have written the poster tag-line "This Time It's Personal"), and *Robocop* (again, the poster tag-line "Part Man, Part Machine, All Cop" came from him he says).

I asked Drazen how he would have approached creating a trailer back in those days of the mid to late 1980's and he was nice enough to explain the process, giving examples from the *Creepshow 2* trailer specifically to illustrate. "I came from a marketing background, so I tried to treat each film like it was a separate product and tried to find what was special about it, or what they called 'market differentiation', and set out that way," he says. "What was wonderful about New World was that they always began with the producer - you got to write the script, pretty

Right: Full page advertisement from Laurel Entertainment to New World Pictures featured in the April 28, 1987 issue of *Variety*.

Hi, I'm from Laurel Entertainment
and I'm here to deliver
CREEPSHOW 2
·New World Pictures·
CREEPSHOW
2
Thank you
New World
Laurel Entertainment Inc.
928 Broadway, N.Y., N.Y. 10010 212-674-3800

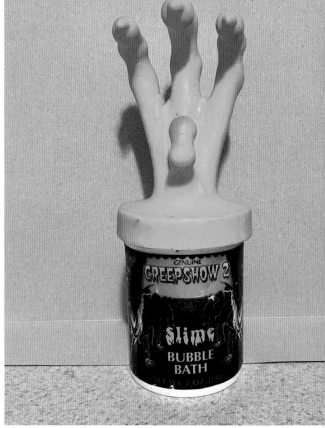

Left: Attendees of the 1987 ShoWest convention in Las Vegas play promotional *Creepshow 2* pinball machines supplied by New World Pictures. The machines were actually *Strange Science* games by Bally Midway. **Right:** Promotional *Creepshow 2* slime bubble bath given out at the 1987 Cannes Film Festival. (courtesy of Lori (Koonin) Schneider)

much decide which direction it was going. You'd have a discussion with a man named Steve Segal, he gave out the jobs, and then you were pretty much on that film all the way through - the trailers first and then the TV. So in that case, then you would write the script. What I typically liked, you didn't have to write...other places you might write eight, ten, twenty other scripts and there might be some places where there would be two or three other people writing similar numbers of scripts. And then they would pick one and go do it and as a writer your job was pretty much done once they picked a script, unless they needed re-writes for something that wasn't working a certain place. But what would happen is they might pick your opening, someone else's ending, a third person's middle, you know, or whatever. What was nice is that we had control at New World, ourselves. So, it was always our beginning, middle, and end. And what I liked to do was write that one script, in general, and the process I liked to use was to give it to the editor and then I would disappear. The script would call out certain scenes and you'll see how in this case the script was written very specific with the scenes that I wanted to follow it in mind. Like, there was a line about being stuck to your chair, I knew that I wanted the guy getting shot through the chest with the arrow when he was sitting in the chair there (Fatso from *Old Chief Wood'nhead*), so I would call out the individual scenes there. And then usually when there was a montage I would say, 'action montage', and let the editor - I don't remember if there is, there must be some montage in this - but the editor would do that. And if he couldn't make my line work, you know, my notion for the visual, then he could put his own in there. But what I did was I got out of the way so that the editor could bring what he was going to bring to it. And I felt if I sat there and micro-managed him that I was no longer going to be

very objective when I had a look at the cut. So, I would get away, let him do his work, bring what he was going to bring to it, then come back and see it when he had a first cut done. And then we would start from there to see what was working, what wasn't working, what we could change, if there were better ideas - things like that. And then we'd talk over the changes and I'd go away and come back each time until we had something that was finished."

As for the process of writing the script in which the editor - in this case Roland Mesa, a friend of star Holt McCallany at the time - would work from, Drazen explains that process for us as well. "For a teaser trailer you might get footage from a movie, whatever they've got shot or whatever. But usually for a trailer you've got a rough cut of the movie because you had to see what footage was available," he says. "In this case I would have sat down and taken, by hand, notes of the movie of every shot that I thought was usable; every line that I might take out - every visual that might be interesting. And it would have been a VHS recorder, without a remote, so I'd have to stop it with my finger, probably in '87, and write down the line and if I couldn't remember, if it was a long line, I'd go back and start it up again. It was a drag; it could take a day of notes. Then you'd write a script."

As for the trailer's narration which Drazen scripted you wanted to have a commanding voice delivering the material, yet at the same time you wanted that voice to convey a bit of a wink to the audience. When you hear: "So don't just

252

sit there. Walk. Run. Swim if you have to. But whatever you do don't take your time 'cause the scares come twice as quickly in...*Creepshow 2*"; that voice belongs to the late, great Percy Rodriguez. "He knew he had 'that' kind of voice that was perfect for scares with tongue planted in cheek and had a great time doing these kinds of trailers," says trailer editor Roland Mesa about Rodriguez.

Canadian born Rodriguez (Rodrigues) was a respected actor appearing in films like *The Heart is a Lonely Hunter*, as well as countless television shows such as *The Man from U.N.C.L.E.*, *Mission Impossible*, and *Sanford and Son.* But it was his work as a voice-over artist for movie trailers for which Rodriguez would be best remembered. Coming attractions for *The Exorcist*, *Taxi Driver*, *The Omen*, *Psycho II*, *Children of the Corn*, *The Return of the Living Dead*, and *Into the Night* all feature the unmistakable and powerful voice of Rodriguez. But perhaps no trailer would come to define his uncanny ability to truly *sell* a motion picture more than this one from 1975: "There is a creature alive today who has survived millions of years of evolution. Without change. Without passion. And without logic. It lives to kill. A mindless eating machine. It will attack and devour...anything. It is as if God created the Devil and gave him...*Jaws*."

"I chose Percy and I directed him during the session," says Marshall Drazen. "We came from a culture of not always having the best, how should I say, the best production value on screen. So, in this case, after looking at the film, though it was very good, it was obviously made on a budget; they did the best they could with the budget they had, but this wasn't going to compete with certain other films that might have been out there at that time, on that basis. So, the challenge seemed to be to make it seem like it was fun and appeal to what might be - it can't be about the movie. So, that's why when we wrote it we didn't talk about the plot or anything because number one there was three or four vignettes. So, it was hard to tell people there was a story; we couldn't sell three different stories. So, what we were selling was the experience of the movie, that you're gonna have fun if you go there. Like I said, the product differentiation would be, 'This is a movie you'll have fun going to see.' So, we didn't promise the best production value or get bogged down in the story. So, anyway, we wanted people to smile or laugh at the trailer to communicate if you're laughing at the trailer and enjoying the trailer you're going to enjoy the experience of the movie. Now, the one thing we could control - this is just a long way of getting back to Percy - the one thing we could control for production value was getting the very best voice we could for the trailer. And someone who could have the horror thing, but drip it with irony. And that's why I chose Percy. As far as Percy Rodriguez, he was as fine a gentleman, as classy a person to work with and his performances always speak for themselves."

Besides the theatrical trailers, *Creepshow 2*'s television spots would also be handled by Drazen and this is where Rusty Citron and New World would show off their flair for creativity. For the TV spots the Creep is seen sitting inside a packed movie theater laughing maniacally at the images on the screen, while the crowd screams and cowers in fear. This inspired advertisement is easily one of the best movie TV spots of all time and is still memorable to genre fans today. "I remember that it was shot in our screening room," laughs Citron. "It was actually done in the New World screening room."

"I wrote that and if memory serves I directed it. I mean, I just don't want...you're writing a book, someone could read the book, I wouldn't want anyone to think I was taking their credit, but I'm pretty sure that I directed it. I think we shot it in the theater screening room there at New World," says Marshall Drazen. "I can't recall if they had done that before. I'm sure when they had the idea, because it had the pedigree going for it and the heritage that it came from another one, I'm sure they wanted to make it more special and so they decided to do this shoot. So, I'm sure that we had to come up with something that would be relatively low budget to shoot, so we came up with that idea. I don't remember if they said shoot with the Creep or if it was my idea or whatever, but the script would have been my script and I then I directed it."

As for the quality of Drazen's work on the TV spot it made a favorable impression on *Creepshow 2*'s director. "I would have loved to been there to see it, just witness it," says Michael Gornick. "Because I thought it was very well done, very well done."

Regarding the mentioning of the spot having been shot in New World's screening room apparently New World did at times take advantage of their screening room for advertising. On the back cover of *Fangoria* #58, October 1986, an advertisement for New World's videocassette release of Lamberto Bava's *Demons* is featured with some very familiar auditorium seats in view. Unfortunately neither Drazen nor Citron could recall who the actor was playing the Creep in the spot or who provided the makeup effects for the character, nor could they remember who the voice-over talent was from it.

One of the oldest means of advertising for a motion picture is, of course, the official one sheet poster. In 1982 Warner Brothers would replace Laurel's fantastic Jack Kamen design, the Creep peering through a window as Billy reads his *Creepshow* comic book by flashlight, with Joann Daley's brilliant version of the Creep selling movie tickets from inside an old fashioned box office booth.

And just as Warner Brothers had done five years prior so too would New World as they would replace Jack Kamen's wonderful design, the Creep selling Billy the latest issue of the *Creepshow* comic at a newsstand, with Greg Winters' serviceable version of the Creep sitting inside a movie theater pointing to the screen. As to why New World decided to change the art it was for reasons you might suspect. "We wanted to keep the same theme with the original poster art and we wanted to obviously make it slightly different so that there would be no question that it was not the same movie being re-released," says Bill Shields, who was responsible for the film's international distribution at New World. "But, yeah, we wanted to keep that going because the first movie had done, you know, some reasonable business; maybe not as much as Warner Brothers would have liked, but certainly we thought the financial rewards were there. And why go out of your way to - and some people would do this - but why go out of your way to make it more difficult for people to know what they were going to see? We wanted to reach the people that liked this kind of movie and reminisce about, 'Oh, yeah! I saw the other one, it was pretty good! Yeah, this looks good!' As well as the younger teenagers growing up and saying, 'Oh, yeah, I saw the other one on TV. Yeah, this looks good!' So, we wanted to keep the same basic thing there because the *Creepshow* character, that monster there, was very good and sold tickets."

I'd love to be able to give you more detail on how Winters' artwork was created for the *Creepshow 2* poster but Winters, through a "representative", requested a substantial fee to be interviewed over the telephone, which I declined to pay. Winters would go on to do some amazing and beautiful artwork for several popular video game titles in the 1990's for both Nintendo and Sega, among other advertising assignments. It's a shame that we couldn't learn a little about his process for *Creepshow 2's* poster art.

As for the poster's tag-lines, "When the curtain goes up the terror begins" and "Good to the last gasp", once again those would fall under the umbrella of Marshall Drazen. "Yeah, I think I wrote both of those," he says. "I wish I had a fresher memory of the things, but I do believe I wrote the posters as well. But just because, you know, the fog of time it wasn't something that I would have put in my 'book'. In terms of the posters, I wrote them and forgot them."

One final form of publicity that New World utilized to help spread the word about *Creepshow 2* was an annual trade convention run by the National Association of Theatre Owners. Among the many stars who appeared at the Las Vegas held event in February 1987, which included Dan Aykroyd, Tom Cruise, and Robin Williams, were a pair of film legends from *Old Chief Wood'nhead*. "We had George Kennedy and Dorothy Lamour at Showest in our hospitality suite," says Lori (Koonin) Schneider.

"Every year there's an event called ShoWest - or there used to be, it's now called CinemaCon - and what we did is that we would host a...it was called like a buffet or cocktail hour, something like that, and that's when most of the studios would bring in their stars and they'd talk about the movies," explains Rusty Citron. "So we decided, especially for exhibitors, because most exhibitors were older guys who had known who Dorothy Lamour was, and certainly George Kennedy. And it wound up being very successful; I don't think it aided that much to the movie itself, but we were able to get some press attention which, at that point, is all that it's about anyway."

"People were lined up. And I tell you the exhibitors at ShoWest, you know, a lot of the exhibitors, at least back then, were older men and to them Dorothy Lamour was, I guess, a sex symbol from their era," Lori (Koonin) Schneider adds. "So, people were anxious to come and take their pictures with her."

One final note regarding the ShoWest convention: in another ingenious marketing move New World brought with them a pair of Bally Midway pinball machines featuring the Greg Winters *Creepshow 2* theatrical poster art on the back-glass for attendees to play at their leisure. Talk about a collector's item! In reality the games were both *Strange Science* pinball machines, recently manufactured in November 1986, which featured comic book type artwork in the game's playfield.

One of the most sensible ideas to promote the release of *Creepshow 2* would sadly never reach the film's intended audience. In 1982 Plume Books, a division of New American Library, released the comic adaptation of *Creepshow* featuring original artwork by the late, great Bernie Wrightson. For its sequel Laurel hoped to do something similar, this time through Marvel Comics. And with Laurel having a prior working relationship with Jim Shooter on the attempted *Copperhead* project this seemed like a no-brainer.

The man who would adapt George Romero's screenplay into a comic book script was David Michelinie. Having had prior experience with movie adaptations such as 1983's *Krull* and 1984's *Indiana Jones and the Temple of Doom*, Michelinie was a smart choice, understanding the material well, considering he was an admirer of Stephen King's work. Working under editor Bob Budiansky's direction Michelinie would handle the writing chores on all three tales, as well as the wraparound story.

As for the artists who would tackle the stories for Marvel they would consist of John Ridgway - who would handle *Old Chief Wood'nhead*, Kelley Jones - who would work on *The Raft*, and Hilary Barta - who would design the adaptation's cover; apparently no one was picked for *The Hitchhiker* or the wraparound story before the project met its untimely fate. "I was never directly involved with the business end of the project," says Michelinie. "What I was *told* was that the production company had granted Marvel the comic book adaptation rights, but when the book was nearly completed Mr. King's representatives advised Mr. Romero's people that their deal did not include those rights. So, the project was canceled."

"I was heartbroken over that. And it was one of those things where I had always felt like the best thing I had done was never gonna see the light of day," laughs Kelley Jones.

Strangely, Jim Shooter had no memory at all as to why the adaptation was axed, or the project even being at Marvel for that matter, so Michelinie's recollection is perhaps the closest thing there is to a legitimate explanation. However, there's a caveat I learned during my research which contradicts the story Michelinie was told, a caveat regarding King's enthusiasm for the comic from Kelley Jones. "They (Marvel) had to run stuff by the company (Laurel/New World); but primarily Stephen King, who was very much into...you know, he loved comics. He had liked what I had done quite a bit and at that point had asked if I would do the whole thing," says Jones. "I never spoke with him, that just came through my editor who had made the comment, 'It's gonna be tough to edit you'; when Stephen King says this is what he wants they really then can't change what you're doing. It was funny, but they said, 'We just ran it by thinking he'd want changes, he didn't, he wants you to do the whole thing', and then they had to tell him that wasn't possible because of the deadline and whatnot; but it was a big coup for me to have that happen."

Right: Full page advertisement for the film on the back cover of the June 1987 double issue of *Cinefantastique* magazine.

THE MASTERS OF THE MACABRE
STEPHEN KING AND GEORGE A. ROMERO WELCOME YOU TO

CREEPSHOW 2

WHEN THE CURTAIN
GOES UP
THE TERROR BEGINS.

GOOD TO
THE LAST GASP.

NEW WORLD PICTURES PRESENTS A LAUREL PRODUCTION

CREEPSHOW 2 STARRING LOIS CHILES GEORGE KENNEDY DOROTHY LAMOUR AND TOM SAVINI AS "THE CREEP"

MUSIC COMPOSED BY LES REED AND RICK WAKEMAN ASSOCIATE PRODUCER MITCHELL GALIN

EXECUTIVE PRODUCER RICHARD P. RUBINSTEIN SCREENPLAY BY GEORGE A. ROMERO BASED ON STORIES BY STEPHEN KING PRODUCED BY DAVID BALL

NEW WORLD PICTURES
© 1987 NEW WORLD PICTURES. ALL RIGHTS RESERVED.

DIRECTED BY MICHAEL GORNICK

R RESTRICTED
UNDER 17 REQUIRES ACCOMPANYING
PARENT OR ADULT GUARDIAN

SPECIAL MIDNIGHT SHOW THURSDAY, APRIL 30

WESTWOOD
Mann Westwood 208-7664

HOLLYWOOD
Hollywood Pacific 464-4111

Regular Engagement STARTS FRIDAY at a Theatre or Drive-In Near You

He didn't know who I was, he just reacted to the fact that he felt that I had captured the spirit of his story and that it felt like a horror comic to him - that's what they told me, that it felt like a horror comic. It had all of the atmosphere and the gruesomeness of an E.C. book, that's what he was looking for. And since I knew that stuff, a lot of guys don't, at that time they were all doing superheroes. I was a big fan of the old E.C. books; I had copies of the E.C. books, so I knew that's how I wanted it to look. And I was a big fan of the first film. So, once he gave his blessing and his endorsement it was full steam ahead."

When it came to Hilary Barta's proposed cover for the doomed adaptation, the artist did his best E.C. homage as he captured, in this writer's opinion, the authentic feel of those classic horror comics from a bygone era. Barta's design showcases a cackling Creep in the foreground as he calls your attention to a freshly dug grave, complete with a R.I.P. headstone, in the background. It was the perfect cover. "Oddly, I recall that I drew this on spec - on my own - without being given the job by the editor," Barta says. "I can't recall much else about it, but outside of, 'What the...?!', it was rare for me to be drawing covers for Marvel."

A final interesting and relevant aspect to this whole fiasco of the comic adaptation being axed is the fact that in late 1986, either right before work on the comic began or shortly afterwards, New World Pictures purchased the Marvel Entertainment Group. The sale, which according to *The Los Angeles Times* was rumored to be in the neighborhood of 40 to 50 million dollars, involved Marvel Comics Group, based out of New York, Marvel Comics Ltd, based in England, and Marvel Productions, which produced animated films and TV shows out of Los Angeles. "We bought Marvel, we wanted to expand, we had the cash and we made an offer on Marvel," says New World Pictures head honcho Bob Rehme. "Marvel was privately owned by a bunch of investors, not big investors, but they had...it was simply a publishing company at that time. Stan Lee was still involved at that time, but the management was some other people; we went and we bought that. I tried to expand Marvel into a company like it is today; we weren't able to do that at that time. It was over thirty years ago, it was before we did *Creepshow 2*. I knew that Marvel had the potential that it has now, what it's doing."

New World would utilize Marvel, to a certain degree, during its marketing of *Creepshow 2*. When the film was featured at ShoWest in Las Vegas decorative balloons featuring Marvel characters such as Captain America were placed alongside the *Creepshow 2* pinball machines on display. In New York, as early as *Creepshow 2*'s opening weekend, New World was publicizing "The Wedding of The Amazing Spider-Man" which was a publicity stunt held before the New York Mets vs. Pittsburgh Pirates baseball game on Friday, June 5, 1987. "Come to a Marvel-ous night at Shea Stadium..." read the baseball graphic which was featured on the giant, full-page *Creepshow 2* ad slick in *The New York Times*.

Left: Full page advertisement in the April 26, 1987 edition of *The Los Angeles Times*.

Speaking of comics I recall during the release of *Creepshow 2* a local comic book store I frequented in my hometown of Savannah, Georgia giving away full size one sheet posters for the film. These one sheets had an additional fold in them that made them roughly the size in diameter of a paperback novel when completely folded and I remember picking one up while in the shop one day. During my interviews with former New World Pictures publicity staff no one could recall the posters being a part of their marketing for the film, but obviously it would have made sense to target comic book shops with some form of advertising at the time.

Another memorable form of promotion for *Creepshow 2* that I vividly remember from my long ago youth was an appearance by Tom Savini on *Late Night with David Letterman* in late April 1987. Unfortunately the amount of attention the film received during the roughly 11 minute segment amounted to a total of about 12 seconds! To be fair Savini was interrupted by Letterman just as he was raising up a photo of himself to discuss his Creep makeup so they could instead see an explosives demonstration Savini had brought along. Towards the end of the appearance, which would turn out to be the final one for the legendary effects artist on Letterman's show, Savini is setting up a demonstration on the late night television host to show how someone is shot in the head in a motion picture. As Savini once again attempts to promote *Creepshow 2* he is hilariously foiled by the agitated Letterman: "Okay, but I do have to mention *Creepshow 2* is opening May 1," Savini said. "Fine, yeah. Before you assassinate the host, get in a plug," scoffed Letterman in response. **(1)**

Incidentally on this very same day that Savini appeared with Letterman Laurel Entertainment would run a full page ad in the daily *Variety* for *Creepshow 2*. In the black and white advertisement the spectral version of the Creep, similar to the one in the Greg Winters poster art, is seen standing outside an office door that says New World Pictures. As the Creep knocks on the door with his left hand he's holding a film cannister in his right with the *Creepshow 2* logo on it. Above the Creep's head is a classic comic word balloon/bubble with the words, "Hi, I'm from Laurel Entertainment and I'm here to deliver *Creepshow 2*". At the bottom of the page just above Laurel's company name and address is another word balloon/bubble which says, "Thank you New World". **(2)**

With *Creepshow 2*'s release date rapidly approaching a special screening of the film for cast and crew was held in New York City, just a day before its May 1 national opening. On April 30, 1987 Laurel hosted a 7 o'clock evening showing at the Eastside Cinema on Third Avenue in midtown Manhattan. Even though the majority of those I interviewed didn't remember much regarding the screening there were a couple of people who did recall attending the event and how fun and jovial the mood was. One of those was "Billy" himself, Domenick John Sportelli. "I didn't know anyone there; I do remember being introduced to various people. But the one thing that I remember about the screening that stands out as being so cool for me as a kid was watching this horror movie with the people that were in it and when their characters were killed or something

New World Pictures
cordially invites you and a guest
to attend a special screening.

 NEW WORLD PICTURES

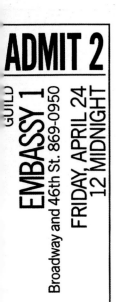

ADMIT 2

GUILD
EMBASSY 1
Broadway and 46th St. 869-0950
FRIDAY, APRIL 24
12 MIDNIGHT

 and New World Pictures
cordially invites you and a guest to a screening

FROM THE MASTERS OF THE MACABRE STEPHEN KING AND GEORGE A. ROMERO

NEW WORLD PICTURES PRESENTS A LAUREL PRODUCTION CREEPSHOW 2
STARRING LOIS CHILES GEORGE KENNEDY DOROTHY LAMOUR AND TOM SAVINI AS "THE CREEP"
MUSIC COMPOSED BY LES REED AND RICK WAKEMAN ASSOCIATE PRODUCER MITCHELL GALIN
EXECUTIVE PRODUCER RICHARD P. RUBINSTEIN SCREENPLAY BY GEORGE A. ROMERO BASED ON STORIES BY STEPHEN KING
NEW WORLD PICTURES PRODUCED BY DAVID BALL DIRECTED BY MICHAEL GORNICK [R] RESTRICTED UNDER 17 REQUIRES ACCOMPANYING PARENT OR ADULT GUARDIAN
1987 NEW WORLD PICTURES ALL RIGHTS RESERVED

THIS INVITATION IS NOT TRANSFERABLE. PLEASE ARRIVE EARLY, SEATING IS LIMITED TO THEATRE CAPACIT

crazy happened in the movie, them just laughing. So, it was more like a comedy experience than it was a horror movie screening," Sportelli says. "One of the girls in *The Raft* - I specifically remember this - when the slime comes up and grabs her face and she was melting I just remember her cracking up, like laughing, 'Oh my god!', like just laughing, that she couldn't believe that was happening to her on screen and it looked so great. But that's what I really recall from the screening and that changed my view a lot about movies and horror movies and stuff; just seeing how these actors and actresses watch themselves get killed and it's actually kind of funny."

"My recollection of that screening was that it was

Above: Advance special screening invitation from New World Pictures at the Embassy 1 in New York City on April 24, 1987. (courtesy of Taso Stavrakis)

primarily cast, crew and some press people, and probably some of the distributor's reps," says author Paul Gagne, who was in town to pick up copies of his soon to be released magnum opus on the career of George Romero, *The Zombies That Ate Pittsburgh*, from his publisher Dodd, Mead & Company. "I think my strongest recollection isn't something specific, but more of a general perception of what was a really upbeat mood among the cast, crew and film-makers in the theater that night. For many of these

PEPSI.
THE CHOICE OF A NEW GENERATION.

Stephen King's
CREEPSHOW II
to Benefit
Red Cross Flood Relief
May 14, 1987
Bangor Cinema 8 — Bangor, Maine
THURSDAY, 7 P.M.
Presented by Z-62, Bangor Cinema 8, Pepsi-Cola Bottling
GENERAL ADMISSION

00006

people, this was the first major film they worked on that wasn't directed by George. I wouldn't quite compare it to college kids being away from home for the first time, but it was a little like that. The first time testing their wings without the parents, finding out they could fly, and feeling really, really good about it. If that makes any sense? Plus a lot of laughing during the film at what I assume were in-jokes from the production."

On May 1, 1987 *Creepshow 2* was unleashed in the United States opening in 867 theaters across the country. Interestingly enough New World decided not to follow up on an opening day promotion that Warner Brothers had run in 1982 in a lot of major U.S. cities: if you came dressed as the Creep you could get in for free if you were one of the first 25 in Atlanta, 50 in Pittsburgh, 98 in Dallas, or 300 in Los Angeles in line that day. However, New World would schedule midnight shows in larger cities for *Creepshow 2* the evening before its opening date. In Los Angeles you could catch it at the Mann Plaza in Westwood and at the Hollywood Pacific in Hollywood, while in New York City you could get an early peek at the Embassy 1 in Manhattan.

The regional release pattern New World utilized - not

Above: Ticket stub from one of two benefit screenings held at the Bangor Mall Cinema 8 on May 14, 1987. The profits went to assist victims of the April 1987 floods which devastated parts of Maine. Stephen King was on hand to introduce the film before each screening. (courtesy of Lori Huckabey)

as limited as the one United Film Distribution Company implemented for George Romero's *Day of the Dead* in 1985 though - had the film opening in major territories across the country such as New York, Los Angeles, Chicago, Atlanta, Dallas, Philadelphia, and San Francisco. However, it wouldn't reach Boston until three weeks later when it premiered on May 22 and incredibly wouldn't open in cities such as Denver, Minneapolis, Indianapolis, Seattle, and Pittsburgh until four weeks afterwards on May 29! The film opened in my little hometown of Savannah, Georgia before it would finally reach Pittsburgh; that's amazing. "At the time it saved money because you had to buy prints. I mean, this was the day where physically you had to buy prints and they had to be shipped and all that sort of stuff to theaters. And when you have an exploitation...you know, let's be honest, as much as I like horror movies they're still exploitation films. So, in the areas that you're going to have the most receptive audiences - which are pretty much the areas that you read off - you wanted to go there first. And then after some of those theaters come off after several weeks you can take those prints, which were in those days costing...I don't remember exactly what they cost but it was quite a number of hundreds of dollars each, you could take those and have them shipped to other theaters. So, you would reuse the prints, otherwise you would have to literally throw them away or have them destroyed. So, rather than putting out a thousand, two thousand screens all at once you went regionally; this saved a certain amount of money," explains New World's Bill Shields. "It also allowed you to adjust. For example, a market like Boston, which was a more highbrow market and didn't respond as well to horror movies, exploitation type movies, as other parts of the country; you know, you would have some success at your back, you would get the good theaters from the exhibitors because you'd say, 'Alright, it had already done a lot of business even though it's not the perfect picture for the Boston area.' So, you'd have some leverage there in terms of what terms the theaters were going to pay you back. And you would have some leverage and then you would move in, hopefully, on a level of success. Initially the picture did a certain amount of business, most of the business in the first week, but it was still respectable the second and third week."

Creepshow 2 would start strong in both New York and L.A. where it would finish number 1 at the box office its opening weekend; New York in particular took to the film where it would gross $1 million of its $3.6 million opening. However, nationwide it would trail behind Michael J. Fox's *The Secret of My Success* which bested the film by a million dollars during the weekend of May 1-3, 1987. A caveat to that number though is *Creepshow 2* opened on 466 fewer screens than *The Secret of My Success*, which was in its fourth week of release, meaning New World's little horror picture earned roughly $700 more per screen than Universal's major release.

The film would eventually stop tracking by the end of June around the $13.5 million mark - with a final total today of $14 million at the box office - which isn't gang-busters business, but it wasn't a dud either. It would make the *Variety* Show Business Annual Edition's rundown of the big films of 1987, which reflected their collected domestic rentals for distributors that year. With total rentals of 4,900,000 it finished well ahead of other genre fare released the same year such as *Evil Dead 2*, *The Monster Squad*, and *Near Dark*. The film was profitable for New World and compares to other well-known genre films they released during that era such as *Children of the Corn* and *Hellraiser*. "Movie speaks for itself in that it was the 2nd highest grossing film for New World while under the new management," says Richard Rubinstein. And while that's not totally accurate - the film's box office would actually trail behind titles such as *Angel*, *Soul Man*, and *Flowers in the Attic* - it certainly fared better than the typical New World release.

As for the film's international distribution, New World partnered with third party distributors who released their films in foreign markets. The international rollout for *Creepshow 2* would begin, depending on the country, as early as the U.S. release in May 1987 with Canada (which surprisingly isn't really considered international) or as late

as January 1988 with France. In England Entertainment Films, a company that specialized in low budget genre fare such as *The Prowler*, *Re-Animator*, and *Troll*, would handle the film's release in November 1987. In Italy Eagle Pictures, a fairly new distributor at the time, would oversee the release, while in Spain Union Films would be responsible for *Creepshow 2*'s exhibition. In Canada - depending on the province in which you lived - the film was distributed by New World Mutual Pictures of Canada, which covered most of English speaking Canada such as Ontario, Alberta, and British Columbia. However in Quebec, a majority French speaking province, Films René Malo would handle the distribution duties. Unfortunately, in the Nordic region of the globe - Sweden, Norway, and Finland - it would have to contend with censorship issues. It would open strong in Sydney, Australia where it took in $71,200 at a dozen locations, finishing on top in its debut "down under".

As for the critical reception the film earned, it wasn't very pretty. Despite the fact that the original itself was met with a lukewarm response, the lack of as much direct involvement this time around from Romero and King, partnered with a lower budget and fewer stories, didn't go unnoticed with critics.

"Tied together with some humdrum animated sequences, three vignettes on offer obviously were produced on the absolute cheap, mostly in the wilderness with a minimal number of actors," read *Variety*. "All are so deficient in imagination and scare quotient they wouldn't even pass as even satisfactory episodes on a TV show like *Amazing Stories* or *The Twilight Zone*." **(3)**

"*Creepshow 2* dredges up two unpublished and one published Stephen King stories for this three-yarn, macabre sequel," *The Hollywood Reporter*'s Duane Byrge said. "Unfortunately, this isn't baseball, and one out of three isn't good - the two never-printed tales are worthy of staying in the vault." **(4)**

"*Creepshow 2* is a cut-rate sequel from those two popular masters of horror, Stephen King and George Romero, that plays like leftovers," said Kevin Thomas in *The Los Angeles Times*. "Fans of both deserve better." **(5)**

"As directed by Michael Gornick, with a screenplay by George A. Romero, *Creepshow 2* has three suitably grisly ideas that are only glancingly developed," wrote Janet Maslin in *The New York Times*. "The episodes are marginally interesting, but each is a little too long. And each could be fully explained in a one-sentence synopsis." **(6)**

"Standing in line for a sold out showing of *Creepshow 2* at the Embassy in Times Square, I was amazed at the huge crowd. It reminded me of a hoard of the dead - milling around in the neon, jostling for position, subject to periodic outbreaks of violence. An auspicious beginning, but I soon discovered the creeps outside were more interesting than the creeps inside," read the opening paragraph of Melanie Pitts' review in *The Village Voice*. And as unfriendly as her opening was, the finale was even harsher. "Fortunately, as the stories died, the audience came viciously to life, booing and hissing with surprising energy. 'What is this shit?!' exclaimed some, and I had to sympathize. After all, the dead know rot when they see it." **(7)**

"King appears as a truck driver in one scene. But those

Left: New World's version of the Creep from their brilliant television spot advertising the film's release. (courtesy of Michael Gornick) **Above:** Box office advertisement from New World featured in the May 9, 1987 issue of *Screen International*.

who want to keep up with the King oeuvre may want to bring a flashlight so they can read one of his novels while watching this film," Ralph Novak of *People* magazine proclaimed. "It's hardly worth devoting a whole attention span to." **(8)**

"But these tales aren't as frightening as they are grisly and hard-edged - no kid (or adult, for that matter) would want to curl up in bed with these," said Patricia Smith of the *Chicago Sun-Times*. "In fact, the only kids I can imagine enjoying these stories in comic-book form are those who enjoy torturing ants with matches." **(9)**

"*Creepshow 2* is a tepid, protracted near-zero of a movie that sells very well its first week only because sequels to horror hits do anyway and because the names Romero and King matter in marketing the genre," wrote Ed Blank of *The Pittsburgh Press*. "The prolific King, who more often than not seems only a hack, has outdone himself in coming up with next to nothing new. Most of *2* is mildewed slew." **(10)**

"Though it's never a bad movie, *Creepshow 2* is amazingly tame and plodding. Even the appearance of several name actors, including George Kennedy, Dorothy Lamour, Lois Chiles, and King himself in a cameo, does little to spiff up this generally lackluster movie," Marylynn Uricchio penned in the *Pittsburgh Post-Gazette*. Despite her negative review Uricchio would manage to throw in an honorable mention at the end of her review for the film's director. "Michael Gornick, who has worked as a cinematographer for Romero, directed the sequel, and though he is obviously restrained by a small budget and

the transparent nature of the individual stories, he adds some nice touches." **(11)**

Even in *The Times Recorder*, a small newspaper in Zanesville, Ohio, whose film critic was Tom Brown, the guy who played the memorable "chef zombie" in *Day of the Dead*, the film couldn't get any respect earning a D- from the former Wampum mine zombie extra. "It is not scary, the pacing is lousy and King's stories here are no example whatsoever of the talent the guy has. In short, it's a get-rich-quick cheapie loaded with unnecessary blood-letting and silly animation in between the three rotten stories," Brown wrote in his review before delivering the coup de grace. "Concluding, I was sorely disappointed in 'Creepshow II'. No humor, imagination, originality, scares and sadly no George Romero directing." **(12)**

Despite the film failing to hit with mainstream critics in America, it would nonetheless find acceptance with others across the country that recognized the film for what it was intended to be.

"Actually, King is the most moral of men. In all his work, the wages of sin is death," wrote Chris Chase in New York's *Daily News*. "Anyone who practices vehicular homicide in a King fable pays dearly for the error, and if you kill a nice old man and his wife, you'll very likely get an arrow through your brain. For what it is - an unpretentious thriller - *Creepshow 2* is just dandy." **(13)** By the way, I would be remiss in not mentioning that part of Chase's review - "As scary as anything you're apt to see" - would be featured at

Above: Daniel Beer, star of *The Raft*, poses in front of the United Artists Twin, formerly the Rivoli Theatre, in New York's Times Square. The once grand theatre would sadly close not long afterwards. (courtesy of Daniel Beer) **Left:** The old Capitol Theatre in Singapore showcasing advertising art for the film's release there, along with *Robocop*. (courtesy of Lee Karr)

the top of upcoming ad slicks and advertising for the film, including the eventual VHS home video release, which was actually Chase referencing *The Hitchhiker* episode, in case you were wondering.

A second review of the film would appear just a few days later in the *Daily News*, this time from "The Phantom of the Movies", Joe Kane. "While it lacks some of *Creepshow*'s freshness and star power (though Lois Chiles, Dorothy Lamour, and George Kennedy are on hand), *Creepshow 2* is a suitably sick crowd-pleaser in its own right," the Phantom proclaimed. "As long as this eerie series sticks with proven format rather than hack formula, the Phantom wouldn't mind seeing a *Creepshow 3*." **(14)**

"*Creepshow 2* is a nice diversion for a hungry horror fan's night out," Daniel Aquilante proclaimed in the *New York Post*. Like the aforementioned review by Chris Chase, a blurb from Aquilante's review - "Made me squirm in my seat" - would make its way into the film's advertising campaign. And if you're curious as to what exactly made Aquilante squirm in his seat it was *The Raft* segment which apparently played into his own fears of being conscious while being eaten alive. "One by one they're sucked down and gobbled up by the goo," Aquilante wrote. "The only lesson I got out of that was it takes a guy like Steve McQueen to beat a blob." **(15)**

"*Creepshow II* is a fast-food film: fatty, half-baked, more salty than tasteful and cooked up for mass consumption," wrote Tony DeSena in the *New Jersey Herald*. "Trouble is, sometimes junk food really hits the spot." **(16)**

"*Creepshow 2* is one of those frivolous, cheap-scare flicks that I really can't slag too much," Mary Ann Murdoch said in the *Ocala Star-Banner*. "Its purpose is singular - to provide a few gasps and squeals - and it achieves that goal." **(17)**

"The movie has a lot going for it. Many parts are morbidly funny, and there are a lot of sick puns," wrote Linda Cook in Davenport, Iowa's *Quad-City Times*. "The exaggerated characters, the none-too-eloquent dialogue and stark camera shots all make the movie seem like a moving comic book." **(18)**

"I found myself laughing more than being 'scared', but perhaps that's the way *Creepshow II* is intended," wrote Jack Kegg in Cumberland, Maryland's *Cumberland News*. "Look closely, kids, amidst the blood and guts there are lessons to be learned in each of these stories. I hope you get the message." **(19)**

"The anthology film comprises three frightening stories that recall *The Twilight Zone*. Of course, the film is bolder and bloodier - with Stephen King and George Romero doing the writing, what would you expect?," said Hal Boedeker of the *Miami Herald*. "But beneath the surface shocks, the storytelling has some of the imagination, humor, and skill that distinguished Rod Serling's work." **(20)**

As for Michael Gornick, while it wasn't exactly enjoyable to see his work so easily disregarded for the most part, it wasn't really a shock either. "It wasn't unexpected, you know. I knew going into it that sequels always suffer from that comparison to the original," he says. "And this one had a lot going against it because George was not involved, it was three stories versus the five...so, was it disappointing? No, I mean, it was making money. I mean, for a brief period of time, that one week, it was top box office. It was all positive. And in general the acceptance was the fact that yes I could do it, I could deliver, even under stress, a motion picture that could make money; that all felt good. So, I was waiting for the next project, which never came."

Regarding the genre print coverage the film received, unlike its predecessor, the spotlight was minimal. In 1982/1983 the original *Creepshow* had numerous genre periodicals

Right top, middle and bottom: Interestingly some of the European lobby cards – like these from Spain, England, and Germany respectively - went with images that were either from rehearsals or were silly publicity shots: the kids lounging on the beach from *The Raft*, Dorothy Lamour wearing glasses in a scene from *Old Chief Wood'nhead* in which she does not, and Tom Wright without makeup appliances menacing Lois Chiles who's wearing a completely different top than the one she wears in *The Hitchhiker*.

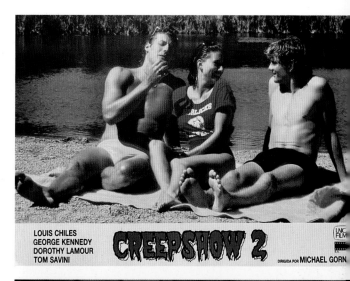

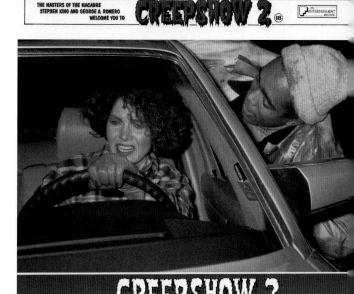

5,- DM 1/88
Phantastische Zeiten
Science Fiction · Horror · Kino · Comic
HORROR
James Herbert
Der neue
Meister des Grauens
KINO
ROBOCOP
CREEPSHOW II
Masters of
the Univers
SCIENCE FICTION
Sex im Weltraum
Neue Serie: Erotik in der Phantastik
FANTASY-COMICS
Über Zeichner und die Szene

Above: One of the rare times *Creepshow 2* was given front cover publicity in a genre periodical. *Phantastische Zeiten*, German for "Fantastic Times", honored the film with a spectacular cover and five pages of coverage inside its pages.

which showered the film with attention: *Fangoria*, *Cinefantastique*, *Fantastic Films*, and *Famous Monsters of Filmland* were all more than happy to cover the dream-team project of Romero and King in detail.

In 1987 the sequel wouldn't fare quite as well with the same media which, frankly, should have done more to promote the picture. "I had been on other sets. Like, I went on the set of *The Fly*. That was my first big *Fangoria* set visit and I did four, maybe five, articles on it. But this one, it just wasn't warranted," says *Fangoria*'s Tony Timpone. "I remember the photos really weren't that good. Most of the pictures I wound up getting for the movie were from Everett Burrell. Yeah, the photos just weren't that good. This was also when *A Nightmare on Elm Street* was all the rage and we were doing constant coverage on that. Empire Pictures was churning out these movies. And it also might be because I saw an early screening of the film and to be honest with you I thought it was a dog, I thought it was really bad. So, I might have cut down on the coverage for that reason, too. You know, I just didn't think it was that good. But, thinking back, I think, the main reason was we didn't get photo support and there really weren't as many angles to cover. It's like we used to do these articles after the movie came out, but the effects in the movie really weren't anything that special to warrant the follow-up article. We did a follow-up with Gornick. But there weren't any really big genre people in the movie either. You had these Hollywood veterans like George Kennedy and Dorothy Lamour who weren't exactly *Fangoria* people. So, there really weren't any other good angles to support for follow-up stories, so that was another reason."

As mentioned back in the Day 26 and Day 27 sections of Chapter 3 writer Wolf Forrest had visited the set of *Creepshow 2* in Arizona as a member of the media working on a freelance piece for *Cinefantastique* magazine. Five years prior writer Paul Gagne, author of *The Zombies That Ate Pittsburgh*, had visited the set of the original *Creepshow* in Pittsburgh and penned a massive 20 page article about the making of that film for *Cinefantastique*. According to Forrest something similar was planned here as well, a large multifaceted piece examining the production in detail, but unfortunately things didn't work out as planned with only a 1 page teaser article appearing in the "Coming" section of the June 1987 issue.

After departing Prescott, with more than 80 behind-the-scenes photographs in hand, and returning to his home in Tucson, Forrest sent a summary of his set visit to the editor, the late Frederick S. Clarke, in Chicago and that's when things started to get complicated. "The first dispute occurred over ownership/copyright issues of the photographs: first-time use for the magazine, then rights reverted to me, unless there was some later publication planned," explains Forrest. "I was not restricted to any word length. The article that appeared was designed specifically as a lead-in to the second article, which I wrote during negotiations with Clarke. When I sent my first article, along with about 20 photographs, only one of which was used, I told him there were others that would be supplied with the second article, but I wanted to resolve the rights issue before any more photos were sent. I sent him dupes of my original slides, telling him so, and he insisted on getting the originals. Mr. Clarke maintained that all photos were property of the magazine and needed to be sent ASAP, and I told him that I would at least need to be paid up front for everything, and then the rest of the photos and the second article would be sent. I was still writing the second article at the time, but then negotiations broke down and I never finished it. None of these particulars was outlined in the first communique he sent me; there was never a real contract, it was relatively casual, done on a virtual handshake, you could say. I don't think any more articles appeared about *Creepshow 2* in subsequent issues - whether it was because I held key components that prevented a complete analysis or coverage got squeezed out by other films, I can only speculate."

For the record, while deciding not to cover the film as in-depth as he had with the original *Creepshow*, Clarke did give the picture a "good" review in the September 1987 issue of his *Cinefantastique* magazine. He also published a full page ad for the film on the back cover of the June 1987 issue.

Quickly I'd like to backtrack for a minute to mention a rather special premiere for the film that took place in Bangor,

Maine. In early April 1987 some of the worst flooding in Maine's history hit the state destroying hundreds of homes - while flooding thousands of others - wiping out roads and bridges, and causing over $100 million dollars in damage. Spearheaded by the local Pine Tree chapter of the American Red Cross a flood relief campaign was organized to help raise money for flood victims. Included in that effort were a pair of special showings on Thursday, May 14, 1987 of *Creepshow 2* at the local Bangor Mall Cinema 8. Appearing at both shows that night to introduce the film was none other than Stephen King himself, whose radio station WZON participated in the relief efforts. "Stephen King was indeed there; he made a short speech before the movie began," remembers lifelong fan Lori Huckabey, who was at the 7 o'clock screening that night. "I remember him, the crowd, and the reporters afterwards. We were asked our favorite segment on the way out and I told them I loved *The Hitchhiker* the most. I now love all the stories equally, but in 1987 and at 14 years old that one had the most scare factor to me. Not to mention King's classic cameo and recognizing the streets where it was filmed! It was an amazing evening...and a school night at that!"

As for the crowd in the theater with Huckabey that night, what did they think? "The place went wild when King's cameo came up! Much clapping and cheering throughout the film, but the cameo put it over the top. It is one of his best in my humble opinion," she says. "*Creepshow 2* has since become one of my favorite King films. It's much too underrated."

And before we move on I should also mention a more personal screening of the film that was shared between two crew members - David Ball and Rebecca Mayo. Back in Arizona that May to do some location scouting for a potential western film project he was looking into, which we'll return to shortly, Ball decided he'd take in a showing of *Creepshow 2* with Mayo, who he had recruited once again to help out with coordinating things for him. "He and I went together in Phoenix, it was May and I believe it was Memorial Day weekend of '87 when the movie came out, and he and I went to a Harkins movie theater in Phoenix and David Ball and I watched *Creepshow 2* on the big screen together, as it came out, as it debuted. We critiqued the whole thing all the way through the movie," laughs Mayo. "We sat in the audience critiquing it like, 'Oh my god! Can you see a shadow there? Oh that camera angle was wrong!' You know, blah, blah, blah...and we were critiquing it the whole time and I'm sure people around us in the theater wanted to kick us out."

The reason I mention wanting to return to the location scouting trip is because of how eventful it turned out to be for Mayo and Ball, their own personal horror story you might say. "We were on a location scout in a helicopter, it had to be late afternoon, flying around Weavers Needle in the Superstition Mountains, that has been such a famous location for many, many western films," Mayo recalls. "And

Above and below: The aborted comic adaptation of *Creepshow 2* from Marvel Comics featured a perfect E.C. inspired cover design by Hilary Barta of the Creep and contained amazing artwork by Kelley Jones for *The Raft* story. It's an absolute shame it was never published. (courtesy of Hilary Barta and Kelley Jones)

we were up in the air and we lost our rotor power up on top and we went spiraling down to earth. I remember we all had headsets on, headphones, and our pilot was a seasoned Vietnam veteran and he was saying, 'Well, it's gonna be a rough landing. I'm gonna try and land us in between two rocky cliffs on the ground and I'm gonna hopefully land us upright. So, just hang on and don't panic.' And he did. We went spiraling down to earth. Our pilot managed to land the producer and I, and himself upright, a little bit at an angle, on a rocky piece of dirt in between mountain ranges and steep cliffs as we went down behind Weavers Needle (laughs). And we survived!"

After the film's release Michael Gornick would begin to hear from some of those involved who were instrumental in helping him bring his sequel to life, and their encouraging and thoughtful words were much appreciated by the veteran film-maker. "Mike, most of the reviews I saw were fairly negative - which I'm sure doesn't bother you much since the film is doing so well, and how often *do* critics like films in this genre?," wrote *Old Chief Wood'nhead* performer Dan Kamin in a June 1987 letter. "But I think a lot of them missed some of your fine, unusual work in the film. I was particularly pleased and impressed with the strong atmosphere you gave to each scene. Some of the establishing shots, particularly in my sequence, were beautiful. The look of the film evokes wonderful, pastoral Americana - maybe that undercuts some of the horrific content, but I found it very sweet." **(21)**

"Well Mike, I'm so glad that 'Creepshow' is doing O.K., it makes all our hard work worth while doesn't it," editor Peter Weatherley penned in a hand written letter from July 1987. "Only hope it brings your name & work to notice and you get a few offers to direct, you deserve it." **(22)**

More than anyone though Gornick had hoped to hear feedback from the two men who conjured up the film's stories for him to direct, Stephen King and George Romero; that particular correspondence, unfortunately, was not as forthcoming. "You know, we never all sat in a room together, discussed this, either before or after the fact and said, 'Did it work? What did I do?' Unfortunately, Stephen was far too busy; he offered his pleasure subsequently to me that it was good and he wanted to work again with me and so I knew that was something positive," explains Gornick. "George and I didn't have a healthy relationship after or during the making of *Creepshow 2* and so I never got his final input. But I did hear subsequently, I don't think in print, but I heard from somebody through the grapevine that he said it didn't work for him."

By the Fall of 1987, roughly six months after its theatrical release, *Creepshow 2* would be released on U.S. home video by New World Video. It would debut in Billboard's Top Video Cassette Rentals the week ending November 14, 1987 at number 16, peaking at number 15 the week ending November 28, 1987. Much like it did in theaters, where it wasn't necessarily a box office bonanza, *Creepshow 2*

Above right: Home video advertisement for the film featured in *Video Business* magazine. **Below right:** Rare promotional "Scream Test" film slate pin from New World Video.

Above: Immediately following the release of *Creepshow 2* Laurel would announce *Creepshow 3* in an advertisement in the May 6, 1987 issue of *Variety*. Ultimately, the world wouldn't see a *Creepshow 3* until 2006 when Taurus Entertainment released it, without the involvement of any of the original film's creators.

would do well enough for itself at the video store where it was a steady title. "I think the movie was profitable. I don't think it was *very* profitable. I mean, it was a low enough budget that it was hard for it not to make money," says Mitchell Galin. "It was also the world of the VHS. I mean, that was the VIG of the studio, was always the VHS deals. It's like they yelled down the hall saying, 'Hey, we're making *Creepshow 2*? Do you want to release it on your label?' And the guy yells back, 'Of course!' And for that they get their twenty-five or thirty percent sales commission and out of that the twenty percent royalty they get paid. So, in those days that's actually the acknowledged place where the studios kind of raped you, in terms of what's going on. And *Creepshow 2* did pretty well on VHS at the time."

So, with *Creepshow 2* now in the books and part of film history, what about a follow-up, a *Creepshow 3*? As early as May 6, 1987 - the week of *Creepshow 2*'s opening - *Creepshow 3* was already being promoted by Laurel in *Variety* along with other titles such as *Tales from the*

Darkside: The Movie, *Pet Sematary*, and *The Stand*. So, how come we never saw *Creepshow 3*, at least from Laurel Entertainment? "Well, we developed the script for it. A part of it was actually a couple of holdover scripts from the second movie," says Mitchell Galin. "We had the bones for the next one and the hope was always that the movie would do well enough that New World would want to do the next one, and it just never materialized. I think that's possibly because it capped out at whatever it capped out at, in terms of theatrically. And I'm not sure where New World was in the equation because they...within a few years after that, I'm not sure when, they went through some corporate re-configurations."

"I don't remember that the picture did all that well. It might have done okay, I don't remember," New World's Bob Rehme says. "This was kind of late in our run; I think we made this picture in '87? So, the results wouldn't have been in until '88 or so and it wasn't something that was right at the top of our list. And then we sold the company."

By the early 1990's talk started percolating again regarding a possible *Creepshow 3*, this time as a fully animated feature, with well-known artist Ralph Bakshi of *Fritz the Cat* and *The Lord of the Rings* fame attached to the project. The news was reported in *Fangoria* #100 in March 1991, but sadly nothing ever came of it. "I remember we explored an animated approach with Ralph, but no specifics," says Richard Rubinstein.

Of note here is that in a search of the U.S. copyright office a registration for a *Creepshow 3* TV promo from 1/2/1992 turned up, featuring the note "Based on the character named The Creep from *Creepshow* feature films". Interesting, what could this be? "The only thing that I personally knew of for a *Creepshow* promo or trailer beyond *Creepshow 2* was that Richard was anxious to get something off the ground in terms of a *Creepshow* series for television. And I personally composed out of the material we had at hand, meaning both *Creepshow* 1 and 2, and some material from *Tales from the Darkside*, a promo that was probably about three to four minutes that promoted this idea of a television series. And it featured the voice of the Creep as a kind of narrator about bringing *Creepshow* to television," Michael Gornick says. "I actually did the Creep because we couldn't afford...and Joe Silver had just passed away. So, I did the narration over top, which wasn't extensive. But, you know, he was the narrator for this trailer piece. So, why it became *Creepshow 3* I don't know, but who knows?"

Chapter 6 Thanks For The Ride

The decades that have followed since *Creepshow 2*'s production have been an interesting ride for so many of the players who fought and struggled to bring it to the big screen. Some went on to tremendous success in the film and television industry, both in front of and behind the camera, while others would decide to take completely different paths with their lives.

When you think of success in Hollywood there's perhaps no better example from *Creepshow 2* than the dynamic duo of Howard Berger and Greg Nicotero. Within a year of the release of *Creepshow 2*, as well as *Evil Dead 2*, Berger and Nicotero would team up with fellow effects artist Robert Kurtzman and open what would go on to become an industry powerhouse in the field of special makeup effects, KNB EFX studio. Since 1988 KNB has worked on countless movies and television shows, earning the two remaining founders, Berger and Nicotero (Kurtzman left after 2003), untold wealth, as well as enormous acclaim. Howard Berger would win both the Academy Award and the BAFTA for his work on 2005's *The Chronicles of Narnia: The Lion, the Witch, and the Wardrobe*, while Greg Nicotero would snag multiple Emmy Awards for his work on AMC's *The Walking Dead*, as well as on the Sci-Fi Channel's 2000 mini-series remake of *Dune*, executive produced by Richard Rubinstein and Mitchell Galin and written and directed by John Harrison. "Look at Greg Nicotero and Howard Berger, who came on to *Creepshow 2*. You know, now they're the biggest special effects makeup house in

Above: Rick Catizone and Michael Gornick at the "Saturday Nightmares" convention in New Jersey – June 2011. (courtesy of Rick Catizone)

Hollywood," says Charles Carroll. "And Greg directs and is an executive producer on *The Walking Dead*. I talk to Greg all the time, if I need something bizarre. I mean, I call those guys up or talk to Howard, 'Hey, can you guys help us out?' And they go, 'Yeah. Hey, man! What's up?' They're cool and they're hugely successful!"

Berger and Nicotero aren't alone though when it comes to awards and respect. Their colleague on *Creepshow 2*, Everett Burrell, would also win an Emmy Award in 1994 for the television show *Babylon 5* with his own makeup effects studio, Optic Nerve, which he formed with the late John Vulich. And dismissed original makeup effects lead Ed French has also nabbed a pair of Emmy Awards since his disastrous departure from *Creepshow 2* for his work on HBO's *Westworld* and Fox's *House, M.D.*

Amazingly the most talented artist, in my humble opinion, from the crew, Mike Trcic, would not win any prestigious awards like those shared by his colleagues as he ended his career in Hollywood prematurely by the mid 1990's. But if you've ever seen the original *Jurassic Park* and were floored by the live action mechanical T-Rex built by Stan Winston's team then you know Trcic's work, as he was the lead sculptor on the T-Rex head. It simply doesn't get any better than that, does it?

Other crew members who would go on to win Emmy

Awards included a pair of friends from the production: Felipe Borrero who won in 1999 for his work on HBO's *The Rat Pack* and Angela Nogaro who won in 2003 for her work on ABC's *Alias*.

Director of photography Tom Hurwitz would also receive an Emmy Award for his cinematography on ABC's After School Special *Just Another Kid: An AIDS Story* in 1988, while Todd Liebler, one of Hurwitz's camera assistants, would go on to win multiple Emmys for his work with the late Anthony Bourdain on *No Reservations* and *Parts Unknown*.

Producer David Ball would take home a BAFTA Cymru Award in 2003 as line producer on *Plots with a View* (aka *Undertaking Betty*), while stuntman Jery Hewitt would win a SAG Award for his stunt contributions for 2007's *The Bourne Ultimatum*. And Maine location manager Henry Nevison would be awarded a Mid-Atlantic Emmy in 2015 for his acclaimed documentary, *On the Other Side of the Fence*.

There are others as well, but the point is you can see there were a lot of talented people who worked on *Creepshow 2*, some of whom were just cutting their teeth in the industry.

Production manager Charles Carroll has become a solid producer and director in television working on shows such as *Criminal Minds*, *Third Watch*, and *Chicago Med*.

Steve Arnold, who was the assistant to production designer Bruce Miller, graduated to art director working on big budget films such as Sam Raimi's *Spider-Man* in 2002. Today he's a sought after production designer showcasing his work on *Castle Rock*, *House of Cards*, and *Mindhunter*.

Nick Mastandrea, who was key grip on the film, is now one of the top first A.D.'s in Hollywood working with some of the biggest names in the business: Christian Bale, Russell Crowe, Tom Cruise, Eddie Murphy, and Meryl Streep. He would go on to form a strong working relationship with writer/director Wes Craven serving as first A.D. on the *Scream* series and *New Nightmare*, among others.

Production designer Bruce Miller has worked as an art director and production designer on well-known films and TV shows such as *Wayne's World*, *Apollo 13*, *Sex and the City*, and *Revenge*. But after *Creepshow 2* he wondered whether he was cut out for the role of production designer. It would be an old friend from the production, from the Pittsburgh crew, who would come in with an assist to show that he was. "The *Creepshow 2* experience for me was so traumatic that I didn't think that I could be a production

Below: Daniel Beer, star of *The Raft*, reunites with his director, Michael Gornick, after 31 years at the "Chiller Theatre" convention in New Jersey – October 2017. (courtesy of Lee Karr)

designer. I needed more experience, which is why I went back to being an art director for so many years," says Miller. "Then Nick Mastandrea, who was working for Wes Craven at the time, told me that they were going to do this movie called *Scary Movie* and that Wes' designer, he was pretty sure she had agreed to do it, but that she was going to back out ultimately, that she didn't want to be a designer of horror movies, which were way down the list of acceptable contracts at that point and that I should put my name in the hat. And I said, 'Well, sure.' It had been ten years since *Creepshow 2* and, yeah, might as well."

That Wes Craven movie, *Scary Movie*, which interestingly enough was originally offered to George Romero, who turned it down, would undergo a title change, *Scream*, becoming one of the biggest hits of 1996, going on to spawn an incredibly popular franchise. "I didn't know what was going to happen. I didn't know if it was going to be another experience like *Creepshow 2*, which was so emotionally draining," Miller says. "But it ended up being a great project to work on, of which none of us thought that anybody would see it, because horror movies were not what they are today. And lo and behold it became this mass hit and my career has taken off since then."

Among the younger, new to the scene cast members from the production by far Don Harvey and Holt McCallany have gone on to have the most success in their profession. Today they're both strong and reliable character actors who have stayed busy on countless productions for film and television. As of late they've become "heartthrobs" for an older generation of female viewers with Harvey gaining attention for his role as Tom Baker on ABC's *General Hospital* and McCallany earning a large female following with his role as Bill Tench on David Fincher's Netflix series *Mindhunter*. They both look back at the experience of *Creepshow 2* fondly, but with a realistic perspective, as well.

"This is the second film I ever did. The first one was *The Untouchables*, which was pretty amazing. But this was a little different because it was a little more low budget, so I got to know everybody. *The Untouchables* I was just kind of in a couple of scenes and I was watching. But *Creepshow 2,* that was more like it felt like I was involved directly with the movie," Harvey says. "I mean, I love horror movies. I never really thought of myself as that kind of an actor. You know, I was like a legitimate actor. I did a lot of theater, stage, Shakespeare, I studied at Yale. I didn't see myself as a guy who would be in a horror movie. But then it's like, 'Hey, a job's a job.' I was just a kid, you know? I went to do it and it was incredible."

"You know, Lee, I'll tell you something, it was one of those...it's a blessing and a curse in some ways. Although there are (Sam) Whitemoon fans out there, it wasn't the kind of performance that was gonna lead to...it's not like I was going to suddenly have a career playing Native Americans. Do you know what I'm trying to say? So, that was kind of a one shot deal and it was always gonna be. So, it really did take me many years after that to find success, it didn't kind of launch me in any way. As a matter of fact there was a long time when I didn't work much. You know, he's a bad guy. He's very intense. You know what I mean? As a screen debut it was not particularly auspicious, but I had a good experience working with Michael (Gornick)," shares

an honest McCallany. "I mean, at the end of the day, it's a horror movie, not a big budget movie, and it was a tricky part for them to cast - I was a very gung-ho, young actor. And, look, I'm grateful to Michael Gornick and I'm grateful to Leonard Finger because they took a chance with me."

These days McCallany enjoys it when fans discover that the same guy who plays FBI agent Bill Tench in *Mindhunter*, the same guy who uttered the famous line from *Fight Club*, "In death, a member of Project Mayhem has a name. His name is Robert Paulsen", also just happens to be the villainous and hilariously vain Sam Whitemoon from *Creepshow 2*. "It's more like, 'That was you? You were the Indian in *Creepshow 2*?' And I'm like, 'Yeah', and they go, 'Dude, I remember that!' So, I do get that. And, look, people seem to remember the film fondly and frankly it's not clear to me why they didn't decide to continue the anthology," he says. "Someone brought to my attention recently the fact that you can buy Sam Whitemoon t-shirts from, I think it's called Teepublic or something. Anyway, I went online and I saw them and there's my face with the wig and it says, 'There ain't no dust in Hollywood, man', and so I bought a couple of them and I wear them to the gym sometimes. But they're great. Yeah, I would say that's my favorite line. Obviously, you know, 'I'm going to Hollywood, this hair's gonna get me paid and laid', I mean, that line will live in infamy (laughs)."

Then you have Dan Kamin, the brilliant mime artist who portrayed Chief Wood'nhead in the film. Kamin would continue his career as a mime, performing to this day in fact, but the opportunity to be associated with motion pictures would still present itself down the road. "In a way it's always been a little bit of a joke in my resume," he says. "You know, it's just such an oddity that I did a horror movie because my career...I perform at symphony orchestras and I've done other movies that were a lot more high profile than *Creepshow 2* in which I had a lot more of a fundamental creative role to play."

Some of those higher profile gigs include training Robert Downey, Jr. for his role as Charlie Chaplin for the 1992 film *Chaplin*, a role for which Downey would be nominated for an Academy Award and take home the BAFTA. He also worked with Johnny Depp for the 1993 film *Benny & Joon,* choreographing some of the physical comedy scenes. And for the 1996 film *Mars Attacks!* Kamin worked with director Tim Burton on the physical movements for the Martian Girl played by Lisa Marie.

Patricia Tallman, who worked performing stunts for *The Raft*, would go on to land the lead role of Barbara in Tom Savini's 1990 remake of *Night of the Living Dead*. "That was nuts," says Tallman. "At first I was calling Savini, 'Why is George redoing this? Why would he redo a classic?' Because we weren't doing all these remakes then, right, it was sort of a new thing. And he sent me the script and wanted me to audition. And then I saw the changes they had made in the script, and Tom was talking about the changes he wanted to make in the effects, and I thought,

'Okay, okay. I get it. Alright, this could be cool.' So, I was very happy to get the part."

And while Tallman would continue acting - she had a nice five year run on *Babylon 5* - her main thrust was performing stunts for big Hollywood productions. She was Laura Dern's stunt double on *Jurassic Park*, she was the possessed witch that battles Bruce Campbell in *Army of Darkness* - "Yo, she-bitch. Let's go." - and she worked on Mike Myers' *Austin Powers* films, among many others.

Matt Marich, who landed his job on *Creepshow 2* courtesy of a John Vulich recommendation, as well as that spot-on Marvin the Martian impression, would utilize the experience to find further work in Hollywood. Again, thanks to an assist from Vulich, as well as from Everett Burrell, Marich would work for Kenny Myers on *Return of the Living Dead Part II*. From there he'd perform a variety of jobs on a range of film productions: mechanical effects assistant on *Bill & Ted's Excellent Adventure*, set dresser on *Tombstone*, and carpenter on *The Sandlot*. He even helped Burrell and Vulich open their makeup effects studio, Optic Nerve. "I tiled their floor in their office," he explains. "I built a stand for their foam latex oven and some tables. I built fiberglass skeletal bodies for re-shoots of the movie *The Dark Half*, another Stephen King film, and was around them at the infancy of starting their business and so forth."

Eventually Marich would start his own company, along with his wife, that catered to large corporations and theme parks such as Universal Studios Hollywood, Knotts Berry Farm, and Carowinds building animatronics, props, and sets. These days he works for Universal Studios in Orlando, Florida in a similar capacity.

Lori Chontos, who worked on *Creepshow 2*'s animation unit in Pittsburgh, would find her way to Orlando as well. Not long after the film's release Chontos took a chance on realizing her dream of working for Disney Animation by moving to Orlando. For two years she pursued a job with the company that she grew up loving, only to be rejected because she was deemed overqualified. However, things were about to start looking up for her as she was hired to work at Universal Studios Orlando, where she's been for the last three decades. In her time there she's worked on some of the park's biggest attractions including *T2-3D*.

For Chontos the chance to work on *Creepshow 2* and achieve that goal of working on an animated film is something she looks back on fondly and with gratefulness. "It was just an incredible experience and it helped me in my career to be where I am today," she says. "If that didn't happen I don't know where I'd be, the path kind of led me to here. But it's still my roots; it's something I'll always be proud of."

As referenced at the start of the chapter some members of the production would choose very different paths for the rest of their lives in the wake of *Creepshow 2*.

Bangor still photographer Richard Greene, while still continuing his photography business, would find himself

Left: *Old Chief Wood'nhead* star Holt McCallany reunites with director Michael Gornick outside PNC Park in Pittsburgh. McCallany was in town to film season 1 of Netflix's *Mindhunter* at the time and was eager to see his first feature film director after 30 years – July 2016. (courtesy of Lee Karr)

involved in local government, eventually becoming the mayor of Bangor.

And speaking of government, Maltbie Napoleon would leave both modeling and acting behind not long after the release of *Creepshow 2* becoming an activist back home in Hawaii. Napoleon argues that the Hawaiian Kingdom was overthrown by the United States well over a century ago and that U.S. state and federal governments are actually illegal in Hawaii, that the U.S. is illegally occupying the Hawaiian Islands. "Now, we know that in 1898 there was a special session in Congress about the military coming to Hawaii to use as a port for the Spanish American War, which would violate Hawaiian neutrality at the time," he explains. "Because the Hawaiian Islands were the Hawaiian Kingdom, they were a legitimate country, and all of the sudden, my grandparents, my parents, and me we're being told that we're U.S. citizens and that Hawaii is a part of the United States. But after learning the actual history and the legal events that took place it never happened, there was never a legitimate treaty of annexation, which provides the legalities of transferring the independence and the sovereignty of the kingdom to somebody else."

Actress Jeremy Green would leave the entertainment industry behind and - continuing our theme here - find herself working in government; in her case, in the city manager's office of a small town on the West Coast.

Green's co-star from *The Raft*, Paul Satterfield, would stick around in the industry for close to 25 years, working predominantly in television, until finally deciding that acting just wasn't where his true passion was any longer. He went back to school, earned his master's degree, and today is a school teacher in the Midwest. "For you to tell me that he became a teacher just touches me, because I always loved Paul so much. His kindness to me was so appreciated, such a sweet young man," says Rebecca Mayo, the Arizona school teacher turned production secretary on *Creepshow 2*. "That doesn't surprise me. He asked me questions about my teaching and how long I had been teaching and where I was teaching and all of that. Good for him; I'm very proud of him."

Like Satterfield two other cast members from the production would go on to very successful careers which allow them to help others, in this case in the field of psychiatry: Domenick John Sportelli and David Vining Holbrook.

"Yeah, you know, the entertainment industry is a tough one, basically; I'm sure you know. I was brought into it at a very young age. And I gotta tell you, I did well, I did a lot of national commercials and a ton of modeling; I was very busy. And as a kid I was going to Manhattan every day after school and my friends were playing sports and doing all that stuff and I would just go every day to Manhattan. And when I had some autonomy in my early teens I said, 'You know what? I just want to be a normal kid. I don't wanna do this anymore.' And that was it! And then I decided to just not pursue acting. However though, I will tell you this, it was such a unique experience growing up it affected me for the rest of my life. When I was in college and graduate school I went back to modeling and I did pretty well at doing commercial print. So, that kind of supported me through college, grad school, and med school," says Dr. Sportelli, who besides his normal medical

Above: Michael Gornick poses with the incredible bust of his late friend and collaborator George Romero at the Monroeville Mall after the close of "The Living Dead Weekend" convention – June 2018. (courtesy of Lee Karr)

practice can be seen on the syndicated television show *The Doctors*, as well as on Fox News as a guest speaker discussing topical issues of the day. "And here's how things kind of come full circle: I did an internship in family medicine and then I decided to go into psychiatry because I loved my background in philosophy and sociology and history; just more a philosophical thinker than a medical thinker. So, I ended up at Robert Wood Johnson University Hospital for residency and it turns out that the assistant program director was a total horror movie buff. When I was interviewing for the residency position I started talking to him about my past and kind of how I grew up, and my life, so when I told him that I had a little part in *Creepshow 2*, that might have gotten me the spot in residency. So, this little tiny part absolutely affected my life, going many years later and gaining...I shouldn't attribute gaining my residency solely to that, but it made an impression on the assistant program director. At least it made me memorable. And then, throughout residency, myself and the program director came up with a teaching protocol to teach medical

students psycho pathology through the use of horror films. So, based on my history, being in the movie industry and my silly claim to fame with *Creepshow 2*, we started this lecture series where we would show medical students horror movies and then talk about the psycho pathology in it to introduce them to psychiatric service. Yeah, and we actually did a research paper on it and everything and had it published in *Academic Psychiatry*. And I'm telling you, it all goes back to *Creepshow 2*."

"I have patients who are real aficionados of *Creepshow 2*! They were before they ever met me. Isn't that funny? They'll be like, 'You were in *Creepshow 2*!?' Which I don't care, as opposed to some people who might think, 'I'm a psychiatrist, I'd rather be real serious.' But I try to be just very human. And even if I have patients who...they're young people who want to be an actor someday, if that becomes some way I think I can reach them and help form a bond with them I'll tell them, 'Hey, I used to be an actor. I was in *Creepshow 2*. You can look on the internet and you can see me getting shot with arrows,'" laughs Dr. Holbrook. "It's a way to humanize myself and step down off the high pedestal or whatever of being the 'doctor' and all that stuff."

And for Dr. Holbrook the choice to help others in his particular field of endeavor harkens back to his former life, which makes him immensely satisfied. "I think of what I'm doing now as really an extension of having been an actor, in a lot of ways," he says. "You know, if you're really lucky as an actor you get a couple of chances in your whole life time to actually do something really good. And in my work, every day is like Shakespeare."

Perhaps no one from the film though would experience a more life-altering change of course than production assistant Billy Kosco. After completing *Creepshow 2*, Kosco would return to Los Angeles - where he had gone to college - looking for work in the film industry. He wound up discovering that he wanted to challenge himself and learn his true purpose in life. He yearned to experience the world and interact with all of the different people that are out there, starting in his own backyard, the U.S. He would begin by bicycling across the country, stopping in occasionally with a distant relative or an old friend. The majority of the time though he was camping in the woods - alone. "It started doing something to me where I think it became a very prayerful experience where I was...you learn how to just sort of...like, I just have to trust God," he says. "I started reading the bible because I was scared at night in my tent and stuff."

Kosco would find himself knocking on church doors looking for a safe place to crash during his travels with no further expectation than perhaps being allowed to camp behind the church. "A lot of times people would say, 'Just come on in', or the priest would say, 'I've got a couch you can crash on.' And I just found that people were good. We read about the horror of this world, it's like, that's just the tantalizing stuff. The world's actually made up of good people," he says. "You know, even your film crews, you hear about Hollywood people, they're all just drugged out and sexed out...that does exist. But in general people are good; they want to have fun, they want to help each other out. The backbiting...like on this show, nah, they're cool; you're talking to the producer and saying, 'Hi', to the director. Nobody acted like their poop didn't stink - it was a good bunch of people."

He would end up working in the Peace Corps, spending time in war-torn Eastern European countries such as Croatia and Bosnia. It was during this period that he began to experience an awakening. "And a lot of that made me just think, like, 'Dang, I can't remove myself from the suffering of the world or people who don't know how to talk about God', like in Romania or Hungary," Kosco explains. "They're like, 'Why do we talk about this god? It's sunny for you, it's sunny for me. You make two dollars an hour, I make two dollars an hour. Okay? Beer is thirty cents for me, it's thirty cents for you. God, how does he figure in? It doesn't matter. You're wasting your time; you're wasting your money. Just live your life!' But I'm like, 'What do you think happens after we die?' I just noticed a bit of an impoverishment, you know, in the way people thought about the purpose of life and it just started meaning more to me. I started finding out that the conversations that I really enjoyed were when people wanted to talk about existence or life after death or suffering. I was like, 'Man, that stuff, that's for real!' And it just attracted me more and maybe it really caused me to pull away from wanting to make movies. I sort of said, 'Yeah, movies I'm really interested in them, but I want to kind of live them. I don't want to actually make stories, I want to live the stories.' It was easier for me to say I'm not going back to L.A., it's okay. And then I worked as a teacher for a while. And then finally just really felt the Lord was saying, 'Hey, what are you gonna do?' - I was 31 - and he was like, 'Why don't you be a priest?' I was like, 'Doggone it!' I was ticked actually. But it fit! It was like pieces of a puzzle that were...your whole life is shaken out and some are upside down and you're like, 'What?' And as soon as I felt that, I was like, 'Oh, god. You're kidding me!' You know, almost married twice - real close, even proposed to a girl and stuff. So, I'm like, 'Well, how does that fit? What about this?' You know, I wasn't an evil guy, but I screwed around, too, like everybody, and stuff. But it all came together."

Indeed, it did all come together for Father Kosco. As of this writing, he's been a priest for over 20 years. He's a fascinating guy. He reminds me very much of the priest that George Romero played in his own film *Martin* from the late 1970's: gregarious, really funny, extremely bright and knowledgeable, but more than anything, approachable. Yes, he's a religious leader, an "elder", but he's a human being who simply wants to make a positive difference in the lives of those that he meets. And his parishioners love him for it. Some of his sermons are available online and you can see and hear the connection they share. In fact, there are several videos on Youtube where Father Kosco shares a special message to the faithful and the quality of those videos is first rate - a bit cinematic, you might say. So, that appreciation for the power of cinema still resides inside this Man of God. But, as far as he's concerned, he made the right choice upon reaching his proverbial fork in the road many years ago. "Even Spielberg, like, on judgement day, God will say, 'Hey, that *Schindler's List*, that was really good'...'Well, what did you think about *Jaws*?'...'That was well done. I don't know if it helped anybody move closer to me,'" jokes Father Kosco as he explains his decision

Above: Michael Gornick meets Rick Wakeman again, 32 years after *Creepshow 2*'s post production ended, at The Palace Theatre in Greensburg, PA – October 2019. (courtesy of Lee Karr)

making in leaving behind those once upon a time dreams of Hollywood. "I'm like, 'What are the odds that you're going to be part of something that's *major*?' And it was, like, pretty low. So, it's like, are you gonna take the gamble to be part of something major or are you actually going to live something major, but it will be in minor though, it will be with a small group of people, it's not going to be a movie. But for those people, it's big. And I was like, 'I'm okay with that.' I'm okay with that. Yep, that's my story."

This brings us full circle to director Michael Gornick. As he mentioned in the previous chapter when discussing the negative reviews the film received, the opportunity to direct another motion picture never did come around again. Before becoming friends and getting to know him really well, I'd always wondered why he never went on to direct more feature films. He had proven he was quite capable of weathering massive storms, both figuratively and literally, during the production of *Creepshow 2*. In fact, one of the film's stars wondered the same thing and mentioned so during our first interview session. "I kept waiting to see more stuff coming from Michael," says Holt McCallany. "I think he's a smart guy and he's got a lot of talent, a lot of ability, and I was just surprised that he never decided to make another film."

Of course, like so many things in life, the answer to that is a complicated one. "I stayed a member of Laurel Entertainment, which was my own personal decision. Because at that point in time I had reached a point where, corporately speaking, there were all the attractions of stock options and insurance. I had a large family at that point and so the ability to write off a whole life insurance and medical insurance policy to a corporation, make a very handsome salary, and have the possibility of some future projects (was enticing). It wasn't the end of my directorial career, you know, we went on to make something called *Monsters* and we did work for CBS on *The Golden Years* - I got to direct. So, it wasn't the end of my career, but it made a lot of sense to stay with them because they had a lot of exciting

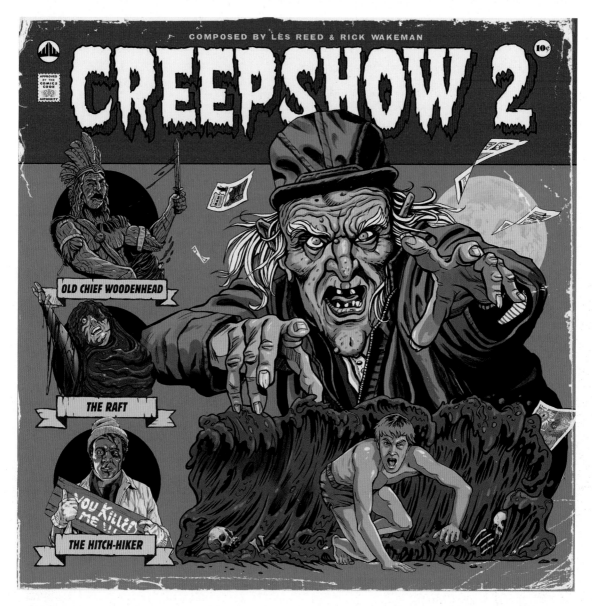

COMPOSED BY LES REED & RICK WAKEMAN

CREEPSHOW 2

10¢

OLD CHIEF WOODENHEAD

THE RAFT

YOU KILLED ME !!!

THE HITCH-HIKER

Left and above: The beautiful cover art for Arrow Video's special edition Blu-ray and Waxwork Records' vinyl soundtrack were met with delight by fans across the globe.

projects. *The Stand* loomed on the horizon, which I knew I'd be involved in some respect; didn't know if I'd direct it, but I knew I'd be involved heavily. So, there were a lot of exciting projects out there that seemed possible," Gornick explains. "But I think by staying on you become staid and you don't get representation. I never had representation which is probably my ultimate mistake in my whole career. You know, people have always advised me, 'Mike, you never had an agent. You should have got an agent at some point.' Because early in the game, even after I'd finished *Dawn* and so forth, I had people like Sean Cunningham (*Friday the 13th*) try to correspond with me to come work for them. And I think if I'd had an agent I probably could have done better from a career standpoint. Would I have been happier? I don't know. I kind of doubt it."

Gornick would go on to work on *The Langoliers* and *The Night Flier*, both based on Stephen King stories and

both produced by Richard Rubinstein and Mitchell Galin, before calling it quits in the late 1990's. No longer would he commute back and forth from New York City to Pittsburgh, instead he would stay home in "The 'Burgh" full time. For a number of years he worked as a "civilian", you might say, in every day type jobs. These days he's retired and enjoys spending time with his wife of forty-five years, Michele, and their many grandchildren, who unquestionably bring them much joy and happiness.

Besides the grand-kids one of the things which keeps Gornick busy these days is the convention circuit. Gornick has created a little cottage industry for himself at shows meeting fans from all around the world who have an appreciation for not only the cinematography work he created with George Romero, but for *Creepshow 2* as well. And it's been a pleasant and gratifying experience, to say the least. "In present day I'm actually stunned by what has transpired because at the time it was not terribly well received," Gornick says. "But what amazed me later though is that into the 90's, and then beyond, something settled in terms of people being able to view it and take it in and not referencing it to a previous production of *Creepshow*; and looking upon it as a singular piece of work that, yes, was a sequel but had its own merits. And that was delightful. It was delightful. I mean, to the point that within my own family, my daughter married a gentleman from Michigan and he told me stories shortly after they were married, he said, 'You know, I watched *Creepshow 2* and I lived near a lake. I couldn't go out on the lake for almost a year.' I said, 'Wow, I'm so sorry to hear that.' He goes, 'No, no. It was so much fun, but I was frightened to death.'"

As for Laurel Entertainment, the company Richard Rubinstein formed back in 1980 with George Romero, less than two years after the release of *Creepshow 2* it would merge with Aaron Spelling's production company to form Spelling Entertainment, Inc. Rubinstein and Mitchell Galin would stay on board producing *Pet Sematary*, *Tales from the Darkside: The Movie*, *The Golden Years*, and *The Stand*. By the mid 1990's they would leave to start a new production company, New Amsterdam Entertainment, which still exists today. New Amsterdam would go on to produce the 2000 mini-series of *Dune* for the Sci-Fi Channel as well as Zack Snyder's 2004 reboot of *Dawn of the Dead* for Universal (Galin was gone by the time the *Dawn* remake came about).

"Richard and I had a really nice run. I mean, we sort of balanced each other in pretty good ways," says Galin. "Richard's a very good business man and understands the ins and outs of deal making and has a love for films. And yet, in a certain sense, he's always needed a creative partner to sort of do what he's doing just because he's not operational in a creative sense. So, we kind of made a good match. And the relationship just developed from my being the vice president of the company to eventually me being a partner with him in the next company that we started together after Laurel ended. We kind of balanced each other out pretty well."

As Michael Gornick discussed, an appreciation for *Creepshow 2* has steadily grown over the decades since its 1987 release. In just the last few years Arrow Video released - then re-released - a fantastic special edition Blu-ray of the film, Waxwork Records pressed the film's soundtrack on vinyl featuring beautiful new original artwork complete with liner notes from composer Les Reed, Fright Rags produced a series of popular t-shirts and enamel pins, and Celebrity Machines released a replica "CREEP" license plate, just like the one seen in the film's opening. But by far the most impressive tribute to the film's legacy occurred in November 2020 when the prestigious Los Angeles auction house Profiles in History, in their Icons & Legends of Hollywood Auction, offered an original screen used prop statue of "Chief Wood'nhead" estimated between $6,0000-$8,000, which was purchased by the amazingly talented makeup effects artist and sculptor Mike Hill for his fiancé, Meg, who is a devoted fan of the film.

In 2015 Slasher Con in Virginia held a mini *Creepshow 2* reunion with Dan Kamin, Daniel Beer, and Tom Wright. And in 2017 your humble author helped organize another mini *Creepshow 2* reunion at Chiller Theatre in Parsippany, New Jersey with Michael Gornick, Daniel Beer, Don Harvey, Domenick John Sportelli, and Rick Catizone in attendance.

Each show featured a panel discussion where the people who worked to bring the film to life got to interact with those who love it. "Slasher Con was not real well attended, but our panel was well attended. And it was evident that people really, really love this film and it's an important film in their lives. And they were so pleased to be able to ask questions and express their appreciation," recalls Dan Kamin. "It is a good film. And it gave me much more respect for it as a film that's had a meaning to people in their lives."

"The afterlife of it is just astonishing to me. Absolutely astonishing," says Daniel Beer. "And I love hearing from people and fans and stuff like that about it. I just love it. And it's not just this lightweight horror movie, people have an emotional thing...they never talk about the gore, that it's about the gore. It's not just an entertainment thing. It's something more to them."

"I was a teenager when I saw the movie, in Charleston, South Carolina with a few friends and at that time I remember it being very gory - for me that is - but also goofy, in a good way. I loved it. We would quote the movie all the time; for me that's why it has its staying power," says mega fan Todd Householder. "My friends and I would go around school quoting the movie but changing up the lines or names. We would pass each other in the hall and say, 'Hagoonee", and the person's name, and they would respond the same way. When we'd drive somewhere and get out, boy or girl driving, with the hitchhiker's voice, 'Thanks lady, thanks for the ride.' After lunch, we'd ask each other if we were full, or do you still want 'Chow' and then shake our heads like they do in the movie. 'Don't tip the raft' and Fatso saying 'Loco' were other gems. The day it came out on VHS I waited at Blockbuster to open so I could rent it. I watched it nonstop until I knew every line from the movie."

"The elements of *Creepshow 2* that make it unique are what have drawn new fans into its clutches over the years. The great thing about *Creepshow 2* is that instead of being a carbon copy of the '82 original - it takes a different approach in terms of musical score, animation, and film length. These differences make *Creepshow 2* an excellent companion piece to the first film - rather than being a boring retread of what had already been done," says online personality Eric Anderson whose review of the film on his Youtube channel "MountainTop9" impressed Michael Gornick so much so that he graciously invited Anderson to be a part of this book project. "While it didn't get the promotion that it so richly deserved upon its initial release - the film has managed to flourish over the years, winning over new viewers with its nostalgic charm and wonderfully entertaining stories. Whether it be the stomach churning special effects, the enchanting electronic score, or the brilliant direction from Michael Gornick, *Creepshow 2* is overflowing with amazing elements that all add up to making a timeless horror film."

"I was proud of it," says Tom Hurwitz. "I still have students who come to me and say, 'That's one of my favorite films.'"

Hearing Tom Hurwitz say that he's proud of the film, which is a little surprising considering the circumstances in which he left the project, brings about the topic of the way people involved in its creation look back on its making and how it all turned out. Some of the feelings have been discussed throughout the book already; however there's always room for a few more. Right, kiddies?

"You know, I have to tell you, since that was the beginning of my career it holds a special place for me," says Angela Nogaro. "First of all it was a cult film and so having that as my second film, which so many people know about in the world of special effects and stuff, it really has a stand out place and makes it special to me.

"I think it turned out really great considering all the obstacles that we had, both in working under very difficult situations, with not a lot of money," Felipe Borrero says. "And I think the film, as a horror film, is a classic. It's one of those things you don't forget."

"It was such a pleasant experience," recalls Jeanne Talbot. "It was great; it was probably one of the best experiences I ever had. And as I got further into my career and I got to work on bigger and bigger films, the attention on these big movies, where there's so much more money and there's also more time, the tension gets very palpable on a film set. And I don't remember any of that. And this was a tough shoot!"

"It was a great experience, but especially for a first major film out of college. I really enjoyed it," says Dex Craig. "That's one of the awesome things about working on *Creepshow 2* in particular was that ideas were welcome and even me, a lowly production assistant/props assistant, I was able to contribute to things that wound up clearly on screen. There was a really good culture."

"I thought it was pretty good! You know, for what it was," says Dr. David Holbrook. "I always liked *The New York Times* film reviewer, Janet Maslin, because she didn't judge a film from some lofty, Ivy League plateau. She would judge every film based on: what kind of film is it? What is it trying to accomplish? And does it accomplish what it's trying to accomplish? And I thought it was a really good, little movie for what it was trying to do."

"It's never comfortable for me to watch my own performance, but I thought the film was really great," Page Hannah says. "And I have to say I love the segment with, 'Thanks for the ride, lady!' I just loved it. I mean I still like that line, it so sticks with me. I love that Stephen King always makes an appearance; I wished it was in our segment! It was an extremely enjoyable experience for me."

"I was actually - despite how difficult it was - I was pretty proud of the way it turned out. And it actually has legs," shares Tom Wright, who hears that famous line which Page Hannah just mentioned constantly from fans. "To this day I get stopped by anyone who's a horror fan and they talk about *Tales from the Hood* and *Creepshow 2*."

"I'm proud of the work that everybody did," says Lois Chiles, who claims that famous line, "Thanks for the ride, lady", has been a part of her life for decades now, with her UPS delivery man being the first to say it to her many years ago. "I enjoyed watching the film. I especially enjoyed Tom's (Wright) work. I think it was shot well. You know, it's always weird to look at yourself, but I think we pulled it off."

Creepshow 2 was a product of its time, no doubt. Like a lot of films made in the 1970's and 1980's, particularly those produced by Laurel, it celebrated the genre. And

Above: Fright Rags would release a series of popular collector t-shirts and enamel pins, while Celebrity Machines produced a fantastic replica of the CREEP license plate.

with its low budget it relied heavily on ingenuity to achieve its goals. It wasn't mean spirited; it was more about just having fun and enjoying some scares mixed in with a few laughs. Personally, I miss those days of yesteryear and they become more precious each year that passes. Out of the one hundred plus people I spoke with for this project it was probably legendary comic book artist Kelley Jones who I believe summed up best what the experience of enjoying a film like *Creepshow 2* is really all about. "Think of all the 'A list' pictures people forget about and jettison," says Jones, whose Marvel adaptation of *The Raft* unfortunately still remains officially unpublished. "You know, I will never go through *Gandhi* again, but I'll watch *Creepshow 2* a couple of times a year. You know what I mean? I am a big believer in that."

And with that, bores and ghouls, as the Creep himself might say, "'Til next issue, try to stay scared. Heh, heh, heh..."

Acknowledgements and Remembrances

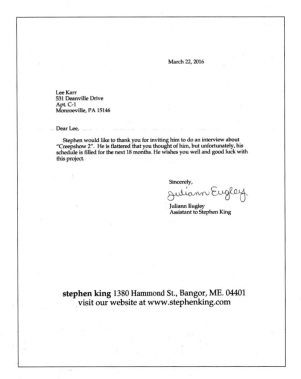

Above: The closest I came to getting an interview with Stephen King for this book project: a rejection letter from his personal assistant. They were kind enough to respond though. (courtesy of Lee Karr)

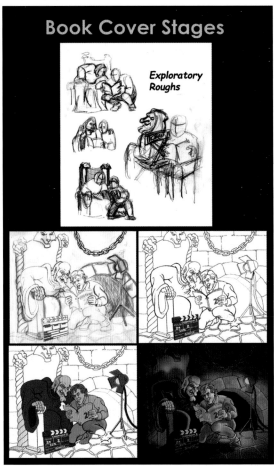

Above: The various stages of progress for this book's original – and absolutely gorgeous, I might add - cover art from animator Rick Catizone. (courtesy of Rick Catizone)

Just like with my previous book, there is absolutely no way I could have completed this labor of love without the assistance of so many. From the cast and crew of Laurel-CST, Inc. to the executives at New World to the wonderful folks associated with De Wolfe Music to those who are simply fans of the film, the contributions made - both large and small - are ones I am sincerely grateful for. Without this collective, the book just doesn't happen...

Jim Allan, Barbara Anderson, Eric Anderson, Ben Barenholtz (R.I.P.), Hilary Barta, George Beahm, Daniel Beer, Logan Berkshire, Andrew Bernard, John Bick, Christopher Blackwell, Felipe Borerro, Tim Broughton, Pat Buba (R.I.P.), Jeff Carney, Charles Carroll, Peter Catalanotto, Lois Chiles, Lori Chontos, Jim Cirronella, Rusty Citron, Mary Jo Claugus, Kevin Clement & Chiller Theatre, Scott Coulter, Dex Craig, George Danby, Edward O. Darling, Marc Stephan Del Gatto, George Demick, Marshall Drazen, Jack Dyer, Barbara Eden, Clark (Utterback)Everitt, Michael Felsher, Stan Obcamp-Fikel, Leonard Finger, Willie Fonfe, Ed Fountain, Wolf Forrest, Ed French, Ron Frenz, Dan Frye, Paul Gagne, Mitchell Galin, Eileen Garrigan, Kim (Yost) Goddard, Charlotte Goodwin, Google Newspaper Archive, Jason Green, Miles and Cindy Greenacre, Richard D. Greene, Garry Greer, Vincent Guastini, Todd Gutner, Page Hannah, John Harrison, Richard Hassanein, Richard Hart, Gary Hartle, Don Harvey, Elfed Hayes, George Higham, Mike Hill, Kathy Hinshaw-David, Rex Hinshaw, Dr. David V. Holbrook, Nathan Hollabaugh, David Holt, Todd Householder, Lori Huckabey, Tom Hurwitz, John Hyde, Eddie Jones, Kelley Jones, Dan Kamin, John Kent & Toyfinity, Father William Kosco, Gary Kosko, Ted Kurdyla, Gloria Lamont, Jason Late, Tom Lauten, Todd Liebler, Jennifer Lurey at SAG-AFTRA, Henry Lynk, Frank Maresca, Matt Marich, Nick Mastandrea, Gerard McMahon (G Tom Mac), Jim Melkonian, Roland Mesa, David Michelinie, Anthony Miletello (R.I.P.) & the *Creepshow* Museum on Facebook, Bruce Miller, Maltbie Napoleon, Bruce & the Needful Things collection at The Dark Tower.org palaver forum, Henry Nevison, Newspapers.com, Aaron Newton, Angela Nogaro, Brian Noodt, Simon Park, Brad Parker, Richard Parks, Vinny Petrosini, Joe Pilato (R.I.P), Plexus

Books (Sandra, Coco, and Nia), Historic Preservation office for the city of Prescott, Arizona, Amy Rabins, Tony Randel, Robert Rehme, Patrick Reid, John Ridgway, Steve Rosie at De Wolfe Music, Gerald and Renee Roy, Ben Rubin and the George A. Romero Archival Collection at the University of Pittsburgh, Richard P. Rubinstein, Andy Sands, Andrew Santagato, Jeff Schechtman, Lori (Koonin) Schneider, Bill Shields, Eileen Sieff-Stroup, Deane Smith, Shirley Sonderegger, Vicki Sorrell, Dr. Domenick J. Sportelli, Christian Stavrakis, Taso Stavrakis, Eric Swanek, Doctors Jim and Mary Lou Talamo, Jeanne Talbot, Patricia Tallman, Debra Tanklow, Bill Teitler, Dr. Arthur Thomas, Anthony Timpone, Alan Toomayan, Jonathan Wacks, Rick Wakeman, Straw Weisman, Joanna Robinson-Weymueller, Steve Werndorf, Steve White, Kevin Williamson, Phil Wilson, Joe Winogradoff, Shawn Winstian, Gerald Winters, Kato Wittich, Tom Wright, Gary Yee, and John Young of the Dewey-Humboldt Historical Society. And there are probably a few names I'm forgetting here, so I apologize if I've somehow left anyone out.

As I touched on in the preface there were some special people who really went the extra mile on behalf of this book - none more so than Michael Gornick. Without his blessing and his invaluable, unending contributions this book would have never happened, it's as simple as that. Mike is one of the kindest and most generous human beings I've ever known and I'm so proud to call him my friend. I hope he's pleased with the outcome of this effort.

David Ball also made significant contributions to this book, including consistently being there if I had a follow-up question. Like Mike, he always had the time for me, even going to the trouble of digging through his files to unearth paperwork regarding the casting fiasco for the Annie character in *The Hitchhiker* segment. David graciously agreed to write the foreword for me late in the game when Michael Gornick decided he wasn't comfortable doing so due to modesty. I just can't say enough good things about David and I hope he's happy with the results here as well.

Rick Catizone worked overtime in answering my many questions regarding the film's animation and I owe a debt to him for making that chapter as detailed as it is. And his original new art for the cover of this book is simply fantastic! Thank you so much, Rick.

My Arizona connections, Rebecca Mayo and Michael Morgan, each took the time to rummage through their personal belongings to locate their production files and then mailed them in large boxes, entrusting me implicitly with them. How wonderful are people like this?

Steve Arnold patiently took multiple trips down memory lane with me providing fantastic anecdotes about such things as the cars featured in the film; just invaluable stuff. Likewise with Beth Kuhn who was so kind and appreciated my love for the film so much that she mailed me her original art designs for some of the creatures featured on the Creep's delivery truck, as well as sending me her original Art Department crew jacket. I can't begin to tell you how generous a thing that was and how much I appreciate it and cherish the gesture. Thank you, Beth.

Star Holt McCallany, more than any actor from the film,

Above: Taking in a Pittsburgh Pirates game with my better half, Renee McLamb(yellow shirt), and Holt McCallany, Eileen Sieff-Stroup, and Michael & Michele Gornick – July 2016. (courtesy of Lee Karr) **Below:** Celebrating our mini *Creepshow 2* reunion at "Chiller Theatre" in New Jersey: Rick Catizone, Dr. Domenick John Sportelli, Daniel Beer, Don Harvey, Michael Gornick, and Lee Karr & Renee McLamb – October 2017. (courtesy of Rick Catizone)

truly collaborated with me to make this book as detailed and accurate as possible. Holt allowed me to interview him multiple times for the project and really took the time to ensure I had my facts about his life and his time on the film accurate. I can't tell you how much that is appreciated. To borrow a phrase from Rebecca Mayo, he's a gentleman and a scholar. Thank you, Holt.

And George Dreisch isn't just a great mechanic, but he's a really funny guy who's fantastic at telling stories as well. He's also a great tour guide to boot. Thank you for the fun trip around Bangor checking out filming locations, George!

Former Marvel Comics Editor-in-Chief Jim Shooter proved to be another generous, helpful ally in this project.

Above left: With the awesome George Dreisch outside the former Dyer estate, which was the exterior of Annie Lansing's home in *The Hitchhiker*. George was nice enough to join me on a tour of Bangor filming locations and provided a wealth of information – April 2017. **Above right:** With the wonderful Father William Kosco at the Pittsburgh International Airport in June 2019. Father Kosco became one of the biggest allies for this book and I'm so thankful for his support. And he signed my *Creepshow 2* poster to boot. How cool is that! **Below left:** Renee and I with Holt McCallany, plus friend and fellow *Creepshow 2* fan Todd Householder, at Morton's in downtown Pittsburgh in November 2018. Holt invited us all to dinner – and graciously picked up the check as well – after allowing us to visit the set of *Mindhunter* earlier that evening. Holt is genuinely one of the classiest and nicest guys you'll ever meet and has been a tremendous supporter of this book project, something I'm eternally grateful for.

He graciously sent me copies of correspondence between Laurel and Marvel from their discussions about the *Copperhead* superhero film project, including early outlines and treatments dating all the way back to 1982 written by George Romero and Shooter himself. Amazing stuff!

Of course, more than anyone, I want to give thanks to my beloved Mother, Katrina Faye Karr. My Mom struggled with Lewy body dementia for five years until that struggle finally ended in late February of 2021. I'm an only child, raised by a single mother, which wasn't easy for either of us. Growing up my Mom never questioned my taste in movies though, never looked down on my interest in horror. She'd drop me off at the movie theater or drive me to the video store ensuring that I'd be able to see these films. She'd run me up to the local convenience store or book shop so I could purchase the newest issue of *Fangoria* or *Cinefantastique* when they hit the shelves. She allowed me to call long distance from Savannah, Georgia to Washington, D.C. one evening in April 1986 so I could speak with Stephen King on *Larry King Live*. She knew I was fascinated by the behind-the-scenes aspect of film-making, just as I had been when I was a child with the early *Star Wars* films. I loved watching movies, of course, but I was even more intrigued by how they were made. I'm lucky that I had a Mom who realized this and allowed me to educate myself on such subjects.

And maybe the horror thing didn't bother her too much because her own mother - my Grandmother, Grace Lindsay, who is a saint to me - LOVED Stephen King. She had all of his early works which she ordered through her book club, two of which she gave to me on my 15th birthday. Over two decades later I had the opportunity to have King sign one of those books, *The Shining*, at a book signing in Washington, D.C. I told him the story of the book and how much it meant to me and I could tell he appreciated hearing it. Having Stephen King's signature right under my Grandmother's is precious, let me tell you.

So, Mom, thank you for everything you did in raising me, you were always in my corner, and I couldn't have been more fortunate to have you as a parent. I love you more than anything in this world.

And to the love of my life, Renee McLamb, I want to thank you for your support. You've put up with me and all of my issues for over 20 years now, which makes you worthy of the Bronze Star! You understood all of those times when I needed to just concentrate on writing, giving me space and allowing the work to unfold. You get me and I'm lucky to have you as my soulmate.

Since the release of *Creepshow 2* in 1987 we've lost some of the people whose talents helped to craft this memorable "little film that could". From the cast, the voice of the Creep himself, Joe Silver, along with Gordon Connell, the voice of Mr. Haig, have both left us. Frank Salsedo, the man who brought such dignity to the role of Benjamin Whitemoon, is also among the departed.

Screen legend Dorothy Lamour, who was nominated for Best Supporting Actress by The Academy of Science

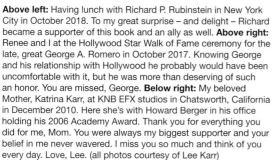

Above left: Having lunch with Richard P. Rubinstein in New York City in October 2018. To my great surprise – and delight – Richard became a supporter of this book and an ally as well. **Above right:** Renee and I at the Hollywood Star Walk of Fame ceremony for the late, great George A. Romero in October 2017. Knowing George and his relationship with Hollywood he probably would have been uncomfortable with it, but he was more than deserving of such an honor. You are missed, George. **Below right:** My beloved Mother, Katrina Karr, at KNB EFX studios in Chatsworth, California in December 2010. Here she's with Howard Berger in his office holding his 2006 Academy Award. Thank you for everything you did for me, Mom. You were always my biggest supporter and your belief in me never wavered. I miss you so much and think of you every day. Love, Lee. (all photos courtesy of Lee Karr)

Fiction, Fantasy and Horror Films at the 15th Saturn Awards ceremony in 1988 for her portrayal of Martha Spruce, is another painful loss. Likewise for her co-star George Kennedy, a titan of the film industry both literally and figuratively. In 2008 I had the opportunity to meet Mr. Kennedy briefly at the Chiller Theatre convention in New Jersey when he was a guest at the show. And yes, of course, I had him sign my official *Creepshow 2* one sheet! "Harem Scare-um!", he wrote on my poster, chuckling after doing so. Mr. Kennedy was still with us when I began research on this book project and I tried to locate him for an interview, however he was already in poor health at the time and passed about six months later. An interview with the legend wasn't meant to be, but I did my best to make his presence felt in these pages.

Behind the scenes, film editor Peter Weatherley and sound editor Jim Shields, as well as generator operator Tom Colston are gone. From the marketing side, the legendary voice of so many film trailers, including this one, Percy Rodriguez, along with New World advertising executive Steve Segal have passed away. And, of course, the legendary E.C. artist who created the initial poster art for both of the *Creepshow* films, Jack Kamen, has left us as well.

Stuntman Jery Hewitt, who graciously granted me an interview for this book and provided key information about *The Hitchhiker* stunts, has passed away, too.

We also lost composer Les Reed. I was fortunate enough to interview Mr. Reed for this project before his passing and he was such a gentleman taking the time to answer in detail all of the questions I had for him regarding the film. And if you've read his liner notes for the Waxwork Records release of the film's soundtrack, you know he felt

genuine affection for *Creepshow 2*.

Finally, that brings us to our biggest loss, the great George A. Romero. What can I say here about George that hasn't been said elsewhere a million times? He was a legend even in his own time, yet he always seemed, to me at least, to be uneasy with that status. His humility as an artist made me love and respect him even more.

Honestly, he wasn't very keen on speaking with me about *Creepshow 2* - I called him up and asked if I could interview him and he basically told me no! However, he did have a thing or two that he wanted to say regarding the film, so I quickly grabbed my recorder and took advantage of the handful of minutes he granted me. He wasn't directly involved this time around with the sequel, so that played a large part in his reluctance to speak on the subject, I believe. George was famous for always signing "Stay Scared" above his signature, but more than anything he loved to laugh. And because of that, I feel, his presence is felt in the film via his screenplay which is filled with his typically silly and at times hilariously sick sense of humor.

How lucky we all were to have had a talent such as George A. Romero making movies during our lifetimes, or "playing with electric trains" as he so often put it. George, you are loved and dearly missed by countless people around the world. And I'm one of them.

Sources and Notes

Chapter 1: Two Creeps Are Better Than One

1) Originally quoted in an article by Jack Matthews, "Novelist Loves His Nightmares", which appeared in the Friday, November, 12 1982 edition of the *Detroit Free Press*, page 31; later reprinted in the 1988 book *Bare Bones: Conversations on Terror with Stephen King*, pages 210 and 211, edited by Tim Underwood and Chuck Miller, published by McGraw-Hill Book Company.

2) Quoted to Paul Gagne in the September/October 1982 issue of *Cinefantastique* magazine, Volume 13 Number 1, *"Creepshow*: Masters of the Macabre", page 21, published and edited by Frederick S. Clarke.

3) Taken from the book *Danse Macabre* by Stephen King, page 22, paperback version published in 1983 by Berkley - originally published in 1981 by Everest House.

4) Taken from a taped segment featured on the television broadcast of "The Horror Hall of Fame II" in 1991 honoring E.C. Comics for publishing.

5) Quoted to Michael Stein and reported by Jessie Horsting in the February 1983 issue of *Fantastic Films* magazine, Volume 5 Number 2, pages 60 and 61.

6) Quoted to John Benson on July 16, 1981 - appeared in *Squa Tront* magazine, issue number 9, 1983, page 4.

7) Taken from the U.S. Senate Subcommittee on Juvenile Delinquency from April 21, 1954. Audio recordings published on www.wnyc.org by Annotations: The NEH Preservation Project, courtesy of the NYC Municipal Archives WNYC Collection.

8) Taken from the U.S. Senate Subcommittee on Juvenile Delinquency from April 21, 1954. Audio recordings published on www.wnyc.org by Annotations: The NEH Preservation Project, courtesy of the NYC Municipal Archives WNYC Collection.

9) Quoted to Dwight R. Decker and Gary Groth in issue number 81 of *The Comics Journal* magazine, May 1983, "An Interview with William M. Gaines", page 74.

10) Quoted to Blake Mitchell and Jim Ferguson in the February 1983 issue of *Fantastic Films* magazine, Volume 5 Number 2, page 63.

11) Quoted to Tony Crawley in issue number 55 of *Starburst* magazine, March 1983, "The King/George Conversations, Part Two", page 28.

12) Quoted in the Spring 1980 double issue of *Cinefantastique* magazine, Volume 9 Number 3/Volume 9 Number 4, "Coming" section - page 78, published and edited by Frederick S. Clarke.

13) Quoted to Patrick Kiger in the October 1981 issue of *Pittsburgh* magazine, volume 12 number 10, "A Deadly Duo", page77.

14) Taken from the December 27, 1979-January, 10 1980 issue *Rolling Stone* magazine, "The Horrors of '79" by Stephen King, page 19.

15) Taken from *Fear Itself: The Horror Fiction of Stephen King* edited by Tim Underwood and Chuck Miller, after-word by George Romero, copyright 1982 by Underwood-Miller Publishers, re-published by Signet 1985, pages 256 & 257.

16) Quoted to Bhob Stewart in the January 1980 issue of *Heavy Metal* magazine, vol. III no. 9, page 84.

17) Taken from Roger Ebert's nationally syndicated review of *Creepshow*, which originally appeared in the *Chicago Sun-Times*, reprinted in *The News Journal* - Wilmington, Delaware - on Friday, November 12, 1982.

18) Taken from Gene Siskel's review, "*Creepshow*: 1 plus 1 makes 5 bad horror stories", which appeared in the Thursday, November 11, 1982 edition of the *Chicago Tribune*, "Tempo", section 3, page 16.

19) Quoted to Bob Martin in the October 1982 issue of *Fangoria* magazine, number 22, page 24.

20) Quoted to Bob Martin in the April 1982 issue of *Fangoria* magazine, number 18, "On the set of *Creepshow* - part 1", page 19.

21) Taken from a letter written by George Romero to Jim Shooter at Marvel Comics – 1983.

22) Quoted to Ed Kelleher in the May 1987 issue of *The Film Journal* (Showsouth Edition), volume 90, number 5, "Florida-Based Romero Eyes 4 New Chillers", page 12.

23) Taken from *Scream Greats: The Fangoria Video Magazine Series Volume One: Tom Savini, Master of Horror Effects* - 1986 O'Quinn Productions, Inc.

24) Taken from a letter written by George Romero to David Vogel at Laurel Entertainment - April 12, 1983.

25) Taken from a letter written by George Romero to David Vogel at Laurel Entertainment - April 12, 1983.

26) Taken from a letter written by George Romero to David

Vogel at Laurel Entertainment - April 12, 1983.

27) Quoted to Bob Martin in the May 1982 issue of *Fangoria* magazine, number 19, "On the set of *Creepshow* - part 2", page 24.

28) Quoted to Stanley Wiater in the book *Dark Visions: Conversations with the Masters of the Horror Film,* page 150, published in 1992 by Avon Books.

29) Quoted to Paul Gagne in the 1989 book *Feast of Fear: Conversations with Stephen King*, edited by Tim Underwood and Chuck Miller, page 177, published by Warner Books.

30) Quoted in *The Twilight Zone* magazine, June 1983, page 6.

31) Taken from the book *Skeleton Crew* by Stephen King, Notes section, page 509, published in 1985 by G.P. Putnam's Sons.

32) Taken from the book *Skeleton Crew* by Stephen King, Notes section, page 510, published in 1985 by G.P. Putnam's Sons.

33) Taken from the book *Skeleton Crew* by Stephen King, Notes section, page 510, published in 1985 by G.P. Putnam's Sons.

34) Taken from the book *Just After Sunset* by Stephen King, Sunset Notes section, page 365, published in 2008 by Scribner.

35) Taken from Orson Welle's introduction of the radio play broadcast of *The Hitch-Hiker* - September 2, 1942 - "Suspense!", CBS (Columbia Broadcasting System).

36) Taken from the comic story *Foul Play*, featured in *The Haunt of Fear*, number 19, published by E.C. Comics, June 1953.

37) Quoted to Gary Wood in the February 1991 issue of *Cinefantastique* magazine, Volume 21 Number 4, "Stephen King: Upcoming Horrors, *Thinner & Others*", page 31 , published and edited by Frederick S. Clarke.

38) Quoted to Robert Stewart in the July 1979 issue of *Fantastic Films* magazine, volume 2, number 3, "From Night until Dawn", page 55.

Chapter 2: Laurel - CST, Inc.

1) Taken from a New World Pictures inter-office memo written by Randy Levinson to Paul Almond, May 19, 1986 - "Creepshow II'.

2) Taken from a letter written by David Ball to Tom Savini on June 19, 1986 - "Creepshow II".

3) Quoted to Dennis Daniel in the June 1988 issue of Chas. Balun's *Deep Red* magazine, number 3, "Savini Speaks: Interview with a Master Illusionist", page 7, published by Fantaco Enterprises, Inc.

4) Taken from the *Creepshow 2* DVD featurette "Nightmares in Foam Rubber" - written, produced, and directed by Perry Martin - Anchor Bay Entertainment, Inc. 2004.

5) Taken from the *Creepshow 2* DVD featurette "Nightmares in Foam Rubber" - written, produced, and directed by Perry Martin - Anchor Bay Entertainment, Inc. 2004.

6) Taken from the *Creepshow 2* Blu-ray featurette "Tales from the Creep with Tom Savini" - edited, shot, and produced by Michael Felsher - Red Shirt Pictures, 2016 & Arrow Video, 2016.

7) Taken from the *Creepshow 2* script - screenplay by George A. Romero, stories by Stephen King - page 4, polish dated July 8, 1986 - Laurel Entertainment, Inc.

8) Taken from the *Los Angeles Daily News*, "Dorothy Lamour: Still going strong, even sans sarong", by Kirk Honeycutt - May 7, 1987.

9) Taken from a letter written by Taso Stavrakis, c/o The New York City Stunt League, to Laurel Entertainment, attn: David Ball and Charles Carroll on July 30, 1986 - "Creepshow II".

10) Quoted to Paul Gagne in the 1989 book *Feast of Fear: Conversations with Stephen King*, edited by Tim Underwood and Chuck Miller, page 178, published by Warner Books.

11) Taken from a letter written by Charles Carroll to David Ball and Michael Morgan on August 29, 1986 - "Drake Location Site".

12) Quoted to Paul Gagne in the 1989 book *Feast of Fear: Conversations with Stephen King*, edited by Tim Underwood and Chuck Miller, page 176, published by Warner Books.

13) Taken from a memo from Taso Stavrakis on September 9, 1986 - "Water Safety Rules".

Chapter 3: Jolting Tales Of Horror

1) Taken from a Western Union Telegram sent to Michael Gornick at the Prescottonian Motel from Bill Teitler on September 16, 1986 - 9:34am EST.

2) Taken from the Friday, September 19, 1986 production call sheet - special note from David Ball.

3) Taken from an 11 page letter written by Edward E.

French to Richard P. Rubinstein on December 8, 1986 - "Creepshow II".

4) Taken from the *Creepshow 2* DVD featurette "Nightmares in Foam Rubber" - written, produced, and directed by Perry Martin - Anchor Bay Entertainment, Inc. 2004.

5) Taken from a memo written by David Ball to Jeff Schechtman on September 20, 1986 - "Creepshow 2 casting".

6) Taken from the *Creepshow 2* DVD featurette "Nightmares in Foam Rubber" - written, produced, and directed by Perry Martin - Anchor Bay Entertainment, Inc. 2004.

7) Taken from a Western Union Mailgram written by David Ball to Jeff Schechtman on September 23, 1986.

8) Taken from the *Creepshow 2* DVD featurette "Nightmares in Foam Rubber" - written, produced, and directed by Perry Martin - Anchor Bay Entertainment, Inc. 2004.

9) Taken from the *Creepshow 2* DVD featurette "Nightmares in Foam Rubber" - written, produced, and directed by Perry Martin - Anchor Bay Entertainment, Inc. 2004.

10) Taken from the *Creepshow 2* DVD featurette "Nightmares in Foam Rubber" - written, produced, and directed by Perry Martin - Anchor Bay Entertainment, Inc. 2004.

11) Taken from the *Creepshow 2* DVD featurette "Nightmares in Foam Rubber" - written, produced, and directed by Perry Martin - Anchor Bay Entertainment, Inc. 2004.

12) Taken from a memo written by David Ball to Charles Carroll on September 27, 1986 - "Dorothy Lamour".

13) Taken from a letter written by Michael Morgan to John & Nora Rubel on September 29, 1986.

14) Taken from a memo written by David Ball to Steve White on October 1, 1986 - "Hitchhiker - Casting of Annie".

15) Taken from the *Creepshow 2* DVD featurette "Nightmares in Foam Rubber" - written, produced, and directed by Perry Martin - Anchor Bay Entertainment, Inc. 2004.

16) Taken from a note to the crew from David Ball attached to the October 6, 1986 call sheet.

17) Taken from the *Creepshow 2* script - screenplay by George A. Romero, stories by Stephen King - Second Draft , page 61 - 1984 - Laurel Entertainment, Inc.

18) Taken from the *Creepshow 2* script - screenplay by George A. Romero, stories by Stephen King - page 52, blue page revision, August 13, 1986 - polish July 8, 1986 - Laurel-CST, Inc. - 1986.

19) Taken from the *Creepshow 2* DVD featurette "Nightmares in Foam Rubber" - written, produced, and directed by Perry Martin - Anchor Bay Entertainment, Inc. 2004.

20) Taken from the *Creepshow 2* DVD featurette "Nightmares in Foam Rubber" - written, produced, and directed by Perry Martin - Anchor Bay Entertainment, Inc. 2004.

21) Taken from the *Creepshow 2* DVD featurette "Nightmares in Foam Rubber" - written, produced, and directed by Perry Martin - Anchor Bay Entertainment, Inc. 2004.

22) Taken from the *Creepshow 2* DVD featurette "Nightmares in Foam Rubber" - written, produced, and directed by Perry Martin - Anchor Bay Entertainment, Inc. 2004.

23) Taken from the *Creepshow 2* DVD featurette "Nightmares in Foam Rubber" - written, produced, and directed by Perry Martin - Anchor Bay Entertainment, Inc. 2004.

24) Taken from the *Creepshow 2* DVD featurette "Nightmares in Foam Rubber" - written, produced, and directed by Perry Martin - Anchor Bay Entertainment, Inc. 2004.

25) Taken from a memo written by David Ball to Jeff Schechtman on October 15, 1986 - "CS2 - Casting of Annie".

26) Taken from a memo written by Richard Rubinstein to Steve White on October 16, 1986 - "Creepshow II Casting/Hitchhiker Segment".

27) Taken from the book *Danse Macabre* by Stephen King, pages 395 & 396, paperback version published in 1983 by Berkley - originally published in 1981 by Everest House.

28) Taken from a letter written by Les Reed to David Ball on October 20, 1986 - "Re: Creepshow II".

29) Taken from a memo written by Howard Berger on October 21, 1986 - "Hitchhiker Make-Up".

30) Taken from a letter of recommendation written by David Ball to Rebecca Mayo on October 25, 1986.

31) Taken from the book *On Writing* by Stephen King, page 94, published in 2000 by Scribner.

32) Taken from a memo written by Richard Rubinstein

to Bob Rehme on October 29, 1986 - "Creepshow II Casting".

33) Taken from the *Creepshow 2* DVD featurette "Nightmares in Foam Rubber" - written, produced, and directed by Perry Martin - Anchor Bay Entertainment, Inc. 2004.

34) Taken from the *Creepshow 2* DVD featurette "Nightmares in Foam Rubber" - written, produced, and directed by Perry Martin - Anchor Bay Entertainment, Inc. 2004.

35) Taken from a memo written by Jeff Schechtman to Richard Rubinstein on October 31, 1986.

36) Taken from a memo written by Jeff Schechtman to Richard Rubinstein on November 3, 1986 - "Creepshow II".

37) Taken from a letter written by Father William Kosco to Michael Morgan on October 31, 1986.

38) Taken from the *Creepshow 2* DVD featurette "Nightmares in Foam Rubber" - written, produced, and directed by Perry Martin - Anchor Bay Entertainment, Inc. 2004.

39) Taken from the *Creepshow 2* DVD featurette "Nightmares in Foam Rubber" - written, produced, and directed by Perry Martin - Anchor Bay Entertainment, Inc. 2004.

40) Taken from the *Creepshow 2* Blu-ray featurette "Tales from the Creep with Tom Savini" - edited, shot, and produced by Michael Felsher - Red Shirt Pictures, 2016 & Arrow Video, 2016.

41) Taken from a memo written by Taso Stavrakis to Charles Carroll on November 3, 1986.

42) Taken from a memo written by Richard Rubinstein to Jeff Schechtman on November 4, 1986 - "Creep II/ Casting Delays".

43) Quoted to Anthony Timpone in issue number 64 of *Fangoria* magazine, June 1987, "On the Road with Creepshow 2", page 29.

44) Taken from a memo written by Charles Carroll to Taso Stavrakis, George Dreisch, and Dean Wiseman on November 6, 1986 - "Brakes on stunt car".

45) Taken from a memo written by Taso Stavrakis to Charles Carroll on November 6, 1986 - "Brakes on stunt car (memo reply)"

46) Taken from a memo written by David Ball on November 6, 1986 - "Pay checks".

47) Taken from the *Creepshow 2* script - screenplay by

George A. Romero, stories by Stephen King - First Draft - page 41, dated January 10, 1984 - Laurel Entertainment, Inc.

48) Taken from the *Creepshow 2* DVD featurette "Nightmares in Foam Rubber" - written, produced, and directed by Perry Martin - Anchor Bay Entertainment, Inc. 2004.

49) Taken from an article by Margaret Warner in the *Bangor Daily News*, Monday, November 17, 1986 - "Moviemakers stress need for Maine film commission", page 7.

50) Taken from an article by T.J. Tremble in the *Bangor Daily News*, Thursday, November 20, 1986 - "Brewer police to crack down on I-395 speeders", page 8.

51) Taken from a letter written by David Ball to Taso Stavrakis on November 20, 1986 - "Your Services as Stunt Coordinator".

52) Taken from a letter written by Taso Stavrakis to David Ball on November 24, 1986 - "DB memo of 11/20/86".

53) Taken from a letter written by David Ball to Taso Stavrakis on December 6, 1986 - "Re: Your Letter of December 1, 1986 ".

54) Taken from a letter written by Taso Stavrakis to David Ball on December 29, 1986 - "Re: Your Letter of December 6, 1986".

55) Taken from the *Creepshow 2* DVD featurette "Nightmares in Foam Rubber" - written, produced, and directed by Perry Martin - Anchor Bay Entertainment, Inc. 2004.

56) Taken from a memo written by David Ball on November 21, 1986 - "Completion of Schedule ".

57) Taken from the *Creepshow 2* DVD featurette "Nightmares in Foam Rubber" - written, produced, and directed by Perry Martin - Anchor Bay Entertainment, Inc. 2004.

Chapter 4: Hagoonee', U.S.A - Ya'at'eeh, U.K

1) Taken from a letter of recommendation written by David Ball on behalf of George Dreisch - December 6, 1986.

2) Taken from letters written by Richard Rubinstein to Ed French on December 10, 1986 - "Re: Yours 12/8"

3) Taken from letters written by Dorothy Lamour to Michael Gornick and Rebecca Mayo - December 1986.

4) Taken from the *Creepshow 2* script - screenplay by George A. Romero, stories by Stephen King - page 2,

polish July 8, 1986 - Laurel Entertainment, Inc.

5) Taken from the *Creepshow 2* script - screenplay by George A. Romero, stories by Stephen King - Second Draft , page 3 - 1984 - Laurel Entertainment, Inc.

6) Taken from early animation concept drawings by Gary Hartle, descriptions by Rick Catizone.

7) Taken from early animation concept drawings by Gary Hartle, descriptions by Rick Catizone.

8) Taken from early animation concept drawings by Gary Hartle, descriptions by Rick Catizone.

9) Taken from a letter written by Les Reed to David Ball on October 20, 1986 - "Re: Creepshow II".

10) Taken from a letter written by David Ball to Les Reed on June 18, 1986 - "Creepshow II".

11) Taken from a letter written by Les Reed to David Ball on October 20, 1986 - "Re: Creepshow II".

12) Quote from Chris Blackwell from the comments section of YouTube video posted by Ty Davies on April 27, 2012 , "Ghettoblaster - *The Living Daylights* Music Found".

13) Taken from the July 9, 1949 issue of *Collier's* magazine - "The Old Folks take it harder than Junior" - page 74 - published by The Crowell-Collier Publishing Company.

Chapter 5: Second Issue Collector's Edition

1) Taken from an appearance by Tom Savini on *Late Night with David Letterman* on April 28, 1987 - National Broadcasting Company, Inc.

2) Taken from an ad in the Tuesday, April 28, 1987 edition of the daily *Variety* - page 13.

3) Taken from the review in the Friday, May 1, 1987 edition of the daily *Variety* - page 3.

4) Taken from Duane Byrge's review in the Friday, May 1, 1987 edition of *The Hollywood Reporter*.

5) Taken from Kevin Thomas' review in the Tuesday, May 5, 1987 edition of *The Los Angeles Times* - part VI, page 5.

6) Taken from Janet Maslin's review in the Monday, May 4, 1987 edition of *The New York Times* - section C, page 17.

7) Taken from Melanie Pitts' review in the Tuesday, May 19, 1987 edition of *The Village Voice - "Stiffs"*.

8) Taken from Ralph Novak's review in the Picks & Pans Screen section of *People* weekly magazine - May 25, 1987 - page 10.

9) Taken from Patricia Smith's review in the Monday, May 4, 1987 edition of the *Chicago Sun-Times* - "'Creepshow 2' beats formula to a pulp".

10) Taken from Ed Blank's review in the Friday, May 29, 1987 edition of *The Pittsburgh Press* - "Tepid 'Creepshow 2' trades on names of Romero, King" - page C3.

11) Taken from Marylynn Uricchio's review in the Saturday, May 30, 1987 edition of the *Pittsburgh Post-Gazette* - "There's no terror in the tame 'Creepshow 2'" - page 21.

12) Taken from Tom Brown's review in the Sunday, May 10, 1987 edition of *The Times Recorder* - "Creepshow II - Romero is Missing" - page 7-C.

13) Taken from Chris Chase's review in the Saturday, May 2, 1987 edition of the *Daily News* - "Stephen King's Trilogy of Terror" - page 11.

14) Taken from Joe Kane's ("The Phantom of the Movie") review in the Wednesday, May 6, 1987 edition of the *Daily News* - "You want gore? They got gore".

15) Taken from Daniel Aquilante's review in the Monday, May 4, 1987 edition of the *New York Post* - page 27.

16) Taken from Tony DeSena's review in the Friday, May 8, 1987 edition of the *New Jersey Herald* - "'Creepshow II' amuses as ghoulish sequel".

17) Taken from Mary Ann Murdoch's review in the Friday, May 8, 1987 edition of the *Ocala Star-Banner* - "'Creepshow 2' A Screen Scream" - page 11B.

18) Taken from Linda Cook's review in the Saturday, June 6, 1987 edition of the *Quad-City Times* - "Film is horribly funny" - page 15.

19) Taken from Jack Kegg's review in the Saturday, May 16, 1987 edition of the *Cumberland News*.

20) Taken from Hal Boedeker's review in the Wednesday, May 13, 1987 edition of the *Miami Herald* - "Creepshow 2 is a scream" - page 7D.

21) Taken from a letter written by Dan Kamin to Michael Gornick - June 8, 1987.

22) Taken from a letter written by Peter Weatherley to Michael Gornick - postmarked July 8, 1987.